Norbert Pohlmann
Helmut Reimer
Wolfgang Schneider

ISSE/SECURE 2007
Securing Electronic
Business Processes

SAP® R/3® Interfacing using BAPIs
by Gerd Moser

The SAP® R/3® Guide to EDI and Interfaces
by Axel Angeli, Ulrich Streit and Robi Gonfalonieri

Computing Fundamentals
by J. Stanley Warford

Process Modeling with ARIS®
by Heinrich Seidlmeier

Understanding MP3
by Martin Ruckert

From Enterprise Architecture to IT Governance
by Klaus D. Niemann

ISSE/SECURE 2007 Securing Electronic Business Processes
by Norbert Pohlmann, Helmut Reimer and Wolfgang Schneider

Norbert Pohlmann
Helmut Reimer
Wolfgang Schneider

ISSE/SECURE 2007 Securing Electronic Business Processes

Highlights of the Information Security Solutions Europe/SECURE 2007 Conference

With 140 illustrations

Bibliographic information published by Die Deutsche Nationalbibliothek
Die Deutsche Nationalbibliothek lists this publication in the Deutsche Nationalbibliografie;
detailed bibliographic data is available in the Internet at <http://dnb.d-nb.de>.

Many of designations used by manufacturers and sellers to distinguish their
products are claimed as trademarks.

1st edition 2007

All rights reserved
© Friedr. Vieweg & Sohn Verlag | GWV Fachverlage GmbH, Wiesbaden 2007

Editorial office: Günter Schulz / Andrea Broßler

Vieweg is a company of Springer Science+Business Media.
www.vieweg.de

Cover design: Ulrike Weigel, www.CorporateDesignGroup.de
Typesetting: Oliver Reimer, Ilmenau
Printing and binding: MercedesDruck, Berlin
Printed on acid-free paper
Printed in Germany

ISBN 978-3-8348-0346-7

Contents

Identity, Information Security and Rights Management ____ 115

Preface

ENISA is proud to be working with eema, TeleTrusT, NASK (the Polish research and development organization and leading Polish data networks operator) and the German Federal Ministry of the Interior as well as the German Federal Office for Information Security for this year's 9th annual Information Security Solutions Europe Conference.

The aim of the ISSE has always been to support the development of a European information security culture and especially a cross-border framework for trustworthy IT applications for citizens, industry and administration. ENISA is committed to these goals. In our work we assist and advise the European Commission, Member States as well as business community on network and information security as well as on legislative requirements, and we are delighted to support the ISSE again this year.

The security of communication networks and information systems is of increasing concern. In order to face today's complex information security challenges it is clear that working collaboratively with one another is the key to generating new strategies to address these problems. It has been an exciting opportunity to facilitate this collaboration at the ISSE 2007, pulling together the wealth of industry knowledge, information and research that we hold in Europe, as well as across the globe.

The success of this event in generating ideas and frank, lively debate around the complex topic of IT security is due also to the independent, varied nature of the programme, which was selected by worldwide specialists in the field.

Some of the key topics explored at this year's conference have been chosen as the basis for this book, which is an invaluable reference point for anyone involved in the IT security industry.

We hope that you will find it a thought-provoking and informative read.

Andrea Pirotti, Executive Director, ENISA

About this Book

The Information Security Solutions Europe Conference (ISSE) was started in 1999 by eema and Tele-TrusT with the support of the European Commission and the German Federal Ministry of Technology and Economics. Today the annual conference is a fixed event in every IT security professional's calendar.

The integration of security in IT applications was initially driven only by the actual security issues considered important by experts in the field; currently, however, the economic aspects of the corresponding solutions are the most important factor in deciding their success. ISSE offers a suitable podium for the discussion of the relationship between these considerations and for the presentation of the practical implementation of concepts with their technical, organisational and economic parameters.

From the beginning ISSE has been carefully prepared. The organisers succeeded in giving the conference a profile that combines a scientifically sophisticated and interdisciplinary discussion of IT security solutions while presenting pragmatic approaches for overcoming current IT security problems.

An enduring documentation of the presentations given at the conference which is available to every interested person thus became important. This year sees the publication of the fifth ISSE book – another mark of the event's success – and with about 50 carefully edited papers it bears witness to the quality of the conference.

An international programme committee is responsible for the selection of the conference contributions and the composition of the programme:

- **Ronny Bjones,** Microsoft (Belgium)
- **Gunter Bitz,** SAP (Germany)
- **Lucas Cardholm,** Ernst&Young (Sweden)
- **Roger Dean,** eema (UK)
- **Ronald De Bruin,** ENISA
- **Jan De Clercq,** HP (Belgium)
- **Marijke De Soete,** NXP Semiconductors (Belgium)
- **Jos Dumortier,** KU Leuven (Belgium)
- **Walter Fumy,** Siemens (Germany)
- **Michael Hange,** BSI (Germany)
- **John Hermans,** KPMG (The Netherlands)
- **Jeremy Hilton,** Cardiff University (United Kingdom)
- **Frank Jorissen,** SafeBoot (Belgium)
- **Matt Landrock,** Cryptomathic (Denmark)

- **Mirosław Maj,** CERT Polska (Poland)
- **Tim Mertens,** ENISA
- **Attila Péterfalvi,** Parliamentary Commissioner for Data Protection and Freedom of Information (Hungary)
- **Norbert Pohlmann,** University of Applied Sciences Gelsenkirchen, Chairman of the Programme Committee (Germany)
- **Bart Preneel,** KU Leuven (Belgium)
- **Helmut Reimer,** TeleTrusT (Germany)
- **Joachim Rieß,** Daimler Chrysler (Germany)
- **Paolo Rossini,** TELSY, Telecom Italia Group (Italy)
- **Wolfgang Schneider,** Fraunhofer Institute SIT (Germany)
- **Jon Shamah,** CoreStreet (UK)
- **Krzysztof Silicki,** NASK (Poland)
- **Robert Temple,** BT (United Kingdom)

The editors have endeavoured to allocate the contributions in these proceedings – which differ from the structure of the conference programme – to topic areas which cover the interests of the readers.

Norbert Pohlmann   *Helmut Reimer*   *Wolfgang Schneider*

eema (www.eema.org):	TeleTrusT Deutschland e.V. (www.teletrust.de)
Established in 1987, eema is an independent association of IT professionals, businesses and governments providing business and technical networking opportunities at both local and regional levels in the broad areas associated with e-Identity and its related applications, such as security. Our mission is to stimulate the growth and effectiveness of our members' business in these areas through increased market awareness, cooperation and opportunity creation.	TeleTrusT Deutschland e.V. was founded in 1989 as a non profit association promoting the trustworthiness of information and communication technology in open system environments. Today, TeleTrusT counts more than 80 institutional members. Within the last 17 years TeleTrusT evolved into a well known and highly regarded competence network for applied cryptography and biometrics.
We aim to bring our 1,500 member representatives together in a neutral environment for education and networking purposes. We enable members to share experiences and best practice by holding meetings and conferences, by facilitating working groups who produce reports on topical subjects, and by helping members to connect with the right person to help them solve business issues or develop beneficial business relationships. All work produced by members is available free to other members, and previous papers include: Towards Understanding Identity, Role Based Access Control – a Users Guide, Secure e-mail within a Corporate Environment and Secure e-mail between Organisations.	In the various working groups of TeleTrusT ICT-security experts, users and interested parties meet frequently at workshops, round-tables and expert talks. The activities focus on reliable and trustworthy solutions complying with international standards, laws and statutory requirements. TeleTrusT is keen to promote the acceptance of solutions supporting identification, authentification and signature (IAS) schemes in electronic business.
	TeleTrusT facilitates the information and knowledge exchange between vendors, users and authorities., This helps innovative ICT-security solutions to enter the market more quickly and effectively. TeleTrusT aims to create standard compliant solutions in interoperable schemes.
Contact: Roger Dean Executive Director of eema roger.dean@eema.org	Keeping in mind the growing importance of the European security market, TeleTrusT seeks the co-operation with European organisations and authorities with similar objectives. Thus, the European Security Conference ISSE is organised in collaboration with eema, ENISA and NASK this year.
	Contact: Dr. Günther Welsch Managing Director of TeleTrusT Deutschland e.V. guenther.welsch@teletrust.de

Welcome

We are honoured to be hosting and co-organising this year's ISSE/ SECURE 2007 Conference in Warsaw.

As Minister of Interior and Administration, I am responsible for the development and diffusion of Information Technology in Poland, especially for implementing e-Administration and for the development of the Information Society.

Aware of the increasing concern for ICT in all the fields of economic and social activity, the Ministry of Interior and Administration plays a highly active role in legislation, strategy development as well as projects implementation.

A high priority has been given to projects aimed at higher personal data protection and secure electronic systems in public administration. As an example, the Electronic Platform of Public Administration Services project provides for a single platform with e-services of public administration for citizens and businesses. One of its tasks will be to provide public administration with common tools for user's authorization and certification.

The Ministry also took over the competences concerning digital signature implementation in reason of activities strongly related to its policy lines concerning implementation of eID and registers security for the forthcoming public e-services.

The Ministry of Interior and Administration's concern for ISSE/SECURE 2007 conference is an excellent prove of its deep interest for issues concerning the European information security challenges.

We look forward to create a good field for effective transfer of ideas, knowledge and best practices among policy makers, experts in ICT security and industrials.

Władysław Stasiak
Minister of Interior and Administration

Microsoft: A Trustworthy Vision for Computing

The continually evolving computing landscape of today has two primary macro-level developments: more people and businesses rely on computing every day, and the threats that can undermine trust in computing are increasingly sophisticated and malicious.

From the customer's perspective, it is increasingly important that sensitive data are protected, that software businesses adhere to business practices that promote trust with users, and that the technology industry renews its focus on solid engineering and best practices to ensure the delivered product or service is more reliable and secure.

Microsoft's approach to this environment is Trustworthy Computing (TwC), a long-term, collaborative effort to create and deliver secure, private, and reliable computing experiences for everyone. Microsoft formed TwC in January 2002, when Bill Gates committed the company to fundamentally changing its mission and strategy in the key areas of Security, Privacy, Reliability, and Business Practices.

TwC's five-year milestone seems an appropriate time to examine our efforts to date and to affirm the promise of TwC. What follows is an update on some of the things we're doing to ensure that customers can count on every one of our new and exciting innovations.

Pricacy

Microsoft is working with policymakers and industry leaders in the United States to encourage federal laws that establish baseline privacy protections for consumers while still allowing commerce to flourish. And, since privacy threats know no borders, we're also working with governments around the world to make privacy laws as consistent as possible.

Security

Microsoft works closely with other software vendors, the research community and security companies to find better ways to build more secure software, locate vulnerabilities, collaboratively address issues as they arise, and establish best practices across the industry. We partner with law enforcement worldwide to help find and catch individuals who write and distribute malicious software. And, when a new issue threatens customers, our Security Response Center mobilizes teams to investigate, fix and learn from security vulnerabilities. We continue to release security updates on a regular schedule.

Reliability

Over the past few years, we've made great progress in improving the reliability of our products, as well as other software built on our platform, through continuous improvement technologies – software that can diagnose, report, and fix problems as they arise. For example, the error-reporting features in Microsoft Office 2007 perform thorough diagnostics when applications hang or crash, including checking the computer's hard disk and memory and verifying that the customer's software is up-to-date and uncorrupted. It can dynamically keep track of system resources, and help avoid performance and reliability issues when running a large number of applications.

Looking Ahead

Microsoft has spent the past five years working to transform the company around TwC, and it has improved by an order of magnitude in each of the areas noted above. But, there's still plenty of work to do. We've only tapped a fraction of computing's vast potential, and the coming years will continue to bring new innovations that transform how we live and work.

The world of PCs and servers is evolving into a rich web of connected devices and services and computing has become enmeshed into the fabric of our lives. This is why TwC has to do more than address today's challenges – it must ensure that the innovations people will rely on tomorrow are designed from the outset to be reliable and secure, respectful of their privacy, and supported by trustworthy and responsive companies.

Legal, Technical and Social Aspects of Security

Regulating Information Security: A Matter of Principle?

Andreas Mitrakas · Silvia Portesi

European Network and Information Security Agency (ENISA)
{andreas.mitrakas | silvia.portesi}@enisa.europa.eu

Abstract

The widespread use of information technology in daily transactions has exacerbated the role of information security to protect information assets. Regulating network and information security has taken place through instruments and instantiations used for most of the time for different purposes than those strictly needed by information security itself. If information security is the answer to such requirements as confidentiality, integrity and availability of resources, setting up appropriate regulation is the means to set up binding frameworks. Regulation in this respect takes into account the requirements for a soft law approach that encompasses self regulatory frameworks and standards. A set of regulatory principles addressing the content and form of regulation in network and information security is an additional means to further enhance the impact of legislation and serve stakeholders.

1 Introduction

The widespread use of information technology in daily transactions has exacerbated the role of information security to protect information assets. The potential vulnerabilities that have been typically associated with transactions in the Public Administration and private enterprise challenge users and legislators alike. While information security is the answer to such requirements as confidentiality, integrity and availability of resources, establishing appropriate policies is the means to set up binding bilateral frameworks [Pfle00]. Furthermore a regulatory framework underpins certain high level requirements that need to be addressed at legislative level and complements the bilateral arrangements of individual users. Further up stream, there is, however, a latent need of principles of information security in order to guide the regulatory process. This paper addresses such questions as *is there a real need to regulate network and information security, under what conditions can it be taken up by the legislator* and *is law is an appropriate means to address regulatory principles in information security?* Input to this paper has been drawn from the working group on regulatory aspects of network and information security that ENISA set up in 2006. The remainder of this paper addresses the following areas: an overview of regulatory principles in the light of legal positivism and their influence in the regulatory process of network and information security; specific regulatory considerations for network and information security; a set of regulatory principles that can be leveraged upon to the benefit of more concrete regulation in network and information security.

2 Working with rules

Positivism has vouched that law is a set of rules used to determine which behaviour will be punished and which will be coerced by the public power. If a specific case is not covered under this assertion, then a specialist, like a judge intervenes to determine the case. A legal right or obligation must directly

N. Pohlmann, H. Reimer, W. Schneider (Editors): Securing Electronic Business Processes, Vieweg (2007), 3-17

fall under a legal rule [Dwor77]. Austin described three types of rules, legal, moral and religious ones. A basic set of legal rules is provided by the sovereign who, subsequently, empowers a judge to make new rules or re-assert known ones [Aust1832]. For H.L.A. Hart there is a system of primary and secondary rules whereby primary rules define what is allowed and what is not [Hart61]. Secondary rules affect the operation of primary rules and address three discreet areas namely, the uncertainty about what law is and whether a rule is valid, the rigidity of rules which addresses rules of change and allows laws to be varied, and how to resolve legal disputes from which rules of adjudication emerge. For Hart a legal system is the union of primary and secondary rules.

According to Dworkin, beyond set rules imposed by a designated authority, in a democracy, rules also include policies and social standards that are promulgated through various channels associated with social functions. A policy sets out a standard to improve a certain feature of the society [Dwor77]. Standards in this sense should not be interpreted as technical standards that will be discussed separately further down in this paper, but rather as social norms that cut across the society. Principles on the other hand set out a social standard that is a requirement of justice, fairness, or morality. As Dworkin argues, positivism is a model of and for a system of rules that forces us to miss the important role of social standards that are not rules. Principles are rules that conflict and interact with each other so that each principle that is relevant to a particular problem and it provides a reason arguing in favour of but without necessarily stipulating a particular solution thereto [Dwor77]. Empowering a judge requires exercising discretion, which can be asserted when someone is charged of making decision as part of social standards set by an authority.

Long before any explicit manufacturer's liability rules came about, a New Jersey (US) Court, in the case *Henningsen v. Bloomfield Motors Inc.* (32 NJ 358, 1961), was faced with an important question of whether and to what extend a car manufacturer may limit its liability for a defective car. The manufacturer in question has set a contract clause signed to by the buyer which said that the manufacturer's liability for defects was limited to "making good" defective parts while "this warranty was in lieu of all other warranties, obligations and liabilities." Faced with a defective product the plaintiff argued that in his case additional expenses should be covered for by the manufacturer due to the defective product that he made available. At the time there was no statute to point to that would allow the plaintiff to support his argument. The Court in its reasoning took into account limitations in the principle of contractual freedom and it suggested that "in a society like ours where the automobile is a common and necessary adjunct of daily life, and where its use is so fraught with danger to the driver, passenger and the public, the manufacturer is under special obligation in connection with the construction promotion and sale of his car". Subsequently the Court refused to be taken as an instrument of inequity that is there to enforce a "bargain" in which one party takes advantage of the economic necessities of the other.

In *Henningsen,* the guidance of the Court was provided not so much from an established and firm background of rules, but rather from a set of social norms or standards that suggest that a Court cannot be used as an instrument to promote unfairness; except in case of fraud and wilful misconduct contractual freedom can be indeed limited to match social needs of the society. In the absence of a set of rules, exercising discretion provided the appropriate interpretation of a social standard and injected input in case law. Luhmann argues that the essence of positive law is that it is a decision; and to that the concept of positive law can be reduced to. A decision entails that law is not only promulgated through decision, but also is valid by the power of decision which subjects it to change [Luhm95]. In an environment where business needs prevail, adapting law enables it to be a powerful instrument for the wilful promotion and regulation of social and economic goals. Luckily, by virtue of an EU regulatory framework for information society services, we do not have to rely on assumptions such as those posed in *Henningsen* any more.

Setting up meta-rules on how to carry our regulation in those areas related to network and information security that has been deemed necessary, we observe the significant role that technical standardisation, for instance, plays in bringing together legal requirements with specific societal needs. Standardisation has emerged as a key EU policy area that complements the legislative process especially in such areas as products and technology. Standardisation policy in the EU goes back to the *Cassis de Dijon* case in which the European Court of Justice ruled that a product meeting the requirements of one member state should be legally made available in another; allowing the emergence of mutual recognition of technical standards as a matter of significant interest in the EU internal market (ECJ 120/78 of 20/02/79). The EU approach to technical harmonisation has resulted in limiting standards to technical specifications and safety requirements while reserving a prominent place for EU standards organisations such as the European Committee for Standardisation (CEN) and European Telecommunications Standards Institute (ETSI). This role for standards has gradually led to a soft approach that contains covers up for limitations emanating from a strict legislative process that can be seen as too narrow to address business and society needs. Technical standards, thus, provide a layer of "soft law" that deviates from a strict legislative approach [Send05] [Send04]. Often technical standards rely on a framework set out through a directive that is complemented by the appropriate standards. These standards are typically promulgated by the industry. The figure below provides an outlook of frequently used soft law instruments and their association with legislative instruments as they are often encountered in an EU context. A co-regulatory process links the requirements at the legislative level with the outcome of the standardization process that remains in line with the stipulations of the legislative framework.

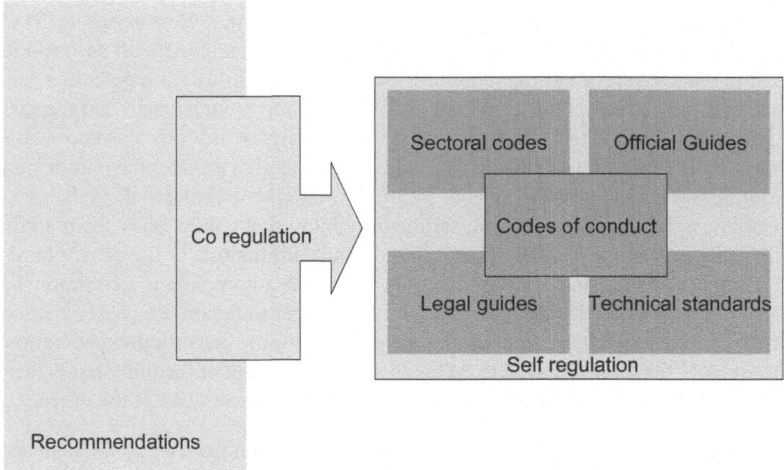

Figure 1: Soft law instruments in a co-regulation approach

In a concrete situation related to network and information security we observe that Directive 1999/93/ EC on a Community framework on electronic signatures, standards establishes a presumption of conformity, meaning that the electronic signature products that meet their requirements also comply with the legal requirements [Mitr06]. This approach has been underlined by the Commission Decision of 14 July 2003 on the publication of reference numbers of generally recognized standards for electronic signature products in accordance with Directive 1999/93/EC of the European Parliament and of the Council. This Decision has endorsed and given legal effect to certain standards promulgated by the industry-led European Electronic Signatures Standardization Initiative (EESSI). Standards assume legal significance in cases where the law mandates them in order to give specific effect to a particular regulation within the EU.

With regard to security standards the ISO 27000 family of standards provides recommendations on information security management to those who are designated to initiate, implement or maintain security in an organization. This standard provides a common basis to pursue security management practices and indirectly to provide confidence in transactions. The ISO 27000 family of standards invokes the general requirement for network and information security and more specifically the requirements for confidentiality, integrity and availability. Integrity in this case encompasses the notions of authentication and non repudiation, which have both been subjected to legislation especially through the electronic signatures directive. The ISO 27000 standard is a self regulatory framework that extends to policies and agreements that all aim at setting up the conditions for network security safeguards within an organisation or in specific transaction frameworks [Mitr07]. The instrument of recommendation can be further used at EU level in order to highlight the significance and role of such standards but also of other instruments such as codes of conduct [Send05].

3 Making rules

Starting from mid-1990s, the technological revolution, characterised by the development and spread of information technologies, has reshaped the material basis of the society. "Economies throughout the world have become globally interdependent, introducing a new form of relationship between economy, state and society, in a system of variable geometry" [Cast04]. Adequate regulatory solutions, at national and supranational level, to face these changes, started to be discussed and adopted. In making rules in network and information society, some regulatory principles are followed. Sometimes, however there could be noted a discrepancy between the desired solution and the one made available by the legislator. Inefficient legislation might have further sipped in and influenced bilateral relationships, leading to regulatory solutions that could be a far cry from what was essentially needed in the first place, when regulation was deemed to be an appropriate solution. Especially at the level of regulatory principles a necessary condition to consider regards the efficiency of the offered solution.

The Coarse theorem gives a notion of what efficiency means when making an agreement. Referring to bilateral relationships, Coarse suggests that a contractual solution must take into account three factors: transaction costs, the efficiency of the outcome and the legal framework to lead to a regulatory solution [Poli89]. The efficiency of a regulatory solution, such as a contract for example also depends upon factors such as the social context, the transaction costs and the legal reality of the environment in which the legal solution is applied [Will05]. A regulatory solution should take such variables into account and include for example the cost of obtaining information, the negotiation cost, the gains of breaching a rule as opposed to possible costs like a reliance remedy or a restitution remedy, etc. If, for example, the cost of obtaining information in order to set up a regulatory framework is quite high such solution might not necessarily be a rational choice [Will05]. Determining the cost of obtaining information on the overall solution is yet another facet of the problem that cannot be easily reached.

There is an additional role, reserved to economic rules, which produces outcomes that are in the interest of everyone [Mitn80]. Economic rules aim at correcting market inefficiencies or failures which is an often appearing feature in a society. In a broad sense, regulation in this regard might include technical and consumer related standards, health and environment standards, competition policies, industry regulations etc [Hix99].

Rules provide incentives and set the limits of human interaction and behaviour with regard to an area of interest. Against this background rules that regard services can be seen as comprising of three general discreet categories being moral, social and economic ones. Economic rules, in specific, focus on these very incentives, in order to establish a system of fines that invokes the approach that recklessness is punished or compliance is rewarded. The flip side of these rules with an economic interest encompasses the concept of using a system of credits that it pays to educate and raise awareness in specific areas of interest. This paper suggests that general rules can be used to enhance the current level of security available to the beneficiaries of the information society as a whole in a way that enhances information society services. There is but limited need for specific formal rules as it is addressed further below. Rules can be based on the three main categories that are mentioned above, being moral, social and economic ones, in order to provide a framework for authorities, users and service providers alike in their efforts to make available or rely upon dependable and robust services that appropriately mitigate network and information security risks.

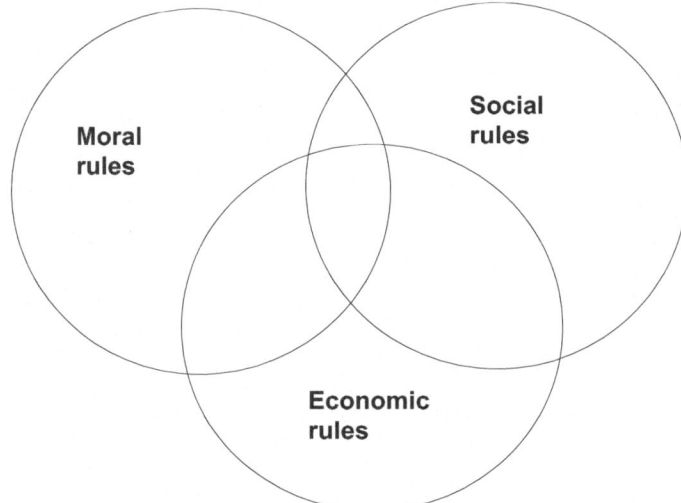

Figure 2: Three types of rules: moral, social and economic

When answering the question "what rules have to do with network and information security?" it is important to highlight the features of the Internet, upon which information society services are largely based in making the most of a secure service and transaction environment. A discreet case that related to information security concerns identity risks in information society that can be epitomised in the motto published along a synonymous cartoon in NY Times on suggesting that "*On the internet nobody knows that you are a dog*", as authored by Peter Steiner who wrote it in his July 1993 cartoon in NY Times. It is questionable whether the age old question regarding social responsibility, which goes: "*could a man resist the temptation of evil if he knew that his acts could not be witnessed*" could be successfully replied in the information age; apparently the reply at least in the real world appears to be 89% of the time [Boas61] [Levitt06]. The shift to avatars made available through the services of Second Life, Second Life is a 3-D virtual world entirely built and owned by its residents demonstrates the significance of this underlying identity drive in information society (http://secondlife.com/). An avatar is an Internet user's own representation in the form of a three-dimensional model used in computer games. Avatars facilitate the need to take up a role, marking or altogether one's real identity and the Internet is a means that predominantly facilitates this need. Avatars can be deemed as an expression of an underlying social desire to act under an assumed identity that allows the user to authenticate itself in a virtual world. However desirable this approach can barely resemble reality and in a real life context it cannot be morally or socially justified as it would undermine trust. Therefore addressing authentication methods to ensure trust in user access or management for example becomes a priority area for information security.

Readjusting our focus on security, however, the relentless exposure of services, service providers and users to network and information society risks has made it an indispensable feature of information society to rely upon rules in order to ensure the confidentiality, integrity and availability of services. What are these rules that have already become available? Are there any principles that could be leveraged upon in order to ensure that acts and omissions do not necessarily leave services out in the cold?

This paper further examines the role of information security as a component of information society.

4 Information security: to serve and protect?

When examining the role of rules in network and information security it is important to highlight the potential role of rules in addressing the requirements of the information security community. This task becomes more apparent if taking a practical case regarding the protection of personal data and the role of its regulatory framework in Europe. The scope of information security measures in information society can be twofold. On one hand information security aims at protecting the interests of the service provider with regard to access the resources, which are necessary in order to deliver a service [FoBa01]. Security, however, can be used in order to ensure the protection of rights, such as privacy, in a way that the end user benefits. End user in this respect might be a natural person in its capacity as citizen or consumer etc. Additionally, legal persons can benefit in terms of legal safety, compliance with regulations in highly regulated environments such as stock markets and the like. Personal data protection is this emblematic area where all stakeholders are better off if they protect data rather that ignore it. To the data controller personal data is an asset that can be leveraged upon in order to deliver meaningful services; as such the data controller has a duty to protect this asset [Ters06]. To the data subjects, on the other hand personal data represents a means to receive personalised services that requires protection due to its vicinity to the personal sphere of the protection of fundamental rights.

This heightened significance of rules in the area of personal data protection emanates from the strong cultural and legislative drive in the early seventies' Western Europe that led to the gradual adoption of data protection legislation. The European Union considered the global reach of certain aspects of data protection law that has led to the currently available European framework on data protection [Buel06].

When examining the needs in terms of rules of network and information society it is important to envisage the potential objectives that these rules might seek to play. Pursuant to the assumption regarding the protection of personal data it is clear that rules of any sort, in network and information security, serve the dual purpose of protecting fundamental rights and ensuring services rendered. Therefore there is a strong societal drive that powers rule making as well as a strong economic drive that sets out a framework of incentives and fines in case of breach as discussed in the previous section. An underlying strong moral element might remain a little out of sight because it might be embedded in the societal requirement that is manifested through legislation at the Member States level. Such moral element associates, however rather with the moral premise of the right "to be left alone", the core element of privacy, rather with the specific mechanics of how such an arrangement might work out in terms of protecting personal data. As the basic requirement on privacy stated in article 8 of the Council of Europe Convention on Human Rights and Fundamental Freedoms and then in articles 7 and 8 of the Charter of Fundamental

Rights of the European Union, has also been enshrined in legislation such as Directive 95/46/EC etc., the associations among the moral and societal elements become apparent.

5 What's law got to do with it?

An emerging legal framework that derives from the role that information plays in modern day transactions is setting up the pace for developments in business and banking. Organizations that implement appropriate security measures mandated by industry regulations or legislation expect to benefit from the mitigation of potential liability of shareholders, employees, customers, trading partners or other third parties involved in a transaction.

The set up of the European Network and Information Security Agency (ENISA) to address selected network and information security matters has emerged as a new element in supporting the approximation of laws in the Member States in the framework of the First Pillar regarding the EU Internal market. To this effect the decision of the European Court of Justice asserted that the principle of article 95 of the Treaty regarding the EU Internal Market is well served just by setting up a measure such as ENISA along with the array of legislative measures undertaken by the European Union over time.

The ENISA case (C-217/04), UK v. EP & Council presents an example of challenging the legal basis of EU Agency based on article 95 of the Treaty on the EU Internal Market. Regulation (EC) No 460/2004 of the European Parliament and of the Council of 10 March 2004 establishing the European Network and Information Security Agency (hereinafter, ENISA Regulation) has been challenged before the European Court of Justice (hereinafter, ECJ) with regard to the legal basis of ENISA servicing EU Internal Market purposes on the basis of article 95 of the Treaty (ex art. 100a). While art. 95, maintains the system of majority voting it involves co-decision between Council and parliament under art. 251 of the Treaty. It has been noted that this approach results in greater intermediary powers to the Commission at the Council level since gaining a qualified majority suffices for a vote [Weil91]. In its ruling ECJ affirmed that the ENISA Regulation was yet another measure in a broader EU framework regarding network and information security. Being far from the only measure regarding the approximation of laws, as the plaintiff had claimed, the ENISA Regulation has been part of a broader set of regulatory measures composed by the framework Directive and including specific Directives that address various aspects of the EU Internal Market in the area of electronic communications. The ECJ decision highlighted the potential divergence in Member State laws that could emanate from differences in transposing Directives in this area. The ECJ ruling also removed uncertainty by linking article 3 of the ENISA Regulation (EC) 460/2004 with the objectives of the framework Directive as well as of specific Directives in the area of network and information security.

Additional requirements associated with the area of specific activity that regulation is called in to serve also influence the way that regulation is promulgated. For example the need for the end user to become aware of risks and measures to mitigate them or the need for security measures to facilitate or at least to refrain from hindering interoperability can be seen as measures of specific interest that could typically sip in regulation. The table below makes some associations between areas of network and network security and types of rules, such as the above.

Table 1: *Ad hoc* substance areas and their relation to types of rules

	Ad hoc sample substance				
	Data protection	Privacy	Awareness	Interoperability	Information society Application
Social rules	X	X	X	X	X
Moral rules		X	X		
Economic rules	X	X		X	X

The table above is a plain indication of the associations that certain *ad hoc* sample substance areas might have with the rules of choice that can be used as regulatory instrument in a network and information security framework. Essentially this table demonstrates that not all areas of interest or instruments available in network and information security merit or require being associated with a need to have formal rules with an economic impact. As discussed above these rules with an economic impact are essential formal rules promulgated by the legislator. Inevitably on several occasions a regulation can rest at the level of bilateral arrangements in the framework of self regulation as a reflection of a moral requirement or a social constraint imposed in the transaction. While moral or social constraints address the needs of portions of the society they might not have a universal interest or create a grand impact that merits the attention of the legislator. In this regard self regulation may produce results that are sufficiently efficient and therefore more desirable.

6 A Working Group

The ENISA Working Group on Regulatory Aspects of network information security (hereinafter, WG-RANIS) carried out an overview of EU legislation as it has become available in the area of network and information security (http://www.enisa.europa.eu/pages/ENISA_Working_group_RANIS.htm). The target of this Working Group has been to compile a list of activities in an effort to represent state-of-art in an inventory-centric approach that addresses legal actions on issues relevant to network and information security.

In their report this Working Group came up with a significant number of legislative instruments (over 65 in total) that cover the period as of 1990. In total more that 65 instruments were collected that cover a broad range of EU policy and law making [RANIS06]. The areas of legislative attention with an interest for network and information security cover for example: security and financial services, intellectual property rights, corporate and IT governance, data authentication, data protection and retention, electronic communications, networks and services. This very broad approach that has yet to be systematically addressed had been spared no legislative instruments in order to meet the regulatory requirements of network and information security. In this regard regulations, directives, recommendations, resolutions etc., had all been invariably used in to promulgate the legislative framework of network and information security. The instruments of choice to give effect to this framework can be seen in the radar table below that was compiled by the Working Group itself [RANIS06]:

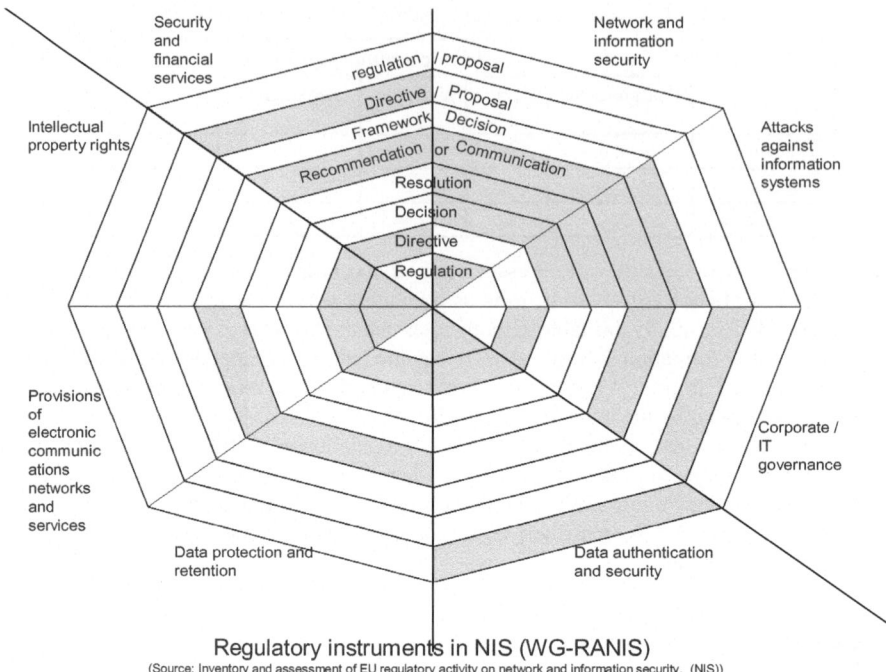

Regulatory instruments in NIS (WG-RANIS)
(Source: Inventory and assessment of EU regulatory activity on network and information security, (NIS))

Figure 3: Regulatory instruments in network and information security

7 Regulatory Principles

A set of underlying principles is necessary to guide legislation towards efficient regulation that is commensurate with societal needs. Such legislation should recognise lateral societal needs that are not necessarily represented in legislation itself but which are, nevertheless represented in the form of standards or bilateral arrangements. The principles that WG-RANIS has seen as looming can be found in the report itself. The section below relies on some of these principles, and provides an overview and explanation regarding the regulatory framework at large.

Multi facet legislation
The network and information security regulatory framework is typically multi faceted comprising of several layers, such as privacy, telecommunication, business applications, authentication and identity, intellectual property protection, competition, taxation and electronic communication emerge as interest areas for network and information security. Therefore, as Matsuura points out, there are several substantive categories of law applying to information and network security, such as intellectual property law, privacy law, law of contracts and commercial transactions, consumer protection law, anti-trust law, property law, etc. [Mats02]. Interlacing the underlying legislative principles of various areas can be challenging for the legislator of network and information security who risks voting potentially conflicting rules. Hence, sufficient consideration could be given to legislation of lateral areas in a way that adapts new legislation to the existing framework.

Moreover, network and information security addresses a framework that benefits directly or indirectly a multitude of business, government and application areas that merit a legislative approach. In developing new regulations or updating those already existing in the field of network and security, regulators could take into account the impact they might have on all the different stakeholders and to consider the different possibilities the various areas of law might offer.

Political background
In the EU, the "Bangemann Report" was one of the first reports on the then new subject area of information and communication technology and its implications for the society; this report was prepared by the High Level Expert Group containing recommendations presented to the Council to ensure competitiveness for European enterprises the international service market [COM94] and [KLP+06]. In March 2000, at the Lisbon Summit meeting "Towards a Europe of Innovation and Knowledge", EU Heads of State and Government agreed to make the EU the most innovative knowledge-based society by 2010. The eEurope 2005 Action Plan was launched at the Seville European Council in June 2002 and aimed to "stimulate secure services, applications and content based on a widely available broadband infrastructure". The eEurope 2005 initiative ended in 2005 and was followed by the i2010 initiative, which is strategic policy framework laying out guidelines for the information society and the media until 2010. The political drive behind eEurope has shaped the legislative framework in several of the areas adjacent to network and information security. The inevitable embracing between politics, policy and law underline that legal initiatives often need to have political support in order to become effective and enforceable, while they maintain the interest of the stakeholders.

A global role for Europe
In a networked world, EU legislation on information security should not be drafted in isolation from the rest of the world. While being a legislative pioneer, as it has been the se for the EU in the area of personal data protection, makes it a hard case to prove to the rest of the world, in the long run the results can span across several countries that adopt the EU promulgated model. Appropriate communication at an international level is necessary along with coordination that advances EU premises in network and information security and asserts that network and information security risks cannot be isolated and dealt with in one region or sector of industry only. It is important that the EU maintains a continuous dialogue, for instance, with the Organization for Economic Co-operation and Development (OECD), the G8, the World Intellectual Property Organization (WIPO), the World Trade Organization (WTO), and International Telecommunication Union (ITU). The immediate effect thereof is to avoid duplications in legislation and regulation and use synergies to reach world-wide an enhanced level of network and information security.

Soft law approach
Since traditional regulatory instruments, such as legislation, in some cases turn out not to be easily applicable or effective (in particular in the on-line environment), other modalities of regulations can be considered as possible alternatives [Send05]. Approaches such as co-regulation and self regulation might service well the set up of requirements for network and information security. Providing a legal mantel under a framework directive or a recommendation is an essential extension to give legal validity to some of those standards, especially the ones having the most far-reached consequences for the stakeholders. It is also important to maintain a view on building the regulatory requirements in the architecture of the security standard at hand, an approach that has the obvious benefit of cutting down on compliance tests and reaffirming trust [Lessi06].

Subsidiarity
Article 5 of the Treaty establishing the European Community states that "In areas which do not fall within its exclusive competence, the Community shall take action, in accordance with the principle of

subsidiarity, only if and in so far as the objectives of the proposed action cannot be sufficiently achieved by the Member States and can therefore, by reason of the scale or effects of the proposed action, be better achieved by the Community. Any action by the Community shall not go beyond what is necessary to achieve the objectives of this Treaty". A protocol annexed to the Treaty of Amsterdam sets the conditions and application criteria of subsidiary and proportionality principles, such as for instance the obligation to justify any EU legislative proposal by providing its compliance with these principles.

Inevitably these principles apply also to EU legislation related to network and information security. For instance, the EU level boasts benefits such as consensus on services needed and the debate on the need to interoperate with each other. However much like in other areas of EU policy, when addressing policy requirements in public administration applications and systems it is critical to adhere to the prevailing principles of proportionality and subsidiarity. For example, in public administration applications and systems cross border cooperation observes the principle of regulation at a national level within a Member State and is coupled with action at EU level where necessary only.

While subsidiarity is a topical principle when regulating network and information security, the EU involvement in the regulation of this area has been longstanding as evidenced through the ENISA case, described above.

The right to network and information security
Information security as such is not a right in itself; there is no such thing as a right to information security. There are, nevertheless, fundamental rights that can be enforced or granted, especially so in the cyber-world, only if network and information security is accepted and enforced. Dworkin argues that instruments that allow citizens exercise and enjoy other basic rights and freedoms, should be encouraged and afforded protection in a meaningful way [Dwor77]. Network and information security is such an instrument as there seems to be an indirect right to network and information security that can be detected through provisions in legislation, such as the Directive on data protection (e.g. art 18 of 95/46/EC) or the emerging rules regarding corporate governance.

Moreover, it appears of interest to consider this principle also from the analogy of security in physical world which is deemed to be of a paramount issue and it is considered to be a fundamental obligation of the state. Public and private sector invest resources and efforts in security in the real world. Legislations and regularity measures are adopted to enforce physical security. Legislators, regulators and policy makers should apply the "what holds on-line should be also hold on-line" approach. This approach is mentioned, for instance, in the Recommendation 22 of the EU Ministerial Conference in Bonn on 7-9 July 1997 and it has been reflected in the G8 Okinawa Charter on Global Information Society, 23 July 2000 as well as in several other national and supranational legislation and soft law. Subsequently enforcing network and information security legislation and regulation should aim at protecting valuable assets and providing them with the same protection they would enjoy in the physical world. In the meantime, a new initiative "should be based on an actual need rather than purely on theoretical considerations" [KLP+06]. Moreover, legislators and regulators should avoid – wherever possible and appropriate – creating situations where parallel legal framework are created to enforce off-line and on-line security.

A final consideration with regard to a "right to information security" should take into account the varying requirements of citizens, organizations, government entities that are all discreet stakeholders in the network and information security sphere. While the market and provision of security services is largely controlled by the private sector legislation could reserve for itself a mere complementary role allowing space to self regulatory frameworks.

Interoperability

Interoperability has been singled out as an essential area of EU competence in order to iron out differences in the prevailing approaches among solutions presented by individual Member States. As discussed, for instance, in ETSI White Paper on "Achieving Technical Interoperability" [ETSI06], there are different levels of interoperability:

- Technical interoperability, which refers to the ability of hardware or software components, systems and platforms that enable the machine-to-machine communication
- Syntactical interoperability which is related to the data formats
- Semantic interoperability, generally associated with the meaning of the content of the communication
- Organizational interoperability, that is the "ability of the organizations to effectively communicate and transfer (meaningful) data (information) even though they may be using different information systems over a widely different infrastructures [...]

Interoperability is a critical requirement for transactions B2B (business to business), B2G (business to government) as well as cross border G2G (government to government) transaction. The figure below represents the various levels of interoperability [ETSI06].

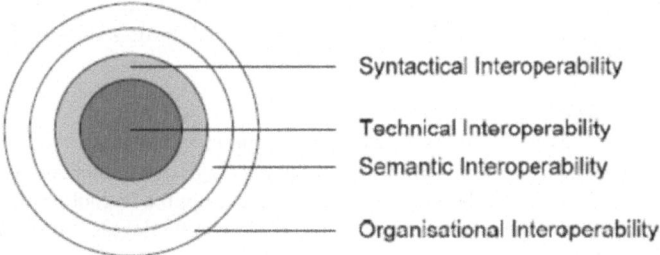

Figure 4: Various levels of interoperability

In shaping legislation, interoperability at all levels is a principle to consider. Furthermore, co-regulation that is promulgated through technical standards or other soft-law instruments as discussed above (see figure 1) can further enhance interoperability as it gives the stakeholders the ability to directly influence the outcome of the outcome of the co-regulatory process.

Technical standards

Co-regulation and the promulgation of technical standards have largely been tantamount to the method of choice for the regulation of various aspects of technology in the EU. The regulation of electronic signatures in the EU for example has been based on a co-regulation approach that encourages the cooperation between the legislator and industry in order to ensure an optimal level of technical standards, while allowing for space in order to take into account the requirements of the market actors when setting out a regulatory framework. This approach could possibly inspire the approach in the areas where regulation might be necessary. The role of technical standards has been sufficiently discussed in this paper already especially in view of the need to inject requirements of the social context in the regulatory process. Technical standards can be relied to address technical and organisational matters, but they should be avoided for matters regarding the regulation of rights, obligations or liability of stakeholders.

IPR protection

An important area where information and network security plays an important role is intellectual property rights (IPR). Computers are often used to store and distribute intellectual property protected material. To use material protected by IPR, the user must obtain permission from the IPR owner, such as licenses. Licenses generally are used to regulate duplication, distribution and modification of IPR protected material. Information and network security helps protecting the use of IPR protected material and ensuring that this material is used in conformity to the relevant licenses [Mats02]. Therefore, the policy to develop copyright and equivalent laws should support the development of security solutions for network and information security in a way that it does not pose excessive constraints on accessing knowledge [Lessi04].

Technology neutrality

The principle of technology neutrality refers to the fact that legislation is shaped in such a way that operators of networks, for instance, are subject to the same rules and obligations regardless of what platform and applications these operators use. This principle is mentioned in several national, supranational and international e-policy documents. For instance, the Ministerial Conference held in Bonn on 6-7 July 1997, declared: "Ministers stress that the general legal framework should be applied on-line as they are off-line. In view of the speed at which new technology are developing, they will strive to frame regulations which are technology-neutral, while bear in mind the need to avoid unnecessary regulation". The European Commission Green Paper on Consumer Protection refers to a "comprehensive, technology neutral, EU framework directive to harmonize national fairness rules for business-consumer commercial practices".

Application-centric regulation for security

If the principle of technology neutrality is a general principle inspiring legislation, there are some exceptions to this principle. In network and information security legislation, there are indeed some developments in the opposite direction: in NIS an application-centric approach could delivered better results and has managed to address the concerns applying to specific technologies. There are applications of specific legislative interest due to the enhanced interest they pose to the society or to the public order. Examples include digital tachographs that are which are electronic devices recording in a trustworthy way a vehicle's speed and the working hours of the driver, or and fishery management whereby a security system is used to report in a trustworthy manner the catch of the day [MHPG07]. In such instances the specific security requirements of the application area merit special attention due to the particular interest they pose. Additionally legislation creates a relatively isolated environment in which the technical solution is developed. Therefore the confidentiality, integrity and availability requirements of such application areas should rather be studied in a stand alone mode rather than fit in a generic approach provided by generalized security methodologies and standards. An application centric approach in tackling regulatory network and information security issues can produce meaningful results for the stakeholders. The obvious delta to cover up the gap between generic models and application specific requirements is an area that merits further examination.

8 Conclusions

Developments in information and communication technologies that have been dubbed as a revolution have challenged the way that regulation is promulgated and applied. Reflecting on regulatory principles in an area of law such as network and information security should ideally be done in the beginning of the line. After almost 20 years of regulatory production and more that 25 of standardisation this process bears fruit to the extent that it leads to coordinated regulation that addresses risks in a meaningful way. Revisiting the way that network and information security regulation is promulgated is a necessity as it has become apparent that inherent shortcomings of technology cannot be necessarily addressed through regulation. Additionally the end user maintains an exposure to risk levels that sometimes could be a reason of concern. Launching a discussion on regulatory principles takes into account the need for a soft law approach that has been typical in the regulation of information security matters this far. Regulation includes both law and self regulatory instruments such as contracts and standards. A set of principles regarding the content of regulation provide the main directions for future legislation. Bringing these two together and matching instruments to principles and areas of interest is a discussion that has yet to be taken up.

References

[Aust1832] Austin, John: The province of jurisprudence determined, London, 1832.

[Boas61]   Boas, George: Rationalism in Greek philosophy, The John Hopkins Press, Baltimore, 1961, p. 162-163.

[Boss00]   Boss, Amelia: Searching for Security in the Law of Electronic Commerce, Nova Law Review, Vol. 23, 2000.

[Buel06]   Alfred Buellesbach: Chapter IV, Transfer of personal data to third countries. In Alfred Buellesbach, Yves Poullet, Corien Prins, Concise European IT Law, Kluwer Law International, 2006, p.102-108.

[Cast04]   Castells, Manuel: The Rise of the Network Society, Blackwell, UK, 2004, p. 28ss.

[COM94]   Recommendations to the European Council Europe and the global information society, European Commission, Brussels 1994.

[COM02]   Communication from the Commission to the Council, the European Parliament, the Economic and Social Committee and the Committee of the Regions – eEurope 2005: An information society for all An Action Plan to be presented in view of the Sevilla European Council, 21/22 June 2002, COM(2002) 263 final, Brussels, 2002.

[Dwor77]   Dworkin, Ronald: Taking rights seriously, Duckworth, London, 1977, p. 17, 22, 72.

[ETSI06]   ETSI (European Telecommunications Standards Institute): White Paper on "Achieving Technical Interoperability", Sophia-Antipolis, October 2006, p. 6.

[FoBa01]   Ford, W., Baum, M.: Secure Electronic Commerce, (2nd edition) Prentice-Hall, 2001.

[Hart61]   Hart, H.L.A.: The concept of Law, Clarendon Press, Oxford, 1961.

[Hix99]   Hix, Simon: The political system of the European Union, Palgrave, London, 1999.

[KLP+06]   Koops, B -J., Lips, M., Prins, C., Schellekens, M. et al.: Starting Points for ICT Regulation, Information Technology and Law Series, The Hague 2006, p. 7, 44, 48, 49ss.

[Lessi04] Lessig, Lawrence: Free Culture, Penguin, NY, 2004.

[Lessi06] Lawrence Lessig: Code, Basic Books, NY, 2006, p. 61.

[Levitt06] Levitt, Steven D.: An economist sells bagels: A case study on profit maximisation, National bureau of economic research working paper, Cambridge, MA, 2006.

[Luhm95]   Luhman, Niklas: Social systems, Stanford University Press, Stanford, CA, 1995.

[Mats02]   Matsuura, J.H.: Security, rights, and liabilities in e-commerce, Artech House, US, (2002), p. 3ss.

[MHPG07] Mitrakas, Andreas, Hengenveld, Pim, Polemi, Despina, Gamper, Johann: Towards secure eGovernment, in Mitrakas, Andreas Pim Hengenveld, Despina Polemi, Johann Gamper, Secure eGovernment web services, IGI Publishing, Hershey, 2007.

[Mitr06] Mitrakas, Andreas: Article 9 [Committee]. In Alfred Buellesbach, Yves Poullet, Corien Prins, Concise European IT Law, Kluwer Law International, 2006, p. 387-389.

[Mitr07] Mitrakas, Andreas: Annex II, Overview of Current Legal and Policy issues, in Christos Douligeris, Dimitris Seripanos (eds.), Network Security: Current status and future directions, John Wiley & Sons (IEEE Publication), Hoboken, NJ, 2007, p 481-506.

[Mitn80] Mitnick, B.M.: The political economy of regulation: creating, designing and removing regulatory forms, Columbia University Press, NY, 1980.

[Pfle00] Pfleeger, C.: Security in Computing, Prentice Hall, 2000.

[Poli89] Mitchell Polinsky, A.: An introduction to law and economics, (2nd edition), Little, Brown & Co., Boston, 1989, pp. 11-14.

[RANIS06] WG-RANIS: Inventory and assessment of EU regulatory activity on network and information security, (NIS), ENISA Working Group Report, 2006.

[Send04] Senden, Linda: Soft law in the European Community Law, Hart Publishing, Oxford, 2004.

[Send05] Senden, Linda: Soft law, self regulation and co-regulation in European Law: Where do they meet? In Electronic Journal of Comparative Law, Vol., 9.1, January 2005, www.ejcl.org

[Ters06] Terstegge, Jeroen: Article 17 [Security of processing]. In Alfred Buellesbach, Yves Poullet, Corien Prins, Concise European IT Law, Kluwer Law International, 2006, p. 76-79.

[Weil91] Weiler, J.H.H.: The Transformation of Europe, 100 Yale law journal 2403 1991, p. 2461.

[Will05] Williamson, Oliver E.: Transaction Cost Economics and Business Administration, Scandinavian Journal of Management, 21 (1), March 2005, p. 19-40.

ISTPA Operational Analysis of International Privacy Requirements

John T. Sabo

1401 Eye Street NW, Suite 1220, Washington DC 20005 USA
Director, Global Government Relations, CA, Inc.
President, International Security Trust and Privacy Alliance
john.t.sabo@ca.com

Abstract

The ISTPA Privacy Framework is an open, policy-configurable model consisting of 10 integrated privacy services, designed to facilitate an operational template for architecting and implementing privacy management solutions. Given the major changes in information privacy since the publication of the Framework in 2002, and because language and context differ across international privacy laws and directives, ISTPA initiated the *Analysis of Privacy Principles: Making Privacy Operational* as a structured review of a set of major privacy instruments to ensure that the ISTPA Framework Services can be used to support any set of common privacy "requirements."

Using direct references extracted from each source law or directive, mapped against basic privacy principles, the *Analysis* compares and correlates the language in each instrument associated with these basic principles and identifies in nine instances where a particular principle is composed of additional, definable components. For example, Notice, based on the requirements expressed in the referenced instruments, is more accurately understood as a set of five related but discrete requirements. As a consequence of this analysis and findings, the study provides a set of composite, operational definitions for each principle. These operational definitions include the sub-components identified in the study. The *Analysis* also identified three additional privacy requirements expressed across these international privacy instruments: anonymity, data flow, and data sensitivity.

In summary, the *Analysis* is a practical first step in framing the huge variations in language and the differing placement of many principles/practices in international privacy law, regulations and directives. It enables ISTPA to test the ISTPA Privacy Framework's completeness and to identify areas for possible revision based on the inherent complexity of data protection laws and directives as well as the evolution of privacy requirements and expectations since the Framework's first publication in 2002. The *Analysis* will also be of use by external audiences: privacy officers, those persons responsible for creating privacy policies and controls in organizations, and standards bodies having an interest in privacy.

1 Introduction and Background

1.1 The ISTPA Privacy Framework

Since its formation in 1999, the International Security Trust and Privacy Alliance (ISTPA) has examined data privacy from an implementation and operational perspective. That is, are there components of data privacy that can be understood and defined in such a way that IT-supported business processes and systems can more easily and effectively deliver policy-driven privacy management and compliance? Can differing privacy policies be more easily integrated into business systems and networks? Can technical "services" be invoked to make this possible? Much effort went into answering these questions, result-

N. Pohlmann, H. Reimer, W. Schneider (Editors): Securing Electronic Business Processes, Vieweg (2007), 18-25

ing in publication of the *ISTPA Privacy Framework*, v.1.1 in 2002. The document is available at www. istpa.org.

Leading to development of the Framework, we discovered that confusion often exists for information technology professionals confronted with demands to build privacy-compliant systems, and that particular misunderstanding about what constitutes information privacy is often evident in the IT security discipline. For example, in the past several years, privacy often has been associated with data confidentiality, and the public policy debate, laws (and attention from vendors and system engineers) is devoted to addressing that particular issue. Little attention is devoted to the breath of privacy principles and issues. This phenomenon is very apparent when we look at the attention paid to data breaches today in the United States and globally. Data breaches are serious matters; but data confidentiality alone is not privacy.

ISTPA understands privacy holistically and in the context of the lifecycle of personal information. In its initial examination of data privacy leading to development of the *ISTPA Privacy Framework*, ISTPA members reviewed existing laws and directives, interviewed international data protection commissioners and privacy practitioners, and attempted to identify basic privacy principles to inform its work. From this review, ISTPA members selected a representative set of privacy principles to guide analysis of data privacy and contribute to development of the Framework structure. We determined that data privacy means that personal information must be handled in accordance with the following principles:

- **Accountability** – the ability to audit the handling of personal information to ensure compliance
- **Collection limitations** – limiting the types of information collected
- **Disclosure** – informing the subject when personal information is collected
- **Participation** – allowing subject choice over collection and distribution
- **Relevance** – collecting only personal information pertinent to the application
- **Security** – protecting personal information from unauthorized access, alteration or destruction
- **Use limitations** – limiting the subsequent use of collected information, and
- **Verification** – checking the validity of personal information.

ISTPA also examined "privacy practices," which were more operational expressions of these principles. We selected notice and awareness, choice and consent, access (by the subject of the personal information), information quality and integrity, update and correction, and enforcement and recourse as key practices. We also included security in our assessment, but determined that a very rich body of security standards, practices and technical frameworks already existed and could be applied to data privacy requirements. Consequently we chose not to specifically incorporate security components – data confidentiality, integrity and availability – in the first version of the ISTPA Privacy Framework.

Generally, we found that the fair information practices could be used as a guide in implementing the privacy principles, since the practices are more operational in nature. However, even the practices we reviewed were missing essential elements to support a technical, programmatic implementation. Missing elements included such functions as agency, interfaces, policy control, and repository. To address this disconnect between "practices" and functional, technical implementation, we developed the ISTPA Privacy Framework. In our view, a framework of services provided a more complete template for an implementation of the practices and principles by incorporating the missing functionality. At a more granular level, we believed that our framework would support the development of mechanisms and technologies needed to enable privacy functionality, and that standards could ultimately emerge.

As noted on page 3 of the Framework document:

- [T]he ISTPA Framework Working Group has evolved the following list of privacy services and capabilities, based on the requirement to support the privacy principles and practices described above, but at a functional level. A system and process design person should be able to integrate these privacy services/capabilities into a functional architecture, with specific mechanisms selected to implement these functions. In fact, the purpose of the ISTPA Privacy Framework is to stimulate design and analysis of the specific functions, both manual and automatic, that are needed to implement the complete set of privacy fair information practices. In that sense, the ISTPA Privacy Framework is an analytic framework.

- To create a usable framework, various system capabilities must be identified that are not explicit at the privacy practices and principles level. For example, a policy management (or control) function is essential to honor the [personal information] usage constraints established by the subject, but such a function is not explicitly called out in the privacy principles. ... Such inferred services are necessary if information systems are to be made "privacy aware." Without them, enforcing privacy requirements in a fully automated environment will not be possible, and both businesses and consumers will be burdened with inefficient and error-prone manual processing.

1.1   ISTPA Framework Services

The ISTPA Privacy Framework v. 1.1 incorporates the following services:

- **Agent:** A software process acting on behalf of a data subject or a requestor (as a persona) to engage with one or more of the other Services defined in this Framework. Agent also refers to the human data subject in the case of a manual process.

- **Interaction:** presentation of proposed agreements from a data collection entity to a data subject; input of the subject's personal information, preferences, and actions; and confirmation of actions. To the extent the data subject is represented by an Agent, this service comprises the interface to the Agent. Generally, Interaction covers all exchanges from the Framework to outside environments.

- **Control:** the role of "repository gatekeeper" to ensure that access to personal information stored by a data collection entity complies with the terms and policies of an agreement and any applicable regulations. Control faithfully enforces privacy policy.

- **Validation:** checks for correctness of personal information at any point in its life cycle.

- **Negotiation:** arbitration of a proposal between a data collection entity and a data subject. Successful negotiation results in an agreement. Negotiation can be handled by humans, by agents, or by any such combination.

- **Usage:** the role of "processing monitor" to ensure that active use of personal information outside of the Control Service complies with the terms and policies of an agreement and any applicable regulations. Such uses further include derivation, aggregation, anonymization, linking, and inference of data.

- **Audit:** the recording and maintenance of events in any Service to capture the data necessary to ensure compliance with the terms and policies of an agreement and any applicable regulations.

- **Certification:** validation of the credentials of any party involved in processing of a personal information transaction.

- **Enforcement:** redress when a data collection entity is not in conformance with the terms and policies of an agreement and any applicable regulations.

Although this set of services is abstract and does not in all cases use the same terminology as that of specific privacy principles and practices, the ISTPA believes that it essentially captured the functionality needed to manage and enforce any set of privacy policies and practices in accordance with internal laws, regulations and policies. We understood the Framework as "policy-configurable," and theoretically it would provide implementers with a basis for interoperable systems and, once standards and mechanisms were available, would allow for management of multiple policy rules.

1.2   Drivers for Framework Analysis and Revision

Given its positive reception in 2002, the ISTPA Privacy Framework was submitted in 2003 as a candidate ISO Publicly Available Specification (PAS) (ISO/IEC (PAS) DIS 20886) by the International System Security Engineering Association (ISSEA – see www.issea.org), an ISTPA member organization. However, the submission raised a number of questions in the international privacy community. At the 26th International Conference of Data Protection and Privacy Commissioners in 2004, convened in Wroclaw, Poland, the delegates formally requested that ISTPA/ISSEA withdraw the Framework from the ISO balloting process to work on certain issues that they considered important to the international data protection community, among them:

- development of a privacy technology standard that would support the implementation of legal rules on privacy and data protection where they exist and the formulation of such rules where they are still lacking, and
- development of an international privacy standard based on the fair information practices as well as the concepts of data scarcity, minimization and anonymity.

ISTPA recognized that the data protection commissioners raised valid questions, and ISSEA formally withdrew the Framework from consideration. ISTPA also understood that any operational privacy framework must support all core privacy principles and their functional implementation. Language and context differ across relevant legislation, directives, conventions and standards, and therefore ISTPA members decided that a structured review of major, representative international privacy instruments was necessary to ensure that the ISTPA Framework Services in fact support all core privacy requirements.

That understanding was the catalyst for our undertaking an in-depth study of international privacy laws and directives which was completed in May 2007 and published by ISTPA. The complete study, *Analysis of Privacy Principles: Making Privacy Operational* is available at http://www.istpa.org and all references below are from that document.

2 The Analysis of Privacy Principles

2.1 Overview

The *Analysis of Privacy Principles: Making Privacy Operational* provides an analysis of major, international information privacy laws, directives and regulations (which the study calls 'instruments' to ensure ease of reference in the document). Members of the ISTPA Framework Working Group reviewed the English version of these instruments, parsed their expressed requirements, developed a set of consistent privacy categories and then cross-mapped their essential requirements. Because the terminology and context differ among these instruments, a key purpose of this approach was to determine if the ISTPA Framework Services can support common "requirements" derived from these instruments.

For purposes of this study, we used the term "requirements" to characterize expressed components of privacy principles.

In our view, this analysis was necessary to test the ISTPA Privacy Framework's completeness and to identify areas for possible revision based on the evolution of privacy and data protection law and practice since the Framework's first publication in 2002, as well as address issues raised in the international data protection community.

2.2 Selected International Laws and Directives

As noted in the *Analysis,* more recent comprehensive data protection laws enacted in Europe, Canada, Japan, Australia and several other jurisdictions incorporate well-accepted principles and practices. Although the most common model is the EU Data Protection Directive (95/46/EC), 25 European Union countries and three additional EEA countries, nine other European countries or dependencies have enacted laws based on the EU Data Protection Directive. Eight other countries and the Hong Kong SAR have enacted comprehensive data protection laws in other regions of the world and there are similar laws (with somewhat narrower scope) in the Canadian provinces and territories and some of the Australian states.

It is important to note that the *Analysis* makes no attempt to select the "ideal" set of privacy requirements or to suggest that one legislative or policy approach to privacy has precedence over another. Those who control the collection, use or disclosure of personal data must make their own determination as to which laws, regulations and policies are applicable to their governmental and business operations. We have conducted what is essentially a descriptive and analytical exercise and have attempted to harmonize disparate language, definitions and expressed requirements in order to provide a common basis for a true operational privacy framework. To ensure that this work was manageable, we:

- selected a set of twelve internationally significant privacy instruments
- illustrated selected subsets of their stated requirements, recognizing that there are many more available for analysis and that in a few instances certain requirements might fit into more than one category
- verified that the more recent sets of information privacy principles are broadly similar to older ones, although we found a few requirements that only appear in newer regulations, such as specific types of data sensitivity
- limited our research to those documents published in English
- analyzed the requirements for commonalities and differences
- used the results of analysis to prepare findings usable for the ISTPA Privacy Framework revision and additional work.

The twelve instruments selected for detailed evaluation include, in chronological order:

- The Privacy Act of 1974 (U.S.)
- OECD Privacy Guidelines
- UN Guidelines Concerning Personalized Computer Files
- EU Data Protection Directive 95/46/EC
- Health Insurance Portability and Accountability Act (HIPAA) Privacy Regulations
- Canadian Standards Association Model Code (incorporated in the Personal Information Protection and Electronic Documents Act [PIPEDA])

- US FTC statement of Fair Information Practice Principles
- US-EU Safe Harbor Privacy Principles
- Australian Privacy Act – National Privacy Principles
- California Senate Bill SB 1386, "Security Breach Notification"
- Japan Personal Information Protection Act
- APEC (Asia-Pacific Economic Cooperation) Privacy Framework

2.3 Study Methodology and Key Findings

The study methodology includes the use of a working set of core privacy principles in order to facilitate cross-instrument mapping while also accommodating their many variations in the twelve instruments. These privacy principles are Accountability, Notice, Consent, Collection Limitation, Use Limitation, Disclosure, Access and Correction, Security/Safeguards, Data Quality, Enforcement, and Openness.

Using direct references extracted from each instrument, mapped against these terms in tabular format, the *Analysis* compares and correlates the language in each instrument associated with these key principles. This analysis provided a number of key findings, including two major findings associated with establishing operational privacy requirements relevant to our privacy Framework.

First, the study determined that three additional privacy requirements are often expressed across these international privacy instruments: anonymity, data flow, and data sensitivity. Anonymity is a state in which information or data are rendered anonymous so that the data subject is no longer identifiable. Data Flow is the communication of personal data across geo-political or policy jurisdictions by private or public entities involved in governmental, economic or social activities. Sensitivity is specified data or information, as defined by law, regulation or policy, which requires specific security controls or special processing.

Second, we determined that privacy principles, as expressed in international law, are in fact more complex than typically recognized, and have a number of clear sub-components. This finding is valuable, because it provides a more granular understanding of privacy principles for practitioners and will lead to a better assessment of the ISTPA Privacy Framework's comprehensiveness and illustrate areas where the Framework will require modification. In addition to integral principles (i.e., principles containing no sub-components) there are nine instances where the *Analysis* has determined that a principle has additional sub-components.

2.4 Illustration of Sub-Components

The following table illustrates a sample of two privacy principles, Notice and Consent, extracted from the *Analysis,* each of which incorporates specific sub-components. These sub-components will need to be managed in IT-enabled business process systems.

Notice	Notice of Collection	Notice must be provided to the Data Subject of the purpose for collecting personal information and the type of data collected
	Policy Notification	Data Subject must be notified of the applicable policies in terms of Consent, Access and Disclosure
	Changes in Policy or Data Use	Notice must be provided if and when any changes are made to the applicable privacy policies or in the event that the information collected is used for any reason other than the originally stated purpose
	Language	Notice must be provided in clear and conspicuous language
	Timing of Notification	Notification will be sent at the time of collection, before the time of collection or reasonably thereafter, by the time of collection and no later, or following a security breach
Consent	Sensitive Information	Data Subjects must be informed of, and explicitly consent to, the collection, use and disclosure of sensitive information (i.e. medical or health conditions, racial or ethnic origins, political views, religious or philosophical beliefs, trade union membership or information regarding sex life) unless a law or regulation specifically requires otherwise
	Informed Consent	The Data Subject must provide *informed* consent to the collection of personal information unless a law or regulation specifically requires otherwise
	Change of Use Consent	Consent must be acquired from the Data Subject to use personal information for purposes other than those originally stated at time of collection
	Consequences of Consent Denial	Data Subjects must be made aware of the consequences of denying consent

Other principles having sub-components include

- Collection Limitation (Limitation of Consent, and Fair and Lawful Means)
- Use Limitation (Acceptable Uses and Data Retention)
- Disclosure (Third Party Disclosure, Third Party Policy Requirements, and Disclosure for Legal and Health Reasons)
- Access and Correction (Access to Information, Proof of Identity, Provision of Data, Denial of Access, and Correcting Information)
- Security/Safeguards (Safeguards and Destruction of Data)
- Enforcement (Ensuring Compliance, Handling Complaints, and Sanctions)
- Openness (Public Policies and Establishing Existence of Personal Data)

2.5 Additional Findings and Observations

In addition to these two key findings, we believe that the *Analysis* also contributes to the privacy community a useful methodology for examining disparate privacy rules across many geographies and jurisdictions. This methodology can be used to develop more detailed findings related to the granularity of privacy requirements contained in other privacy laws and policy statements. We recognize that judgment is needed when analyzing legal statements and expressions of policy in many different privacy instruments. However, ISTPA did not intend to produce an exhaustive study, nor make claims that other interpretations are not possible. Rather it is our belief that unless privacy receives the kind of attention and technical analysis which is used for many other aspects of IT-enabled systems and business processes, privacy will not benefit from standardized approaches to management and compliance.

There are three other observations included in the study that reinforce the value of this approach.

First, the content of diverse privacy instruments and even specific language look more alike in progression over time; more recent legislation (excluding focused legislation such as California SB 1386) reflects expanded privacy expectations and tends to incorporate more requirements seen in prior legislation. More specialized requirements (such as identity anonymity) tend to appear in more recent legislation.

Second, legislation often tends to be expressed as disconnected requirements (e.g., practices), with no cohesive or overall "system design" focused on the life cycle of personal information. The personal information "life cycle" (collection, sharing, distribution, policy components) and ultimate destruction is typically not addressed in a uniform way.

Third, a useful comparison of the many imprecise concepts contained in privacy practices/principles depends on language interpretation. However, if the legislative instruments are 'abstracted' to a high level (as done within the restricted scope of the *Analysis*), we see clear commonality of requirements.

3 Conclusion and Next Steps for Using the Analysis

The *Analysis of Privacy Principles: Making Privacy Operational* offers an unusual and useful perspective on information privacy: the sub-components of privacy principles expressed as requirements. It uses those requirements as the basis for a set of operational definitions of value in to practitioners responsible for operational privacy management and privacy compliance systems. What are some "next steps" following publication of the *Analysis*? Clearly, as noted in the paper, ISTPA intends to use the *Analysis* findings to improve the v 1.1 Framework and develop version 2.0. A working group has been formed to start this process and the Framework functionality is being analyzed for completeness and support for the newly-articulated requirements.

More work is also needed to explore development of a common privacy vocabulary and taxonomy. We believe the identification of more granular requirements and operational definitions offered in the *Analysis* represent a solid step in this direction, but ultimately standardized operational systems will need more clarity in the meaning of privacy terms and structure to achieve improved policy support, especially where multiple laws and jurisdictions complicate privacy management and compliance.

We also believe that more work is needed to address the intersection of security and privacy in both policy and operational services. For example, many if not most privacy requirements, such as correcting personal information, informed consent, data minimization, and data accuracy will require security controls. Mapping security controls to all relevant privacy requirements will be an interesting challenge. The ISSEA is now leading an initiative to map security controls to the ISTPA Privacy Framework services.

The International Security Trust and Privacy Alliance extends a welcome to technologists interested in data privacy who wish to join us in these initiatives. We believe that the *ISTPA Privacy Framework* **v1.1** and *Analysis of Privacy Principle: Making Privacy Operational* are important contributions to the literature of privacy management and compliance, but we recognize that much work remains to be done, by many communities of interest.

For additional information, and to learn more about this study and ISTPA, please contact John Sabo at john.t.sabo@ca.com. Or visit the ISTPA Web site at www.istpa.org.

The Legal Conflict between Security and Privacy in Addressing Crime and Terrorism on the Internet

Murdoch Watney

University of Johannesburg
South Africa
mwatney@uj.ac.za

Abstract

Internet security aimed at addressing terrorism and crime is not only a technological issue, it invariably impacts on the legal system, such as the right to privacy. Many information security professionals focus on security and pay little or no regard to the privacy rights of the Internet user whereas the opposite can be said of privacy activists. Countries face the challenge of applying new approaches to the Internet in the prevention, detection and investigation of crime and terrorism and the prosecution of the perpetrator. Commission of crimes and terrorism as well as securing the Internet against terrorism and other crimes result in a conflict between security, a technical issue and privacy, a legal aspect. A perplexing question is whether an Internet user can expect online privacy and whether globalisation in respect of the use of the Internet and the approaches in combating crime and especially terrorism have not resulted in an online environment that is incompatible with privacy rights.

1 Introduction

Most governments introduced the Internet to their countries with unbridled enthusiasm without paying much regard to the effect the Internet would have on their legal system. Today the Internet confronts all countries on a global level – United States of America (USA), United Kingdom (UK), France, India, China, Poland and South Africa – with the same problems. They all have to fight the growth of child pornography websites, work together to dismantle terrorist networks, combat cybercrime such as organised crime and protect their cultural industries against piracy [Pain06]. Governments today realize the power of the Internet and although the enthusiasm for this medium may have been tempered, many governments realize that the advantages of the Internet outweigh the disadvantages.

Governments therefore seek solutions to effectively address the disadvantages associated with the Internet, such as the abuse of the Internet in the format of crime and now, the threat of terrorism. The evolution of laws regulating the Internet aimed at addressing crime and terrorism illustrate the problems governments face when deciding upon the form and feasibility of securing the Internet. Although the aim of the solutions are above reproach, namely the securing of the Internet for purposes of, initially crime prevention, detection, investigation and prosecution and lately, national security, the form of the solution in achieving this aim is open to debate. The solution a government has implemented to address crime and terrorism on the Internet, has resulted in many questions, such as: Is securing the Internet the same as policing the Internet? Would Internet state control by means of state surveillance and the use of surveillance methods such as interception, monitoring, data retention or data preservation and decryption provide the solution to terrorism and other crime or should governments even go further and apply ultra-state regulation in the form of censorship?

It is clear from the aforesaid that securing the Internet to combat terrorism and crime bring about many concerns such as the conflict between security and privacy, and in some instances, the right to freedom of expression. How do we reconcile the conflict between security and privacy? Should the conflict be an issue of concern? If affirmative, can we reconcile two such opposite concepts at all, since security falls within the ambit of information security technology and the right to privacy resort within the legal system?

Globally most legal systems recognise an individual's right to Internet privacy. Yet, statements abound that online privacy is nothing but an illusion that does not exist in an electronic medium such as the Internet [Dave06]. How much truth exists in such statements? Does privacy protection differ in an electronic medium such as the Internet compared to the physical world?

These issues are of special relevance since the terrorist attack on 11 September 2001 (referred to as 9/11) on the USA served as a catalyst for implementing state control of information in the format of surveillance technology in respect of the Internet [Lyon03]. The pressure to secure the Internet has not diminished since 9/11; if anything, it has intensified.

The control governments apply to information on the Internet impact on privacy and security. Monitoring and debating governmental control of the Internet by privacy groups, the Internet user, information security professionals and lawyers are fundamental in preventing abuse of governmental control and in upholding human rights such as the right to privacy. Many questions flow from state control of the Internet and the conduct of for example, ISPs in ensuring state control. Should search engines reveal user's search terms to a government in conducting research for the possible implementation of legislation or reveal information of an Internet user who criticised a government or filter search terms to comply with a country's laws and regulations, thereby negating the right to privacy and freedom of expression? [Flin06]

Now is the time to scrutinise the impact of Internet state control on the right to privacy as countries implement or are in the process of implementing legal and technical measures to exert control of information on the Internet in addressing security issues such as the abuse of the Internet for terrorism and serious crime.

2 A brief summary of the evolution of Internet laws in addressing crime and terrorism

2.1 Introduction

The tension between privacy and security (par. 3) can only be fully appreciated against the background of

- The origin of the Internet;
- The global impact and consequences of the USA's decision to commercialize the Internet; and
- The different phases of legal development that characterize the evolution of laws regulating the Internet in addressing crime and terrorism.

2.2 The origin of the Internet and the impact and consequences of the commercialization of the Internet

The Internet originates from the early 1960's in the USA as a result of a project referred to as ARPAN-ET. The United States Defence Department wanted to link its network, ARPANET to various radio and satellite networks to ensure that the United States defence communications system could withstand a nuclear strike [RuDa02].

The historic decision of the USA to commercialize the Internet in 1992 resulted in many unforeseen and far-reaching consequences, such as:

- It not only brought about a new medium, an electronic medium but it also introduced the information age. The electronic medium now co-exist with the physical medium but little, if any, attention was initially focused on the characteristics of the electronic medium or the effect the Internet would have on the legal system and specifically, human rights.
- The Internet was one of the factors that contributed to globalization [Lyon03]. For the purpose of this discussion it is important to define the meaning of the term 'globalization'. The term 'globalization' only gained widespread use in the 1990's and was brought about by improvement in transport and communication. It encompasses a world in which things are increasingly done at a distance and is characterised by the quick and easy, and in many instances, cheap transfer of technology, data, information and now terrorist networks. 9/11 was a product of globalization [Lyon03].
- It resulted in an unexpected prodigious growth of Internet-connected countries. Each Internet-connected country has its own sociological, economic, political and cultural perspective. As the Internet is a global communication and information medium, it can only be effectively regulated by means of harmonised laws. However, taking into account the different perspectives of the Internet-connected countries, it is not always so easy to reach consensus regarding the required global uniform laws to address crime and ultimately terrorism on the Internet (see par. 2.3 hereafter).

2.3 The phases of evolution of Internet legal regulation

The evolution of laws regulating the Internet in addressing crime and terrorism may be divided into 3 developmental phases, namely self-regulation, conduct regulation and extending conduct regulation to include control of information on the Internet.

Governments were initially not concerned with Internet legal regulation and the Internet was left to **self-regulation**. This can be seen as the first phase of the Internet evolution. Self-regulation soon proved unsuccessful in addressing crime as illustrated by the release in the USA in 1988 of the first worm, the Morris worm (named after its creator) [RuDa02]. It is interesting to note that this worm was released prior to the commercialization of the Internet when the Internet was used by a small trusted group of people, mostly from a military and educational environment. The release of the Morris worm by a member of this trusted group was therefore met with not only dismay but also with a growing realization that self-regulation is not effective in enforcing compliance of ethical conduct on the Internet.

As Internet usage increased, the exploitation of the Internet by means of online crimes increased. The Internet was not created with security as its main objective, but had been designed to be open with distributed control and mutual trust among users [Alex06]. The wake-up call for legal regulation came with the release of the 'I love you' virus in 2000 [HiCo02]. Although the Federal Bureau of Investigation

(FBI) and the Central Intelligence agency (CIA) traced the origin of the 'I love you' virus to the Philippines within 24 hours after its release, the conduct was not a crime in the Philippines at that stage and therefore the perpetrator could not be prosecuted or extradited to the USA to stand trial [Carr03]. This illustrates the effect of globalization on crime, namely that crime is increasingly committed outside a country's borders. Furthermore, even if a country which experiences the effect of the crime committed outside its borders, has legislation in place that criminalizes such conduct, such legislation is powerless if the perpetrator resides in a country which does not have the necessary legislation criminalizing such conduct. Cybercrime can therefore only be effectively addressed on the Internet if the various Internet-connected countries have harmonised legislation that will assist each other in the investigation and prosecution of crime.

Governments realised that they needed a solution in addressing crime on the Internet, or differently put, in securing the Internet. Western governments also acknowledged that there should be an international treaty, which outlines guidelines in addressing cybercrimes aimed at establishing harmonized legislation in the various Internet-connected countries. This would assist with the international combat and investigation of cybercrime. In 2001 the Council of Europe Convention on Cybercrime introduced the one and only treaty on cybercrime which was signed by all the Council of Europe member countries and four non-European member countries, namely Japan, Canada, USA and South Africa [Watn03].

Legal regulation of conduct on the Internet brought about the second phase in the evolution of legal regulation. This solution was however only partially successful. The effectiveness of conduct regulation was hindered by the application of the traditional law enforcement methods, tools and approach to crime within an electronic medium. Traditionally a re-active approach, in terms of which the crime is only investigated once it has been reported, has been applied. In some instances this approach fails to address the deterrence, prevention and investigation of crime on the Internet and/or prosecution of the perpetrator. This can be illustrated with reference to 'identity theft'. By the time that the commission of the crime has been detected, it is difficult to establish the identity of the perpetrator, since the evidence identifying the perpetrator are in many instances not available anymore. Information is vital in crime prevention and detection. Traditionally the police carry the responsibility of ensuring compliance and enforcement of laws. The Internet however, brings about challenges that necessitate the involvement of third parties, such as the Internet Service Provider (ISP). For example, Internet users may gain access to child pornography unless a statutory obligation is placed on the ISP to prevent access to child pornography. If the ISP does not have such a statutory obligation, then law enforcement becomes very difficult. Furthermore, countries make laws applicable within their borders but this does not address the challenge of the borderless nature of cybercrime. International harmonization of laws is therefore required to effectively and successfully address cybercrime.

Due to the problems experienced with the traditional law enforcement methods, tools and approach, governments were already prior to 9/11, looking for more effective enforcement of Internet laws. 9/11 served as a catalyst to move from conduct regulation to the next phase of Internet legal regulation, namely extending the laws regulating conduct to include **laws aimed at state control of information** available, accessed and distributed on the Internet.

The third phase, which is now in the early stages of development and refining, is characterized by governments facing the dilemma of deciding which form such Internet state control should take. The following forms of governmental control exist:
- No access to the Internet as practiced by countries such as Cuba; or
- Surveillance: most western countries such as the EU member countries, USA and South Africa apply or are in the process of applying surveillance technology and legislation regulating the use

of surveillance technology (bearing in mind that different surveillance methods may be used); or

- Censorship: practiced by countries such as China, Saudi Arabia and Singapore. These countries have adopted technological apparatus to monitor Internet messages, censor websites and prosecute those who speak out against government policies as undermining 'state security' [Pain06, Bowr05].

It is important to draw a distinction between state surveillance and censorship. Censorship is an ultra form of governmental control and includes surveillance of the Internet user as well as information available, distributed and accessed on the Internet such as monitoring content of websites. Contrary to state surveillance, censorship affects the free flow of information and access to information globally. Censorship not only affects the right to privacy but freedom of expression. The purpose for extensive censorship is in some instances wider than addressing crime and may have political motivation. Censorship is in general applicable to all information. Censorship in respect of specific information may in some instances be justifiable, for example in South Africa; the Internet Service Provider (ISP) must use filtering technology to prevent the distribution of child pornography [Watn06]. Whether the use of filtering technology is successful or not, is not under discussion here.

2.4 The 'driving force' behind the evolution of Internet legal regulation

As already indicated, the Internet was not designed as a central entity with a main governing authority, nor was it designed with security as its main focus (par 2.2). In a short time, the Internet became in many countries an integral part of society on different spheres, such as e-commerce, e-governance and socially. Unfortunately the increased Internet usage resulted also in the exploitation of the Internet in different formats and specifically for purposes of this discussion, crime and terrorism.

Internet-connected countries (specifically westernized countries) realize that addressing initially crime and now, terrorism, is of paramount importance to ensure the exploitation of the advantages of the Internet as well as the growth of trust and confidence in respect of the use of the Internet. Although no central entity is responsible for the drafting of legislation, various factors contribute to the development of legislation, such as international treaties, the influence of dominating 'powers', social and political circumstances.

Technology alone cannot address security concerns. Compliance and enforcement of technology can only be achieved by means of legislation. In some instances, crimes not known in the physical world were created by the implementation of the Internet (such as hacking, denial of service attacks) and such conduct is criminalized by means of legislation. Legislation also prevents abuse of technology by ensuring safeguards, which is especially important in respect of the third phase, Internet state control of information.

The Council of Europe (CoE) realized the importance of harmonised laws in respect of cybercrime and spearheaded the Treaty on Cybercrime (par 2.3). The Treaty on Cybercrime, although it provides for surveillance, is mainly aimed at conduct regulation of crime and embodies a re-active approach to crime detection. It was not drafted against the background of terrorism and was signed in November 2001, approximately 2 months after 9/11.

Governments soon realised that due to the deficiencies experienced with the traditional law enforcement tools, approach and methods, they could only address serious crime effectively if there was some form of control of information on the Internet. The gathering of information is the key in fighting crime and terrorism on the Internet [Lyon03].

The terrorist attack on the USA (9/11) served as motivation for the USA government to implement in 2001 the first Internet state control of information legislation in the form of surveillance, namely the USA Patriot Act. The USA Patriot Act brought about the third phase of Internet legal regulation. This act provides for surveillance methods such as interception, monitoring and data preservation. 'Data preservation' is applicable to the preservation of specific traffic data of an identified traffic user for a specific criminal investigation for a very limited period of time. Data preservation is an example of a re-active law enforcement approach.

EU members have also been subjected to terrorism and/or the threat of terrorism. On 15 March 2006, the European Union (EU) implemented the mandatory Data Retention Directive 2006/24/EC making it compulsory for the 27 EU member states to implement national legislation providing for European Internet Service Providers (ISPs) to retain the traffic data of all Internet users. The Data Retention Directive deviates from the proposed data preservation set out in the Convention on Cybercrime. This deviation is easily explained with reference to the time period when the Convention was passed, the traditional law enforcement deficiencies and bearing in mind that terrorism can only be prevented and/or detected by means of a pro-active approach, in other words the gathering and retention of information for a period of time, irrespective of whether a crime has been reported or detected. The Directive does not prescribe the serious crimes to which the traffic data directive is applicable and this allows EU members the freedom to prescribe the serious crimes in national legislation.

Although the westernized Internet-connected countries have used the threat of terrorism as key motivator for the implementation of surveillance on the Internet, surveillance applies to other serious crimes besides terrorism. Most countries favour the use of the surveillance method, data retention as opposed to data preservation. The USA is giving serious consideration to the use of data retention, especially in respect of the investigation of child pornography [McCu06; Morp06].

As already illustrated, the different forms of governmental control of information on the Internet and the purpose of securing the Internet bear testimony to the difficulty countries from different perspectives experience in reaching consensus. The only consensus reached by the different Internet-connected countries appears to relate to the necessity of the third developmental phase, namely control of information.

3 Privacy and security on the Internet

3.1 Introduction

Most countries recognize the right to privacy. From an international perspective the United Nations Universal Declaration of Human Rights of 1948 protects the right to privacy against arbitrary interference. The degree and extent of privacy protection however, depend on the government of a country (see par. 3.2 hereafter).

As indicated, western governments realize that the gathering of information is the key in fighting crime and terrorism [par 2.4]. Two types of information are affected by the gathering of information:

- Content information: communication that includes information concerning the substance, purport or meaning of that communications (as defined in section 1 of the South African Regulation of Communications and Provision of Communication-related Information Act 70 of 2002); and

- 'Traffic data' refers to the records of transactions kept by ISPs when a user engages in online activity [Nico03]. ISPs must retain the following traffic data (as outlined in the EU Mandatory Data Retention Directive 2006/24/EC):
  - To trace and identify the source of a communication;
  - To trace and identify the destination of a communication;
  - To identify the date, time and duration of a communication;
  - To identify the type of communication; and
  - To identify the communication device.

An Internet user will reveal above-given information when going online. This raises the question whether the Internet user has a right to privacy regarding this information?

Much has been written on the nature and meaning of the right to privacy [EdHo03]. Privacy is not an abstract term and has only meaning within the context of a national culture, a particular political system and a specific time [McCl76]. One of the earliest definitions of privacy in the USA referred to privacy as "the right to be let alone" (termed by Brandeis and Warren in 1890) [McCl76; Deig03; EdHo03]. Due to the commercialization of the Internet and the impact of the Internet on privacy, privacy extends wider than merely "the right to be let alone" and can be divided into categories [EdHo03].

Internet privacy may be divided into two components:

- Data (information) privacy means the control of an Internet user in respect of who has access to his/her personal information, when and how; no personal information may be processed without the permission of the affected Internet user. Personal information is any information that can identify a person.
- Communications privacy means protection against interference and/or intrusion regarding his/her communications such as websites visited, e-mails sent and received and use of search terms.

The right to privacy developed within a physical medium and subsequently it should be asked whether the privacy right applies to an electronic medium such as the Internet. If answered in the affirmative, the question arises how privacy is protected in an electronic medium taking into account that the Internet faces challenges unknown to that of the physical world, such as the fact that there are virtually no online activities or services that guarantee absolute privacy [EdHo03]. ISPs and websites may for example monitor online activities. The ISP can determine which search engine terms were used, which websites were visited and the dates, times and duration of online activity. The Internet user can ensure privacy by means of privacy-enhancing technology such as encryption, using anonymous re-mailers. As the Internet was not designed with security as a priority, these tools can also secure the communications of the Internet user.

If the Internet user does not utilise privacy-enhancing technology, does it imply forfeiture of the legal right to Internet privacy enjoyed in the physical world?

Ellison, the CEO of Oracle said in 2001 that Internet privacy is "largely an illusion". This was confirmed by McNeally, builder of Sun computers [Dawe06]. I cannot support these sentiments. The right to privacy is a legal right to which every Internet user is entitled, irrespective of the communication medium used and/or whether the user makes use of privacy-enhancing technology (some may say that this technology may also be used to hide criminal activities).

The third phase of Internet legal regulation, namely governmental control of information and more specifically the use of surveillance technology, affects both the Internet user's data and communications privacy. Differently put, the right to privacy protects the Internet user's right to freedom from processing of personal information without consent and/or the right to freedom against interference of communications without consent. However, this does not imply that the right to data and communications privacy is an absolute right that may never be restricted (see par. 3.2 and 3.3).

3.2 The European Union and United States of America's approach to Internet privacy and security

As indicated, governments differ in their approach to Internet privacy protection. Since the EU and the USA are identified as the two major 'western powers' regarding their influence on the development of laws, it is relevant to look at their approach. The EU and the USA approach the protection of the right to privacy very differently. The EU has general legislation in place that guarantees privacy protection against governmental and commercial intrusion, referred to as so-called 'hard' data protection laws as opposed to the 'soft' laws of the USA [EdHo03]. The view in the USA has been that the rights of the government should be limited (the Privacy Act of 1974 protects the personal information against govermental intrusion) but in respect of commercial entities, the emphasis has been on self-regulation with the implementation of sector specific legislation to deal with privacy violation (such as the Gramm-Leach-Bliley Act of 1999 that imposes privacy requirements on financial institutions) [EdHo03].

The **EU** protects the right to privacy in article 8 of the Council of Europe Convention of the Protection of Human Rights and Fundamental Freedoms of 1950. The right to privacy is not absolute, but may be restricted in terms of article 8 paragraph 2. Article 8 paragraph 2 states "there shall be no interference by a public authority with the exercise of this right except such as is

- in accordance with the law;
- necessary in a democratic society; and
- in the interests of national security, or public safety, or the economic well-being of the country, or for the prevention of disorder or crime, or for the protection of the rights and freedoms of others."

The European Union implemented two data (information) protection directives, namely a general directive, Directive 95/46/EC on the protection of individuals with regard to the processing of personal information and on the free flow of information and a specific directive, 2002/58/EC (the Directive on Privacy and Electronic Communications) in respect of processing of data specifically on an electronic medium such as the Internet. 'Processing' is defined in Directive 95/46/EC as the collection, recording, storage, retrieval, use, disclosure by transmission or making available, blocking or destruction. Both directives provide for obtaining consent before processing personal information of an Internet user.

Problems with the prevention, detection and investigation of crime and terrorism led in 2006 to the EU implementing a mandatory Data Retention Directive 2006/24/EC and thereby amending article 15 of Directive 2002/58/EC that provided for voluntary data retention. By 15 March 2009 all EU member states must have national legislation that provides for traffic data retention of all Internet users. The EU Data retention legislation represents pro-active policing. Traditionally laws in the physical world are re-active: a perpetrator is apprehended after a crime is committed. Pro-active legislation is pre-emptive with every citizen being a target for suspicion and observation. In other words, the crime is prevented before it is perpetrated or if a crime is committed, the evidence gained before the commission of the crime can be reconstructed.

Although data retention is a privacy-destroying tool, it serves as a security mechanism to protect all Internet users against crimes such as 'identity theft' and where committed, it assists in the investigation and possible prosecution of the criminals. The ultimate aim of the general retention of traffic data is to ensure harmonised European data retention laws that can assist in tracing the source of the communication, namely the perpetrator of a crime in across border investigations of serious crimes and terrorism [GoDu03]. From the perspective of the law enforcement authorities, erasing the 'electronic footprints' (traffic data) would have the same effect as wiping off the fingerprints at a crime scene in the physical world. It is for these reasons that the Internet user's privacy is restricted or 'curtailed' (not abolished). The law enforcement benefits derived from the surveillance method, data retention have not escaped criticism [GoDu03]. Some have perceived the retention of the electronic 'fingerprints' (traffic data) of Internet users as excessive as all Internet users are now treated as potential criminal suspects [ElBC06]. Doubts have been raised in respect of the effectiveness of data retention in addressing crime and national security abuse. Criminals may for example find back doors to keep communications free from state surveillance, such as the use of stenography and peer-to-peer systems. Personal information may include traffic data such as the IP number as it may reveal personal information and therefore, fall under the protection of the data protection directive [GoDu03]. It has also been said that in some instances retention of traffic data may be more privacy invasive than content data retention. Problematic may be the application of data protection rules to the traffic data warehouses, such as the security of data storage, usefulness of the data and the evidential value of retained traffic data [GoDu03].

Regarding the justifiability of traffic data retention as an exception to Internet privacy in terms of article 8 of paragraph 2 of the European Convention on Human Rights, Goemans and Dumortier [GoDu03] refer to case law of the European Court of Human Rights. The case law found traffic data retention not justifiable as an exception because it was not necessary, appropriate and proportionate. The authors state "…it seems quite doubtful that general regulations on mandatory retention of traffic data would succeed the challenge of the proportionality test taking into account the immense and undifferentiated scope of intrusion into the private lives of individuals, irrespective of whether or not they are under suspicion." One should bear in mind that the case law referred to, were all decided prior to 9/11 and other subsequent terrorist attacks in Europe. Furthermore, as stated earlier, the meaning of 'privacy' is not static but must reflect the circumstances at a specific time period (par.3.1). It is quite probable that in future an EU member's national court as well as the European Court of Human Rights may debate a constitutional challenge to the justifiability of traffic data retention as an exception to Internet privacy. The outcome of such a challenge is not so obvious (see par 3.3). The court will have to balance the security benefits derived from Internet state control of information against the infringement of data and communications privacy and determine which one outweighs the other and whether the infringement of Internet privacy for national security and law enforcement purposes qualify as an exception to Internet privacy in terms of article 8 paragraph 2 of the European Convention on Human Rights.

Contrary to the EU where the right to privacy is a fundamental right protected in the European Convention on Human Rights, the Constitution of the **USA** does not explicitly mention a right to privacy [McCl76, HiCo02; Agra02]. The USA Supreme Court has stated that the Constitution implies a right to privacy in certain circumstances [ElBC06; Agra02]. Privacy rights have developed as a mixture of state common law, federal and state legislation and constitutional law [Agra02]. There have been calls for general Internet privacy legislation in the USA as a means of addressing for example the escalating problem of 'identity theft' [Schu05].

Since the Internet itself is not a privacy protecting medium, the best approach to privacy protection would be comprehensive Internet privacy legislation as implemented by the EU [EdHo03].

3.3 Effect of Internet state control of information on Internet privacy and security

At what price do we secure the Internet? Control of the Internet affects the core elements of western democracies, namely the right to privacy and freedom of expression [GoDu03]. The degree and extent of privacy infringement depends on the form of government control, namely surveillance or censorship (includes surveillance), the surveillance methods employed and the purpose for Internet state control of information.

It should be borne in mind that it is not only governmental control but also the threat of online crime and terrorism that affects the Internet user's right to privacy. The Internet user wants – in some instances – demands, governments to protect them against crime and terrorism. The question is how far may government protection of the Internet go before it becomes an unjustifiable invasion of Internet user's privacy?

The challenges of the Internet in the combating, investigation of crime and terrorism and prosecution of the perpetrator necessitate new law enforcement and national security approaches. Reliance on technology alone will not protect the Internet user's human rights effectively. Legislation safeguards Internet users against governments moving towards a police state or applying surveillance technology excessively without any justification.

The ideal is to balance national security and law enforcement needs with Internet privacy [Lyon03; HiCo02]. However, in a world changing due to globalisation and defined by the Internet, the continuous threat of terrorism and the abuse of the Internet for the commission of serious crimes, it appears that the erosion of Internet privacy is the price we pay for Internet security.

4 Conclusion

New approaches must be applied to effectively address crime and terrorism on the Internet. Laws that were effective in the physical world must adjust to provide for the characteristics of the Internet, such as pro-active policing. The western world has always jealously guarded the protection of human rights, yet new technological and political developments often challenge the human rights culture.

The exploitation of the Internet for the commission of serious crimes and terrorism challenges countries to find ways of controlling cyberspace, whilst at the same time encouraging the continuous growth of the Internet, stimulating technological innovation and enjoying the benefits brought by the Internet.

> *"Our interconnectivity through the Internet enables cost effective data transmission to almost any point on the planet. When the data facilitates lawful commerce or promote human rights the enchanting magic validates the technology. When the data facilitates murder and mayhem or governmental oppression, the baneful condemns the technology. A complete free society – if it is to survive –requires citizens who exercise self-restraint and who are willing to accept the consequences of failures of that self-restraint. At some threshold of failures, however, citizens demand of their government protection from each other. At some point, such protection curtails the freedom of citizens and the citizens find themselves in a police state. Thus the pendulum swings between anarchy and totalitarianism, between unbridled freedom and censorship, between anonymity (i.e. no accountability and Big Brother (i.e., no privacy). To achieve the balance of costs and benefits, we must first understand the problems we hope to solve"* [Poor02].

Internet policies for effective crime prevention and individual privacy are in conflict. The phases of the evolution of Internet legal regulation illustrate the tension between security and privacy: initially at the first phase, self-regulation, too little emphasis was placed on security. As self-regulation involved into conduct regulation and now state control of information, the emphasis increasingly moved to security resulting in the erosion of Internet privacy.

Internet state control requires debate on the justifiability of Internet state control in securing the Internet against serious crimes and terrorism, the forms employed and the consequence of the forms employed to enforce Internet state control.

We are at a crossroad in respect of securing the Internet. Obviously the ideal is to achieve a balance between the cost (privacy violation) and the benefit (Internet security). This balance can only be achieved once we fully appreciate the problems that must be addressed. If we conclude that the solution lies with Internet state control of information, the challenge of implementation still remains.

Edwards and Howells state "what the Internet gives with one hand it often takes away with the other" [EdHo03]. The Internet user has a right to Internet privacy and this right is best protected by comprehensive Internet privacy legislation, similar to that of the EU Directives. In respect of commercial transactions and governmental intrusion on the Internet, the privacy rights of the Internet user is protected, bearing in mind that the EU and USA have different approaches to the protection of Internet privacy.

Due to the continuous threat of crime and terrorism on the Internet, governments have implemented or are in the process of implementing Internet state control of information legislation to secure the Internet. This legislation impacts negatively on privacy protection and erodes privacy. It is difficult to achieve a balance between security and privacy infringement. Legislation must therefore ensure checks and balances to prevent privacy violation without justification and/or excessive privacy infringement. The privacy erosion is the price we pay for securing the Internet. The Internet user must decide whether the privacy erosion is a too steep prize to pay for Internet security. Obviously governments don't think so.

References

[Agra02]   Agranoff, Michael: E-mail: Balancing Corporate Assets and Employee Privacy; The Privacy Papers: Policies for Secure Personal Data. In: R. Herold: The Privacy Papers Managing Technology, Consumer, Employee, and Legislative Actions. CRC Press LLC, USA, 2002, p. 5 and 41 – 42.

[Bowr05]   Bowrey, Kathy: Law and Internet Culture. Cambridge University Press, 2005, p. 8 – 9, 194 – 197.

[Dave06]   Daves, Nic: A right to privacy? Get over it. In: http://www.mg.co.za/printPage.aspx?area=/insight/insight_comment_and_analysis/&art... (May 23, 2006).

[Carr03]   Carr, Indira: Anonymity, the Internet and Criminal Law Issues. In: C. Nicoll, JEJ Prins and van Dellen, MJM: TMC Asser Press, The Hague, 2003, p.188.

[Deig03]   Deighton, John: Market Solutions to Privacy Problems? In: C. Nicoll, JEJ Prins and van Dellen, MJM: TMC Asser Press, The Hague, 2003, p. 137, 140.

[EdHo03]   Edwards Lilian and Howells, Geraint: Digital Anonymity and the Law. In: C. Nicoll, JEJ Prins and van Dellen, MJM: TMC Asser Press, The Hague, 2003, p. 208- 209, 214, 216 – 217, 228 – 239, 245.

[ElBC06]   Eleftheriou, Demetrios; Berliri, Marco and Coraggio, Giulio: Data Protection and E-Commerce in the United States and the European Union. In: The International Lawyer, Vol 40, No 2, 2006, p. 398 – 400.

[Flin06]   Flint, David: Don't be Evil. In: Business Law Review, April 2006, p. 102 – 104.

[GoDu03]   Goemans, Caroline and Dumortier, Jos: Enforcement Issues – Mandatory Retention of Traffic Data in the EU: Possible Impact on Privacy and On-line Anonymity. In: Nicoll, C; Prins J.E.J. and van Dellen,

M.J.M: Digital Anonymity and the Law. TMC Asser Press, The Hague, 2003, p. 161, 164, 167 – 169, 172 – 183.

[HiCo02]   Hiller, Janine and Cohen, Ronnie: Internet Law and Policy. Pearson Education, Inc., New Jersey, 2002, p.75 – 76, 95, 98 – 100, 169, 170 – 171.

[Lyon03]   Lyon, David: Surveillance after September 11. Polity Press, Cambridge, 2003, p. 15, 29, 89, 109 – 112.

[McCu06]   McCullagh, Declan: America debates data retention. In: http://insight.zdnet.co.uk/ ,39020415,39263973,00.htm. (April 18, 2006).

[McCl76]   McClellan, Grant S: The Right to Privacy. HW Wilson Company, New York, 1976, p. 3, 14, 25.

[Morp06]   Morphy, Erica: AG wants law compelling ISPs to hold customer Data. In: http://www.exommerce-times.com/story/53`42.html?u=crbuysc&p=ENNSS_0be3a1d63b9517... (30 September 2006).

[Nico03]   Nicoll, Chris: Digital Anonymity and the Law. In: C. Nicoll, J.E.J. Prins and M.J.M. van Dellen. TMC Asser Press, The Hague, 2003, p. 116 – 119.

[Pain06]   Pain, Julian: Let's not forget 10 September 2001. In: http://www.rsf.org/article.php3?id_article=10760 (June 12, 2006).

[Poor02]   Poore, Ralph, Spencer: Computer Forensics and Privacy: At what price do we police the Internet? In: R. Herold: The Privacy Papers Managing Technology, Consumer, Employee, and Legislative Actions. CRC Press LLC, USA, 2002, p. 33 – 34.

[RuDa02]   Rustad, Michael and Daftary, Cyrus: E-Business Legal Handbook. Aspen Publishers, Inc, New York, 2002, p. 5 – 6.

[Schu05]   Schulz, Eugene: Personal information comprises: It is time for the U.S. Government to wake up. In: Computers and Security, 2005, p. 261 – 262.

[Watn03]   Watney, Murdoch: Criminal and Procedural Aspects in the Prevention of Cyber Crime. In: Journal of South African Law. JUTA, South Africa, 2003, p. 56 – 74, 241 – 257.

[Watn06]   Watney, Murdoch: Regulation of Internet Pornography in South Africa. In: Journal of Contemporary Roman Dutch Law, Butterworths, South Aftica, 2006, p. 227 – 237, 381 – 395.

Data Encryption on File Servers

Janusz Gebusia

Hewlett-Packard, Consulting & Integration
Orteliuslaan 1000, 3528 BD Utrecht, The Netherlands
Janusz.Gebusia@HP.com

Abstract

A lot has been said about methods of protecting data stored on local computers. A very interesting question raised by many organizations is whether data stored on central file servers requires special protection. Does this data need encryption? What are the risks? What are the mitigation techniques? This paper tries to provide a brief answer to these questions. It also gives a few examples of different encryption solutions and technologies.

1 Introduction

Protecting data stored on local computers has become a high priority for many organisations. This is primarily due to the enormous popularity of notebook computers. Losing a notebook that holds sensitive information is a very realistic threat. Also unrestricted access to office desktop systems that are left unattended increases the risk of losing confidential data. A lot has been said about methods to mitigate these types of risks. There are dozens of products that can be used to protect data residing on local computer hard disk drives. Some of the solutions encrypt the whole device; others are used to protect particular files and folders.

A very interesting question raised by many organisations is whether data stored on central file servers should be protected. Does this data need encryption? What are the risks? What are the mitigation techniques? For several reasons central servers are generally regarded as being more secure than workstations. The central computers are usually placed in a relatively secure physical environment. Often these servers are hardened. Customers also pay a lot of attention to the access permissions that are set on the system files and folders. An intranet is usually well protected against access from the external world. The servers are usually placed in separated networks. So what is the business case of using encryption on central file servers? What kind of products can be used?

This goal of this paper is to provide a brief answer to these questions. It will also discuss the possibility of using Microsoft EFS and will give a few examples of different encryption solutions that can be used to protect data on central servers.

2 Why Encrypt Files on Central File Servers?

Most of the organisations focus on the physical and logical protection of their IT environment, and the confidentiality of data-in-transit and data-at-rest that are stored on local computers. Confidentiality of data stored centrally can be in many cases sufficiently guaranteed by using a correct set of access permissions on files and folders. All these countermeasures can significantly reduce the risks but still cannot completely eliminate vulnerabilities and threats such as:

N. Pohlmann, H. Reimer, W. Schneider (Editors): Securing Electronic Business Processes, Vieweg (2007), 38-48

- Theft or loss of the disks or the backup media;
- Access granted by mistakes to unauthorized users;
- Attacks against file servers and theft of information;
- Attacks against authentication services, such as Active Directory (AD) and taking control over accounts or groups that have access to a confidential data (elevation of privilege);
- Unauthorized access by malicious system administrators.

When the value of the data is very high (highly confidential information) then the risks are also proportionally very high. In such cases, organisations start looking for additional countermeasures to eliminate vulnerabilities or simply reduce threats.

The very interesting conclusion drawn from the many discussions I had with customers is that the threat of unauthorized access to confidential data by domain, system or storage administrators seems to be one of the most recurring issues. This is not astonishing if you remember that, for example, in a standard Windows environment without any additional countermeasures it is practically impossible to protect an object from being accessed by domain administrators. The administrator can always override permissions on objects by using the default right of taking ownership of all domain objects. He can also create Group Policy Objects that change user rights and apply them to different computers. The administrator can also change the membership of different groups. In summary, using these and many other methods the administrators can very quickly and relatively easily access confidential data which should be strictly restricted to some pockets of users.

Below there are some examples of organisations that intended to implement protection mechanisms for centrally stored data:

1. Police department
   Although all of the data stored on the police computers is regarded as sensitive, it is difficult to compare the confidentiality of information about speeding fines with information about organized crime, drug dealers or money laundering. The police departments that are responsible for these want to have the strict guarantee that their data is only accessible by authorized users. In such a scenario, the administrators of the IT environment can not be given access to the files. These departments require the data to be protected using strong encryption technologies.

2. Bank
   One of the biggest European banks outsourced one of their datacenters to HP. From their perspective HP was an external party. The bank wanted to protect confidential data about its customers from being accessed by HP staff. The bank decided to deploy a storage encryption solution.

3. Local Parliament
   HP was building a new IT environment based on Windows Server 2003 for a local Parliament. Although one AD structure for all the members of the Parliament and the staff was an attractive solution from the cost and efficiency perspective, a question was raised about how to protect data of one caucus from being accessed by members of another one. The customer was planning to apply an encryption technology to guarantee the confidentiality of the files stored in the datacenter.

When discussing with customers the methods of protecting sensitive data that reside on centrally controlled servers I could clearly identify the following basic common requirements:

- The data should be protected against non-authorized access.
- The data should be protected by a strong encryption solution.
- Application of a "four-eye principle" should be possible.

- Sharing the data among strictly controlled group of users must be possible.
- The applied solution should be as transparent as possible for the users.
- The administration of the solution should be relatively easy.
- The applied solution should be flexible and scalable.
- The impact of the solution on the overall systems performance should be acceptable.

3 Possible Solutions

Having in mind the requirements, we can now start to investigate the possible solutions. There are a number of available solutions that provide file encryption on different levels, using certificates or password-derived keys. However, there are some limitations to most of these solution approaches such as manual encryption and decryption on each use, leaks on the level of temporary and paging files, weak encryption algorithms, no data recovery, high price or high costs of key management.

This paper briefly describes a few examples of data encryption solutions, which do not have most of such disadvantages:

- Microsoft Encrypting File System (EFS);
- Decru DataFort;
- Utimaco SafeGuard LAN Crypt.

These three products provide file and folder level encryption.

The available data encryption solutions can be divided in two groups: software-based and hardware-based. The latter offer usually a very good performance but can be quite expensive. During our discussions with customers we also discovered that these hardware-based solutions were "psychologically" harder to accept for customers than software-based ones. Decru DataFort is an example of a hardware-based solution.

4 Microsoft Encrypting File System

Those of you who know the features and disadvantages of Microsoft Encrypting File System (EFS) may be surprised that I put the product on a list of possible file server encryption products. EFS is usually used to protect files on notebook PCs. Because of the fact that EFS is an out-of-the-box product that comes bundled with the Windows platform, EFS is often a very natural starting point for discussions about encryption solutions. A customer typically asks: "When I purchased my Windows system I implicitly purchased EFS too, so what can I do with the product? Can I use it for my purposes? What are the advantages and disadvantages?". In this paper I will briefly mention those features of EFS, which are particularly important for the purpose of encrypting files on the file servers.

4.1 EFS Principles

Encrypting File System is a standard out-of-the-box feature of Windows 2000, Windows Server 2003, Windows XP, and Windows Vista machines. EFS provides users with privacy, transparent operation, and the potential of data recovery. EFS is tightly integrated with the NTFS version 5 file system, which is the native file system of Windows 2000 and later operating systems.

4.1.1 EFS Certificates

EFS utilizes a public/private key pair that is universally unique to a specific user. EFS supports X.509 certificates. The certificates can be issued in two ways:

- By a Windows machine itself as a self-generated, self-signed certificate;
- By a Public Key Infrastructure (PKI) Certification Authority (CA).

If a PKI does not exist in an organization, EFS will use self-signed certificates. A server or workstation, that hosts the encrypted files for a particular user, will generate a self-signed certificate. As long as EFS is used for purposes of an individual user (no sharing), this solution is acceptable. Sharing encrypted files among multiple users on a single workstation is also possible and easy to manage. However, sharing encrypted files on centrally managed servers is a very difficult issue. The difficulties are caused by the way the self-signed certificates and corresponding private keys are generated and stored.

The recommended method of a certificate generation is to utilize a PKI. The most suitable PKI for the purposes of EFS is an infrastructure that is based on Windows Certification Authorities integrated with AD. The advantages are:

- Automatic enrolment of the EFS certificates;
- Automatic certificate publishing in Active Directory;
- Backup and restore of user private keys, which is important for file recovery purposes;
- The possibility to defining multiple Recovery Agents that can perform file recovery.

4.1.2 User Profiles

To be able to encrypt and decrypt, the user EFS certificate and the corresponding private key must be locally present on the machine that performs the EFS encryption and decryption operations. The certificate and key are stored in a local user profile. The roaming profile mechanism is used to distribute private keys among the computers (local workstations and remote file servers), where a particular user uses EFS. Although the roaming user profiles simplifies the process of private key distribution among all workstations and servers that are used for the EFS purposes, the concept has some significant disadvantages, which discourage many customers from using it. The profile size can grow to several or hundreds of Mbytes. This can have a significant impact on the required storage, user logon time, network bandwidth etc.

4.1.3 EFS File Sharing

In Windows XP and Windows Server 2003 Microsoft added support for EFS encrypted file sharing. As described above, this feature is required by customers that want to store and share their files on file servers. Although this functionality looks very attractive, it has some significant disadvantages. These are:

- Using groups on encrypted files is not supported
- Sharing on the folder level is not supported

The lack of support for groups is caused by the fact that EFS utilizes X.509 certificates. This standard supports only individual user certificates. Group certificates are not supported. As a result, a user who wants to share a file has to select each individual user certificate for each of the users that must have access to that file. Sharing of files among a few users is not a significant problem. However, sharing files between several or hundreds of users can become an administrative nightmare and is virtually impossible.

Support for sharing a folder with multiple users is also not provided. That means that a user cannot select a group of users to share a folder. He/she must set EFS file sharing separately on each individual file that resides in the folder.

4.2 General EFS Recommendations

Using EFS to encrypt files on remote servers in highly secure environments is a quite challenging option and definitely not recommended. All issues and challenges are described in the above sections. The summary of the most important disadvantages and other complicating factors is:

- PKI strongly recommended.
- Roaming profiles or roaming credential feature strongly recommended.
- Sharing files is difficult.
- No sharing on a folder level possible.
- No sharing for groups possible.
- Too high risks of data exposure by unintentional file decryption.

5 Decru DataFort

Decru DataFort™ storage security appliances use wire-speed encryption and strong authentication to protect stored data. The appliances can be deployed transparently in Storage Area Network (SAN), Network Attached Storage (NAS), Direct Attached Storage (DAS) or Tape Backup environments. DataFort is available in several models:

- DataFort E-series supports CIFS, NFS file systems and iSCSI connectivity;
- DataFort FC-series supports Fibre Channel for disk and tape;
- DataFort S-series supports SCSI tape environments.

DataFort E-series ('E' means Ethernet version) E510 was designed to transparently encrypt data flowing from clients to file servers and to decrypt on the way back. The appliance is built as a fully protected 19" rack mountable device equipped with tamper resistant features. The internal, hardened operating system is called DecruOS, which is based on FreeBSD UNIX. DataFort is designed to meet the FIPS 140-2 security level 2 requirements. The most important internal components of DataFort are described in the following sections.

5.1 Storage Encryption Processor

Storage Encryption Processor (SEP) is the kernel of all the DataFort appliances. It is a Decru-designed hardware engine performing wire-speed (multi-gigabit) full-duplex encryption. SEP implements AES-256 encryption, a True Random Number Generator (TRNG) to generate keys, and a key management unit protecting the encryption keys. Thanks to the gathering of these features in a single processor unit, the keys never leave SEP in an unprotected format. This makes attempts to compromise the keys extremely difficult.

5.2 Cryptainer™ Storage Vaults

Cryptainer™ is an encrypted storage container. In the DataFort NAS version the cryptainer is a folder on a file server. On a SAN version, the cryptainer is a storage disk volume. Thanks to the support for encryption, user authentication and user authorization on each cryptainer access, DataFort delivers a secure compartmentalization solution that can be used to logically segment the data and to guarantee data confidentiality.

Each cryptainer in the DataFort NAS environment can be defined as:

- Windows Common Internet File System (CIFS) share, known also as Server Message Block (SMB) share;
- UNIX Network File System (NFS) export.

Cryptainers are equipped with the Access Control Lists (ACL) to control access to the data stored inside the cryptainers. A basic configuration of DataFort is shown in Figure 1.

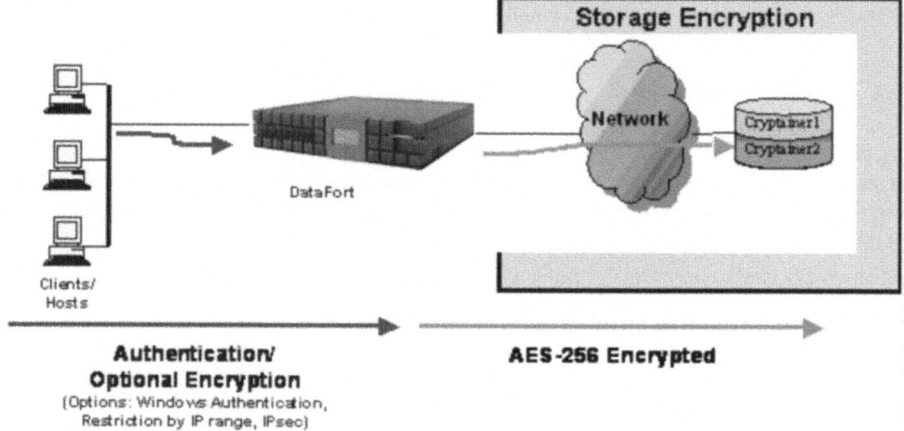

Figure 1: DataFort NAS Version Configuration (Source: Decru)

DataFort can be optionally equipped with an IPSec accelerator to encrypt the client-to-DataFort communication. The implemented IPSec protocol uses Kerberos or a pre-shared secret as an authentication method.

5.3 Levels of Virtualization

DataFort provides three levels of virtualization. These are: virtual server, virtual share and cryptainer. Virtual server is the highest virtualization level. DataFort can host multiple virtual severs. Each virtual server is mapped to one physical file server. One virtual server can hold multiple defined virtual shares. Each virtual share is mapped to one physical share on a file server. Each virtual share can define multiple cryptainers. The cryptainers are mapped to physical folders on the physical share on the file server. Each physical folder can contain multiple subfolders. The folder structure is not virtualized so the whole structure can be directly seen inside a cryptainer. All files in the cryptainer and all its subfolders are encrypted. Cryptainers cannot be nested. Using this virtualization scheme encrypted files can be accessed using the following UNC format:

\\Virtual_Server\Virtual_Share\Cryptainer\Subfolder\Encrypted_file

5.4 Clustering

DataFort NAS appliances can be deployed in clusters to provide disaster recovery capabilities. Currently two-node clusters are supported. Both nodes of the cluster share the same configuration data and the key material. The failover operations are transparent to users. If a crash occurs on one cluster node, the second takes over operations transparently. The administrator can also initiate a cluster failover manually. DataFort supports an active/active cluster configuration with load-balancing of operations between the cluster nodes. One node can host one group of virtual servers while the second one can concurrently perform operations for another group. The distribution of virtual servers among the cluster nodes is not automatic and has to be performed manually by an administrator.

The key material and configuration changes are synchronized between the cluster nodes. To provide confidentiality for the synchronization traffic DataFort uses an IPSec tunnel.

5.5 Active Directory Integration

DataFort can be integrated with AD to authenticate and authorize users for cryptainer access. The CIFS cryptainers are equipped with ACLs. Access control is based on the standard Windows access control mechanism, using a combination of a user id and group memberships. To control access DataFort queries AD Domain Controllers regularly for changes to user group memberships. The appliance can also query the cryptainer on file servers for the ACLs. The combined information about the users, group membership and the user permissions on the cryptainers is stored within DataFort SEP.

6 Utimaco SafeGuard LAN Crypt

SafeGuard LAN Crypt is a member of SafeGuard product family from the Utimaco Safeware company. It is an interesting example of a software-based content encryption product providing security on the file and folder level. Using a combination of asymmetric and symmetric cryptography SafeGuard LAN Crypt provides fully automated encryption of files and folders residing on local computers or remote file servers. SafeGuard LAN Crypt is a popular product especially in Europe and particularly among governmental and financial institutions.

6.1 SafeGuard LAN Crypt Main Features

SafeGuard LAN Crypt (sometimes abbreviated to SGLC) is a fully automated and transparent encryption product. Unlike solutions that were presented earlier in this paper the SGLC encryption takes place exclusively on the client computer. This makes the product independent of a data medium. It can be used to protect files on local computers and remote file servers. It can also be used to encrypt data in offline folders and on removable media such as USB memory sticks, floppy disks or CD-ROMs. The important advantage of the fact that the data is being encrypted and decrypted not remotely on file servers but locally on a client computer is the confidentiality of information that is transported over the network. To protect the transported data in the case of EFS or DataFort, some network encryption technologies must be used. This feature of SafeGuard LAN Crypt has some consequences. Although no special software on the file server side is required, is necessary to install software component on the client computers. This fact is sometimes regarded by customers as a disadvantage. However, a client-based solution is not necessarily a disadvantage. The effective choice of client-based or server-based solutions depends on customer specific considerations, such as complexity, costs, migration scenario or deployment.

The basic encryption unit of SafeGuard LAN Crypt is a file. However, the administrator can define rules forcing encryption of not only individual files identified by their name, but also of group of files identified by parts of the file name (using wildcards), file types identified by their extension, directories, subdirectories or even all files on drives. It is necessary to emphasize that although the file-level encryption makes the product enormously flexible, some customers just require encryption on the folder-level, so having encryption policies on the file-level may increase the integration and management complexity of the solution. Also, maintaining the encryption keys per individual file may also have some performance impact. The encrypted files can be shared among multiple users. Similarly to many other solutions, SGLC utilizes symmetric cryptography to encrypt files using uniquely generated encryption keys – Data Encryption Keys (DEK). The DEKs are encrypted by encryption keys, which are generated by administrators. These keys can be shared by users that are members of logical user groups defined by the administrators. All users who share a particular encryption key have access to encrypted files.

All encryption rules and encryption keys assigned to a particular user are placed in a special user encryption profile. Profiles are protected with another encryption key – the Profile Encryption Key (PEK). The PEKs are protected by Public Key cryptography. The profiles are stored centrally in user policy files.

Administration of the SafeGuard LAN Crypt configuration, encryption information, user encryption profiles, etc. is done from a management workstation. Most of the objects are stored in a separate database. Policy files containing the encryption profiles are stored centrally on a server, which must be available to users during a logon process. During this process the encryption profiles are retrieved, loaded locally to the client computers and cached for a predefined time in the Windows registry for the future use.

For management purposes, the concept of Security Officers (SO) is introduced. The administration tasks are performed with a standard Microsoft Management Console (MMC).

SafeGuard LAN Crypt can be integrated with Active Directory (AD) to a certain degree. The AD can be a source of user and group information that is used to define encryption rules. Group Policy Objects (GPO) technology can be used to distribute configuration settings to the client computers. These setting include, for example, the path to the centrally stored policy files or some PKI-related data.

6.2 Keys and Algorithms

SafeGuard LAN Crypt uses a combination of symmetric and asymmetric cryptography to protect files, encryption keys and user profiles. Similarly to many other solutions, SGLC utilizes symmetric cryptography to encrypt files using uniquely generated encryption keys – Data Encryption Keys (DEK). The DEKs are encrypted by encryption keys, which are generated by administrators. These keys can be shared by users that are members of logical user groups defined by the administrators. All users who share a particular encryption key have access to encrypted files. The following symmetric algorithms are supported: AES 128-bit end 256-bit, 3DES, DES, IDEA, XOR.

All encryption rules and encryption keys assigned to a particular user are placed in a special user encryption profile. Profiles are protected with another encryption key – the Profile Encryption Key (PEK). The PEKs are protected by Public Key cryptography. The profiles are stored centrally in user policy files. The SGLC asymmetric cryptography requires certificates. The certificates can be provided by a company internal or a commercial Public Key Infrastructure (PKI). The product can also utilize self-signed certificates issued by the SGLC Administration component. These are simple X.509 Class-1 compatible certificates which can only be used by SafeGuard LAN Crypt. SafeGuard LAN Crypt supports certificates stored on smart cards, USB tokens or other devices.

The functionality and the hierarchy of the keys used by SGLC are illustrated in Figure 2.

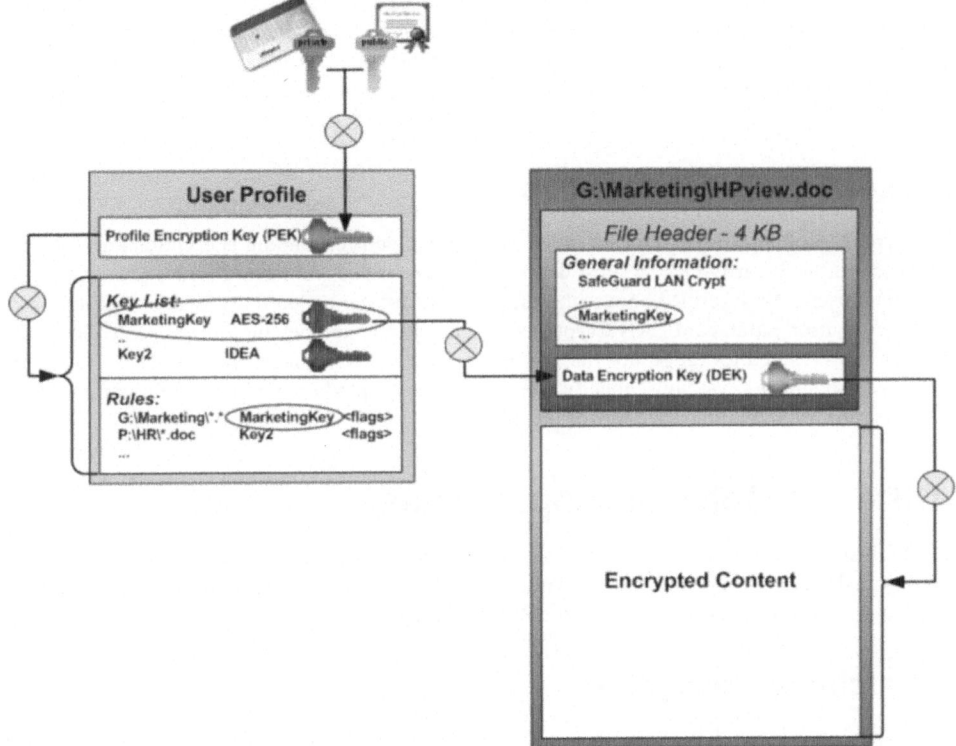

Figure 2: Key Hierarchy

6.3 Encryption Rules

Encryption rules define how data should be encrypted. A rule consists of an encryption path, a group key and options. Since a key is generated for a particular algorithm, an encryption rule implicitly defines the algorithm to be used for encrypting the files.

The encryption path defines which files have to be encrypted. SafeGuard LAN Crypt supports absolute and relative path definitions. An absolute path definition specifies a full path to the encrypted files, including a drive letter or an UNC path. A relative path contains no drive letter or share name. It specifies only part of a path so the system can match it to multiple directories located in different parts of the infrastructure.

The second item in an encryption rule is a key. The rule specifies only a logical key name, but not the value. The latter will be added to the user encryption profile together with the rule.

6.4 Transparent encryption

Files, for which encryption rules are specified, are automatically encrypted by a client component without any user intervention. The client component is called a filter driver. When a user wants to open a file, the filter driver analyses the user encryption profile, searches for a rule that could be applied, and if found, derives the encryption key and decrypts the encrypted file in the memory. When a file is being saved, the filter driver encrypts it according to the specified rule. The encryption/decryption process is transparent to the user. However, the user can has the possibility to explicitly encrypt or decrypt the file.

6.5 User Encryption Profiles

The encryption profiles contain the encryption rules and the corresponding encryption keys. Prior to a profile creation the Security Officer must define both items: rules and keys. Profiles are always linked to individual users. As described above, the rules are always generated per group. To create a profile for a particular user, SafeGuard LAN Crypt analyses the group membership of the user, collects all the encryption rules defined for all groups the user is a member of, and places them in the profile together with the corresponding keys. Subsequently, the profile is encrypted with a Profile Encryption Key. The PEK is then protected by the public key of the user.

7 Different Solution Approaches

File and folder encryption is, however, not the only solution that can be used to protect data in a shared environment. There are other specific encryption technologies that can be used to serve the same purpose, such as database encryption, Enterprise Rights Management or SAN encryption.

7.1 Database encryption

Database protection technologies usually use a sophisticated combination of symmetric and asymmetric cryptography, and hardware and software components that are implemented inside or outside the protected databases. The existing solutions can be divided into few groups:

- Application-level encryption
- Centralized encryption servers
- Database-level encryption
- File or media-level encryption

Some examples of the players in the database encryption market are: Application Security, Cryptix Foundation, Ingrian Networks, nCipher, NetLib, RSA, Vormetric.

7.2 Enterprise Rights Management

Rights Management uses a completely different approach for data protection: the persistent protection of information throughout the information lifecycle. It does so by attaching the entitlements to the protected content. The entitlements, which are called digital "rights", are no longer applied to the environment where the data rests or moves but to the data itself, no matter where the data is. Rights Management systems usually use a complex combination of symmetric and asymmetric cryptography to protect the content and to ensure that the adjusted rights cannot be removed or changed. The major players in the Enterprise Rights Management market are: Adobe Systems, Authentica, Liquid Machines, Microsoft, SealedMedia

7.3 SAN encryption

Due to market analysts the majority of data resides on networked and distributed storage. Since SAN is the environment where the vital data rests and moves, it is a potential target for different types of attacks. The security aspects and requirements of a SAN environment are very specific. The biggest source of threats is personnel having physical access to the SAN components. When taking decisions about the countermeasures to protect the SAN environment, it is necessary to analyze not only the SAN threats but also the data protection mechanisms applied on the different layers of the infrastructure. A quite obvious principle is that if you protect the confidentiality of data on the file or the database levels, you will probably not need to apply any specific SAN security measures. If you don't encrypt the database on either the file or database levels and if the estimated threats to the SAN environment are high, then you may need to investigate how to protect the storage. A very interesting class of solutions is the encryption of data on a SAN volume level. Decru DataFort and NeoScale CryptoStor are good examples of these solutions.

8 Conclusion

Protecting files on centrally managed files servers is a very important issue for highly secure environments even if the servers are placed in a physically strongly protected datacenters. Organizations start looking for additional countermeasures such as file and folder level encryption solutions on central file servers to eliminate vulnerabilities or reduce threats. Microsoft Encrypting File System, Decru DataFort and Utimaco SafeGuard LAN Crypt are examples of such solutions. Other solution categories which can help protecting information are database encryption, Enterprise Rights Management, and SAN encryption.

References

[Decr05]   Decru: DataFort Administration Guide for E-Series DataFort, 2005

[Utim05]   Utimaco Safeware A.G.: SafeGuard LAN Crypt Administration, version 3.21, 2005

[Cohe04]   Cohen, Fred: Database Security: Protecting the Critical Content of the Enterprise, Burton Group, 2004

[RsaS02]   RSA Security: Securing Data at Rest: Developing a Database Encryption Strategy, 2002

[Henr06]   Henry, Trent: Rights Management: Driving Security to the Data, Burton Group, 2006

[GrKo03]   Gruener, Jamie and Kovar, Matthew: Abridged Report, The Emerging Storage Security Challenge, The Yankee Group, 2003

Setting up an Effective Information Security Awareness Programme

Dirk De Maeyer

KPMG Advisory
ddemaeyer@kpmg.com

Abstract

The security group of a large insurance company in Belgium wanted to set-up and conduct a successful security awareness programme for all employees. Before designing the programme, the group performed field research (including discussing with security peers) into what constitutes a successful awareness programme. The security group also made an inventory of available awareness material, both internally (within the company and the group to which the company belongs) and externally. Based on the various input received a conceptual approach for an effective security awareness programme was drafted on which the insurance information security awareness programme was built. Measuring the results of the programme proved that the approach was effective.

1 Introduction

To start off we need to define what makes up information security awareness and why organisations create awareness programmes. Several **definitions** can be found ranging from IT security oriented towards the broader information security orientation.

The Sans Institute defines security awareness training as *"educating the users on the appropriate use, protection and security of information, individual user responsibilities and ongoing maintenance necessary to protect the confidentiality, integrity, and availability of information assets, resources, and systems from unauthorized access, use, misuse, disclosure, destruction, modification, or disruption."*

NIST states *"An effective IT security awareness and training programme explains proper rules of behaviour for the use of agency IT systems and information. Security awareness efforts are designed to change behaviour or reinforce good security practices."*

In the Standard of Good Practice ISF defines information security awareness as *"the degree or extent to which every member of staff understands*

- *the importance of information security*
- *the levels of information security appropriate to the organisation*
- *their individual security responsibilities*

... and acts accordingly".

Especially the last part of this definition "acts accordingly" is very crucial. Indeed the main objective of security awareness is to create and maintain an information security-positive environment reflected by the behaviour of the organisations' employees.

N. Pohlmann, H. Reimer, W. Schneider (Editors): Securing Electronic Business Processes, Vieweg (2007), 49-58

A security awareness programme can then be defined as an organised and ongoing effort to guide the behaviour and culture of an organisation in regard to security issues.

Why do we need security awareness ? When we talk about information security management, we think in terms of technical and procedural controls that protect information assets with respect to confidentiality, integrity and availability. However, many of these controls can miss their effect when employees act in a security-negative manner, this is to say they are not aware of the risks of their current insecure behaviour and/or they set aside the organisation's policy and standards because it is more convenient to work like that. So, implementing effective security controls will depend on creating an information security-positive environment, in which employees understand and act according to the behaviour that is expected of them. Creating information security awareness is exactly that: create and maintain a security-positive behaviour amongst your employees. Common expressions such as *"People issues are the biggest security concerns"* underpin this idea.

2 Organising an effective security awareness programme

Input from peer security officers and security consultants indicated that although many organisations conducted security awareness programmes with the aim to change the behaviour of their employees into the desired security-positive behaviour, those programmes often failed to deliver any lasting value. The reasons given were:

- The awareness programmes were not managed as a formal project, lacking formal objectives, business sponsors or the necessary resources for successful completion. As a consequence such awareness programmes were often not correctly prioritised against other security projects/activities and because of the lack of formal milestones and correct assignment of resources the programmes did not maintain the initial pace of delivery.

- The awareness programmes were not targeted at specific business issues, but they were designed and conducted from a belief that awareness needed to be raised. Indeed if the need for awareness is not clearly defined, than it is difficult to construct a good business case.

- The awareness programmes did not use specialised awareness materials.

- The awareness programmes did not include a mechanism for assessing security behaviour, but – if any assessments were performed at all – they measured security knowledge. It is clear that programmes should measure their effectiveness; this is whether the awareness message actually changed the employees' behaviour, in stead of measuring the security knowledge, which only shows that the employees received the messages.

- Most awareness programmes were sponsored by the security management teams. This had as consequences that line managers were reluctant to let their employees follow awareness training, that employees following the training did not appreciate the importance of security or its relevance to their functions because their line managers had not communicated the need for security, and that the programmes failed to achieve a culture change because employees did not see senior management acting more securely.

The approach depicted in figure 1 will counter these raised issues.

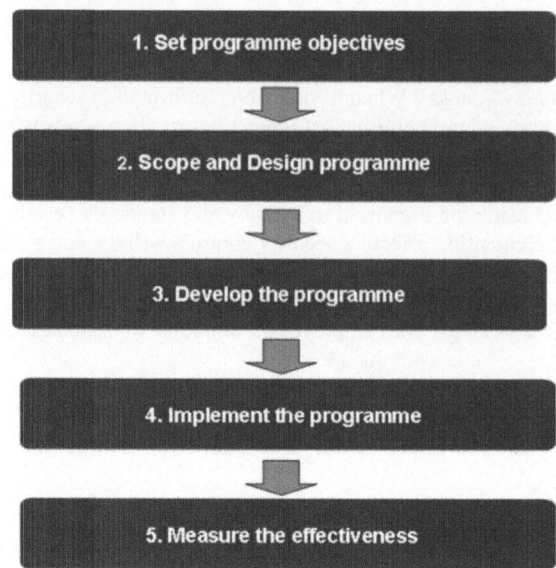

Figure 1: An approach for an effective information security awareness programme

The key phases in this approach are

1. **Set clear, defined and measurable objectives** and goals for security awareness that address the problems of security-negative behaviour.

2. **Scope and design the security awareness programme** by creating a formal project. The programme can contain one or more awareness campaigns. Each campaign should have its own specific goal to change a specific aspect of security-negative behaviour. After developing the awareness plan organisational buy-in needs to be sought and secured.

3. **Develop the security awareness campaigns** that support the business needs of the organisation and are relevant to the organisation's culture.

4. **Implement the security awareness campaigns** that deliver the awareness messages in a meaningful way to the employees. Employees should get the feeling that the messages were developed specifically for them.

5. **Measure the effectiveness of the campaigns** so that effective activities can be repeated, if necessary, and other activities can be revised. Monitoring compliance and effectiveness should lead to continuous improvement. After all, for security awareness you never can do enough.

In the following paragraphs we will discuss in more detail some of the important aspects of these phases.

A common way to define measurable objectives is to apply the **SMART** principle:

- **Specific:** the objective must be well-defined with a single key result. Clear objectives are easier to achieve.
- **Measurable:** the objective should be quantifiable. This allows more easily to evaluate whether the objective is reached or not.
- **Attainable:** the objective must be feasible, do-able.

- **Realistic:** the objective must be attainable with the available or planned resources (budget, time, people).
- **Time-delimited:** the objective should clearly state when it has to be met.

Some examples of suggested **metrics** are the ratio of business versus personal Internet use (for the topic Internet misuse), the number of password resets (for the topic password management), and the number of clear desks or of locked workstations (for the topic physical security).

Very often organisations use **awareness slogans** in their security awareness programmes to reinforce the messages of the individual awareness campaigns.

Some tips for **delivering awareness messages** are
- Use a mix of existing and new channels for delivering the message
- Provide awards for security-positive behaviour
- Enforce security policies. For example perform spot checks of offices with notes left for employees in both good and bad situations.
- Use peer pressure to encourage security-positive behaviour. For example publish policy breaches by department.
- Make security simple. Assist employees in getting security right in stead of saying "You should not do this" without giving them the correct solution.

The barriers to implementing an information security awareness programme are primarily resistance to change and lack of commitment. Resistance to change has to do with cognitive dissonance. Namely, individuals try to rationalise undesired behaviour and are blind for their own faults. Ever heard of statements like "My grandfather lived until the age of 92, so smoking is not unhealthy" and "Everybody drives 160 here, so why should not I drive too fast as well".

For breaking resistance to change mechanisms such as telling about really occurred security incidents, showing security vulnerabilities and how these can impact the organisation's business if they get exploited, etc. are useful. Some other examples are:
- Show how poor security negatively impacts the budget in the long run.
- Threat of disciplinary actions for breaches of policy.
- Show cost savings due to less time spent on security incidents.
- Show why security is required.
- Develop communications plans and training packages to reduce long term resource requirements.

Another crucial element is that once the behaviour is changed, it should be maintained. After all, if the change does not hold and employees return to their previous security-negative behaviour, the awareness programme has not been effective. The NIST SP 800-16 describes exactly that "*people tend to practice a tuning out process called acclimation. If a stimulus is used repeatedly, the recipient will selectively ignore it. Thus, awareness campaigns must be ongoing, creative and motivational, with the objective of focusing the employees' attention so that the learning will be incorporated into conscious decision making. This is called assimilation, a process whereby an individual incorporates new experiences into an existing behaviour pattern.*"

One way to enforce the desired security-positive behaviour is performing assessments on a continuous basis. If employees know that their behaviour will be evaluated, they may adopt their behaviour to ensure that the evaluation result is positive. Other mechanisms are for example:

- Publish success stories.
- Make the role of security coordinator within departments desirable, so that there are plenty of volunteers keen to assist in maintaining security within their department/team.
- Include security responsibilities in job descriptions and ensure that security behaviour is taken into account during annual job/performance evaluations.

Many organisations included within their programme the measurement of what was learned by their employees. Typically when using a Computer-Based Training (CBT) a questionnaire is included at the end of the training module to assess what the employees have learned. Although this is useful for registering who completed the training and with what success, it does not measure the actual behaviour of the employees. Nor does it indicate, if their behaviour is changed into security-positive behaviour, that it will remain that way. To obtain that information measurement of behaviour over time is needed, for example by measuring on regular intervals, for example before the specific awareness campaign on Internet usage, 4 weeks after the campaign is received by employees and then bi-monthly, whether there is a positive change in the ratio of business versus personal Internet use.

In the following chapter we describe how this approach was applied to the information security awareness programme for the insurance company.

3 Organising an awareness programme in practice

The security team of the insurance company structured the programme in the following steps

1. Define objective and scope,
2. Set up the project plan,
3. Obtain senior management commitment,
4. Prepare the deliverables,
5. Organise road shows to obtain employee participation,
6. Roll-out the programme,
7. Track the programme and its effectiveness.

During the initial field research phase, the available information at the insurance company was also inventoried in order to evaluate its use for the awareness programme. Available materials were among others topical posters in 3 languages, awareness brochures, and a series of 5 computer-based training (CBT) courses available in the local languages French and Dutch.

3.1 Defining objective and scope

Given that the insurance company in Belgium resulted from the merger of 3 Belgian insurance companies and that there had not been any formal awareness training for all employees, causing security-negative behaviour of employees, such as sharing passwords, leaving active workstations unattended, discussing confidential information in public locations, etc., the main objective was an **awareness raising for general employees with as desired target a more security-positive behaviour during the**

execution of their day-to-day tasks. Also in scope was the development of an adapted induction program for new joiners.

Another objective was to measure in an objective manner the effectiveness of the security awareness program at the insurance company, including its evolution over time. This should be done via objective metrics.

3.2 Setting up the project plan

Taking into account the available material and the culture of communication within the insurance company, a good **mix of different awareness media** was incorporated in the programme. The plan also specified the necessary resources (material and staff) to roll-out the various deliverables.

The security team split the awareness programme into **5 awareness campaigns**. These matched the 5 topics of the already available CBT courses, namely:

1. Security basics, physical access, clean desk;
2. User ids and passwords;
3. Internet and email usage;
4. Portable equipment;
5. Security incidents and social engineering.

The security team also defined a general awareness slogan for the programme: "Security is (Y)Our business". The reasoning behind: security is the domain of security officers, but moreover every employee's responsibility.

An important factor for the execution of the awareness programme was the creation of so-called security coaches. They were motivated to become within their department the main security motivators, as well as the first contact point for security questions or issues for their direct colleagues. They would also support measuring the effectiveness of the awareness programme by performing various practical samples.

The project plan was based on the project management methodology currently applied within the insurance company.

3.3 Obtaining senior management commitment

As soon as the project plan was defined, a proper and visual presentation to top management was given. As figure 2 shows the security group obtained formal commitment from multiple management levels: the board of directors, the management forum, as well as from the workers council (including the active support of trade unions).

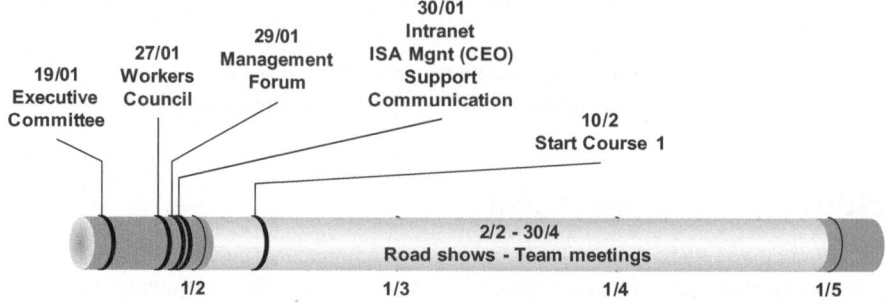

Figure 2: Obtaining management support and general timeline for the programme

The commitment from the board of directors resulted in an Intranet publication from the CEO explaining the importance of the security awareness training and demanding each employee to actively participate in the road shows and the presented courses. Additionally the CEO distributed a communication to all line managers asking them to allow time for their employees to take the courses (15-20 minutes per month), to include security responsibilities in the job descriptions within their department and to include security as an element in the annual performance management evaluation of their employees, as well as to appoint a security coach within their department. Both communications were prepared in advance by the security group in full cooperation with legal counsel, internal communications and marketing.

This formal commitment was also found back in the minutes of meeting.

3.4 Preparing the deliverables

As previously described the security awareness programme was focused around the 5 existing CBT courses. In the CBT courses practical information was given on how to do security right. Examples of make security simple are instructing employees how to create strong passwords and how to clean your desk before lunch time and before leaving for home.

Practically the most time was spent during the preparation of the deliverables, namely enhancing the computer-based training courses with a pre and post assessment, and developing Intranet pages containing additional (explanatory) information on the course topics.

These options were taken based on practicality and internal questions raised by IT and some end users during an initial pilot of the training courses.

3.5 Program roll-out

The actual roll-out of the programme is shown in figures 2 and 3.

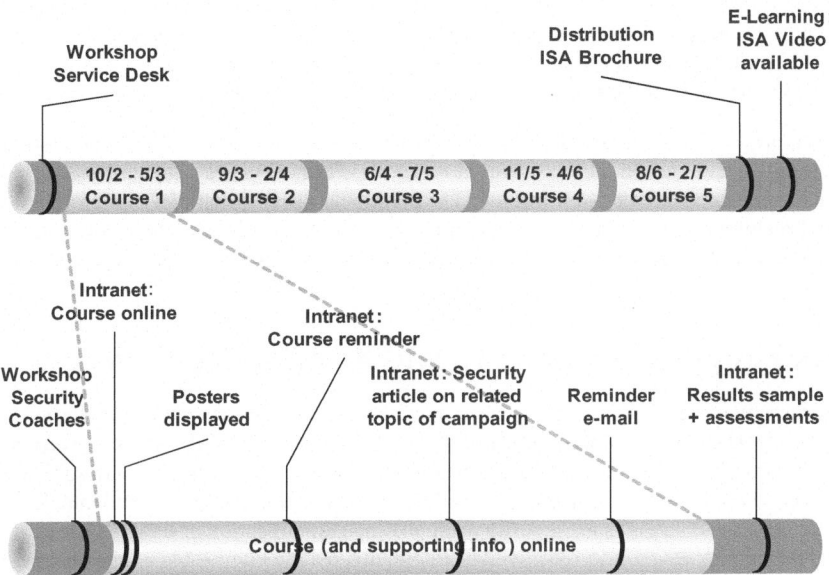

Figure 3: Timeline programme roll-out

As shown in figure 2 the roll-out started with road shows to which small groups of employees were invited – participation was mandatory as communicated by the CEO and traced via attendance sheets (metric!). In these 30 minutes sessions the employees were informed about the necessity of the security awareness training – by showing examples of security incidents and by showing their impact to the organisation, and by indicating the necessity for compliance with regulations – and were persuaded to participate.

Figure 3 shows the timeline for the awareness activities related to the training courses and the awareness activities that are repeated per campaign (training course).

Prior to the launch of the courses, a session with the service desk was organized resulting in pragmatic feedback for fine-tuning the relevant content. At the same time the service desk was made aware of potential questions / issues that might be raised by employees.

Just before launching a course, a workshop with the security coaches was conducted on the upcoming campaign. The security group did this to make the security coaches aware of the upcoming messages, so they were able to react to questions from colleagues directly addressed to them and to get more feedback on the content to further refine the campaigns if deemed necessary.

Then a publication on the Intranet invited employees to take the course. In parallel to the launch supporting posters were displayed at various locations, such as coffee corners and print/copy rooms. During the courses collective reminders were published on the Intranet. These also included indirect invitations, such as security articles related to the campaign topic and with reference towards the training course, publication of participation degree per department and per employee category, and publication of the answers to the assessments (after a participation degree of 85%). Just before the launch of the next course personal e-mail reminders were sent for those that had not yet participated.

After the course series, an information security awareness brochure was distributed summarising the information brought forward in the courses. Somewhat later videos were made available in the e-learning environments showing interviews detailing some specific topics. Employees were free to enrol themselves to watch the video at their convenience.

As induction programme a presentation was developed focusing on the most important topics from the general awareness training. In the presentation video clips of interviews with staff talking about security incidents they encountered were included. As additional reading material the information security awareness brochure was distributed at the end of the induction training. These awareness induction trainings were incorporated within a one-day joiners' workshop that was typically organized every 2 to 3 months.

3.6 Tracking the programme and its effectiveness

For the learning management system there was a choice between an external and an in-house development. For budget reasons the choice fell on in-house development. The LMS was based on a mix of end-user computing tools. In the assessments a registration/feedback form was included, so that employees could be tracked upon their participation, as well as on their scores on the assessments. By comparing post with pre assessment results the security team obtained an indication of how the course contributed in learning the employees security-positive behaviour, at least the knowledge of such behaviour.

For those employees lacking participation personal e-mail reminders were sent. The security group actively replied to any questions or feedback submitted by the employees. For the latter staff showed a high appreciation.

The security coaches were involved to perform a sample on workstation log-off after business hours. Good behaviour was awarded with a security gadget (whoopie). Results of (non-) compliance to the procedure were published per department and location on the Intranet. It was initially also the intention to organize the same sample again 2 months later, as well as to organize other samples such as security spot checks on clean desk, and to have personalized follow-up on the results of the assessments by the security coaches. However during the programme top management withdrew the commitment of having security coaches in every department.

3.7 Results

The CBT training courses showed an overall participation of nearly 88 %, so participation was a success. This success was obtained thanks to the

- road shows targeted at all employees motivating them to participate,
- enhanced CBT courses with various media support (posters, Intranet, brochure, video),
- Intranet messages (related security articles, publication of participation degree and of the correct answers),
- personal email reminders,
- possibility for feedback on course content, actively replied to by the security group.

The comparison of post and pre assessments showed a significant improvement of the knowledge of security-positive behaviour.

The sample on workstation log-off showed very little cases of non-compliance to the procedure, so the CBT training course that covered this topic can be considered effective. Another metric used by the security team was to monthly retrieve the number of and to calculate the percentages of Internet use per defined subject categories which can be linked to business and personal Internet use. Again the percentage of non-compliance to procedures dropped over time, hence proving effectiveness of the campaign on Internet use.

4 Conclusion

This case study shows how a successful information security awareness programme can be constructed with a good mix of scarce resources and a relatively small budget by applying an approach as described in chapter 2.

Following the general security awareness programme, more advanced training sessions for targeted groups such as service desk, IT engineering, software developers, sales and marketing, and management were envisaged.

As yearly refreshment for the general awareness training awareness quizzes would be organized, as well as regular security publications on the Intranet. Every 4 years a more extended awareness programme would have to be organized.

References

The Standard of Good Practice, Information Security Forum, January 2005, http://www.isfsecuritystandard.com/ pdf/standard.pdf

Security Awareness Training, Sans Institute, http://www.sans.org/security_awareness.php

National Institute of Standards and Technology Special Publication 800-16, Information Technology Security Training Requirements: A Role- and Performance-Based Model, April 1998.

National Institute of Standards and Technology Special Publication 800-50, Building an Information Technology Security Awareness and Training Program, October 2003.

National Institute of Standards and Technology Special Publication 800-55, Security Metrics Guide for Information Technology Systems, July 2003

National Institute of Standards and Technology Special Publication 800-100, Information Security Handbook: A Guide for Managers, October 2006

Saferinternet.pl Project – Educational Activities for Internet Safety in Poland

Anna Rywczyńska[1] · Agnieszka Wrzesień[2]

[1]Research and Academic Computer Network (NASK)
anna.rywczynska@nask.pl

[2]Nobody's Children Foundation (FDN)
awrzesien@fdn.pl

Abstract

In the following article the Consortium NASK (Research and Academic Computer Network)-FDN (Nobody's Children Foundation) has a pleasure to present the report[1] of its activities connected with conducted since 2005 European's Commission Programme Safer Internet. The topic of this paper is not only reporting past actions but also presenting planned operations in the next years.

1 Introduction

Since January 2005 Nobody's Children Foundation and NASK (*Research and Academic Computer Network*) have been involved in the Awareness project, which is realized within Safer Internet Programme run by the European Commission. Both organizations constitute Awareness node for Poland. In October 2006 the NASK-FDN Consortium began to implement another two-year edition of the European's Commission's Programme – Safer Internet Plus. Since then a part of the node became a Polish Hotline "Dyżurnet.pl" that had been launched at NASK in 2005 to receive reports concerning illegal content on the Internet. An overall coordinator of the combined node is NASK.

Polish Awareness Node has been involved in comprehensive activities aimed at the following goals:

- To assess and diagnose threats related to new media in Poland;
- To educate children and their parents on safe Internet use;
- To enhance professionals' competence in improving Internet safety;
- To initiate activities aimed at improving safety on the Web;
- To promote the NIFC Hotline in Poland (Dyżurnet.pl – the Polish contact point for combating illegal content on the Internet).

---

1 Safer Internet programme In Poland – report on implementation of Awareness and Hotline projects 2005-2006.

N. Pohlmann, H. Reimer, W. Schneider (Editors): Securing Electronic Business Processes, Vieweg (2007), 59-64

1.1 Conferences and trainings

The major goals of the Awareness programme in Poland involve publicizing the problem of Internet threats and improving the competence of professionals who work with children or deal with Internet offending. To meet these goals in 2005 and 2006 the FDN-NASK Consortium organized several conferences and training programmes addressed to professionals such as teachers, childcare providers, psychologists, law enforcement staff, ISPs and ICP's.

The FDN-NASK consortium and its local partners have organized through 2005-06 conferences on children's safety on the Internet, under the banner of "Safer Internet". Such conferences have been held in all provincial capitals in Poland. They provided an opportunity to present the activities undertaken within Safer Internet in Poland, and to discuss problems related to children's safety on the Internet. These conferences have been held under the patronage of the Polish Minister of National Education and Sport, the Minister of Internal Affairs and Administration, the Minister of Justice, the Minister of Science and Information Technology, the Children's Ombudsman, the Office of Competition and Consumer Protection, the National Police Headquarters, the Polish Committee for UNESCO, and the Polish National Committee for UNICEF. The conferences consisted of plenary sessions and workshop sessions. The educational workshops on safe Internet use were addressed to teachers and guidance counsellors, while the workshops on combating harmful and illegal content on the Internet were targeted at law enforcement staff. Furthermore, each conference was accompanied by educational events for children and their parents, co-organized by the consortium's local partners.

The 16 "Safer Internet" conferences were attended by nearly 3000 professionals from all over Poland. The provincial conferences were also accompanied by outdoor educational events for children and their parents.

On the 16th and 17th of October 2007 the Polish Awareness node and British organization CEOP within EC Safer Internet Programme in Poland will organize the international conference "Protecting children online" in Warsaw . The conference participants will be mainly people from education sector, psychologists, pedagogues, police, and representatives of NGOs working with children. Apart from Polish participants we invited also people from eastern European countries (outside EU), who are interested in conducting projects on Internet safety or have just initiated their efforts in this fields.

1.2 Child in The Web – Social Campaign

In 2004 Nobody's Children Foundation launched a nationwide social campaign "Child in the Web" addressing Internet safety and the problem of Internet-based paedophilia. It was the first attempt to convey messages on Internet safety to the Polish society. The media part of the campaign was carried out under the slogan: "You never know who is on the other side". Since January 2005 the campaign has been carried out by the FDN-NASK consortium within Awareness project. The campaign has been conducted under the patronage of the Minister of National Education and Sport.

In 2005 the campaign focused on educational activities conducted by teachers and volunteers among elementary and secondary school students across Poland. For campaign purposes class scenarios on Internet safety were created, drawing on the storyline of the educational Web project for children www. sieciaki.pl. By the end of 2006 the organizers of the campaign distributed more than 4260 class scenarios and the organizers of the Child in the Web campaign were informed about educational sessions conducted among more than 70 thousand elementary and secondary school students and nearly 17 thousand parents.

In September 2006 the second stage of the Child in the Web media campaign was launched under the slogan: "Internet is a window on the world. The whole world". The main goal of this part of the campaign was to draw adults' attention to dangerous content children may be exposed to when using the Internet on their own (pornography, drastic scenes, xenophobia, racism, etc.). The campaign was developed in cooperation with McCann Erickson Agency. Apart from messages targeted at adults, concerning children's exposure to dangerous

content on the Internet, advertisements for children were developed within the campaign. The slogan: "Give safe answers to dangerous questions" was supposed to remind children about the safety rules in online interactions. The following advertisements were created within the campaign: three TV ads, two radio spots, a press ad (three designs) and a citylight. One of the radio spots – warning against racist content present on the Internet – won a prestigious award in the „social advertising" category of the "Golden Eagles" National Advertising Festival.

1.3 Sieciaki.pl – educational project for children

Sieciaki.pl is an educational project run by the Nobody's Children Foundation that was launched on Safer Internet Day 2005. The project comprises two major elements: a website and a desktop application to be installed on registered users' PCs. Additionally, the project involved meetings with children, open-air events, concerts, and educational sessions. Films, songs, and multimedia materials have been prepared as well.

The Sieciaki.pl project pursues the following major goals:
- to educate children on safety on the Internet,
- to educate children on how to use the Web,
- to promote safe Internet use,
- to certify and promote safe websites.

The website was initially designed for children aged 9–15, but its registered users include younger children and older youth as well. The website's storyline is based on characters called Sieciaki (which could be loosely translated into "Web Kids") – children knowing the principles of safe Internet use and fighting the Web evil embodied by black creatures called Sieciuchy ("Web Goblins"). Endowed with special powers, Sieciaki have the fundamental task of disseminating knowledge about safe, efficient, and constructive use of the Internet. Designed to be attractive for children, Sieciaki are supposed to encourage the website user to become one of them. Children are asked to help NetRobi, a robot constructed to fight with the Web Goblins. The robot communicates messages, gives instructions, and looks after the team of Sieciaki and all the children wishing to join the team. The robot can communicate with Sieciaki, thus helping the website characters to fight the evil powers in the Web, and conveying guidelines and task instructions related to safe Internet use to all users of the website. By the end of 2006 www.sieciaki.pl had 50 142 registered users. The website was accessed more than 4 million times. The website administrators sent 755 messages and 112 guidelines, and organized 76 competitions.

1.4 Safer Internet Day in Poland

Initiated by the European Commission, the Safer Internet Day (SID) has been celebrated since 2004. This initiative aims at drawing the public's attention to the issue of children and youth's safe access to Internet resources. On **8 of February 2005** Poland organized the Safer Internet Day celebrations for the first time. On this occasion the **www.dbi.pl** website was launched (DBI is the Polish acronym for Safer

Internet Day), presenting the idea of SID and the available ways of joining its celebrations. The organizers encouraged schools, local social/civic organizations, cultural centres, local authorities, owners of cyber cafes, etc. to undertake initiatives for Internet safety. As a part of the SID celebrations, the Nobody's Children Foundation and NASK organized a conference on the youngest Internet users' safety. Strong media coverage of the conference contributed to the success of the SID initiative. By the end of February 2005 more than 200 local initiatives were implemented across Poland.

In 2006 Safer Internet Day was celebrated on 7 February. Just as in the preceding year, the University Library in Warsaw hosted a conference for the media and stakeholders of the Safer Internet programme in Poland. Special conference guests were Terry Jones and Paul Griffiths from the National Crime Squad UK. They presented the British system of combating Internet-based paedophilia, and the following day they conducted a training session at the Police Academy in Szczytno for 60 police officers representing provincial police headquarters from all over Poland. Moreover, in 2006 nearly 400 local initiatives were implemented across Poland within the SID celebrations.

Almost 40 countries participated in SID 2007 that took place on 6 February. In Poland main event – press conference – was organized in the Warsaw University Library – host of the event from the very beginning. During the conference Saferinternet.pl Consortium and project Partners presented their activities on fields of Internet safety and prepared many prizes for schools and other educational institutions that took part in national and international competitions. There was a streaming from the conference to the Internet and the transmission is available on the www.dbi.pl webside. (polish lan*guage)*

1.5 The National Coalition for Internet Safety

The National Coalition for Internet Safety is a platform of cooperation between government agencies, NGOs, schools and other educational institutions, and industry organizations for children and youth's safety on the Internet. The launch of OKBI was announced during the Safer Internet Day celebrations, on 7 February 2006.

The Coalition's main goals include:
- to raise public awareness of Internet-related threats;
- to exchange experiences related to efforts for Internet safety efforts;
- to cooperate in the implementation of initiatives aimed at raising the level of Internet users' safety;
- to distribute information about activities undertaken in Poland and in Europe within the Safer Internet programme.

Information about the National Coalition for Internet Safety (OKBI) and the application form are available at www.saferinternet.pl. Members of OKBI have a chance to promote their initiatives for Web safety, are invited to conferences and specialist trainings organized within the project, receive a monthly bulletin and have access to a discussion forum.

1.6 The Consultation Committee

The Consultation Committee was established in January 2006, as an advisory body supporting the implementation of the Safer Internet programme in Poland. The Committee's tasks include providing help in planning activities aimed at improving safety on the Internet, the evaluation of the Awareness and Hotline projects, and contributing to the optimization of efforts. Moreover, members of the Committee actively participate in selected components of the two projects. In 2006 the Consultative Committee had 4 sessions. Apart from the executors of the Safer Internet programme, the Nobody's Children Foundation and NASK, representatives of the following institutions and organizations contributed to the Committee's work:

- Central Teachers' Training Centre,
- National Police Headquarters,
- Warsaw Police Headquarters,
- Ministry of Education and Sport,
- Ministry of Science and Information Technology,
- Ministry of Justice,
- Ministry of Internal Affairs and Administration,
- Ministry of Labour and Social Policy,
- Polish Chamber of Information Technology and Telecommunications,
- Children's Ombudsman,
- Polish Committee for UNESCO,
- Office of Competition and Consumer Protection,
- Association of Audio-Video Producers.1 Coalition for Internet Safety (OKBI)
- Children's Ombudsman,
- Polish Committee for UNESCO,
- Office of Competition and Consumer Protection,
- Association of Audio-Video Producers.

1.7 Research

Within the Safer Internet Programme in Poland, the Nobody's Children Foundation and the Gemius S.A. agency conducted two online studies on children's behaviours on the Internet. The respondents in those studies were children aged 12–17. Some of the questions in the survey were also addressed to the parents of young Internet users. The findings were used to plan educational programmes and media campaigns and proved helpful in the evaluation of projects.

The research programme, conducted in January 2006[2], concerned children's risky behaviours on the Web, especially online and real-world interactions with persons met on the Internet (N=1779 children, N=687 parents). The studies found that a vast majority (68%) of young Internet users were invited to meetings with persons known from the Internet, and often accepted such proposals (44%), failing to observe the fundamental safety rules. The study also showed that nearly 30% of parents could not see any threats to children on the Internet!

The results of this survey were used to verify the underlying assumptions of the educational part of the Child in the Web campaign and to draw more attention to safety issues related to children's meetings with people on the Internet.

The other research project was conducted in September 2006[3] and focused on the problem of dangerous content on the Internet (N=2559 children). The study found that young Internet users were very

---

2 FDN/Gemius, January 2006
3 FDN/Gemius, September 2006

frequently exposed to pornographic and erotic images and to violent content on the Web. A vast majority of the respondents reported that this was mostly casual contact. The subject of the studies was related to the problems emphasized at the second stage of the Child in the Web media campaign, carried out under the slogan: „Internet is a window on the world. The whole world". The research findings were first presented during the press conference that inaugurated the campaign.

2 Conclusions

Basing on our previous experience, until the end of 2008 FDN–NASK Consortium will conduct our activities involved mainly in education efforts leading to help young Internet users, for whom the new media play increasingly important role and who are often unaware of the threats that may result from combining two worlds – the virtual and the real one. Among our actions are:

International Safer Internet conferences
The FDN-NASK Consortium – in cooperation with its foreign partners – will organize two international highprofile events devoted to a wide range of issues related to children's safety on the Internet. Groups invited to participate in the conference will include teachers, educational counsellors, social workers, police officers, and representatives of the justice system. The first one will take place on 16-17 October.

Safer Internet Day
In 2008, just as in the preceding years, national celebrations of the Safer Internet Day will beorganized.

Educational campaign
Educational activities addressed to children, youth, teachers, and parents will be continued, including the development of e-learning modules on Internet Safety, and a social campaign targeted at upper secondary school students.

Research
The FDN–NASK Consortium will continue its research on children and youth's behaviour on the Internet. Furthermore, a national study will be conducted into the security level provided by cyber cafes, and filter software will be tested.

Hotline
Established within NASK, the Polish hotline Dyżutnet.pl will continue its efforts to combat illegal content on the Internet. A media campaign will be carried out to promote the hotline.

Helpline
Helpline.org.pl – a helpline established by the Nobody's Children Foundation – will provide advice concerning Internet-related risks for children, parents, and professionals.

Sieciaki.pl
The Nobody's Children Foundation will continue the Sieciaki.pl project designed to educate children and youth on safe Internet use. These plans include further development of the www.sieciaki.pl website, continuing the "Sieciaki on Holidays" campaign, as well as other educational and media activities.

Is Cyber Tribalism Winning
Online Information Warfare?

Godfried Williams · Johnnes Arreymbi

University of East London
Dockland Campus, UK
{g.williams | j.arreymbi}@uel.ac.uk

Abstract

Cyber tribalism is the term that defines alliances and associations formed by Cyber tribes usually a group of people in a virtual community that have attributes such as a common language, similar belief systems, culture, traditions, practices and interest. The purpose of such a tribe, just like any tribe is formed to communicate, disseminates information and build relationships. In such an alliance, people who communicate do not necessarily know each other, although this is not always the case. Communication is done in a virtual manner. There is no assurance of personal interest protection, control and safeguards. Tribesmen have autonomy with respect to their activities. Members can each converse or relate to total strangers for social or business purposes. Examples of such communities are news groups, electronic chat rooms, and search engines such as Google, subject interest based communities and many more. Although there are several challenges and issues arising as a result of these associations, the immediate ones are spoofing and spam attacks, malware trace, theft, sabotage and sale of critical business information and more recently cyber terrorism.

This paper explores the role of Cyber tribalism in modern information warfare techniques and assesses the impact of this phenomenon on business critical information infrastructure. The paper covers paradigms and theoretical concepts underlying information warfare, On-line systems vulnerabilities, and attack methods used by Cyber tribes. The latter part of the paper examines countermeasures for managing security threats posed by cyber tribes, and cost implications.

Keywords: Cyber tribes, Information warfare, online communities, Cyber terrorism, Security, economics of Security

1 Introduction

Cyber communities have increasingly developed over the years to serve many functions. In all, these communities so-called 'Cyber tribes' are formed essentially for communication and relationships building in virtual space. Many virtual communities are built around tribal lines and on certain issues that are common to them, such as believes, culture, traditions, religion, shared-interests, and/or common language. The Internet and World Wide Web technologies have created societies that rely so much on immediacy, access and connections; a world of cyber spatial relations which is increasingly affecting human-human interaction or relationships. As would later be seen in this paper, the intentions of the cyber tribes or communities can be for 'the good, the bad and/or the ugly'. Their activities may involve social, economical, political and security elements.

N. Pohlmann, H. Reimer, W. Schneider (Editors): Securing Electronic Business Processes, Vieweg (2007), 65-72

1.1 Social elements:

- Socialising – chat rooms, bloggers, etc.
- Communication – email, YouTube
- Entertainment – Music distribution/download, game play etc
- Social Engineering – identity theft, spoofing and spamming, bullying, incitation (suicides)

1.2 Economic Elements:

- Money scams
- Money Laundering,
- Information Theft,

1.3 Political Elements:

- Radicalisation
- Confrontation
- Intimidation
- Terrorism

1.4 Security Elements:

- Paedophilia,
- Cryptography
- Crime concealment etc.

In cyberspace, the 'good' communities interact to communicate, socialise, entertainment and/or share good practices amongst members of their tribes. For example, some propagate role playing games tribes, chat-forums, discussions or simple one-to-one communication. The 'bad' communities are formed either intentionally or unintentionally, with a purpose to push for sabotage or destruction, and culminate information warfare on both the individual or business communities in the cyber world. For example hackers, social engineers or virus writers fall into this category and can include bullying and intimidation. Interestingly, the secondary intentions of some of the information warfare may trickle outside the cyberspace to affect real life communities. The worst case scenario is when such communities develop and degenerate into intense intimidation and cyber terrorism. The tribes push for some kind of hidden agenda for a course only best known to their community; such is the case with Hizbulla/Hezbollah and Al-Qaeda groups in Middle-Eastern region.

2 The shift

2.1 Physical vs. Virtual Environments

2.1.1 Physical

The physical environment is where communities live and work together. The people have everything in common and everybody knows everybody. Individuals or groups could sit and chat or make physical interactions with one another. Such a community work to protect and serve the interests of one another – i.e. everybody is (was) everybody's guardian.

2.1.2 Virtual

The environment has been influenced by technologies – such as internet and WWW – cyberspace. In such communities, not everybody knows everybody; and everything including communication is done in virtual space. In most cases, very little of personal interest is served and/or protected by another and members are on their own. The dilemma is that, anyone can chat with or be related to total strangers for social or business reasons. Some cyber tribes have developed into very large communities and boasting about 8 million members or users. For example Second Life community (www.secondlife.com) Second Life is an online 3D digital world, where avatar or residents interact and do business virtually. Recent figures show an impressive 8 million residents, with more than 40,000 online at any one time. The community does business to the tune of L$1.7 million daily).

Total Residents:	8,011,051
Logged In Last 60 Days:	1,732,159
Online Now:	36,918
US$ Spent Last 24h:	$1,667,039
LindeX Activity Last 24h:	$243,619

Source: (http://www.secondlife.com/whatis/economy_stats.php) [Accessed July 10 2007]

3 The Issues

Information warfare is the use and management of information in pursuit of a competitive advantage over an opponent (Borden, 1999). It may involve the collection of tactical information, assurance that one's own information is valid, spreading of propaganda or disinformation among the enemy, undermining the quality of opposing force information and denial of service or of information collection opportunities to opposing forces. The rationale for information warfare can be strategic for economic, military and/or other non-military objectives. Most of the techniques are not new and security services in many countries around the physical world have used them in fighting both real life wars, especially during World wars 1 & 2 and the present Iraq war which also involves online warfare.

Arreymbi, (2005) reported issues in the use of social engineering – phishing, pharming, identity theft etc, – spoofing and spamming as a form of information warfare in cyberspace. The Anti Phishing working Group (APWG, 2007) have also reported an increase in activities in the phishing and pharming domain. Therefore it could be said that the shift whether intentional or unintentional, is moving towards online information warfare and cyber terrorism.

This phase of online information warfare is coming from avatars who are bent on intimidation and destruction of the world and its people. Mostly religious fanatics and/or so-called freedom fighters, who have become very sophisticated in their manipulation and use of technology to serve their interests. They use cyberspace and online media to preach, recruit and train fighters for their course and also propagate anti-western propaganda and warfare – for example, Al-Qaeda using the internet and Aljazeera network media to incite hatred and terror on Westerners. Recently, there have been many devastating effects on the public, economies and general world security. The other issues involve paedophiles using online systems with highly coded information to undercut police monitoring. They sell or pass on abused children's photographs and other paedophilia information to their network members all over the world and for profit.

4 Costs Implications

Online activities such as information warfare come at a very high cost to stake holders. In the UK, the police, security services, the public, Government officials and the economy have suffered enormous financial and human costs. Other factors in Europe and USA have mounted increasing pressure on the population in the physical environment to curb cyber terror, compared to the risk free online virtual environment. Online information warfare is moving into other areas such as airlines operations and utilities such as gas, electricity and telephone networks etc.

Arreymbi and Williams (2005) examined the economics of electronic security and reported areas where flaws emanated. They also suggested some fixes to the problems given access to malicious cyber tribes. They argue the fact that advanced technologies are not providing adequate protection or safeguards to vital online information systems increases the risks factors. More cyber groups are finding easier means to access and capture business critical information and using them for competitive advantage or selling for profit to fund terror. For example, the South Korean and the Irish public have both experienced alarming suicides rates of stars and politicians due to internet chat room bullies and online peer pressure in organised mass brawls respectively. On sites such as Bebo, Facebook and Myspace are being monitored by UK police to stem the organised social crimes that are using such media and damaging lives and properties.

5 The challenges

The challenges involved in the operation and management of such dynamic environment is building intelligence, tracing attack sources, identifying users and protecting business critical data suing both hard and soft techniques in the physical and/or virtual infrastructures – such as the botnets etc.

5.1 Revealing Cyber Identities Techniques, countermeasures for meeting challenges and weaponry

5.1.1 Personalisation

This section is an extract from the monograph Artificial Intelligence Existing and Emerging Techniques Williams (2007). Refer to chapter 4 of the Monograph. It also highlights techniques and sources of weaponry for revealing Cyber Identities as well as for attacking vulnerable people who use the Internet.

(Peppers and Rogers, 1993, 1997) define *personalisation* as a process that allows the relationship with customers on the Internet to migrate from anonymous mass marketing and sales to 'one to one' marketing.

Kobsa also defines personalisation as a form of user modelling Kobsa(2000). The paper does not explicitly state that personalisation is different from user modelling. The interpretation given to his definition is that, *personalisation* is a process that helps user modelling. It is not synonymous to the process of modelling the requirements of users. User modelling seems to encompass other generic user requirement that sometimes transcends the boundaries of the characteristics and attributes of the user.

5.1.2 Personalisation Tools and Information retrieval

Personalisation tools are user behaviour oriented bias. They rarely capture the physical attributes of the user. This is a distinct feature of personalisation. Personalisation tools in most cases serve the interest of service providers and product vendors rather than for example persons who use their services or buy their products. The primary design goals of personalisation tools are to support management information systems of service providers. The tools attempt to capture user features such as interest, knowledge, habits etc. that could help in explaining the behaviour of a particular user. It is also dependent on external factors that are not easy to control. These factors constitute uncontrolled variables when formulating solutions to problems. It also seems to focus on user *preferences* rather than *needs*.

5.1.3 Predictive statistical models for information retrieval

Predictive statistical models use observed samples as the rationale for creating user models. They could also anticipate behaviour through information gathering from likeminded people. This notion was introduced by Zukerman and Albrecht (2000) as a *collaborative approach*. This section briefly highlights issues of predictive statistical models as introduced by Zukerman and Albrecht.

Predictive statistical models discussed here are linear models, TFDF (Term frequency inverse document frequency). A weighting scheme commonly used in information retrieval, Markov Models, Neural networks and Bayesian Networks. User's interest and behaviour could change over a period of time. Physical attributes and characteristics will not change in the short and midterm.

The models do not focus very much on the present. Most efforts seem to be devoted to addressing problems that occur as a result of changes, rather than focusing on the present needs of the user which is physical and could be modelled. User profiling technique focuses on the primary needs of the user.

Although techniques such as content based filtering is ideal for customising a system's functionality to specific requirements of a particular user, the approach requires each user to provide relatively large amount of data to enable the construction of a statistical model. This is an example of how user modelling over relies on user's input in real time.

The models also seem to be user dependent rather than self dependent. Self dependence means the capability to fulfil a given task on the basis of current information available to any entities or objects which possess functionality.

5.1.4 Subscriber and Mass Emailing Networks

Group and mass emailing systems serve as a social network. People with specific affiliations and interest belong to these networks. Membership usually takes informal forms. There are no fees paid for membership. It is rather based on the individual interest and information hotspots. Mass emailing systems and networks have the following characteristics;

- Membership is uncontrolled
- Members are of different age range
- Members are geographically dispersed
- Members originate from different social and cultural background
- A cross section of members will have met at seminar, workshop, conference or some form of meeting in a formal setting

5.1.5 Chat rooms

Chat rooms are virtual based auditorium where people log in to engage other people on challenging topics and themes as well as highly informal interactions. In communication parlance chat room interaction is full duplex and asynchronous. Chat rooms can also take the form of electronic and online workshops as well as Webinar and discussion groups.

5.1.6 SMS (Short message Service or Simple Messaging Service)

Short message service also known as text messaging is a way of sending short messages across mobile phones at a cheaper cost. Cyber tribes employ cellular networks to communicate. Although SMS can serve as a source of information for militating against attacks, it can also be exploited to the advantage of the attacker by denying voice services to large communities. SMS can also take advantage of zombie networks by using them as unprotected communication channel. Distributed denial of service attack can also be launched on SMS networks. The open functionality platform nature of SMS applications also makes it becomes a tool for information warfare Enck (2005)

5.1.7 Cyber language

A Cyber language is the language used for interaction on the Internet. Without doubt or question the Internet has its own language and linguistics. Internet users have to be familiar and conversant with the language in order to communicate effectively as well as use the system. The internet has its own vocabulary, grammar and lexical structure. As mentioned earlier at the beginning of this paragraph, effective communication is mainly based on the individuals experience and knowledge of common vocabulary. Poor language comprehension can be a form of vulnerability that could be exploited to the advantage of an attacker.

5.1.8 Online Gamers

Online gamers are tribe indicators. Online and computer game players could be drawn into Cyber tribalism, for the simple reason that gamers belong to special communities. These communities are so large in number that, members of the communities eventually develop and build new set of characters and principles. Game systems can be exploited as a source of weaponry. Tribes who want to control and manage information dissemination on the Internet are very likely to use game systems and communities as an operational base.

6 Who is winning the war?

Winners of the new age of information warfare are more likely to be in the hands of users or systems that have maximum control. Factors influencing this phenomena are:

- Control of Network
  The free access to information tools on the Internet sets the grounds for a battle of control. The war for control is mainly on how much access one protagonist has to information. Given that at present there are several utility programs that allow network traffic analysis and management without any external regulation, control of the network much often is in the hands of the public. Until some form of regulation and monitoring system is enforced it will be a losing battle.

- Effectiveness of Cyber Policing
  Cyber Policing are systems for monitoring and managing Internet activities. These systems can range from human to computer intelligent systems that provide alerts in cases of intrusion, exceptional and out of order network behaviour. They can also be described as behaviour monitoring systems. The intelligent systems supporting these activities have human interfaces that could be vulnerable. In theory they are designed to provide holistic information to security and safety personnel, however in practice their scope of geographical coverage is limited. This is partly due to the heterogeneous nature of networks.

- Information Depot is unprotected
  The Internet is like an ammunition depot which is unprotected and accessible by the public. Without a doubt it is a public network. There are vast amount of ammunition that could be used in information warfare. " These cuts across 22 tools and methods for attacks such as; Brute Force, Masquerading, Traffic Analysis, Profiling, Scavenging, Roaming and Scouting, Spoofing (Web, DNS, IP), Stealth Attacks, Denial of Service(DOS) (SYN Flood, Smurf, TCP ACK Flooding etc), Distributed Denial of Service (DDOS), Malware propagation(Worms, Viruses, Bots, Spyware) Man in the Middle, Replay, TCP Session Hijacking, ARP (Address Resolution Protocol) pollution, IP Fragmentation, Replay, TCP Session Hijacking, Password conjecture and guesswork, Backdoor, Mobile codes and electronic bombs, Ping, Permutation Analysis. Software tools and utility computer programs used by hackers to exploit vulnerabilities" Williams (2007). These tools make security systems vulnerable as such tilts the balance of strength in favour of attackers.

- Effective Internet based Geographic Information Systems (GIS)
  There is a lack of Internet based (GIS) capable of tracking locations with vulnerable networks. An Internet based GIS will help in managing weaker platforms within Global Networks. Integrated Location based services will be an enhancement of such a platform.

7 Conclusions

This paper discussed issues with respect to Cyber tribalism. The paper focused on social elements such as chat rooms, bloggers, Communication, email, U-Tube, Entertainment, Music distribution/download, game play, Social Engineering, identity theft, spoofing and spamming, bullying, incitation (suicides. Economic elements including money scams, money Laundering, Information theft form part of the review. The political elements highlighted covered radicalisation, confrontation, intimidation and terrorism. The main security elements covered paedophilia, cryptography and crime concealment.

Cyber Identities Techniques, countermeasures should focus on the application of personalisation tools, tracking of subscriber and mass emailing systems, chat rooms, SMS. There is the need for game saw enforcement agencies to be very conversant with different language paradigms. Online and computer game communities are sources of threat and power for attackers and info Ackers.

The battle of the new age of information warfare from our preliminary investigation is tilting in favour of end users, attackers and criminals due to maximum control of information and information management systems Factors influencing this phenomena are network control, ineffectiveness of cyber policing, unprotected information depot and infective internet based GIS. In other for law enforcement agencies to gain leverage there is the need to put up systems that will effectively address the issues identified and reviewed in sections 5 and 6. In our next work we will explore the appropriate strategies and model solutions in addressing the issues highlighted.

References

Arquilla, J. and Ronfeldt, D. (2001) Networks and Netwars: The future of Terror, Crime and Militancy, RAND (2001) (ISBN: 0833030302).

Arreymbi, J. (2005) Phishing Attack – A Socially Engineered Threat to e-Business. Proceedings of the International Conference on Internet Computing, Las Vegas, USA, CSREA Press.

Arreymbi, J. and Williams, G. (2005) Assessing the Economics of Electronic Security. ISSE 2005, Paulus, S., Pohlmann, N. and Reimer, H. (Eds). Vieweg. (ISBN 3834800112)

Borden, A. Col. (Ret). (1999) What is Information Warfare? Aerospace Power Chronicles, USAF.

Cordesman, A. H. (2002) Cyber-threats Information Warfare, and Critical infrastructure Protection: Defending the US Homeland (2002) (ISBN: 0275974235)

Denning, D. (1998) Information warfare and Security, Addison –Wesley (ISBN: 0201433036)

Rattray, G. J. (2001) Strategic Warfare in Cyberspace, MIT Press (2001) (ISBN: 0262182092).

Enacket al (2005), 12th ACM Conference on Computer and Communication Security

Williams G.B (2004), Synchronizing E-Security, Kluwer Academic Publishers

Williams G.B(2007), Artificial Intelligence, Existing and Emerging Techniques. Google Partner Programme, Kobsa and Powl (1995, 2000), (1997)Peppers and Rogers (1993, 1997), Zukerman and Albrecht (2000)

Williams G.B (2007), Online Business Security Systems, Springer-Verlag

Phishing Across Interaction Channels: Methods, Experience and Best Practice

Philip Hoyer

Senior Architect – Office of CTO
ActivIdentity (UK)
109 Borough High St, London SE1 1NL
philip.hoyer@actividentity.com

Abstract

This paper will draw on the experience gathered from years of working closely with banks and the current trends to combat phishing and online fraud threats. It will detail the renewed emphasis that strong authentication is not enough but a form of transaction authentication is needed. It makes a call to make the user more aware of the security process asked to perform a specific action and the concept of security process ergonomics. It details some aspects of the important decisions banks need to make when considering the use of anti phishing and anti fraud techniques across different interaction channels such as web, call centre, IVR, branch..

1 Banking channels – not only the internet

When considering phishing and online fraud attacks it is important to consider all interaction channels a user has with the bank, some of these channels are often overlooked in phishing analysis that focuses only on the internet channel:

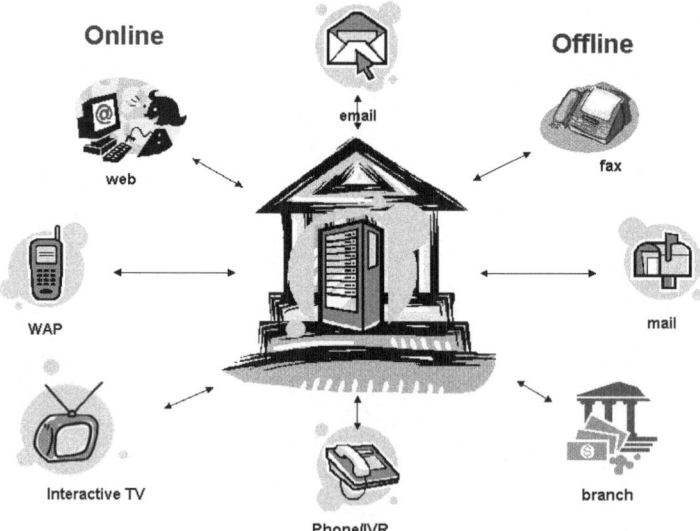

Figure 1: The possible interaction channels with a bank

N. Pohlmann, H. Reimer, W. Schneider (Editors): Securing Electronic Business Processes, Vieweg (2007), 73-81

As we will see not all channels behave the same or can be protected the same manner against phishing and online fraud attacks. Channels vary in three important respects:

1. Element of human involvement. Channels such as call centre or branch usually involve direct interaction with another human being. This reduces the potential for a brute force attack and increases the level of flexibility. However it also opens potential for a social engineering attack and may expose the bank to an attack from the inside.

2. Scale of usage. Phishing, unlike hacking, is a business. Hence phishers are most interested in channels with high levels of usage since it increases the odds of a successful attack.

3. Secure communication. Some channels are unprotected in terms of the data they transport (the phone for example or the fax), these carry additional challenges.

2 Phishing the aim and fundamental steps

The prime aim for a phisher is to get to your money, period. This takes normally the following steps:

1. Log on as you by using your logon credential (historically a harvested password)

2. transfer your money into the phisher's account or more often into an intermediary account

Now transferring money can either be done directly or it can be further broken up into:

a. setting up the phisher's target account / beneficiary

b. performing a transfer to the newly set up target account

It is important to understand these to see where the attack vectors are.

The first approach is to strengthen the door, meaning to make it more secure to log onto the banking web site. This has some benefits but does not mitigate against attacks where a user might have already logged in, for example from their computer at work while going for a tea break without locking their workstation.

Since most strong authentication mechanism to log on can somehow be attacked it is as important if not more so to protect step 2 of the phishing process.

2.1 Why strong authentication is not enough

In the context of this paper we define strong authentication as a two-factor authentication mechanism, often implemented by something you know (static credential, either a password or a PIN to unlock a device, similar to the PIN on a banking card) and something that you have (proof of possession achieved by some cryptographic mean, often as one time passwords that are generated via an algorithm using a moving factor and a symmetric key).

Considering the steps above, let's assume that MyBank protects the web banking channel with strong authentication. Lets also assume that for cost reasons and technical reasons the authentication technology is not PKI protected by TPM or smartcard but a device that is capable of generating one-time passwords (OTPs) and capable of generating a response to a challenge (Challenge/Response). As also pointed out by Bruce Schneier [Schn05] this protects against simple phishing attacks but not against the more sophisticated attacks, such as man in the middle:

"Here are two new active attacks we're starting to see:

1. **Man-in-the-Middle attack**. An attacker puts up a fake bank website and entices user to that website. User types in his password, and the attacker in turn uses it to access the bank's real website. Done right, the user will never realize that he isn't at the bank's website. Then the attacker either disconnects the user and makes any fraudulent transactions he wants, or passes along the user's banking transactions while making his own transactions at the same time.

2. **Trojan attack**. Attacker gets Trojan installed on user's computer. When user logs into his bank's website, the attacker piggybacks on that session via the Trojan to make any fraudulent transaction he wants.

See how two-factor authentication doesn't solve anything? In the first case, the attacker can pass the ever-changing part of the password to the bank along with the never-changing part. And in the second case, the attacker is relying on the user to log in." [Schn05]

For this reason and others explained below, a more in depth user aware security model is needed. Additionally, steps need to be taken to protect the static credential (password or PIN) when used over an unprotected channel or staffed channel such as a call centre.

2.2 Channel specific challenges of strong authentication

Some channels require different usage of credentials (factors)

Assume a 2 factor mechanism:
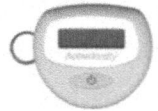
- an 8 digit OTP generated by a simple token
- a 6 digit PIN managed on the server

Over the internet since the channel is transport protected the user enters OTP + PIN (appended)

Over a phone (IVR) the PIN cannot be entered in its entirety because the channel is not protected

The use of the PIN (static credential or second factor) is different between channels
- Internet – entire PIN
- Phone – partial PIN (eg 3rd and 5th digit)

From a user and support perspective it is highly desirable though to have the same mechanism to protect all channels, but not all strong authentication mechanisms can be used across all interaction channels. The following matrix analyses commonly used strong authentication mechanisms and how applicable they are for each channel:

	WEB 	IVR 	Phone 	WAP 	iTV
Static credentials	Y	Insecure	Insecure	Y	Y
Partial Credentials	Y	Y	Y	Y	Y
Question & Answers	Y	Complex / Impractical	Y	Complex / Impractical	Y
OTP	Y	Y	Y	Y	Y
Challenge Response	Y	Requires numeric	Y	Y	Y
Certificates (PKI)	Y	N	N	Partial	Complex
Biometric (voice)	Complex	Y	Y	Complex	N

Figure 2: Strong authentication mechanisms applicability by interaction channel

As one can clearly see some very strong protection mechanism, such as a certificate cannot be used over phone (call centre).

2.3 A technical social engineering phishing attack

The following attack although not exactly a classic phishing attack in terms of password harvesting prepares the ground for the fundamental argument of the paper to raise the user awareness of the security processes both for initial authentication but more so for transaction authentication.

MyBank decided to deploy strong authentication based on devices capable of OTP and Challenge/Response. Both logon and transaction authentication are based on challenge/response. In the case of transaction authentication the 'challenge' is the target account number. This was deemed very strong protection since the challenge was also based on part of the transaction details.

The attack redirected a user to a pass-through phishing site. The clever bit, of the phisher, to be able to get 2 valid responses to subsequent challenges, to be able to perform all the necessary steps to get to your money (logon and transfer), was to fake a technical problem with the logon page.

The phishing pass-though site claimed that the logon had failed and asked the userto try again while capturing a valid challenge-response from the user and covertly logging into the user's account.

The phishing pass-through site now presented the logon page with the challenge given by the banking site to perform the transfer.

A user that wants to do banking and sees that there was problem on logon, will without much second thought try again because he wants to use the service.

After the user entered the response the phishing site can now perform the transfer. The user was successfully phished.

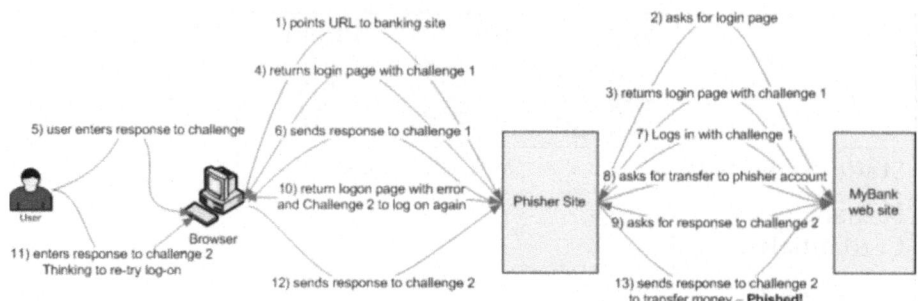

Figure 3: Phishing attack sequence

2.4 User awareness – a call for security ergonomics

The above attack highlights the problem with the disconnect in user awareness between the process necessary to perform the task (making a transfer) and the security process to allow it to happen.

Since both logging in and performing transfers use the same mechanism the user does not associate one security process with one specific task.

This user awareness is not linked to a specific user group either as described in [Dhamija06], even experienced computer users can be fooled by a sophisticated phishing site.

Furthermore the above attack exploits one of the basic human approaches to a problem, that of trial and error. This is augmented by the innate distrust in technology that some user groups manifest and the standard user response in case of failure. How many of us try again to start a car, or would re-press a button if there was no response the first time.

Combine that with some of the early experiences with teething problems around basic network connectivity and one would have an almost 100% success rate of people re-trying the login if faced with a technical error message (Again [Dhamija06] demonstrated that most users do not distinguish between messages from the browser or operating system and messages from the site itself).

Since the user is a fundamental part of the phishing equation, any anti-phishing technique of note must take the user element into consideration.

The way to take the user into account is to have different security processes for the different actions and steps.

This has many similarities to the discipline of ergonomics and hence this is a call for improved security ergonomics. As Alphonse Chapanis discovered in 1943, whilst studying why pilots of B-17 bombers sometimes crashed on landing (two identical levers one for the flaps one for the landing gear next to each other confusing the pilots under stress and tiredness) [Roscoe97], a user that cannot distinguish between the security processes for different actions will be confused and hence easily tricked.

As much as one does not perform the same security processes when entering a car (normally by inserting a key or more recently by presenting a fingerprint) and when driving it, the user of a banking internet site should have to go through two distinct security processes when accessing the interaction channel (for example presenting an OTP on internet logon) and when performing a transfer (e.g. a challenge response or other appropriate transaction authentication process).

If two different processes would have been in place, the above attack would not have worked because the phisher would not have been able to gather the challenge response by faking a technical problem with the login page.

Since we have established the reason for securing the transaction process via a different security process lets see more closely what this involves.

2.5 Strength in depth – Securing the transaction

To secure the transaction there are several aspects to take into consideration:

1. **The transaction context** – this analyses the context in which the transaction is happening and is often referred to as risk based authentication. This will for example take into consideration factors such as the time of day a transaction is happening the IP geo-location etc and based on a number of these factors calculate a risk score. If the score is below a threshold defined by the risk policy of the transaction it can be refused or additional credential confirmation can be asked from the user. The in-depth discussion of this topic is out of scope of this paper.

2. **Transaction Fraud Event data sharing** [MRaihi07] – This approach means that financial institutions share description of fraudulent events. Since fraudsters sometimes use the same payee instructions (including the amount) for multiple fraudulent payment attempts. By reporting the payment instructions used in the fraud, other institutions may be able to stop future fraudulent payment attempts to the same payee. The in-depth discussion of this topic is out of scope of this paper.

3. **Transaction data authentication** – this method applies a cryptographic process over part or the whole of the data of transaction that can be verified by the bank and not modified or regenerated by an attacker. One of the examples could be a PKI signature, the author prefers the term transaction authentication because of the common association between signatures and the use of asymmetric (PKI) cryptography. There are very good symmetric transaction signature algorithms (such as CAP Mode 1 with amount and currency or CAP Mode 2 with TDS [Mas07], or Ansi X9.9 [ANSI86]). The advantage of the symmetric key based algorithms is that the resulting authentication code or signature can be of a length that can be transcribed by humans or entered into other interaction channel access devices such as a phone.

Let's see transaction data authentication in more detail:

2.6 Transaction data authentication

As defined above transaction data authentication method applies a cryptographic process over part or the whole of the data of transaction that can be verified by the bank and not modified or re-generated by an attacker.

Let's analyse the advantages of using a cryptographic process based on a symmetric algorithm. This analysis uses the form factor of an EMV debit card that has a second authentication application on the card (CAP application) and can be used with a disconnected reader to generate both One Time Passwords (OTPs) and responses to an 8 digit challenge (Challenge/Response).

The use of symmetric algorithms running on an unconnected separate security device (hardware security anchor such as the EMV Card together with the reader) for transaction authentication has the following advantages (non exhaustive list):

- The resulting transaction authentication code (TAC) can be compressed to a size that a person can transcribe (under 16 characters or digits in length)
- The TAC can be entered in other channel access devices used by financial institutions such as phone for phone banking, can be spoken to an automated phone banking channel such as Interactive Voice Response systems (IVR) or to the operator of the bank's call centre.
- The TAC can be written down and used in complete offline channels such as the FAX for offshore transaction instructions.
- The devices that will generate the TAC having to perform only symmetric cryptography can be implemented on relatively cheap microcontrollers. This means the possibility of producing a cheap relatively tamper proof hardware security anchor that by being unconnected is resistant to the usual attacks of the most common of internet access channel devices, read the PC.

There are also some disadvantages (non exhaustive list):

- the cryptographic entropy of the TAC is limited (to the number of digits of the response) hence it needs to be assessed against the risk profile of the transaction itself
- the device needs to be carried around and provisioned separately to the channel access device (note that the separation from the channel access device can also be seen as an advantage, by allowing the user access to services from different channel access devices)
- the user needs to enter the response
- the user needs to enter the transaction data

Let's analyse the last disadvantage in more detail especially with respect to the user awareness problem and attack described above.

If one thinks of a standard banking transaction of transferring money (the one the phisher is most likely to use to get your money into their hands) one does have distinct transaction data elements (not exhaustive list):

- unique transaction id
- date of transaction
- source account number
- target account number
- amount
- currency

Now assuming we want to protect the transaction and create a transaction authentication code (TAC) we could use all of the above data to generate the code. If the device that generates the TAC is an unconnected device we would have to ask the user to type in all the data, something that will for sure backfire since a too cumbersome security process will not be used by the user.

Some institutions have hence taken the approach of minimal data entry by making the user enter just the unique transaction id into devices capable of generating a response from a challenge (the transaction id in this case). This is relatively user friendly but presents one problem.

Since the unique transaction id is generated by the banking system, the user has no relationship to it and does not associate it with the other transaction data. Hence it will be impossible for the user to distinguish between a real transaction id (challenge) or a transaction id (challenge) presented by a phishing site for the phisher's transaction to get to the user's money = Bad security ergonomics.

The key to effective transaction authentication, and thus protection against man in the middle and Trojan attacks, is to make it blindingly obvious to the user that the data which he is signing (i.e. the challenge) is a parameter of the transaction. The objective is for the process to be so simple, obvious and sensible that the user is immediately suspicious when asked to deviate from it. Arguably the best approach is to require the user to enter the number of the target account. This offers good protection against attack, provided that the challenge-response process is reserved solely for this purpose (see earlier example).

It's tempting to leverage the signature used for transaction authentication to also introduce an element of non-repudiation, to provide a proof that the user did indeed request the transaction. However this can complicate the process by introducing additional parameters that need to be signed, such as an amount. Strictly speaking a signature generated with a symmetric key does not provide non-repudiable proof and this may be better addressed with strong audit logging.

If the transaction authentication code (signature) does need to be a function of a second piece of transaction data then it is important to make the user aware of how the challenge he has to enter to generate the TAC is constructed, this can be done even through visual aid for example by using partial digits from the amount to be transferred and the last part of the target account number:

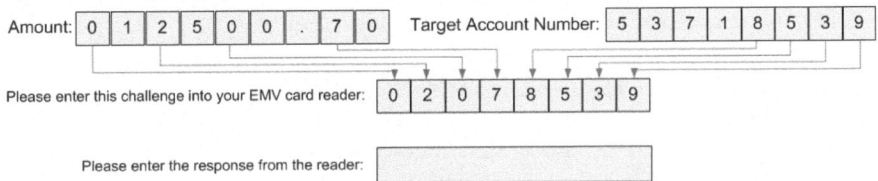

Figure 4: User meaningful challenge based on partial amount and last digits of account number

In this way:

1. the user uses an OTP for accessing a channel bit not for a transaction

2. the user only enters challenges when making transactions but not when accessing a channel (and a short challenge at that)

3. the user can associate the challenge with the transaction data relative to the transaction being performed

4. The security processes can be used by non-internet channels such as the phone and the call centre

The bank has created two cross-channel security processes with good security ergonomics that will likely be used and make the life of the phisher that much more difficult.

3 Conclusion

Hopefully it has become clearer that institutions that are targets of phishing attacks and online fraud and offer different interaction channels to their services, when choosing the right security mechanisms must take into consideration:

1. The user and the security ergonomics of the processes that will be implemented

2. Clear user aware association of the security process required for the action to be performed will fend off sophisticated attacks (e.g. OTP for log-on and challenge response for a transfer)

3. Different interaction channels present their own challenges – the best security mechanisms might not even work for some channels

4. There are viable solutions that allow for a high level of security without compromising the user experience that are truly cross-channel (e.g. EMV CAP enabled debit cards with unconnected readers or hardware tokens capable of both OTP and challenge/response).

As the attacks become more sophisticated the defence from them must stay user security ergonomically friendly and cross channel capable, otherwise the attacks will migrate to the channel with least defences.

References

[Schn05]   Schneier Bruce, "The Failure of Two-Factor Authentication", March 2005, http://www.schneier.com/blog/archives/2005/03/the_failure_of.html

[Dhamija06] Dhamija, Rachna – Tyger, J.D. – Hearst, Marti : Why Phishing Works: http://people.deas.harvard.edu/~rachna/papers/why_phishing_works.pdf , 2006

[Roscoe97] Roscoe Stanley, "Adolescence of Aviation Psychology", Human Factors and Ergonomics Society, 1997, ISBN 0-945289-10-3, http://www.aero.ca/e_adolescence.html

[Mas07]   MasterCard Worldwide, "Chip Authentication Program – Functional Architecture", February 2007

[ANSI86]   American National Standards Institute, ANSI X9.9: Financial Institution Message Authentication (Wholesale), 1986.

[MRaihi07] David M'Raihi et al , IETF," How to Share Transaction Fraud (Thraud) Report Data", http://www.ietf.org/internet-drafts/draft-mraihi-inch-thraud-02.txt

IT-Security Beyond Borders – an Assessment of Trust Levels Across Europe

Christian Wernberg-Tougaard

Innovation and Transformation, Unisys EMEA
Lejrvej 17, DK-3500 Værløse
christian.wernberg-tougaard@unisys.com

Abstract

The world is changing – faster and faster. Every now and then we realize that if we had planned, if we had envisioned the transformation of the society's use of technology, we would have been much more prepared for fighting IT-security threats and challenges.

At the same time several indicators point at disrust to digital service among both citizens and companies. The studies cited in the paper indicate that society needs to raise the awareness – not only of IT-security – but of the culture associated with being citizens and companies in the digitized service society – otherwise we might risk a new generation of people who suffer from techno-fear.

This paper discusses two subjects: (1) the outcome of an expert group appointed by the Danish Board of Technology on behalf of the Danish Parliament to examine future IT-security threats and challenges that needed international action to prevent damage to Denmark. This section will inherently be biased toward telling the Danish case, although its applicability is far wider internationally. The outcome has been presented to a parliamentary committee which together with Government will focus on the long term pan-European actions that need to be done/coordinated in order to avoid damaging IT-security threats in the future. (2) the current level of trust as evidenced by the "wheel of distrust" (the mechanism creating greater and greater uncertainty and disbelief of the digital services – something that will be pivotal to overcome for the growth of countries) and research.

The paper concludes with recommendations for the joint actions that the European Commission (EC) and the Member States need to take in order to preserve the advanced digital community that we are on the edge of realizing.

1 Trust – and "wheel of distrust"

One of the classical examples of identification of a threat to the digital service society is the "junk mail problem" – in a 1975 research paper Jon Postel [Post75] identified that the mail protocol of the would-be internet based e-mail system had an inherent "flaw" that enabled anyone to send unlimited and/or unsolicited mail to anyone – if just the mail address was know.

In 1975 this was not a problem as the mail systems operated akin to a peer-to-peer system – as everybody knew everybody they were e-mailing. However, today e-mail communication is global – and the ability to spam millions of people at effectively no cost to the sender has made the "junk mail problem" a real and serious issue – which has demanded global regulation and costly effort eventually leading to building up an entire industry to fight spam.

N. Pohlmann, H. Reimer, W. Schneider (Editors): Securing Electronic Business Processes, Vieweg (2007), 82-92

The moral of this story is that a lack of envisioning of full impact of implementation of (otherwise beneficial) IT solutions can have severe unforeseen consequences. With respect to spam the key error was adaptation of a physical security scheme in the virtual world – putting power to an existing process does not always yield the desired results. Unwanted or unintended side effects can and will happen with future IT related decisions.

Many threats have been previously identified and dealt with – but how do we ensure that the impact of what we do today does not have unwanted future side effects? In truth – we can not. Like the computer theoretical "halt problem"[1], we can not tell from some implementation of IT whether it will be completely "good" or completely "bad" – in an IT-security sense. But by utilizing past knowledge and the combined skills of research, private and public experts we will be able to at least predict some of the challenges and consider counter measures.

1.1 Declining Trust

In one sense – the phrase 'declining trust' has an inherent flaw in that we don't actually know the exact trend line as to date there exists no reliable time series data measuring trust. Having said that, there exist are some useful indicators that suggest individuals are becoming more trust diluted – or that trust in general is eroding in the Digital Society of the 21st century.

In a global research effort to probe this key question, Unisys created the TEI (Trusted Enterprise Index) which is focused on measuring trust among citizens and companies. As always, such indexes are only high level indicators; but nevertheless they tell a worrisome story. IT-security – measured via TEI – does not actually measure whether people are *in-fact threatened* – rather whether they *feel threatened* which consequently affects their behaviors and actions. Nordic banks have been overwhelmed by phishing attacks. The greatest concern has not been the loss of actual money – rather the loss of customer confidence and faith; at risk is people distrust the banks' Internet services, and that they would revert to analogue services and undermine the previous efficiency gains earned by self-service digitalization. Such behavior would be very difficult to reverse quickly; putting it another way trust is easily lost but hard won (or regained).

The Trusted Enterprise Index (TEI) surveys trust in a multi-dimensional way: the trust to basic societal functions (such as democracy), the fear of dislocations such as pandemics and of course whether digitalization makes people anxious or distrustful. As this research is the first in a continued global study of trust, it is difficult to assess the transformation of trust over time – and the impact of different tools and policies on trust. But the findings are nonetheless interesting as a baseline, and clearly show that there are significant levels of concern and anxiety among European citizens[2] towards security. It is impractical to review the entire research findings in this paper, so instead I will extract some of the trust identifiers for discussion – interested readers can consult www.unisys.com for white papers, background information etc.

Typically a statistically significant subset of the European citizens and companies have been asked about their view on trust – gauging their reaction as: "Are you extremely concerned, very concerned, somewhat concerned or not concerned with …".

---

1 The stop problem is the mathematical proof – by Alan Turing – that you can not determine whether a program will stop or not. See Wikipidia under „Halting Problem".

2 Unisys has – through the Ponemon- Institute – analyzed 7 EU member states (2007) [France, Germany, Holland, Sweden, Italy, Spain and Belgium] and asked citizens and company-representatives about degree of concern about "Threat of terrorism", "Pandemics", "Environmental disasters", "IT-security" and many other trust-related areas. See more: http://www.unisys.com/about__unisys/trusted_enterprise_index.htm

One of the questions asked is: "Your computer security and the threat of viruses, spyware or spam" (see figure 1) – among the surveyed European countries the "Extremely concerned" and "Very concerned" range from 27% (France) to 53% (Holland).

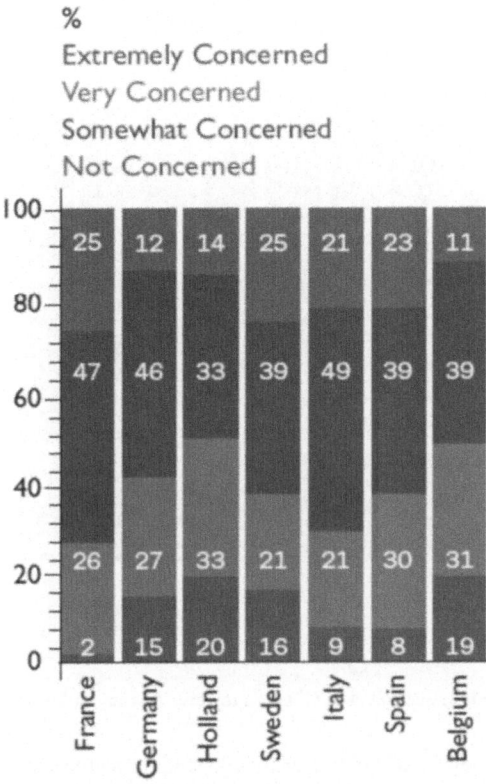

Figure 1: Level of Concern for IT-security in Europe

Another major topic is the protection of the individual information integrity – via privacy protection. The European commission has focused on the privacy issue in a number of areas – from RFID-technology to in-depth personal information exchange on air travelers between EU and US. But do the citizens feel their privacy as being endangered today? The overwhelming response is – *Yes*. When asked about "Others having unauthorized access to your personal information" on average +50% answered "Extremely concerned" and "Very concerned" (see figure 2). It seems appropriate therefore that the European Commission takes privacy serious.

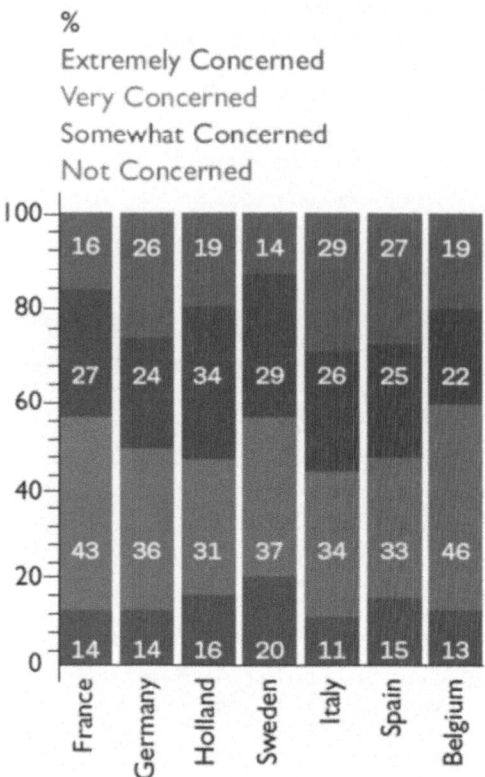

Figure 2: Level of Concern towards privacy in Europe.

The Trusted Enterprise Survey clearly indicates that depending on the survey country, a range between large minority to clear majority of European citizens are filled with uncertainty and distrust in respect to digital services today. On other areas like terrorism and pandemics, the fear is even more outspoken in the survey feedback.

Naturally the study gives rise to numerous interesting questions – to which, we do not as yet, have answers. For example: Are highly digitized societies more likely to have trust issues? – and therefore more vulnerable to trust erosion? What factors drive the transformation of trust? Taking a more theoretical perspective it is possible to envision some of the consequences of trust erosion – a mechanism that is part of what an be termed the"wheel of distrust"[3] which is discussed in the next section.

1.2 The Wheel of Distrust

The "wheel of distrust" is a description of a mechanism that is escalating the collapse of trust in the digitized service society. One of the prime reasons the "wheel of distrust" exists is, that we live in a world of duality – where we are in-between the analogue and the digital world – so as individuals can elect to

---

3 The wheel of distrust was presented at the German Presidencies conference on „Innovation and Responsibility" Berlin, June 4-5, 2007. You can read more and see the presentation at my blog: http://blog.wernberg.org

choose whether we want to be remain part of the analogue regime or join or exit the digitized regime. One of the determinants of shift is trust; another is convenience[4].

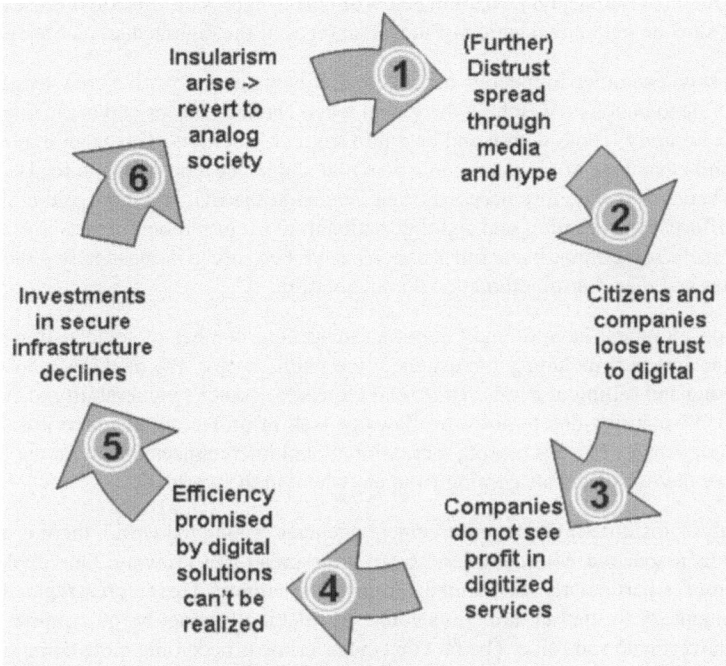

Figure 3: The Wheel of Distrust

(1) The Wheel of Distrust starts by rumors, media and hype that creates fear, uncertainty and doubt (FUD). **(2)** Citizens lose trust to digital services – the same occurs with companies; I appears citizens are more FUD-sensitive than companies, therefore likely that citizens will act on their distrust before that of companies – however skepticism will escalate. **(3)** Companies (to a certain extent including Public Sector companies) lose faith in the efficiency gains embedded in digitalization (efficient work processes, automation, reduction of labor intensity etc.) and hence **(4)** the full realization of the promised benefits of digitalization becomes unachievable – as citizens opt out of self-service due to fear of privacy loss (if the fear / distrust is greater than the convenience) etc. **(5)** As companies do not see profit in digitized services there is no need to protect the infrastructure – to make it more safe – and hence disinvestments in infrastructure occur which in turn **(6)** causes even more citizens to revert back to the analogue society which will **(1)** further erode the trust to the digital service infrastructure.

Every country in the digital age – must face the "wheel of distrust" and the associated consequences that are triggered. Citizens world-wide are generally becoming more and more distrustful of the digitized service society. This erosion of trust can lead to an escalating distrust of digital solutions – thereby fueling further erosion.

In order to utilize the power of the digitized service society, the trust among citizens (and companies) to digital services must be restored – this calls for a combination of heightened awareness and collabo-

---

4 In a research study by Unisys, consumers were documented to have willingness to hand over privacy to gain convenience (Global study of biometric authentication, Unisys [Unis06]).

ration between research-public-private groups to proactively address the next generation IT-security threats. Currently the benefits of e-Services surpass the actual problems experienced by users – supporting continued growth in e-trade, home banking etc – but the danger is the erosion of trust will undermine or dramatically slow down the realization of the advantages of the digitized service society.

Take Denmark as an example: To meet its official goal of being an innovative knowledge and entrepreneurial society able to punch its weight at the global level, Danish citizens and companies must be able to communicate securely – both within and beyond Denmark's borders. This is an important prerequisite for taking full advantage of globalization's potential and hence a prerequisite for Denmark's future economic well being. It is therefore necessary that Denmark, the EU, and the world at large, seriously increase their efforts in preventing and fighting national and transnational cyber-crime. Many of the security problems facing Denmark and other nations cannot be solved domestically – they require multilateral solutions and meaningful international collaboration.

Technological development have brought about an increasing number of societal functions being integrated with the Internet; including for instance, the public sector, the banking industry, as well as widespread buying and selling of goods. This trend increases society's vulnerability to cyber-crime and means that poor IT-security, due to software flaws or lack of protection against viruses and hackers, has serious consequences. For this reason, increasing global interconnectedness via the Internet consequently increases the risk of threats coming from anywhere in the world.

Among the analysis institutes and law enforcement agencies around the world, there is a clear consensus that problems associated with cyber-crime are widespread and growing. One explanation is that the global Internet is particularly well suited for criminal activity. The culprits typically hide behind networks of computers, located in numerous countries, making Internet-borne criminal action incredibly difficult to investigate and solve. The fact that cyber-crime is becoming more complex and criminal action harder to detect, also points to the fact that cyber-criminals are also becoming increasingly skilled in their trade.

Though the problems continue to exponentially grow over time, IT-security issues are as a whole poorly addressed in both Denmark and internationally, as compared to other forms of crime. The amount of scientific investigation and publicly available statistics regarding cyber-crime is highly limited; just as concrete initiatives to prevent and confront cyber-crime are characterized by a lack of resources, focus and understanding.

1.3 Consequence of "wheel of distrust"

So what? – the world has been analogue for millennia, so why the sudden this fear of distrust?. That's exactly the point – if you compare the paradigm shift from an agricultural society to an industrialized society over the past 200 years, it meant more efficient production methods – where investments were tied to machines, not people. The weak link in this system was the production apparatus and processes itself. No spare parts or no fuel, meant no value creation.

During the transformation toward the post-industrial knowledge society people became more and more an asset than a cost. But, in a knowledge society – people, and what they know, are the tangible asset to the corporation.

When moving from the knowledge society towards the digitized service society, people become – not irrelevant – but assume another role. As information is stored in a collaborative environment, describing processes, procedures, methods etc. the value of people is measured by their ability to access and assess information and create new insight and outcomes – they become knowledge-innovators. But this role – and the society associated with it – demands resilient and available infrastructure and systems, as the workforce effectivity is directly contingent on the ICT infrastructure. Therefore, the criticality of the ICT-infrastructure is dramatically rising in our increasingly inter-connected world of structured and unstructured data, information and knowledge. This increasing degree of interconnectivity makes even small disruptions locally more likely to trigger larger impacts regionally – or even globally.

But why should Governments worry? – is this really a governmental issue and not a private issue? No – European governments do need to act – and act quickly. The rate of transformation of the analogue society into the digitized services society is accelerating; more and more technology becomes IP-enabled – therefore reachable through the internet. Machine to machine interactions already far outnumber human to machine interactions today. In our new everything wireless and inter-connected world, BOTnets with everything from domestic appliances such televisions and refrigerators to new communication and entertainment devices such as iPhones – will create a new sensory and interactive world of the 21st century with new rules, new opportunities and new threats.

In order to have a future society that is based on a sound socio-economic foundation, governments need to ensure that citizen actions and experiences are as good or better in the digital world as compared to the analogue world. One way to ensure this is through "e-citizen training" as well as effective protection of critical or vulnerable IT-infrastructures – all in order to preserve and regain the trust of the citizens. At the same time, other studies have indicated that there is a tight connection between ICT-investments, innovation and GDP growth. Examining the infrastructure backbone of the globalization – the outsourcing and off shoring etc of labour and services would have been impossible without ICT innovations fuelling that transformation. You can examine the last poorly connected sub-region of the world to cost-effective high speed data connections – East Africa – to see how lack of competitive infrastructure hampers economic growth and competitiveness.

I would postulate that a society that is consequently seen as less secure and as less trusted, will experience lower growth in GDP – everything else equal – than those not such limited. This means – in traditional applications of economics – that if you could evaluate the effect of a policy segregated from any other influence, then the countries that have focus on protecting the digitized service society will in the long run have higher growth and economic sustainability than those not protecting the digitized service society.

2 The Danish IT-security policy frame

The challenge was taken up recently by an expert working group examining "IT-security Beyond Borders", under the auspices of the Danish Board of Technology (DBT) [DBT07]. The mandate was to look at what could threaten Denmark that would require international action for an adequate response. The group suggested actions that would go significantly farther than previous efforts in the arena of IT-security in Denmark. We are resolute that it is now time to take concrete and well-aimed steps in the form legislation, certification, and labeling programs among other things.

Our working process included a brainstorming effort among 40+ leading holistically thinking IT-security experts of Denmark to make a prioritized list of themes – then to reduce this down to 6 concrete problems with associated solutions. These were discussed with global IT-security leaders[5] within differ-

---

5 The International advisors to the Working Group: Former White House IT-security advisor: **Howard Schmidt** , Chief Information Officer for the Government of Austria: Prof. dr. **Reinhard Posch**,. IT-security economist: Ph.d. **Tyler Moore** and Chairman

ent fields of knowledge and finally validating the meta-problems and their solutions with industry and public sector interest groups.

2.1 Problems identified by the working group

The working group sought to develop and present internationally-focused recommendations for cross-border IT-security problem areas that are seen to be among the most problematic now and in the near future for the Danish society – and even though the policy recommendations are specific for the Danish context, it has relevancy and significant impact on other EC member states as well as the wider international community.

The goal is for all the recommendations presented to be realizable in practice. The group advises that the recommended solutions should be set in motion as soon as possible and simultaneously in the outlined six problem areas. It is furthermore the working group's intention that the recommendations should contribute to improving Danish and international IT-security – a prerequisite to citizens and firms being able to harvest the many benefits that a digitally connected world has to offer. The six areas of focus are:

1. Vulnerabilities in software and hardware
2. Inadequate knowledge of IT-security
3. The inability to differentiate between secure and insecure products and services
4. The lack of concerted, transnational police efforts and prosecution in the cyber-crime arena
5. Lack of secure identification
6. The lack of focus on IT-security in public procurement

The aim of identifying the six problem areas – and the accompanying suggested actions, has come from realizing that most of the current and future dangers to the digitized service society that Denmark actually originate outside Denmark rather than inside the country. Only 0.04% of the spam in Denmark originates there, China and US are the biggest sources. The same trend appears to be true for many other IT security areas.

It is also important to stress that the expert group recommended actions regardless of associated implementation complexity – an example being the suggestion of automated updates[6] or a Europe wide "white list" of secure products. Many of the suggestions will take significant pan-European discussions – or even global discussions – to identify the right scheme of operations. However, the basic requirement is the need to drive concrete actions in order to make a safer future digitized service society.

The key driver of the expert group has been to make sure that, citizens and companies in the digitized service society will continue to believe that the digitized service society is relevant and trusted society to actively engage with in the future – that it is the "trustee" of innovation and development of the welfare society. Many of the measures suggested have a "trust"-improving dimension – such as ensuring that people can use technology without fear of becoming part of a BOT-net, or that everyday citizens remain as trustful in using the digitized information super-highway as they would be in the analogue equivalent (where one exists). Future purchase scenarios might mean fewer consumer product choices with certain products and services, with more limited features but inherently much more secure and trustworthy than equivalent offerings today.

---

of ENISA's ad hoc working group on Regulatory Aspects of Network and Information Security and member of the United Nations CEFACT Steering Group: **David Marsh**. We are very thankful for the valuable input provided by the experts.
6   The German BSI has recently suggested this action as well.

2.2 Overview over solutions suggested.

Problem area	Solutions suggested
1. Vulnerabilities in software and hardware Problem: Vulnerabilities in hardware and software, such as operating systems and packaged programs were the most serious of all IT-security problems in 2006, as measured in the number of instances and their consequences. The consequences of these vulnerabilities are of greater consequence for small and medium-sized enterprises (SME's), public institutions and private citizens, rather than large firms.	Solution 1: Develop a model that ensures security updates in software are installed on the users' computers directly after a security flaw is found. The process should be imperceptible for the basic user while advanced users should be given the option to steer their own update process. Solution 2: There should be EU regulation that vendors of electronic, network-based (IP based) hardware such as computers, telephones, MP3-players, alarm-systems, and in the future even domestic white goods (such as refrigerators), must deliver their products with the latest firmware and software updates pre-installed. Solution 3: Denmark/EU should create a "white-list" for software and hardware. The public sector could then set the example and drive the market by only using white-listed IT-products. Solution 4: A certification program for Internet Service Providers (ISPs). All ISPs in the EU are obliged to follow a code that at least meets the standard set by the Danish ISP Security forum's code of conduct. Within 3-5 years, it should be made law that all ISP's are ISO 27001-certified (or meet an equivalent thereof).
2. Inadequate knowledge of IT-security Problem: Inadequate knowledge is a significant cause of the lack of security. The human factor is. important in relation to "phishing", identity theft and the spread of harmful programs that can "crash" a computer. This can obviously cause the loss of data from the hard disk including documents, photos, films, music, etc.; and for companies, the loss of client records and intellectual capital. The lack of IT-security knowledge is rarely an isolated problem for the firms and citizens who are ill-secured. The consequences of poor security can spread to a firm's customers, partners, etc., and the people listed in private user's address list – in total, causing exponential damage and economic loss.	Solution 1: A greater focus on IT-security in school. The security aspect should be connected with students' use of computers throughout the course of their education. Solution 2: Establishing "The Board for Greater IT-Security" focusing on citizen awareness – Solution 3: Regulation against "*Cyber-pollution*".
3. The inability to differentiate between secure and insecure products and services Problem: An ever greater number of products and services contain an element of connectivity (Internet Protocol – IP-based) and thus it is ever more relevant to offer secure products and services to users with the aim of improving the general security level. This includes computers, mobile phones, hard disk recorders in TV's, media centers, refrigerators, and similar items in a private home. In the near future nearly all consumer goods, including cars, boats and planes, will contain IP technology and be connected to the net.	Solution: Denmark should take the initiative to develop a concept for labeling internet-connected products, meaning that private persons and companies are given the ability to see the security level of a given product. For example, a star-rating as in the auto-industry's "crash-test" scheme, could be implemented. The labeling program should include the entire EU, and thereafter spread to the global market. The reason for the global focus is that the security problems are expected to increase further because these products will continue to be produced around the world by numerous manufacturers, making it evermore difficult for end-users and companies to comprehend and handle the security aspect.

4. The lack of concerted, transnational police efforts and prosecution in the cyber-crime arena Problem: Cyber-crime is a difficult arena for law enforcement agencies in Denmark as well as the EU and world at large. Interpol is largely absent from the fight against IT-related crimes and Europol's roll is relatively small due to limited resources. The growing amount of cyber-crime on a global basis is fraught with inadequate police efforts. It is problematic that the prevention and investigation of cyber-crime is generally prioritized very low in comparison with other police investigations, that the sector receives few resources and therefore has an acute lack of personnel with the competency to make a change in and outside of Denmark.	Solution 1: Structuring the efforts: acknowledging cyber-crime as a new law enforcement specialization. Appointing at least one unit responsible for cyber-crime in each police district, and establishing a central authority that can address complex cases concerning cyber-crime professionally – nationally and internationally. Prioritizing cyber-crime should not come at the cost of other police activities. Rather budget increases are needed to supplement the efforts. Solution 2: Increasing the knowledge level: Law enforcement authorities must be equipped with greater competency across the board – from the education of specialists in the various sectors of cyber-crime, to increasing the knowledge of prosecutors and judges. Solution 3: Further development of international cooperation agreements, which can ensure more efficient and effective processing of transnational cyber-crime cases.
5. Lack of secure identification Problem: Communication security is a prerequisite for the free flow of information, efficient eGovernment, and thus better public service in the future. Citizens' usage of the increasingly integrated economic service infrastructure in the EU and around the world, can be halted by the lack of a clear identification mechanism, nationally and across the EU. This could minimize the risk of the abuse of personal data.	Solution: Denmark should establish a long-term strategy for the further development of the existing "Digital signature" into a "citizen service passport", seen as a 'digital identity, which then helps to minimize the risks involved in eGovernment, eTrade, and other forms of electronic communication. The goal is that, in the long run, all EU citizens should have an interoperable digital ID. The working group points to a project under development in Austria, as a source of inspiration. The Danish development work should be coordinated in relation to the entire EU, with the goal of building a secure, EU-interoperable "citizen service infrastructure", using common and open communication standards.
6. The lack of focus on IT-security in public procurement Problem: Under 5% of the criteria found in contracts for the public procurement of IT account for security. The working group finds that IT-security is not taken seriously when the EU and its member countries take bids on infrastructure and systems contracts. It is problematic that technical specifications for IT-security and privacy in the public procurement of IT products are either lacking or non-existent, and that these contracts seldom contain a "connectedness analysis", meaning an assessment of the consequences of a security breach on all of the interconnected public units, many of which are not themselves a part of the procurement agreement.	Solution: Regulation stating that IT-security must be a key parameter in all public procurement contracts, where IT is a component. Specification sheets and bids should contain both a security and connectedness analysis that assesses the consequences of a security breach for interconnected sectors.

3 Conclusion

An examination of the 6 identified key issues of future IT-security problems which need international action or collaboration is needed in order to protect the business resilience of the future digitized service society has led to some rather cunning proposals. They will be difficult to agree upon internationally, as well as challenging and costly to implement. I and my colleagues in the expert group are convinced that addressing the identified problems should be a major European Community effort in order to prepare for a safe and secure economic future. Some of our suggestions might be impractical, some might show to be outdated due to technologic development – but most of the recommendations should and can be undertaken today.

The creation of a pan-European understanding of the need to educate and train citizens and companies to understand the digital society – to make them become effective digital citizens and digital companies – will not only make them better able to protect themselves against internet wrong-doers, but will also fuel innovation and applicability of digital solutions and content.

What is needed is a much stronger holistic approach to the concept of being a "digitized citizen" compared to being an analogue citizen (or company). Governments should invest in preparedness, in training, in awareness – and in creating incentive models for embedded protection of the digitized service societies citizens and companies.

In conclusion, for governments there is no way back – most governments have used the digital dividend (the surplus created by using more efficient IT that people/processes) on other spending – and going back to a lesser digital world is not an option: **There is only one way – forward**. There is a carrot so we don't have to use the whip. *Ceteris paribus:* countries that become more trusted in the digitized service society will have higher GDP growth. Countries with higher amount of digital-prepared citizens and companies will more easily fit into the next generation of society, and hence more easily protect their competitive advantages. So Governments should take the trust issue real seriously – and act quickly to their national advantage and that of their citizens.

References

[Post75]   Postel, Johnatan: "RFC 706 – On the junk mail problem". Network Working Group, Request for Comments: 706, NIC #33861, Nov 1975. http://www.faqs.org/rfcs/rfc706.html

[DBT07]   The Danish Board of Technology: "IT-security beyond borders" – the findings and recommendation to the Danish Parliament and the Ministry of Science by an independent expert group, 2007.http://www.tekno.dk/subpage.php3?article=1288&toppic=kategori11&language=uk&category=11

[Unis06]   Unisys: Global Study on the Public's Perceptions about Identity Management, May 2006. http://www.unisys.com/eprise/main/admin/corporate/doc/ID_Research_w_paper.pdf

Analyzing and Improving the Security of Internet Elections

Adam Wierzbicki · Krzystof Pietrzak

Polish-Japanese Institute of Information Technology
{adamw | peki}@pjwstk.edu.pl

Abstract

Internet elections are one of the tools of e-Government that seems a natural application of the increasingly ubiqui-tous computer networks. The possibility of voting from your own home would decrease the costs of elections, and as a consequence, elections could be carried out more frequently. This would increase the participation of citizens in the democratic state, enabling a transition from a representational to a direct democracy. Yet, Internet elections are vulnerable to a large number of security threats, and the risk of failing to provide security is the disruption of democratic society. For this reason, many previous attempts to provide Internet elections have failed, and their use has been discouraged by security experts. In this article, the conclusions of previous security analyses – the SERVE security report and the experiences from the Estonian Internet elections – are updated to take into account recent technological developments. The article presents new methods that can be used to increase the security of Internet elections.

1 Introduction

Internet elections remain an elusive myth, the "Holy Grail" of ITC security experts. The implementation of Internet elections today is technically simple. However, it is very difficult to design and implement an Internet election system that would have a level of security comparable with traditional elections. Additionally, the main potential advantages of Internet elections: increased election participation and decreased cost, are very hard to achieve without sacrificing security.

In democratic societies, the increase of citizen participation in the decision making process is of funda-mental importance. The existence of secure Internet elections would enable a transition from the repre-sentational democracy to a participating democracy, where most significant decisions would be carried out on a majority basis. At the same time, the increasing adoption of the information society causes an increased confidence in ITC technology, and a desire to reuse working solutions in new application areas, such as elections.

Yet, even electronic elections – without the use of the Internet, but using dedicated electronic devices that act as terminals for voters, and a fully electronic vote counting system – have basic security prob-lems. Such systems must assure vote confidentiality, integrality, and anonymity; they must have working access control that allows only authorized voters to vote; and they require a comprehensive audit trail. The cost of failing to realize these security requirements is immense: the compromising of an election can lead to severe social problems. In a traditional election system, all of these security requirements are met using a complex system of security procedures, including trusted, impartial third parties.

N. Pohlmann, H. Reimer, W. Schneider (Editors): Securing Electronic Business Processes, Vieweg (2007), 93-101

Internet elections create even more security challenges than electronic elections without Internet access. The majority of these challenges can be attributed to the openness of the Internet (its geographical distribution, lack of administrative control, etc) and to the lack of control over the hosts of voters. A final reason for the difficulty of implementing Internet elections in many countries is the still limited Internet access of voters.

Note that it is not necessary to aim for perfect security, but merely for a security level that is comparable with traditional systems. Yet even this goal seems elusive. It is difficult to judge whether an Internet election system is sufficiently secure. There are two ways in which this could be attempted: the first is a security audit of proposed Internet election systems by independent, impartial security experts. The second way would be a statistical comparison of election results that would be carried out using Internet elections and traditional elections. Yet, for this approach to work, Internet elections would already have to be sufficiently popular in order to yield a representative outcome.

This article attempts to address the question: has the progress since 2004 in the area of information security been sufficient to justify the introduction of Internet elections? In other words, **are the conclusions of previous analyses (mainly, the SERVE security report) still valid today? What are the new security technologies that could be used today to implement secure Internet elections?** Is the Estonian approach a new development in the area?

A second goal of the article is to propose new technological methods and new election procedures that could mitigate some of the described security threats. In the next section, we give a brief overview of the most important attempts to implement Internet elections: the SERVE system, the Estonian Internet election system, and of a recent proposal of an Internet election system in Poland. The third section contains a security analysis of Internet election systems. The fourth section discusses new methods of improving Internet election security. The last section concludes, presenting our recommendations for Internet elections that are compared with the results of the SERVE security report and with the implementation details of the Estonian Internet election system.

2 Overview of Internet Election Systems

In this section, we give a brief overview of chosen Internet election systems. A security analysis of these systems is presented in the next section.

2.1 The SERVE system

The idea of carrying out Internet elections has been undertaken by the US Department of Defense (DoD) in 2003. The goal of the project has been to reduce the barriers of election participation for voters that were American citizens living outside the U.S., including military personnel and their dependents. The project has been called SERVE: the Secure Electronic and Voting Experiment. The project has been carried out by Accenture and had a budged of about 20 million US dollars. The deployment of SERVE has been planned for the 2004 elections in the USA.

SERVE was never deployed, and the DoD has discontinued further efforts of creating an Internet election system. This decision was a result of the conclusions of a report about the security of SERVE, written by a panel of experts in computerized election security assembled by the DoD. As a result of the expert's analysis, it became clear that **the use of Internet elections could create a real threat to election security** – and, as a consequence, to national security. Because of the critical nature of the report and of the spectacular failure of the SERVE project, Internet elections have attracted attention from leading professionals in information security [1].

In the SERVE system, it was possible to vote for 30 days before Election day, until closing of the polls. Every eligible voter had to register at an election office, received a *password using traditional mail* and could vote *only once* from his own personal computer, using a Web browser that could run ActiveX or Java. The Web browser had to enable cookies and JavaScript. (A drawback of SERVE was that the prepared application worked only on a Windows system.)

The main system components of SERVE were: the Voting Application running on a Windows PC in a Web browser, an online Network Server, a Vote Storing Server and many Vote Counting Servers. The voter used the Voting Application that encrypted its communication using SSL/TLS, and send the ballot and personal voter information the Network Server. Next, the Network Server encrypted this data and sent it to the Vote Storing Server. This server decrypted the information and verified the access rights (franchise) of the voter. The Vote Storing Server retains a copy of the encrypted ballot and voter personal data, and sends a copy of the ballot to the Vote Counting Servers (in the Local Election Offices). There, the anonymous votes are counted and stored in a database.

2.2 The Estonian Internet election system

Since the failure of SERVE, the idea of Internet elections has been adopted by other nations. The small European country of Estonia (about 1 million eligible voters) is so far advanced in its adoption of Internet elections that a national election has been carried out in this country through the Internet on March 4th, 2007 [3]. This decision followed the success of a pilot deployment that was used in a local election in Estonia in 2005. Yet, due to concerns about security, the Estonian voting project is not a true Internet election: the legislators have decided that the Internet election would be followed by another phase, during which all voters could use the traditional ballots. More importantly, votes cast in the second phase *override* votes cast over the Internet.

In its structure, the Estonian election system superficially resembles SERVE; however, there are several important improvements. Like in SERVE, voters could vote for some time before Election Day of the traditional elections: from the sixth to the fourth day before Election Day. The Estonian Internet voting system has the following characteristics [8] that differ significantly from the SERVE system:

- each eligible voter is able to revote. In this case the older votes are deleted.
- classical voting in polling box cancels the voters' electronic votes.
- if considerable attacks against e-voting have been detected, the Electoral Committee might stop e-voting and cancel the results of voting.

The Estonian Internet voting system has the following components [9]: a Web-based Voting Application that communicates with an online Network Server using SSL/TLS; a Votes Storing Server and offline Votes Counting Servers. The Voting Application is able to run on Windows, Linux and MacOS operating systems. It contains an integrated public key used to encrypt communicated ballots.

In the Estonian Internet Election system, voters were authenticated using personal IDs that were stored on Smartcards, together with a personal PKI. This approach allowed to solve authentication and integrality problems. The access control (checking of voter franchise) could be performed easily due to the voter signature that was made using a public ID issued by the Estonian government. The Network Server performs authentication and access control, sends a list of candidates to a voter and receives the encrypted ballot. The ballot is not decrypted, but immediately transferred to the Votes Storing Server.

The role of the Network Server ends after the user has cast a vote. The Votes Storing Server stores votes until the end of the voting period. After that, the received votes are counted by an offline Vote Counting Server. The electoral committee can use the encrypted logs of the system to resolve problems.

2.3 The proposed Polish Internet election system

In Poland, the question of Internet voting is especially relevant because of the recent proposal of the initiative "Polska Młodych" to introduce Internet elections [4, 5]. The proposal is quite naïve from the point of view of information security and has received well-deserved criticism [6, 7]. While the proposal in its current shape is hard to defend (it is rather a draft than a complete description of an Internet election system), it has received a lot of media attention in Poland. The promise of realizing Internet elections is attractive to all users of such technologies as e-banking, e-commerce or e-learning. Yet, the level of public awareness of the associated security problems is very low.

The proposed system repeats the mistakes of the SERVE system, such as using ordinary passwords. It does not use applets or ActiveX components, but instead a simple Web form that is sent to a server. The Internet elections are carried out on the Election Day. In addition, the system does not specify any procedures for vote storage, anonymizing and counting. The description of the system finishes with the submission of the ballot. The proposal has very little technical content; instead, it focuses on a draft of legal regulations of Internet elections.

A further limiting factor of using Internet elections in Poland or in other countries is that there exists no method of strong cryptographic authentication of citizens. In this aspect, Estonia is unique, since all its citizens are equipped with PKI certificates stored in their public IDs.

2.4 Research on new Internet election protocols

The basic problems of providing anonymity and authorization of voters have been approached by researchers that use new cryptographic protocols that provide controllable anonymity and full privacy of the votes [13]. This and other research solutions can be seen as important steps towards realizing the goal of securing Internet election, yet they usually do not propose a comprehensive security solution for an Internet election system that would take into account all realistic vulnerabilities.

3 Security Analysis of Internet Elections

In this section, we present a security analysis of Internet elections that builds upon the experiences of the previously described Internet election systems. We also present a critique of the described systems.

3.1 General requirements of Internet elections' security

These requirements can be summarized in the following points:

1. Only eligible voters are able to cast ballots that participate in the computation of the final election result
2. Eligible voters are not able to cast more than one ballot that would all participate in the computation of the final election result
3. Votes are anonymous. To fulfill this requirement, votes must be private when they are transmitted together with personal voter information that is required to check voter eligibility.

4. All correct and valid votes must be counted in the final election result. It must be possible to repeat the calculation of the election result.

5. It must be possible for independent auditors to check that all correct and valid votes were correctly counted in the computation of the election result.

6. The results of the election must be secret until the end of the election.

7. The voting system must enable all eligible voters to cast a vote during the Internet election.

Note that this list includes only the requirements that are fulfilled by a traditional voting system. An example of a requirement that is desirable for elections, but is not fulfilled by traditional elections is the enforcement of a ban on selling and buying of votes.

3.2 General vulnerabilities of Internet elections

The vulnerabilities of Internet elections can be classified into the following broad categories (we give some example vulnerabilities for each category, without attempting to classify all vulnerabilities):

A. Vulnerabilities and attacks on the Internet election software.
1. Backdoors of Internet election software
2. Malicious bugs in the Internet election software
3. Revealing of the software's cryptographic keys

B. Vulnerabilities and attacks on the Internet election execution environment.
1. Trojan horses, viruses and malicious software that block voting, spy on votes, or modify votes
2. Sabotage of the client's Web browser by modification of its configuration
3. Hacking of the Internet election servers

C. Infrastructure vulnerabilities.
1. (Distributed) Denial of Service attacks on Internet election servers, clients, the DNS system, or network infrastructure
2. Phishing and spoofing of the Internet voting servers
3. Man-in-the-middle attacks
4. Attacks on the Public Key Infrastructure

The above-mentioned attacks can be carried out by many types of attackers, some of which may be equipped with significant resources and technological know-how. Among others, potential attackers are: local political organizations, political organizations in other countries, terrorists, criminals, individual or organized hackers. Some of these attackers may have very high funding and infrastructural support.

3.3 Vulnerabilities and attacks on the Internet election software

The SERVE system was a close-source system and has been criticized for its lack of software audit. The certification process of Internet voting software is often insufficient. In 2006, the American Election Assistance Commission revoked the certification right of Ciber, Inc., a company that tested the American electronic voting systems. The reason for revoking certification rights were lax procedures [10]. The case of Clinton Curtis [12], who was a developer of software for an electronic voting machine who was asked to include a backdoor in the code, is warning enough that the danger of malicious bugs and backdoors is real. All documented attacks on electronic voting system (such as the vulnerabilities of the DIEBOLD system documented by the Open Voting Foundation) could also occur in the case of Internet voting systems [11].

A particular drawback of the SERVE system has been the fact that the ballot was decrypted on the Vote Storing Server, along with the voter's personal information. This problem has been solved in the Estonian Internet election system.

3.4 Vulnerabilities and attacks on the Internet election execution environment

One of the reasons for the critique of Internet election security is the low security of personal computers owned by the voters. These computers often have out-of-date and insecure operating systems; do not have updated antivirus software; are not adequately protected using firewalls and Intrusion Detection Systems. One of the conclusions of the SERVE security report has been that Internet elections could be more secure if the voters would use specially prepared computers installed at election points (a "*kiosk*" approach) [2]. Yet, this approach practically destroys the advantages of Internet voting and actually significantly increases the cost of an election.

3.5 Infrastructure vulnerabilities

A very good example of infrastructure vulnerability is the Distributed Denial of Service attack that was carried out by Russian hackers against Estonia shortly after the Internet election. The attack was provoked by a decision of the Estonian government to move a public monument of the Soviet army soldiers. The decision was highly unpopular among the Russian minority in Estonia, and consequently in Russia. The DDoS attack started on 27 April, 2007. Data gathered by Arbor Networks showed that sources of attack were worldwide, rather than concentrated in a few locations. Attack bandwidth changed from under 10 Mb per second to 95 Mb per second. 25% of the attacks lasted no longer than one hour, and about 5% lasted over 10 hours. The peak of the attacks was executed by a botnet with a throughput of 100 Mb per second, which reaches the capacity of Estonia's Internet connectivity. Targets of the attacks were government and parliament sites. Many of these sites had to close down; some reverted to text-only pages. While this attack has not targeted an Internet election system, it demonstrates how easily the Internet election in Estonia that took place a few months earlier could have been sabotaged by an external political organization. The described DDoS attacks would have made it impossible for voters outside Estonia to use the Internet voting system, and therefore the entire Internet election would be compromised.

The proposed Polish Internet election system is particularly vulnerable to DDoS, since the procedures propose using the Internet voting system on Election Day only.

4 Methods For Improving Internet Election Security

In this section, we propose a few methods for the improvement of Internet election security. The proposed methods mainly focus on mitigating the vulnerabilities of the Internet execution environment.

4.1 Distribution of operating systems and applications on Live-CD

The simplest approach to provide a secure runtime environment for Internet voting system would be a Live CD containing a hardened Linux or BSD-based operating system. Such a system would guarantee that the runtime environment is secure, without any malicious software.

There are some issues regarding running Live CD systems. The first problem is network connectivity. A majority of Internet users posses only one PC that often is connected through a USB ADSL modem to the Internet. Using Live CDs in such an environment will require users to manually configure the Internet connection. The problem is even bigger with a wireless connection, due to the fact that a vast group of wireless network adapters are not supported in Linux systems, and if they are supported, they commonly lack advanced security mechanisms like WPA or WPA2. This will prevent users from using a wireless Internet connection with enabled WPA encryption.

4.2 Virtual machines on voter hosts

The problems of running Live CD versions of operating systems are partially resolved by using virtualization technologies. Instead of running an Internet voting application in a clean environment from a Live CD, the user can run it inside a virtual machine.

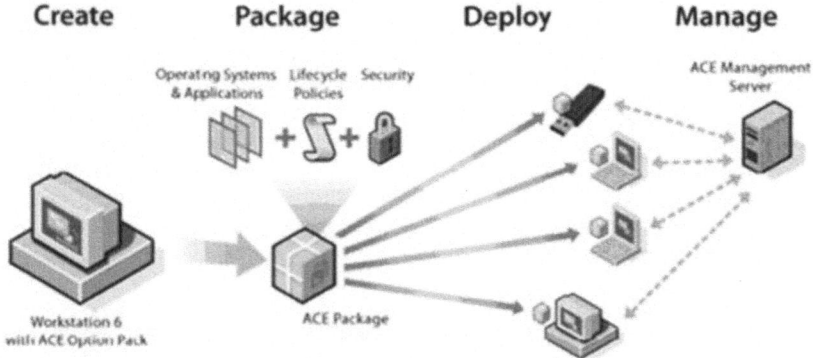

Figure 1: Secured Virtual Machine Technology (source: www.vmware.com)

The virtual machine can use the Internet connection configured for the host. The machine is started by running an application, relieving the user of having to manually restart the computer and to change the BIOS boot order.

By using software like VMWare ACE (demonstrated on Figure 1), we can push security of virtual machines even further. The virtual machine can be encrypted, the integrity of the virtual machine image can be checked, and policies regarding virtual machine usage can be expressed and enforced. This enables to provide secure operating systems with built-in cryptographic keys. Consequently, the virtual machine can provide a secure communications channel. Using the keys distributed with the machine will prevent spoofing and man-in-the-middle attacks.

Currently, a license of VMWare ACE is between 10 and 50 dollars for an individual user (a VMWare virtual machine without the advanced security mechanisms is free). The purchase of a large number of licenses for Internet voting applications would require a negotiation that would probably considerably reduce the price. Alternatively, there are virtual machine technologies that are available as Open Source, like XEN or QEMU.

The use of secured virtual machines does not prevent all attacks on the voter's execution environment. A Trojan horse or spyware could still create screen dumps that compromise vote anonymity. Malicious software could take control over the keyboard or mouse, attempting to select the wrong candidates in the voting application. Such an intervention, however, would be noticed by the voter. The advantage of using virtualization technologies lies in the fact that malicious software cannot interfere with the voting application and prevents compromising privacy and integrity of the communicated ballot.

4.3 Remote execution of voting applications

Instead of using Virtual Machines, voters can use virtual desktops that provide users with remote execution of an operating system with the Internet voting application. By using software like Terminal Services RemoteApp, we can provide the voter with a simple application that is executed on the voter's personal computer and connects securely to a terminal server. Once the connection is made, the terminal server creates a virtual desktop for the user and starts the Internet voting application. Terminal Services RemoteApp and Citrix Metaframe allow to make a single application (instead of a full virtual desktop) available for the user. This solution does not require Virtual Machine installation on the voter's PC; on the other hand, the remote execution of voting applications is less scalable than the Virtual Machine approach.

Another advantage of using remote execution is that voter authorization is carried out by the terminal server (it can be based on Smartcards, as in the Estonian solution), but the Internet voting application itself need not be aware of the voter identity. This also implies that it becomes impossible to check which ballot has been cast by which voter. On the other hand, the logs of the terminal server and of the Internet voting server are sufficient for future audit.

5 Conclusion

The SERVE security report recommended using an expensive "kiosk" infrastructure as the only secure alternative to the Internet voting system based on voter's personal computers. **In this article, we have demonstrated that this conclusion of the SERVE security report is no longer valid**. The use of virtualization technologies makes it possible to create a secure execution environment on voter's personal computers, and to overcome several infrastructural vulnerabilities, such as the man-in-the-middle attack or the spoofing of Internet voting servers.

Most of the security threats listed in the SERVE security report are still valid today. However, a much larger emphasis should be placed on selective Distributed Denial of Service attacks, as indicated by the events that have taken place in Estonia. On the other hand, Estonia's example also shows that the popularity of Internet elections is still very low: only about 9000 voters (1.84%) cast an electronic ballot in the Internet election in Estonia. This is a result of the low trust of voters in such technology, since over 80% of people in Estonia responded that they were in favor of Internet elections in a previous opinion poll.

True Internet elections are still a mythical goal. The Estonian election can be called a success mainly because it used a very conservative voting procedure that allowed voters to override their decisions made in the Internet election through a second vote in the traditional election. Other attempts of Internet elections have been usually carried out only at a local, and not at a national level. The current state of security technology still does not enable fully secure Internet elections, yet the use of new technology – such as virtualization – increases Internet election security.

We recommend the cautious use of Internet elections that should be preceded by a national political debate and by a thorough security analysis of the Internet election system by independent security experts. This analysis should focus on providing a sufficient level of security, not perfect security that exceeds the security requirements of traditional elections. The potential use of Internet elections should be accompanied by a development of appropriate election procedures, such as the procedures used in the Estonian election. We recommend the use of virtualization technology to create secure execution environments and communication channels for Internet election applications.

6 References

[1]   D. Jefferson, A. Rubin, B. Simons, D, Wagner et. al; "Analyzing Internet Voting Security"; Communications of the ACM; October 2004, vo. 47, no. 10, pp. 59-64

[2]   D. Jefferson, A. Rubin, B. Simons, D, Wagner; "A Security Analysis of the Secure Electronic Registration and Voting Experiment (SERVE)"; January, 2004; www.servesecurityreport.org

[3]   Estonia to hold first national Internet election; Reuters; February 21, 2007

[4]   Głosowanie przez Internet, a project of "Polska Młodych", 2007, Poland, http://www.polskamlodych.pl/

[5]   A. Pach, Schemat rozwiązania e-voting, an opinion for "Polska Młodych", 2007, Poland, http://www.polskamlodych.pl/dokumenty/schemat_rozwiazan.pdf

[6]   M. Kutyłowski, Opinia na temat projektu głosowania przez Internet Stowarzyszenia Polska Młodych, 2007, http://www.polskamlodych.pl/dokumenty/opinia-kutylowski.pdf

[7]   Stanowisko w sprawie głosowania elektronicznego w wyborach powszechnych, Internet Society Poland, 2007, http://www.isoc.org.pl/200701/wybory

[8]   T. Magi, Practical Security Analysis of E-voting Systems, Master thesis, Tallin University of Technology, 2007

[9]   Estonian National Electoral Committee; General Description of the E-voting System; 2004; http://www.vvk.ee/elektr/docs/Yldkirjeldus-02.pdf

[10]   C. Drew, U.S. Bars Lab From Testing Electronic Voting, The New York Times, January 4, 2007; http://www.nytimes.com/2007/01/04/washington/04voting.html

[11]   Risk Assessment Report Diebold AccuVote-TS Voting System and Processes, September 2, 2003, http://www.verifiedvoting.org/downloads/votingsystemreportfinal.pdf

[12]   Clint Curtis, hasło w Wikipedii, Wolnej Encyklopedii: http://en.wikipedia.org/wiki/Clint_Curtis

[13]   A. Zwierno and Z. Kotulski, A Light-Weight e-Voting System with Distributed Trust, Electronic Notes in Theoretical Computer Science 168 (2007) 109–126

Remote Access Mechanics as a Source of Threats to Enterprise Network Infrastructure

Paulina Januszkiewicz · Marek Pyka

Wyższa Szkoła Biznesu w Dąbrowie Górniczej
(Academy of Business in Dąbrowa Górnicza, POLAND)
{mpyka | pjanuszkiewicz}@wsb.edu.pl

Abstract

The issue of providing secure communication between mobile users and enterprise infrastructure is currently regarded as one of the main tasks for administrators. In the presented article the authors will conduct a discussion concerning remote access mechanics. For a significant number of enterprises information is the key element of business activity. Such information often proves to be the base of market activity and one of the most vital assets of an enterprise. The interest in the area of remote access solutions is growing rapidly, mainly due to organizational requirements and the necessity to maintain a position within the market.

Nowadays, many dynamically developing companies rely on IT systems to process information, which in many cases lacks appropriate protection. The authors shall attempt to introduce the issues of virtual private networks in the aspect of their significance for business, as well as the subject of Network Access Protection. Arguments in favor of using remote access shall be presented, based on the susceptibility analysis for various methods conducted by the authors.

1 Introductory information

Along with the technological and business development, many large and medium sized enterprises face the necessity of a higher degree of integration in the terms of IT systems, which in turn enables more efficient resource management. The changes of sales procedures, as well as the current fashion for mobility are forcing the enterprise IT departments to design and implement remote access methods for a wide range of users. Enterprises are using VPN (Virtual Private Networks) solutions in order to guarantee the integrity of internal business resources and ensure confidentiality of communication between the client and the enterprise network. The popularity of such methods created a false sense of confidence for this solution and an overall sense of security within the infrastructure in which it is implemented. Three types of private networks are being employed in practice [Lam, LeBlanc, Smith 2005]:

- Trusted – when the Internet Service Provider guarantees that no third party besides the selected company will be able to access the wiring used for confidential information transmission.
- Secure – when data is subject to encryption at both ends of the tunnel, which renders any attempts of listening virtually impossible.
- Hybrid – when the network meets the requirements of both trusted and secure solutions.

N. Pohlmann, H. Reimer, W. Schneider (Editors): Securing Electronic Business Processes, Vieweg (2007), 102-109

One should bear in mind that even a properly implemented private network solution cannot completely prevent the possibility of unauthorized access. the protocols used in the creation of secure VPN networks are mainly focused on providing a secure communication channel with authorization on both ends – or without it (depending on the implemented remote access protocols). What they fail to provide, is the possibility to examine the status of a client system before establishing connection. Unfortunately, the lack of control over the client system before establishing the secure channel might often lead to serious issues within the internal enterprise network.

Introduction of appropriate security measures is usually involving additional financial effort – such concept leads the majority of enterprises into realization that access mechanics security is nothing more than a needless cost generation. The administrators' attempts to limit and condition the remote access rules are often regarded as needles resource access handicapping and an impediment to the business process. However, many VPN users do not recognize the issue of information security as focusing on the aspect of availability. The following diagram illustrates the relation between information availability, the degree of security and cost efficiency of implemented technologies.

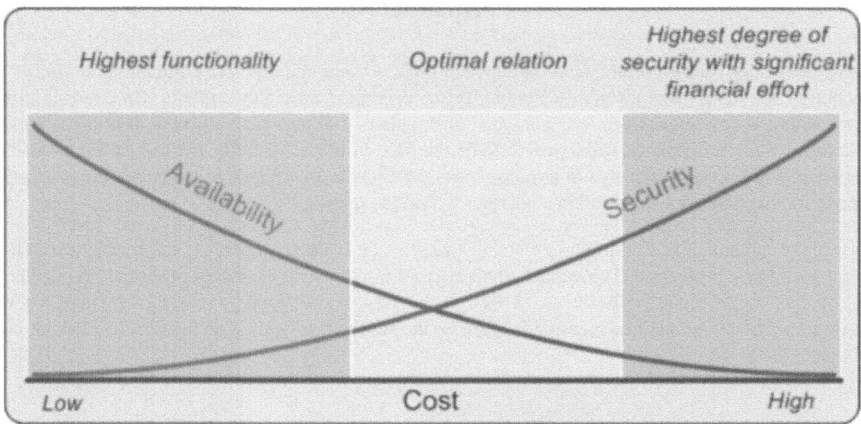

Figure 1: the relation between availability, security level and cost of information protection.

2 Threats and Chosen Remote Access Mechanics

One of the most important issues concerning data access security is the awareness of external threats, which makes approximately 30% of all threats. There are many scenarios which are known to include a threat to a remote access network, ranging from interception of VPN authorization data to standard methods of password breaking or configuration errors made by the administrators. However, the biggest of current threats to VPN communications is malicious code that can penetrate the internal network through the secure channels. the data control measures protecting the enterprise against malicious software are unable to react and protect the infrastructure, because the whole traffic going through the VPN channel is encrypted, making it impossible to intercept by third parties, as well as our own security systems. The recent analysis of attacks conducted against companies shows that the main goals of the attackers are information gathering and financial profit (replacing the widely discussed motivation of 'proving one's worth' [Smith, Komar 2005]) and the main target of attacks is a user workstation. By analyzing the reports of antivirus software manufacturers, one should notice that 80% of malicious software infiltrates the enterprise infrastructure through spam or secure communication channels (Symantec, Kaspersky, Sophos). The threat of malicious software becomes even more immediate, when the clients of VPN networks are mobile computers belonging to users who are not aware of the threats, do not follow basic security guidelines, do not use firewall systems or work on accounts with administrator privileges. Computers that are not sufficiently protected by their users should be treated as not trusted by the access control systems and be subject to strict verification principles. The issue becomes even more intensified when employees are forced to rely on public access points (HotSpot, Kiosk, Internet-café) to establish communication with enterprise infrastructure. In order to mitigate the threats it is required to maintain constant control over the client status: making sure that he is not working with administrator privileges, ensuring that he is using firewall services and current versions of antivirus software etc. Within the Internet, one might come across specialized malware applications that listen for specific VPN traffic and after it takes place, they establish a session with a remote server and transfer entire or filtered traffic from the victim computer. Verification of client computer configuration and its critical applications status may protect a company from information leaking or its loss altogether.

During the implementation of client station control mechanisms one should consider several factors, such as the procedures of action in case when it is impossible to verify the client, when the client fails to meet the security policy requirements, when it is possible to reconfigure the client station etc. Building remote access control systems is not an easy task and certainly not a cheap one. It requires the administrators to develop w wide range of policies and control principles, as well as to enforce intensive log gathering and analysis procedures. There are already some technological solutions available on the market (they shall be discussed later) that aim to help building secure remote access infrastructures for VPN networks and Terminal Services. While searching for an adequate enterprise solution, one should bear in mind that the access method should be versatile enough to allow client access regardless of the applied communication mechanics or types of shared applications.

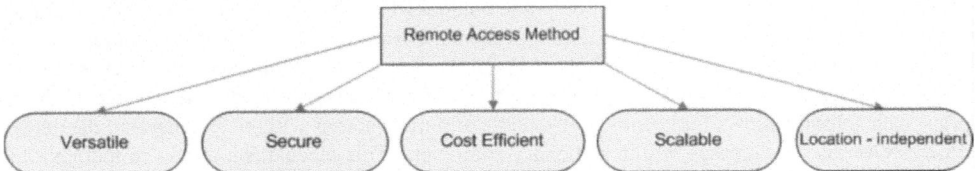

Figure 2. Perfect remote access method characteristics.

Access method security is conditioned by the access device, the client and the resources – therefore it is necessary to verify user identity, the location form which the connection is being established and the connection method. These elements brought together with the remaining aspects of communication security, all contribute to the confidentiality of information processed within an enterprise. It is important to allow users to connect through mobile devices such as laptops, PDAs, as well as stationary PCs. the only limitation should be the installed software or the configuration itself.

Network access control is solely dependant on electronic measures of security – that is ever since the additional physical control disappeared. According to Infonetics Research forecasts for years 2006-2008, the market turnover for Network Access Control solutions might reach 3.9 billion USD (Figure 3).

Access control is one of the most vital elements of security – it allows to identify users, as well as the devices handled by them. Resource access is usually gained from various locations, based on the policies attributed to each access method. NAC helps to enforce security principles, ensures protection, improves keeping track of principle violations, perfectly integrates itself with virtual private networks and works similarly to VPN quarantine.

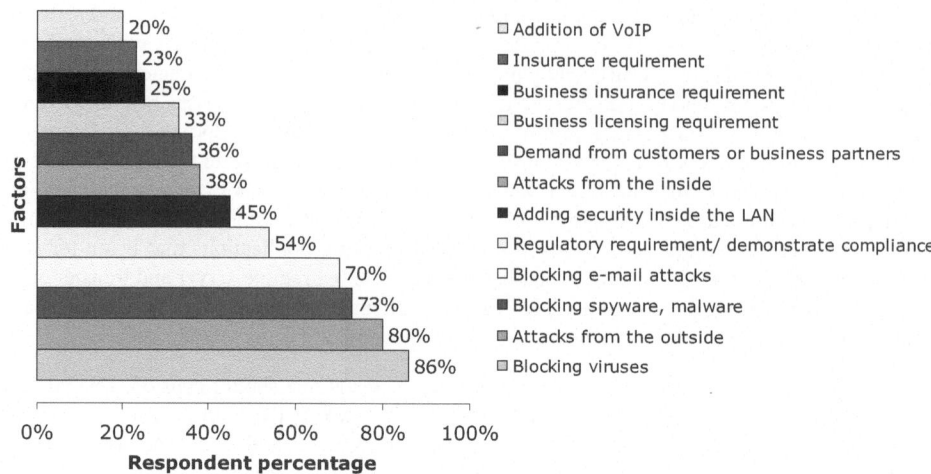

Figure 3. Factors contributing to enterprise security development [Infonetics Research 2006].

NAP (Network Access Protection) (further description in 3.1) is another solution for improving net-work security. It has been recently developed by Microsoft, which integrated it with Windows Vista and Windows Server 2008 Codename 'Longhorn'. With NAP, computers connecting to the enterprise network can automatically be subject to an update – during this process their access to the network will be severely limited or blocked altogether only to be unlocked when the computer meets the determined requirements. This platform enables validation of the used security policies, keeps computers in a con-dition agreeing with the access rules – thanks to update servers (Remediation Servers). NAP is also used for mobile device control, since it verifies the condition of each device as soon as it connects to the net-work – such solution allows for keeping the benefits of remote access without endangering the network security. NAP also finds usage within stationary computers. This mechanism allows to maintain high levels of efficiency and working comfort, without stepping down in the field of security.

NAP is a brand new technology and has not yet taken root in the majority of enterprise security systems. RAS, IPSec or VPN are still being used, however, RAS requires to maintain access points, leading to needless cost generation, while IPSec and VPN require to maintain and manage client-side software, effectively limiting access from stations outside enterprise control. The organizational issues of remote access can be solved by enabling application access through a web browser. On the other hand, in case of a high number of shared applications, one should take account for expenses associated with a regular audit and security tests of the servers hosting the service. It is also a good idea to implement a technol-ogy that will handle threats of malicious software coming from stations that establish remote access.

VPN solutions involve a variety of standards: L2FP/ L2F (Layer 2 Forwarding Protocol), L2TP (Layer 2 Tunneling Protocol), PPTP (Point-to-Point Tunneling Protocol), MPLS (Multi Protocol Label Switch-ing) and the most common: IPSec, VPN and SSL VPN (Secure Socket Layer VPN). According to Garter Research 2007 reports, SSL VPN begins to outstrip IPSec and the 2/3 of mobile users will choose this solution in 2008. Several years after the introduction of the SSL protocol, the TLS (Transport Layer Security) protocol was launched, providing slightly more advanced security mechanisms. The differ-ences are quite significant, since the hashing algorithm MAC got replaced with HMAC, the amount of generated alarms was increased and the requirement of DSS/DH algorithm support was implemented. The issue of compatibility between those two algorithms has not been resolved yet; however, the major-ity of solutions supports both protocols.

SSL VPN is one of the methods of gaining remote access to enterprise resources. In comparison to IPSec, which is located in the network layer of the OSI model, SSL operates on a higher, transport layer. The role of SSL is to secure communication, therefore ensuring confidentiality and integrity of the transferred data and perform authentication of both ends. Virtual private networks operate on similar principles. SSL allows to encapsulate information flowing on higher layers (for example – application layer). The SSL protocol also allows to create site-to-site virtual private networks tunnels, as wells as client-to-site, known as 'clientless VPN'. The SSL VPN solution is commonly associated with client access, which is an incorrect assumption. It is believed that client-to-site does not require installation on client workstation – this is incorrect, because performing certain actions requires a Java or ActiveX applet.

Solutions involving similar general ideas were being used some time ago in Unix remote access text systems. Even today SSH (Secure Shell) is commonly used, providing connection encryption. Such solutions are applied particularly in server technologies, where other connection methods are not possible (for example modem access). With this method, the risk of a threat between the sever and the client is relatively low, only the possibility of intercepting the authentication data is the element that weakens this method. Considering the fact that authentication process will be enhanced by the mechanism of the One Time Password, that leaves the communication still not sufficiently protected, which can lead to attempts of modifying it by man-in-the-middle attacks.

Remote access enhanced by a graphical interface is a whole different approach to working 'remotely'. First of all, a slightly higher bandwidth is required in comparison to the console. Within the Unix systems, it had been attempted to solve the bandwidth availability issue and the Window X system was developed. It is based on a 'client – server' architecture, where applications run on a remote server are the clients and a graphical terminal is the server. Today, similar techniques can be seen in Windows 2003 Server or in the client technology of Windows XP/Vista – the well known Remote Desktop. In such solutions, API is designed in a way that allows to transmit only the data vital for communication, for example only the window coordinates, not the whole pictures.

Apart from software that is a part of the operating system, some third party solutions exist. These technologies integrate themselves with the available system platform and use the system API. By making remote access services available, one brings about the risk of exposing the internal network to unauthorized access, effectively exposing confidential enterprise data. One should ensure at least a basic level of security, software and hardware-wise. The variety of available market solutions, gives one the freedom of choosing a method that will agree with the location, time and expenses. Latest solutions in the area of remote access based on Microsoft technology shall be presented below.

3 Inteligent Network Access Protection

3.1 Network Access Protection (NAP)

NAP is a built-in solution for Windows Vista, Windows Server 2008 Codename 'Longhorn' and Windows XP SP2 (with NAP for Windows XP client) systems. The aim of NAP is to protect enterprise systems against threats, enforce the security guidelines and help maintaining the client status according to the institutions policy. Depending on the rules governing this solution, client computers can be automatically updated and their access to the network can be limited or blocked until they meet the requirements. NAP is a versatile solution – it can integrate itself with third party technologies through the API interface.

3.1.1 Action scenarios

Network Access Protection cooperates with software that supports: System Health Agent (SHA) and System Health Validator (SHV) solutions, such as antivirus scanners or update servers. NAP can be employed in following circumstances:

1. Health status control for stationary computers and mobile devices.
    The solution allows for constant status monitoring of stationary computers and updating stations that fail to meet the security requirements. As far as mobile devices are concerned, their health status cannot me controlled outside the company, which could pose a threat for standard VPN solutions. With NAP technology, the health status of a connecting device is always verified. Thanks to this approach, one is able to keep the benefits of mobile operation, without hindering security.

2. Limitation of network access.
    By using the available policies one can determine whether a given mobile device has the correct access privileges for strictly limited network fragments, without compliance with the internal enterprise policy or it can access the entire network, but under the condition of having the correct configuration and the latest antivirus signatures.

3. Health status verification for personal computers.
    NAP allows one to verify at each connection attempt whether a given personal computer fails to meet health status requirements, for example by lacking certain software or by incorrect registry entries.

3.1.2 NAP Platform Components

The NAP platform allows to use many components for network protection [Microsoft 2007], which are as follows:

*   Internet Protocol security (IPsec), which is responsible for host authentication
*   IEEE 802.1X – access point control
*   Virtual Private Networks
*   DHCP servers

Those technologies can be merged together and their correct operation is supervised by the Network Policy Server (NPS) (the successor of IAS server in Windows Server 2003), which is analyzing the binding access rules within the enterprise. IPsec protocol enforcement is conducted by a certificate server and IPsec NAP Enforcement Client (EC). Client receives authentication certificates from the server, testifying to their compliance with the enterprise policy. The usage of IPsec can be defined for port numbers and IP addresses (for each one), such approach seriously limits network communication – only the nodes that are mentioned in the policy are active. On the other hand, this is the most secure access limitation method, since only known units are involved.

The usage of limitation mechanics enforced by 802.1X access points allows to cut the client on from the network on a determined switch or access point, assign him a profile in which IP filtering is conducted and then move him to the correct network. Only after performing certain remediation functions the client is able to access the network. In the case of VPN servers, the server responsible for policy enforcement (VPN NAP Enforcement Server) is forcing certain settings every time a client attempts to access enterprise network. DHCP enforcement is conducted every time a client desires to reserve or renew IP address. This is the weakest form of protection, because it is based on routing table entries. The NPS server is responsible for users connecting remotely (RADIUS), works as a NAP policy server in cooperation with the described components, coordinating their actions and verifying client health status. Apart from the described built-in NAP mechanisms it is possible to use additional, third party components.

Figure 4 depicts a network, where NAP technology with the components described above is applied. The way NAP works can be summarized in several steps:

1. Client connects to the network, requests network access and presents his health status.

2. Technology that is processing the request (for example VPN) forwards the client status to NPS.

3. NPS verifies client status according to the enterprise policy.

4. If the connecting client fails to meet the requirements, he is being redirected to a separate VLAN and gains access to selected resources (depending on the policy). In this phase the computer is being adapted to the policy requirements.

5. If the client meets the requirements, he gains full access to the network.

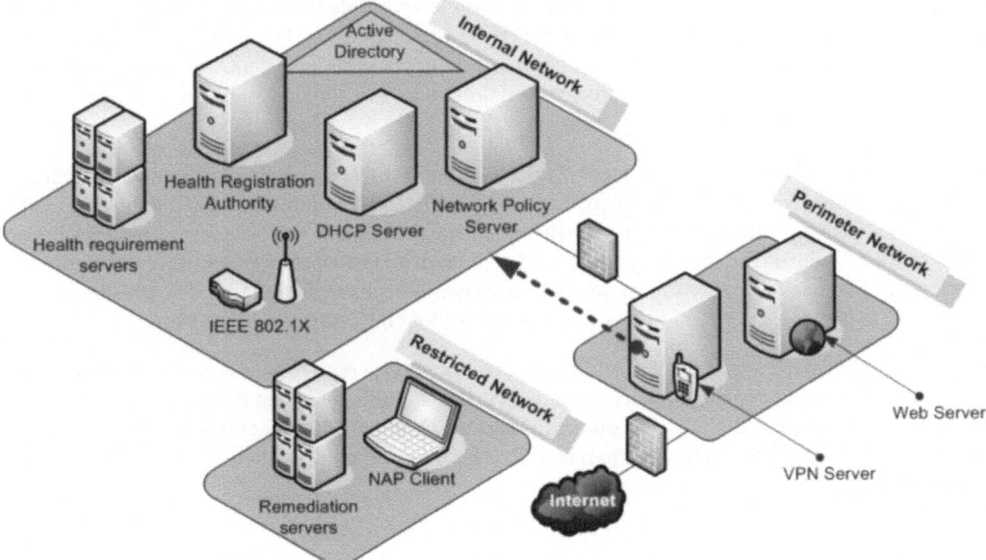

Figure 4. An example architecture involving NAP technology.

3.2 Terminal Services

Windows Server 2008 Codename 'Longhorn' introduces new terminal services functionality, which allows to connect with remote computers, as well as applications. The Remote Programs (TS Remote-App) service enables integration between the application launched on the terminal server and the user's desktop as if the user was running the application locally. Web Access service has similar functionality, but the particular elements are run in a web browser. Application sharing greatly improves work versatility, however, one should keep in mind that users with incorrectly assigned privileges will gain access to all functions offered by the application. File saving which is the result of user's work on a remote application might be conducted on the remote server, which means that the user gains access to server hard-drives.

One should never make an application available without knowing its privileges. In the case when a domain user is accessing the server, a proper policy should be applied on him, forbidding him to access data. The TS technology can be integrated with NAP – thanks to this the administrators will be able to ensure that terminal services users have the correct health status according to the enterprise policy.

4 Conclusion

The possibilities offered by remote access methods are vast. A dynamically developing enterprise is unable to avoid them and sooner or later, they will become one of the key mechanisms of resource access. The Carter Group report, concerning the recent trends in infrastructure development for 2007 – 2008, is emphasizing that remote access will be a major development direction of enterprise infrastructure. However, it should be kept in mind that the additional functionality might unintentionally threaten network security.

The issue mostly involves administrators, making them responsible for the health status of the clients that attempt to establish connection. The market offers a wide range of solutions that allow to manipulate the settings of user stations, install required software, perform virus scans and edit the registry. While pondering the issue of choosing a remote access solution, an institution should determine the tasks of such technology, as well as who will be using it.

Remote access is a solution that enhances work flexibility; however, one should remember that even sufficiently secured data transmission between the networks cannot eliminate threats that reside within user stations, such as viruses or rootkits. It will not help against threats resulting from careless behavior, like password disclosure or spam-oriented social engineering. The existing threats force us to use such solutions as NAC or NAP that supervise client access privileges. Additionally, it is possible to track down users that pose a threat and to report information about the current network status.

Summarizing, it can be stated that the additional functionality of remote access carries certain risks, in the same way as connecting computers into a network or to the Internet. In the case of remote access, the risks are serious, but the business process practically enforces this functionality. This is why it is worthwhile to know how to mitigate the risk and reach intended goals without exposing the system to needles threats.

References

[Lam, LeBlanc, Smith 2005] Lam K., LeBlanc D., Smith B.: Ocena bezpieczeństwa sieciowego (Assessing Network Security). APN Promise, Warsaw 2005.

[Infonetics Research 2006] Infonetics Research, "User Plans for Security Products and Services: North America 2006".

[Smith, Komar 2005] Smith B, Komar B, Microsoft Security Team: Microsoft Windows Security Resource Kit, Second Edition. Microsoft Press, October 2005

[Microsoft 2007] Microsoft Technet: Platforma Network Access Protection w systemie Windows Server "Longhorn" (Network Access Protection platform in Windows Server "Longhorn"). 6th September 2006.

"Private Investigation" in the Computer Environment: Legal Aspects

Arkadiusz Lach

Nicolaus Copernicus University
Department of Criminal Procedure
arkadl@uni.torun.pl

Abstract

The presentation will focuse on tracing incidents and gathering evidence by private persons. Such persons may be victims of incidents, network administrators, persons responsible for IT security in companies. Reacting on incidents by them is unavoidable and often it is their action which enable to trace the perpatrators of the abuse nd punish them. As an abuse we can regard computer hacking as well as for example acts of unfair competition. Beside that, in the recent years we can observe in Poland development of so called cyber forensics. It could be regarded as a real legal mine field as private gathering of evidence was not generally regulated by the Polish lawmaker. That's why the person reacting for incident may easily cross thin line between legal and illegal acivity which may result in civil or criminal responsibility.

The problems which should be discussed in the presentation are:
1. Introducing to the problem and its scale
2. The possibility of gathering evidence by private persons in the Polish law
3. Methods which may be used by private perons
4. Actions to the most common incidents
5. Evidential value of gathered materials
6. Civil and criminal responsibility for acts contrary to the law

This topic will be presented in comparative law context, taking into consideration opinions expressed in law journals and by the judiciary. Beside estimating the present situation it would be interesting to try to pose some propositions as to possible changes in the law.

1 Introduction to the problem

The subject of this paper is conducting investigatory activities by private individuals and collecting information that could become a piece of evidence. Such individuals may be e.g. victims, aggrieved persons, network administrators, persons responsible for IT security in companies. Their reaction to incidents is unavoidable and, frequently, it is their actions that allow us to detect offenders and bring them to justice. The incidents of abuse may involve, e.g. hacking into servers, unfair competition acts or abuse done by employees.

Private gathering of evidence becomes more and more common and – as one may say – "trendy". Expansion of modern technologies certainly contribute to it, as well as activities of detective agencies and availability of technical means that enable such gathering of information. One may also add the lack of faith in effectiveness of the law enforcement and a preference to deal with issues without unnecessary publicity, which could damage the company's reputation. Moreover, in the last few years we have observed the growth of the cyber forensics in Poland.

N. Pohlmann, H. Reimer, W. Schneider (Editors): Securing Electronic Business Processes, Vieweg (2007), 110-113

It is however a legal "mine field", since gathering of evidence by private individuals has not been in fact regulated by the Polish legislators. This means that the person responding to the incident can easily cross that thin line between what's legal and what's not, bringing upon themselves civil or criminal liability.

2 Gathering evidence by private individuals in the light of the Polish law

The basic question to be asked first is whether the Polish law allows private individuals to gather information constituting a body of evidence. Responding to that question, one must point out, that the Polish code of criminal procedure (CCP) contains no provisions on the subject matter. This resulted in disputes between law professors. Legislators, however, refrained from any action.

We should assume that the provisions of law do not generally prohibit private individuals to gather information constituting a body of evidence, provided that such gathering does not contravene provisions of the criminal code, civil code and other acts.

3 Available methods

A method to be used more and more frequently nowadays is certainly the wiretapping. Well-known corruption cases, such as the Gudzowaty tapes, are the best example of it. Thus, a question arises, whether the wiretapping is in fact legal. First, it should be noted that violation of confidentiality of correspondence is protected by both the Constitution and the criminal code. So, there must be a legal exception to this prohibition, which would cancel the illegality of such action. Such exceptions were defined in the code of criminal procedure and in other acts of parliament for the so called legal interception. There is no single regulation pertaining to private persons.

We can resort to several court decisions relevant to the subject matter.

In the judgment of 10.05.2002 [1] the Supreme Court stated, that a magnetic tape containing a telephone call between the defendant and the victim, recorded by the latter, may constitute a body of evidence. According to the Supreme Court there are no legal impediments, and failure to accept such evidence would be an unjustified reduction of the body of evidence. Neither the provisions of the CCP apply since such interception was not conducted by public authorities. While agreeing with those theses one must point out, that in this case it is rather difficult to speak of the wiretapping, since the recording was made by one of the parties involved in the conversation. And it is assumed that the wiretapping involves actions of a third party. We must admit however, that in the foreign legislations this issue is approached in various ways.

On the other hand, in the judgement of 13.11.2002[2] relating to a typical direct surveillance (installed in the room), the Supreme Court pointed out that "the provisions, which regulate lawful interception, commonly recognized as removing the illegality of interception, should be treated as a vital guideline, when evaluating the annulment of illegality in other interception cases, since they indicate in which situations the legislator allows exclusion of confidentiality of communication." The Court indicated that annulment of the interception's illegality may occur, when the intercepting person acts in defence of the justified legal interest. However, the catalogue of crimes listed in the CCP and in the Police Act 1990 should be treated as indication as to whether such annulment of illegality actually occurred. Thus,

---

1 Ref.. WA 22/02, OSNKW 2002, no. 9 – 10, item 77.
2 Ref.. I CKN 1150/00, LEX no. 75292.

the Supreme Court applied the principle of proportionality, which enforced the balance of the protected rights and the sacrificed rights.

Substantial doubts may be raised by the decision of the Supreme Court of 14.11.2006[3], in which the Court expresses a view, that private gathering of evidence takes place, when a law enforcement officer delivers the wiretap equipment and provides operational instruction, and without whose cooperation the whole wiretapping operation would not be possible. This thesis seems to contravene the line of judicial decisions of the European Court of Human Rights and allows one to get around the provisions on the judicial control of the surveillance operations by taking advantage of people outside of the Police.

It should be underlined, that persons rendering detective services do not possess special authorization for interception of communications. By virtue of art. 7 of the law dated 6 July 2001 on detective services[4], a detective – when rendering services mentioned in art. 2 par. 1 of this law – may not use the technical means and methods, as well as conduct operational and intelligence activities reserved for authorized bodies, pursuant to separate regulations. Violation of this prohibition is subject to up to 3 years' imprisonment (art. 45 of the law). In practice however, this article is rarely observed.

Another frequently used method of gathering evidence is the real-time analysis of traffic data. It must be assumed, that the entity conducting such analysis (e.g. an employer) should prove, that it has a justified interest in such actions, and the receiver & sender of information were informed about application or a possibility of application of such procedure[5].

It's worth to point out at this time, that in one of the recent judgements the European Court of Human Rights decided, that employers do not have the right to analyze in detail the calls made by their employees, even considering the fact, that they are authorized to receive the billing data[6].

Besides acquiring data in real-time, there is also an issue of accessing the stored data by searching through the equipment or media in an employee's possession. Also in this case there is a need to create clear procedures allowing data browsing in a manner, that would be justified as to its purpose and be in accordance with the principle of proportionality. Regardless of the above, if the data captured by the system constitutes the private life material (e.g. pictures, private correspondence) their browsing should not take place.

4 Evidential value of the collected information

The Polish law is very liberal as to the admissibility and evaluation of evidence. Also, the fruits of the poisonous tree theory does not exist in Poland, although its implementation, at least partial, would be welcomed. At this time however, the evidence obtained by private individuals with violation of the current law, even through criminal acts, is accepted by courts.

5 Criminal and civil liability for actions that contravene the law

In accordance with art. 23 of the Civil Code, the man' personals rights, especially health, freedom, honour, freedom of conscience, name or pseudonym, image, confidentiality of correspondence, immunity

---

3 V KK 52/06, LEX no. 202271.
4 Journal of Laws [Dz. U.] No 12, item 110.
5 More on the subject A .Lach, *Employee monitoring at the workplace*, Monitor Prawniczy no. 10/2004, p. 264 – 268.
6 See the judgement of the European Court of Human Rights dated 3.04.2007 on Copland versus the United Kingdom (application no. 62617/00).

of residence, scientific, artistic, inventive and improvement work, remain under protection of the civil law, regardless of the protection granted by other regulations. Whereas art. 24 § 1 of the civil code provides, that he, whose personal rights are threatened by other person's action, may demand ceasing this action, unless it is legal. In case of the violation, he can also demand that the person, who had committed the violation, performed the activities necessary to remove its effects, especially that this person made a statement of appropriate content and form. By virtue of the rules defined in the code, he can also demand a pecuniary compensation or payment of appropriate sum of money for indicated social purposes. On the other hand, § 2 of this article states, that if the pecuniary damage was done as the result of violation of personals rights, the aggrieved party may demand indemnification on general terms.

For the sake of supplementation it should be added, that according to the Supreme Court "illegal activity is the activity that contravenes legal standards or rules of social co-existence, and the illegality is cancelled by actions complying with the provisions of law, conforming to the rules of social co-existence, actions by consent of the aggrieved party and in execution of the legal rights."[7]

Naturally, except for the civil liability, the criminal liability may occur as well. We can quote here especially art. 267 of the penal code:

§ 1. Whoever, without being authorised to do so, acquires information not intended for him, by opening a sealed letter, or connecting to a wire that transmits information or by breaching electronic, magnetic or other special protection for that information, shall be subject to a fine, the penalty of restriction of liberty or the penalty of deprivation of liberty for up to 2 years.

§ 2. The same penalty applies to a person, who – in order to acquire information, which is not intended for him – installs or uses a tapping device for audio or vision or any other special device.

§ 3. The same penalty applies to a person, who discloses information acquired in the manner described in § 1 or 2 to other person.

§ 4. Persecution of the crime defined in § 1-3 proceeds at the request of the aggrieved.

This provision prohibits both direct surveillance (e.g. analysis of screen radiation, hidden monitoring of the screen's activity) and the indirect surveillance (installing devices to control transmission of information in the networks). Moreover, we should put emphasis on the fact, that in order for the criminal liability to occur, one condition has to be met – intercepted information must not be intended for a person intercepting it or that person may not be authorized to acquire it. This provides an opportunity for various interpretations, especially in the context of employers.

6 Conclusion

The issue presented here shall certainly continue to grow in significance. The life brings new problems all the time. Problems, which legal experts will have to deal with. As the chance may have, some famous and controversial case may contribute to at least partial regulation of the issue of gathering evidence by private individuals, especially employers. However, the chances for that are slim at best. What remains for now is interpretation of the current law, taking into consideration especially the principle of proportionality, and analysis of judicial decisions.

---

7 Judgement of 4.06.2003, Ref. I CKN 480/01, LEX no. 137619.

Identity,
Information
Security and
Rights Management

Design Rationale behind the Identity Metasystem Architecture

Kim Cameron · Michael B. Jones

Microsoft
{kcameron | mbj}@microsoft.com
http://www.identityblog.com/, http://research.microsoft.com/~mbj/

Abstract

Many of the problems facing the Internet today stem from the lack of a widely deployed, easily

understood, secure identity solution. Microsoft's "InfoCard" project and the Identity Metasystem vision underlying it are aimed at filling this gap using technology all can adopt and solutions

all can endorse, putting users in control of their identity interactions on the Internet. The design decisions presented in this paper are intended to result in a widely accepted, broadly applicable, inclusive, comprehensible, privacy-enhancing, security-enhancing identity solution for the Internet. We present them and the rationale behind them to facilitate review of these design decisions by the security, privacy, and policy communities, so that people will better understand Microsoft's implementations, and to help guide others when building interoperating implementations.

1 Introduction

1.1 The Challenge: A Ubiquitous Digital Identity Solution for the Internet

By definition, for a digital identity solution to be successful, it needs to be understood in all the contexts where you might want to use it to identify yourself. Identity systems are about identifying you self (and your things) in environments that are not yours. For this to be possible, both your systems and the systems that are not yours – those where you need to digitally identity yourself – must be able to speak the same digital identity protocols, even if they are running different software on different platforms. In the case of an identity solution for the entire Internet, this is a tall order. It means that, to succeed, the solution will need to be adopted by the wide variety of operating systems, browsers, and web servers that collectively implement the phenomenon we know of as "the Internet". ".

1.2 Practical Considerations

To have any hope of such widespread adoption, we believe that any Internet-scale identity solution will need to satisfy these practical considerations:

N. Pohlmann, H. Reimer, W. Schneider (Editors): Securing Electronic Business Processes, Vieweg (2007), 117-129

- **Improved Security and Privacy:**
  To be widely adopted, platform and software vendors will need to be convinced that the solution results in improvements in the overall Internet security landscape. Likewise, consumers (and their advocates) will need to be convinced that the solution improves the consumer privacy landscape.

- **Inclusive of Technologies:**
  There are a number of identity technologies in widespread use today (Kerberos, X.509, SAML, etc.) with more being invented all the time. To gain wide acceptance, the solution should be able to leverage existing identity technologies and deployments, incorporating them as part of the solution and building upon their strengths, rather than calling for their wholesale replacement.

- **Inclusive of Scenarios:**
  The solution must be broadly applicable across a wide range of use cases, even accommodating those with conflicting requirements. For instance, in many cases users will want guarantees that their identity providers can't accumulate a record of the sites they visit. However, in some governmental and financial settings, an audit record of sites visited using an identity may be required. Both kinds of identities should be able to be accommodated. At an even more basic level, the solution must be applicable not just on workstations but also on different devices such as wireless mobile devices and cell phones.

- **Incrementally Deployable:**
  The solution must coexist with and complement existing authentication systems, rather than calling for a "forklift upgrade" or "flag day" where existing solutions must be replaced by the new one all at once.

1.3 Architecture of a Proposed Solution

Such a solution, the Identity Metasystem [Microsoft 05a], has been proposed and some implementations are under way. The Identity Metasystem is based upon a set of principles called the "Laws of Identity" [Cameron 05b]. The Laws are summarized in Appendix A. The

Laws are intended to codify a set of fundamental principles to which a universally adopted, sustainable identity architecture must conform. The Laws were proposed, debated, and refined through a long-running, open, and continuing dialogue on the Internet [Cameron 05a]. Taken together, the Laws were key to defining the overall architecture of the Identity Metasystem.

While the Laws of Identity have undergone broad review and been met with significant acceptance, that's certainly not the end of the story. While the Identity Metasystem is designed in accordance with the Laws, there are also numerous practical design decisions that had to be made to translate the vision into working, interoperable systems. The purpose of this paper is to publish the design decisions underlying the Identity Metasystem architecture and the rationale behind them. This is intended both to enable a deeper understanding of the problems that this solution addresses and to enable discussion of these design decisions by the security, privacy, and policy communities.

2 Identity Problems on the Internet and an Overview of the Proposed Solution

The section briefly describes the problems motivating the need for a new identity solution for the Internet and gives an overview of the mechanisms that the Identity Metasystem employs to do so.

2.1 The Internet's Problems are often Identity Problems.

Many of the problems facing the Internet today stem from the lack of a widely deployed, easily understood, secure identity solution. Microsoft's "InfoCard" project and the Identity Metasystem vision underlying it are aimed at filling this gap using technology all can adopt and solutions all can endorse, putting users in control of their identity interactions on the Internet. A comparison between the brick-and-mortar world and the online world is illustrative: In the brick-and-mortar world you can tell when you are at a branch of your bank. It would be very difficult to set up a fake bank branch and convince people to do transactions there. But in today's online world it's trivial to set up a fake banking site (or e-commerce site …) and convince a significant portion of the population that it's the real thing. This is an identity problem. Web sites currently don't have reliable ways of identifying themselves to people, enabling imposters to flourish. One goal of InfoCard is reliable site-touser authentication, which aims to make it as difficult to produce counterfeit services on the online world as it is to produce them in the physical world. Conversely, problems identifying users to sites also abound. Username/password authentication is the prevailing paradigm, but its weaknesses are all too evident on today's Internet. Password reuse, insecure passwords, and poor password management practices open a world of attacks by themselves. Combine that with the password theft attacks enabled by counterfeit web sites and man-in-the-middle attacks and today's Internet is an attacker's paradise. The consequences of these problems are severe and growing. Last year the number of "phishing" sites was growing at over 1000% per year [Anti-Phishing 05]. Online banking activity is declining [Gartner 05]. The recent FFIEC guidance on authentication in online banking reports that "Account fraud and identity theft are frequently the result of single-factor (e.g., ID/password) authentication exploitation" [FFIEC 05]. Consumer trust of the Internet is low and dropping. The status quo is no longer a viable option.

2.2 "InfoCard" and the Identity Metasystem

The code-named "InfoCard" project at Microsoft is a joint effort with a diverse coalition of contributors across the computer industry to produce an authentication solution for the Internet that can:

- be widely accepted,
- work in a broad range of identity contexts,
- utilize existing authentication technologies, including multiple factors,
- incorporate new authentication technologies as they are invented, and possibly most importantly,
- enable users to simply and consistently make informed and positive authentication decisions on their own behalf.

The result of this effort is known as the Identity Metasystem [Microsoft 05a], an overview of which is contained in this section. As previously mentioned, the Identity Metasystem is based upon a set of principles developed through an open industry dialog [Cameron 05a] called the Laws of Identity [Cameron 05b]. What do we mean by an "Identity Metasystem"?

This concept is probably most easily introduced through an analogy.

Before 1982, the networking world was fragmented. If you wanted to write a networkenabled application you had to choose what network to write it for: Ethernet, Token Ring, ArcNet, X.25, etc. The invention of a Network Metasystem, the Internet Protocol (IP), changed all that. It made it possible to write networking applications that worked across networks without knowing the particulars of each network.

It even enabled those applications to work with new networks that hadn't been invented yet, such as 802.11 wireless networks.

Digital identity is similarly fragmented today. If you want to write an identity-enabled application, you have to choose which identity system to write it for, such as Kerberos, SAML, X.509, Liberty, custom username/password systems, etc. The Identity Metasystem is intended change all that, just as IP did for networking. It will make it possible to write identity-enabled applications that can work across multiple identity systems and can even use new identity systems as they are invented and connected to the Identity Metasystem. This analogy holds true in another way. IP didn't compete with or replace the individual networks such as Ethernet — it used them. Similarly, the Identity Metasystem doesn't compete with or replace individual identity technologies such as Kerberos, Liberty, X.509, SAML, etc. — it uses them. That's why it's called an identity metasystem —it's a system of systems, tying individual identity systems into a larger interoperable metasystem (see Law 5). By allowing different identity systems to work in concert, with a single user experience, and a unified programming paradigm, the metasystem shields users and developers from concern about the evolution and market dominance of specific underlying systems, reducing everyone's risk and increasing the speed with which technology can evolve.

2.3 Roles within the Identity Metasystem

Different parties participate in the metasystem in different ways. The three roles within the metasystem are:

- **Identity Providers,** which issue digital identities. For example, credit card providers might issue identities enabling payment, businesses might issue identities to their customers, governments might issue identities to citizens, and individuals might use self-issued identities in contexts like signing on to web sites.
- **Relying Parties,** which require identities. For example, a web site or online service that utilizes identities offered by other parties.
- **Subjects,** which are the individuals and other entities about whom claims are made. Examples of subjects include people, companies, and organizations.

2.4 Claims-Based Identities and InfoCards

In the Metasystem, digital identities consist of sets of claims made about the subject of the identity, where "claims" are pieces of information about the subject that the issuer asserts are valid. This parallels identities used in the real world. For example, the claims on a driver's license might include the issuing state, the driver's license number, name, address, sex, birth date, organ donor status, signature, and photograph, the types of vehicles the subject is eligible to drive, and restrictions on driving rights. The issuing state asserts that these claims are valid. The claims on a credit card might include the issuer's identity, the subject's name, the account number, the expiration date, the validation code, and a signature. The card issuer asserts that these claims are valid. The claims on a self-issued identity, where the identity provider and subject are one and the same entity, might include the subject's name, address, telephone number, and e-mail address, or perhaps just the knowledge of a secret. For self-issued identities, the subject asserts that these claims are valid.

In the client user interface, each of the user's digital identities used within the metasystem is represented by a visual "Information Card" (a.k.a. "InfoCard", the source of this technology's codename). The user selects identities represented by InfoCards to authenticate to participating services. The cards themselves represent references to identity providers that are contacted to produce the needed claim data for an identity when requested, rather than claims data stored on the local machine. Only the claim values actually requested by the relying party are released, rather than all claims that the identity possesses (see Law 2).

2.5 Putting the User in Control

One of the fundamental tenets of the Info- Card work is that users must be in control of their identity interactions (see Laws 1 & 2). Among other things, this means that users must be given the choice of which identities to use at which services, they must know what information (which claims) will be disclosed to those services if they use them, and they must be informed how those services will use the information disclosed. In the offline world, people carry multiple forms of identification in their wallets, such as driver's licenses or other government-issued identity cards, credit cards, and affinity cards such as frequent flyer cards. People control which card to use and how much information to reveal in any given situation.

Similarly, the Identity Metasystem makes it easier for users to stay safe and in control when accessing resources on the Internet. It lets users select from among a portfolio of their digital identities and use them at Internet services of their choice where they are accepted. The met system enables identities provided by one identity system technology to be used within systems based on different technologies, provided an intermediary exists that understands both technologies and is willing and trusted to do the needed translations. Part of being in control that's all too often overlooked is that to be in control, you must be able to understand the choices you're presented with (see Laws 6 & 7). Unless we can bring users into the identity solution as informed, functioning components of the solution, able to consistently make good choices on their own behalf, we won't have solved the problem. Many identity attacks succeed because the user was fooled by something presented on the screen, not because of ins cure communication technologies. For example, phishing attacks occur not in the secured channel between web servers and browsers — a channel that might extend thousands of miles — but in the two or three feet between the browser and the human who uses it.

The Identity Metasystem, therefore, seeks to empower users to make informed and reasonable identity decisions by enabling the use of a consistent, comprehensible, and self-explanatory user interface for making those choices. One key to securing the whole system is presenting an easy-to-learn, predictable user interface that looks and works the same no matter which underlying identity technologies are employed. Another key is making important information obvious — for instance, displaying the identity of the site you're authenticating to in a way that makes spoofing attempts apparent. Likewise, the user must be clearly informed which items of personal information relying parties are requesting, and for what purposes. This allows users to make informed choices about whether or not to disclose this information.

2.6 Authenticating Sites to Users

To prevent users from being fooled by counterfeit sites, there must be a reliable mechanism enabling them to distinguish between genuine sites and imposters. Our solution utilizes a new class of higher-value X.509 site certificates being developed jointly with VeriSign and other leading certificate authorities. These higher-value certificates differ from existing SSL certificates in several respects. First, these certificates contain a digitally signed bitmap of the company logo. This bitmap is displayed when the user is asked whether or not they want to enter into a relationship with the site, the first time that the site requests an InfoCard from the user.

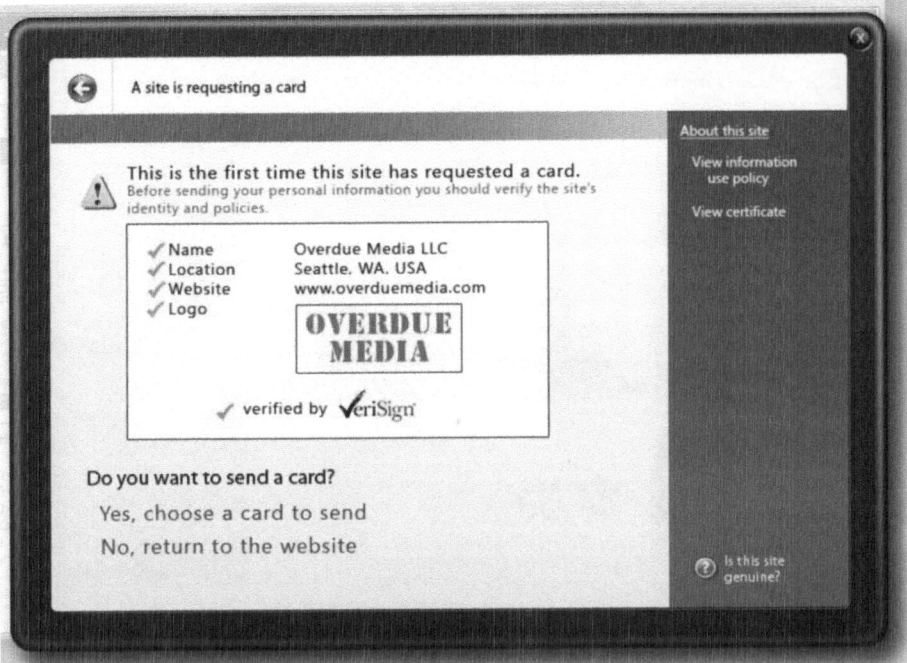

Figure 1: Site Verification Screen

Second, these certificates represent higher legal and fiduciary guarantees than standard certificates. In many cases, all that having a standard site certificate guarantees is that someone was once able to respond to e-mail sent to that site. In contrast, a higher-value certificate is the certificate authority saying, in effect, "We stake our reputation on the fact that this is a reputable merchant and they are who they claim to be". Users can visit sites displaying these certificates with confidence and will be clearly warned when a site does not present a certificate of this caliber. Only after a site successfully authenticates itself to a user is the user asked to authenticate himself or herself to the site. To make this all more concrete, Figure 1 shows an example of what a screen displayed upon a user's first access to a relying party accepting "InfoCards" might look like. As this example shows, the screen can include the name, location, web site URL, and logo of the organization whose identity is being approved (such as Overdue Media). It can also include the name and logo of the organization that has verified this information (such as VeriSign). To help the user make good decisions, what's shown on the screen varies depending on what kind of certificate is provided by the identity provider or relying party. If a higher-assurance certificate is provided, the screen can indicate that the organization's name, location, website, and logo have been verified, as shown in Figure 1. This indicates to a user that this organization deserves more trust. If only an SSL certificate is provided, the screen would indicate that a lower level of trust is warranted. And if an even weaker certificate or no certificate at all is provided, the screen would indicate that there's no evidence whatsoever that this site actually is who it claims to be. The goal is to help users make good decisions about which identity providers they'll let provide them with digital identities and which relying parties are allowed to receive those digital identities.

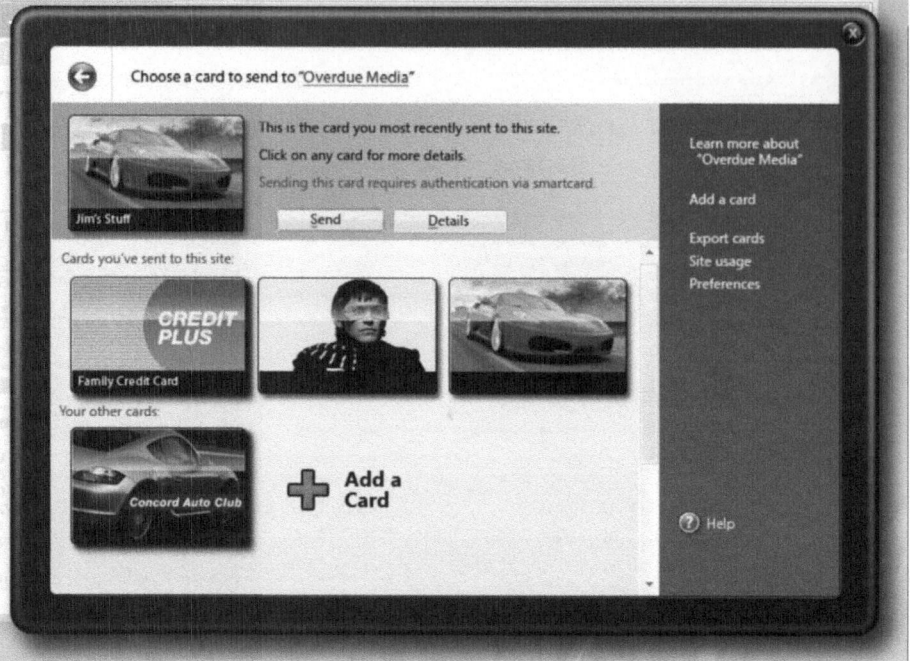

Figure 2: Identity Selector Screen

2.7 Authenticating Users to Sites

InfoCards have several key advantages over username/password credentials:

- Because no password is typed or sent, by definition, your password can not be stolen or forgotten.
- Because authentication is based on unique keys generated for every InfoCard/site pair (unless using a card explicitly designed to enable cross-site collaboration), the keys known by one site are useless for authentication at another, even for the same InfoCard.
- Because InfoCards will resupply claim values (for example, name, address, and e-mail address) to relying parties that the user had previously furnished them to, relying parties do not need to store this data between sessions. Retaining less data means that sites have fewer vulnerabilities. (See Law 2.)

InfoCard implements a standard user interface for working with digital identities. Perhaps the most important part of this interface, the screen used to select an identity to present to a site, is shown in Figure 2. As this screen shot illustrates, each digital identity is displayed as an InfoCard. Each card represents a digital identity that the user can potentially present to a relying party. Along with the visual representation shown above, each card also contains information about a particular digital identity. This information includes what identity provider to contact to acquire a security token for this identity, what kind of tokens this identity provider can issue, and exactly what claims these tokens can contain. By choosing to use a particular card, the user is actually choosing to request a specific security token with a specific set of claims created by a specific identity provider. But from the user's perspective, they're simply selecting an InfoCard to use at a site.

2.8 Protocols Behind the Identity Metasystem

The Identity Metasystem is built on a small number of interoperable Web Services (WS-*) protocols. Specifically, the encapsulating protocol used for claims transformation within the Metasystem is WS-Trust [WS-Trust 05]. Format and claims negotiations between participants are conducted using WS-MetadataExchange [WSMetadataExchange 04] and WS-SecurityPolicy [WS-SecurityPolicy 05]. Finally, messages are secured using WS-Security [WS-Security 04]. These protocols enable building a platform independent Identity Metasystem and form its "backplane". Like other Web services protocols, they also allow new kinds of identities and technologies to be incorporated and utilized as they are developed and adopted by the industry. To foster the interoperability necessary for broad adoption, the spec fications for these (and other) WS-* protocols are published and are freely available, have been or will be submitted to open standards bodies, and allow implementations to be developed royalty-free. Deployments of existing identity technologies can be leveraged in the metasystem by implementing support for the small number of WS-* protocols above. Examples of technologies that could be utilized via the metasystem include LDAP claims schemas; X.509, which is used in Smartcards; Kerberos, which is used in Active Directory and some UNIX environments; and SAML, a standard used in inter-corporate federation scenarios.

3 Design Decisions behind the Identity Metasystem

This section lists many of the key design decisions behind the Identity Metasystem architecture and gives the rationale for them.

3.1 Protocol ≠ Payload

There are a number of forms of digital identity in use today such as Kerberos, X.509, SAML, and user-name/password systems, with more being invented all the time. Each typically represents identities in a different manner, and yet it is highly desirable to be able to utilize all these kinds of identities within the same identity solution. While some identity systems have developed custom communication protocols tied to particular identity formats, doing so results in little or no interoperability between the different systems using those incompatible protocols. Instead, we decided to employ a single encapsulating protocol set capable of utilizing all identity payload formats in a common manner. Specifically, the protocol set was chosen to enable specification of requirements, negotiation of capabilities, transmission of payloads, and transformation of payloads, all in a format independent manner. This means that the encapsulating protocol remains stable even as the types of payloads used evolve.

3.2 Identity Selector ≠ Identity Provider

The Identity Metasystem employs software on each platform that lets users choose an identity from among their portfolio of identities to use for each authentication. This software is called the Identity Selector, and is invoked each time the user needs to make a choice of identities.

(Figure 2 shows a screen shot of an Identity Selector.) A key decision was to implement an Identity Selector that is independent of any specific identity provider, technology, or operator.

This enables an open architecture in which multiple identity providers using potentially multiple different identity technologies can all participate, with the user experience being the same each time. This open architecture allows both existing identity technologies and those yet to be invented to be used in the same ways. Because identity providers are not tied to the identity selector but are instead communicated with by the selector using standard protocols, the identity providers can live anywhere: "in the cloud", at ISPs, on devices such as smart cards or USB keys, media players, cell phones, or on your PC, … anywhere reachable via the identity provider protocols. A corollary of this decision is that the simple self-issued identity provider that runs on your PC "out of the box" is just one among many and not "special" in any way.

3.3 Identity Selector ≠ Metadata Store

The identity selector software allows users to choose from among the identities in their portfolio of identities. This portfolio is represented by what we call the Metadata Store – the store of configuration info telling the identity selector how to contact an identity provider to obtain actual identity information. This metadata store also contains the pictorial representation of each identity, each "InfoCard". We made the design decision to have the identity selector user interface software be separate from the metadata store software, with communication protocols connecting them. This decision provides significant flexibility that would otherwise not exist. Specifically, it means that the identity selector user interface can run anywhere – not just on your workstation, but also on devices like your mobile phone or your media player. It also means that the metadata store can live wherever you want, for instance, on your phone, your media player, in the cloud, on a smart card or USB device supporting roaming, or on your PC. All of this contributes to giving the user control over how their identity is represented, stored, and released.

3.4 Guarantee Separation of Contexts

Many relying parties need a consistent handle to be presented each time an identity is used so they know that each use represents the same entity. But if this same handle is used at different relying parties, that gives them the opportunity to share data between them about how the same user has been using the different sites – all without the knowledge or agreement of the user. A design decision was to mitigate this danger by supporting the use of "unidirectional identifiers" (see Law 4) so that the identifiers given to each relying party can be distinct from the identifiers given to others. The system is able to automatically generate pairwise identifiers for each combination of identity provider and relying party that is used. No common URL, GUID, etc. is sent that could serve as a correlation handle between sites. Another way in which separation of contexts is facilitated is by ensuring that only those claims explicitly requested by a relying party are provided to it (as per Law 2). So, for instance, even though an identity provider might be capable of furnishing claims containing a subject's postal address and telephone numbers, unless they are requested the identity provider will not supply them to that relying party. Thus, the set of claims released varies on a per relying party basis.

3.5 Facilitate "Data Rejection"

Currently most sites retain a dossier of information about you: your "Customer Record". In the metasystem, a design decision was to have the selector remember what the user has released to a given site, and resupply that same information to the site whenever it requests it. The result of this decision is that sites can safely discard this information about you between sessions because it will be resupplied when next needed. Besides having privacy benefits for users, this option also has liability benefits for relying parties: Information that is not retained cannot be stolen, meaning there cannot be data breaches for which a site can be held accountable.

3.6 Claims ≠ "Trust"

A design decision was to factor out trust decisions and not bundle them into the identity metasystem protocols and payloads. Unlike the X.509 PKIX [IETF 05], for example, the metasystem design verifies the cryptography but leaves trust analysis for a higher layer that runs on top of the identity metasystem.

3.7 Human Token ≠ Computational Token

For a human user to meaningfully control the information that would be released by selecting an identity, he or she must be able to view a human-readable and comprehensible representation of those claims. Hence, the identity selector must be able to display representations of claim values. However, because claims can be represented using any payload format, including new ones yet to be invented, it would be impossible to write identity selector code to meaningfully display claim values based only upon the payload's native representation of those claim values (unless we implemented potentially dangerous extension mechanisms, significantly increasing the vulnerability of the system). Therefore a design decision was to have identity providers send claim values both in their native format and in a human-readable format (the "display token"), with the two sets of values cryptographically bound together to allow auditing of an identity provider either by users or by relying parties that understand the claims.

3.8 Auditing ≠ Non-auditing Identity Providers

In many cases users will want guarantees that their identity providers can't accumulate a record of the sites they visit. Yet in some governmental and financial settings, an audit record of sites visited using an identity is absolutely required; both kinds of identities should be able to be accommodated. A design decision was to architect the identity metasystem such that it could accommodate identity providers exhibiting either of these mutually-exclusive requirements. As a result, the system supports release of the identity of the relying party to "auditing" identity providers. But when interacting with non-auditing providers, it only releases a one-way function of the relying party's identity – computed on a per-user basis so the identity provider cannot deduce the identity of the relying party.

3.9 Authentication Goes Both Ways

Identity systems are typically used to prove the identity of the user to the relying party. But many forms of "phraud" are possible because the identity of the relying party is not adequately proven to users, meaning that imposter sites can pass as the real thing. A key design decision for the identity metasystem is to require that a site prove its identity to a user before the user ever supplies any information to the site.

3.10 Predictable, Protected Human Communication

Human beings are bad at handling complexity. Faced with unfamiliar choices, some fraction of the population will make the wrong decisions, even when those decisions are not in their best interests. Thus, a key design decision is to make the interactions that the metasystem has with its users as simple, familiar, self-explanatory, and predictable as possible. This is achieved, in part, by making the communication channel with the user as narrow and constrained as possible, thus eliminating noise on the channel (complexity) that could increase the likelihood of the user misunderstanding the communication. Our user studies show that familiarity is a powerful weapon against social engineering attacks. When faced with the unfamiliar interactions caused by many forms of attacks within an otherwise familiar and predictable channel, the studies show that users will quickly and reliably realize that "something's not right here", decline to continue down the attack's path of choices, and thus thwart the attack. Part of the familiarity comes from the design decision to represent all identities using the same InfoCard metaphor on the desktop, no matter what underlying identity technologies their providers use. Another kind of familiarity derives from the user recognizing his or her portfolio of identities. Consider an analogy. If someone were to hand you a wallet that wasn't yours and try to get you to use it, you'd quickly look inside, see that the cards in the wallet were not your cards, and recognize that this wasn't your wallet. Similarly, if an attacker was to try to spoof the InfoCard user interface, they would be unlikely to convince many users to use it, because while they could put up the right sets of decorations on the window, the attacker wouldn't know your set of cards. Finally, the InfoCard user interface is protected on the Windows implementation by running it in a separate secure desktop under a different user account. This means that unless malicious code is running with administrative privileges, it can't even see the InfoCard process, let alone control or communicate with it. All local secrets are stored in an encrypted form and no programmatic interface to the card store is provided. Some might argue that these technical measures aren't foolproof (which is true). But compared to entering identity information such as passwords in a browser running in the user's context, they do significantly raise the bar.

4 Status and Plans

Microsoft has been actively working with innovators and industry players since 2004 developing both the principles behind the Identity Metasystem and interoperable implementations. For instance, in May 2005, we demonstrated interoperation with an open source Java identity pro10 vider written by Ping Identity [PingID 05]. Implementation guides [Microsoft 05b] have been published enabling (and encouraging) people on non-Windows platforms to build interoperable Identity Metasystem implementations. Several beta versions of Microsoft's implementations have been released [Microsoft 05b], with more to come.

Microsoft recognizes that, for the Identity Metasystem to succeed, it must be widely adopted, including on non-Windows platforms and by non-Microsoft browsers and web servers. We are heartened by the widespread recognition that, while Microsoft may be competing with other platforms and others' software offerings, we all share a common interest in seeing a viable, ubiquitous Internet authentication solution deployed. Microsoft will be shipping its "InfoCard" client implementation as part of WinFX [Microsoft 06] — a set of managed code APIs that will be available on all of Windows Vista, Windows XP, and Windows Server 2003. WinFX will ship at the same time as Windows Vista. While we are not at liberty to disclose others' implementation plans, we are excited at the possibilities of implementations on non-Microsoft platforms as well. Stay tuned for future developments!

5 Conclusions

Many of the problems on the Internet today, from phishing attacks to inconsistent user experiences, stem from the patchwork nature of digital identity solutions that software makers have built in the absence of a unifying and architected system of digital identity. The Identity Metasystem, as defined by the Laws of Identity, would supply a unifying fabric of digital identity, utilizing existing and future identity systems, providing interoperability between them, and enabling the creation of a consistent and straightforward user interface to them all. Basing our efforts on the Laws of Identity, Microsoft is working with others in the industry to build the Identity Metasystem using published WS-* protocols that render Microsoft's implementations fully interoperable with those produced by others. The design decisions presented in this paper are intended to result in a widely accepted, broadly applicable, inclusive, comprehensible, privacy-enhancing, security-enhancing identity solution for the Internet. We present them and the rationale behind them to facilitate review of these design decisions by the security, privacy,

and policy communities, so that people will better understand Microsoft's implementations, and to help guide others when building interoperating implementations. We believe that many of the dangers, complications, annoyances, and uncertainties of today's online experiences can be a thing of the past. Widespread deployment of the Identity Metasystem has the potential to solve many of these problems, benefiting everyone and accelerating the long-term growth of the Internet by making the online world safer, more trustworthy, and easier to use. Microsoft is working with others in the industry to define and deploy the Identity Metasystem. We hope that you will join us!

References

[Anti-Phishing 05] Anti-Phishing Working Group. Phishing Activity Trends Report, February 2005. http://anti-phishing.org/APWG_Phishing_Activity_Report_Feb05.pdf.

[Cameron 05a] Kim Cameron. Kim Cameron's Identity Weblog, May 2005. http://www.identityblog.com/.

[Cameron 05b] Kim Cameron. The Laws of Identity. Microsoft Whitepaper, May 2005. http://msdn.microsoft.com/webservices/understanding/advancedwebservices/default.aspx?pull=/library/en-us/dnwebsrv/html/lawsofidentity.asp.

[FFIEC 05] Federal Financial Institutions Examination Council. Authentication in an Internet Banking Environment, October 2005. http://www.ffiec.gov/press/pr101205.htm And http://www.ffiec.gov/pdf/authentication_guidance.pdf.

[Gartner 05] Gartner. Gartner Survey Shows Frequent Data Security Lapses and Increased Cyber Attacks Damage Consumer Trust in Online Commerce, June 2005. http://www.gartner.com/press_releases/asset_129754_11.html.11

[IETF 05] ETF. Public-Key Infrastructure (X.509) (pkix), December 2005. http://www.ietf.org/html.charters/pkix-charter.html.

[Microsoft 05a] Microsoft. Microsoft's Vision for an Identity Metasystem. Microsoft Whitepaper, May 2005. http://msdn.microsoft.com/webservices/unde rstanding/advancedwebservices/default.aspx?pull=/library/en-us/dnwebsrv/html/identitymetasystem.asp.

[Microsoft 05b] Microsoft. Windows Vista Developer Center: InfoCard. http://msdn.microsoft.com/windowsvista/building/infocard/.

[Microsoft 06] Microsoft. WinFX Developer Center, January 2006. http://msdn.microsoft.com/winfx/.

[PingID 05] Ping Identity. SourceID InfoCard STS Toolkit for Java, August 2005. http://www.sourceid.org/projects/infocards/.

[WS-MetadataExchange 04] Web Services Metadata Exchange (WS-MetadataExchange), September 2004. http://specs.xmlsoap.org/ws/2004/09/mex/WS-MetadataExchange.pdf.

[WS-Security 04] Web Services Security: SOAP Message Security 1.0 (WS-Security 2004), March 2004. http://docs.oasis-open.org/wss/2004/01/oasis-200401-wss-soap-message-security-1.0.pdf.

[WS-SecurityPolicy 05] Web Services Security Policy Language (WS-SecurityPolicy), July 2005. http://specs.xmlsoap.org/ws/2005/07/securitypolicy/ws-securitypolicy.pdf.

[WS-Trust 05] Web Services Trust Language (WS-Trust), February 2005. http://specs.xmlsoap.org/ws/2005/02/trust/WSTrust.pdf.

6 Appendix A – The Laws of Identity

The "Laws of Identity" [Cameron 05b] are intended to codify a set of fundamental principles to which a universally adopted, sustainable identity architecture must conform. The Laws were proposed, debated, and refined through a longrunning, open, and continuing dialogue on the Internet [Cameron 05]. Taken together, the Laws were key to defining the overall architecture of the Identity Metasystem. They are:

- **User Control and Consent:** Identity systems must only reveal information identifying a user with the user's consent.

- **Minimal Disclosure for a Constrained Use:** The identity system must disclose the least identifying information possible, as this is the most stable, long-term solution.

- **Justifiable Parties:** Identity systems must be designed so the disclosure of identifying information is limited to parties having a necessary and justifiable place in a given identity relationship.

- **Directed Identity:** A universal identity system must support both "omnidirectional" identifiers for use by public entities and "unidirectional" identifiers for use by private entities, thus facilitating discovery while preventing unnecessary release of correlation handles.

- **Pluralism of Operators and Technologies:** A universal identity solution must utilize and enable the interoperation of multiple identity technologies run by multiple identity providers.

- **Human Integration:** Identity systems must define the human user to be a component of the distributed system, integrated through unambiguous human-machine communication mechanisms offering protection against identity attacks.

- **Consistent Experience across Contexts:** The unifying identity metasystem must guarantee its users a simple, consistent experience while enabling separation of contexts through multiple operators and technologies. The Laws of Identity are discussed in more detail in The Laws of Identity whitepaper [Cameron 05b]. To join in the discussion of the Laws of Identity, visit www. identityblog.com.

Federated ID Management – Tackling Risk and Credentialing Users

Marc Speltens[1] · Patrick Patterson[2]

[1]Transglobal Secure Collaboration Program
CertiPath LLC
marc.speltens@certipath.com

[2]Carillon Information Security Inc.
ppatterson@carillon.ca

Abstract

This presentation will outline the approach taken by the International Aerospace and Defense Industry (IADI) to address the lack of common Identity Management policy and practice "standards," and the deployment of PKI and Federated Identity Management with the goal of decreasing risk and cost in collaborative programs across the entire supply chain.

ID management is one of the most challenging security issues in business today. As collaboration moves quickly across geographies, organisational boundaries and more, security is increasingly important. More business is done online, but companies are unable to absolutely confirm the identity of those they are doing business with. Businesses relying solely on user ID/password combinations for authentication are at grave risk – and digging themselves deeper every day as hackers work to break codes into secure data.

The most secure means of multi-enterprise collaboration is achievable through Federated Identity Management.

Leading organisations are taking steps toward Federation – the single best source of authority to vouch for an individual's identity. These businesses no longer have to manage identities and do password resets for customers, supply chain members, and collaboration partners. Instead, only those with issued credentials are allowed access to specified applications and databases.

Audience members will leave this workshop session with the following:
- A better understanding of the approach that has been taken by IADI to implement Federated Identity Management
- Techniques and lessons learned for implementing Federated Identity Management
- An understanding of issues that remain to be solved before the full value of Federated Identity can be achieved.

1 Federation

1.1 What is it?

Conceptually, a Federated Identity is simply the re-use of a single credential to gain access to multiple resources (or, in federation jargon, Service Providers (SP)). An early example of this is already practised in many different places, under the auspices of "Single Sign On" (SSO). However, in most SSO implementations, the resources are usually all within the same entity, be it business or government.

Efforts have been under way over the last several years to expand this capability, so that one may use a single login within a community of entities (a Federation). This adds a layer of complexity, as each entity within the Federation may have their own distinct security rules, privacy guidelines, and requirements for obtaining a credential. Frequently, this complexity is compounded by the fact that these rules, guidelines and requirements are not synchronised, and may even conflict.

In the remainder of this paper, we will examine the Federation work being done by the Transglobal Secure Collaboration Program (TSCP) to enable collaboration and supply-chain management, explore the technical, business and policy challenges, and propose some solutions based on this work.

1.2 Why the TSCP is interested in Federation

The TSCP was formed by leading companies in the IADI, and is comprised at the time of writing of The Boeing Company, Lockheed-Martin, Northrop-Grumman, EADS, Rolls-Royce, BAE Systems, and Raytheon as well as the Governments of the US, UK, and the Netherlands. Collectively, the company participants have a supply chain that comprises over two hundred thousand companies, and they all form parts of programs that require them to collaborate efficiently, while preserving their own intellectual property interests, and adhere to export control regulations. Today, these companies generally manage their supply chain collaborative programs by handling user account management for partner employees internally. As they are not "canonical" for these external users, i.e. they do not know for certain the employment status or the proofing and vetting of these users, this situation exposes these organisations to a level of risk that is increasingly becoming unacceptable. Additionally, most of these accounts use relatively weak authentication mechanisms such as username/password for access, adding both security concerns and administrative overhead, arising from lost or forgotten passwords, to the risk.

Given this background, the TSCP has been working over the last several years to establish a strong, PKI-based credentialing system for users, and, more recently, to establish a FIM-based access-control scheme, allowing user account information to be maintained canonically by the companies that employ those users. This system also provides a managed collaboration infrastructure where protection profiles for export control and intellectual property protection are more easily established and maintained.

2 First Problem – Credentialing

2.1 Common Policy is the Beginning

One of the most difficult requirements for Federation to be possible is to build a common credentialing policy that allows all members of the Federation, from different organisations, to be issued a trusted ID. Projects such as [GUIDE] and [eAUTH] have spent much time working on the problems inherent in establishing these policies. The differences in national privacy, labour, and disclosure laws make it a non-trivial exercise to build a proofing and vetting scheme that will be accepted across multiple jurisdictions. In the case of the TSCP, this task was made somewhat easier because the customer community, which includes the US Department of Defence, and the UK Ministry of Defence, had already made some progress in establishing a common proofing and vetting regime. As access to and from those organisations is one of the major drivers of the TSCP, the participants felt that adopting a set of policies based on those of the US Federal Bridge CA, with certain modifications for the European community, was the best way forward.

This choice of proofing and vetting regime laid the foundations for the IADI's acceptance of the TSCP's single credentialing policy for all aerospace users. This in turn has led to the founding of CertiPath LLC, a joint venture between SITA, ARINC, and Exostar, which provides a PKI bridge to allow credentials issued by one enterprise to be validated by any other member of the bridge. An added value of CertiPath is that they have obtained cross-certification with the US Federal Bridge, and are working on cross-certification with the UKMoD. This will allow CertiPath members to propagate and accept credentials to and from their major clients.

2.2 One Size Does Not Fit All

The very nature of CertiPath as a joint venture has become an important feature. It is unrealistic to expect organisations with less than several thousand employees to set up their own PKI and cross-certify with CertiPath. However, as a joint venture between three certificate-issuing companies, the three partners are the natural vendors to issue certificates to companies that, for whatever reason, do not wish to issue their own certificates. This leads to a large degree of flexibility, and although it implies a tight binding between the company purchasing certificates and the issuer of the certificates, to ensure that there are not incorrectly valid certificates in the system, it appears that the model being deployed by the members of the TSCP is going to work.

2.3 Already a Risk Reduction

If the efforts of the TSCP were to stop now, they would already have enabled significant reduction in risk. Even though it is still necessary to provision each user's account on the service provider, the PKI credential allows the proofing and vetting level of the user to be enforced. That is, the user will only be authorized if he uses a PKI crendential that is issued in compliance with a certain Certificate Policy. Furthermore, PKI provides notice when a user has had his credential revoked, such as for example when he is no longer employed by a particular company. This is not perfect, since it doesn't accommodate re-assignment within a company, nor is there a facility for more complex trust decisions, but at least the necessity for maintaining passwords on the service provider side for each user has been removed.

3 Federation Sets the Stage for Scalability

3.1 Federation Introduces a New Set of Policies

PKI proponents may sometimes claim that PKI will solve all of your credentialing issues, because it can categorically prove the user of a credential is who they say they are. The latter may be true, but the former is a falacy. In reality, it is rarely the identity of the user that is actually interesting to someone making an access control decision. More likely, they want to make a decision based on facts about that person. For instance, what is their citizenship, who do they work for, and do they work on a particular project? In the Federation world, these are most often referred to as attributes and claims.

For an attribute to be meaningful, however, it must come from an authoritative source, and, furthermore, must be expressed in such a way that all members of the Federation agree to the attribute's semantics and usage. To do this, one or more Federation Policies needs to be developed.

3.2 Federation Policy and Attribute Profiles

Developing Federation policy turns out to be a rather complicated affair. With PKI, we have over twenty years of prior experience with the creation and audit of the policies surrounding credentials. There are even certain audit programs, such as WebTrust, which are internationally recognised and allow validation of equivalence of trust between multiple certificate authorities. The very concept of Federation, however, is so new that the each implementation is left with the task of answering critical questions such as „how to trust that an Identity or Attribute provider is canonical and trustworthy for the claims it issues", and, more fundamentally, „what are the common attributes that need to be expressed within this Federation". This is unsurprising, as these very questions are the ones that are supposed to be answered in PKI certificate policies, according to [RFC3647]. The difference is that there hasn't been a formalised body of work like [RFC3647] that establishes how the answers to these questions should be expressed.

Setting aside questions of policy for a moment, PKI has the advantage that there is a large set of standards ([PKIX]) that specify how all the components of a PKI will express their values. With Federation, there is currently only sparse coverage of attributes and values that may need to be expressed. [SAML] does give us ways to express the security context of a particular set of assertions, and [CardSpace] gives us an „Identity" namespace, but there are not yet any standardised ways the authors are aware of to express some attributes the TSCP requires, such as „Citizenship", „Group Membership", „Proofing level", „Is a member of the users covered by NDA or contract number ##", and so on. Admittedly, some of these are very specific to the application to which the TSCP would like Federation to be put. However, they are also so fundamental to generic concepts of the use cases, particularily for export control and intellectual property protection, that a standardised schema covering attributes such as these would be highly desirable.

Now, before we standardise a schema for various necessary attributes, one fundamental question needs an answer: How does one go about determining what the necessary attributes are? In the case of the TSCP, this is an ongoing activity; the participants have been collectively searching within their organisations for the data models and flows that are used to express the primary use cases of intellectual property protection (IPP) and export control (EC). Input from the TSCP members is used to model the generic process flow of a project where data must be protected for IPP or EC reasons. For each such process, a set of prerequisite attributes can be constructed for each decision. Where such an attribute must come from a Federated Identity, this has been noted, the source of authority identified, and an encoding for the attribute proposed. The collection of attributes thus identified for each use case is then brought into a single profile for that use case.

3.3 Radical Shift for Access Control

Current implementations of Federation suffer from one major limitation. Most are simply dedicated to passing rather rudimentary information around, and still require at least some *a priori* knowledge about the actual user upon whom the access control decision is being based. That is, most current deployments are limited to role-based Federation, where the SP doesn't have or need an account for each person, but has something like a group account (with audit trail to allow for individual accountability) for each task, and the permissions for each data object are based on these „group permissions". Now, this is certainly much better than having to provision for each user and manage user-account lifecycles within each SP, so even with this limitation there are already several large economies being realised.

The true „holy grail" of Federation, though, is for each application to become truly claims-aware, and to base all access control decisions on the claims being made by the IdP on behalf of the user seeking access to the data. The impediments to this are twofold:

1. The current lack of availabile mechanisms to autmatically process multiple claims and make complex access control decisions based on a set of rules. e.g.: Is this user a party to this NDA, are they a citizen of Canada, and are they in a country where they are allowed to view this data?; and

2. Difficulty in shifting the thinking of data owners such that they realise they will still have individual accountability for each access, without managing individual access.

The first item is being addressed by such standards as [XACML], but the second is rather more difficult. Within the TSCP the second is being addressed by the ongoing education of the participant members, as well as by providing all of the members with examples which show how to maintain accountability in each of their environments. However, it will take some time for the full impact of this new way of thinking about credentialing to permeate the industry.

3.4 Data Tagging Enables Claims Awareness

Governments and industry have been pining for data tagging for a very long time now. XML has been maturing and gaining popularity for a while, and while it's true that this makes it possible to have a standardised encapsulation of data that allows attributes to be applied, there are still some problems. These problems lie in the fact that the data is not editable in this tagged format, and so, once a document is taken out of the repository where these attributes are applied, the attributes are lost. With [OOXML] and [ODF] emerging as the new document standards, we may finally be able to finally embed these attributes into the documents themselves. This will require a rights management scheme of some sort to ensure that the user will not strip out the tags; however, the very act of placing the documents into a usable form such as [OOXML] or [ODF] will at least preserve this tagging.

It is the tagging of data in the repository that is of interest for Federation. If each data entity is stored with pertinent attributes in a format that is readable by the access control system, then the access control system will be able to use those tags to build the rules determining the access in a way that most accurately reflects the intent of the data owner. This will eliminate the need to manage access control rules in a non-intuitive way. For instance, it would surprise the authors if most users could create a correct set of access control rules using the Microsoft access management control; however, we believe that most users will be able to accurately determine that the document they are working on is to be used only by members of their own program or group, or if the document is need-to-know for a business or technical audience, for example.

4 Technology

The reader may notice that there has been no reference to specific Federation technologies in the preceeding discussion. With the exception of a passing reference to SAML, the authors have decided to avoid making specific reference to WS-Federation, Liberty-Alliance, Shibolleth, and many of the other standards that exist to varying degrees of completeness in the Federation world today. This is mainly because, as discovered in the TSCP activities, by and large the products that implement these standards today work. Instead it is the larger questions concerning policy and profile development that are more difficult, more pressing, and currently need the most attention.It is evident to the authors that before we can truly realise the benefits of Federation, or even begin to implement claims-aware SPs in a truly scalable fashion, organisations and enterprises will need to significantly upgrade their technology platforms. For example, today, there are very few applications which are truly „claims aware", and there are even fewer that allow the seamless integration of PKI and Federation. However, as some of the more interesting capabilities are just now starting to appear on the roadmaps of various technology providers, the authors would like to temper that last statement with „upgrade, but wait just a bit longer before you do".

5 Conclusion – Through Federation to Scalable Compliance

The members of the TSCP strongly believe that the only way to ensure all their partners respect its various compliance domains is through Federation. Just as CertiPath has enabled them to need to manage only a single trust relationship for their PKI credentials, the TSCP hopes that the creation of an International Aerospace and Defence Federation will allow them to need to manage only a single relationship with the Federation enabler. This, and the other benefits previously outlined, will result in a substantially reduced cost of managing supply chains, while achieving a level of IPP and EC compliance that has previously eluded the industry.

There is a long way to go before this enabler is established, all of the PKI credentials issued, all of the data tagged, and all of the access rules written. Much work remains to be done, and many questions to be resolved. However, the authors are confident that the path forward is known, and that in the near future we will see the convergence of technology and policy that will fully realise the goals of the program.

References

[GUIDE]   See: http://www.guide-project.org

[eAUTH]   See: http://cio.gov/eauthentication

[RFC3647] S. Chokhani, W. Ford, R. Sabett, C. Merrill, S. Wu, *Internet X.509 Public Key Infrastructure Certificate Policy and Certification Practices Framework, Request for Comments 3647*, <http://www.ietf.org/rfc/rfc3647.txt>, November 2003.

[PKIX]   See: http://www.ietf.org/html.charters/pkix-charter.html

[SAML]   See: http://www.oasis-open.org/committees/tc_home.php?wg_abbrev=security

[CardSpace] See: http://cardspace.netfx3.com

[XACML]   See: http://www.oasis-open.org/committees/xacml/

[OOXML]   See: http://www.ecma-international.org/memento/TC45.htm

[ODF]   *ISO/IEC 26300:2006 Information technology -- Open Document Format for Office Applications (OpenDocument)*, November 30, 2006, International Organization for Standardization, Geneva, Switzerland.

Information Security Governance for Executive Management

Yves Le Roux

CA
25 Quai Paul Doumer
F-92408 COURBEVOIE CEDEX
Yves.leroux@ca.com

Abstract

As an educational resource for boards of directors, executive management and IT security professionals, the IT Governance Institute has designed and created a publication, titled "Information Security Governance: Guidance for Boards of Directors and Executive Management, 2nd Edition" [ITGI06] . This paper is based upon this publication. This paper starts by a definition of the Information Security Governance and its six basic outcomes: Strategic alignment, Risk management, Resource management, Performance measurement, Value, Integration. It will continue by presenting an information security governance framework presenting the necessary people components in developing a security strategy aligned with business objectives and their roles and responsibilities. A more detailed "must do" list is given for the two levels of executive management considered in this paper: Board of directors (or Trustees) and Executive Committee (or Information Security Steering Committee). Relationships amongst the outcomes of effective information security governance and management directives will be explained for the various management levels involved.

In conclusion, the success of an information security program rests on the willingness of top management to stress its importance, to act in line with the principles enacted in policies, on the precision in which security responsibilities are assigned, on the effectiveness of security training, and on the attitudes and daily practices of every man and woman of the organization. Every level of management, starting with the board of directors, must play a vital role in this effort.

1 Information Security Governance Definition

In "A Board Culture of Corporate Governance" business author Gabrielle O'Donovan defines corporate governance as 'an internal system encompassing policies, processes and people, which serves the needs of shareholders and other stakeholders, by directing and controlling management activities with good business savvy, objectivity and integrity. Sound corporate governance is reliant on external marketplace commitment and legislation, plus a healthy board culture which safeguards policies and processes. [CGIJ03]

All employees, whether in the public or private sector, are inextricably dependent on information in the workplace. Therefore, an organization's information assets, whether tangible or intangible, are essential. They are necessary for day-to-day productivity and for the ongoing viability of missions. Information assets are pervasive in contemporary organizations.

N. Pohlmann, H. Reimer, W. Schneider (Editors): Securing Electronic Business Processes, Vieweg (2007), 136-146

Furthermore, the current economic climate is one in which legislative and regulatory obligations on each organisation are steadily scaling upwards, and this trend will continue. The demand for effective use of information is crucial to satisfying these external demands

Consequently, information security governance is a subset of corporate governance that provides strategic direction, ensures that objectives are achieved, manages risks appropriately, uses organisational resources responsibly, and monitors the success or failure of the enterprise security programme. Information security deals with all aspects of information (spoken, written, printed, electronic or any other medium) and information handling (created, viewed, transported, stored or destroyed).

The six basic outcomes of information security governance should include:

- **Strategic alignment** of information security with business strategy to support organisational objectives
- **Risk management** by executing appropriate measures to manage and mitigate risks and reduce potential impacts on information resources to an acceptable level
- **Resource management** by utilising information security knowledge and infrastructure efficiently and effectively
- **Performance measurement** by measuring, monitoring and reporting information security governance metrics to ensure that organizational objectives are achieved
- **Value delivery** by optimising information security investments in support of organisational objectives
- **Integration** with the business process. Security functions are integrated at the design stage.

As with any other business-critical activity, Information security must be thoroughly planned, effectively executed and constantly monitored at the highest levels of the organization. Information security is a top down process requiring a comprehensive security strategy that is explicitly linked to the organisation's business processes and objectives. For security to be effective, it must address entire organisational processes from end to end, physical, operational and technical.

In 2002, was published the "OECD Guidelines for the Security of Information Systems and Networks: Towards a Culture of Security" [OECD02]. These voluntary Guidelines constitute a foundation for work towards a culture of security. They clearly states that

- The principles of Awareness, Responsibility, Response, Ethics, Democracy, Risk Assessment, Security Design and Implementation, Security Management, and Reassessment apply to all participants, but differently, depending on their roles in relation to information systems and networks.
- Leadership in pursuit of policies that will support the aims and objectives of these principles is essential and should encourage all participants to adopt and promote a culture of security as a way of thinking about, assessing, and acting on, the operations of information systems and networks.

2 The Information Security Governance Framework

To achieve effective information security governance, management must establish and maintain a framework to guide the development and maintenance of a comprehensive information security program.

The governance framework will generally consist of:

- A comprehensive security strategy explicitly linked with IT and organisational business objectives
- An effective security organisational structure void of conflicts of interest with appropriate authority and resources
- Governing security policies that address each aspect of strategy, controls and regulation
- A complete set of security standards for each policy to ensure procedures and guidelines comply with policy
- Institutionalised monitoring processes to ensure compliance and provide ongoing feedback on effectiveness
- A process to ensure continued evaluation and update of security policies, standards and procedures
- Implementation of effective information security risk assessment methodology

This framework in turn provides the basis for the development of a cost-effective information security program that supports the organisation's goals. The overall objective of the program is to provide assurance that information assets are given a level of protection commensurate with their value or risk their compromise poses to the organisation. The framework generates a set of activities that support fulfillment of this objective

Figure 1 indicates the necessary people components in developing a security strategy aligned with business objectives. To promote alignment, the business strategy provides one of the inputs into risk management and information security strategy developments. Other inputs are the business processes, risk assessments, business input analyses and the information resources critical for their success. Regulatory requirements must also be considered in developing the security strategy.

Security requirements are the output of the risk management activity and are input to the planning activity together with the current state of the enterprise relative to these security requirements. Other inputs to the planning stage are the available resources and applicable constraints for achieving the desired state of security. The strategy provides the basis for an action plan comprised of one or more security programmes that, as implemented, achieve the security objectives. The strategy and action plans must contain provisions for monitoring as well as defined metrics to determine the level of success.

Figure 1 — Information Security Governance Conceptual Framework

We see clearly that information security governance requires strategic direction and impetus. It requires commitment, resources and assignment of responsibility for information security management, as well as a means for the board to determine that its intent has been met.

The tone at the top must be conducive to effective security governance. It is unreasonable to expect lower-level personnel to abide by security policies if senior management does not.

3 Information Security Governance and Executive Management

As stated in the title of this paper, we will focus on two entities which are part of this process:

- Board of directors or Trustees
- Executive Committee or Information Security Steering Committee

3.1 What the Boards of Directors/Trustees must do?

The 'Information Security Oversight: Essential Board Practices' published by National Association of Corporate Directors, states as essential security practices for directors:

- Place information security on the board's agenda.
- Identify information security leaders, hold them accountable and ensure support for them.

- Ensure the effectiveness of the corporation's information security policy through review and approval.
- Assign information security to a key committee.
- In this section, we will try to see in more details what the Board of directors must do

3.1.1 Become informed about Information Security.

For many Directors, information security is hard, often annoying, and something most of them wish they didn't have to deal with, as individuals and in their organizations. There are formidable disincentives to addressing security at more than just a tactical, technical level.

One of the greatest barriers is a generational disconnect: the difference between the "digital natives," people who grew up with computers and IT, and who often have an inherent understanding of IT security issues, and the "digital immigrants," the people who grew up before computers were a common household appliance, and who often find it harder to understand the impact of these issues.

Directors understand that they are accountable for protecting stakeholder interests in a demonstrable manner as part of responsible enterprise governance. We must remind them that stakeholder interests are most effectively protected by selecting a broad set of security principles interpreting and tailoring these for the enterprise, and ensuring their use and enforcement in the normal course of business.

Furthermore, we must explain them how investment in security can enable an organization to act on new opportunities to better achieve business objectives.

3.1.2 Set direction, i.e., drive policy and strategy and define a global risk profile.

Governance and risk management are inextricably linked, with governance action being an expression of responsible risk management and effective risk management requiring efficient governance. Inserting security into ongoing governance and risk management conversations is an effective and sustainable approach for enterprise-wide security governance.

It is essential to discuss risk in the context of a company's desired levels of return and growth.

Hunger for returns without a defined appetite for risk can lead to disaster. Many apparent risk management failures have been caused by profits being chased and risks being assumed that were poorly understood. The implication for management is clear: identify the risks that the organization faces, measure them and articulate the appetite for them. This needs to be done in a comprehensive and balanced way where quantitative measures are combined with qualitative measures, as well as those for which the institution may have zero tolerance.

3.1.3 Provide resources to information security efforts.

Selecting protection and prevention actions based on risk helps determine how much to invest, where to invest it, and how fast. When this selection has been done, Directors must ensure that sufficient resources (people, time, equipment, facilities, budget) are authorized and allocated to achieve and sustain an adequate level of security.

3.1.4 Set priorities.

Directors must validate/ratify the key assets they want to protected and define the priorities

3.1.5 Support change.

Educational and cultural change efforts are important themes in driving information security responsibility throughout the organization. One important component encompasses developing skills and capabilities and establishing a more rigorous, coordinated approach to information security. Other elements focused on building awareness of individual and collective responsibilities, getting people to move from observing information security in a passive role to seeing themselves as an active player on the corporate information security team.

3.1.6 Obtain assurance from internal or external auditors.

It is very important for the Board to have confidence that the security features, practices, procedures, and architecture of an information system accurately mediates and enforces the security policy. This has to be done by an independent review and examination of records and activities to assess the adequacy of system controls, to ensure compliance with established policies and operational procedures, and to recommend necessary changes in controls, policies, or procedures.

3.1.7 Insist that management makes security investments and security improvements measurable, and monitors and reports on programme effectiveness.

Measuring, monitoring and reporting on information security processes is a requirement to ensure organisational objectives are achieved. As previously stated, 'you cannot manage what you cannot measure'. Methods to monitor security related events across the organisation must be developed and it is critical to design metrics that provide an indication of the performance of the security 'machinery'.

3.1.8 Assign responsibilities to management.

Information security and designating responsibilities are not technical problems. They are business and managerial issues that must be addressed at the highest levels of management.

Creating the right "tone at the top" means management's first job is to convey how important security is to the organization. Consequently, the Board must assign information security to the executive Committee or in large organizations to a Information Security Steering Committee with correspondent responsibilities and authorities.

3.1.9 Insure compliance with laws and regulations.

Executive-level personnel can be held liable and fined or imprisoned if losses or damage to information assets occur due to fraudulent or damaging actions, and they cannot demonstrate that they have an effective program to prevent and detect violations of law. The main issue for multi-national organization is a potential conflict of law. As an example, SWIFT is stuck between the US intelligence rock (US Patriot Act) and the EU privacy hard place (EU directive 95/46). In this case, the Board will have to set direction and, if needed, decide an action plan.

3.1.10 Define and promote a code of ethics.

What is done with information collected during the normal course of business is often a question of ethics. Beyond what is legal, an organization must ask itself what is right. To be successful, an ethics policy should be:

- Given the unequivocal support of top management, by both word and example.

- Explained in writing and orally, with periodic reinforcement.
- Understood and performed by all employees.
- Monitored by top management, with routine inspections for compliance and improvement.
- Backed up by clearly stated consequences in the case of disobedience.
- Remain neutral and nonsexist.

3.2 What the Executive Management /Information Security Steering Committee must do?

Implementing effective security governance and defining the strategic security objectives of an organisation is a complex, arduous task. It requires leadership and ongoing support from executive management to succeed. Developing and implementing an effective information security strategy also requires integration with, and cooperation of, business process owners. It is imperative that senior and executive management ensure appropriate governance structures that include clarity of intent and direction, clear delineation of roles and responsibilities, adequate and effective monitoring, and suitable compliance enforcement.

3.2.1 Provide oversight for the development of a security and control framework that consists of standards, measures, practices and procedures.

Policies, standards, baselines, and procedures are key elements in ensuring that personnel understand how to handle specific job tasks. The policy lays out the general requirements, the standard specifies the tools required, the baseline designates the parameters to be used, and the procedures provide the step-by-step process required in routine activities.

3.2.2 Set direction for the creation of a security policy, with business input.

An information security policy contains senior management's directives to create an information security program, establish its goals, measures, and target and assign responsibilities. This policy defines an organization's high-level information security philosophy. Policies are brief, technology and solution independent documents. In general, policies remain relevant and applicable for a substantial period of time, and only require revisions when there is a fundamental change to an organization's business or operational objectives and environment. Functional policies implement the high-level policy and further define the information security objectives in topical areas.

3.2.3 Ensure that individual roles, responsibilities and authority are clearly communicated and understood by all.

Security is not a function of a single person nor of one group or team. Everyone must be aware of their responsibility and role in creating a secure environment. A security program contains many important elements. Each must be addressed through the security program and not overlooked or forgotten. They must be clearly communicated and must be clearly understood by all.

Specific security functions must be assigned to designated security professionals as their primary duty.

3.2.4 Require that threats and vulnerabilities be identified, analysed and monitored, and industry practices used for due care.

Organizations need a continuous program of risk assessments on things you can protect. Information security is an ongoing process, and multiple areas require attention. Threats and vulnerabilities evolved. It is important to have a function following the various weakness in a system allowing an attacker to violate the confidentiality, integrity, availability, access control, consistency or audit mechanisms of the system or the data and applications it hosts. The only way to reduce the chance of a vulnerability being used against a system is through constant vigilance, including careful system maintenance, best practices in deployment and auditing.

Due care may be considered a formalization of the implicit responsibilities held by an individual towards another individual within society. Action or omissions of skilled professionals might lead to a tort of negligence. Consequently it is important to follow the best industry practices which are considered as the "State of art".

3.2.5 Require the set-up of a security infrastructure.

Security infrastructure will include the hardware and software components which provide basic security services:

- Maintaining integrity of the computing processes.
- Controlling access to system resources and data.
- Provide consistent and predictable computing services.

3.2.6 Set direction to ensure that resources are available to allow for prioritization of possible controls and countermeasures implement accordingly on a timely basis, and maintained effectively.

Not only, have we had to implement controls and countermeasures but also to be sure they continue on the same level of effectiveness across the time. As an example, in many places, guards at the entry gate don't check carefully the ID of people they see everyday during a long period.

3.2.7 Establish monitoring measures to detect and ensure correction of security breaches.

Monitoring measures need to be established to detect and ensure correction of security breaches, such that all actual and suspected breaches are promptly identified, investigated, and acted upon, and to ensure ongoing compliance with policy, standards, and minimum acceptable security practices.

3.2.8 Require that periodic reviews and tests be conducted.

To maintain the level of security in a changing environment, you must periodically review the implementation of your information security strategy

Tests are used to evaluate the effectiveness of security countermeasures currently in place. The countermeasures may be technical, administrative or physical. They can also add to the credibility and, therefore, position of an enterprise in the marketplace if they show that the management exercises due diligence. On the other hand, tests can bring to the attention of top management that security weaknesses exist.

3.2.9 Institute processes that will help implement intrusion detection and incident response.

The organization's local policies and procedures should have detailed information about what types of activity should be reported, as well as the appropriate person to whom you should report.

3.2.10 Require monitoring and metrics to ensure that information is protected, correct skills are on hand to operate information systems securely and security incidents are responded to on a timely basis.

The success of an information security program implementation should be judged by the degree to which meaningful results are produced. A comprehensive security metrics analysis program should provide substantive justification for decisions that directly affect the security posture of an organization. These decisions include budget and personnel requests and allocation of available resources. A security metrics program should provide a precise basis for preparation of required security performance-related reports. The results of consistent periodic analysis of the metrics data are used to apply lessons learned, improve the effectiveness of existing security controls, and plan future controls to meet new security requirements as they occur.

3.2.11 Ensure that security is considered an integral part of the systems life cycle process and is explicitly addressed during each phase of the process.

Building an information system requires a balance among various requirements, such as capability, flexibility, performance, ease of use, cost, business requirements, and security. Security should be considered a requirement from the beginning — it is simply another feature that needs to be included. Attempting to retrofit the required and desired security controls after the fact can lead to user frustration, a lowered security posture, and significantly increased implementation costs. Based on the importance of each requirement, various trade-offs may be necessary during the design of the system. Thus, it is important to identify what security features must be included. Then if a performance or flexibility requirement means downgrading or not including a security feature, the architecture designers can keep the primary goals of the system in check and make compromises on the nonessential points.

It is important to notice that security professionals are concerned not only with the development phases but also with the operation and maintenance phases (after the application has been developed) as well.

4 Illustrative Matrix of Outcomes and Directives

The relationships amongst the outcomes of effective information security governance and management directives are shown in figure 2.

Figure 2 — Relationships of Security Governance Outcomes to Management Responsibilities

Management Level	Strategic Alignment	Risk Management	Value Delivery	Performance Measurement	Resource Management	Integration
Board of Directors	Require demonstrable alignment	Policy of risk management in all activities, ensure regulatory compliance	Require reporting of security activity costs	Require reporting of security effectiveness	Policy of knowledge management and resource utilisation	Policy of assurance process integration
Executive Management	Institute processes to integrate security with business objectives	Ensure roles and responsibilities include risk management in all activities, monitor regulatory compliance	Require business case studies of security initiatives	Require monitoring and metrics for security activities	Ensure processes for knowledge capture and efficiency metrics	Provide oversight of all management functions and plans for integration
Steering Committee	Review and assist security strategy and integration efforts, ensure business owners support integration	Identify emerging risks, promote business unit security practices, identify compliance issues	Review and advise adequateness of security initiatives to serve business functions	Review and advise *vis-à-vis* security initiatives meet business objectives	Review processes for knowledge capture and dissemination	Identify critical business processes and assurance providers, direct assurance integration efforts
Chief Information Security Officer	Develop security strategy, oversee security program and initiatives, liaise with business process owners for ongoing alignment	Ensure risk and business impact assessments, develop risk mitigation strategies, enforce policy and regulatory compliance	Monitor utilisation and effectiveness of security resources	Develop and implement monitoring and metrics approaches, direct and monitor security activities	Develop methods for knowledge capture and dissemination, develop metrics for effectiveness and efficiency	Liaise with other management providers, ensure gaps and overlaps are identified and addressed

5 Conclusion

Implementing effective information security governance for most organisation will require a major initiative given the often fragmented, tactical nature of typical security efforts. It will require committed support of senior management and adequate resources. It will require the elevation of security management to positions of authority equivalent to its responsibilities. This has been the trend in recent years as organisation's grow totally dependent on their information assets and resources and the threats and disruptions continue to escalate and become ever more costly.

Yet the success of a sound information security program rests not only on technical proficiency but, more importantly, upon people, especially the employees of an organization. It rests on the willingness of top management to stress its importance, to act in line with the principles enacted in policies, on the precision in which security responsibilities are assigned, on the effectiveness of security training, and on the attitudes and daily practices of every man and woman of the organization. Every level of management, starting with the board of directors, must play a vital role in this effort.

References

[CGIJ03] Corporate Governance International Journal, "A Board Culture of Corporate Governance", Vol 6 Issue 3 (2003)

[ITGI06] IT Governance Institute, Information Security Governance: Guidance for Boards of Directors and Executive Management, 2nd Edition, 2006

[OECD02] Organization for Economic Co-operation and Development (OECD), Guidelines for the Security of Information Systems and Networks—Towards a Culture of Security, Recommendation of the OECD Council at its 1037th Session on 25 July 2002.

[NACD 01] National Association of Corporate Directors, 'Information Security Oversight: Essential Board Practices', USA, 2001

Model Driven Security
for Agile SOA-Style Environments

Ulrich Lang · Rudolf Schreiner

ObjectSecurity Ltd.
St. John's Innovation Centre
Cowley Road, Cambridge CB4 0WS, UK
{ulrich.lang | rudolf.schreiner@objectsecurity.com}

Abstract

There is evidence that many IT security vulnerabilities are caused by incorrect security policies and configurations (i.e. human errors) rather than by inherent weaknesses in the attacked IT systems. Security administrators need to have an in-depth understanding of the security features and vulnerabilities of a multitude of ever-changing and different IT "silos". Moreover, in complex, large, networked IT environments such policies quickly become confusing and error-prone because administrators cannot specify and maintain the correct policy anymore. Agile service oriented architecture (SOA) style environments further complicate this scenario for a number of reasons, including: security policies may need to be reconfigured whenever the IT infrastructure gets re-orchestrated; security at the business process management layer is at a different semantic level than in the infrastructure; semantic mappings between the layers and well-adopted standardised notations are not available. This paper explores how the concepts of security policy management at a high, more intuitive (graphical) level of abstraction and model-driven security (tied in with model driven software engineering) can be used for more effective and simplified security management/enforcement for the agile IT environments that organisations are faced with today. In this paper, we illustrate in SecureMDA™ how model driven security can be applied to automatically generate security policies from abstract models. Using this approach, human errors are minimised and policy updates can be automatically generated whenever the underlying infrastructure gets re-orchestrated, updated etc. The generated security policies are consistent across the entire distributed environment using the OpenPMF policy management framework. This approach is better than having administrators go from IT system to IT system and change policies for many reasons (including security, cost, effort, error-proneness, and consistency). The paper also outlines why meta-modelling and a flexible enforcement plug-in model are useful concepts for security model flexibility.

1 Unmanageable security

Today's IT environments are simply not manageable anymore using traditional security policies and policy management approaches because of the complexity, heterogeneity and size of the IT landscape. This is especially true for service oriented architecture (SOA) style environments where agility and re-use of IT services (in whatever technical incarnation) are maximised. Maintaining security policies and models in line with rapidly changing IT systems and services orchestration (with confidence in system trustworthiness) requires new ways of managing agile policies.

There is evidence that many IT security vulnerabilities are caused by incorrect security policies and configurations (i.e. human errors) rather than by inherent weaknesses in the attacked IT systems. Security administrators need to have an in-depth understanding of the security features and vulnerabilities of a multitude of ever-changing and different IT systems and versions.

N. Pohlmann, H. Reimer, W. Schneider (Editors): Securing Electronic Business Processes, Vieweg (2007), 147-156

Traditionally, security policy administrators manually enter a technology-driven policy based on users/ identities and often some form of rights/roles (and other attributes) into the various systems (and possibly into a central "identity and access management" solution). Such policies have the advantage that access to systems is explicitly defined with little scope for semantic confusion. However, in complex, large, networked IT environments such policies quickly become confusing and error-prone because administrators cannot specify and maintain a correct and consistent policy anymore.

More recently, some tools can deal with security policies at a higher level of abstraction, which is therefore closer to the way in which humans reason about security policies (including standards such as Sarbanes-Oxley – SOX – and HIPAA).

This paper explores how the concepts of security policy management at a high (graphical) level of abstraction and model-driven security (tied in with software engineering) can be used for more effective and simplified security management/enforcement for the agile IT environments that organisations are faced with today (e.g. SOA).

Model driven security is concerned with the application of model driven engineering to security. The idea behind model driven software development (Model Driven Architecture, MDA) is that the application logic is specified and maintained undistorted by details of underlying technologies and can therefore be migrated to new technologies with less effort. The MDA process consists of three basic steps, the Platform-Independent Model (PIM) application specification in UML, the conversion of the PIM into a Platform-Specific Model (PSM), and the application code generation.

In this case study, we use model driven security to automatically generate security policies from UML application models, from abstract SOX/HIPAA models, and from BPEL/BPMN SOA orchestration models. Using this approach, human errors are minimised and policy updates can be automatically generated whenever the underlying infrastructure gets re-orchestrated, updated etc. The generated security policies are consistent across the entire distributed environment.

In order to make run-time policy administration and policy violation detection less cumbersome and error-prone, policies are managed in a graphical central security policy manager. For many reasons (including security, cost, effort, error-proneness, and consistency), this approach is better than having administrators go from IT system to IT system and manually change policies. In our case studies, the policies are automatically enforced via local OpenPMF policy enforcement points (PEPs). Furthermore, policies can be updated in our case study without restarting the system or redeploying PEPs, which allows fast incident response. This also allows automatic policy reconfiguration if SOA-style IT environments are re-orchestrated (i.e. if communications are changing).

Meta-modelling is another useful concept to achieve a high degree of policy model flexibility. A policy repository based on meta-modelling allows security attributes and policy model features to be added as required.

To allow enforcement based on the maximum number of security attributes available, PEPs can be flexibly linked into the communications path at any layer that is accessible (customisation may be required), such as the network, firewall, middleware, database/directory, and the application itself.

We will show the viability of these concepts and its benefits using prototype demonstrators for SOA based IT environments (and other distributed environments)

2 Model driven development

Software development for large-scale distributed software systems is a difficult and error prone process. Model Driven Development (MDD) is considered a useful emerging approach for the development of business applications. Many existing MDD solutions and tools support this domain, and existing MDA solutions are very well suited to describe the structural parts of an application, e.g. components, classes or interfaces. The model is often mapped to a standard business platform like EJB or Web Services.

However, the handling of the non-functional aspects like flexibility, Quality of Service, adaptability, assurance and security are often not sufficiently covered. Security is mainly implemented directly at the platform level, e.g. by configuring roles. If this is not sufficient, e.g. if more complex security policies have to be enforced, it has to be done as part of the implementation of the business logic. This of course is a large obstacle to one of the main principles of component based software development, namely component reusability. In such cases the component implements not only its business functionality, but also a hard coded security policy. The component can only be reused if both the functional and the non-functional requirements match.

In recent years, more advanced middleware platforms became available, which were specifically tailored to meet the demanding requirements like adaptability, flexibility, robustness and security. In contrast to standard business platforms, these new advanced platforms also offer support for non-functional aspects. Functional and non-functional aspects are clearly separated from each other. Like in EJB, the business functionality is implemented in a component. The non-functional aspects such as access control rules are handled by the container, the component's runtime environment, and are described by policies expressed in policy definition languages like PDL. The CORBA Component Model (CCM) [OMG02] is one of the best platforms for developing large scale distributed systems. It is based on the mature CORBA middleware and adds some more advanced concepts. It also simplifies the usage of some CORBA Services. The SecureMiddleware platform [Obje07a] we use for realising systems is an implementation of the CORBA Component Model called Qedo [Qedo Team 2006) combined with an extended security framework called OpenPMF [Obje2007b, Lang04] and running on top of MICO, an open source CORBA ORB with enhanced security functionality [MICO07].

Since the MDA approach improves the overall software development process so significantly, it would be most beneficial to also use it for the development of applications based on these advanced middleware platforms, with particular emphasis on the non-functional aspects. In another paper [LaSc07] we describe the integration of the non-functional aspects with the focus on security into the overall MDA development process and tool chain, which is used to build a virtual airspace management system (applicable to both defence and civilian IT environments) with stringent security requirements. This paper focuses more on the applicability of these concepts to SOA.

We will otline how security can be embedded into the model driven engineering process to automatically generate (most of the) security policy for the deployed application using our SecureMDA. We will also show how the generated security policies can be enforced and maintained in OpenPMF, a consistent, central repository. OpenPMF uses local policy enforcement points and central monitoring. Federation of OpenPMFs across several organisations may be useful in the case of inter-organisation collaboration (for example, to exchange policy details and authorisation tokens).

In addition to typical commercial SOA environments, security also plays a critical role in distributed systems for acute situational awareness and collaborative decision making in defence and crisis management, because information must be accurate (which is also related to reliability/robustness) and must be protected from eavesdropping. It is extremely difficult to specify, manage, and monitor a useful security policy in such dynamic environments. Model driven security can also help here to maintain a consistent security policy even in the face of frequent changes to the distributed system.

2.1 Policies and Meta Policies in OpenPMF

OpenPMF has been designed to integrate with almost any distributed systems platform and security technology. It borrows some concepts of model driven software engineering and applies them to security. OpenPMF has a very modular design with well-defined interfaces that allow flexibly replaceability and code reuse. It is therefore easily to integrate into a Qedo QoS Enabler for security enforcement at the component level.

One of the key concepts of OpenPMF is using the OMG Meta Object Facilities [OMG07) for the definition of an abstract information model of security policies. The benefits of using UML/MOF standard are extensibility, flexibility, XMI policy interchange, and automatic generation of the repository code and interfaces/descriptors. It also allows the usage of model transformations. The security meta-model describes how to express policy hierarchies, rules and entities used for rules. Meta-policies can be defined in very different ways. For example it is possible to describe specific security models, e.g. Mandatory Access Control. For role based access control (RBAC) this was proposed by Lodderstedt et al. [Lodd02]. Such semantically rich meta-policies have the advantage that the policy described can easily be mapped to existing enforcement functionality, if it is based on the same security model. It also gives certain guarantees about the correctness of the policies, because only well formed rules can be stored. On the flipside, this approach it is not very flexible. Therefore we decided to define a more flexible repository which is not based on a particular security model, but on a description of rules. The big advantage (but also the challenge) of this semantically poor model is the possibility to define arbitrary rules (both correct and incorrect, however). It is therefore necessary to pay great attention to the policy definition.

When the OpenPMF policy management framework is initiated, the technology-neutral policy, written in a policy definition language (PDL), is loaded into the policy repository. It is then obtained by the different systems, servers or applications and transformed into an efficient internal representation optimised for the evaluation of abstract attributes obtained from the underlying security technology and platform. At runtime, each incoming invocation triggers the evaluation process, after which the resulting decision is enforced on the particular underlying platform. In SecureMiddleware, the policy evaluation is done in an OpenPMF QoS Enabler.

OpenPMF is administered through the management daemon and the management GUI. In addition, the policy violation detection daemon collects relevant information from various layers of the underlying IT infrastructure and detects intrusions.

The current way of specifying the policy is by using our human-readable, technology-independent Policy Definition Language (PDL), which supports different security models. PDL uses concepts of the Principal Calculus [LABW92] which theorises about principals and its two different privilege delegation relations. PDL supports rules that are expressed in terms of requests and replies (i.e. initiating invokers, intermediaries, actions, targets etc.). Some of the features supported by the language are wildcards, multiple sets, several (arbitrary) actions, sets of clients/targets, groups and roles, and hierarchical nesting. PDL also provides advanced support for delegation.

3 MDA Tool Chain

The SecureMiddleware MDA tool chain has been produced for the rapid model based development of CCM based security-critical software systems based on SecureMiddleware. It supports a platform independent modelling of systems there is no need to model, e.g., platform-specific data types, or to decide early in the development process which particular platform to use. By using transformers, Platform independent models (PIM) can be automatically transformed into the platform specific models (PSM) which then can be used for further steps (e.g. C++ code or security policy generation). The tool chain is a set modelling and other development tools with adaptations to additionally support the security domain; its architecture is shown in figure 1.

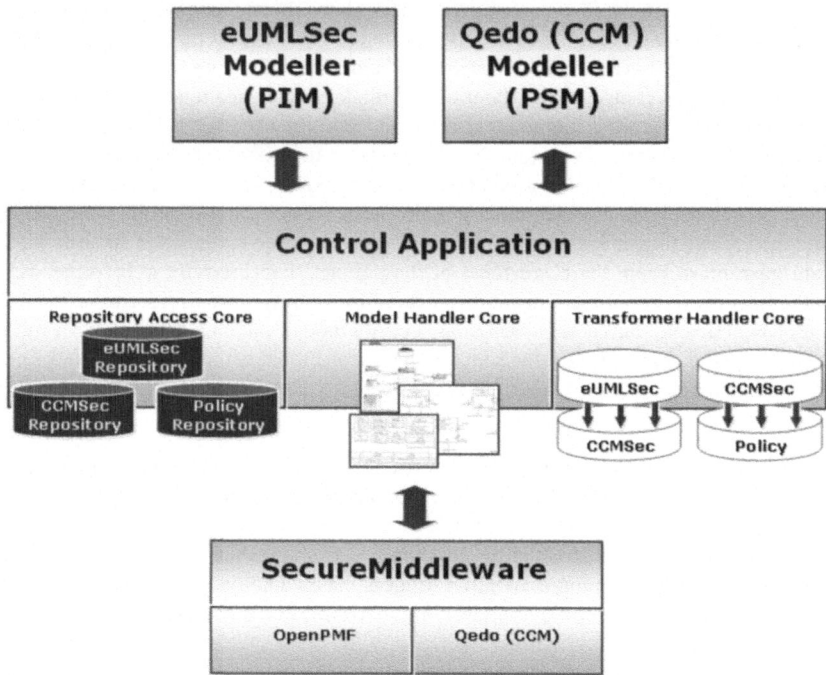

Figure 1: Overview of the tool chain architecture

For system design we use the Unified Modelling Language (UML) [OMG04, OMG03] as the foundation in our tool chain. In fact, UML is the standard for object-oriented modelling, many modelling tools support UML and a great number of developers use the language.

Since UML 2 as a whole is a language with a very broad scope and has a less precisely semantic definition (when it shall be used for automatic transformation or code generation) SecureMidleware uses a subset of UML 2 together with a specialised and absolutely clear semantics. This subset is called eUML (essential UML). The eUML metamodel includes only the required UML2 metamodel elements which formally define modelling elements, their semantic and relations. The eUML language concentrates on the most important diagram types of the 13 diagram types supported by UML 2, including structure diagrams, activity diagrams and package diagrams as the most important elements.

Similar to UML, the eUML supports user-defined UML profiles. We can extend the eUML metamodel by using profiles to customise the language for particular domains like security (as done in our SecureMDA technology [Obje07b] for OpenPMF. For modelling our security policies we have defined a security profile for eUML, called the extended eUML language eUMLSec. The profile definition includes a stereotype <<Security_Role>> that extends the eUML metaclass Class. This stereotype is used for modelling roles for role-based access control of the system. From eUMLSec we automatically generated the eUMLSec repository shown in the figure 4.

As already mentioned, we start modelling with the eUMLSec and use the eUMLSec Modeller Tool, which is a Plug-In implementation for Sparx Enterprise Architect [Spar07]. This Plug-in is synchronised with the eUMLSec repository in both directions (load and store of eUMLSec models), including the synchronisation of graphical information of the stored in the repository models. Furthermore, the eUML Plug-in contains dialogs and wizards specific for the eUMLSec language to specify details of language elements. At this level, the model shall not contain any specific platform dependent information.

The next step in the tool chain is to transform designed model into the platform specific model, in our example the SecureMiddleware platform. As already mentioned in this paper, SecureMiddleware is an extended CCM implementation provided by Qedo with security support provided by OpenPMF. Thus, we need two additional repositories for further transformation steps: The CCMSec repository for the management of platform specific information, and the Policy repository for management of policies defined in the platform. These repositories are automatically generated from metamodels (CCM metamodel, Policy metamodel) and are parts of the tool chain architecture.

The heart of our tool chain architecture is a generic control application component which is used to manage and control the various components of the tool chain. The management of repositories, transformers and models is done via the control application GUI. In the standard configuration of the tool chain control application loads three repositories: the eUMLSec, the CCMSec and Policy, and two transformers: The eUMLSec2CCMSec and CCMSec2Policy[1].

The eUMLSec2CCMSec transformer transforms an eUMLSec model from the eUMLSec repository into the CCM based specific model with security information. This transformed model will be stored in the CCMSec repository after the transformation has been done. The second transformer in the tool chain transforms CCMSec models into the policies stored in the Policy repository. After the last transformation, the OpenPMF Policy Evaluators, here embedded in QoS Enablers and CORBA Portable Interceptors, can obtain the security policy from the policy repository and enforce it at runtime.

CCMSec models can be modified or completed (e.g. by adding deployment information or other nonfunctional aspects like QoS) by using the Qedo Modeller Tool implemented as an Eclipse plug-in. The Qedo Modeller handles the connection to the CCMSec repository to propagate models into the repository and also load models from the repository and display them graphically.

4 SecureMDA™ model driven security

The overall complexity of the systems is the reason why is the manual development of security policies so difficult, even for skilled security and middleware specialists. Therefore, to make security manageable, it is necessary to reduce the complexity the persons in charge of security have to deal with. Using a model driven approach for development of security policies brings a number of advantages: 1) abstraction and reduction of complexity: Policies can be defined and integrated into system designs at a high

---

1 Related work: Another, more academic UML security notation that is not MDA based was proposed by Jürjens [Jürj04].

level of abstraction; the "hard work" is done by transformers. 2) well defined and structured procedures help to avoid overseeing something. 3) UML models can be used to detect and correct design errors or to verify the correctness of transformations.

Using SecureMDA in our tool chain, we are able to generate automatically platform specific security policies out of UML PIMs, and enforce them consistently using OpenPMF. This process is depicted in figure 2, and a demo video is available [Obje07b]:

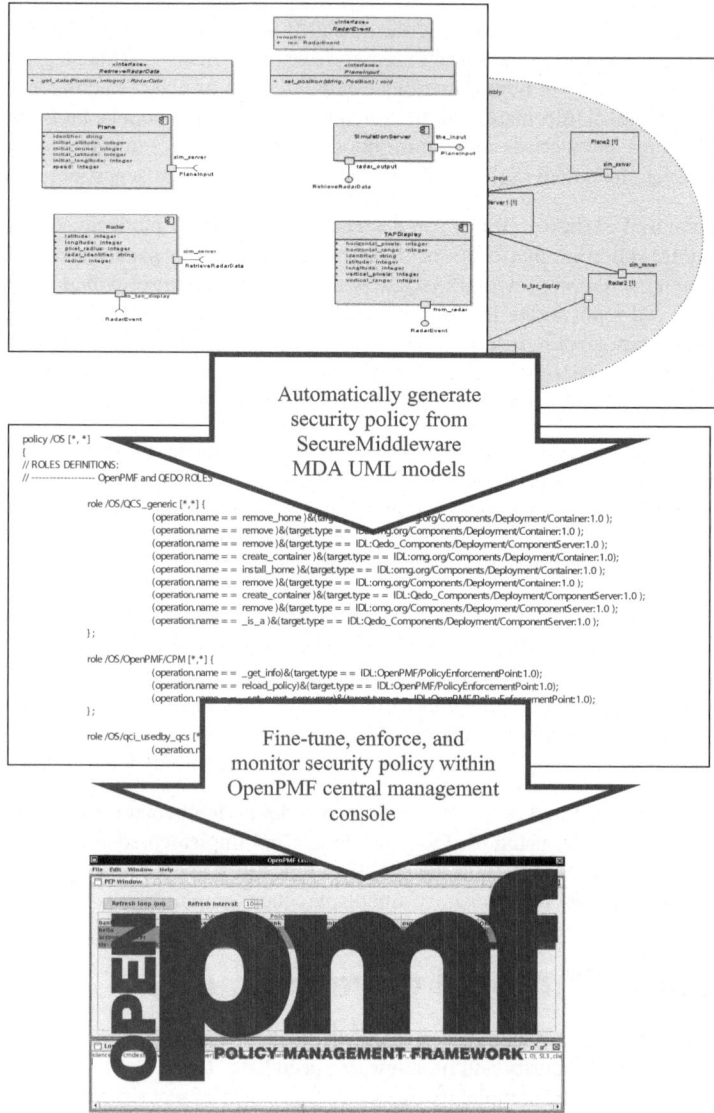

Figure 2: Overview of the security tool chain architecture

A very good and proven approach of reducing complexity is grouping things, for example by using Role Bases Access Control (RBAC). A role is a job or function within a system. The role comprises all operations on a set of targets that can be executed from the user (person or system component). Another paper [LaSc07] shows how UML can be used to specify information related to role-based access control in the overall design of an application and how this information can be used to automatically generate policies we present a simplified and small fraction of a secure air traffic management system we have worked on as part of an EU FP 6 project [AD4C07].

Using the mentioned above profile definition for security we defined following roles as stereotyped with <<Security_Role>> UML classes. In this paper, we just give a very simple example for Role Based Access Control (RBAC), a security model which is well suited for a large number of applications, esp. for protecting operations. In addition to RBAC, our tool chain current (July 2007) also supports additional security models, for example Mandatory Access Control (MAC) for controlling information flow between components, and a notation of delegation. Our framework can also easily be extended to support other security models, like Chinese Wall, thanks to the flexibility of the transformers and meta policy used. Both for MAC and Chinese Wall, the transformer generate a complex set of security rules for each simple annotation of security properties in the eUMLSec model. In addition to the generation of the rules for the application component interaction, our tool chain is also able to automatically generate the complex rules sets for the underlying Qedo infrastructure daemons.

5 TrustedSOA™ model driven security for SOA

Security for Service Oriented Architecture (SOA) is currently a big question and in many cases even a show-stopper. The fundamental problem is that agile SOA style re-orchestration of service (provider/ consumer) interactions makes security policy management a "moving target". Should security administrators manually reconfigure the security policy for each system and each user whenever a business process changes and the IT infrastructure is re-orchestrated? The maintenance cost and the human error potential would be enormous.

Model driven security as outlined in our SecureMDA approach helps solve this problem in a very innovative and elegant way: whenever the models of the application changes (these could be BPMN or UML models), the security policy simply gets automatically re-generated and redeployed dynamically on the underlying infrastructure. This way the error potential and human overhead is minimal.

We have successfully shown in our TrustedSOA [Obje07c] technology that this approach works: SecureMDA generates security policies from various models (including UML and high-level HIPAA security models), which are loaded into OpenPMF and automatically enforced acros an XML web service based SOA through matching OpenPMF plug-ins (so far BEA Web Logic and Sun Glassfish):

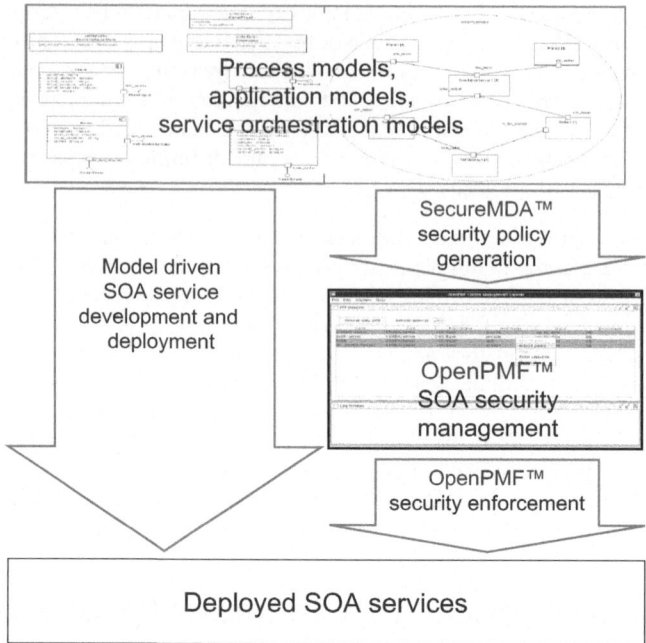

Figure 3: Overview of the TrustedSOA security architecture

6 Conclusion

Model Driven Architecture (MDA) greatly improved the development of large scale distributed applications. In this paper we have described how the concepts of Model Driven Development are applied to build a security aware tool chain called SecureMDA [Obje07b], which allows the automatic generation of security policies form application models during the MDA process. The tool-supported, graphical definition of security policies at a high level of abstraction reduces the complexity of the task of definition of security policies. The automated transformation of high level system and security models to platform specific artefacts greatly simplifies development, deployment, and maintenance.

Security for Service Oriented Architecture (SOA) is currently an extensively discussed topic [Lang07a, Lang07b], both in defence and civilian organisations (e.g. [Lang07c]). The touted benefits of SOA are in particular business agility and IT reuse, and SecureMDA model driven security is a way to achieve agile, ad-hoc, but at the same time secure IT environments.

The presented tool chain has been successfully used for the development of a secure prototypical Air Traffic Control visualisation application as part of the European AD4 project [AD4C07]. The tool chain and the secure middleware platform currently supports two very commonly used security models, Role Base Access Control for the invocation of operations and Mandatory Access Control for controlling information flow, but can be easily extended to other security models as well. First evaluation of first iterations of the system shows the generated security policy is in line with the permitted interactions of the system, as defined by the system and security design and has the expected level of assurance. Therefore, our approach for the integration of security greatly improves the development of complex and secure distributed systems.

7 Acknowledgements

The authors would like to thank Julia Reznik and Tom Ritter from Fraunhofer FOKUS for their input as part of our EU FP6 AD4 project.

References

[AD4C07] AD4 Consortium, "EU FP6 R&D project AD4 – 4D Virtual Airspace Management System" web page [online], http://www.ad4-project.com/

[Jürj04] Jan Jürjens, Security Modeling with UMLsec, Workshop regarding Security in Information Systems, SISBD2004, Málaga (Spain), Nov. 9, 2004

[LABW92] Lampson, B. et al Lampson, B., Abadi, M., Burrows, M., Wobber, E., "Authentication in Distributed Systems: Theory and Practice". *ACM Transactions on Computer Systems 10*, 4, pp 265-310, November 1992

[LaSc04] Lang, U., Schreiner, R., "OpenPMF Security Policy Framework for Distributed Systems". Proceedings of the Information Security Solutions Europe (ISSE 2004) Conference, Berlin, Germany, September 2004

[LaSc07] Lang, U., Schreiner, R., "Simplifying security management of cross-organisation collaborative decision making". Proceedings of the 6th European Conference on Information Warfare and Security, Defence College of Management and Technology, Shrivenham, UK, 2-3 July 2007

[Lang07a] Lang, U. et al, "TrustedSOA. SOA security and assurance" blog [online], www.trustedsoa.org, 2007

[Lang07b] Lang, U. et al, "Model Driven Security" blog [online], www.modeldrivensecurity.org, 2007

[Lang07c] Lang, U. et al, "Secure Air Traffic Management and CDM-A" blog [online], www.secure-airtrafficmanagement.org, 2007

[Lodd02] Lodderstedt T., "SecureUML: A UML-Based Modelling Language for Model-Driven Security. In UML 2002 – The Unified Modelling Language. Model Engineering, Languages, Concepts, and Tools". 5th International Conference, Dresden, Germany, September/October 2002, Proceedings, volume 2460 of LNCS p. 426-441, Springer, 2002

[MICO07] MICO project team, "MICO CORBA project" web page [online], www.mico.org

[OMG02] Object Management Group, "CORBA Component Model" [online], OMG document number formal/02-06-65, www.omg.org

[OMG03] Object Management Group, OMG ptc/03-09-15:"UML 2.0 Infrastructure Final Adopted Specification" [online], www.omg.org

[OMG04] Object Management Group, OMG ptc/04-10-02: "UML 2.0 Superstructure Revised Final Adopted Specification" [online], www.omg.org

[OMG06] Object Management Group, "Meta Object Facility Core Specification 2.0" [online], OMG document number, formal/2006-01-01, www.omg.org

[Obje07a] SecureMiddleware project team, "SecureMiddleware Project" web page [online], http://www.securemiddleware.org

[Obje07b] ObjectSecurity Ltd., "OpenPMF project" web page [online]. http://www.openpmf.com (with SecureMDA, http://www.securemda.com), 2007

[Obje07c] ObjectSecurity Ltd., "TrustedSOA" web page [online]. http://www.trustedsoa.com, 2007

[Qedo06] Qedo project team, "Qedo (Quality of Service Enabled Distributed Objects) CCM Implementation" web page [online], http://www.qedo.org/, March 2006

[RiLS05] Ritter, T., Lang U., Schreiner R., "Integrating Security Policies via Container Portable Interceptors", Adaptive and Reflective Middleware Workshop (ARM2005) at Middleware 2005.

[Spar07] Sparx Systems, "Enterprise Architect" web page [online], http://sparxsystems.com.au

The Business Perspective on Roles Including Root Causes of Implementation Problems and Proven Ways to Overcome them

Marc Sel

PricewaterhouseCoopers
marc.sel@pwc.be

Abstract

We present a new way for addressing the business aspects of roles and provisioning. We will quickly outline what is meant by roles and provisioning. We will then discuss what is commonly understood by 'business aspects'. Subsequently root-causes for identity management project failures are analysed. A dual track/multi-layer approach to overcome the major hurdles is then introduced, and learning from a case study is discussed.

These six 'root causes' are: (1) language (different stakeholders speak different languages), (2) lack of distinction between accountability and responsibility, (3) mismatch between expectations of centralised top-down control models such as COSO and today's mainly distributed organisations, (4) technical incompatibilities of most of today's systems, (5) SOD is inherently hard to achieve with the current technical state-of-the-art, and (6) low visibility of access control issues makes it hard to obtain adequate funding,

The innovative aspects of our approach can be summed up as:
- three layers of activities (coordination, business and technical)
- adaptation of various software-based techniques from such as 'Use Cases' combined with distributed email campaigns to translate requirements into tangible solutions that can immediately be appreciated.

We illustrate how we addressed these six ‚root causes‘ during a project.

1 Roles and provisioning

1.1 Introduction

Most medium to large sized organisations today built up and manage what could be referred to as their 'authorisation space'. This space is essentially structured into three dimensions: the different user communities (subjects), the ICT services and applications (objects), and the processes allocating users authorisations onto these services. In the real-world, this space can be impressively large. For one particular company with 40.000 employees (and excluding the authorisations of customers on company systems) we estimated the total number of authorisations that were managed around 35 million. Since that organisation's authorisations were decided by a core team of 10 persons, this meant that on average, every authorisation manager was dealing with approximately 3,5 million authorisations. Most of these

N. Pohlmann, H. Reimer, W. Schneider (Editors): Securing Electronic Business Processes, Vieweg (2007), 157-165

authorisations have been built up over the years, often surviving multiple rounds of business reorganisation. Ensuring that authorisations are configured appropriately and stay that way is a challenge.

1.2 IdM initiatives often fall short of meeting expectations

Many vendors tout Identity Management (IdM) systems as the overarching solution to the management of user identification and authorisation. Such systems are aiming essentially at quicker turnaround time for user-id and authorisation provisioning. These systems typically address the aspects of authentication, directories, provisioning and access control. While the actual success rate of such Identity Management projects varies, their approach with regard to access control is typically incomplete. Furthermore there is a clear increase in regulation resulting in ever more complex compliance requirements. So most organisations find themselves confronted with both a complex authorisation space to manage and the requirement to do this in a sufficiently transparent and understandable way. The onus of demonstrating this is imposed on the organisation.

1.3 Roles and provisioning

1.3.1 Roles

With 'roles' we refer by default to roles as defined in the RBAC standard.

The word role as in ‚Role Based Access Control' means different things to different people. The RBAC movement picked up a big momentum, and much work has been done, both theoretical and practical. The original theoretical model has greatly been expanded, and the NIST (National Institute of Standards and Technology – US) published an ANSI standard. Vendors implemented role or RBAC functionality (at least this became common terminology) in relational databases, in operating system and application security, and even in Windows2003. The basic model is based on a 'User-Role-Permission' paradigm. Since users typically access a system via (multiple) sessions, this is also reflected.

1.3.2 Rules

A number of products claim they can provide RBAC functionality through their rule-based approach. A rule-based approach essentially allows to express a security policy in terms of groups and ACL's (access control lists). The minimal approach is to use regular groups ('static' groups) – this is what has been done by Unix for decades. These groups can be structured in hierarchical fashion, allowing inheritance. Furthermore dynamic groups are added, which are constructed 'on the fly' on the basis of filters working on attributes (e.g. LDAP-based), applied to users or groups. You can then express access as "allow (or deny)" for members of particular groups (static or dynamic). You can further add constraints on the basis of e.g. time, context or IP address. This approach has also been referred to as EDAC (Enterprise Dynamic Access Control).

1.3.3 Provisioning

Originally the term 'provisioning' was used restrictively to refer to the provisioning of users on platforms only. Key aspects were provisioning policy and rules engine, workflow, repository and connections to target systems. As provisioning systems extended their functionality, they added possibilities to relate provisioned users to groups on the target systems. In this way they evolved towards Identity and Access Management systems. However, creating hierarchical group-structures and relating groups to actual resources on the target system can also be considered as part of the provisioning challenge. Given the technical diversity of platforms and applications, this is significantly more difficult.

2 The business aspects

2.1 Business aspects of roles and provisioning

Business aspects are typically oriented towards business concepts such as 'Competitive Advantage', 'Compliance', 'Cash flow', 'Delegation and Empowerment' and 'Time to Market'. Alternatively, there is also a 'downside' where problems or negative consequences are categorized. We will first briefly touch upon the 'downside', before discussing the more positive business aspects in the 'upside'.

2.1.1 Downside – negative consequences

The following elements are often identified within larger scale organisations:

- Since it's very difficult to know which 'old' privileges are no longer needed when a person changes position, it is common for 'collectors' to appear in the organisation – people that collect privileges over their career without ever dropping any privilege
- It is common to copy privileges from an existing employee to a newly hired person, taking on the same or similar role. However, this will have dire consequences if the former employee is such a 'collector'.
- Unidentified or unresolved 'SOD' (segregation of duties) issues – leading to compliance violation;
- Access control problems at the level of Operating System or Database infrastructure, supporting financial applications (people with too many/too few authorisations, orphan (unused) definitions in the system etc) – leading to security exposures;
- Development staff can run business transactions in production – leading to security exposures or operational errors;
- Large number of users with access to all kinds of 'super user' transactions in production – leading to security exposures;
- Terminated employees or departed consultants still have access – leading to unacceptable accesses;
- Posting periods not restricted within GL application – leading to lack of financial integrity;
- Custom programs, tables & interfaces are not secured (since they cannot be covered via a standard access control solution) – leading to security exposures;
- Procedures for manual processes do not exist or are not followed – leading to a lack of mitigating controls.

2.1.2 Upside – roles and provisioning as a business enabler

Business aspects are typically expressed in terms of 'Competitive Advantage', 'Compliance', 'Cash flow', and 'Time to Market'. We are convinced that by identifying and addressing the right IAM challenges, the IAM solution allows an organisation be in tune with 'the business'. Let us briefly review each of the above aspects:

- 'Competitive Advantage' – differentiating products come from differentiated business processes – hence IAM should facilitate taking responsibility within the business processes to enable differentiation;
- 'Compliance' – hence IAM should help demonstrate that appropriate controls are in place and complied with, preferably in a repeatable and cost-effective way;

- 'Cash flow' – IAM automation should translate to cost reduction due to having more effective management;
- 'Time to market' – IAM internal process speed should facilitate having the right people with the right authorisations at the right time.

Furthermore, having appropriate roles and provisioning in place helps to combat the many possible 'leakage' scenarios where employees may see increased opportunities for "small theft" of goods and services.

2.2 The business case

The ‚Business Case' is a description that presents a comprehensive view of a project or programme and:

- Verifies the solution to a business problem that meets the needs of the organisation;
- Provides measures of success; and
- Provides a consistent message to communicate to many different audiences.

There is no single best way to describe a Business Case. We make use of the model illustrated below.

The business case for roles and provisioning

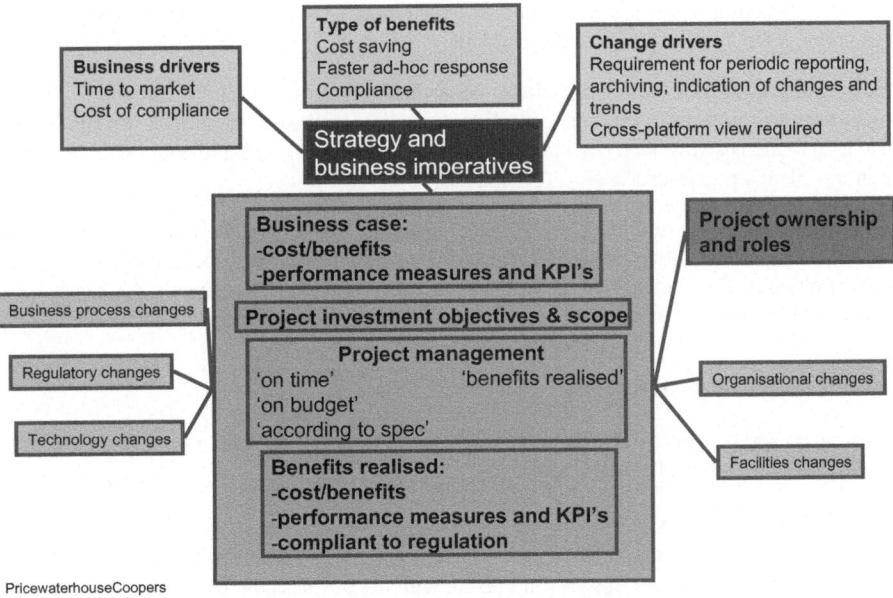

PricewaterhouseCoopers

Figure 1: Structure of a possible 'Business Case' for roles and provisioning

3 Solution and case study

3.1 The challenge

The case study organisation is a European company that is subject to both national competition regulation and the US Sarbanes-Oxley act. They employ approximately 30.000 employees. They recognised the need to strictly manage authorisations, and initiated a company-wide identity and access management project to address the roles and provisioning issues.

3.2 The Business Case

This particular organisation was confronted with structural changes in its liberalised market. This led to significant organisational alignments both for business and IT. As a consequence of reorganisations and outsourcing, their identity and access control landscape had been somewhat neglected. This led to the situation that there was no longer clear accountability over identities and access control, and there was no clear ownership of the corresponding processes. However, under regulatory pressure, this had to be addressed or the company faced potential removal from the US stock exchange and fines from the national regulator.

This situation was rectified in two phases. In a first phase, measures were taken to demonstrate regulatory compliance via cleaning of data and authorisations, and reporting/resolving any SOD issues. In a second phase, a structural approach was followed to bring the IAM (Identity and Access Management) processes under control of the business departments.

The strategic intent was to enable the business departments to structure authorisations to their needs, under their responsibility. Furthermore, compliance requirements should be met. And there was the additional goal to increase productivity by shortening the cycle to get staff and contractors fully up-and-running in the client's processes.

The consequences of doing nothing were considered as undesirable, since both the operational and regulatory pressure would only increase. Hence a business sponsor who is accountable for the delivery of the project objectives was identified, as well as a project manager. Subsequently the key internal and external stakeholders were identified, and a technical solution was selected in line with the IT strategy.

3.3 Root-cause analysis

We witnessed on various occasions the outcome of unsuccessful or only partially successful IAM projects. On this basis, we performed a root-cause analysis.

We identified the following six 'root causes'

1. Language: different stakeholders speak different languages. While the final accountability over access and segregations of duty should reside with the business owners, IAM implementation is a very technical issue, across different systems and technologies. Business owners speak in terms of 'Order-to-Cash', 'Procure-to-Pay', 'Acquisition', 'Year-end Closing' etc. The implementation of these processes resides finally with people making use of programs, transaction codes and tables. IT people speak in terms of transaction codes, program names, database tables, or application objects. Despite their name, Service Oriented Architectures or Web Services are not going to bridge this language gap.

2. Lack of distinction between accountability and responsibility. In an organisation, the CFO typically assumes final accountability for the integrity of the financial statements. Business-line executes assume final accountability for the profitability of their line-of-service. When it comes to IAM, the final accountability for authorisations will reside with the various executives. However, they cannot be bothered with the technicalities of the IAM solution, or intervene in the low-level workflows.

3. Mismatch between expectations of centralised top-down control models such as COSO and today's mainly distributed organisations. While COSO is probably the most influential internal control model, it is inherently assuming that control is centralised. Today's organisations are often very networked and distributed, making it hard to achieve such a control model.

4. Technical incompatibilities of most of today's systems. Many systems have been built to perform business processes. Unfortunately, their identity and access control components are widely incompatible. The simple notion of 'group' for example is widely different in implementation between Unix, RACF and Windows. The applicative authorisation concept of mySAP is different from that of the Oracle E-Business Suite. One level down, the authorisation concepts of a database are different from those at the Application Server (e.g. J2EE) or Operating System level.

5. SOD (segregation of duty) is inherently hard to achieve with the current technical state-of-the-art. Original access control models implemented in the typical commercial products did not allow this. While it is possible to restrict authorisations via e.g. platform groups, application tables or SAP profiles, it is typically not technically feasible (or at least not trivial) to implement SOD. For this reason many company resorted to procedural controls.

6. Low visibility of access control issues makes it hard to obtain adequate funding. As access control is inherently technical and sometimes even rather complex, it can be labour intensive. This makes it often quite expensive, and investments are harder to justify unless you're a major player in e.g. the Financial Services industry.

We subsequently identified mitigating measures that address these various causes.

3.4 The solution

The innovative aspects of our approach can be summed up as:

- three layers of activities (coordination, business and technical); and
- adaptation of software techniques such as 'Use Cases' combined with distributed email campaigns to translate requirements into tangible solutions that can immediately be appreciated.

In each layer many different activities take place. We highlight those that we believe add most value.

3.4.1 Three layers of activities

Coordination – addressing root cause 1: the language issue
The language spoken by the various stakeholders is different which leads to misconceptions and inappropriate assumptions. As solutions, we used workshops, and documents that contain a clearly defined vocabulary, linking the business language to the IT security language.

We found it important to make the distinction between 'business roles' that are allocated by the 'business application owner' to users, and the 'technical roles', which are descendant roles of those 'business roles'. These 'technical roles' contain the technical resources required for business process execution.

Coordination – addressing root cause 2: the lack of RACI

With regard to responsibility for identity and access control, the distinction is often not made between being accountable and being operationally in charge – for this reason business departments are often reluctant to take up their real responsibilities

A clear segregation between final accountability and responsibility is required. We prefer to align on the well-known RACI-model (**R**esponsible, **A**ccountable, **C**onsulted, **I**nformed). We use the term 'account-ability' to refer to the single party that assumes final responsibility. We use the term 'responsibility' to refer to the more day-to-day exercising of the related activities. The party that is responsible reports to the party that is accountable. Both accountability and responsibility can be delegated. However, a clear hierarchical structure is required, including reporting.

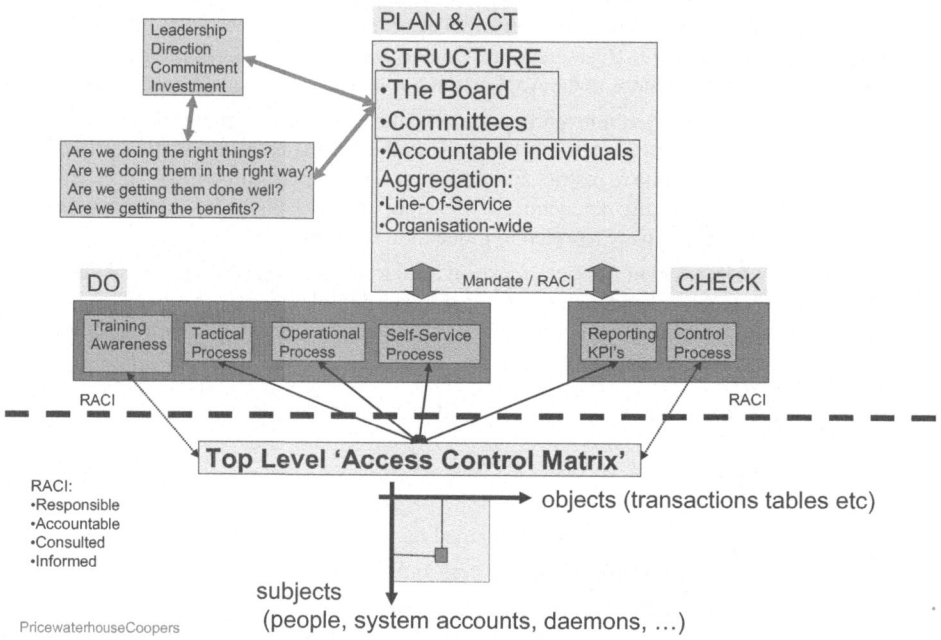

Figure 2: Use of governance model with RACI.

The overall model is divided into two halves. Above the 'dotted line' the managing domain defines structures and processes for the 'Plan, Do, Check, Act'. Below the 'dotted line', the managed domain contains the actual identity and access repositories. We tied the RACI attributes to the IAM data model, and used them to govern the workflow. Owners receive the mandate to be 'accountable', but they can delegate 'responsibility' to lower levels. However, they remain finally accountable. Resource or privilege owners are accountable for granting access to their resources. This means they are accountable for establishing an appropriate role structure, and assigning users to those roles. Obviously, for a large scale public or private organisation, a sound delegation model is required.

Business – addressing root cause 6: the lack of funding
Low visibility of access control issues makes it hard to obtain adequate funding, while addressing e.g. SOD is inherently difficult and hence expensive. Hence we used a business case approach structured as per figure 1 to obtain attention and secure adequate funding.

3.4.2 Software-based techniques

Addressing root cause 3: balancing centralised/decentralised aspects
We observed a certain degree of mismatch between the expectations of centralised top-down control models such as COSO and today's mainly distributed organisations.

Hence we use automated email campaigns to efficiently confirm the RACI assumptions. We used different types of campaigns. User-based campaigns invite the owners of organisational units (or cost centres) to approve the identity of actors in the authorisation model. Role-based campaigns invite the owners of the roles (i.e. the responsible parties) to first accept their ownership over the roles, and subsequently to validate the access of users onto those roles. This can be achieved e.g. by using automatically generated emails to provide access to workflow on a central authorisation portal. In a later phase, also Segregations-of-Duty can be defined, can receive an owner, and their violations can be accounted for via (signed) emails. Violations can be 'accepted' if e.g. sufficient mitigating controls can be demonstrated, or can be 'resolved', i.e. their causes removed. We found email to be a great facilitator for reaching out into today's distributed organisations.

Addressing root cause 4: technical incompatibilities
Technical incompatibilities of most of today's systems make it hard to build up a view on the complete authorisation landscape. For this purpose we introduce what we refer to as 'unification'. We use a simple NIST RBAC 'user-role-permission' model to establish a minimal common denominator for all the different systems. We established a single role-repository, split between 'business roles' and 'technical roles'. Within these technical roles, the different authorisation modes of the various platforms are accounted for.

Addressing root cause 5 – hard to achieve SOD's
SOD (Segregation-Of-Duty) is inherently hard to achieve with the current technical state-of-the-art. Many legacy access control technologies such as ACL's, groups, SAP authorisation objects etc do not allow to express an SOD constraint. To mitigate this weakness, SOD has often been incorporated in subsequent complementary products. However, this meant additional implementation costs and more difficult of integration.

In the SAP world, VIRSA and similar products emerged as enablers for the solution. However, many companies are confronted with having to manage more SOD's that just in SAP. Proprietary legacy systems have particular needs for managing their SOD's.

We decided to use a database as the major repository for the role model of the IAM solution, but store SOD constraints in a dedicated engine from Eurekify. We let the IAM solution validate its actions with regard to SOD in the dedicated engine via Web Services.

Overall architectural model
We used the following overall architectural model.

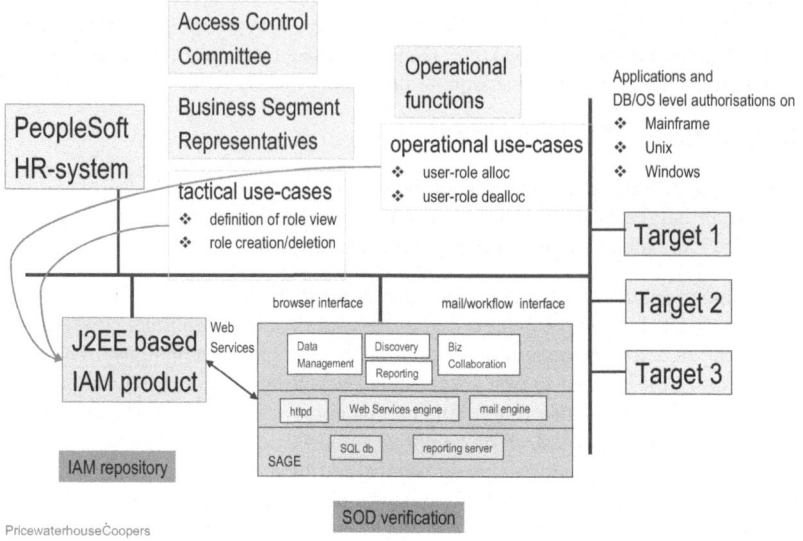

Figure 3: Architectural model

Role creation and allocation is implemented in workflow. By making use of the RACI-attributes of the users, roles and resources in the various use-cases implemented in the workflows, we made sure the final accountability of the authorisations was allocated to the right organisational function (representatives, committees, etc).

4 Conclusion

We presented a new way for addressing the business aspects of roles and provisioning. We identified six 'root causes' for failures of large scale IAM projects: (1) language (different stakeholders speak different languages), (2) lack of distinction between accountability and responsibility, (3) mismatch between expectations of centralised top-down control models such as COSO and today's mainly distributed organisations, (4) technical incompatibilities of most of today's systems, (5) SOD is inherently hard to achieve with the current technical state-of-the-art, and (6) low visibility of access control issues makes it hard to obtain adequate funding,

During the Case Study project, we overcame these 'root causes' by introducing three layers of activities (coordination, business and technical), and by making use of various software-based techniques from such as 'Use Cases' and workflow, combined with distributed email campaigns. Furthermore the use of RACI-attributes enabled us to allocate final responsibility within the business community through the workflow.

We are now looking into ways to further formalise, automate and improve our way of working.

References

[NIST2001] ACM Transactions on Information and System Security, Vol. 4, No. 3, August 2001, pages 224-274.

A Security Architecture for Enterprise Rights Management

Ammar Alkassar[1] · Rani Husseiki[1] · Christian Stüble[1]
Michael Hartmann[2]

[1]Sirrix AG Security Technologies
{a.alkassar | r.husseiki | stueble}@sirrix.com

[2]SAP AG
michael.hartmann@sap.com

Abstract

Securing electronic business documents is an increasing necessity nowadays. Enterprise Rights Management (ERM) is a comparatively new technical approach aimed at enforcing access and usage rights policies to sensitive electronic documents throughout their lifecycles within and across organizations [YuCh05]. While ERM systems in the market are increasingly deployed in today's enterprises, they still lack fundamental security properties. One important security weakness is the ERM client software running on the end-user's machine [TuCh04]. Users can always circumvent the rights enforcement by running exploits and manipulating their operating system or particular components of the ERM client application, thereby obtaining an unprotected copy of the document's content [SeSt06, ReCa05]. In this paper, we emphasize this particular security weakness, and propose a security infrastructure based on Trusted Computing technology that can thwart most possible attacks on an ERM client, preventing therefore any circumvention of the policy enforcement over the document.

1 Introduction

As business tasks become more collaborative, requiring sensitive information exchange between organizations, partners and suppliers, securing business electronic documents become an increasing necessity [LiMi06]. A document's content is subject to leakage or unauthorized modification especially from insiders who contribute to the document's workflow [YuCh05, LiMi06]. Enterprise Rights Management (ERM) is a relatively new technical approach aiming at enforcing access and usage rights policies to sensitive electronic documents as they move between users within and across organizations. ERM systems allow a content provider to define access rights over his document and bind the policy with the document in a way to secure its content from being used in an unprivileged way.

The usage control on the e-document can be defined by rights such as read, print, copy, modify, transfer and other types of rights policies that travel with the document to ensure confidentiality and integrity of the content. Associated to those rights are attributes that specify the users or classes of users for which those rights are granted [YuCh05].

From a business perspective, ERM provides a tremendous advantage with regard to secure e-documents workflow and management, among other applications [LiMi06]. The distributed enforcement of the security policies throughout the e-document's lifecycle provides better protection against content loss,

N. Pohlmann, H. Reimer, W. Schneider (Editors): Securing Electronic Business Processes, Vieweg (2007), 166-177

theft or modification, allowing therefore a more confident exchange and management of e-documents in an enterprise's workflow. By customizing the set of usage rights corresponding to the e-document's addressee(s), ERM systems can enforce a full-scale security policy throughout the whole lifecycle of the e-document within and across the concerned organizations. Leakage, fraud or theft of corporate confidential information can therefore be strongly limited [Liqu06].

Unfortunately, ERM systems currently available in the market still suffer from serious security weaknesses. Some security experts argue that complementary technologies and techniques for ERM systems play a big role in their weakness [SeSt06]. Lack of trustworthy and scalable authentication mechanisms or difficulty in mapping organizational policies to fine-grained access rights can have serious effect on the security level of an ERM system [SeSt06]. However, for a general ERM system, the fundamental threat on the ERM client software operation seems to be more relevant [YuCh05]. In fact, the ERM client software can not be avoided to run on proprietary clients' platforms which remain hostile environments. This is a common threat to any ERM system.

In this paper, we describe ongoing work on a secure architecture for ERM systems. We address the threat on the ERM client software running on clients' open platforms. The architecture proposed in this paper is at the basis of a joint development between Sirrix AG and SAP AG in the context of a secure ERM infrastructure based on Turaya, a security platform developed within the EMSCB project.

2 ERM in enterprises

ERM systems are being integrated in enterprises and organizations document workflows. There security level of ERM systems is becoming more crucial considering the value of the information being exchanged in electronic documents. An unauthorized flaw of business information to insiders or outsiders can have a great impact on the enterprise's value assets, reputation and business competency.

As ERM systems involve many technological aspects – such as policy enforcement and management, users and roles management, policy definition, audit trails management, digital signatures – enterprises tend to acquire the solution that fits best with their goals and incentives to deploy ERM. For this reasons, many enterprises tend to acquire ERM market solutions, others design and implement in-house ERM solutions, an option considered by SAP AG.

3 Market Solutions

While many ERM solutions exist in the market [Liqu06], a short description of few of the most widely used ERM solutions is presented in this section.

3.0.1 Microsoft Windows Rights Management Service (RMS)

Microsoft Windows RMS [YuCh05, Micr03] works with RMS-enabled applications and consists of three main components: RMS server, RMS client software and RMS-enabled applications. A publishing license is created by the content provider or the RMS server and bound to the document. It contains the rights policy expressed in XrML as well as the symmetric decryption key for the content which is encrypted itself by the public key of the recipient. The recipient has to apply at the RMS server for a use license in order to access the document. For this purpose, he has to authorize himself by Windows authentication, Active Directory or a .Net Passport. The use license contains the symmetric key used to decrypt the package, and might contain expiration restrictions. The RMS-enabled application is responsible for retrieving the key from the use license, decrypting the content and rendering it to the user according to the rights defined in the publishing license.

3.0.2 EMC IRM/Authentica

In Authentica's solutions [YuCh05, Auth02] the encryption keys of the content and the rights policies are both saved on a central server. Three main components of the solution are: Authentica Policy Server, Clients authoring component and Client viewing component. Both components are based on application plugins which work with Adobe PDF or MS Office documents and support Digital Rights Management (DRM) functionalities. They have to authenticate to the Policy Server in order to authenticate and exchange keys. The authoring component encrypts the content and computes a message digest for future integrity verification, and publishes the rights policy on the server, where the encryption keys are also stored. The viewing component authenticates to the server, downloads the decryption keys, and can optionally obtain a temporary lease of the rights policy in case the policy allows an offline access to the document.

3.0.3 Adobe

The Adobe ERM solution [Adob06] is based on the Adobe LifeCycle Policy Server which handles all the documents' policies. It allows a definition and dynamic management of usage rights on Adobe PDF documents in addition to Microsoft Word and Excel documents. The author can specify the usage rights for each of the recipients through a drop-down menu in his authoring environment. The Adobe Solution integrates the LifeCycle Policy Server with Microsoft Active Directory and LDAP environments for authentication purposes. Since the policy is always stored and managed at the server, the end-user needs to have an online connection to the server at the time of accessing the document. In order for a user to have offline access to the document, he needs to be assigned an "offline lease" which typically has an expiration time. Policy enforcement in the Adobe ERM infrastructure relies also on DRM technology. Adobe has already acquired Fileline DRM division of Navisware [Gart06] to support its ERM solution.

3.1 ERM in SAP AG

SAP AG envisions a tailored ERM solution [Kuba05] to provide protection of digital content (documents, files, etc…). The envisioned solution is based on DRM mechanisms. The protection is available on a document basis, as well as the creation and preparation of the protection policy at each client's side. The ERM system targets SAP critical areas such as projects, patents, sales, consultancy, legal department, research and development. The ERM system is mainly used to protect MS Office, in addition to PDF files, text documents, HTML and XML files. The exchange of these documents takes place internally and externally the SAP network. Therefore a possibility exists to exchange these documents with external customer and partners, with the ability to protect the sensitive data they include from unauthorized persons by associating permanent digital rights over the documents.

The ERM solution provides encryption of the documents with both online and offline access capabilities. The protection is tightly connected to the document to ensure access restrictions.

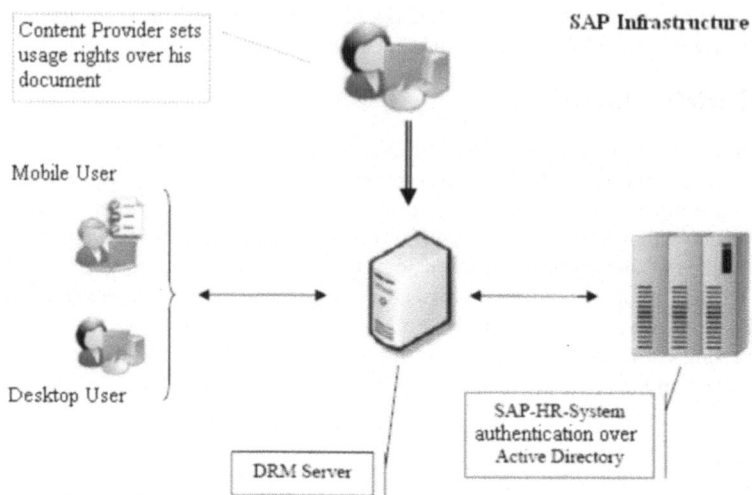

Figure 1: SAP proprietary ERM system infrastructure

The solution also supports audit trails, watermarking, and "disaster recovery" mechanisms for the cryptographic keys. Those are not cached at the client-PC but rather supplied upon authentication. As for external access to document, a conversion to PDF file is securely provided. The ERM solution also supports integration with other SAP systems especially for authentication and identity management purposes.

The access rights policy can be changed in "real-time". It can prevent forwarding of documents, copy/ paste, printing, print-screens, desktop-sharing... It also supports automatic expiration of the access rights.

The implementation supports both Microsoft and Linux platforms, for the Server and Clients. In the case of mobiles, Palm, PocketPC and Blackberry are also supported. The policy definition of the ERM solution is based on the XrML language. The solution aims at restricting installation of crypto-software.

3.2 Security Shortcomings

In addition to many other ERM solutions in the market, the solutions described above do not provide real protection of the client software – whether a separate ERM client or an integrated plug-in in native applications – which remains subject to various attacks. The client software used to access the document relies on a DRM controller which is responsible for enforcing the policy on the document. However, the self-protection of the ERM client software is still weak enough to motivate an attacker to take advantage of the architectural flaws in the underlying operating system [ReCa05] and manipulate the client software (which are both under his control). Such an attacker would be able to circumvent the policy enforcement [YuCh05] or to run processes that can access the encryption keys or plain document content saved in memory [ReCa05], or even processes that can intercept the rendered document content [Stam03].

4 Turaya Security Kernel – Concepts and Terms

Our solution is based on the Turaya security kernel that is currently developed in the context of the European Multilaterally Secure Computing Base (EMSCB) project [Emsc06]. This project which is partly funded by the German Federal Ministry of Economics and Technology aims at developing a trustworthy computing platform, based on open standards and open source that solves many security problems of conventional platforms. The EMSCB consortium includes several scientific and industrial partners. In the following, we shortly describe the basic concepts and terms in the context of the Turaya security kernel (see Figure 1).

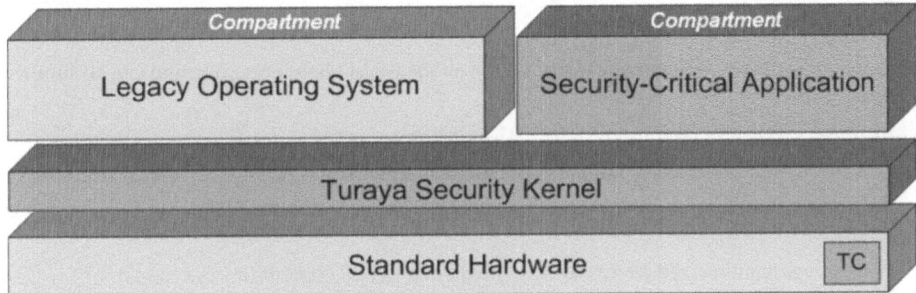

Figure 2: Turaya Architecture Overview

Virtualization: Virtualization technology allows the execution of legacy operating systems on top of a so-called hypervisor or virtual machine monitor (VMM) [Univ06]. Therefore, security kernels like Turaya that provide virtualization are also denoted as secure hypervisor or secure virtual machine monitor. Virtualization is a very efficient mechanism to build secure IT-system, since it allows the reuse of existing operating systems and applications. Finally, Turaya is prepared to take use of emerging hardware virtualization technologies [Adva06, Inte06].

Compartment: Compartments are the isolated virtual machines executed on top of the Turaya security kernel. Compartments can be virtualized operating systems, e.g., Windows or Linux, or lightweight processes directly executed on top of Turaya.

Trusted Channel: In contrast to the well-known secure channels that can be established, e.g. using SSL, a trusted channel not only authenticates the channel end-points, but also provides information about the configuration of that end-point. Configuration in this context means information about the concrete software stack running on that platform.

Domain: A domain is a group of compartments and an attached security policy defining the compartments and users that are allowed to join the domain and the security requirement to be fulfilled in the context of persistent storage (e.g., harddisks) and network connections. Examples of such security requirements are confidentiality, integrity, or freshness (prevention of replay attacks). Since security properties are realized based on trusted channels, it is ensured that security policies attached to domains cannot be bypassed by shutting down the whole system or by maliciously modifying the security kernel or the compartments. By connecting domains of different platforms, so-called Trusted Virtual Domains (TVD) [BGJ+05] can be realized that enforce a certain security policy in a distributed environment.

Turaya assumes an IT-environment that ensures that only authorized configurations can access kernel data. This assumption can either be realized by a secure IT-environment, or by using Turaya's optional feature to support Trusted Computing (TC) technology, e.g., a TPM.

The security kernel provides a management interface to hardware resources and compartments. Moreover, it guarantees strong isolation of compartments. When focussing encryption systems, the isolation feature of the security kernel can be used to prevent potentially malicious software from accessing cryptographic keys and operations. Additionally, the security kernel integrates security-critical services such as a secure user interface, network access, and persistent storage.

5 Solution

5.1 Security Goals

The security goals of the system address the threats on the ERM client operation and can be summarized as follows:

1. Ensuring consistent operation of the ERM client as to enforce the document's policy
2. Preventing unauthorized modification of the document's policy
3. Preventing interception or faking of output data between the rendering application and user's screen
4. Preventing unauthorized access to decrypted document's content or keys in memory

The proposed security architecture, components and protocols to achieve those goals are presented in the following sections.

5.2 ERM policy enforcement problem

We address the security problems emphasized in [ReCa05] with regard to enforcing information rights policy on clients' open platforms. In [ReCa05] the authors argue that *"the protection architecture and access control model of mainstream operating systems makes them inappropriate as a platform for a DRM content rendering client because decrypted content cannot be protected against a privileged process"*. They explain that enforcing Digital Rights Management policy on platforms supporting only Discretionary Access Control features is subject to circumvention, even if tamper resistant hardware like a TPM is integrated in the system. They also argue that Trusted Computing based functionalities such as *Remote Attestation* and *Sealed Storage* are inefficient when employed for policy enforcement on client platforms with mainstream operating systems, first since they can not avoid malicious modifications of the computing platform at run-time, and second because the execution order of code after the operating system loader is not deterministic which would make it impossible to pre-define a set of PCR values reflecting the integrity of all software on the platform. A considerably more secure approach, according to [ReCa05], requires a client platform that combines Mandatory Access Control policies and Trusted Computing functionalities.

5.3 ERM Security Architecture

Based on the conclusions drawn in [ReCa05], and on the advantages of TVDs [BGJ+05], we propose an ERM security architecture that can enforce a security policy on two levels:

1. A mandatory security policy that applies to all platforms on which protected documents and corresponding licenses or keys are going to be accessed.
2. A discretionary security policy that refines the mandatory security policy and applies to a specific document or document class.

While the mandatory security policy is defined based on hardware and software configuration requirements for a secure ERM system operation, the discretionary security policy is defined based on the
document provider's requirements for protecting the document information.

The security architecture makes use of our Turaya Security Kernel and is enhanced by Trusted Computing technology, namely a TPM. In the following, we describe the architecture and how it can enforce
both policy levels.

5.3.1 Mandatory security policy enforcement

The architecture we propose is based on Turaya security kernel for achieving virtualization. It aims at
isolating the ERM client software, the protected document, the usage rights and encryption keys in a
local Domain (cf. 3.1) connected with other ERM-related domains of other hosts to create a distributed
Virtual Domain, e.g., "patent filing". Attached to this virtual ERM Domain is a mandatory security policy that defines some properties of that Domain that are security critical and necessary for a guaranteed
enforcement of the mandatory security policy. Such properties include – but are not limited to – special
hardware configuration such as Trusted Computing support by means of a TPM with proper PCR configuration, secure persistent storage, secure VPN connections between the local Domains creating the
Virtual Domain, special compartments' configuration, and user authentication requirements.

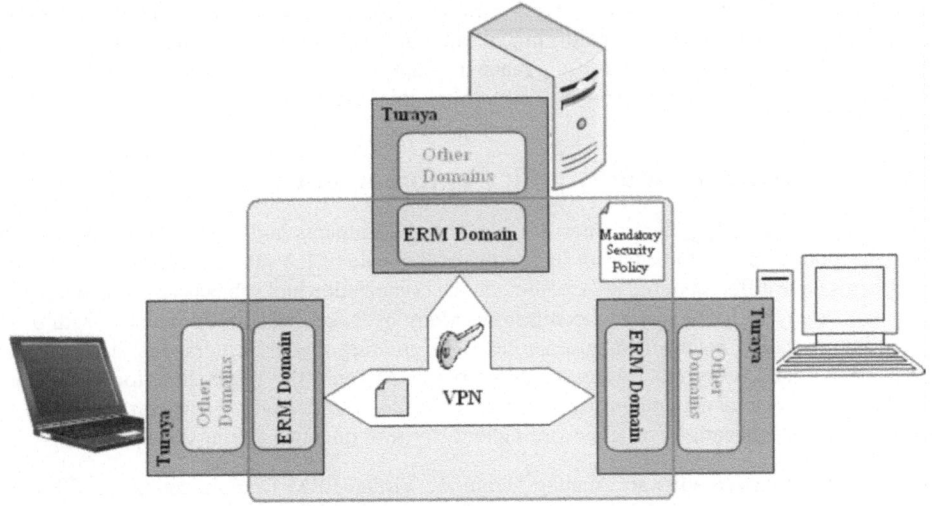

Figure 3: Local ERM Domains inter-connected

The term "mandatory" given to such a security policy stems from the fact that the only deployment of
Turaya security kernel on the client's platform, enhanced by a TPM, provides the elementary security
properties of the policy. Thanks to the efficiency of isolation provided by the Turaya security kernel,
the compartments belonging to such a local Domain are strictly isolated from compartments of other
Domains even if they are running on the same machine. This prevents other processes running on the
client's platform from interfering with the ERM client software operations or accessing the decrypted
document content or keys in the ERM Domain. Moreover, the other Turaya services such as the secure
user interface, network access restrictions, and persistent storage are inherent in the architecture. Only
some configurations of the architecture, components and services are flexible.

This is where Trusted Computing functionalities can be used to enforce a generic security policy that the document provider defines in order to ensure a suitable configuration of the ERM Domain on the client's platform. As explained in Section 3, Turaya inherently provides an interface to Trusted Computing hardware (TPM), with the capability to perform *Sealed Binding*, which is more efficient in the case of the ERM Domain. Sealed Binding is used by the document provider to bind the keys used for encrypting the document package (content, license, usage rights, metadata…) with the suitable configuration of core components of the ERM domain. This means that, while the mandatory security policy of the ERM domain is enforced by the security kernel, the TPM integrated in the client's platform can only unbind those keys if core components of the platform within the ERM Domain can prove their suitable configuration defined by the document provider. Since the ERM Domain is by default isolated from other Domains, the suitable configuration does not need to reflect the nature of all executable (run-time) code on the platform, but only that of the ERM client software and the mechanisms and services provided by Turaya. This avoids the drawback explained in [ReCa05].

Now taking into consideration the need for transferring the document package to more than one client platform, we can identify a Virtual ERM Domain that includes more than one compartment on more than one platform. In other words, we can imagine the Virtual ERM Domain as a virtual trusted realm encompassing all compartments running on different clients' platforms and enforcing the mandatory security policy (i.e. deploying Turaya with isolated compartments with suitable configuration). The protected document, its usage policy and encryption keys can only travel between compartments belonging to this specific Virtual Domain. Any platform that can join the Virtual ERM Domain is therefore trusted to handle the document package in a secure manner. What is left is to ensure enforcement of the usage rights defined over the document. This is done through the Discretionary Security Policy explained in the next section.

5.3.2 Discretionary security policy enforcement

The discretionary security policy relates directly to the documents and the way their corresponding usage rights policies are enforced according to the user or role of the subject accessing the document. ERM systems have different purposes according to the organization and subjects needs, and this reflects itself in the variety of ERM systems architecture. Many of those exists in the market, with different types of authentication mechanisms, users/roles right granting models, centralized/distributed usage policy [Avoc07], and many other aspects. Hence, the ERM controller responsible for decryption and rendering of the document's content can have different tasks to perform. Moreover, the ERM client software (or ERM application) varies according to the type of document being accessed.

Although only authorized software running within the Virtual ERM Domain can access ERM documents, our architecture allows that an ERM controller enforcing a specific policy runs apart from the ERM application in an isolated compartment with specific configuration. This requirement is usually included in the mandatory security policy; however, its details depend on the ERM system specifications and document provider's decision. In order to enforce the discretionary security policy, the content provider profits from the advantages of the mandatory security policy to verify this requirement by including it in the binding of the document package keys. The discretionary security policy will hence be securely enforced by the ERM controller, and the document content rendered according to the usage rights in the policy and the authenticated user or role accessing the document. The ERM controller compartment and the ERM application compartment communicate by means of a Trusted Channel.

5.4 ERM security architecture realization

Our architecture concepts are realized based on the following components:

Turaya security kernel: The high-level concepts of the security kernel have already been discussed in Section 3. The realization is a small security software layer which can be logically divided into a hypervisor layer and a trusted software layer (Figure 2). It is able to achieve isolated compartments based on virtualization technique.

The main task of the hypervisor layer is to provide an abstract interface of the underlying hardware resources like interrupts, memory and hardware devices[1]. Moreover, this layer allows sharing these resources and realizes access control enforcement on the object types known to this layer. Currently we are supporting a microkernel[2] and the Xen hypervisor as the foundation of the hypervisor layer.

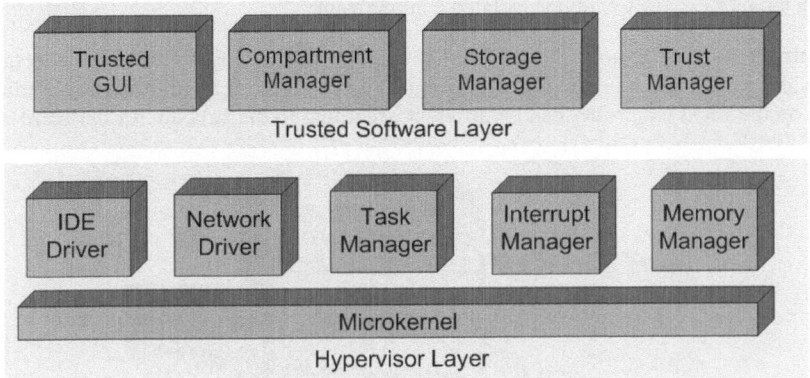

Figure 4: Turaya Security Kernel

The trusted software layer builds on the hypervisor layer and includes security components (particularly the Trusted Manager, Storage Manager and Compartment Manager) which operation is hence considered trustworthy. They communicate over *Trusted Channels* between each other. The components are:

1. ***Trusted GUI:*** controls the graphic adapter and the input devices, i.e., mouse and keyboard, to establish a trusted path between the user and an application. The Trusted GUI labels application windows with unique application names. Moreover, the Trusted GUI enforces a strong isolation between applications on the GUI level. Unauthorized applications cannot, for instance, access the graphical output of other applications or fake their interface to look like the usual password dialog.

2. ***Compartment Manager:*** loads compartments and measures their integrity. These integrity measurements can then be reported to local applications as well as to remote applications. In cooperation with Trusted Computing hardware this functionality constitutes the basis for elaborate Digital Rights Management applications. The advantage of this approach in contrast to other integrity measurement architectures (e.g., [SZJv04]) lies in enhanced end-user privacy protection and improved manageability, e.g., of software updates.

3. ***Storage Manager:*** enables applications to persistently store their local states (user data). It preserves the integrity, confidentiality, and freshness of the managed data and enforces isolation such that only the application or the user having produced the data may later re-access it. The

---

1 Device drivers that are able to directly access the main memory (DMA-enabled drivers) must be outsourced from the legacy operating system for security reasons.

2 A microkernel is a minimized operating system kernel that provides only essential services such as logical address spaces and inter-process communication (IPC). Processes on top of the microkernel run in their own address space and are therefore strongly isolated from each other.

SM ensures isolation of memory storage corresponding to the ERM compartments, and binds the data (content, keys, states…) to the specific ERM compartment's configuration.

4. **Trust Manager:** for interfacing Trusted Computing hardware [ScSW06]. The TM is responsible for handling the necessary protocols for creation of attestation certificates reporting the configuration of the PE compartment, or invoking other compartments or hardware to communicate bound/unbound symmetric keys with which the document/license is encrypted.

ERM Client: an application invoked by the user to access the documents. A Policy Manager application can be either a part or the ERM client, or a separate application. The ERM client and Policy Manager both run on top of a Legacy OS in one isolated compartment.

ERM Controller: running in another isolated compartment. The ERM Controller is responsible of encryption, decryption and rendering of the document content according to the policy. Particular tasks performed by the ERM Controller can be different according to the structure of the ERM system (cf. 5.2.2).

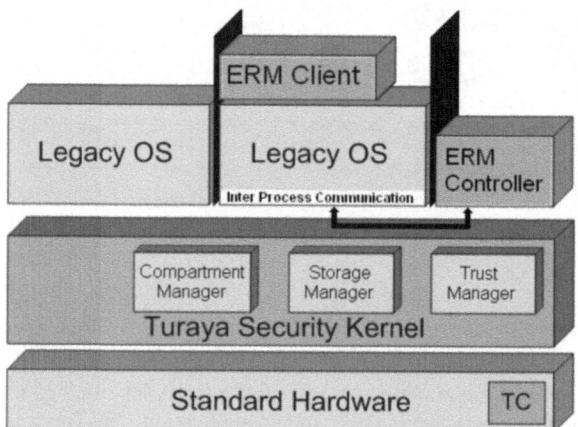

Figure 5: ERM security architecture of client's platform

6 Proof of concept

In this section, we explain how the security architecture and protocols proposed in Section 6.2 and Section 6.3 can achieve the security goals mentioned in Section 6.1.

6.1 Rights Policy Enforcement

The enforcement of the policy that the content provider has already defined and associated to his document is achieved by means of:

Confidentiality of the document content until it reaches the ERM Controller on the user's platform, and this is achieved by symmetric encryption of the license/document. The symmetric key is itself encrypted by a *Sealed Binding Key*, which means that it can only be unbound by the TPM if the configuration of critical components of the user's platform is conformant with "know-good" values defined by the content provider in the mandatory security policy. The unbinding procedure is handled by the Trust

Manager which is part of the Trusted Software layer (cf. Turaya). Hence, both the document policy and its encryption key are delivered securely to the Policy Enforcer.

The Compartment Manager, which is responsible for loading and measuring the configuration of the corresponding compartment, is also a part of the Trusted Software Layer (cf. Turaya). This protects the ERM Controller from manipulation, in particular the correct configuration and integrity measurement of the compartment in which the ERM Controller protects the latter from any attacks on its operation. Therefore, the ERM Controller can securely enforce the policy on the document.

6.2 Secure Document Rendering

Preventing interception or faking of the decrypted data that is rendered to the ERM client application is ensured since the two compartments can only communicate through trusted channels. Therefore, the ERM Controller can also verify some properties of the ERM client compartment proving its trustworthiness. The Trusted GUI, which is also a trusted component within the Trusted Software Layer, can isolate the graphical output of the ERM client from other applications and guaranteeing therefore its authenticity.

6.3 Secure Content and Keys Storage

The Storage Manager ensures secure storage of the data corresponding to any of the compartments, particularly the e-document and the ERM Controller compartment. This means that the decrypted document content, rights policy and keys are stored at run-time in an isolated memory space corresponding to the specific Domain. When the decrypted data has to be persistently stored in memory, the Storage Manager is able to bind the data to specific compartment configuration, which would preserve its confidentiality and integrity. Therefore, no compartment of another Domain can have access to the plain data, neither at run-time nor during persistent storage. The plain data is hence protected from leakage and modification in memory.

7 Conclusion

In this paper, we proposed a security architecture that is able to significantly improve the security of ERM systems by protecting the ERM client running on end-user's proprietary platforms. The architecture makes use of our Turaya security platform, which is based on Virtualization techniques, an open source security kernel, and Trusted Computing technology. It achieves isolation of the ERM software, protected document and keys in a Virtual ERM Domain, ensuring correct operation of the ERM Controller in order to avoid circumvention of the usage rights enforcement over the document. It also protects the plain document content and decrypted keys from leakage or modification both on the GUI and memory levels. Furthermore, the proposed solution suits both centralized and distributed ERM systems architectures.

References

[Avoc07]   Avoco Secure: Choosing an Enterprise Rights Management System: Architectural Approaches. http://www.windowsecurity.com/uplarticle/Authentication_and_Access_Control/ERM-architectural-approaches.pdf, 2007

[SeSt06]   Sebes, J., Stamp, M.: Solvable Problems in Enterprise Digital Rights Management. http://www.cs.sjsu.edu/faculty/stamp/papers/DRM_IMCS2.doc, 2006

[YuCh05]   Yu, Y., Chiueh, T.: Enterprise Digital Rights Management: Solutions against Information Theft by Insiders. http://www.ecsl.cs.sunysb.edu/tr/TR169.pdf, 2005

[Stam03]   Stamp, M.: Digital Rights Management: The Technology Behind the Hype. http://www.csulb.edu/web/journals/jecr/issues/20033/paper3.pdf, 2003

[Kuba05]   Kubasch, B-O.: Informations und Documentschutz im Unternehmen, SAP AG – Corporate Security, 2005, p. 45-47.

[ScSW06]   Scheibel, M., Stueble, C., Wolf, M.: Design and Implementation of an Architecture for Vehicular Software Protection. Embedded Security in Cars Workshop (escar ,06), 2006

[ReCa05]   Reid, J. Caelli, W.: DRM, Trusted Computing and Operating System Architecture. http://crpit.com/confpapers/CRPITV44Reid.pdf, 2005

[TuCh04]   Yu, Y., Chiueh, T.: Display-Only File Server: A Solution against Information Theft Due to Insider Attack. http://www.ecsl.cs.sunysb.edu/tr/TR170.pdf, 2004

[LiMi06]   Liquid Machines, Inc. Microsoft Windows Rights Management Services: Liquid Machines and Microsoft RMS: End-to-end Rights Management for the Enterprise, 2006.

[Liqu06]   Liquid Machines: Enterprise Rights Management: A Superior Approach to Confidential Data Security. Enterprise Strategy Group, 2006.

[Micr03]   Microsoft Corporation: Microsoft Windows Rights Management Services for Windows Server 2003 – Helping Organizations Safeguard Digital Information from Unauthorized Use. Whitepaper, 2003.

[Auth02]   Authentica Inc.: Page Recall: The Key to Document Protection, 2002

[Adob06]   Adobe Systems Inc.: Adobe LiveCycle Policy Server: Document-level persistent protection and dynamic control for multiformat enterprise rights management. http://www.adobe.com/de/products/server/policy/pdfs/ps_datasheet.pdf, 2006

[Gart06]   Gartner, Inc.: Navisware E-DRM Buy Could Give Adobe a One-Stop-Shopping Solution. http://www.adobe.com/manufacturing/pdfs/gartner_1691.pdf, 2006

[Emsc06]   EMSCB Project Consortium: The EMSCB project. http://www.emscb.org, 2006.

[Univ06]   University of Cambridge Computer Laboratory: Xen virtual machine monitor. http://www.cl.cam.ac.uk/Research/SRG/netos/xen, 2006.

[Adva06]   Advanced Micro Devices, Inc.: AMD virtualization solutions. http://enterprise.amd.com/us-en/Solutions/Consolidation/virtualization.aspx, 2006.

[Inte06]   Intel Corporation: Intel virtualization technology. http://www.intel.com/technology/computing/vptech/, 2006.

[SZJv04]   Sailer, R., Zhang, X., Jaeger, T., and van Doorn, L.: Design and implementation of a tcg-based integrity measurement architecture. 13th Usenix Security Symposium, San Diego, California, August 2004.

[BGJ+05]   Bussani, A., Griffin, J.L., Jansen, B., Julisch, K., Karjoth, G., Maruyama, H., Nakamura, M., Perez, R., Schunter, M., Tanner, A., Van Doorn, L., Van Herreweghen, E.A., Waidner, M., Yoshihama, S., Trusted Virtual Domains: Secure Foundations for Business and IT Services (Whitepaper, RC23792), 2005.

Rights Management Technologies: A Good Choice for Securing Electronic Health Records?

Milan Petković · Stefan Katzenbeisser · Klaus Kursawe

Information and System Security Department
Philips Research
{milan.petkovic | stefan.katzenbeisser | klaus.kursawe}@philips.com

Abstract

Advances in healthcare IT bring new concerns with respect to privacy and security. Security critical patient data no longer resides on mainframes physically isolated within an organization, where physical security measures can be taken to defend the data and the system. Modern solutions are heading towards open, interconnected environments where storage outsourcing and operations on untrusted servers happen frequently. In order to allow secure sharing of health records between different healthcare providers, Rights Management Techniques facilitating a data-centric protection model can be employed: data is cryptographically protected and allowed to be outsourced or even freely float on the network. Rather than relying on different networks to provide confidentiality, integrity and authenticity, data is protected at the end points of the communication. In this paper we compare Enterprise/Digital Rights Management with traditional security techniques and discuss how Rights Management can be applied to secure Electronic Health Records.

1 Introduction

Advances in information and communication technologies are expected to bring large benefits in the healthcare domain: the introduction of interoperable Electronic Health Record (EHR) systems can reduce the cost of the healthcare system and enhance the overall quality of treatments, whereas Remote Patient Management (RPM) services will limit the time a patient stays in hospital. Nevertheless, to date EHRs and RPMs are being used on a rather small scale. Besides problems with regard to the integration of different systems and logistic issues, concerns about information security and privacy are primary reasons for the lack of deployed systems. For example, EHR systems are facing strict security and privacy regulations (such as EU Directive 95/46 or HIPAA in the US) to which they have to comply.

Modern healthcare communication architectures tend to be open, interconnected environments: sensitive patient records no longer reside on mainframes physically isolated within a healthcare provider, where physical security measures can be taken to defend the data and the system. Patient files are rather kept in an environment where data is outsourced to or processed on partially untrusted servers in order to allow de-centralized access for family doctors, medical specialists and even non-medical care providers. The currently employed server-centric protection model, which locks the data in a database server and uses a traditional access control model to permit access to data, cannot efficiently deal with the requirements of the new healthcare infrastructures.

N. Pohlmann, H. Reimer, W. Schneider (Editors): Securing Electronic Business Processes, Vieweg (2007), 178-187

In order to allow sharing of records among different healthcare providers or with external parties, end-to-end security techniques facilitating data-centric protection can be employed: data is cryptographically protected and allowed to be outsourced or even freely float on the network. Rather than relying on different networks to provide confidentiality, integrity and authenticity, data is protected at the end points of the communication. However, this is not straightforward to achieve. A system may consist of a number of devices with different constrains and limitations which require specific lightweight cryptographic techniques that have to be interoperable. Furthermore, it may be necessary to perform operations while data is on transit at a specific node of the network. Finally, in emergency cases, access to electronic patient records must be instantaneously available, irrespective of the employed protection model. This opens a number of questions including key management, trust management and secure auditing.

In this work, we compare Enterprise/Digital Rights Management with traditional security techniques and discuss how Rights Management can be applied to secure Electronic Health Records. Instead of securing the flow of information by imposing security requirements at each link/component of the system, Rights Management technologies provide protection by enforcing the use of data according to granted rights or licenses. Using a set of additional technologies, such as encryption, user authentication, logging, and decentralized trust management, it enables protecting critical information and maintains control over its distribution and access. Furthermore, those techniques allow addressing conflicting privacy requirements: e.g., making data available in life-threatening emergency situations, while keeping it confidential to unauthorized people.

2 EHR Security and Privacy Requirements

The Healthcare Information and Management Systems Society[1] [HIMSS03] defines EHRs as follows:

"The Electronic Health Record (EHR) is a secure, real-time, point-of-care, patient centric information resource *for clinicians*.

- The EHR aids clinicians decision making by providing access to patient health record information *where and when they need* it and by incorporating evidence-based decision support.
- The EHR *automates and streamlines the clinician's workflow*, closing loops in communication and response that result in delays or gaps in care.
- The EHR also *supports the collection of data for uses other than direct clinical care*, such as billing, quality management, outcomes reporting, resource planning, and public health disease surveillance and reporting."

Digital health records are used at different levels in healthcare. First, they are used in hospitals at the departmental level (e.g., at a radiology department) where medical data on examinations or treatments are stored in Electronic Medical Records (EMR). To improve sharing of information within institutions, different departmental systems are increasingly integrated into Hospital Information Systems (HIS) such that digital patient records can span over different departments. Such records, which also include administrative data, are called Electronic Health Records (EHR).

The next step after implementation of EMR and HIS systems is the integration of information systems of larger institutions that have multiple sites, or systems of co-operating care-providers in a region. This is an important first step towards the creation of a real EHR, as it increases the availability of patient

---

1 HIMSS is the "healthcare industry's membership organization exclusively focused on providing global leadership for the optimal use of healthcare information technology (IT) and management systems for the betterment of healthcare".

records and allows sharing data among different healthcare providers and organizations. Sometimes this intermediate step is referred to as Continuity of Care Records (CCR), because it support care chains (also known as care pathways) within a region.

Finally, the term EHR is often used in relation with national Electronic Health Record infrastructures. These systems are currently under development in several countries of the European Union and the US [Char06]. A national EHR infrastructure connects all health records of a patient stored in various hospital EHR and/or departmental EMR systems deployed by different healthcare providers. The EHR is meant to provide an integrated, holistic, patient-centric and life-long view on the contents of all these systems[2].

The growth of EHRs from EMRs over HIS and CCRs requires the use of technologies that allow the integration of a plethora of systems into a coherent framework. For this reason, most EHR systems use web service standards like SOAP, ebXML or WSDL. In the context of health records, HL7 provides additional technology that builds on the strengths of the web-service suite of standards [HL7].

From the security point of view, the earliest departmental and hospital centric solutions were based on the "walled fortress" paradigm (firewalls, physical isolation, etc.). As these systems are opening to regional or national EHR systems, this paradigm no longer suffices. Therefore, early versions of EHR systems (that do not yet offer full functionality) utilized a selection of security mechanisms designed to complement web services, such as Transport Level Security, Security Assertion Markup Language, intra-enterprise Role-Based-Access Control, cross-enterprise user authentication, and XML digital signatures.

Around 2010-2015, many countries expect their national EHR infrastructure to be fully functional, connecting all healthcare providers in one distributed system. According to their plans, the national systems will at that time provide functionality for patient-controlled access to EHR systems, where patient policies (such as exceptions or sealed envelopes that hide certain critical information), as well as care provider policies may be integrated with default policies in order to govern access to electronic patient records.

In general, we can state the following central requirements for the security and privacy of EHRs, stemming from legal requirements:

- **Data Integrity**
  The general requirement of the HIPAA Security Rule can be stated as "Covered entities must ensure the confidentiality, integrity, and availability of all protected health information (PHI) the covered entity creates, receives, maintains, or transmits." HIPAA refers to data integrity as to the condition that PHI has not been altered or destroyed in an unauthorized manner. This includes prevention of authorized individuals making unauthorized changes to PHI as well as unauthorized people altering PHI.

- **Data Confidentiality**
  A further crucial aspect is data confidentiality: healthcare data should be effectively protected against improper disclosure when it is stored, transmitted and processed. Moreover, the data should be available only to authorized parties. As with data integrity, data confidentiality is also a HIPAA requirement as part of the HIPAA *Security* Rule. Since confidentiality is closely related to privacy, it is also the focus of the HIPAA *Privacy* Rule. This rule sets standards for how PHI should be controlled. Covered entities are required to describe in general terms how health data

---

2 Sometimes a national EHR infrastructure is also called a "virtual HER". In this highly distributed system different pieces of health records are maintained by a community of different healthcare providers (such as hospitals, pharmacies, general practices, and laboratories).

will be protected; in addition, they have to specify the patients' rights to obtain information on and enforce control over the confidentiality of their data. This includes receiving an account of how information has been used, requesting limits on access to and additional protections for particularly sensitive information, and requesting confidential communications relating to that information. HIPAA does not require consent from patients to use or disclose health data for routine healthcare operations (such as treatment and payment) or to fulfil legal requirements (such as protection of public health). However, a patient's consent is needed for the use of the data for other purposes such as research, marketing and fundraising.

- **Data Availability**
  The availability of information resources in the healthcare environment is another aspect of security which is of utmost importance. It refers to the assurance that up-to-date information is available when needed at a required level of performance and at the appropriate place. Data confidentiality, while being an essential requirement of any healthcare system, is contradictory to data availability. A clear example of this conflict is a medical emergency situation, where data confidentiality is much less important than data availability.

- **User Awareness and Control**
  Recent trends in the healthcare sector towards personal, user-focused healthcare also demand more patient involvement. Patients are taking a more active role, obtaining disease information, discussing diagnoses with doctors, tracking symptoms and managing their illnesses. This also has some backing in the legislation such as HIPAA, according to which patients have, among others, the rights to request additional restrictions on the PHI, or the right to amend and inspect the stored data.

3 Traditional Solutions

Currently, most healthcare related IT-systems are "islands", i.e., all data resides within one administrative domain. This domain is not or hardly accessible from the outside, and the set of users operating on the data is reasonably small and static. In those settings, data is usually protected by a combination of access control and system security.

3.1 Access Control

An access control system matches the data, the accessing party, and the data policy to determine whether or not access to the data should be granted. To this end, the user first needs to be *authenticated*, i.e., the users' identity (or alternatively a special property such as membership in a special group or the role of the party) is established. Secondly, the system evaluates the data policy to determine if access should be granted; this can be by means of a simple table, or by a complex access control language like EPAL or XACML.

Special challenges in a medical environment are that access to the data is very context dependent, and roles of medical personnel may change quickly – an expert on a certain disease can rapidly turn from visitor to acting doctor. While under normal circumstances medical personnel not involved in the treatment of a patient should not be able to access arbitrary data (as sadly demonstrated recently, this may be a substantial security factor), a doctor also should never be blocked from data access in an emergency. Other context information that applies in a highly dynamic and heterogeneous environment such as in healthcare are the security settings and the location of the user (e.g., a doctor may not see certain information if working from home).

3.2 System Security

To provide meaningful protection, access control mechanisms need to be flanked with a number of security measures. Data needs to be protected both during transport and storage; the operating system needs to ensure that access control cannot easily be circumvented; users must be reliably authenticated; and finally, communicating devices must be able to assess the trustworthiness of platforms they communicate with.

While solutions to all those issues exist, it is hard to create a secure system in a practical environment, and many subtle problems remain. While encryption and authentication methods can be considered reasonably safe (assuming the devices get access to cryptographic keys), platform security is still a hard to solve problem.

User authentication – especially in a hospital environment – must be efficient and secure; in practice, it has often turned out that inefficient solutions are circumvented altogether, for example by the party with the highest authority logging in the morning and everybody using that account.

Platform security is an inherently hard problem as long as standard operating systems are used; given the number of known attacks on such operating systems, maintaining a secure configuration requires substantial expertise. As long as the system is not connected to the outside world and centrally managed, a reasonable secure configuration can be maintained. If, however, the system is opened up to allow communication with remote systems, new approaches such as Trusted Computing are needed to solve some of the issues. Security mechanisms like remote attestation of software allow detection of remote security properties, and also allow to give some evidence that a remote platform will enforce agreeable policies.

3.3 Web Service Security Technologies

Once large heterogeneous systems are interconnected, the interoperability between the systems starts playing a major role. One option for an interoperable communication standard is the use of emerging web service technologies. They bring together several standards to cover security aspects. Here, we briefly survey the most important standards, mainly meant to improve XML security. This is because XML is considered the universal format for structured documents on the Internet and is playing an increasingly important role in the exchange of data.

Several tools have been developed to improve the security of XML files, which basically fall into two groups. The first improves XML document security itself by using encryption and digital signatures within a document. The second provides this functionality outside the XML document.

In the first category we find standards such as XML Signatures and XML Encryption; in the second category we find, among others, XKMS and SAML. These standards are briefly described in this section.

XML Signatures
The XML Signature [XMLSi] specification provides a very flexible digital signature mechanism. A requirement of this specification is that signatures should apply either to a part or to a complete XML document. This is very relevant in the healthcare domain when a single XML document may have a long history, in which the different components are authored at different times by different parties.

XML Encryption
XML Encryption is generally performed using a combination of public key cryptography and symmetric key cryptography. Typically, a symmetric key is used to encrypt the content, and is then encrypted

using public key cryptography. Both the encrypted content and encrypted symmetric key are then sent to the recipient. The recipient may obtain the original content by first decrypting the symmetric key with his private key and then the content with the obtained symmetric key. In this way, end-to-end security for applications that require secure exchange of structured data is provided [XMLEn].

XKMS
XML Key Management Specification (XKMS) [Ford01] is a standard that provides an interface between an XML application and a Public Key Infrastructure. XKMS greatly simplifies the deployment of Public Key Infrastructures by transferring complex processing tasks from the client application to a Trust Service. It is designed to help the distribution of public keys to enable signature verification and encryption for recipients. It makes it possible to revoke or update information associated with the key pair if the circumstances change.

SAML
The Security Assertion Markup Language (SAML) standard [SAML] defines a framework for exchanging security information between online business partners. More precisely, SAML defines a common XML framework for exchanging security assertions between entities. An assertion is a package of verified security information concerning subject's (entity or human) authentication status, or access rights.

4 Rights Management Technologies

Digital Rights Management (DRM) is mainly visible in the domain of entertainment and copyright enforcement. To fulfil the needs of content providers, a number of DRM systems have been developed, such as Microsoft Windows Media DRM, IBM's Electronic Music Management System (EMMS), Sony's Open MagicGate or Thomson's SmartRight. Early DRM systems have been device-based, binding obtained content to one device on which it could be consumed. Current research is focussed on overcoming usage barriers as well as making DRM personalized and interoperable. Thanks to the pervasiveness of DRM clients (auch as Microsoft Windows DRM or the Apple iPod) as well as ongoing standardization efforts, Rights Management Technologies are becoming commodity, present in many professional and consumer devices. Consequently, this opens a door for applications of DRM in other domains such as e-Business, e-Government, and in healthcare.

Rights Management Technologies or Enterprise Rights Management (ERM) are increasingly used to protect business documents in order to counter the threat of unauthorized access and distribution of corporate data. ERM has a long-term potential for automating compliance with new regulations, rules and policies, applying among others to the financial and healthcare domain (e.g. HIPAA, the Graham-Leach-Bliley Act for preserving confidentiality of consumer financial information, and the Sarbanes-Oxley Act for integrity of accounting information). Examples of ERM systems are Microsoft's Rights Management Services (RMS) platform, Authentica and SealedMedia.

In contrast to DRM, ERM applications encapsulate sensitive data objects (rather than entertainment content) and protect, control, and monitor their use and dissemination. Data confidentiality and integrity are fundamental requirements inherently supported by ERM systems. Furthermore, ERM provides means for tracing use of the data (e.g. who, when and where was the data accessed, how the data was used, etc.)[3]. Finally, by putting the user of the ERM system into the role of the data owner, ERM gives the data owner control of data dissemination paths.

---

3 Note that a DRM system is a distributed system which involves, in addition to servers at the site of the data owner, also clients deployed at the user. Therefore, it can provide a complete log on the data use.

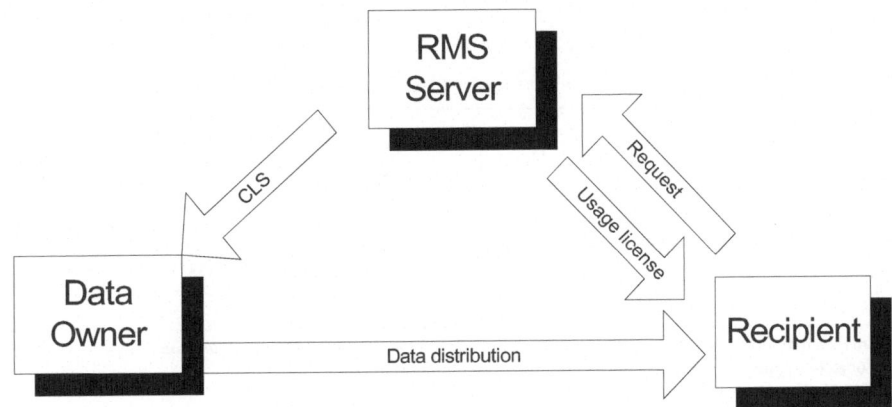

Figure 1. Creating and viewing protected information.

Microsoft Rights Management Service is an example of an Enterprise Rights Management system. Its architecture is briefly sketched in Figure 1. The system enables protection of sensitive information from unauthorized use by allowing the data owner to define usage rights and conditions. In particular, the data owner, who has a client licensor certificate (CLS), protects the data by encrypting it within a protected data container. He also defines a publishing license containing a set of usage rights and conditions for that data container. Technically, a RMS-enabled application encrypts a data file with a symmetric key; the symmetric key is then in turn encrypted with the public key of the author's Windows RMS server and inserted into the publishing license which is bound to the data container. Once this process is finished, the author can start distributing the protected data. When a recipient receives protected data, he needs an RMS-enabled application or browser to access it. This application sends a request for a usage license to the author's RMS server. Next, the Windows RMS licensing server authenticates the recipient and checks if the recipient is authorized (RMS checks the publishing license to see if the recipient requesting a usage license has been granted rights). If the recipient is authorized, the RMS server creates a usage license (including the required decryption key) for the recipient and sends it to the recipient's RMS-enabled application. The application checks the validity of required chains of certificates and revocation lists, decrypts the content and enforces the rights that have been granted.

In the domain of healthcare, some pilots have already been set up to control distribution and usage of Electronic Health Records with existing ERM architectures. The aim is that healthcare providers can securely share confidential patient files with business associates and patients in accordance with HIPAA using the protection of the underlying ERM technology. The ERM framework enforces policies governing access to sensitive information, but also ensures protection if information is distributed beyond organizational boundaries.

5 Rights Management Technologies in the Healthcare Domain

With the increasing role of IT in the healthcare industry as well as more networked applications, medical IT systems can less and less be considered as "islands"; rather, they become a large, heterogeneous network of systems with different security requirements, guarantees, and access policies. Thus, the classical "walled fortress" approach is no longer applicable; data management solutions must take into account that data moves between different domains. This naturally leads to a data-centric protection model as already deployed in DRM and ERM systems.

Table 1: Comparison of classical security technologies and ERM technology.

Enterprise Rights Management Systems	Classic protection technologies
Usage control: Data access/usage is controlled by the object owner wherever the data is physically located.	*Access Control:* Data access is controlled by the owner of the system where the data resides. If data is disseminated, the object owner loses control.
Homogenous end-to-end protection due to a single licensing authority.	*Heterogeneous end-to-end protection* due to a plethora of methods, such as link protection (TLS, IPSec), database security (DAC, RBAC), authentication (PKI) and storage protection.
Inherently distributed architecture. Distributed security architecture (object-centric protection), supporting offline operations with the same security levels.	*Predominantly centralized architecture.*
Requires trusted ERM clients, lower dependence on overall system integrity.	Security heavily depends on operating system security.

Table 1 compares ERM technology to data protection technologies as currently employed in small-scale EHR systems. The main advantage of ERM lies in its implicit access and usage control. In traditional access control approaches, the system owner controls access to data. When information leaves the system, it is up to the receiving party to set up new access control policies. On the other hand, ERM technologies make sure that data is accompanied with a license that defines who can access it, wherever the data is physically located. Therefore, the data owner always controls the data access, even on remote systems. In addition to access control, ERM provides means for usage control, i.e., the data can be used only as specified by the data owner (for example printing a document could be forbidden). Consequently, ERM provides homogenous end-to-end protection that is data-centric, while classical technologies need different security techniques and complex security architectures to reach the same goal. Furthermore, the data-centric protection approach increases data availability and allows off-line access and use of data which are important functional requirements in the healthcare domain: the proper elements of a patient data could be accessible anywhere and anytime only by entitled (authorized) persons, as well as the patient himself. Moreover, ERM enforces that access to off-line data is also granted based on predefined rights. With respect to audit control, their homogeneous security architecture allows for an easy supplement that can support auditing in the full system of distributed devices.

However, deployment of ERM/DRM technology in the healthcare domain is not straightforward. We can identify, among others, the following special requirements for healthcare ERM systems:

- Many parties from different domains and with different rights may be involved in accessing and modifying the documents. It is thus implausible to implement central management. Furthermore, there is a large uncertainty in who will eventually need to access a data object. While normal ERM protected documents are usually meant to be read by a mostly fixed set of parties in the first place, almost every employee in the healthcare system may potentially need to see every piece of data; nevertheless, most of those employees never need – or should get – access to the data.

- There is no clearly defined data ownership; for example, the patient must not be able to self-prescribe drugs, while the doctor in charge has no right to change the patients' home address. Consequently, even the definition of access rules/policies can come from different parties.

- Data access rights are extremely context dependent. For example, a doctor that normally should not see any data may need full access in an emergency, or the doctor may need to see normally blocked data because she suspects a particular disease. In many cases, this context cannot be determined automatically, but only verified by a human after the incident; this requires careful auditing and some automated verification procedures.

- Access control must be extremely efficient to fit into the standard processes in medical care; given the short time doctors currently have to spent with the patients, it is unacceptable to build a system that significantly slows down the doctor.

- Even small fragments of patient records (such as the outcome of an HIV test) may be critical; as opposed to multimedia DRM, it is not even acceptable that partial information leaks.

- Roles can change quickly; doctors routinely call in external experts for advice, which then need access to the patient data. Furthermore, these experts may be at home working on their personal PCs, which hamper efficient transfer of access rights.

- In some cases, hospitals need to work with medical data for research purposes; thus, it should be possible to export anonymised data for such applications.

- Data needs to be protected while being used in a highly distributed way by different systems with complex and maybe legacy architectures, some of which may not have a trustworthy data management system.

- Medical data is rather side channel prone, i.e., a data item may reveal substantial information about its context. For example, the fact that someone takes an HIV test demonstrates that he considers himself at risk, and the fact that a teenage girl had repeated visits to her gynecologist may be revealing her pregnancy. Defining rules that cover the side information without disrupting normal healthcare is not straightforward.

6 Conclusions

Due to their construction, Enterprise Rights Management technologies are already able to satisfy many of the privacy and security requirements related to Electronic Health Records, such as data confidentiality and data integrity. ERM technology goes beyond the classical security technologies and provides a data-centric protection allowing the data owner to stay in control of data access and usage independently of the way in which data is distributed and where it is physically located. By protecting the data itself, ERM allows for highly distributed models and the off-line usage of data. In turn, this increases data availability which is one of the most important requirements in healthcare. Finally, by giving the patient the role of data owner, the ERM technology could provide means for patients to have more control on data sharing (e.g., allowing the patients to share their records with family and friends), as well as give them more awareness on how their data is used.

However, neither ERM nor DRM technologies can be, as such, straightforwardly applied in the healthcare domain. The new domain brings some additional security requirements. For example, a new requirement is to be able to cope with Role-Based Access Control, which is usually applied in the healthcare domain. Although a simple notion of roles, groups and domains exists in ERM, it is still challenging to provide for the required dynamics and context awareness. Therefore, ERM must be enhanced with techniques that address a number of open issues in order to be successfully applied in the healthcare domain.

References

[Char06]   R. Charette, Dying for Data, IEEE Spectrum, October 2006, pp. 16-21

[Ford01]   W. Ford, P. Hallam-Baker, B. Fox, B. Dillaway, B. LaMacchia, J. Epstein, J. Lapp, XML Key Management Specification (XKMS), 2001, W3C http://www.w3.org/TR/xkms

[HIMSS03]Healthcare Information and Management Systems Society (HIMSS), EHR Definition, Attributes and Essential Requirements; 2003; http://www.himss.org/content/files/EHRAttributes.pdf

[HL7]   Health Level Seven (HL7), http://www.hl7.org

[SAML]   Security Assertion Markup Language, Version 2.0, OASIS Security Service TC, http://www.oasis-open.org/specs/index.php#saml2.0

[XMLEn]   XML Encryption, http://www.w3.org/Encryption/2001

[XMLSi]   XML Signatures, http://www.w3.org/Signature

Case Studies from Fuzzing Bluetooth, WiFi and WiMAX

Sami Petäjäsoja · Ari Takanen · Mikko Varpiola · Heikki Kortti

Codenomicon Ltd.
{sami | art | mvarpio | hkortti}@codenomicon.com

Abstract

New wireless technologies such as WiMAX, RFID and ZigBee are rapidly being adopted along with existing wireless standards such as Bluetooth and WiFi. Bluetooth and WiFi have already become notorious for severe security shortcomings during their relatively short existence. New vulnerabilities and exploits are reported and demonstrated every week on live, public networks. The credibility of these wireless technologies has been damaged by security incidents, stemming from fundamental problems in requirements gathering, implementation quality and protocol design. Despite boasts of hardened security measures, security researchers and black-hat hackers keep constantly humiliating vendors. What can be done to avoid making the same mistakes all over again with new, emerging wireless technologies such as WiMAX? This paper draw experiences from the past and current problems in Bluetooth and WiFi and describe how fuzzing techniques can be used to assess the security of the available implementations. Quality and reliability improvements in these implementations will lead directly to decreased development and deployment costs, as well as increase public acceptance and ensure faster adoption.

1 Introduction

WiMAX is an emerging wireless technology that was originally intended for solving the "last-mile" problem in the areas where the wired connections were not desirable. This was the so-called "Fixed WiMAX" (802.16-2004), or 802.16d. With the emergence of "Mobile WiMAX" (802.16e-2005), or 802.16e, carriers are looking WiMAX as one of the technologies for delivering broadband content for the mobile users. At the same time WiMAX security is getting a front stage in public discussions. There are two schools at the moment: one is expecting to see security issues similar to WiFi and Bluetooth, and another one believes that the threats are not severe as security is built-in to WiMAX. We will explain what kind of threats malicious fuzzing could pose to wireless technologies, and how the very same technology can be used for ensuring the security proactively. Bluetooth, WiFi and WiMAX will be used as case studies. Some necessary background information both for the fuzzing and its applicability for the WiMAX will be given and the potential attack vectors are examined. We will present a case study of base station fuzzing using some of the identified attack vectors.

This paper is not about features of the wireless technologies, and therefore we are not going to discuss optimal bandwidth allocation, about various PHY transmission techniques, radio jamming, and performance of wireless networks in varying weather conditions, frequency hopping techniques or Quality of Service. The purpose is not to undermine Bluetooth, 802.11, and most certainly 802.16 technologies. The main focus of this paper is to explore what went wrong when implementing some of the current wireless access technologies, and explore that only through one security assessment technology, namely fuzzing [MiFS90]. This is because most security attacks do not exploit features in wireless technologies, but they abuse various implementation mistakes in the products. Fuzzing is one of the most effective black-box assessment technologies for robustness and security problems.

N. Pohlmann, H. Reimer, W. Schneider (Editors): Securing Electronic Business Processes, Vieweg (2007), 188-195

All tests have been conducted with commercially available fuzzing solutions, and can be repeated by third parties to verify the research results. Although examples are drawn from case studies using Codenomicon robustness testing suites [KaLT00] [LäKH06], they should apply equally well to any other fuzzing technology. Differences in results are probably due to differences in test coverage between various testing tools. This research is based on the work of various security personnel working at Codenomicon and the OUSPG/PROTOS research preceding Codenomicon. These studies been conducted during the past ten years, between 1996-2007. Still, the individual test results are not older than two years, and therefore should indicate the current state of maturity in wireless products. To protect the reputation of the manufacturers, we will not disclose details of individual vulnerabilities, nor the names of any products tested in these assessments.

1.1 Software Security and Robustness

Nowadays, security problems plague the software products used to access the vast Internet. Operating systems, WWW-browsers, e-mail programs all have had their share of the reported problems. Significant portions of these vulnerabilities are robustness problems caused by careless or misguided programming. The Internet "underground community" searches for these flaws using non-systematic ad-hoc methods and publishes their results for "fun and profit". The large number of reported problems from some software packages can be explained by the huge attention they have received and, on the other hand, by the clearly the numerous flaws they contain. Although reports of serious damages caused by exploitation of these vulnerabilities are sparse, they pose a threat to the networked society. Security assessment of software by source code auditing is expensive and laborious. Methods for security analysis without access to the source code have been few and usually limited in scope. This may be one reason why many major software vendors have been stuck in the loop of fixing vulnerabilities that have been found in the wild and providing countless patches to their clients to keep the systems protected. This is also known as the "patch-and-penetrate" race.

The robustness testing, or fuzzing, is based on systematic (or random) creation of a very large number of protocol messages, from thousands to several million test cases, containing exceptional elements simulating malicious attacks [KaLT00]. The method provides a low-cost proactive way of assessing software robustness. The security assessment of a software component is based on robustness analysis of the component. Robustness is the ability of software to tolerate exceptional input and stressful environment conditions. A piece of software that is not robust fails when facing such circumstances. A malicious intruder can easily take advantage of robustness shortcomings to compromise the system running the piece of software. In fact, a large portion of information security vulnerabilities reported in the public is caused by robustness weaknesses. All robustness problems can be exploited by causing denial-of-service conditions by feeding the vulnerable component with maliciously formatted input. There are no false positives in fuzzing or robustness testing. A found failure is always a critical failure, such as a crash or a memory leak. Some of the mistakes are exploitable in a fashion where an attacker can execute malicious code on the target system. An example is a buffer overflow type of robustness flaw that can almost always be exploited to run externally supplied code in the vulnerable component. This report will only recognize this possibility, but not make judgment calls if any of the found issues could be exploited as such.

In addition to increased information security, software robustness promotes software quality in general. A robust piece of software has fewer bugs, and that increases user satisfaction and provides more undisturbed uptime. Robustness analysis provides tools for assessing software quality as a complementary method with traditional process based quality systems and code audits. Robustness weaknesses are introduced during programming implementation) of the vulnerable software component. These kinds of errors easily slip through ordinary code auditing and testing since robustness problems generally do not manifest themselves during normal operations. They become visible only when someone or something presents the implementation with a carefully constructed "malicious piece of input", or corrupted data.

The used security assessment technique, robustness testing, is based on the systematic creation of a large set of exceptional input data fed into the tested component. Due to avoiding any randomness in the tests, the number of input data units causing problems provides a quantitative figure about the robustness, quality and information security of the component. We can assume that the assessment provides information to estimate the maturity of the tested software component. Also, robustness testing is likely to find out various vulnerabilities that would be found by the "underground community". We can assume that hackers will eventually find all the same found issues, unless they are fixed before that. This would support our assumption that these test results can indicate and measure the current security of the tested devices, and the future expenses created by the lack-of security.

1.2 Wireless Vulnerabilities and Incidents

With wireless technologies we have all the same threats, attacks and vulnerabilities as we do in the wireless space. Malicious people will exploit any known weaknesses with the implementations with denial of service attacks, worms, spam, malware and man-in-the-middle attacks.

Wireless networks have three additional aspects that make the security of wireless networks even more challenging than the security of fixed networks:

- Wireless networks are always open
- Attackers can connect into the network from anywhere, and from any distance
- Attackers are always anonymous

Wireless is always open. Physical media does not protect wireless networks. Any device that implements the same radio interface can access a wireless network.

Attacks are not limited by location or distance. The distance from where the attacker can reach the wireless network is only limited by the power of the transmitter. For example, Bluetooth attack tools are known to have several mile radiuses, although valid usage scenarios would never attempt such range of coverage for Bluetooth.

Attackers are always anonymous. Although a valid user can be pinpointed with good accuracy, an attacker can use directed antennas that will only target a selected victim. It is impossible to guarantee detection of malicious users in wireless networks. Attacker can also always attack the message sequences that happen before the authentication of the device.

Some examples of media coverage of wireless problems are given in Fig. 1.

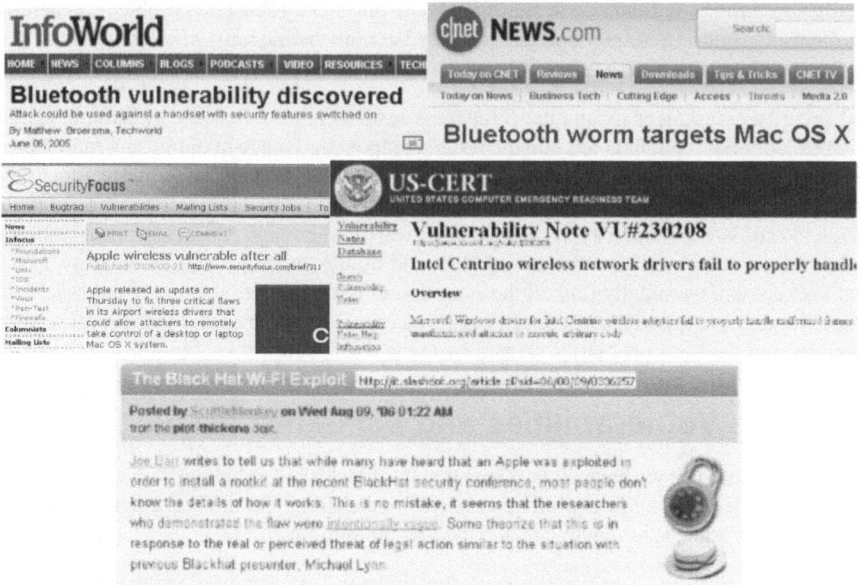

Fig. 1: Examples of attacks and vulnerabilities in wireless technologies, drawn from public media such as Lashdot, US-CERT, SecurityFocus, News.Com and InfoWorld.

2 Case Studies

2.1 Bluetooth Fuzzing

Bluetooth is implemented in a variety of different equipment, some security critical and some less so. Table 1 shows an example set of different Bluetooth devices based on the number of Bluetooth SIG website.[1]

Table 1: Bluetooth devices

Product Type	Number of Products
Audio and Visual	258
Automotive	261
Gaming	21
Handheld	227
Headset	334
Home Environment	203
Input Devices	61
Medical	25
(Mobile) Phone	695
Mobile Phone Accessory	474
Office Equipment	273
Personal Computer	150
Other/Unique	263

---

1 http://www.bluetooth.com/Bluetooth/Connect/Products/

Bluetooth consists of various profiles that implement the different features used in the various devices. These profiles can be implemented on different layers on the protocol stack. Table 2 shows the results of fuzzing different profiles from 31 Bluetooth implementations.

Table 2: Test results from fuzzing Bluetooth

Interface/Profile	Number of implementations tested with a fuzzer	Number of implementations that failed in the test	Percentage of failed products
L2CAP	31	26	84%
SDP	31	24	77%
RFCOMM	31	28	90%
A2DP	2	2	100%
AVRCP	3	3	100%
HCRP	1	1	100%
HID	1	1	100%
OPP	15	12	80%
FTP	5	5	100%
IRMC Synch	1	1	100%
BIP	1	1	100%
BPP	1	1	100%
HFP	5	2	40%
HSP	5	2	40%
FAX	2	0	0%
DUN	5	2	40%
SAP	4	4	100%

Only three implementations survived all tests that were executed, and all other products had problems with at least one profile. Failure-modes varied. Most of the Bluetooth-enabled embedded products simply crashed when tested with any level of fuzzing. Sometimes the result from the fuzzing is that the device ends up totally corrupt, requiring re-programming of its corrupt flash memory to become operable.

2.2 WiFi Fuzzing

Wireless protocols are just like any other packet-based protocols. They can be fuzzed on various different layers, starting from Layer 2, up and including IPv4 and IPv6, and all application protocols that the wireless infrastructure depends on. The example on Fig. 2 shows a test case drawn from a fuzzer that systematically breaks the packets in 802.11 frames.

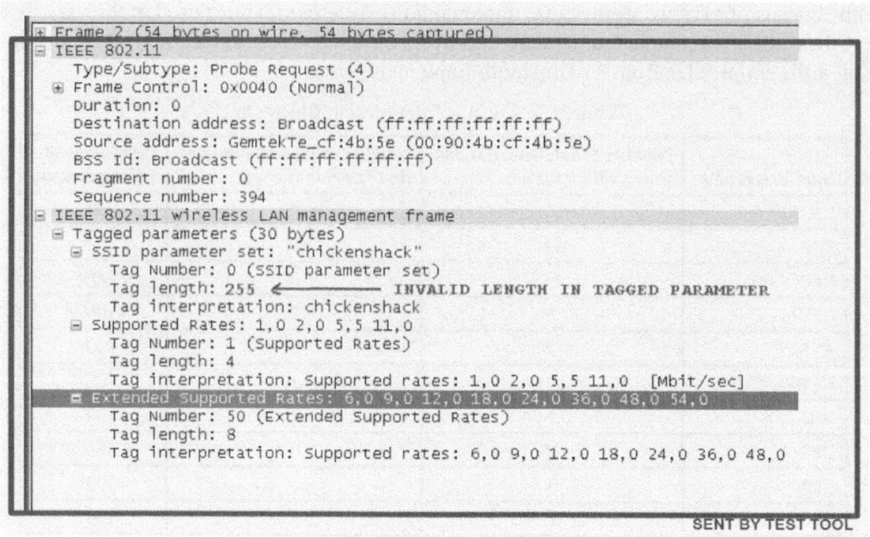

Fig. 2: Fuzzing 802.11 frames with Codenomicon fuzzer

A fuzzing tool can torture 802.11 from various perspectives. Examples of interesting management frames include:

- Probe request
- Association request
- Re-association request
- ATIM
- Disassociation
- De-authentication
- Authentication
- Beacon
- Response, Data and Control messages

Other 802.11 features and resulting messages and elements that can be fuzzed include:

- Open authentication
- WEP
- WPA1
- WPA2
- IEEE 802.1X / EAPOL

Fuzzing tests against WiFi is still work-in-progress, and the results are only preliminary. In the presentation, we will summarize our final findings on fuzzing various WiFi implementations.

2.3 WiMAX Fuzzing

During the assessment of one WiMAX 802.16d base-station (BS) equipment, our assessment found several failures resulting into at least seven separate robustness defects. The defects were verified as real problems, causing denial-of-service and service disruption level problems. These defects are such that they could manifest themselves without being explicitly exploited. E.g. resulting as receiving badly formatted network message as part of normal operation. Furthermore it appears that anyone being able to access the device would be able to trigger some of the found issues. As a mitigating factor, it is noted that found issues are likely to be exploitable only if user has direct IP address to the base stations management interface or IP address.

The purpose of this engagement was to demonstrate the capability and value of fuzzing tools for the purpose of testing IEEE 802.16d WiMAX equipment and the general feasibility of using fuzzing against WiMAX equipment. Due to timing constraints in the assessment, we only ran approximately 50-75% of the tools overall capability. All failures found were repeatable, and we were able to verify all the found problems as valid errors. The objective here is to show you that fuzzing solutions are applicable to the software and equipment verification, in both development and deployment of WiMAX.

At this stage we decided to focus on the application protocols. First, an interface analysis was conducted. The interface analysis indicated that at least the following interfaces are open on the tested platform. To guarantee robust and secure operation of the tested platform under all conditions it is recommended that all of the located interfaces should be tested using available fuzzing tools. The recognized open interfaces were as follows:

- Basic Communications: Ipv4 (ARP, ICMP, IGMP, TCP, UDP, IP), DNS, BOOTP/DHCP, TFTP, SunRPC
- Trunking: IEEE 802.1q
- Remote Access: Telnet, SNMPv1, SNMPv2c

As a metric here, full test space coverage would be achieved by executing all of the tests inside a single test tool. The tool vendor defines the metric in this assessment, and therefore it is not a real attack surface based metric. But as the used tool is a model-based fuzzer, the metric is directly proportional to the protocol specification complexity, and it can provide adequate indication of the test thoroughness. If a single test tool provides a way to run the tests in different message sequences, messages or carrier protocols (UDP, TCP), the total amount of available tests may be larger than the amount of test cases in a test tool. This and other factor of complexity were not considered with the used.

The following tests were executed:[2]

- 12% of the IPv4 tests
- 100% of the telnet tests
- 100% of the SNMP tests
- 100% of the TFTP tests
- 8% of the SunRPC tests

The following suspicious problems were found from the WiMAX equipment:

1. Reboot of IPv4 stack in system under test that repeatedly caused state of denial of service when receiving large amount of abnormal IPv4 packets.

---

2 Percentages are calculated from the systematic tests included in the fuzzer used in the tests.

2. Crash and reboot of system under test when receiving SunRPC request packet with length anomalies.

3. Crash and reboot of system under test when receiving RPC request packet with overflow anomalies.

4. Possible degradation of service when processing certain SNMPv1 and SNMPv2c requests.

During the 2-days of test execution, several security defects from the tested platform were evident. These defects will result in decreased dependability and security of the system. Three out of five assessed interfaces has security problems. The tests were executed against application protocols, and not against IEEE 802.16d link layer (802.16d MAC PDU). The duration of the assessment was limited to two office days, and due to timing constraints only approximately 50-75% of the robustness test tools overall capability was exercised. This would give an estimate of 3-4 work days for a total security analysis using fuzzing tools.

3 Conclusions

To understand the effectiveness of wireless fuzzing, we collected results from three different use cases, namely Bluetooth, WiFi and WiMAX. WiMAX has similarities to both Bluetooth and WiFi, and should have the same frequency of flaws as other wireless technologies have. Fuzzing was found to be extremely cost-effective, and fast security assessment tool. On average, fuzzing found problems in 90% of the devices tested. In light of the test results from WiMAX tests, there is no reason to believe that other WiMAX interfaces including those used on the physical layer would be any less free of bugs than the tested, classical IP based interfaces tested in the WiMAX study. Besides testing the application interfaces, using any available tools to verify and guarantee the robustness of 802.16d and 802.16e MAC layer is highly recommended when similar fuzzers will be available than what we currently have for Bluetooth and WiFi.

References

[MiFS90] Miller, Barton; Fredriksen, Lars; and So, Bryan: An Empirical Study of the Reliability of UNIX Utilities. In: Communications of the ACM 33, 12. 1990.

[LäKH06] Lämsä, Jarkko; Kaksonen, Rauli; and Kortti, Heikki. Codenomicon Robustness Testing – handling the infinite input space while breaking software. Codenomicon White paper.

[KaLT00] Kaksonen, Rauli; Laakso, Marko; and Takanen, Ari: Vulnerability Analysis of Software through Syntax Testing. University of Oulu, White paper. 2000.

[Thom06] Thomson, Fiona: The Worldwide Market for Bluetooth. IMS Research. 2006.

Evaluation of the Possible Utilization of anti-spam Mechanisms Against spit

Christian Dietrich · Malte Hesse

Institute for Internet Security
University of Applied Sciences Gelsenkirchen, Germany
{Dietrich | Hesse}@internet-sicherheit.de

Abstract

Voice over IP can be compared to email in a number of different aspects. Both, email and VoIP are wide-spread communication technologies in the internet. First of all, basic usage scenarios are described, such as hosted VoIP solution, campus VoIP solution and the role of VoIP in core networks. These scenarios are then distinguished by how they are affected by spam over internet telephony (spit).

In a comparative analysis, we evaluate well-proven countermeasures for email spam in the context of VoIP. A three-year-covering survey about email security in Germany serves as an empirical basis in order to provide facts about distribution and effectiveness of antispam measures. Blacklisting of IP addresses turns out to be effective in order to prevent spam and could be as effective for spit. White- and Greylisting can be adapted to fit VoIP. Additional techniques such as CAPTCHAs are described as well. These measures could be used to feed reputation services.

Finally, a combination of mechanisms which might make up a spit prevention system is presented.

1 Introduction

The idea of voice transmitted over IP networks (VoIP) has been fascinating and frustrating developers ever since ARPANET times. The first actual experimental Network Voice Protocol was released in 1973 [WikiENa]. The first commercial breakthrough came in February 1995 with the Internet-Phone Software of the Company Vocaltec [Foth01]. Unfortunately with dropping connection fees in Public Switched Telephone Networks (PSTN) the rapid success did not last. For a long time VoIP was therefore mainly used as a voice call campus solution for enterprises as a substitute for more expensive and less flexible switched Private Branch Exchange (PBX) solutions. Due to the benefit of emerging real-time capable all-IP networks the transmission of speech over public IP networks will develop a great impact over the next couple of years. These networks are developed by operators to improve the convergence of speech and data networks. The hoped for long-term effect for the operators is characterized by a re-duction of maintenance and operating cost for only one single all-IP network. The short-term benefit is believed to be the capability to offer existing and developing all-IP services to customers, like speech, data, television or games services, over just one single network. The terms Voice over IP and Internet Telephony are used as synonyms throughout the paper.

At first an introduction to related work will be given. This will help to define the scope of this document. As a next step the paper examines the possible usage scenarios for VoIP. This discussion is followed by a general introduction to spit. Then we will determine which of the introduced scenarios are actually at risk of spit. With this groundwork up our sleeve the paper discusses the possible utilization of anti-spam

N. Pohlmann, H. Reimer, W. Schneider (Editors): Securing Electronic Business Processes, Vieweg (2007), 196-206

mechanisms against the arising threat developing from spit. Therefore we need to demonstrate which anti-spam mechanisms have been proven effective. The paper closes with conclusions and a view on further work.

2 Related Work

This document aims to evaluate the possible utilization of effective and well-proven anti-spam mechanisms against the developing threat of spam over internet telephony (spit). Similar work has been done by [RoJe07] and [QNTS06]. For this evaluation the focus will be on the general idea of speech transmitted via IP networks and not just on particular protocols like SIP. Therefore we will not discuss video or instant messaging spam which may also be enabled by using SIP and has been discussed in [RoJe07]. Our evaluation is also based on an empirical study about the effectiveness of anti-spam mechanisms which was conducted the third time by request of the German Federal Office for Information Security (BSI). This study as well as other contributions have led to the development of a proof-of-concept of a IP reputation service, which may also be utilized against spit in the future.

Ideas for anti-spit systems have been given in [RTH+06] and [QNTS06] based on a scoring system which evaluates incoming calls at various stages, depending on various sources of information from databases to the feedback of a user. Therefore we will not try to develop our own ideas for an anti-spit system, but we will clarify which methods of information gathering and blocking spit we found to be effective. For a detailed overview on the entire VoIP and spit topic [Rade05] (a diploma thesis) may be used. This paper does not discuss general VoIP security or Quality of Service aspects. Due to the public awareness of these aspects there are various publications available.

3 VoIP usage scenarios

Since VoIP is not presenting one single technology, but stands for the idea of speech transmitted over data networks, there are several possible implementation scenarios. An overview can be found in **Fig. 1**. These scenarios are impacted by the actual user. These users can be categorized by consumers, enterprises and telecommunication service providers (operators).

3.1 Hosted VoIP solutions

Hosted solutions are offered by a service provider for a fee. These services are most of the time used by consumers, but they can also be used by an enterprise. In general the users can be reached by a regular PSTN telephone number and sometimes in addition by a certain internet telephone address. Both are assigned by the provider. The internet telephone address may be addressable throughout the entire internet or only from within the provider's or certain other domains. Hosted VoIP can be used as a substitute to a fixed telephone line since the connectivity with the PSTN can still established. A great advantage is that the user is not bound to a certain location, like he is in a fixed PSTN. All that is required in order to use the service is to have a half-decent connection to the internet. Some users prefer self hosted VoIP solutions by setting up their own VoIP server at home.

3.2 Campus VoIP solutions

Enterprises have great expenses setting up a telephone system with a Private Branch Exchange (PBX). IP based solutions are supposed to be more cost effective and flexible because they can reuse the data network infrastructure. Simple forms of campus VoIP solutions use IP within the internal network and PSTN on the outside.

Some enterprises tend to combine campus solutions with hosted and self hosted VoIP solutions. We want to call this scenario "enabled campus VoIP solution", because they are enabled to receive incoming and place outgoing VoIP calls over the internet. This scenario is potentially cost saving due to reduced external communication costs by using the internet.

Enterprises with distributed offices sometimes connect different campus VoIP solutions over the internet by using an encrypted tunnel. Therefore it is no longer necessary to use a PSTN to talk to someone at a different location of the same enterprise. We want to refer to this as "connected campus VoIP solution". Outgoing calls can still be placed using PSTN.

3.3 Trunk VoIP solutions and VoIP in core networks

Telecommunication service providers replace switched network technology by more flexible packet based technology. This trend can be identified for trunk lines between switching centers but also for entire core networks; so called Next Generation Networks (NGN). Using all-IP networks for the entire core network and within the access subsystem up to the access device of a customer will hopefully reduce operational costs. Up to now the access line to the customer is multiplexed for telephone and internet data splitting it up into bands using different frequencies. This requires separate core networks and a lot of additional hardware. The new attempt is to use IP on the access line and use only one Integrated Access Device (IAD) in the home of the consumer. This device could even be combined with set-top-boxes offering a customer a wide range of services. One of these services is VoIP, what is supposed to look and feel like the same telephone service the customer has always been served.

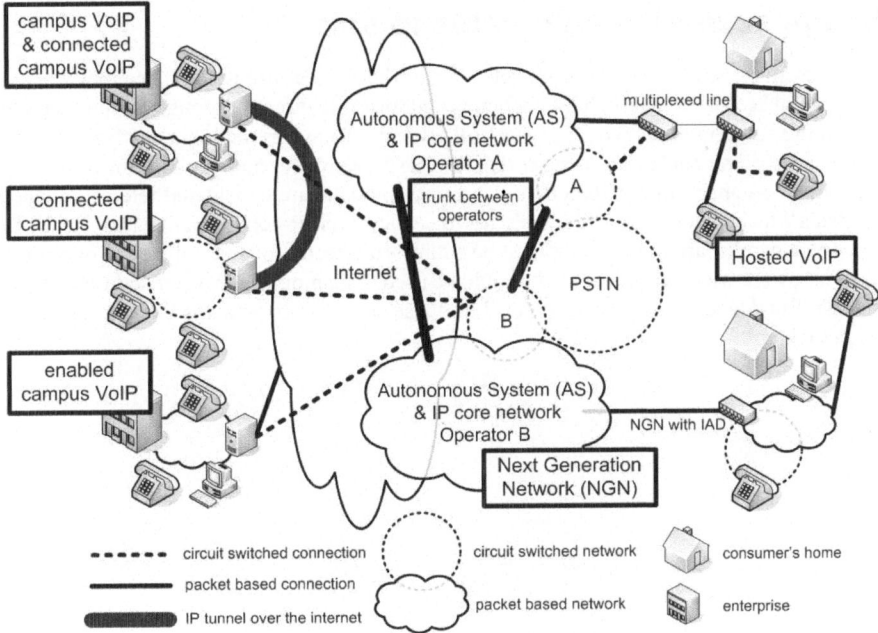

Fig. 1: collection of various VoIP scenarios

4 Spit – a threat arising from VoIP

Besides cost reduction on the provider's side and new services for the users, the convergence of speech and data networks also transfers a series of well proven threats and very effective attack-tools from the IP-world to the redesigned world of telecommunications. This creates a substantial basis for the development of new threats like spam over internet telephony (spit).

4.1 Spit introduction

Spit stands for the abuse of VoIP to initiate unwanted communication. The motivation can be versatile, ranging from telemarketing to social engineering techniques used for phishing. Due to the nature of synchronous voice communication, spit is more likely to get the user's immediate and full attention other than spam, keeping him/her from performing productive work. Some spit is initiated by machines using recordings the rest is placed directly by call centers using human resources. The general problem which makes spam and spit to a large degree possible is the lack of global identification of users in the internet. If users were reliably identifiable, misuse would lead to its originator. As a consequence, blocking unwanted communication would be easier.

From our point of view we only consider telemarketing calls as spit when the callee is connected via internet using VoIP. Telemarketing calls using VoIP as a cost saving access technology to place calls in regular PSTN are from our point of view no spit-calls. This is equivalent for example to the scenario of telemarketers using an internet fax-gateway to send messages to fax-machines all over the world. These faxes would not be considered e-mail spam, just because the internet was used as an access technology.

4.2 Usage scenarios vulnerable to spit

We will now evaluate which scenarios are relevant for the further discussion since they are at risk of spit. These are all scenarios in which a telephone is addressable directly through an internet telephone address from the entire internet and – less but still critical – from certain domains. Scenarios in which a telephone can only be addressed using a regular PSTN telephone number can not receive spit, but of course regular telemarketing calls. Of course some spit calls are considered telemarketing calls as well. Scenarios which are only used to transit the voice data over IP-networks, like they can be found in trunks or core networks, are not vulnerable to be addressed directly for spit. Of course one could argue that hacked hardware within these networks could be used to manipulate or insert additional transit data including spit. But due to the high security level for these networks an attack is likely to be detected and eliminated quickly.

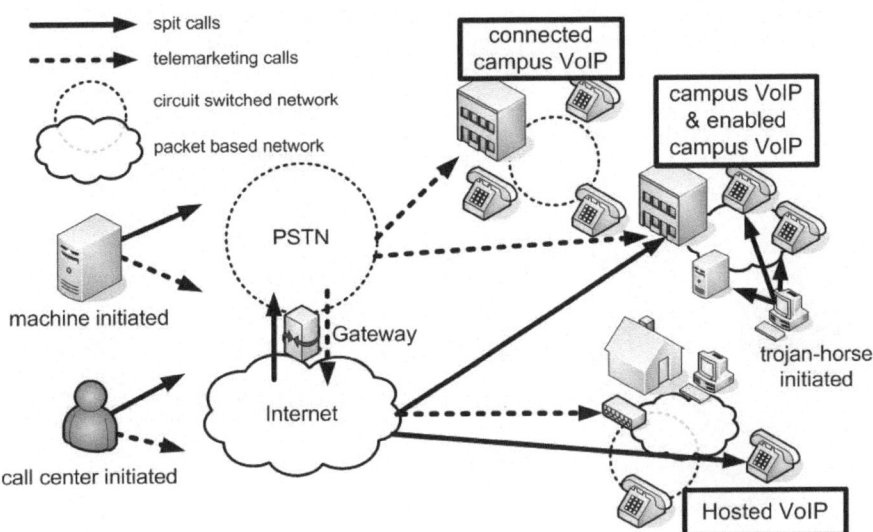

Fig. 2: VoIP scenarios vulnerable to spit

Campus solutions which are not enabled with a hosted connection with the internet are usually not vulnerable to spit. But it is imaginable that a trojan-horse infected computer within the company network, which is used for voice and data communication, could be utilized to address the company's VoIP telephones. This scenario is not as unlikely as it sounds, since trojan-horse infected computers, so called zombies, are the main source for spam today [Iron06]. An attacker broadcasts malware randomly infecting a certain number of systems. These systems might be located within companies' networks. This is one more example why IT security should be taken seriously. This threat needs to be prevented through working IT security solutions and not by an additional anti-spit system.

The relevant scenarios for our further discussion are therefore only hosted and enabled campus VoIP solutions that are addressable directly through an internet telephone address.

5 "Spit on" SPIT

Furthermore we will cover an analysis of anti-spam measures and their distribution based on an empirical study which was conducted the third time by request of the German Federal Office for Information Security (BSI) ([DiPo07]). Our key findings present effective ways of combating spam and give an impression on the future development of email spam. This evaluation will be the first time these results are presented to an English speaking public.

5.1 Email spam and its countermeasures

The survey has been carried out among German companies and institutions. It represents a total email volume of about 1 billion emails per month. This corresponds to about 12.8 million email accounts. The evaluation and interpretation of the survey results can be performed from different perspectives. We consider the perspective of a service provider the most important one in this context. Another perspective is the user's view which is omitted here. The distribution of email portions of a typical German company or service provider is reflected on average by the following figure:

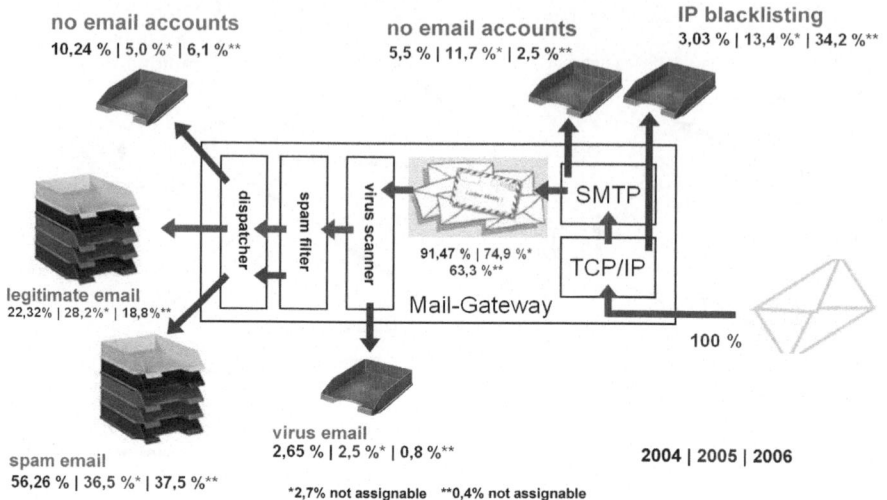

Fig. 3: results of the empirical study ([DiPo07])

For an email service provider, for example, the amount of email that is rejected during the SMTP dialogue plays an important role. Unwanted mail which is rejected during the SMTP dialogue is a big advantage in terms of saving resources. The provider does not need to spend bandwidth, computational power and storage space if an unwanted email is blocked as early as during inbound delivery.

Fig. 3 shows that blacklisting based on IP addresses has become much more important as antispam measure throughout the years 2004-2006. In 2004, only 3% of all incoming mail was blocked due to a blacklisted IP address of the sender. In 2005, this amount increased to about 13%. Last year, on average about 34% of all emails have already been blocked based on IP blacklisting. Some participants of the survey achieve block rates as high as 90%. Combined with a total false positive rate of 0.6% (on average), blacklisting seems to be the most efficient technique in order to prevent from email spam. IP blacklisting prevents an email gateway from an unwanted email entering and thus provides the same resource advantages as described above.

In the context of spit, blacklisting as such has been interpreted mostly as a means to block certain internet telephone addresses, such as VoIP URIs of the form user@domain. [RoJe07] mention blacklisting only in this sense. A spammer (or "spitter") can easily create a number of fresh sender-URIs and thus circumvent URI blacklisting. Getting a new, fresh domain in order to use as sender domain for spit is easy and the amount of available domains is practically limitless. Whereas blacklisting URIs clearly seems ineffective, we need to look at blacklisting IP addresses. Learning from email, the following question arises: Can blacklisting on an IP level be an effective anti-spit technique?

5.2 Possible utilization of spam countermeasures against SPIT

The next part of this evaluation will cover the consideration of the possible utilization of network-level anti-spam mechanisms against the arising threat developing from spit.

5.2.1 Blacklisting

In order to answer the question, we need to subdivide VoIP communication in two major parts: signaling and user data. It is important to understand that the signaling path may be different from the user data path, i.e. the media path. As a consequence, IP packets that carry signaling information may originate from a different IP address than media packets. Usually signaling is performed by some kind of VoIP server or proxy. The media path is setup between the end nodes, i.e. the user devices. The reason for splitting up signaling and media path is simple: IP packet processing in routers needs time. In order to avoid delays in the media stream, processing time is reduced by setting up a direct 'peer-to-peer' path with a minimal number of hops in-between. This results in less media stream delay and jitter.

In terms of blocking spit, it is most important to block the signaling of unwanted calls due to the synchronous nature of VoIP. Once signaling of an unwanted call is avoided, the call will not be established and the user will not even be interrupted. In this case, blocking the source IP address of the media stream is not required. Thus, a countermeasure against spit could be blacklisting of VoIP servers that initiate unwanted calls.

However, blacklisting IP addresses of VoIP servers has a disadvantage. Some servers perform signaling for a huge amount of users. If one user turns out to be a spammer and gets blacklisted, all users that use the same VoIP server will be prevented from doing VoIP. A side-effect of a server being blacklisted is that the service provider that operates the blacklisted server is put under pressure to take action concerning his presumably spamming/spitting client. On the other hand, if contracts between service provider and customer contain acceptable use policies which exclude spitting – and this is encouraged – the service provider has a legal means of taking action against a spitting client. Examples of such actions might be rate-limiting the number of calls or even blocking VoIP service for the customer in question.

An important challenge before blacklisting can be used as an effective countermeasure for spit is gathering information about those IP addresses that make up the VoIP infrastructure. Concerning email, reputation services play an important role as sources for blacklists. IP addresses can be categorized as good or bad, based on their behavior concerning email traffic. The same applies to VoIP. IP addresses should be categorized by their likelihood of being a legitimate VoIP server. To a large degree, email spammers use zombie computers, i.e. infected PCs, to deliver spam (see [Iron06]). We assume that the same will apply to spit. Those zombie computers usually have dialup, often even dynamic IP addresses, whereas VoIP servers are mainly operated at static, "well-known" IP addresses. This difference in type of IP address might be one criterion for a reputation service concerning VoIP.

Proprietary systems might have an advantage due to the fact that they can monitor signaling behavior at a central place. Misuse can be detected easier if a central collection point is available in order to perform frequency analysis. Frequency analysis could be used to find out supposable sources of spit. An example of a behavior of spit sources is a high number of outgoing calls and a low number of incoming calls.

5.2.2 Whitelisting

Making use of a blacklist usually requires whitelisting certain legitimate hosts and thus preventing them from ever being blocked. In our email survey, whitelisting is used at about 25% of all participants. This corresponds to the distribution of blacklisting, which is also in use at about one fourth of all participants. It is clear, from the distribution, that black- and whitelists go together well. Usually whitelists have a higher priority than blacklists and thus an entry of the whitelist overrides one of a blacklist.

As is the case with blacklisting, whitelisting can be understood in several ways. Unfortunately, in the context of email, email addresses can easily be forged. This is due to missing and weak identity authentication mechanisms. With VoIP, usually authentication is stronger and performed across domains. Thus the problem of easily generating new, fresh VoIP addresses is not relevant to whitelisting if the VoIP system provides solid authentication.

Using a whitelist alone produces the so called introduction problem. New addresses cannot enter the system if they are not added to the whitelist. Using IP address blacklists and VoIP address whitelists at the same time turns out to be advantageous in case of a legitimate host being blacklisted. If the whitelist overrides the blacklist, mail from certain whitelisted source VoIP addresses will be let through. This mechanism is seldom used in email due to the source address forging problem.

5.2.3 Greylisting

Greylisting has evolved to a wide-spread countermeasure of email spam. Our survey reveals: In 2005, only 10% of all participants used greylisting. Only one year later, in 2006, the percentage increased to 26%. As a result, one in four email systems uses greylisting. In the context of email, greylisting is a measure to test the RFC-compliance of email sender. An unknown sender gets a temporary error on first delivery. The sender is then supposed to retry after a short, but not too short period of time. However, zombies that send spam usually do not provide this kind of error handling and just skip sending the current message.

Typically, greylisting makes use of the following three properties:

- IP address of the sending host
- Sender and recipient email addresses

One major drawback of email greylisting is the fact, that there exist major legitimate email systems which cannot cope with servers that use greylisting.

In the context of VoIP, greylisting could be implemented as follows. A caller from an unknown source would receive a busy-signal on the first call, expecting the caller to try again some pre-defined time later. This is expected to be effective, because an attacker will not reserve resources to determine which call has to be reinitiated later. On the other hand, this mechanism is not very user-friendly and might conflict with local laws. It may also not be used in time critical environments like for the emergency infrastructure of an enterprise or city emergency service [Rade05].

[QNTS06] present a slightly altered idea of greylisting, which they call Progressive Multi Grey-leveling (PMG): "This method monitors calls and attribute a grey level to each caller. If a caller keeps trying to place calls in a certain time span the grey level increases. If the caller stops placing calls the grey level slowly decreases." Therefore this mechanism tries to analyses how aggressive a caller tries to place calls.

5.2.4 Additional mechanisms

The references give a number of additional mechanisms. We will introduce and comment on some of these and then we will present our idea of a fraud protection mechanism. A different approach to protect the user from unsolicited and time wasting spit calls could be to let an unknown caller take tests before being connected to the user. This test could ask for the recognition of voice which is supplemented by heavy background noise. These kinds of mechanisms will work as long as it is possible to tell the human user apart from a machine, but might be a problem for some challenged people (compare to so called "turing test" or CAPTCHAs). This would keep machine initiated spit from getting through to the callee, but would not prevent call center initiated spit. Of course call center spit is more expensive, but one should not forget that a call center might be placed in countries with cheap labour [RoJe07].

A rate limit for callers will help to reduce the total damage by putting e.g. a limit on calls a person or IP-address might place per day. To keep the reachability up an announcement with an alternative PSTN phone number could be played to the caller. This number will of course create a higher cost than VoIP would.

On a totally different level of mechanisms we can find anti-virus programs, which are scanning email messages for fraud spam and viruses. Due to the real-time nature of voice communication, this kind of scanning, e.g. by pattern matching, is of course not possible in order to completely block an unwanted call. But similar to a virus scanner a voice scanning tool could be implemented to protect users against social engineering attacks. We want to call this idea "fraud protection scanner". Whenever the scanner finds a signature of a known attack message this could be signalized to the user and the call could be disconnected or put on hold, leaving the decision to disconnect the call to the user. Of course this will only work for machine initiated spit using the same message over and over again. In addition the user could report abuse directly through add-ons to phone hardware or softphones, to protect other users from future fraud. This feedback would be used to feed the blacklist and other databases with additional input. We consider this as VoIP equivalents to already existing or evolving email reputation services. This could soon create a new market for the anti-spam and anti-virus industry.

5.3 Combination of mechanisms to a spit prevention system

[QNTS06] and [RTH+06] present their ideas on a spit prevention system which evaluates incoming calls at various stages to detect spit. At a very first stage – at network level – blacklists and other databases with IP-Addresses can be used, to block spit even before the VoIP signaling is started. We have shown that this stage is proven successful in the fight against spam. Sometimes data at his stage might only be an indication, making further evaluation necessary. In this case a scoring is done for the incoming call, raising the score for each negative indication. On a second stage the signaling might be analyzed looking for anomalies and looking up internet phone addresses in databases. At this stage, in case the score is inconspicuous the call would be connected to the callee. The alternative is to block the call completely, to use greylisting to make the caller call again or perform a Turing test to find out if a machine or a person is calling. In addition it would be possible to announce an alternative PSTN phone number which needs to be called in order to reach the desired person.

In case the call is connected a fraud protection scanner as described in section 5.2.4 could be used. Feedback given by the callee and collected through the analyzing process is used to update various databases.

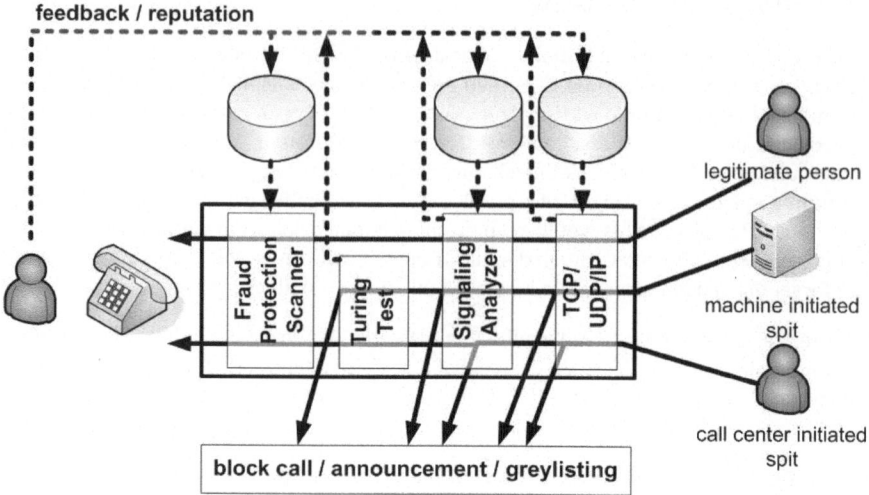

Fig. 4: spit prevention system

For a more efficient spit protection it would be very much necessary to exchange black- and whitelists between different but well selected and trusted partners. Of course these lists would need to be evaluated by each organisation and rated with a trust factor for each partner. The own list would be trusted the most and the trust level for other organisations would be based on experience and company policies. The exchange process needs to be automated, frequent and reliable. This kind of distributed reputation system could be used on VoIP gateways to block spit before it is passed to the callee VoIP server.

6 Conclusions and further work

Closing this evaluation, we will phrase our request to the different stakeholders. Expecting most spit coming from trojan-horse infected computers, we expect internet service providers (ISP) to honor their chair of responsibility in finding acceptable mechanisms to fight spit before it becomes an unacceptable threat. Secure operating systems might help to reduce the amount of trojan-horse infected computers some day, but the past has shown that we cannot rely on the user to make computers more secure. The ISPs can act on a technical level by offering VoIP proxies to all customers and blocking outgoing VoIP traffic not using the proxy. The past has shown that spammers adjust well and quickly to new mechanisms. This evolution process might of course one day lead to zombies using legitimate credentials to sign on to a smart host in order to spam or spit. But with a centralized architecture the ISPs will have an improved basis for diagnoses and defense, for example by means of rate limiting of messages or calls that can be placed by each customer per day. On an organizational level ISPs will need to make sure that they have the legal potential, due to their contracts, to handle customers that spit and spam in an appropriate and restrictive manner. ISPs will be encouraged by avoiding to be added to a blacklist which would endanger the VoIP service for all their customers.

We also need to include attorneys and representatives from governments like policy/law makers in this process, in order to straighten all legal problems at this point of time. A basis for their work could be the EU paper [00451/06]. Global identification of users should be discussed in this environment as well.

Scientific work needs to be done in order to get an understanding of the global VoIP infrastructure and (rough) numbers about VoIP server and client amounts.

References

[00451/06] Working Party 29 Opinion 2/2006 on privacy issues related to the provision of email screening services, adopted on 21 February 2006. Available online: http://ec.europa.eu/justice_home/fsj/privacy/working-group/wpdocs/2006_en.htm Last Access: July 8. 2007.

[DiPo07]   Christian Dietrich, Dr. Norbert Pohlmann: Knackpunkt Spam – Umfrage zur E-Mail-Verlässlichkeit (in German). heise, iX. June 2007, p. 113-115.

[Foth01]   Foth, Egmont: Handbuch IP-Telefonie. Fossil Verlag Köln, 2001.

[Iron06]   IronPort: "Spammers continue innovation: IronPort study shows image-based spam, hit&run and increased volumes latest threat to your inbox", June 28, 2006. Available online: http://www.ironport.com/company/ironport_pr_2006-06-28.html. Last Access: July 8. 2007.

[QNTS06]   Quittek, Juergen, Niccolini, Saverio, Tartarelli, Sandra, Schlegel, Roman: Prevention of Spam over IP Telephony (SPIT). In: NEC Technical Journal Vol. 1 No. 2, 2006, p. 114-119.

[Rade05]   Radermacher, Till Andreas: Spam Prevention in Voice over IP Networks. In: Diploma Thesis, 2005.

[RoJe07]   Rosenberg, Jonathan, Jennings, Cullen: The Session Initiation Protocol (SIP) and Spam. draft-ietf-sipping-spam-04.txt. Internet-Draft, February 2007. work in progress.

[RTH+06]   Rohwer, Thomas, Tolkmit, Carsten, Hansen, Marit, Hansen, Markus, Möller, Jan, Waack, Henning: White Paper: Abwehr von "Spam over Internet Telephony" (SPIT-AL), January 2006.

[WikiENa] Wikipedia, The Free Encyclopedia: Voice over IP. Available online: http://en.wikipedia.org/wiki/VoIP. Last Access: June 28. 2007.

Modeling Trust Management and Security of Information

Anna Felkner · Tomasz Jordan Kruk

Research and Academic Computer Network
{anna.felkner | tomasz.kruk}@nask.pl

Abstract

This paper is a survey of studies of modeling access control and trust management. Access control is an important requirement of information systems. Role Based Access Control (RBAC) is the most flexible type of access control policy. It is a model of access control in enterprise information systems. It uses a user role to control which users have access to given resources. Access rights are grouped by a role name, and access to resources is restricted to these users who are assigned to appropriate roles. Each user can be assigned to one or more roles, which itself can be associated with one or more privileges. Conventional access control models are suitable for regulating access to resources by recognized users. Unfortunately, these models have often been inadequate for decentralized and open systems where the identity of the users is not known and users are changing constantly. To overcome the short-comings of conventional access control models, like RBAC, credential-based access control has been proposed. Credential-based systems implement a notion of binary trust. However, due to the monotonicity requirement, these models will be more appropriate for a theoretical analysis than for real use. Non monotonic Trust Management system for P2P applications is also described.

1 Introduction

Access control is an important requirement of information systems. The data whether in electronic, paper or other form must be properly protected. The protection is provided by using an access control system. Conventional access control systems make authorization decision based on the users identity. Thus, they may be not suitable for decentralized distributed and open systems, where the users identity is not always known.

Trust management is a form of decentralized access control with access control decisions based on policy statement made by multiple principals. It is an approach to scalable and flexible access control in decentralized systems.

In trust management system an entity's privilege is based on its attributes instead of its identities. An entity's attributes are demonstrated through digitally signed credentials.

2 Access control

Access control system is a logical or physical control mechanism designed to protect against an unauthorized data access and usage. Access control includes the supervision of which participants (persons, processes, machines, etc.) have access to given computer system resources and how they share common data with each other. It concerns both applications, a middleware, operating systems and hardware.

N. Pohlmann, H. Reimer, W. Schneider (Editors): Securing Electronic Business Processes, Vieweg (2007), 207-216

2.1 Access Control Models

In any access control model, the entities that can perform actions in the system are called *subjects* (operator, user, process, domain), and the entities representing resources to which access may need to be controlled are called *objects* (data, procedures, files, applications). There are also operation on the object (access to object) and a so-called reference monitor, which makes access control decisions.

We can distinguish three types of conventional access control models: Discretionary Access Control (DAC), Mandatory Access Control (MAC) and Role based Access Control (RBAC). The most popular access control models are: Bell-La Padula (1973), Biba (1977) and Harrisona-Ruzzo-Ullmana (1976).

2.1.1 Discretionary Access Control (DAC)

In discretionary access control model creator of a resource determines who can access the resources. A subject has complete control over the objects that it owns and the programs that it executes. It is restrictive access to information based on the identity of users. Owners of objects can allow or deny access to these objects at their own discretion (thus the name) – it makes control over sensitive data difficult. From practical point of view systems with discretionary access control can be implemented in environments in which sensitive information is not processed, and users give access to their resources responsibly. DAC is not considered as an appropriate solution for most nowadays computer applications.

2.1.2 Mandatory Access Control (MAC)

In the mandatory access control models, every object in the system must be labeled by a security level and each subject has a clearance level. MAC mechanism ensures that all users only have access to that data for which they have a clearance. This policy if often used in systems, in which constant control over information distribution is essential. In this system the information can flow to only one direction – from lower secrecy level objects to higher secrecy level objects. This assures impossibility of secret information delivery to an object with lower secrecy level. The administrator manages access controls, defines a policy, which users cannot modify.

2.1.3 Role Based Access Control (RBAC)

In the role-based access control (RBAC) [Sandhu96, Ferraiolo01] access permissions to resources are defined for roles instead of for single users. Users have assigned roles and access is granted or denied to them based on these roles. Each user can be assigned to one or more roles, which itself can be associated with one or more privileges. This increases scalability of the access control mechanism because there are usually fewer roles than users and privileges in the system, and the permissions associated with the given role tend to change much less frequently than the users who fulfil the job function represented by the role. This is the most general model, because it helps to simulate both discretionary and mandatory access control.

2.2 Role Based Access Control Model

RBAC example is shown in Figure 1.

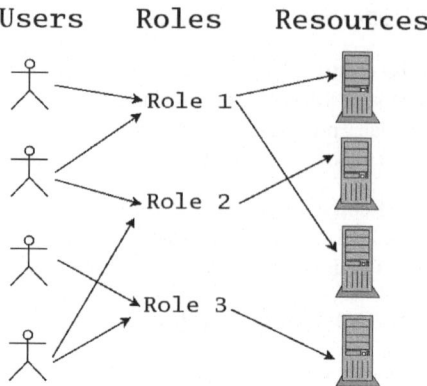

Figure 1: General outline of role-based access control

RBAC is the most flexible type of the access control policy, often met in enterprise information systems. A model is susceptible of modifications suitable for concrete needs. It is often a starting point for further extensions through introduction of new features or improvements in existing ones.

2.2.1 Basic RBAC model

According to Sandhu et al. [Sandhu96] the basic RBAC model has the following components:

- U, R, P, S, users, roles, permissions and sessions respectively,
- $PA \subseteq P \times R$, a many-to-many permission to role assignment relation,
- $UA \subseteq U \times R$, a many-to-many user to role assignment relation,
- user : $S \rightarrow U$, a function mapping each session s_i to the single user $u = user(s_i)$ (constant for the session's lifetime), and
- roles: $S \rightarrow 2^R$, a function mapping each session s_i to a set of roles $roles(s_i) \subseteq \{r \in R: (user(s_i),r) \in$

$UA\}$ (which can change with time) and session s_i has the permissions $\bigcup_{r \in roles(s_i)} \{p \in P : (p,r) \in PA\}$.

For the above definition, a set of permissions assigned to the role $r \in R$ is of the form:

$$\{p \in P : (p,r) \in PA\}.$$

and a set of roles assigned to the user $u \in U$ is of the form:

$$\{r \in R : (u,r) \in UA\}.$$

A user establishes a session during which he activates a subset of the roles assigned to him. Each user can activate multiple sessions, but each session is associated with only one user. The above $RBAC_0$ elements and their relationships are shown in Figure 2.

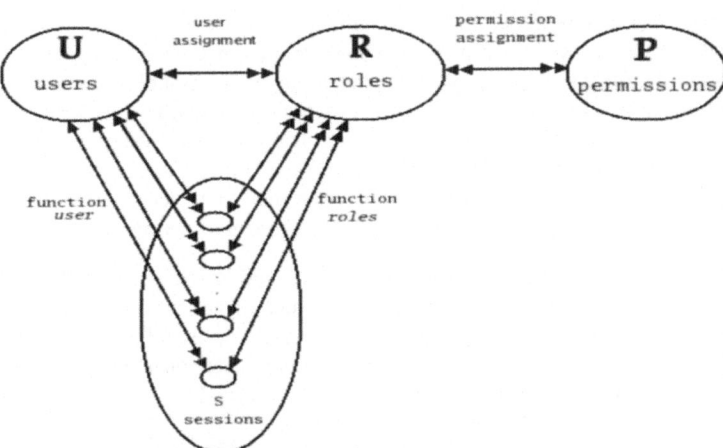

Figure 2: RBAC$_0$ elements and their relationships.

2.2.2 A family of RBAC models

In [Sandhu96] a family of different RBAC models is defined. The basic model described above is called RBAC$_0$. RBAC$_1$ adds the concept of role hierarchies, which refer to situations where roles can inherit permissions from other roles. Hierarchy defines a partial order among roles. An example of a role hierarchy is shown in Figure 3.

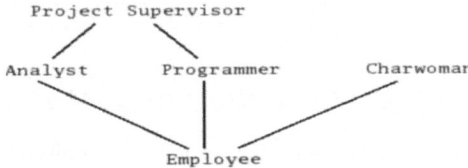

Figure 3: An example of a role hierarchy.

RBAC$_2$ adds constraints, which impose restrictions on acceptable configurations of different RBAC components. The example of role constraints can be the limitation of the number of roles which can be performed by a single user, or roles which must be mutually disjoint, such as purchasing manager and accounts payable manager. The latter is a so-called separation of duties principle. The RBAC$_1$ and RBAC$_2$ models are incomparable to one another. The consolidated model, called RBAC$_3$, includes both RBAC$_1$ and RBAC$_2$. This is the full role-based access control model, which is often called simply RBAC. The comparison of RBAC models is shown in following table.

Table1: The comparison of RBAC models.

Model	Role hierarchy	Constraints
RBAC$_0$	No	No
RBAC$_1$	Yes	No
RBAC$_2$	No	Yes
RBAC$_3$	Yes	Yes

The RBAC model, because of its generality, can be used to express a very wide range of security policies including discretionary and mandatory, as well as user-defined organizational specific policies. Binding permissions to roles and assignment of individual employees to suitable roles simplifies permission administration. It separates the stage of allotting rights, which are necessary to execute given tasks, from determination, who has to execute these tasks. As needs change users can be easily reassigned to different roles. These features have made RBAC very attractive and numerous software products currently support it. RBAC increasingly attracts attention because it reduces the complexity and cost of security administration by interposing the notion of role in the assignment of permissions to users.

The conventional access control models, like MAC, DAC and RBAC, make authorization decisions based on the identity of requester. They are suitable for regulating access to resources by recognized users. Unfortunately, these models have often been inadequate for decentralized and open systems where the identity of the users is not known and the set of registered users changes constantly. To overcome this shortcoming, credential-based access control has been proposed.

3 Trust Management (TM)

Trust management is a distinct and important component of security in network services. It is a promising framework for decentralized security related decisions. It is a form of distributed access control that allows one principal to delegate some access decisions to other principals. Delegation – ability to transfer limited authority over one or more resources to other principals – is an important mechanism for scalable and flexible trust management. The term of decentralized trust management was first introduced in 1996 by Blaze et al. [Blaze96], who defined it as a unified approach to specify and interpret security policies, credentials and trust relationships. A trust relationship between two entities was only based upon credential verification, and was used to control access to services and resources.

3.1 Elements of a Trust Management System

A trust management system according to [Blaze99] has five basic components:
- A language for describing *actions*, which are operations with security consequences that are to be controlled by the system.
- A mechanism for identifying *principals*, which are entities that can be authorized to perform actions.
- A language for specifying *application policies*, which govern the actions that principals are authorized to perform.
- A language for specifying *credentials*, which allow principals to delegate authorization to other principals.
- A *compliance checker*, which provides a service to applications for determining how an action requested by principals should be handled, given a policy and a set of credentials.

3.2 Trust management systems

To overcome the shortcomings of conventional access control models, like RBAC, credential-based access control has been proposed. Credential-based systems implement a notion of binary trust. The credential provides information about the keys, rights and qualifications by one or more trusted authorities.

In trust management systems access control decisions are based on attributes of requests, which are established by digitally signed certificates. A trust management system helps answer questions of the following form: "Can I perform this (potentially dangerous) operation?". The credential-based access control models (PolicyMaker and KeyNote) and credential-based access control integrated with role-based access control models (a family of Role-based Trust-management languages and Non monotonic Trust Management for P2P Applications) will be discussed below.

3.2.1 PolicyMaker

PolicyMaker is a very general model, that is more appropriate for a theoretical analysis than for practical use. Here, a kind of intermediate level key was introduced. These keys are dedicated to execute a concrete action by user. System allows managing key access to actions and assigning keys to users. Authors declare that their solution is flexible from the point of view of introducing changes, and is very safe thanks to the intermediate level keys. It enforces the necessary coordination of the design of policy, credentials, and trust relationships. PolicyMaker is flexible but with minimal functionality.

In general, the models and systems, which are discussed here can be very complex. For the sake of simplicity, only basic examples are presented here.

PolicyMaker example [Blaze96]

We might trust the public key belonging to Bob (Bob Labs president) to tell us which public keys belong to his employees. The local policy would connect his public key with the statement which only checks that "Organization:" field indeed says "Bob Labs". Bob can sign statements on behalf of his employees that check their names in the "From:" field. Bob is trustworthy as the "certificate authority" but only in the connection to his own employees. A policy to trust Bob (whose key is "pgp:"0x01234567") in this role is simple to set:

policy ASSERTS
        pgp:"0x01234567"
                WHERE PREDICATE=regexp:"Organization: Bob Labs";

This policy allows us to trust certificates from Bob (which are just messages signed with his PGP key):
        pgp:"0x01234567"
                ASSERTS
                pgp:"0x7654321"
                        WHERE PREDICATE=regexp:"From: Alice";

The query:
        pgp:"0x7654321"
                REQUESTS "From: Alice
                Organization: Bob Labs";

would succeed, but
        pgp:"0x7654321"
                REQUESTS "From: Alice
                Organization: Matt Labs";

and
        pgp:"0x7654321"
        REQUESTS "From: John
        Organization: Bob Labs";

would both fail.

This example shows how to use PolicyMaker to support authenticity of e-mail messages.

3.2.2 KeyNote

KeyNote [Blaze99] was defined in RFC 2704. It provides a simple mechanism for describing security policy and representing credentials. The policy and credential language is highly expressive and human readable and writeable. KeyNote includes a well-defined format and semantics for credentials and policies. Unfortunately KeyNote does not itself provide credential revocation services, and assertions are monotonic, what results in the lack of practical use of this system.

KeyNote example [Blaze99]

A credential assertion in which RSA Key abc123 trusts either DSA key 3390ee81 (called 'Alice') or RSA key c0123e (called 'Bob') to perform actions in which the "app_domain" is "RFC822-EMAIL", where the "address" matches the regular expression "^.*@keynote\.research\.att\.com$". In other words, abc123 trusts Alice and Bob as certification authorities for the keynote.research.att.com domain.

```
KeyNote-Version:  2
Local-Constants:  Alice="DSA:3390ee81"        # Alice's key
                  Bob="RSA:c0123e"            # Bob's key
Authorizer:       "RSA:abc123"
Licensees:        Alice || Bob
Conditions:       (app_domain == "RFC822-EMAIL") &&
                  (address ~= # only applies to one domain
                  "^.*@keynote\\.research\\.att\\.com$");
Signature:        "RSA-SHA1:213354f9"
```

3.2.3 Attribute–based access control (ABAC)

In attribute-based access control (ABAC) system, access control decisions are based on authenticated attributes of the subjects. Attribute authority is decentralized. ABAC avoids the need for permissions to be assigned to individual requesters before the request is made. According to [Li02] an expressive ABAC system should be able to express the following:

1. Decentralized attributes: an entity asserts that another entity has a certain attribute.

2. Delegation of attribute authority: an entity delegates the authority over an attribute to another entity.

3. Inference of attributes: an entity uses one attribute to make inferences about another attribute.

4. Attribute fields, like age and credit limit.

5. Attribute-based delegation of attribute authority. A key to ABAC's scalability is the ability to delegate to strangers whose trustworthiness is determined based on their own certified attributes.

3.2.4 Role-based Trust Management (RT)

A family of Role-based Trust Management (RT) languages is used for representing policies and credentials in distributed authorization. RT combines features from trust management and role-based access control. RT provides localized authority over roles, delegation in role definition, linked roles, parametrized roles and manifold roles. It is a proposition to fulfil the ABAC requirements. It uses a role term to introduce attributes. A role in RT defines a set of entities who are members of this role. This notion of roles resembles the notions of groups in many systems.

An overview to the role-based trust management family framework was introduced in [Li02]. The most basic part of RT is RT_0, which meets four of the five ABAC requirements (it does not support attribute fields). RT_1 adds to RT_0 parametrized roles, which can express attribute fields. The next one is RT_2, which adds to RT_1 logical objects, which can group logically related objects together so that permissions about them can be assigned together. RT^T provides manifold roles and role-product operators, which can express threshold and separation-of-duty policies. RT^D provides delegation of role activations, which can express selective use of capacities and delegation of these capacities. RT^T and RT^D can be used, together or separately, with each of RT_0 and RT_1. Entities in RT correspond to users in RBAC. Roles in RT can represent both roles and permissions from RBAC.

A few examples of RT

RT_0 example

A person has a right to participate in subject p, when he or she is a student in some department. To be able to fulfil the role of the department, institution ought to be both the organizational unit and conduct scientific / research and didactic activity. Jas is a student in the WEiTI department, which is both the organizational unit and conducts scientific / research and didactic activity. The following credentials prove that Jas have a right to participate subject p:

$$P.p \leftarrow U.p$$
$$U.p \leftarrow U.department.student$$
$$U.department \leftarrow U.orgUnit \cap U.researchAct$$
$$U.orgUnit \leftarrow WEiTI$$
$$U.\ researchAct \leftarrow WEiTI$$
$$WEiTI.student \leftarrow Jas$$

RT_1 examples

The following examples from [Li02] illustrate the use of RT_1

1) A company Alpha allows the manager of an employee to evaluate an employee.
$$Alfa.evaluatorOf(?Y) \leftarrow Alfa.managerOf(?Y)$$

This policy cannot be expressed in RT_0, because the parametrized roles do not occur there.

2) A University StateU gives special privileges to graduates from the first four years of its operation, no matter which degree was conferred.
$$StateU.foundingAlumni \leftarrow StateU.diploma(?, ?Year:[1955..1958])$$

Here, diploma is a role identifier that takes two parameters, a degree and a year, and "?" is an anonymous variable.

3) As part of its annual review process, Alpha company gives a pay raise to an employee if someone authorized to evaluate the employee says that his performance was good.
$$Alfa.payRaise \leftarrow Alfa.evaluatorOf(this).goodPerformance$$

RT^T example [Li02]

There were two operators, $\otimes$ and o, introduced here. They are used to define manifold roles and role-product operators, and can express threshold and separation-of-duty policies.

A says that an entity has attribute R if one member of $A.R_1$ and two different members of $A.R_2$ all say so. This can be represented using the following credentials:
$$A.R_3 \leftarrow A.R_2 \otimes A.R_2, \qquad A.R_4 \leftarrow A.R_1 \ o \ A.R_3, \qquad A.R \leftarrow A.R_4.R.$$

Suppose that:

$$A.R_1 \leftarrow B, \qquad A.R_1 \leftarrow E, \qquad A.R_2 \leftarrow B, \qquad A.R_2 \leftarrow C, \qquad A.R_2 \leftarrow D.$$

Then one can conclude the following:

members($A.R_1$) $\supseteq$ {B, E}
members($A.R_2$) $\supseteq$ {B, C, D}
members($A.R_3$) $\supseteq$ {{B, C}, {B, D}, {C, D}},
members($A.R_4$) $\supseteq$ {{B, C}, {B, D}, {B, C, D}, {B, C, E}, {B, D, E}, {C, D, E}}

Now suppose one further has the following credentials:

B.R $\leftarrow$ B, B.R $\leftarrow$ C,
C.R $\leftarrow$ C, C.R $\leftarrow$ D, C.R $\leftarrow$ E,
D.R $\leftarrow$ D, D.R $\leftarrow$ E,
E.R $\leftarrow$ E.

Then one can conclude that members(A.R) $\supseteq$ {C, E}, but one cannot conclude members(A.R) $\supseteq$ {B} or members(A.R) $\supseteq$ {D}.

3.3 Monotonicity

Despite the fact that the credentials-based models do, to a large degree, solve the access control problem in open systems, they still have some shortcomings. PolicyMaker, KeyNote and languages from the family of role-based trust management framework (RT) are like most trust management languages monotonic: adding new assertion to a query can never result in cancelling an action, which was accepted before. It is a problem, because each policy statement or credential added to the system can only increase the capabilities and privileges granted to others. The monotonicity property can simplify the design and analysis of complex network-based security protocols. It is a good property for researching, analysing and proving, but causes limited usability, because privileges revocation is not possible to assert. Models creators like to give monotonicity as condition, but banishing negation from an access control language is not a realistic option.

3.4 Nonmonotonic Trust Management for P2P Applications

Like it was said before, most trust management languages are monotonic. Non monotonic RTθ system, an extension of RT_0, which was created to manage trust in P2P applications and access control in virtual communities, is the answer to the problem of monotonicity. It introduces a single new statement type adding negation-in-context to standard RT. The authors of [Czenko05] defined a new role-exclusion operator θ.

Modeling access control decisions by a community cannot be done without some form of negation. It is not possible that all community members know each other, so a group of coordinators must be selected. To become a member of a community all the existing coordinators of a given community must approve it. Trust management languages do not support queries of this kind directly. If one wants to know if every coordinators approve we have to ask whether there is a coordinator that does not approve. Role-based trust management languages are monotonic, thus do not allow for negation.

RTθ example [Czenko05]

Company.verifycode $\leftarrow$ Company.tester θ Company.developer.

Suppose that both Alice and Bob are testers and Alice is also a developer of the code:

    Company.tester ← Alice
    Company.tester ← Bob
    Company.developer ← Alice

It shows that this credential does not make Alice to be a member of the Company.verifycode role. Thus, only Bob can verify the code.

4 Conclusion

In this paper, the issues of the access control (MAC, DAC, and RBAC) and trust management modeling (PolicyMaker, KeyNote, and RT) have been presented. These models are strictly monotonic, what is comfortable to proving, modeling and theoretical analysing, but is not appropriate for real use. To create a model, which in its requirements does not have monotonicity is a difficult task. Modeling system, in which credentials could be revoked is very difficult. The goal of our further work is to create a non monotonic trust management model, which will reflect the reality and will be suitable for practical use.

References

[Blaze96] Blaze M., Feigenbaum J., Lacy J.: *Decentralized Trust Management.* In Proceedings of 17th IEEE Symposium on Security and Privacy, Oakland, 1996.

[Blaze99] Blaze M., Feigenbaum J., Ioannidis J.: The KeyNote Trust Management System Version 2. Internet Society, Network Working Group. RFC 2704, 1999.

[Chadwick03] Chadwick D., Otenko A., Ball E.: *Role-Based Access Control with X.509 Attribute Certificates.* IEEE Internet Computing 7(2): 62--69,March/April 2003.

[Czenko05] Czenko M. R., Tran H. M., Doumen J. M., Etalle S., Hartel P. H., den Hartog J. I.: Nonmonotonic Trust Management for P2P Applications. In 1st Int. Workshop on Security and Trust Management (STM), September 2005.

[Felkner06] Felkner A.: Model kontroli dostępu opartej na rolach i jego rozszerzenia, Młodzi Naukowcy Wobec Wyzwań Współczesnej Techniki, 2006.

[Felkner06a] Felkner A.: Applications of RBAC in new Internet technologies, Proc. of VIII International PhD Workshop OWD 2006, Conference Archives PTETiS, 2006.

[Ferraiolo01] Ferraiolo D., Sandhu R., Gavrila S., Kuhn D. R., Chandramoult R.: Proposed NIST Standard for Role-Based Access Control, ACM Transactions on Information and System Security, Vol. 4, No. 3, August 2001, pp. 224-274.

[Li03]   Li N., Mitchell J.: *Datalog with Constraints: A Foundation for Trust-management Languages.* In Proceedings of the 5th International Symposium on Practical Aspects of Declarative Languages, New Orleans, January 2003.

[Li02]   Li N., Mitchell J., Winsborough W.: *Design of a Role-Based Trust-Management Framework.* In Proceedings of the 2002 IEEE Symposium on Security and Privacy, pages 114-130, Oakland, California, May 2002.

[Li03a]   Li N., Mitchell J.: *RT: A Role-based Trust Management Framework.* In Proceedings of the 3rd DARPA Information Survivability Conference and Exposition, Washington D.C., April 2003.

[Sandhu96] Sandhu R. S., Coyne E. J., Feinstein H. L., Youman C. E.: Role-Based Access Control Models, IEEE Computer, Volume 29, Nr 2, s. 38-47, 1996.

Smart Tokens, eID Cards, Infrastructure Solutions and Interoperability

Infrastructure for Trusted Environment: In Search of a Solution

Claire Vishik · Simon Johnson · David Hoffman

Intel Corporation
{claire.vishik | simon.johnson | david.hoffman}@intel.com

Abstract

Millions of PCs are currently sold equipped with a Trusted Platform Module, TPM, serving as a root of trust on the platform. Trusted Computing as an area of security has acquired significant visibility, and many new products and a growing number of research projects in areas ranging from virtualization to network security are based on Trusted Computing technologies and vision. In order to fully realize the vision of the Trusted Computing community, dedicated or compatible trust infrastructure for verification and attestation is required. Similar to other trust-enabling technologies, Trusted Computing needs an infrastructure that can verify the claim that a device is genuine and can be trusted to take part in a transaction, in which it is involved. Such an infrastructure will enable an environment where individuals can use the technology for protected transactions and potentially employ less risky authentication methods. This paper explores the role of infrastructure in Trusted Computing, starting with the discussion of the infrastructure's importance and issues in trust establishment, followed by the description of the basics of Trusted Computing functionality requiring infrastructure support. We use examples of other trust enabling infrastructures, such as general-purpose PKI and infrastructure for Identity Federation to highlight common approaches. Finally, we touch upon economics of trust and intermediation, in order to define potential models for building enabling infrastructure for Trusted Computing.. While the paper doesn't propose concrete solutions for the infrastructure problem in Trusted Computing, some possible avenues of building the necessary framework are outlined.

1 The Problem of Trust Establishment

Establishing and verifying identity of an individual or a device in a networked environment has always presented a serious problem [CHHD06, FRKH00]. Although access control is instrumental in permitting the use of networks or access to data only to the accounts that have proper authorization and have been authenticated, there are numerous open issues. One of the premises of Trusted Computing is to provide a foundation of a trusted platform and trusted environment, thus enabling the users to trust their own devices and other devices on the network In order for a user or device to be trusted, it is not sufficient to be successfully authenticated or to possess a valid key or credential. An authorized user can access restricted resources from a compromised device or network. Or an unauthorized user may be using legitimate credentials belonging to a different individual as well as a compromised platform. While some protocols make it possible to identify a device accessing the network, outside of Trusted Computing, there is no standard procedure to ascertain that the device is running an expected configuration or that the platform has not been compromised. Increased protection of the network helps protect the users of the network and information stored and processed by the users of the network.

N. Pohlmann, H. Reimer, W. Schneider (Editors): Securing Electronic Business Processes, Vieweg (2007), 219-227

Trusted Computing Group defines technical trust as the assurance that the "entity behaves in an expected manner for the intended purpose.[1]" In a more narrow sense, we can say that a platform can be trusted if it is running an expected configuration

In order for advanced platforms to deliver real business value and leverage usage models benefiting from a trusted environment and interaction with other trusted devices and users, we need to devise supporting protocols helping platforms and services to identify themselves, trust identification provided by the other parties, and engage in activities within the framework where security risks are well understood [KALP05]. To achieve this level of trust, users, platforms, and services have to use more detailed profiles and ensure information in those profiles can be validated by the infrastructure that is trusted by the participants.

Software can be hacked by software, and parameters and messages within software systems can be misrepresented with greater ease. Therefore, hardware-based trust is typically considered as providing greater assurance due to its greater resistance to tampering. Hardware-based trust has always been a strong advantage of Trusted Computing. But because hardware platforms use software systems for user-focused functionality, in a truly trusted environment it is important to be able to share information about the state of various components, both hardware and software, and create a mechanism to trust the information contained in these reports.

TCG (Trusted Computing Group) defined platform credentials (Endorsement Credentials) to establish that the platform has a genuine TPM. By signing this credential, TPM manufacturer, platform OEM, or organizational IT can make an assertion that a TPM with certain properties has been installed on a platform. This assertion allows those interacting with the platform to evaluate the level of trust the platform in question should be accorded. For example, if the TPM manufacturer signed the credential, it will be necessary to determine if the manufacturer can be trusted. If an attestation protocol is used, it will be important to establish if the Certificate Authority (Privacy CA) involved in the process is trustworthy. The credential can contain additional information about functionality that can help establish if the capabilities are adequate to support the necessary level of trust.

In many cases, more information may be necessary to provide greater assurance and elicit greater trust. In a simplified case, if we know that a platform from Company X network is accessing an application at Company Y with a user account that is properly authorized and authenticated, trust developed in the course of the transaction may be limited. But if we know that platform from Company X is running an expected configuration, has a hardware root of trust, and the user is biometrically authenticated, a higher level of trust is possible.

Yet greater disclosure of facts is likely to have an impact on users' privacy, and therefore an additional set of requirements for privacy protection is necessary for trust infrastructure that supports more advanced usage models. In this environment, platforms and services need to apply the principle of the least privilege, meaning that every module, user, or program must be able to access only information and resources that are necessary for their legitimate purpose. A related requirement for platforms and infrastructure in the environment requiring greater disclosure is to be able to apply policies in order to carry out minimal levels of disclosure necessary to establish the necessary level of trust [FLLU05]. If, in addition to the principle of the least privilege applied consistently, platforms and infrastructure can exchange messages including varying levels of detail, the resulting variable disclosure will provide greater privacy protection and support higher levels of trust in cases when it is mutually necessary for the participants in the attestation process. More flexible policies associated with disclosure can support

---

1 Definition of technical trust used by the Trusted Computing Group (TCG).

multiple levels of trust, ranging from a confirmation of the membership in a large group to details of the state of the components on a platform.

Finally, in a complex environment characterized by varying levels of trust and multiple types of trusted devices, the use of standard protocols to establish trust will have to be adopted, in order to enable the participants to understand and interpret policies and reports provided in a trusted network.

It is evident that trust establishment for advanced platforms requires intelligent infrastructure that can evaluate evidence of trust from a variety of sources and in accordance with flexible context-driven policies.

2 Background: Trusted Computing and TPM

Among recognized attributes of a trusted device, some are internal to the device (e.g. isolation or user and supervisor processes, isolation of programs, protected long term storage and identification of the current configurations), but other attributes require supporting infrastructure (e.g. ability to obtain verifiable reports of the platform identity using an attestation mechanism for the external observer to confirm the validity of these reports) [GRAW06]

Some important capabilities of TPMs defined in TCG specifications rely on trust infrastructure – a Certificate Authority (Privacy CA) or a CA serving as a verifier for DAA (Direct Anonymous Attestation) protocol. Although TPMs have become ubiquitous on branded PCs, with many models including a TPM as a standard component and some organizations, e.g. in the financial sector, standardizing on platforms with TPMs, two factors precluded the vision of Trusted Computing from being realized completely. One is the lack of consistent support in standard business operating systems, although XEN, Microsoft Vista, and improved TPM drivers are ushering in a more favourable environment. The other is the lack of dedicated or compatible trust infrastructure of CAs supporting attestation, authentication, and, in some cases, verification. The sections below describe TPM components and functions, highlighting the role of the trust infrastructure.

2.1 TPM Functions: Attestation

TPMs are self-contained computing environments that have perimeter protection and can perform certain computations without relying on external resources. A TPM consists of a Program Code Segment (PCS), a small CPU that executes the PCS, non-volatile memory where persistent keys and secrets are stored, and active memory used to store non-persistent secrets that are lost on power-off.

Attestation refers to a set of functions and protocols that enable a TPM to prove to a remote entity that the platform is using a particular configuration. This assertion can constitute a foundation for trust establishment. The attestation claim must be supported by a trustworthy source. To perform attestation, a TPM uses an Attestation Identity Key (AIK) to quote, or sign, platform measurements sent as a part of the attestation process. A TPM has a unique Endorsement Key (EK) pair and an Endorsement Credential signed by its manufacturer, platform OEM, or the IT department, asserting the validity of the EK and the TPM. The public portion of the EK and the Endorsement Credential are used to convince the trusted third party (Privacy CA) of the genuine nature of a TPM.[TCGS07]

The TCG has defined protocols to extend the trust from the EK to an AIK after a Privacy CA evaluates the evidence provided by a TPM on a platform. The EK is not used as a proof of the platform configuration directly, but AIKs, which can be created and destroyed by TPM owners, are instead used for platform attestation. The Privacy CA creates Identity Credentials for AIKs associated with a TPM.. After an Identity Credential is acquired, any AIK operation accompanied by that credential is an assertion of trust validated by the Privacy CA .If the Privacy CA trusts the manufacturer of the TPM (or OEM or the IT department) and the root of trust for measurement (RTM) on the platform, and a remote entity trusts the Privacy CA, a quote signed by a valid AIK accompanied by an Identity Credential constitutes a cryptographic proof of the current state of the platform. Thus, we can see that in order to establish trust and perform attestation for multi-organizational use of TPM-enabled platforms, external trust infrastructure is necessary.

With the growing importance of virtualization, the need for infrastructure that supports trustworthiness of a TPM enabled platform continues since the same level of assurance is needed for virtual TPMs, and the need for trusted third parties is only enhanced by virtualization [GORS06]. TPM virtualization takes place when several domains need access to the same set of resources in a "physical" TPM, as opposed to several partitions sharing resources in one TPM allocated to each. . Each virtual TPM manages its own set of TPM resources, including its own Endorsement Key (EK), Storage Root Key (SRK), PCRs (Platform Configuration Registers), monotonic counter, and general purpose NVRAM. TPM virtualization offers a range of implementation options that can support either greater assurance or greater flexibility and performance, thereby permitting to design systems for a wider variety of use models [BECG+05].

In order for a virtual TPM to function identically to hardware TPMs, a certain level of assurance based on the validation by a trusted third party (Privacy CA) is necessary. Similarly to the hardware TPM, a virtual TPM needs evidence of its identity and genuine nature obtained from the Privacy CA or through a less stringent procedure, still rooted in the reliance on a CA [BECG+05]. Even in less strict environments, the challengers have to know the criteria for the issuance of credentials by the signer in order to trust that signer. The details and capabilities of the virtual TPMs may be either explicitly or implicitly stated in the credential, potentially enabling sophisticated policies based on the functionality described.

Although virtual TPMs may offer greater flexibility in defining the appropriate level of assurance and performance needed in a trusted environment, their reliance on infrastructure is not diminished by virtualization. CAs or equivalent third parties necessary for trust establishment continue to be indispensable.

3 Other Environments

Trusted Computing is not the only technology requiring infrastructure to enable some of the core capabilities. In today's age of ubiquitous connectivity, external infrastructure is required to carry out essential functions in most protocols. The necessary infrastructure is built by various stakeholders to support functionality that brings definite benefits. The stakeholders vary from governments and international organizations to private companies.

Infrastructure for trust establishment has additional restrictions and requirements: it needs to provide a certain level of assurance while assuming the risks for breaches and deficiencies. Below we present brief illustrations of infrastructure efforts associated with some technologies.

3.1 General Purpose PKI

Public Key Infrastructure or PKI is an arrangement that connects users' public keys with their digital identities through a Certificate Authority or a CA, also called "Trusted Third Party". Trusted Computing as well as other technologies based on asymmetric cryptography requires a CA as part of the verification and validation processes. The user identity is unique for each CA. CA issues certificates that bind various attributes together, asserting to the validity of a public key and to the truth of other properties referenced. A PKI enables the users to establish trust through the CA without having to exchange confidential information directly. Early in the Internet age, PKI was considered as a foundation for creating a trusted environment on public networks [WAWU99]. Although many security conscious enterprises and most governments have built PKI, the vision of a global PKI used for reliable authentication on the Internet has not been realized. In practice, over time the reach of most PKI projects has been reduced, and a large proportion has not been successful [LOOP05]. There are numerous reasons for the failure. Technical reasons include general complexity of the certificates, associated policies, and related protocols; difficulties in carrying out lifecycle management of credentials, lack of automation for certificate and key exchange among users of different PKIs; lack of pragmatic procedures for PKI cross certification. Semi-proprietary implementations of CAs make integration with applications, already challenging because of the underlying complexity, practically impossible. But more than technical reasons, it is the business environment that is responsible for the failure of PKI to become as wide-spread as the early technologists had hoped. After all, if there was a valid market reason for the technology to thrive, technical problems would probably have been resolved due to strong economic incentives to achieve success. In reality, it is very expensive to establish and run a PKI, and it proved impossible to charge the users for the certificates, since the benefits of using certificates are unclear to a lay person. Only models that rely on charging enterprises in need of state-of-the-art e-commerce environments have been successful, with Verisign emerging as a leader in this area.

3.2 Federated Identity

It is also useful to mention briefly the Liberty Alliance, a standards consortium formed in 2001 to promote open standards for federated identity management. The Liberty Alliance specifications are designed to ensure that a user does not need to re-authenticate when accessing linked accounts. Because of the linkage of accounts and use of standard protocols, privacy and other policies can be enforced in a more consistent manner. In the six years of its existence, Liberty Alliance scored numerous successes as the organization grew and its specifications enjoyed a good level of adoption.

However, the full vision of the Federated Identity Framework requires significant infrastructure investment by establishing Identity Providers, organizations that maintain and ensure the validity of "registries of identities" as part of the federated system and are trusted by the users and owners of these identities. Although there are numerous successful implementations of systems with federated identity features on a smaller scale, global identity services have not emerged, due to reasons similar to those outlined in the section on PKI: underlying complexity of specifications and lack of economic incentives that would compensate the organizations for assuming the risks acting as Identity Providers.

3.3 DNS

The creation of the DNS (Domain Name Service) was a successful effort to establish a global infrastructure for an indispensable service. Unlike the two previous examples, though, trust establishment is not its main function. DNS serves as a phone book for the Internet by associating domain names with other information necessary to carry out services on the Internet. Its most basic service is to translate host name to IP addresses. In this brief section, we attempt to summarize the reasons for the success of DNS as opposed to many other infrastructure efforts that could create significant benefits for the users, but nonetheless failed.

From the technical point of view, DNS is very simple and flexible. A resolver sends a request for DNS resolution to DNS name servers, but caching on the client is also allowed in order to minimize the number of direct requests to the servers. A DNS resolver is embedded in the operating system, and applications requiring DNS resolution (e.g. Web browsers) are adapted to handle DNS requests. Because of the technical simplicity, several proposals were made to adapt the DNS model as a foundation for PKI services, e.g. certificate set up [NIVI98, GUTM03].

DNS administrators collect payments from those who benefit directly from DNS name assignment. The value of a good domain name is indisputable, and some memorable and simple names were sold for millions of dollars. The domain owners, predominantly organizations and enterprises, but also individual users, pay the fees for domain registration. ICANN, Internet Corporation for Assigned Names and Numbers, is a non-profit organization that has been overseeing DNS since 1998. Prior to that, the function was performed directly on behalf of the US government through organizations such as IANA (Internet Assigned Number Authority)

Although the need to trust the DNS servers is indisputable, the level of assurance and risks that may have to be assumed by operating entities are very different than those needed in a trust infrastructure. Regardless of the differences, DNS highlights some features of a successful infrastructure intermediary: the specification is technically simple, the technology is based on viable business models with clear benefits to the participants, and the establishment of the infrastructure was facilitated by government sponsorship of the initial stages of operations.

4 Trusted Intermediaries: Economics and Technology

Although the examples in the previous section do not attempt to provide a comprehensive analysis of the factors contributing to the success and failure of infrastructure intermediaries, they seem to indicate that success in establishing a technology infrastructure is contingent on the nature of the technology, and, to a larger degree, on the viability of the economic models and attractiveness of economic incentives for potential infrastructure builders.

The following sections briefly outline roles of trusted intermediaries and efficiencies they bring to the market and address fundamental requirements for building infrastructure for Trusted Computing. There are cases when building an infrastructure is essential for reasons other than market related, e.g., national security, but these situations are not considered in the discussion below.

4.1 Market Roles of Intermediaries

Technology infrastructure intermediaries bring a definite market advantage to infrastructure intensive fields that also require a significant level of assurance. The role of intermediaries for the market has intrigued researchers in economics and technology for many years, resulting in a significant body of literature describing various models of intermediation.

In order to understand the economic value of intermediaries, it is useful to start with double coincidence of wants, first described by Jevons in 1875 [JEVO20]. In exchange economies when there is no universal value equivalent (money) in a market, double coincidence of wants leads to increased search efforts for the acceptable exchange that also requires consent of both parties. More importantly than the increased search effort, the value of products in an exchange market is not as readily recognized because of the issue of asymmetric information, unequal knowledge of buyers and sellers about the value of products and transactions. Market efficiency is greater in monetary economies when the universal equivalent of value exists [BAMA95]. But for some products and services, valuation through the universal value equivalent is not very efficient. Numerous studies have shown that it is very difficult to assign a specific value to trust, especially in digital markets, and because of this difficulty, it is hard to define viable business models where trust is monetized [ZHGH05]. But other reports have demonstrated that users tend to reject risks and are willing to pay more for a risk-free environment. These observations indicate that there is a market opportunity for intermediaries engaged in trust establishment [VIWH99].

Intermediaries are viewed in economics as organizations favorably affecting the efficiency of transactions through aggregation to create economies of scale and scope [CHSW97] and by reducing or eliminating friction in markets [WILL87]. A related role of intermediaries is to serve as regulators between participants in a market [SABS96]. These functions are especially important in situations where services provided are difficult to monetize and where the environment is too diverse to provide uniform access to resources, in our case artifacts and protocols of the trust infrastructure.

From the point of view of technology, business models based on intermediation tend to support standards or at least uniform technical environments. They are also more successful in enforcing policies, for example those associated with privacy. There are no competing DNS standards, although some providers are lax with DNS rules, but there are numerous proprietary implementations for internal PKI. It is wrong to explain the differences by stressing only the absence of strong stakeholders to take ownership of multi-organizational PKI, since the situation is much more complex. However, it is important to note that the successful generic PKI model represented by Verisign is characterized by less complexity and greater uniformity than implementations aimed at organizational deployment.

To summarize, there seem to be some conditions associated with successful emergence of the infrastructure intermediaries, especially in areas that facilitate trust and provide assurance. Adherence to standards, simplification of procedures for enrolment and operations, viable market models that rely on economies of scale and scope, and strong stakeholders that are capable of supporting the initial stages of operation all seem to be characteristics playing some role in determining the success of the emerging infrastructure

5 Conclusions: Infrastructure for Trusted Computing

While describing issues in trust establishment and infrastructure-supported features for Trusted Computing, we have noted that there is a continuum of requirements with regard to the release of information details necessary to establish trust, the level of assurance necessary to support various use models, and requirements for performance. The differentiation in requirements calls for several different infrastructure implementations or for intelligent infrastructure capable of operating within several models that the market seems to support.

For very secure environments with the highest assurance, breadth of coverage may not be necessary, while requirements for trust establishment and certification may be very stringent. To support the models of this nature, building a strong and feature-rich organizational infrastructure may be the best approach.

In situations where the breadth of coverage is of importance, but the highest level of assurance is not required, a different model can be used. In these cases, requiring validation rather than identification and authentication, trust may be established simply by confirming the membership of a TPM in a group, with no further information required or establishing that communicating platforms have been equipped with genuine TPMs. A more generic global trusted service provider (similar to Verisign) or an Internet Service Provider may be good candidates to support the needs of users in this group.

In situations where only internal device authentication and attestation are needed, the IT department can act as the owner and maintainer of the infrastructure for Trusted Computing.

For novel advanced applications that require a certain breadth of coverage combined with a high level of assurance as well as support for remote attestation with flexible disclosure rules, new providers will need to emerge. It is not unlikely that these new infrastructure providers may start operating in certain market segments, such as financial services.

While it is impossible to predict how and even whether the infrastructure that can support the full vision of Trusted Computing will emerge, the topic should become a subject of serious discussion in the Trusted Computing community. The technologists will need to consider a wider range of requirements, from simplified protocols to the diversification of viable business models that can combine the required level of assurance with other features necessary to allow Trusted Computing technologies to thrive.

References

[FRKH00] Batya Friedman, Peter H. Kahn, Jr.,and Daniel C. Howe, Trust Online. Communications of the ACM, 43(12), 34-40.

[CHHD06] Elizabeth Chang, Farook Hussain, Tharam Dillon. Trust and Reputation for Service-Oriented Environments: Technologies For Building Business Intelligence And Consumer Confidence. New York: Wiley, 2006.

[KALP05] Katsikas, S.K., Lopez, J., Pernul, G.: Trust, Privacy and Security in E-business: Requirements and Solutions. Proc. of the 10th Panhellenic Conference on Informatics (PCI'2005), pp.548-558. Volos, Greece, November 2005.

[GRAW06] David Grawrock. The Intel Safer Computing Initiative: Building Blocks for Trusted Computing. Intel Press, 2006

[FLLU05] Scott Flinn and Joanna Lumsden, User Perceptions of Privacy and Security on the Web. Third Annual Conference on Privacy, Security and Trust, October 12-14, 2005

[BECG+05] Stefan Berger, Ramón Cáceres, Kenneth A. Goldman, Ronald Perez, Reiner Sailer, Leendert van Doorn. vTPM: Virtualizing the Trusted Platform Module. IBM Research Report. Available at: http://domino.research.ibm.com/library/cyberdig.nsf/1e4115aea78b6e7c85256b360066f0d4/a0163fff5b1a61fe85257178004eee39?OpenDocument&Highlight=0,RC23879

[TCGS07] Trusted Computing Group. TCG Specification Architecture Overview, version 1.3, May 2007. Available at: https://www.trustedcomputinggroup.org/groups/TCG_1_3_Architecture_Overview.pdf

[GORS06] Hari Govind, V. Ramasamy and Matthias Schunter. Architecting Dependable Systems Using Virtualization. Available at: http://www.opentc.net/publications/OTC_Architecting_Dependable_Systems.pdf

[WAWU99] Chenxi Wang Wulf, W.A. Towards a scalable PKI for electronic commerce systems. In Advance Issues of E-Commerce and Web-Based Information Systems, WECWIS, 1999.

[LOOP05] Lopez, J., Oppliger, R., Pernul, G.: Why have Public Key Infrastructures failed so far. Internet Research, Vol. 15, Issue 5, Emerald, Bradford, England, 2005.

[NIVI98] Pekka Nikandre and Lea Viljanen. Storing and Retrieving Internet Certificates. Available at: http://www.tml.tkk.fi/Research/TeSSA/Papers/Nikander-Viljanen/nikander-viljanen-nordsec-98-submission.pdf

[GUTM03] Peter Gootman. Plug and Play PKI: A PKI Your Mother Can Use. In Proceedings of the 12th USENIX Security Symposium. Washington, D.C., USA, August 4–8, 2003

[JEVO20] William S. Jevons. Money and the mechanism of exchange. New York : D. Appleton, 1920.

[BAMA95] A. Bannerjee and E. Maskin. Fiat Money in the Kitoyaka-Wright Model. Quarterly Journal of Economics, 111 (4) 1996, p. 9551005.

[ZHGH05} Jie Zhang and Ali. A. Ghorbani. Value-Centric Trust Model with Improved Familiarity Measurement. Available at: http://www.ijcai.org/papers/post-0233.pdf

[VIWH99] Claire Vishik and Andrew B. Whinston. Knowledge Sharing, Quality, and Intermediation. In WACC 1999: p. 157-166

[WILL87] S. D. Williamson. Recent developments in modeling financial intermediation. Federal Reserve Bank of Minneapolis, Quarterly Review, 11, Summer (1987),19-29.

[CHSW97] S. Choi, D. Stahl, D., and A. Whinston. Economics of Electronic Commerce. Indianapolis: Addison/Wesley, 1997.

[SABS96] M. Sarkar, B. Butler, and C. Steinfield. Intermediaries and Cybermediaries: A Continuing Role for Mediating Players in the Electronic Marketplace. JCMC l(3), 1996. Available at http:///shum.cc.huji.ac.il/jcmc/voll/issue3/sarkar.html.

Integrity Check of Remote Computer Systems
Trusted Network Connect

Marian Jungbauer · Norbert Pohlmann

Fachhochschule Gelsenkirchen
{jungbauer | pohlmann}@internet-sicherheit.de

Abstract

The economic dependence on fast and inexpensive exchange of information that has arisen as a result of globalisation is leading to ever increasing levels of networking. The internet provides a communication infrastructure that is available worldwide. However, it does not provide for trustworthy communication, as it is not possible to assess the computer systems in the network with respect to their system integrity and trustworthiness. The same also applies to intranets. Visitors and field workers who use their computer systems both inside and outside the company network represent a threat to the company through these computer systems. By using the computer systems outside the company network they are also working outside the protective measures and control area of the company's IT. Solution approaches such as Trusted Network Connect (TNC) provide methods for determining the integrity of end points which serve as a basis for trustworthy communication. The configurations of the end points can be measured on both the software and hardware level. It is possible to realise policy-controlled access control through the reconciliation of defined safety rules.

1 Introduction

Only a few decades ago data and documents were exchanged both within and between firms either personally or by post. For the transport of sensitive data it was necessary to use trustworthy communication pathways, such as the company's own postal service.

Subsequently initial forms of electronic data transmission, e.g. transmission by fax or the first networks offered the opportunity of transmitting documents quickly from A to B. However, it was not possible to guarantee the confidential transmission of sensitive data.

Today, in the age of globalisation, the distances, quantity and importance of the information that is to be exchanged are increasing. Furthermore, there is increasing cost and time pressure on all operational processes. Classical, locally restricted networks (intranets) throughout the world are therefore becoming ever more intensively integrated into large, locally unrestricted company networks. Home and field workers require rapid and secure access to data in the company's network from any location. Transactions with other organisations, in particular in the B2B field, are increasingly made by electronic means.

Former static network infrastructures with clear system limits are therefore giving way more and more to heterogeneous and dynamic networks [Hart05].

N. Pohlmann, H. Reimer, W. Schneider (Editors): Securing Electronic Business Processes, Vieweg (2007), 228-237

1.1 The Problem

The flexibility and inexpensive use of the Internet is diminished by a lack of security which currently only permits restricted use by public authorities and industry in fields where security is critical.

Fieldworkers use their computer systems in many environments with various security requirements. Home workers use their PCs for private purposes. Employees take their notebooks home with them. These computer systems which are removed either temporarily or permanently from the protective measures of the company networks are exposed to considerably greater hazards. If they are compromised by malware, their reintegration into the company network (either directly or via the Internet) allows them to circumvent the company's own safety mechanisms and therefore jeopardise the company itself through the company network.

Today Virtual Private Networks (VPNs) are mainly used for connecting external computer systems to company networks. These offer both encoding and user authentication, but no analysis of system statuses and therefore of the trustworthiness of the accessing computer systems.

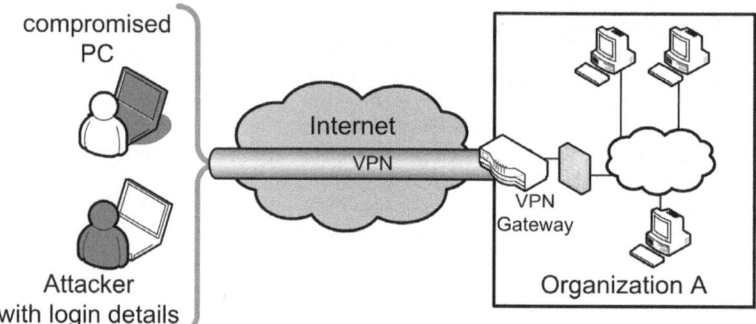

Fig. 1 Possible dangers by VPN

Figure 1 shows two possible dangers to a network from computer systems accessing via VPN:

- Due to the absence of an integrity analysis it is not possible to protect the computer network with its services against a computer system compromised by malware.
- It cannot be ascertained whether the computer system which is being communicated with is also the computer system that it claims to be. If an attacker obtains the access data of a VPN, he can use them for unauthorised access.

1.2 Requirements Placed on Today's Computer Networks

Current and future networks must be flexible and open in terms of their expansion. At the same time they should make trusted communication possible.

Even today possibilities exist to expand networks in a flexible manner and equip them with security services – for example via VPNs. However, there is a lack of security mechanisms which guarantee the trustworthiness of the computer systems employed by the user.

The aim of new security systems must be the verifiability of the trustworthiness of the participating computer systems and the creation of secure communication.

2 Trusted Network Communications

One speaks of trusted communication when the trustworthiness of all communication partners involved can be ascertained. Here it is important that the trustworthiness is considered separately for each communication direction. It is possible to conduct a confidential discussion with an individual whom one trusts without the other person having the same level of trust in oneself. In addition to the individuals concerned, the environment in which the communication takes place must also be trusted. If the communication takes place locally, the location must be classified as trustworthy, i.e. free of listening devices, for example. If the communication takes place over a certain distance, the transmission route – for example a postal service with all its employees and premises – must be trustworthy. Additionally, the trustworthiness depends on the requirements of the communication partner, who defines the requirements he places on confidential communication with the help of a policy. This policy might define which messenger service he considers to be trustworthy and how the delivery must be packaged in order to be able to detect compromised consignments.

With respect to communication via computer networks, all individuals involved in the communication must be reliably authenticated on the one hand, and on the other hand the integrity of all computer systems involved in the communication must be guaranteed.

Techniques already in existence, such as VPN, offer reliable verification of the identity of the individuals involved in the communication and the secure transmission of data via networks. However, there is a lack of appropriate security mechanisms which allow integrity verification of the endpoints used for the communication (computer systems).

The trustworthiness of a computer system depends on the overall status of all hardware and software components with their configurations. Measured integrity does not represent a standardised status of a computer system. Whether the trustworthiness of a computer system exists or not depends rather on the security guidelines (policies) of the communication partners. For example, an operator of a network can consider the trustworthiness of a computer system to be evidenced by the use of an up-to-date operating system, while another operator also demands up-to-date user software, for example the latest browser.

Only when all of the system components, i.e. hardware and software, defined in the policy of the network operator are in a desired and uncompromised state is the trustworthiness of the system considered to be secure. The problem here is that today any compromising – particularly of the operating systems – cannot be measured directly, but only indirectly through the existence of further software. This occurs, for example, through the use of an up-to-date virus scanner and an optimally adjusted personal firewall. Only if these programmes are installed, correctly configured and kept right up-to-date in terms of data can the probability of their being compromised be considered low.

This is the very point at which the new concepts for the establishment of integrity-tested network connections come in. Under the generic term "Network Access Control" (NAC) these concepts make it possible to verify the configuration of the end points when building up a network connection. Which configurations of the hardware and software of a computer system are permitted in a network is defined by the network operator by means of policies. For example, these policies stipulate the presence of a virus scanner with up-to-date virus signature, an installed and well-configured personal firewall and the latest patch level for the operating system and applications. Only if the policies are fulfilled is an enquiring end device granted access to the network and its services.

With respect to these new security concepts, one also speaks of a change to the protection strategy of networks and their services [JuPo06]. As a result of the verification of the computer systems before network access, there is a changeover from the reaction to a threat to its prevention. While attempts are made today through the use of Intrusion Detection Systems (IDS) to detect compromised computer systems on the basis of abnormal measurement readings in network traffic – i.e. a computer system infected by malware must first behave "incorrectly" (reaction) before it can be discovered – preventive security concepts stop computer systems with a faulty or undesirable system configuration – which may therefore be compromised – from entering the network in the first place and using the services present there.

3 Trusted Network Connect

With the Trusted Network Connect (TNC) specification the Trusted Computing Group is developing its own NAC approach. The development is taking place through the Trusted Network Connect Subgroup [Trus06] with over 75 firms represented and is currently available (May 2007) in version 1.2 [Tru+06].

The aim is the development of an open, producer-independent specification for verifying endpoint integrity. This verification is fundamental to ascertaining the trustworthiness of a computer system.

TNC makes use of current security technologies for network access ("802.1x" and "VPN"), for the transport of messages ("EAP", "TLS" and "HTTPS") and for authentication ("Radius" and "Diameter") in order to enable easy integration into existing network infrastructures.

3.1 Phases

All functions provided by TNC can be classified into three phases:

The **Assessment Phase** comprises all actions from the attempt at establishing a connection with a TNC network to the decision on its integrity. The measured values of a computer system are compared by a server in the network on the basis of policies. This comparison makes it possible to take a decision on the integrity of the computer system.

If upon non-fulfilment of the policies the computer system is categorised as not having the required integrity, it moves to the **Isolation Phase**, in which the accessing computer system is isolated in a protected network area. Therefore any computer systems that are compromised with malware do not gain access to the network and the services offered there.

The **Remediation Phase** offers the isolated computer systems the opportunity to restore their integrity, for example through the installation of missing security software, and – after renewed verification – access to the network.

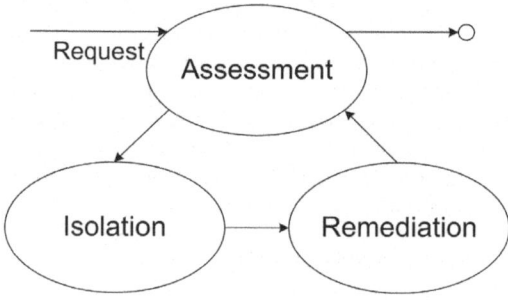

Fig. 2: Connection of the TNC phases

3.2 Structure

A fundamental distinction is made between three elements in the TNC specification.

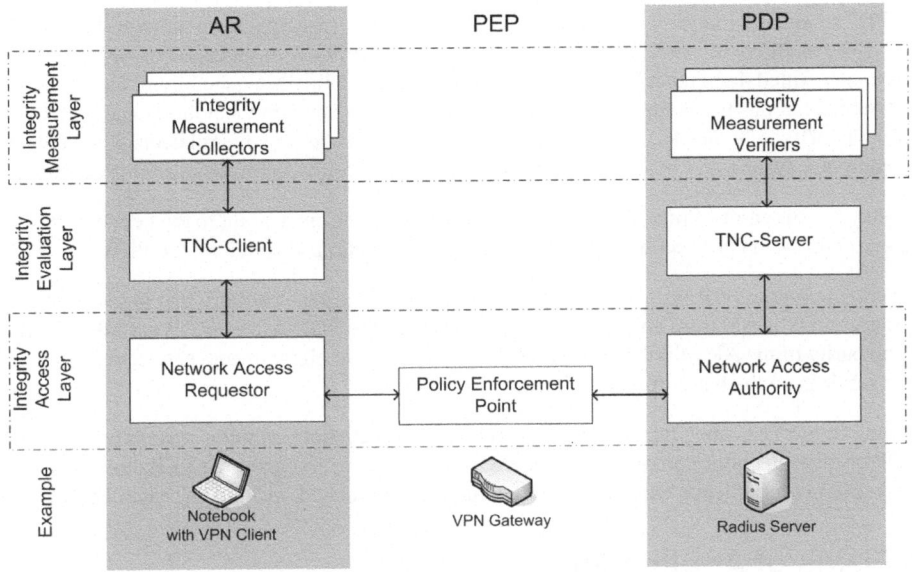

Fig. 3: Structure of TNC

The computer system by which a network connection to a TNC network is to be established is called the **Access Requestor** (AR). On the Access Requestor there are TNC components for a connection request, the transmission of measurement readings and the measurement itself.

Measurement of the individual components of the computer system is carried out by so-called "Integrity Measurement Collectors" (IMC). For each component to be measured there is a suitable IMC, for example one for virus scanners and one for the personal firewall. During the start-up of the system the IMCs are initialised by the TNC client on the accessing computer system in order to be able to collect measurement readings from the respective components during the establishment of a connection. The type of possible measurement readings is not initially restricted. For example, in the case of a virus scanner, information on the producer and the age of the virus signature may be important, whereas for a connected printer the version of the firmware and whether the printer has a fax function may be relevant. In order that an IMC can collect such detailed measurement readings it requires very precise knowledge of the hardware/software to be measured. Mostly such knowledge is only available to the producer of the hardware or software. The collaboration of the producer in the compilation or provision of an IMC is therefore essential.

On the network side there are two TNC elements:

The **Policy Decision Point** (PDP) represents the counterpart to the Access Requestor (AR). This is a server whose task it is to collect the measured readings of an Access Requestor and formulate an access decision with the help of policies. This decision is then passed to the point executing the access.

The Network Access Authority (NAA) in the Policy Decision Point decides whether an AR should be given access or not. To this purpose the NAA asks the TNC server whether the integrity measurements of the AR conform to the security policy.

At the PDP so-called "Integrity Measurement Verifiers" (IMV) represent the counterpart to the IMCs of the AR. Here too there are several IMVs for the different security components. For each security component to be verified there must be a suitable IMV in addition to the IMC (see Figure 3). These compare the measured readings transmitted on the basis of the rules laid down in the policies and notify the TNC server in the PDP of the result. With the partial results this then takes an overall decision on the integrity of the computer system and informs the Policy Enforcement Point via the NAA of this decision.

The **Policy Enforcement Point** (PEP) is the TNC element at the entry point to the network. Its tasks are to receive and pass on connection requests and execute the actions decided by the PDP.

As the entry point the PEP represents the first connection point to the network that is addressed. Incoming connection requests from an AR are passed directly to the PDP. After a PDP has taken its decision on the integrity of the AR, it informs the PEP, which then has to allow or prevent access to the network with its services on the basis of this decision.

According to the TNC specification, a PEP can be an independent computer system or integrated into the PDP or other network equipment. It is therefore possible to integrate the PEP directly into a VPN gateway or, in order to leave existing network structures untouched, in front of or behind this gateway.

3.3 Fields of Application

TNC's specifications have been kept general in order that it can be used as flexibly as possible in many applications. The two most important fields of application are presented below in brief.

- **Protection of the Intranet against Attacks from Outside**
  Through the expansion of a network connection, e.g. VPNs, it is possible with TNC to verify the integrity of the computer systems before access to the network in order to prevent this in the case of non-fulfilment of the security policy. Additionally, it is possible to bind access data to certain computer systems in order to prevent access by third-party computer systems with stolen access data.

- **Protection of the Intranet against Attacks from Inside**
  TNC supports 802.1x, a widespread method of authentication. By equipping all computer systems in the intranet with 802.1x supplicants that have been expanded with TNC functions it is possible to reliably analyse the own computer systems and those of guests with respect to their integrity, and therefore minimise possible dangers from compromised computer systems.

4 Alternative Approaches

Besides TNC there are further NAC approaches in existence. The most prominent representatives are Microsoft NAP and Cisco NAC, which are explained here in more detail. The alternative solutions, including those of Microsoft and Cisco, are – in contrast to the open TNC specification – proprietary and therefore not interoperable as a matter of principle (for more information see section 5).

4.1 Microsoft NAP

With "Microsoft Network Access Protection" (Microsoft NAP) Microsoft are developing their own NAC solution [Micr06a]. The intention is for Microsoft NAP to be available with the server version built up on Microsoft Vista. Client software is being developed for both Vista and Windows XP. Network access is controlled by means of existing technologies such as 802.1x and offers (amongst other things) support for VPNs. It is therefore largely hardware-independent. On the software side, software products from Microsoft are essential for use with the Network Policy Server (NPS) and the required clients.

4.2 Cisco NAC

Cisco Network Admission Control (Cisco NAC) is part of the "Self-Defending Network" strategy and is also one of the policy-based access control systems [Cisc04]. Here Cisco uses its own hardware entirely, i.e. special NAC-compatible hardware is required in the entire network, resulting in the enforced use of Cisco hardware. Cisco NAC is already available on the market.

4.3 Further Solutions

In addition to the three "major" solutions presented, there are many further approaches from firms such as Check Point, Juniper Networks, StillSecure, Symantec and Vernier Networks

5 Critical Consideration

Some aspects of the NAC concepts are discussed critically below. These include the trustworthiness of the measurement readings recorded, administration and – in particular – interoperability.

5.1 Trustworthiness of the Measurement Readings

The security of NAC solutions depends on the trustworthiness of the measurement readings. These must be correctly measured and transmitted without modification to the NAC server.

With today's systems there is no possibility of guaranteeing correct measurement of the system status and its correct transmission. If the hardware or operating system of a computer system has been compromised, the measurement readings must also be considered as being no longer trustworthy, as they can be influenced by the malware at any time. However, as the measured values are to be used to discover the lack of integrity, the permanent risk of unnoticed falsification gives rise to long-term mistrust with respect to the measured values. This was demonstrated recently at the Black Hat Conference 2007 using Cisco NAC. By means of a modified Cisco Trust Agent (CTA) it was possible at all times – irrespective of the computer status – to gain access to a NAC-protected network [Heis07].

In order to get round this paradox, TNC offers a certain level of protection against manipulation of the hardware and the possibility of signing and therefore securing the transmission of the measured values through its optional and direct support for the Trusted Platform Module (TPM). However, without trustworthy determination of the measured values the level of security reached by the use of TPM is still limited.

Only with the introduction of suitable security platforms, such as the Turaya security platform of the EMSCB project [Emsc07] is it also possible to reliably determine the measurement readings for all security components.

However, this problem does not represent a specific problem of NAC approaches, but a general problem of today's computer systems that can be solved through the future use of security platforms built up on Trusted Computing.

5.2 Administration

Policy-based approaches involve an increased administration effort not only during the planning, but also during the operation of the network. This applies in particular to heterogeneous networks, as rules have to be defined for all end points located in the network with every imaginable configuration. Furthermore, there is also a danger that if the rules are too strict this will produce further side-effects. If two companies stipulate a virus scanner that is not a general product, i.e. producer-independent, but require special virus scanners from different producers, this may lead to incompatibilities on the notebook of an employee who works at both firms.

A further important point is the theme of patch management. It must be determined how the data of the policies can be kept up-to-date in an optimum manner. For example, it must be known at all times which version number the current virus signature of a virus scanner has, whether the personal firewall used is up-to-date (i.e. free from known gaps in security) and what the status of the patch database of the operating system and applications being used is. This information must be provided by the producers of the individual components and transmitted to the network operator. A network operator is therefore not only dependent on the producers – who have to equip their software with IMC and IMV functions – when building up the networks, but also during network operation. Here new forms of cooperation need to be found and contractual aspects of liability clarified.

It also has to be clarified how the patches that are to be incorporated can be obtained and installed. It would be possible to have a central patch server within the firm or to purchase them directly from the producers. On the one hand a central patch server minimises data traffic with the Internet. On the other hand it is difficult to keep all patches up-to-date. In practice a combination of both possibilities would therefore be ideal.

Further problems are imaginable in changing environments. If for reasons of compatibility (with other programs) an organisation stipulates an obsolescent software version and another organisation a later version, it is not possible to fulfil both policies. Constant up and downgrading of the versions is either not acceptable due to the effort involved, or simply not possible.

5.3 Interoperability and Standardisation

In spite of their similar structures and in most cases commonly used basic technologies, all of the NAC solutions on the market and under development are mostly proprietary and not compatible with one another. This is an obstacle to the increased use of such solutions, as the firms who decide on a solution that is on the market today have no guarantee that the selected solution will assert itself on the market. Through the selection of the solutions of producers that dominate the market there is therefore a particularly significant risk of the formation of de facto standards which will squeeze other competitors out of the market.

Furthermore, computer systems that are used in frequently changing environments, for example by fieldworkers, involve additional expenditure. These devices have to be prepared for all imaginable solutions.

Since the middle of 2006 several different attempts have been made to guarantee the interoperability of various solutions. These efforts are explained and discussed in brief below:

- In September 2006 Cisco and Microsoft announced their support for each other's solution [Micr06b]. This announcement does not mean that there is any direct adaptation of the architectures, but mainly instead support for both technologies on the client side. This means that the clients of both producers support networks with both Cisco NAC and Microsoft NAP. On the network side the network operators still have to decide on one of the two solutions.

- Various producers of NAC products (note: not Cisco NAC) design their products so that they are compatible with several solutions (example: Complete NAC from StillSecure). Here there is usually a concentration on the three „major" solutions of Cisco NAC, Microsoft NAP and TNC. This results in a competitive disadvantage for the solutions of other producers.

- Microsoft has made the Statement of Health (SoH) protocol available to the Trusted Computing Group. This specifies SoH as an additional interface (IF-TNCCS-SOH) between the TNC client and the TNC server [Trus07a] [Trus07b]. First of all this step offers the TNC-protected networks which support the new interface the advantage that as a client on the part of the AR the NAP clients supplied with the Windows Vista/Longhorn Server can be used. On the other hand it remains to be seen to what extent both interfaces can be administered jointly. If the administration effort should increase substantially, the two interfaces will probably not be able to coexist. Furthermore, there has been no statement so far concerning how new versions of the SoH protocol will be developed (i.e. whether together with other providers or by Microsoft alone) and whether these protocols will be published as an open specification.

- The only effort at standardisation in the NAC sector is currently being undertaken by the IETF with the „Network Endpoint Assessment Working Group". At the beginning of May 2007 the second version of the „Overview and Requirements" paper appeared [Ietf07] for the „Network Endpoint Assessment" (NEA), in which amongst other items a reference model based on TNC, Cisco NAC and Microsoft NAP is described for concept formation. Members of this working group include Cisco and Symantec.

6 Conclusion

Within the framework of increasingly stronger networking within and between firms over unsecured networks, an increase in the trustworthiness of network communication is essential. NAC solutions such as the TNC specification of the Trusted Computing Group provide the opportunity to analyse end points with respect to their integrity, and therefore contribute to an increase in trustworthiness. In contrast to other, proprietary solution approaches, TNC has a major advantage due to its openness. As a result of this openness, TNC is bound neither to the hardware nor to the software of specific producers. This increases its acceptance and adaptation by all producers of system components and network technology, which represents an important factor in its success.

It should be borne in mind however that in all approaches the trustworthiness of the components is not sufficiently guaranteed without the use of secure operating system structures and that therefore the level of trustworthiness that can currently be attained is limited.

As TNC does not require specific hardware such as TPMs or special operating system structures and also supports existing network infrastructures (or builds on them), it can already be readily integrated into existing networks.

References

[Cisc04]   Cisco Systems GmbH, Die Evolution des Self-Defending Network, 2004http://www.cisco.com/global/ AT/pdfs/prospekte/Securtiy_CNAC_032004.pdf

[Emsc07]   Das EMSCB-Projekt, www.emscb.de

[Heis07]   News: Ciscos Netzwerkzugangskontrolle NAC ausgetrickst – März 2007 http://www.heise.de/ newsticker/meldung/mail/87663

[Hart05]   Michael Hartmann, Trusted Network Connect – Netzwerkhygiene auf hohem Niveau, 2005, Datenschutz und Datensicherheit (DuD)

[Ietf07]   Network Endpoint Assessment (NEA): Overview and Requirements, Mai 2007 http://www.ietf.org/ internet-drafts/draft-ietf-nea-requirements-02.txt

[JuPo06]   M. Jungbauer, N. Pohlmann: „Vertrauenswürdige Netzwerkverbindungen mit Trusted Computing – Sicher vernetzt?" IT-Sicherheit – Management und Praxis, DATAKONTEXT-Fachverlag, 6/2006

[Micr06a]   Microsoft Corporation, Network Access Protection – Homepage 2006http://www.microsoft.com/ technet/network/nap/default.mspx

[Micr06b]   Microsoft Corporation, Cisco and Microsoft Unveil Joint Architecture for NAC-NAP Interoperability, 2006 http://www.microsoft.com/presspass/press/2006/sep06/09-06SecStandardNACNAPPR.mspx

[Trus06]   Trusted Computing Group: Trusted Network connect Subgroup, 2006 https://www.trustedcomputing-group.org/groups/network

[Tru+06]   Trusted Computing Group, TCG Trusted Network Connect TNC Architecture for Interoperability, 2006 https://www.trustedcomputinggroup.org/specs/TNC/TNC_Architecture_v1_2_r4.pdf

[Trus07a]   Microsoft and Trusted Computing Group Announce Interoperability, Mai 2007https://www.trusted-computinggroup.org/news/press/TNC_NAP_interop_release_final_may_18.pdf

[Trus07b]   TCG TNC IF-TNCCS: Protocol Bindings for SoH, Mai 2007https://www.trustedcomputinggroup.org/ specs/TNC/IF-TNCCS-SOH_v1.0_r8.pdf

Technical Guidelines for Implementation and Utilization of RFID-based Systems

Cord Bartels · Harald Kelter

NXP Semiconductors
cord.bartels@nxp.com

German Federal Office for Information Security (BSI)
harald.kelter@bsi.bund.de

Abstract

The last years saw the introduction of contactless smartcard technology in prominent projects like ticketing for WC2006, nation-wide public transport solutions and electronic Passports. Currently major implementations of RFID in logistics and NFC-based ticketing and payment solutions are under preparation.

Especially above mentioned prominent projects have been confronted with significant public criticism. Influencial parts of the society and the authorities had and still have the perception that contactless chip technology and RFID may not be secure and mature. This leads to the following situation:

1. Uncertainties concerning public response and customer acceptance are hampering the introduction of RFID systems

2. The data protection authorities are proposing dedicated legal rules for RFID usage.

By launching the project „Technical Guidelines RFID" the German Federal Office for Information Security (BSI) suggests an approach that considers and fulfills the legitimate interest of all involved parties: Citizens resp. customers, service providers and suppliers of RFID systems.

This year BSI will issue 4 Technical Guidelines for usage of contactless chip technology and RFID in major application areas: Event Ticketing, Ticketing in Public Transport, NFC-based Ticketing and Logistics.

These Technical Guidelines will contain technical advice on how to implement a system in a functional, secure and economically viable way. Potential threats for the system owner and the users are depicted, discussed and countered by appropriate security measures. Remaining risks will be described. All proposed solutions are based on standards or open specifications.

Gaining the acceptance from all parties is the most important project goal. An open discussion and integration of all potential contributors is a corner stone of BSI's concept.

Therefore the Technical Guidelines are currently being drafted in close cooperations with leading companies from the respective application domains. These drafts have been discussed in dedicated expert workshops where all relevant groups –incl. the critics- were present. The final versions will include the comments gathered in these sessions.

In future BSI and probably also accredited evaluation facilities will offer a certification service / quality seal for implementations that follow the guidelines.

N. Pohlmann, H. Reimer, W. Schneider (Editors): Securing Electronic Business Processes, Vieweg (2007), 238-250

The Technical Guidelines will serve as comprehensive and neutral information source for German citizens, service providers and industry. This will build transparency and trust.

NXP Semiconductors is working the project on behalf of BSI.

1 Project Description

1.1 Tender Process and Project Setup

Germany's Federal Office for Information Security (BSI) defined the project "TR RFID" in order to generate Technical Guidelines for secure usage of RFID technology in 4 different application areas.

BSI ran a Europe-wide tender process in which some 40 bidders participated. NXP Semiconductors won the tender and is now working the Technical Guidelines. T-Systems has been selected as an additional partner. T-Systems covers the role of an evaluation entity. Their focus tasks are threat analysis, definition of counter measures and definition of remaining risks.

1.2 Project Targets

The project „TR RFID" which is currently being conducted by Germany's Federal Office for Information Security targets the following purposes:

1. Creation of Technical Guidelines for secure implementation and usage of RFID systems in four relevant application areas.

2. Active support for secure usage of RFID in Germany and beyond.

3. Conformity assessments by neutral entities and award of a „quality seal" for conforming implementations by BSI.

4. Consideration of international activities related to technical guidelines for RFID

    a. NIST: Guidelines for Securing Radio Frequency Identification Systems [NIST07]

    b. European commission: Activities for creation of European Guidelines for usage of RFID.

1.1 Target Audience

The Technical Guidelines shall serve as information source and toolkit to entities that are deploying, operating or using RFID Technology. Examples are:

1. System Vendors

2. System operators / service providers

3. Clients / Citizens and their representatives

2 Considerations for the Implementation of Technical Guidelines

2.1 Selection of relevant application areas

The Technical Guidelines shall serve as practical aid for implementation of RFID-based solutions in existing meaningful application areas. The following have been identified:

1. RFID-usage in eTicketing for Public Transport
2. RFID-usage in eTicketing for stadiums and events
3. NFC-based mobile eTicketing
4. RFID-usage in Logistics and Retail

All these application areas saw implementations of the RFID-technology over the last years and are currently preparing major roll-outs.

2.2 Consideration of specific user demands

The target audience of the Technical Guidelines includes entities that may have different expectations and views concerning the described solutions. As an example: In many cases end customers may be mainly interested in privacy protection whereas service providers will probably focus on economic viability and information security.

The Technical Guidelines name and consider the specific objectives for all relevant entities in the described application area.

2.3 Reference Solutions

In all selected application areas and especially in eTicketing there are a number of existing implementations. Some of these are being used as references for the definition of the Technical Guidelines. These reference systems serve as benchmarks for the proposed implementation schemes in order to come to solutions that are secure as well as market-oriented:

1. Existing and planned business processes, products and services of a reference implementation for the particular applications area must be supported.
2. The solution proposal must allow adaptation to specific user needs in a scalable and flexible way.
3. It must be possible to implement secure compliant solution with existing, openly available technologies and products.
4. The proposed solution must consider existing system implementations and provide integration scenarios for feasible existing components or a migration to new systems.

Table 1 provides an overview on the application areas that are currently covered by Technical Guidelines, the reference systems that have been used as benchmark and the supporting entities that provided information about these systems.

Table 1: Reference solutions and supporters

Application Area	Reference Solution	Supported by
eTicketing for Public Transport	VDV Kernapplikation	VDV (Association of German Transport Undertakings)
eTicketing for Events (Stadium, fairs, concerts, etc)	eTicketing FIFA WC2006	DFB (German football association), 1. FC Köln
NFC-based eTicketing	Touch & Travel	Deutsche Bahn AG, Vodafone Germany
Logistics and Retail	EPC Global	GS1, Metro AG

2.4 Open Specifications and Standards

In order to allow the market entry of all interested suppliers, all security measures and implementation proposals given in the Technical Guidelines will be based on open specifications or standards (e.g. [NIST07] and [BSI_05]) if possible.

2.5 Review and consulting by Experts

At the first glance some application areas seem to have the same requirements and usage processes for RFID technology. Examples are the domains of eTicketing in public transport and event ticketing. However, a closer look shows that there are a few significant differences in objectives, role model and some other boundary conditions for implementations.

It is important to understand these specialities and to consider them in the security evaluation and the proposition of security measures. This requires an expert knowledge that can only come from experts from the application domain.

For that reason BSI hosted specific workshops where the draft of an application specific guideline was reviewed and discussed in detail. Experts from service providers, data protection, customer organizations, industry and government participated in these workshops. The results from the discussions have been incorporated into the final versions of the Guidelines.

2.6 Transparency and Trust

The RFID-technology will only be accepted and successful if all entities that are getting in contact with it are convinced that their particular objectives and security targets are obeyed.

This project wants to help generating trust among the entities by providing a set of information –the Technical Guideline- that describes openly and fully transparent all relevant aspects of the implementation. This includes the security targets, the potential threats, the countermeasures that should be put in place and the risk, that may potentially remain after security measures have been applied.

The entities that participate in the RFID system (e.g. system operator, service provider, customer, etc) can review and decide if the proposed solution fit's their expectations. They can also use the guideline to set different priorities than described in current examples. As a result e.g. the protection level for a particular threat may be increased by applying a stronger counter measure.

Of course it is not enough to specify a system in a way that all involved parties are content. It has to be certain that the implementation into a real system is in line with the specification. In order to support this goal, the approach of BSI offers the following options:

1. Declaration of conformity by the system owner
2. Evaluation of the system implementation by an independent evaluator
3. Conformity certificates by BSI based on results of an independent evaluation.

2.7 Scope of System Considerations

RFID-based systems can be very complex. In most cases a lot of IT-components that have no direct relation to RFID are part of the system solution. On the other hand it is not sufficient to look only at media /tag and reader in order to safeguard the system security.

The Technical Guidelines need to consider all security aspects that are relevant for RFID in detail. These aspects are strongly depending on the application area and the specific implementation of the system solution. Therefore the Technical Guidelines are containing detailed descriptions of the application area, the relations operations processes (including e.g. sales channels and processes). Based on this information RFID-relevant uses cases are identified. Processes and use cases shall cover the entire life cycle of a RFID-media or RFID tag. These use cases are then used as basis for the identification of threats and a detailed system specific security assessment for RFID-related parts of the system. Figure 1 shows this approach for the example eTicketing in Public Transport.

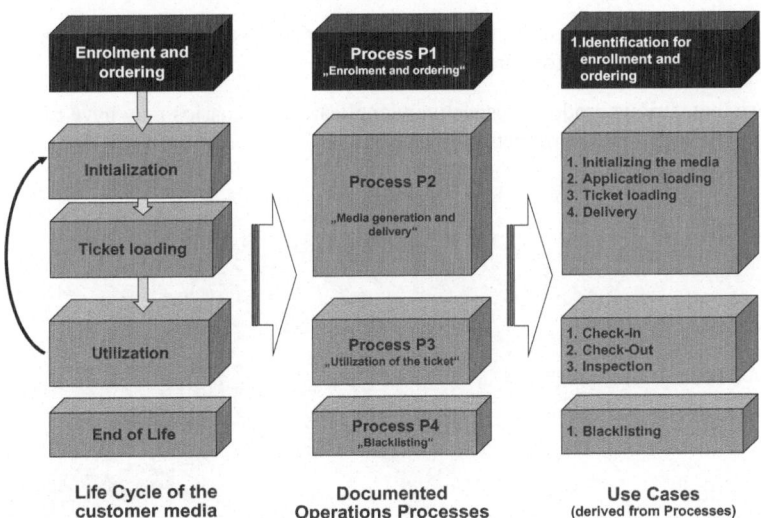

Figure 1: Example: Identification of RFID-relevant Use Cases for eTicketing

All other system components are only considered in a quite general way. Proposed safeguards just follow known standards of IT security.

This concept helps to focus on those system parts that are relevant for RFID and makes sure that all aspects of security are considered. On the other hand the Technical Guidelines leave space for individual and proprietary IT implementations (back-offices, sales systems, logistic systems, etc). This supports in particular the enhancement of existing systems with RFID-technology.

2.8 Scalability and Flexibility

The Technical Guidelines have to address security questions. In parallel economic viability must be achieved for all implementations based on these guidelines. This means that the following requirements have to be considered when laying down the concept of the guidelines:

1. It must be possible to scale systems in a way that cost and benefit fit together. This means in practice that e.g. safeguards must scale with the protection demand. Example: If only low cost products which have a relatively low protection demand are used, the safeguards should be designed accordingly. This may e.g. allow using low-cost media and -by that- reducing the cost of system implementation and operations.

2. The application areas that are selected for the Technical Guidelines include a huge range from small to nation-wide of even cross-border implementations. It is important that the concept that is used in the guidelines can be used for system solutions of any size and complexity.

3. In many cases the economic viability of a system solution can be reached much easier if cooperating with business partners is supported. This applies specifically for eTicketing applications where it can be very beneficial when media that are already available with the client (e.g. multi-application cards or NFC-enable phones) can be re-used for additional applications, products and related services.

The following figures provide examples from eTicketing for cross-system and cross-application utilization of customer media and infrastructure.

Figure 2 shows that various products respectively applications scenarios may have to be supported in one system. On top of that these products may be hosted by various types of RFID- media.

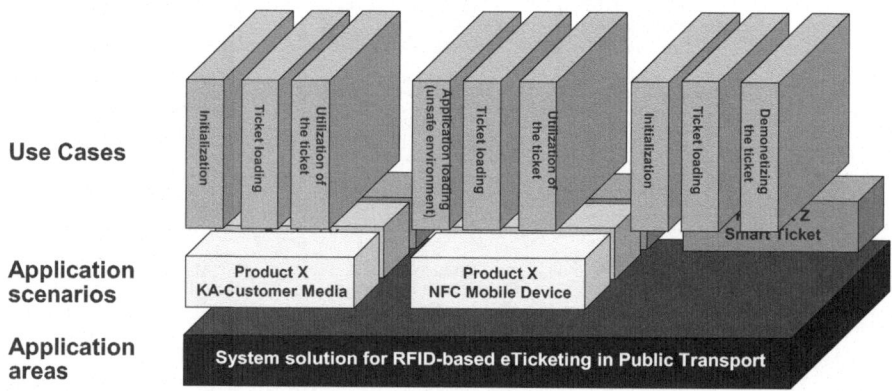

Figure 2: Example for application scenarios, and RFID-relevant use cases for eTicketing in PT

Figure 3 gives an example of a customer media for eTicketing that supports applications from two application areas.

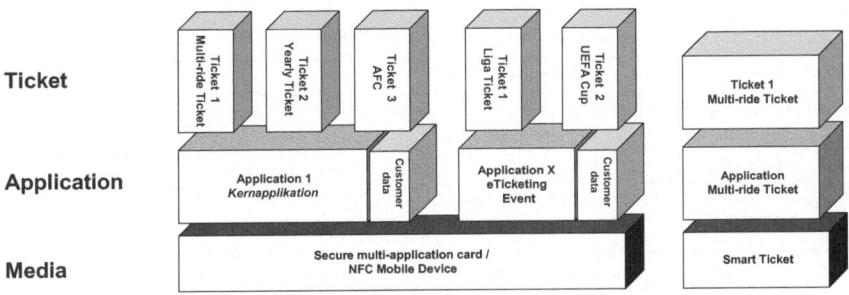

Figure 3: Hierarchical concept for media, applications and tickets in eTicketing

In order to address the mentioned requirements, the following concepts have been used for the Technical Guidelines:

1. A feasible role model and structure of key components (products, applications, and media) will be defined for every application area. These models support a granular and scalable approach.

2. The Technical Guideline has to provide security concepts that cover also combinations of application scenarios and media that are used on the same infrastructure. This is achieved by individual security assessments based on the RFID-relevant use cases.

3. Similar application areas (i.e. eTicketing), that provide a chance for cross-application partnerships, will be addressed by the respective Technical Guidelines with as many communality as possible. Especially the security assessment and the safeguards are using the same technical basis.

4. A special challenge occurs for partnerships across systems and applications from the system security. It must be ensured that the security of one system is not undermined by leakages coming from the other. Normally this requires extensive security assessments in both systems.

The Technical Guidelines are addressing this by introducing a scalable and transparent concept for applying safeguards to the identified threats, the "Protection Demand Categories". In total 3 classes from 1 (normal demand) to 3 (high demand) are in use. All safeguards are defined accordingly in 3 levels from normal protection strength to extended protection strength.

For every individual system implementation first of all the Protection Demand Category will be defined for every security target. This finding will be used for selecting the right level of the related safeguards.

This concept provides an easy way to install secure system cooperation. It has just to be made sure that the Protection Demand Categories of both systems match.

3 Structure of the Technical Guideline

Table 2 shows the structure of all Technical Guidelines that have been created so far.

Table 2: Structure of the Technical Guidelines

Chapter	Contents
Description of the application area	Description of the application area: Structure, services, special boundary conditions, etc
Products and services	Description of e.g. products, services and sales channels
Definitions	Role model, definition of terms
Introduction to the methodology	Introduction the concept and methods that are used for the security assessment.
General requirements	General requirements of involved parties, attention points, etc
Operations Processes	Description of Operations Processes that are relevant for the life cycle of the RFID media
Use Cases	Definition of RFID-relevant Uses Cases
Security assessment	Introduction IT-security. Definition of specific security targets, Protection Demand Categories and threats. Proposed safeguards
Definition of application scenarios	Definition of examples for application scenarios. These examples shall cover the entire range of relevant parameters that may occur in the specific application area. The user of the technical guideline may adapt these scenarios according to own needs.
Implementation proposal for the system solution	Generic system description incl. examples on how to perform a threat analysis and come to feasible safeguards for the system components.
Implementation proposal per application scenario	Examples for using the concept for security assessment in an application-specific way.

4 Explanation of the security concept

The Technical Guideline contains complete examples on how the security assessment should be used for specific application scenarios. These can be adapted to the requirements and boundary conditions of the specific system implementation. In order to explain this concept, this chapter provides a brief walkthrough for one case.

Figure 4 shows the concept for the security assessment that has been used in all Technical Guidelines.

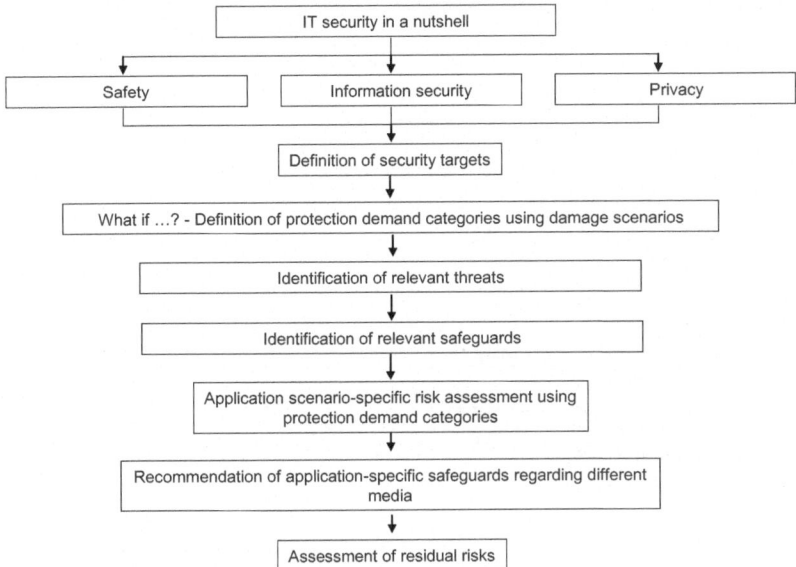

Figure 4: Concept of the security assessment

All considerations are based on the classical definition of security targets that is given in **Figure 5**.

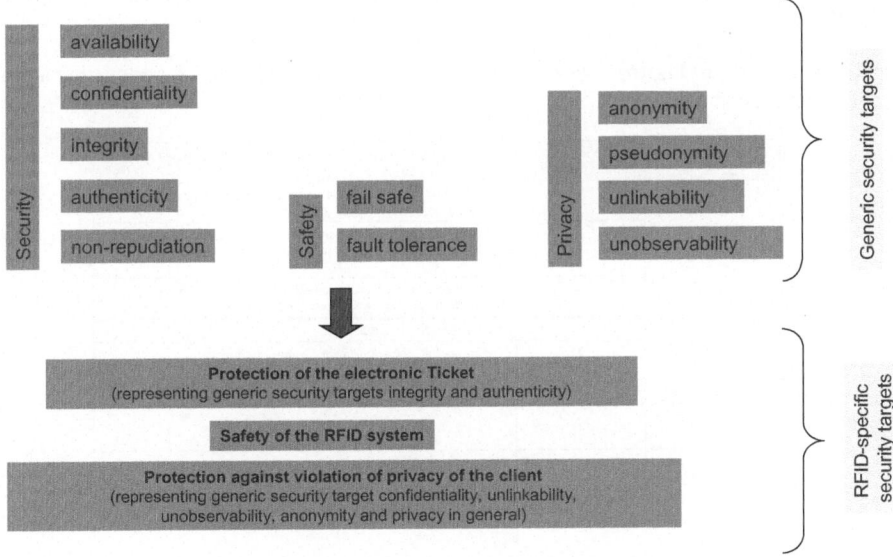

Figure 5: Generic security targets

As next step the specific security targets of all relevant parties from the application area are identified and laid down. These will be the basis for all further steps.

Figure 6 shows the security targets for the example "eTicketing for public Transport".

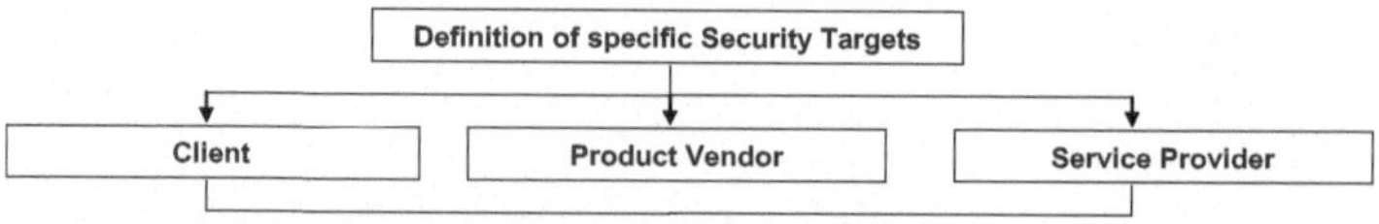

Ref-No.	Security Target	Client's targets	Product Vendor's targets	Service provider's targets
SF1	Technical compatibility	SKF1	SPF1	SDF1
SF2	Back-up solution in case of system malfunction	SKF2	SPF2	SDF2
SF3	Intuitive, user-friendly and fault-tolerant operation	SKF3	SPF3	SDF3
SI1	Protection of client-related data	SKI1, SDP1	SPI1, SPP1	SDI1, SDP1
SI2	Protection of the ticket	SKI2	SPI2	SDI2
SI3	Protection of anonymous data from operations	SKI3	SPI3	SDI3
SI4	Protection of billing data	SKI4, SDP2	SPI4, SPP2	SDI4, SDP2
SI5	Protection of applications and tickets	SKI5	SPI5	SDI5
SP3	Protection against profiling	SKP3		

Figure 6: Application-specific security targets for example eTicketing

In this example the client (i.e. the public transport passenger), the product vendor and the service provider (e.g. the railway company) are the relevant entities. The reference numbers given in the respective colums in **Figure 6** are pointing to the specific security targets of these entities. These are described in the Guideline as well.

The next step is shown in **Figure 7**. For every security target specific criteria for allocating a protection demand category are laid down.

Security target		Protection demand category	Criteria for allocation to a protection demand category
SF1	Technical compatibility	1	All System components are delivered by the same supplier. Supplier guarantees interoperability.
		2	System is build from components from a few, known suppliers. A System Integrator and the System Manager are safeguarding interoperability.
		3	Open system. No restrictions concerning suppliers wanted or allowed (e.g. purchasing via open tender process)
SF2	Back-up solution in case of system malfunction	1	Malfunction affects some clients.
		2	Malfunction affects a significant number of clients.
		3	Malfunction affects a huge number of clients.
SI4	Protection of billing data	1	Data is not available.
		2	Data is lost.
		3	Data was manipulated, abused, etc.
SP3	Protection against profiling	1	Client's reputation is affected.
		2	Client's social status is affected.
		3	Client gets injured or physically harmed.

Figure 7: Definition of Protection Demand Categories

It is important to understand that the criteria may lead to different results for different system components.

Example eTicketing:

1. SF2 will probably become Protection Demand Category 1 if the security target is looking at threats related to the customer media because usually only a few clients will be affected at the same time.

2. SF2 will probably become Protection Demand Category 2 or even 3 if the security target is looking at threats related to the readers or the key management system because this would probably affect a majority of customers in a station or a stadium.

The security assessment starts with the identification of relevant threats. The threats are determined for every security target as identified in **Figure 6**. In practice this threat analysis has to be carried out for every relevant system component (i.e. media/tag, reader, key management system, enrolment system, etc). **Figure 8** shows an example for the customer media for eTicketing. The relevant threat GT1 describes the unauthorized reading of ticket data. This affects the security targets S12 and SI5 and consequently –next to security targets of the other parties that are not shown in this example- also the specific security target SDI2 of the service provider.

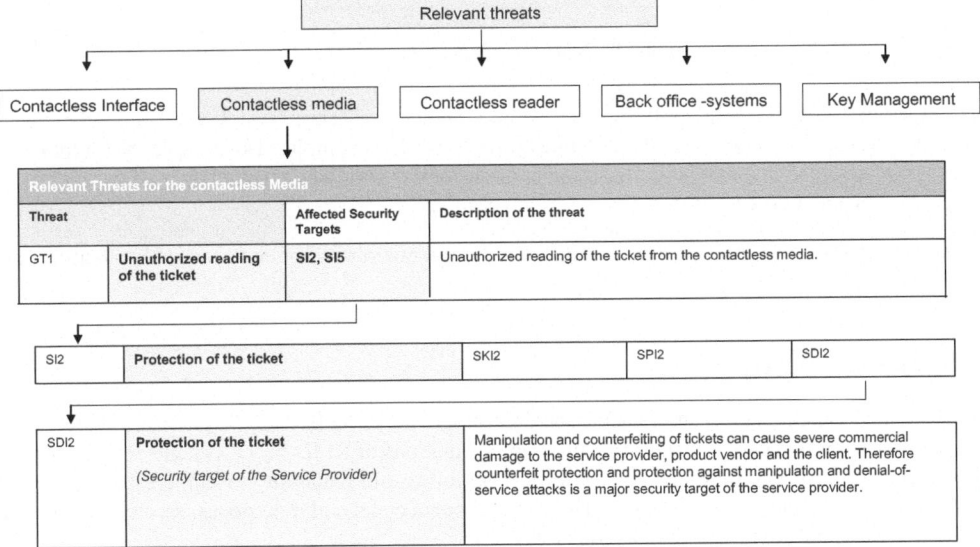

Figure 8: Identification of relevant threats

Threat GT1 can be countered by specific safeguards which are given in the Technical guideline. These safeguards are specific to the relevant system components. One of them –MT1- is shown in **Figure 9**.

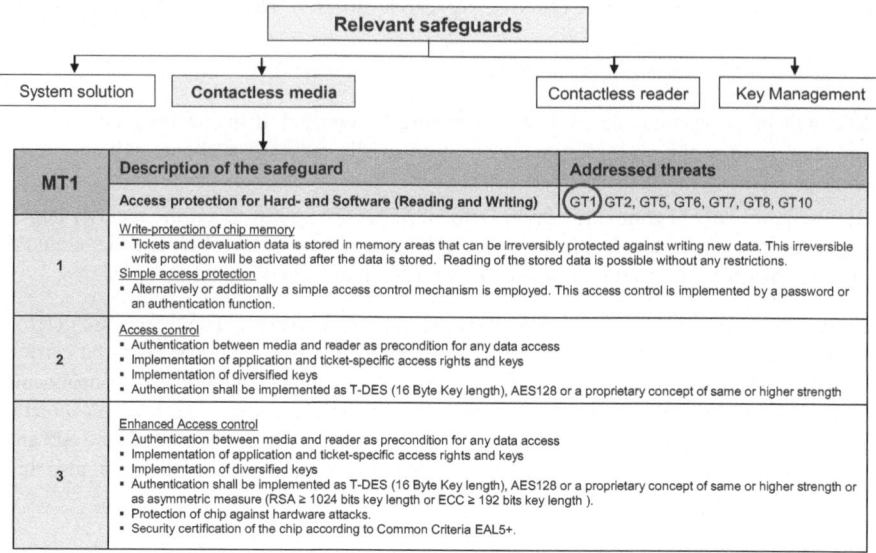

Figure 9: Proposed safeguard for threat GT1

MT1 describes measures that apply for the customer media in eTicketing in 3 levels that relate to the Protection Demand Categories as defined in **Figure 7**. For the example eTicketing level 1 applies because it was assumed that only a limited number of customers would be affected by malfunctions of the customer media at a time.

As the final step the residual risk that remains after the safeguard was applied needs to be identified and described.

5 Conclusion

The Technical Guidelines for Implementation and utilization of RFID-based Systems provide a comprehensive toolkit that can be used for secure implementations of RFID-based systems in a specific application area. This toolkit provides the necessary flexibility and scalability to support the entire range from local implementations to systems that span and connect several enterprises, service providers or even different applications and application areas.

The adaptation to the specific needs of a system can be carried out by the system integrator or the system operator.

All information that is relevant to the specific objectives and security targets of all involved parties is given in the technical guideline or has to be documented in the system specification. The benefits and also the residual risks of the solution are described in detail and fully transparent to all parties participating in the system. The optional evaluation and certification service provides additional confidence into the implemented solution. Clients, Service providers and System Operators will benefit from a high level of confidence and trust in the RFID-based system solution.

The Technical Guidelines will improve the customer acceptance of RFID-based systems and will help service providers and system operators to implement secure systems according to their needs in a cost-efficient way.

If required, additional Technical Guidelines for new application areas will be developed over time.

References

[BSI_04]   Britta Oertel, Michaela Wölk, Lorenz Hilty, Andreas Köhler, Harald Kelter, Markus Ullmann, Stefan Wittmann: RFID – Security Aspects and Prospective Applications of RFID Systems. In: http://www. bsi.de/fachthem/rfid/RIKCHA_englisch_Layout.pdf. Bundesamt für Sicherheit in der Information-stechnik (BSI), SecuMedia Verlag Ingelheim, 2004.

[BSI_05]   Bundesamt für Sicherheit in der Informationstechnik (BSI): BSI Standard 100-3 – Risk Analysis based on IT Grundschutz, Version 2.0. In: http://www.bsi.de/english/publications/bsi_standards/ standard_1003_e.pdf, 2005.

[NIST07]   Tom Karygiannis, Bernard Eydt, Greg Barber, Lynn Bunn, Ted Phillips: Guidelines for Securing Radio Frequency Identification (RFID) Systems. In: http://csrc.nist.gov/publications/nistpubs/800-98/SP800-98_RFID-2007.pdf, National Institute of Standards and Technology, 2007.

High Density Smart Cards: New Security Challenges and Applications

Helena Handschuh[1] · Elena Trichina[2]

[1]Spansion EMEA, 105 rue Anatole France
F-92684 Levallois-Perret, France
Helena.Handschuh@spansion.com

[2]Spansion International Inc., Willi-Brandt-Allee 4
D-81829 Munich, Germany
Elena.Trichina@spansion.com

Abstract

High Density cards represent the next generation of secure portable and removable tokens for the mobile and wireless markets. What makes these cards so particular is that, in addition to the traditional ISO 7816 interface to the Subscriber Identity Module, there are hundreds of megabytes of non-volatile Flash Memory available on the same token. This is a small revolution when compared to current EEPROM cards which allow for only a few hundreds of kilobytes of memory both for applications and data. Flash memory can be accessed either via a USB (Universal Serial Bus) or an MMC (MultiMediaCard) high speed interface. Therefore two different ecosystems co-exist on the same chip, which makes the security aspects of these cards particularly interesting and challenging.

In this paper we examine the specific security aspects of such high density cards and explain what potential security issues a manufacturer has to face and how he can overcome them. We discuss specifically how flash memory interacts with other memory on board, how it is organised, what it is used for. We contrast this approach with the memory architecture and organization of conventional smart cards such as those used in GSM and EMV payment applications. Since there is no ROM memory at all on these cards, we explain where the proprietary and highly sensitive operating system of the card manufacturer and the proprietary algorithms of the telecommunications operators will reside, how they can be protected and what the challenges are for initializing the whole system. Current secure smart card personalization techniques will have to be revisited and new procedures need to be put in place to securely instantiate this new generation of (SIM) cards. New algorithms for EEPROM emulation and anti-tearing (the fact that data is not lost when power is lost abruptly) need to be developped, one-time programmable areas need to be provided to boot-up securely. Initial program loader techniques and public key schemes are required for secure personalization. The high speed interface has to be secured and separated from access to the main memory on chip.

We also discuss security aspects of single die architectures, platform security for flash memory cards and security aspects of cryptographic hardware cores including the necessity to protect them against side-channel attacks as on traditional smart cards. These security features in turn allow considering high density cards for enhanced security applications such as secure data storage thanks to on-the-fly encryption at the megabyte rate, enterprise DRM, DRM agents for mobile TV, mobile payment and m-commerce. New applications which require huge storage capacity and sophisticated security features at the same time are enabled with this new generation of smart removable devices.

N. Pohlmann, H. Reimer, W. Schneider (Editors): Securing Electronic Business Processes, Vieweg (2007), 251-259

1 Introduction

High Density cards such as the new High-Capacity SIM cards (Subscriber Identity Module) [HC-SIM] represent the next generation of secure portable and removable tokens for the mobile and wireless markets. SIM cards are removable chip cards which are issued by a telecommunications operator and inserted into a GSM or 3G handset when a user buys a wireless telephone. They allow accessing the wireless network and provide the only billable link between the operator and the user. The chip contained in a SIM card typically holds a secure and proprietary operating system developed by the smart card manufacturer and some operator specific cryptographic algorithms for network authentication and for key generation for the voice/signalling data encryption algorithm residing in the handset. The card also holds a user-specific secret key K_i which is the operator's most valuable secret on board the chip.

Compared to traditional SIM cards, the new generation of high density cards, contain several **tens to hundreds of megabytes** of non-volatile Flash Memory where previous generations only had a few **tens to hundreds of kilobytes** of non-volatile ROM (Read-Only Memory) and EEPROM (Electrically Erasable Programmable ROM) memory. This is a small revolution in the smart card world. Another aspect which makes these cards so particular is that, in addition to the traditional ISO 7816 [ISO 7816] interface to the module running at 9600 bits per second, the flash memory can be accessed either via a USB (Universal Serial Bus) or an MMC (MultiMediaCard) high speed interface, respectively running at 12 and 26 Mbit/s. Therefore two different ecosystems co-exist on the same chip, which makes the security aspects of these cards particularly interesting and challenging.

1.1 Main Smart Card Characteristics

In a traditional smart card architecture, one finds the following elements: an 8-bit up to 32-bit processor, up to 512 KB of ROM which is used to store the proprietary operating system of the issuer, 64 to 256 KB of non-volatile EEPROM memory which allows to store some additional application data and secret keys, user data, or software patches to the operating system in ROM (such as operator specific cryptographic algorithms), and for high end cards up to 4KB of RAM memory in which the processor stores temporary data while running computations and applications.

In the new generation of high density cards, the memory features turn out to have significant differences. Basically, everything is replaced with Flash memory, which allows achieving much higher densities in a still reasonable die size. Typical smart cards have to fit within 25 mm², whereas high density cards are expected to fit into less than 80 mm², depending on how many additional megabytes of flash memory they contain. Table 1 below provides an overview of the main differences between a traditional smart card such as a SIM card or an EMV card used for banking applications, and a high-density card.

Table 1: Technical characteristics of traditional vs. high density cards

	Typical Card	High Density Card
Confidential Operating system	ROM (512 KB)	CodeFlash (512 KB NOR Flash)
Application Data, Secret Keys	EEPROM (256 KB)	Emulated EEPROM (128 KB NOR FLASH)
RAM	5 KB	24, 48, 64 KB
User Data	In EEPROM	4 to 256 MB (OR)NAND FLASH
Interface	ISO 9600 bit/s	+ USB, MMC High-speed protocols
Die Size	25 mm² in 0,13µm technology	Less than 80 mm² in 90nm technology

1.2 The Operating System

From a manufacturer's perspective, the main challenge is that there is no embedded ROM memory anymore since high density flash memory gradually replaces both ROM and EEPROM on board the chip. This means, that the proprietary and highly sensitive operating system of the card manufacturer and the proprietary algorithms of the telecommunications operators need to reside in non-volatile programmable memory. They cannot be permanently burnt onto the chip as is the case for ROM-based smart cards: in such cards, the smart card manufacturer writes and compiles the whole operating system and securely sends it to the chip manufacturer who subsequently masks it on silicon. The fact that the operating system can now be downloaded into the card after it has been manufactured and that it resides in programmable flash memory implies that new security measures have to be taken onboard the chip. The contents of the so called CodeFlash area need to be protected against unauthorized modification and reading. In other words, the memory needs to be scrambled at the hardware level so that its contents become physically unreadable when someone tries to hack into the system and probe individual memory bits, but it also has to be locked by a secure flash memory WP (Write Protection) mechanism which makes sure that certain areas of the memory can only be programmed and erased by authorized people.

On the positive side, the masking step which previously required about 6 months time can now be replaced by an initialization stage requiring a few seconds to a few minutes, depending on the size of the operating system.

The initialization process however has to be carefully thought through. Where transport keys and secret codes were sufficient to protect a masked chip from being intercepted and used by a malicious attacker in the previous world, new techniques allowing securely booting from the chip and securely installing the first operating system need to be put in place. Typically the chip is manufactured with a small piece of code already stored in flash memory called the initial program loader. This program loader recognises genuine operating systems which can be installed into memory by verifying a public key signature attached to such downloadable pieces of code. Once the operating system is in place, it erases the initial program loader and locks down the card into normal use.

This new initialization process presents a few challenges in itself. The chip manufacturer cannot personalize every smart card manufacturer's individual public key into the chip during the production phase; only one or a few such keys can be installed. This means that the first step is to download a smart card manufacturer's certificate securely into the chip. This certificate, issued by the chip manufacturer should contain the public key of the smart card manufacturer which subsequently allows checking the signature generated by the smart card manufacturer on his operating system before installation. In this setting, only one initial public key, namely the chip manufacturer's own public key, needs to be injected during the production phase.

The next interesting challenge is that the smart card manufacturer, and also the issuer may wish to have the high density card initialized by a third party, but may not wish to allow such third party to have access to the plaintext of the operating system. Therefore an additional encryption/decryption layer needs to be considered during initialization. The question then becomes how to securely transfer the decryption key into the chip, and at which stage. Solutions to this problem include using the chip's onboard symmetric or public key generation or key-exchange capacity, or initializing the chip with a set of secret keys which could be diversified into a smart card manufacturer specific encryption key by the card itself.

1.3 Emulated EEPROM and OTP areas

An additional new feature of high density cards is that they also replace traditional EEPROM with flash memory. Both of these are non-volatile programmable memories, but the main difference between them is that they are not read and programmed in the same way. EEPROM can be read, programmed and erased byte by byte, by providing the address of the byte to be written or erased and the value to be written. Flash can typically be programmed byte by byte (or page by page, a page being defined as a set of 16 or 32 consecutive bytes) but can only be erased by entire sectors (or blocks), meaning a huge set of consecutive bytes, typically 16 or 64 kilobytes at a time. This is of course much less flexible when we want to personalize or update secret keys of say 16 bytes into this memory. Therefore new algorithms for **EEPROM emulation** and **anti-tearing** (the fact that data is not lost when power is lost abruptly) need to be developed. Such algorithms generally start by copying some content into a new page in a sector and continue doing so until the whole sector is full. When the sector is full, a new one is created and partially written with information from the previous sector while the previous sector is fully erased. This comes of course with a performance penalty when compared to traditional EEPROM, but the timing of the full sector erase cycle can be controlled by the operating system and performed when time is not crucial.

One more characteristic is that flash memory is programmable and thus openly accessible. Therefore, OTP (One-Time-Programmable) and WP (Write Protection) sectors need to be defined which can only be written once and/or which allow locking some areas of the flash memory in order to simulate the behaviour of ROM. This is required for securely booting from a flash-based chip card. OTP mechanisms come in different flavours and include the possibility to have such OTP feature defined and controlled by the embedded software, i.e. the operating system. This means that we can define areas which have some OTP lock bits attached to them and which the operating system can overwrite if necessary. Some permanent OTP bits are also available which securely lock access to invisible parts of the memory in which master secrets are held, or in which unique chip-dependent numbers are written for traceability purposes.

2 Smart Card Platform Security

2.1 Single Die Architecture

A very important feature of high density cards is the fact that both the flash memory and the microprocessor and peripherals need to be securely implemented on a single die; having a two-die architecture automatically introduces a security weakness since an external bus needs to somehow link the two dies in a multi-chip package. This bus would be extraordinarily sensitive to probing attacks or more advanced attacks using focused ion beams or similar heavy equipment in order to read out the bus lines. Therefore, a single-die architecture is the preferred choice for a high density card. In Figure 1 below we provide an overview of a typical single-die high capacity SIM architecture. One notices that this chip inherits all traditional items form the smart card chip architecture together with some additional features. These include high speed protocol interfaces, a specific AES encryption engine for on-the-fly encryption capability of megabytes of data flash, a secure 32-bit ARM CPU, cryptographic accelerators for public key computations, symmetric encryption and hashing, and a random number generator. One can also find the previously mentioned OTP areas, and a huge Flash Memory array comprising CodeFlash, Emulated EEPROM and Data Flash altogether. The system RAM in this architecture is up to 64 KB and there is a dedicated CryptoRAM of up to 4KB.

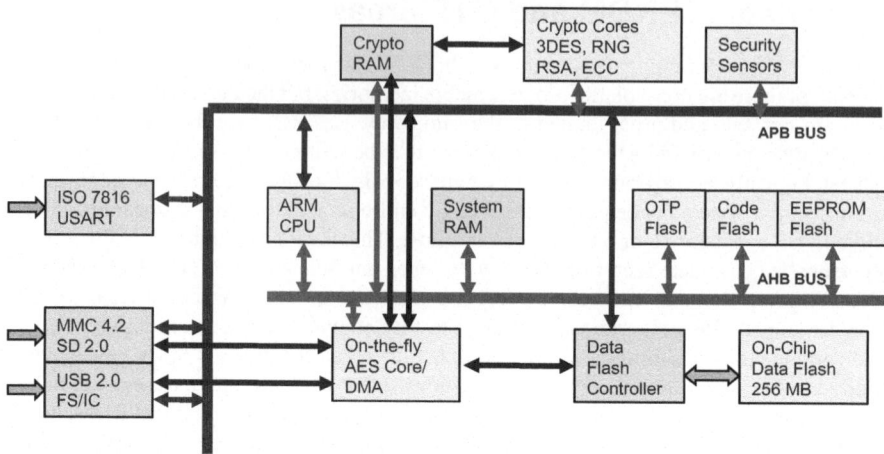

Figure 1. HD-SIM™ system architecture

As in traditional secure smart card design, one finds security sensors which allow protecting against fault attacks at the hardware level. They detect when the chip is being tampered with. Among the many other hardware security features inherited from smart card design we cite the following:

- An independent internal clock allows protecting against fault attacks on the clock frequency.
- The fact that several metal layers compose the design allows burying the most sensitive elements (such as the bus) and signals at the bottom of the chip.
- A protective metal shield is installed on top of the chip to detect when the chip is decapsulated and invasive attacks are performed.
- Several bus and memory scrambling mechanisms are implemented in order to defeat invasive attack strategies in which someone tries to read out the contents by using a probe-station or a focused ion beam.

2.2 Cryptographic Cores

Also inherited from traditional secure smart card principles are the security aspects of cryptographic hardware cores including the necessity to protect them against side-channel attacks as on traditional smart cards. This means that specific hardware design techniques and embedded software coding techniques need to be applied to provide actual tamper-resistance of these peripherals. Traditional cryptographic cores only provide certain confidentiality and authenticity functionalities such as encryption, signature computation and verification, message and entity authentication. But if these functionalities have to be securely implemented in hardware or in software, one has to add countermeasures into the design which make them immune to typical side-channel attacks such as power attacks, electromagnetic attacks, timing attacks, and fault attacks. There exists extensive literature on the topic and the question of how to achieve complete tamper-resistance is still a somewhat open and evolving topic. Every year new side-channel attacks are published and the designers need to make sure to come up with efficient and secure countermeasures.

Luckily, side-channel attacks on fielded devices are much more difficult than they appear on paper. The reasons for this are numerous. First it is very difficult to get open access to smart card devices to set-up template attacks in which one models the behaviour of the chip under known keys and plaintexts.

Second there are many concurrent countermeasures which make the analysis a very noisy process and require many more curves than expected. Third, published successful attacks are usually and mostly performed on open dedicated hardware designed for evaluation purposes. There is a step before one can attack real devices. Common criteria evaluation labs always perform white box analysis in which they have access to all the implementation details, including the countermeasures; this is not the case in an attack on a fielded device. Last but not least, smart cards are not the only link in the security chain; there are often back-end fraud detection systems which allow disabling a card as soon as required. Therefore tamper-resistance needs only equate the cost of fraud. As long as the gain in attacking the system is low, attackers will focus on more lucrative targets.

3 Applications

Advanced security features in turn allow considering high density cards for enhanced security applications such as secure data storage thanks to on-the-fly encryption at the megabyte rate, enterprise DRM, DRM agents for mobile TV, mobile payment and m-commerce. New applications which require large storage capacity and sophisticated security features at the same time are enabled with this new generation of smart removable devices.

Applications related to Digital Right Management schemes (DRM) are evolving with the mobile industry [OMA]. DRM refers to the technologies and processes that are applied to digital content to describe and identify it and to define, apply and enforce usage rules in a secure manner. Thus, along with copy prevention and access protection technologies, modern DRM includes definition of "rights" (e.g., play 10 times) specified using an XML-based rights expression language (REL), rights management information, and all usage rules. In addition, DRM defines protection mechanisms, authentication and authorisation protocols, and how protected content and rights objects are transported to devices using a number of transport mechanisms.

A (very simplified) scheme for applying DRM to protect digital content works as follows: the content is encrypted with a secret key and packaged in a DRM content format (DCF). During customer purchase, permissions and constraints are assigned to the content in the form of a rights object (RO) which is encrypted with the customer's public key. Among other things, RO contains a secret key to decrypt DCF. A customer receives the content and can start using it on a DRM-compliant device. To be DRM compliant, a device must contain a so-called DRM agent that executes all security functions and manages the RO on the device (extracts semantics of the REL, represents it as a state of RO and rules how the state is updated when content is consumed). The most important function of the DRM agent is to ensure that content is consumed according to the rights.

As one can see, for the DRM scheme to be truly robust, the DRM agent must reside in a tamper-resistant (trusted) environment. Obviously, high density smart (SIM) cards with high-speed interfaces provide such an environment.

In addition, high density smart cards can be used as "Secure Removable Media" tokens which may store, update and disable rights objects as well as store and play back DRM protected content. With a high density smart card as secure removable media, a mobile user can easily transfer content while still being able to consume it according to the rules defined by the RO on different devices. This not only reduces embedded memory and tamper-resistance requirements on the mobile device (thus, reduces its cost) but widens the OMA DRM area to various types of devices, e.g., home consumer electronics, and allows users to enjoy purchased DRM-protected content freely. The concept of secure removable media is popular with flash device manufacturers; and there are a number of standards, such as Secure

MMC and Trusted Flash already available. The advantage of high density SIM cards over other solutions is that they can be used natively with any GSM phone, and thus do not require dual card or dual slot phones.

Of course, the distribution of ring tones does not require such sophisticated mechanisms; and indeed, low-end mobile phones are most likely to support OMA DRM v.1 (which prevents content, and more importantly, the RO, from leaving the device, unless it is copied on a secure removable media after which access to this content on the device is not allowed).

There are (still emerging) interesting developments which extend the horizon of smart card applications and may even bring these devices into an "IT mainstream". To integrate the card tightly with other IT networks, smart card developers have been putting the main Internet protocol, TCP/IP, on prototype smart cards for some years in an attempt to allow smart card applications and the Internet to "speak the same language". But other pieces were missing: the communication speed was too slow; for, say, a PC to recognise a smart card, special software had to be loaded on the PC to "hook up" smart card readers; programming of Web servers was also required in order for them to recognise the card. With silicon vendors giving smart (SIM) cards large amount of memory and high speed (USB or MMC) interfaces and with smart card vendors putting TCP/IP on it, the SIM card is now equipped with technical capabilities which open up a number of new applications – from allowing the SIM card to communicate directly with online banks or Web merchants to securing the rights to download music on a mobile phone and store the rights objects (along with the MP3 file) on the SIM.

Such prototypes as the Network Card incorporate the USB protocol which is instantly recognised by computer desktops and sends and receives data at 12 Mbps. However, in 2006 the Network Card was still a prototype because chips with USB interface and large enough non-volatile random access programmable memory were not available on the market yet. This would allow, for example, a user to plug his card into a USB connector and then by-pass the un-trusted and vulnerable PC to link directly with his bank or with his enterprise Web sites. In fact, he may have these Web sites stored on his SIM card, as well as his credentials in order to avoid the log-in page.

Smart Card Web Server (SCWS) is one of the applications which can be hosted by high-density SIM cards. It is being standardised by OMA [OMA] and is defined as an HTTP server implemented in the smart card embedded in the mobile device (e.g., SIM, (U)SIM, UICC or R-UIM). It allows mobile network operators (MNO) to offer SIM card based services to their customers by using the widely deployed HTTP/1.1 protocol. The simplified architectural model is as follows. The smart card (SC) provides a local Web server for the user to browse using the phone (called ME or mobile equipment in specification documents) WAP browser. The Web server is accessible via a gateway (on the phone) which translates the TCP/IP protocol into a simplified local protocol between ME and SIM. One such protocol is already standardised by 3GPP, the so-called Bearer Independent Protocol; but it need not be only BIP. The HTTP requests and responses are then sent directly to the SCWS over the local ME-SC protocol.

The default home page (retrieved when typing a standardised URL) may contain a "personalised" content for an individual customer provided by the MNO. Among other things, it can contain links to customised phone books, FAQs, offers and promotions; it may also contain a list of favourite Web sites (e.g., customer's bank, local restaurants), customer's archive, portals of mobile commerce applications... The amount and variety of applications which can be enabled by the SCWS is limited only by imagination. The SCWS is capable of serving static and dynamic content to the Web browser in the phone; and it is also possible to provide data (such as queries and parameters) in the URL to access smart card entities or applications.

The property that it is possible for the SCWS to invoke smart card applications is extremely important (for example, currently there is no way for software on the mobile phone to address applications on a SIM card directly): by providing parameters to SC applications, the SCWS will return the application response. This property, when available, will benefit many applications which "span" over ME, SIM card, and the Internet, such as secure mobile commerce (see below) or DRM. To provide secure transport of data between the SC and ME and between ME and the rest of the world, HTTPS is also implemented on SCWS. The SCWS gateway, apart from the Protocol Adapter, contains an Access Control Policy Enforcer which filters HTTP(S) requests to smart card applications according to the access and filtering rules which are specified in the SC and read by the Enforcer during the communication session. For some client applications the SCWS port can be blocked by the rules; in this case the HTTP(S) message cannot reach the SCWS.

As SCWS opens up a possibility for the smart card and the Internet to speak the same language (via TCP/IP), multi-application smart cards will eventually become commonplace. HTTP provides a familiar "look and feel" interface to the applications stored in separate domains in the card's memory. With a large amount of programmable memory on board, the applications may vary – even from customer to customer. Potentially even OTA (over the air) downloads of digitally signed (by trusted authorities) applications by mobile subscribers themselves will become a reality. Initially, though, a more restrictive scenario of multi-application smart cards gets some traction, for example, in Japan, where mobile network operators led by DoCoMo allow subscribers to choose from a list of services to download to the smart cards embedded in their phones. The bank cards in Turkey combine loyalty programs and bank cards with some success and already roll out programs which involve numerous dual-interface smart cards. The technology is available, but the commercial or inter-industry relationships needed to make multi-applications happen are not there yet.

As card memory capacity and microcontroller capability grow, the number and complexity of applications on a SIM card will grow as well. Among potential front runners are DRM (see above), national electronic identity cards and mobile commerce and payment applications.

National electronic identity cards along with supported PKI infrastructures are at different stages of realisation in most of the EU countries and some of the Asia-Pacific countries. The card is a usual smart card which, apart from standard information and security marking, contains at least two Citizen Certificates: the authentication certificate of the cardholder and the signature certificate of the card holder. Private keys of the certificates are usually generated by the smart card itself; the related public keys are signed by the Certification Authority (some appropriate governmental body) during the registration phase, and the private keys never leave the card.

In some countries, for example, in Finland and Germany, a mobile subscription customer may request a national ID-compatible PKI-SIM card from a mobile network operator. As digital documents signed by such cards are legally valid (at least in Finland), the cards can be used for all mobile payment services and secure mobile commerce which require, apart from end-to-end security with strong customer authentication, also strong non-repudiation (binding parties to the transaction). What is missing, actually, is the services! To address this issue, paper [HHT07] describes an open mobile payment platform based on FINEID-enabled PKI_SIM card supported by a national PKI infrastructure. As a proof of concept implementation, the train ticket mobile commerce service was implemented and described in details. The implementation includes phone-based m-payment client which is responsible for product selection, creation of payment order, and all other communication with the merchant's Web gateway (or virtual POS). The FINEID PKI-SIM based applet communicates with the m-payment client and provides authentication services (certificate verification) and a digital signature of the transaction details. Simulation software for a virtual POS (or merchant) terminal and a bank was also created.

The developed platform is independent of the mobile network operator, service provider and payment institution and can be used by all of them. Such applications will benefit from high capacity SIM cards which can store on board digital certificate directories and certificate revocation lists (which can be periodically updated via "push" services – a possibility when SCWS will allow a SIM card to talk to the Internet freely). Using a national electronic ID card as an enabler for many services which require strong authentication inspires not only academics. In Malaysia, the "Mycad" citizen ID card is well-known for allowing to pack up to nine applications – from the cardholder's passport to his toll-collection account – into the same card.

Biometrics (and especially storing and processing of biometric information in the smart card rather than on centrally administrated databases/servers) provides yet another case for high capacity smart cards. Combined with sensor terminals (which can be even on the phone itself) biometry will provide strong identification of the end-user which may be further combined with strong authentication by PKI-SIM with national ID (or electronic passport). In general, biometrics in e-passports (facial images, fingerprints, iris scan, may be other biometrics) require large amounts of memory; high density smart cards can answer the challenge. It is not a futuristic scenario anymore: it is already being implemented on a trial basis, e.g., a "registered traveller" program at Schiphol Airport in the Netherlands, where an iris scan is stored on a (contactless) smart card.

The convergence of the Internet, mobile payment, electronic identity, DRM services and local area networks with a secure SIM card at the nexus is reasonable. As we have seen, the high-density card technology is already quite capable of playing a central role in safeguarding fixed, mobile and broadband wireless networks; what is mostly lacking is cooperation between all parties involved to overcome legislative and business issues.

4 Conclusion

High Density cards represent the next generation of secure portable and removable tokens for the mobile and wireless markets. In addition to standard smart card properties, they offer megabytes of storage space for user and application data, and for the smart card operating system itself. The new architecture introduces new challenges for securing the system which call for innovative solutions. New applications which require large storage capacity, sophisticated cryptographic functionalities and tamper-resistance at the same time are enabled with this new generation of smart removable devices.

References

[HC-SIM] Constantinou, A.: High Capacity SIMs : A White Paper. Informa Telecoms and Media. 2006. http://visionmobile.com/whitepapers.html

[ISO 7816] International Standards Organization, ISO 7816 Identification Cards – Integrated circuit(s) cards with contacts. Parts 1 to 4.

[HHT07] Hassinen, Marko, Hypponen, Konstantin, Trichina, Elena: Utilizing National Public-key Infrastructure in Mobile Payment Systems. In: Electron. Comm. Res. Appl., Elsevier, 2007, doi:10.1016/j.elerap.2007.03.006. Available online at www.sciencedirect.com

[OMA] http://www.openmobilealliance.org

ID Cards in Practice

Detlef Houdeau

Infineon Technologies AG
Munich Germany
Detlef.Houdeau@infineon.com

Abstract

This article focuses on electronic travel identity documents in international applications that are compliant with the worldwide ICAO 9303 standard and on registered travel programs to enable a "fast lane" process for frequent travellers. This article also discusses the standardization aspects and interoperability aspects similar to technical roll-out programs and its target user groups.

1 Travel Documents In Accordance with ICAO 9303

1.1 Implementation of ePassports in the European Union [1]

When the Council Regulation of the European Commission (EC) 2252/2004 met on December 13th 2004 on standards for security features and biometrics in passports and travel documents, the European Union adopted provisions governing the introduction of ePassports for all member states. With August 2006 as the latest date for this roll-out, these ePassports require a digital photo of the passport holder, along with other data such as name, date of birth, nationality etc., to be stored on a chip within the travel document. This electronic data is protected by security protocols called Basic Access Control (BAC) – a protocol being mandated by ICAO – through Passive Authentication (PA). By applying BAC to the first generation of electronic passport booklets through an inspection system, it then reads the printed MRZ (Machine Readable Zone) information from the data page which is the key to gaining access to data on the chip. At the same time, the stored data is not alterable since there is a unique digital signature from the issuing authority to confirm data authenticity (Passive Authentication).

In June 2006, this Council Regulation was followed by the EC decision to introduce two fingerprints as additional biometric identifiers in European member states' passports, which is required to be implemented no later than until June 2009. The fingerprints, which represent more sensitive biometrical data, are protected from unauthorized access through the advanced data protection protocol Extended Access Control (EAC). Moreover, EAC meets additional data protection requirements for the introduction of fingerprints in several ways. First, the EAC mechanism performs the BAC protocol and checks the authenticity of the chip and inspection systems by running the latest versions of PKI (Public Key Infrastructure) protocols on asymmetric key pairs. Then, for inspection, systems at various border control areas are required to be equipped with certificates from the issuing state as a precondition to gain the fingerprint access stored on the chip. The EAC also grants the most secure data encryption by establishing strong session keys during data transmission. Therefore, European citizens receive the highest possible security and privacy for their sensitive data stored on tamper-proof travel documents.

N. Pohlmann, H. Reimer, W. Schneider (Editors): Securing Electronic Business Processes, Vieweg (2007), 260-265

1.2 Market

In CY (calendar year) 2005, less than 10 countries started issuing ePassports. In CY 2006, the number of countries increased to 40 countries. By the end of CY 2007, it is expected that there will be 55 countries issuing ePassports. The annual run-rate in 2006 increased to 11 million pieces in the US, 24 – 34 million pieces in the Visa Waiver Program (VWP) Europe, 8 – 14 million pieces in VWP Asia and 6 – 10 million pieces in all non-VWP countries [3].

1.3 ICAO Framework [1]

The ICAO (International Civil Aviation Organization) has defined the use of contact-less chips, with biometric identification embedded in passport booklets to be based on proven technology standards within the smart card industry that are currently available. The final specifications were adopted in May 2005 on ICAO/PKI/BAC and in June 2006 on ICAO/PKI/EAC.

The ICAO TAG/MRTD drafts adopt specifications to design MRTDs with the specifications published by ICAO in Document 9303. The ICAO TAG/MRTD specifications comply with the ISO (International Organization for Standards). As illustrated in Figure 1, the latest version of document 9303 contains 3 Parts:

- Part 1, sixth edition provides specifications for Machine Readable Passports (MRPs)
- Part 2 provides specifications for Machine Readable Visas (MRVs) – no revision to the chip
- Part 3 provides specifications for various card format types of official travel identity documents (e.g. ID cards)

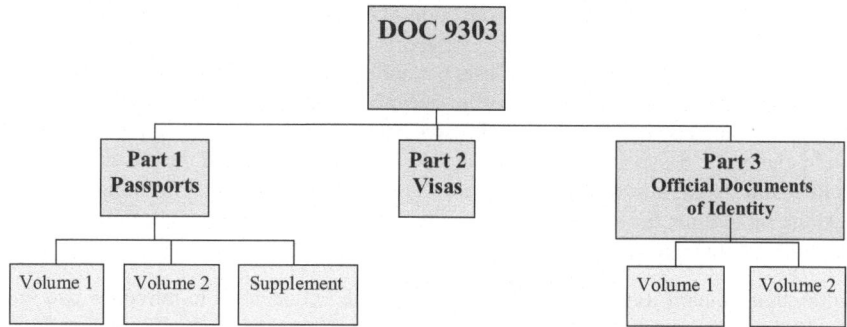

Figure 1: ICAO DOC 9303, overview

Passports are ruled within **3 volumes of document 9303 – part 1**:

- Part 1 – Volume 1 *Machine Readable Passports without Additional Data Storage*, 2005
- Part 1 – Volume 2 *Specifications for Electronically Enabled Passports (E-Passports) with Biometric Identification Capability*, 2005
- Part 1 – Supplement is entitled *Supplement to Doc9303-part 1-sixth edition*

To meet the challenge of deploying biometrics in MRTDs, ICAO assessed the following technical factors when selecting technologies and considering interoperability:

- Booklet, data format, contents, and storage requirements
- Durability and reliability specifications, and performance (speed, accuracy and related attributes)
- E-passport reader specification and data retrieval standards
- Data protection protocols
- Biometric data standards
- Compatibility with MRTD enrolment, renewal, border control, automated recognition systems
- Redundancy (ability to fall back to similar manual methods to support inspection of identifying the document holder when the machine-assisted technique fails)
- Backward compatibility (i.e., for use in environments without ePassport readers)

ICAO has endorsed face recognition as the mandatory biometric identifier and allows its member states to use fingerprint and/or iris recognition as optional biometrics. The storage format of those biometric data must be optimally compressed. Images are compressed using JPEG, JPEG2000 or WSQ formats, with the following minimal sizes for optimal matching rates:

- 15-20 Kbyte for a compressed face image of standardized format
- 10 Kbyte for a compressed fingerprint image of standardized format
- 30 Kbyte for a compressed iris image of standardized format

The image formats of biometric data are considered interoperable storage formats whereas feature formats are considered less reliable. Therefore, storage and the use of feature data formats are only allowed in addition to image data "at the discretion of the issuing state."

1.4 The Electronic Identity in the Future [1]

In addition to issuing the new generation of ePassports (since August 2006 was the official deadline for all member states of the EU), there are two additional programs in progress for all member states between the years 2007-2009:

1. Implementation of border control system based on the new technology at the "Schengen" borders
2. Implementation of fingerprint technology for data collection in the issuing offices

Implementing border control systems based on new technologies increase security with the identification and verification process using the biometric process. Implementing fingerprint technology for data collection is a pre-condition before the state can issue the second generation of ePassports.

Many governments of the EU member states believe that issuing a national electronic ID (eID) card, only after the second generation ePassport is issued, should be implemented. The eID card would use similar technology to the ePassport. There are two key reasons for this approach:

- Reuse of infrastructure, such as data capturing, PKI, IT-Network, border control systems, will be more efficient and cost effective
- By increasing security at border control inside the Schengen area, as ID cards will be more difficult to counterfeit

In Europe, about 20% of residents have the ePassports and about 80-90% of residents hold ID cards. In most of the member states, ID cards are mandatory. For travelling in Europe, the ID card is the typical and most popular travel document. Therefore, to increase security at borders the ePassport should be combined with the eID card for EU residents when the new border control process is required.

In the autumn of 2005, the EC published a recommendation for minimal security for programs such as the national eID card in its regulation 14351/2005. These travel programs are typically controlled by the Ministry of Interior (MoI) in each member states. The main three pillars of these programs are:

- Schengen Visa for foreigners who stay for a maximum 90 of days in Europe, according to the regulation 0269/2006; chip-less with biometric data, security print and MRZ-line, in an ID2 format, inside of a visa page of the foreigner's passport

- ePassport for European residents according to the regulation 14351/2005; chip-based with biometric data in an ID1 format

- Residence permits cards for foreigners who stay for extended periods in Europe, such as students, works and tourists, according to the regulation 1030/2002; chip- based with biometric data in an ID1 format (a new specification is in progress)

2 Registered Traveller Programs for "Fast Lane" Process

2.1 View from the Top [2]

The increasing number of passengers going through airports in Europe, North America and parts of Asia, in combination with an improvement in aviation security, calls for new automatic border procedures. Airlines require right-on-time departures, ground handlers need to assist frequent flyers in connections and transferring at airport hubs, and the border police continue to look for "the needle in the haystack." This "haystack" needs to be split into two parts – risk assessment, and focusing limited resources in the right programs. In the US, a program developed to establish common business rules and technical standards to create a permanent, interoperable and vendor-neutral RT Program – the Registered Traveller Interoperability Consortium (RTIC) – was developed over 18 months ago. This is a joint venture between the government (TSA) and the security industry, with focus on airport security. The EU Commission, meanwhile, published a tender in the autumn of 2006 on the technical, political and financial impact of such programs in the European Union under TREN/J2/114-2006.

2.2 Status of RT Programs

There are four pilots running in Europe, with Heathrow in the UK, Schiphol in the Netherlands, Fraport in Germany and Charles de Gaulle in France, which are all host airports. The main focus of these pilots is on the Schengen border and the exit/entry control process. In the US, six airports have introduced RT program with an expedited secure lane and a registered traveller card price of USD $100. The participating airports are Orlando, Los Angeles, Minneapolis-St.Paul, Boston, Washington Reagan National and George Bush Interconti-nental airport in Houston. The previous focus was on domestic flights. With the expanding of the CLEAR program, the Nexus program is designed to expedite the border clearance process for low-risk, pre-approved travellers into Canada and the US. One of the well-known programs in Asia would be run between the two mega-cities of Tokyo (Japan, specifically Narita International

Airport) and Seoul in South Korea (Incheon International Airport), one of the most frequently travelled routes in Asia.

2.3 RT Program Technologies

The preferred biometric technologies, as seen in the table 1 below, are iris and fingerprint template recognition. So far, the use of these technologies in RT programs is not compatible with the ICAO 9303 scheme for ePassports, EU regulations 2252/2004 or the US VISIT framework. Matching is done 1:1 and sometimes 1: many. Most programs have this process running in combination with a smart card as a secure token. Both contact-based (e.g. in US) and contact-less (e.g. in France) cards are used. Each program has its own data register combined with specific data content and scheme. Interoperability among biometrics, secure tokens and data registration is a goal, although current reality tells a different story. The total cycle for such automatic border control is 12-20 seconds.

Table 1: Overview on the Registered Traveller Programs in Europe, US and Asia. Source: [5].

Country	Program Title	Participating Countries	Biometrics	Smart card solution	Total cycle time
France	P.E.G.A.S.E.		Fingerprint	Yes	15 sec.
UK	miSense	Hong Kong, Dubai	Fingerprint, Iris	Yes	10-12 sec.
Netherlands	Saphire	Indonesia	Iris	Yes	12 sec.
Germany	ABG		Iris	No	20 sec.
USA	CLEAR/NEXUS	Canada	Fingerprint, Iris	Yes	t.b.d.
Japan	iPass	South Korea	Fingerprint	Yes	t.b.d.

2.4 Outlook [4]

The international interoperable and scalable architecture of an RT program, with a focus on logical data structure, overall security architecture, biometric technology, cross-border data exchange, and airport process realignment, are the keys in terming the citizen's acceptance of these programs. This includes adapting passenger flow, appropriately channelling, separating and sorting travellers, and correctly verifying their identity against strongly authenticated enrolment data. Boundary conditions include separate flows for EU and non-EU citizens, registered and non-registered persons, and increasing passenger clearing rates in the next two years. This comes at the exact time when the new generation A350 and A380 Airbus aircrafts, which allow up to three times the capacity of passengers compared to today's aircraft, is rolled out.

Typically 5 to 7% of passengers in each EU member state are frequent travellers with a business share for the airline of around 50%. This would be the potential user group and market for this application. In the US, there will be an increase in the number of airports participating in this program. The number of members will also grow.

3 Comparison between Travel Documents According to ICAO and Registered Traveller Programs

The following table gives a short view on both parallel programs:

Table 2: Comparison on the electronic travel documents, according the new international standard ICAO 9303 and the registered traveller program for automatic border control process (ABC)

Program	Electronic travel documents	Registered traveller program
Application standard	ICAO 9303	US: RTIC EU: t.b.d.
Biometrics	Face, Image Fingerprint, Image Iris: not in use Standard: ISO 19794	Face: not in use Fingerprint, Template Iris, Template Standard: t.b.d.
Logical data structure	ICAO 9303, LDS	US: RTIC, data structure EU: t.b.d.
Security Architecture	ICAO 9303, PKI, BAC (for Fingerprint EAC)	US: RTIC, security architecture EU: t.b.d.
Secure Token Interface	Contact-less (ISO 14443)	US: contact based EU: t.b.d.
User group	All travellers US: all borders EU: Schengen border	Frequent travellers US: domestic flights EU: inner EU flights
Lifetime secure token	Typical 10 years	Typical 1 year
Document format	ID3	ID1

The key difference between the electronic travel document, according ICAO 9303 and the registered traveller program is the biometric technology and the matching process.

In the ICAO framework is only an image of a face and in future the image of two index fingerprint stored. Only technology according ISO 19794 are in use. The border terminal need time to read the big data set and need times for converting in templates for the metric verification. The matching is running on the terminal (MoT). Beside the 1:1 verification of document and document holder are in future a check with the wanted-list and/or a check with the no-fly-list possible and required.

In the registered traveller programs are templates of fingerprints and/or templates of iris in use. The data size is smaller and the matching could be running on the card (MoC). This allows a speed process and can significant increase passenger clearing. Additional checks, like with the wanted-list and/or no-fly-list are not in the scope.

References

[1]   EUROSMART, position paper 2007, www.eurosmart.com

[2]   ID World magazine, July 2007, page 32-34

[3]   Keesing, Annual Report 2006

[4]   Silicon Trust, press release, 5th of July 2007, www.silicon-trust.com

[5]   Registered Traveller Forum, ID WORLD, Paris, France, 28th of February '07.
        see www.wisemedia.it

Large Scale Fingerprint Applications: Which Technology Should be Used?

Andreas M. Wolf

Cross Match Technologies GmbH
Unstrutweg 4, 07743 Jena, Germany
Andreas.Wolf@CrossMatch.com

Abstract

This paper wants to support parties deploying large scale fingerprint based systems. Several issues on how to select the technology that is the appropriate one for their needs are discussed and recommendations are given; with special emphasis to the application of standards to ensure "global" interoperability.

What technology is available today? What can be used for large scale projects? What is necessary for different parts of these projects?

In real world applications, especially in cost intensive applications with a long life span, what ID applications tend to be, the application requirements should determine the technology to be used. What technology is available to address the needs of all these applications and programs? Which requirements should be fulfilled? Which standards should be applied? Which standards exist at all? Are there experiences in the filed that could and should be reused? This paper gives an overview on existing fingerprint standards and characterizes existing large scale projects which include biometric fingerprint subsystems.

1 Introduction

Fingerprint scanners are used in large scale biometric systems for decades, in the so called AFIS systems (Automated Fingerprint Identification Systems). Widely accepted standards are in place for this application domain. Today, new applications with probably even more enrolled users and within even more heterogeneous environments enter the market that also deploy finger print scanners. Here, we want to discuss several aspects, especially, but not only considering standards in those ID technology projects. Beginning with an overview on important applications and projects, applicable standards (especially for the fingerprint domain) are cited, and requirements and recommendations are given, followed by a short assessment.

Access control protocol, IT security, and privacy protection aspects which also have very high importance in the context of large scale biometric applications are only sketched, but not considered in detail.

Any project definitions for large scale projects that plan to make use of fingerprint biometrics should probably consider the structure and size of the user group, interoperability, reliability of the overall system, and system security aspects. These aspects are analyzed in more detail later.

Cross Match Technologies is engaged in several international standardization groups organized below the roof of the International Standards Organisation (ISO), via DIN NIA-37 and INCITS M1 the

N. Pohlmann, H. Reimer, W. Schneider (Editors): Securing Electronic Business Processes, Vieweg (2007), 266-275

company sends delegates to ISO/IEC JTC1 SC37, the biometrics standardisation organization that is responsible for the definition of standards for which compliance is required, e.g., by the International Civil Aviation Organization (ICAO) recommendations for electronic Machine Readable Travel Documents (eMRTD).

2 Applications & Projects

Fingerprint devices that are available in the market include

- **Tenprinter:** Scanners that are intended to capture fingerprints for criminal booking stations, including rolled finger imprints. Booking stations provide input to AFIS systems. This input includes fingerprint images as well as biographic data.

- **Palmprinter**: Scanners that are intended to capture fingerprints and palmprints for criminal booking stations. Rolled prints of all fingers are usually captured, too.

- **ID flats** devices: Scanners which are able to capture images of four fingers at the same time. These scanners capture so called flat images, in contrast to systems that capture images of fingers rolled from nail to nail. ID flats scanners are also available in versions allowing to capture rolled prints.

- **Two-finger** scanners: This is a comparatively new scanner concept. Especially for applications where more than one fingerprint shall be captured at the same time due to efficiency or other reasons and larger scanners are too expensive two-finger devices can be used.

- **Single finger** scanners: Devices that capture one finger per step. Usually, this scanner type captures flat finger impressions, but there are also scanners that can capture rolled imprints. Single finger scanners are that class of devices people usually have in mind speaking on fingerprint scanners.

Physical principles that are used to capture fingerprint data include

- **Optical** scanners, typically applying the frustrated total reflection (FTR) principle. In these scanners the person to be fingerprinted has to put the finger on a prism and the image is taken by a camera. Other optical principles do not use a prism. Such scanners usually take images of the presented finger directly, in some of these systems no direct contact between finger and scanner is required. In high end criminal applications like AFIS only optical FTR scanners are used today.

- **Semiconductor** based technologies. This includes capacitive, thermal, and pressure sensitive devices. These scanners can capture flat imprints of a single finger or combine small image strips to an overall image of a finger in the case of the so called swipe scanners.

- **Other principles**. Other scanner principles are also available or in development. Examples are infrasound based devices.

In real world applications, especially in cost intensive applications with a long life span, like ID applications tend to be, the application requirements should determine the technology to be used. From physical access control systems cheap swipe sensors are well known. Obviously high quality optical scanners are more expensive, but the quality of images generated by them is superior. So for every application and every new use case a new compromise between quality and costs has to be found.

What are the most important large scale projects today where fingerprint scanners are involved? Some example projects that can be seen in the field are the following. This list may not be complete, but refers to some projects that have a certain importance for Europe as well as the USA.

- The meanwhile very common **Automated Fingerprint Identification Systems** (AFIS). AFIS systems are in place for more than ten years now. Paper card based fingerprint databases have been in use for more than a century. Following revenue figures presented by the market research institutions, business with and around AFIS systems is one quarter to one third of the overall biometrics revenues. AFIS technology is very mature today. The next generation of criminal fingerprint scanners to be introduced in the next few years will have optical resolutions of 1000 points per inch (ppi). This high resolution allows even the automated inspection of third level details of fingerprints like pores. Criminal AFIS systems have reached a global interoperability. AFIS operators maintain huge databases of tens or hundreds of millions of fingerprints. Standards to be applied in AFIS systems are in place for many years. Experiences from this application field should be reused whenever this is appropriate or should be used as a starting point for any large scale fingerprint based project. For AFIS systems, in most cases tenprinter and palmprinter devices are used.

- **Civil Background Checks**. Some countries not having a citizen register, run systems for, e.g., screening applicants for sensitive jobs that is based on fingerprints. Here, in many cases flat imprints of all ten fingers are captured and compared with the criminal AFIS databases of suspects. Obviously, as civil background check systems must connect with AFIS data, they must be able to provide fingerprint images fulfilling the AFIS requirements, especially on image quality. For background checks, ID flats scanners are usually deployed.

- **US-VISIT** program. In US-VISIT, from every foreigner entering the US a facial image and images of the two index fingers are captured. It is planned to extend the program to capture ten flat imprints and to improve the capturing of biometric data at the time of departure. Currently, in the program optical single finger scanners are used. For capturing ten flats, ID flats scanners are expected to be used.

- **Electronic Passports** are issued meanwhile by many countries, especially by all EU Member States and Visa Waiver countries. All electronic passports, following ICAO recommendations, must contain an electronically stored facial image of the passport holder, and they may contain electronically stored images of a secondary biometric modality. The secondary modality may be the two index finger images or the two iris images. The EU law requires fingerprint images to be stored in EU passports starting latest in 2009. These fingerprints will be access protected by a procedure called Extended Access Control (EAC) consisting of a set of cryptographic protocols ensuring the integrity of the passport as well as of the document reader device. Facial images do not need to be protected by access restrictions according to ICAO Doc 9303, but, however, it is best recommended practice to use Basic Access Control (BAC), a scheme where the access key can be derived from the data contained in the lower line of the Machine Readable Zone (MRZ) of a travel document.

- The **Schengen Information System II** (SIS II) is the common search system for collection and exchange of immigration and law enforcement information throughout the Schengen zone. This system allows participating countries to drop border controls between countries inside the zone. SIS, the former version, has been in place since 1995 and is currently moving toward SIS II, a biometric-based system. The Schengen zone now includes 15 States: Austria, Belgium, Denmark, Finland, France, Germany, Greece, Iceland, Italy, Luxembourg, the Netherlands, Norway, Portugal, Spain and Sweden. Slovakia, Slovenia, Estonia, Hungary, Latvia, Lithuania, Malta, Poland and Czech Republic are invited to join in the near future. The UK and Ireland are not full members of the Schengen zone, they maintain their own border controls. The biometric data in SIS II is based on ten flat fingerprints and on a facial image. It can be used for identity verification as well as for identification purposes.

- The **EU Visa Information System** (VIS) will enable consular authorities to share information on all visa requests for entry to the Schengen zone. The system will be interoperable among more than 3000 issuing posts for EU visas.

- The **Personal Identity Verification** (PIV, HSPD 12, FIPS 201). PIV will ensure that all contractors and employees of the US government with an ID card carrying secure credentials allowing a reliable verification of the identity of the holder of that card. This project is fully regulated by the US government. In HSPD (Homeland Security Presidential Directive) 12 is given a "Policy for a Common Identification Standard for Federal Employees and Contractors". All parts of this program are completely regulated by US standards and specifications. The user group of this project is huge but closed what allows total control of all applied equipment making the interoperability task much easier. For enrolment purposes, ten flat fingerprints are required. This data then is used, e.g., for background checks. On the issued access/ID cards only minutiae of two fingers are stored. For verification purposes, e.g., in systems for physical access control, the technical requirements to be fulfilled by the images provided by the fingerprint scanners have been relaxed compared to the enrolment, where AFIS quality is required.

- Upcoming **trusted traveller programs**. As not all countries issue or will issue electronic passports, and only a few will incorporate fingerprints in their documents, biometric registered traveller programs are in place or planned. These programs so far are isolated to certain airports, certain airlines or certain countries. Usually, there is no interoperability between these programs and therefore no mutual acceptance of enrolments, not only due to possible different political standpoints of the owners. As the access to fingerprints stemming from the passports is restricted by law, at least in the EU, additional systems based on fingerprints enrolled by volunteers might be useful. If such systems really shall speed up airport and airline processes, global interoperability would be required, technically seen. Of course, a common political understanding on the concept of the trusted traveller must also be reached. As the technical requirements are common to those of the global e-passport system, the same technical requirements should be addressed.

In the following, some of these applications shall be considered in more detail.

2.1 AFIS

AFIS stands for Automated Fingerprint Identification System. This is the domain of the biometrics industry generating the largest revenue compared with all other applications. AFIS systems are in place in many countries in the world, and some countries already introduce the third generation of devices. That is, this application domain is most mature among all applications that make use of biometric technology. This also includes that there is a series of internationally accepted and applied standards that ensure global comparability and interoperability of AFIS data. This is a feature which is widely used by police organizations all over the world.

The scanner equipment to be used by AFIS installations shall comply with the FBI Electronic Fingerprint Transmission Specification (EFTS) for all scanners, especially with the appendix F of this standard. The data format to be used for storage of fingerprint as well as biographic information is described in ANSI/NIST ITL 1-2007. For quality assurance of captured images many algorithms are available. The most popular one of them is the NIST Fingerprint Image Quality (NFIQ) methodology.

2.2 EU Visa Information System

The EU Council Decision of 8 June 2004 established the Visa Information System (VIS) (2004/512/EC). In this regulation a common technical platform together with SIS II is recommended. The Commission Decision of 22 September 2006 defined the technical specifications on the standards for biometric features related to the development of the Visa Information System (2006/648/EC). The CS-VIS systems of the Member States will be compatible and interoperable with live scan devices. They will be used at the national level, and are capable of capturing and segmenting up to ten flat individual fingerprints.

For the enrollment (Visa application) it is planned to use live scan devices for ten flat fingerprints, i.e., EFTS/F compliant scanners; for the verification side, that is, for border inspection systems, there are no specifications given so far.

VIS will enable consular authorities to share information on all visa requests for entry to the Schengen zone. This will prevent the practice known as "visa shopping" – when applicants rejected at one nation's office try to obtain visas at another nation's office. Even if an individual presents false biographic information, the biometric system will reveal that he or she already applied and was rejected at another office. The system will be interoperable among the more than 3000 Schengen visa issuing posts.

The VIS incorporates a facial image and ten flat fingerprints, as well as biographic information. The fingerprint data will be managed via the so called Biometric Matching System. The facial image is currently not be used for biometric identification, but this might change in the future.

VIS will handle more than 20 million visa requests annually, as well as 45 million requests to check the validity of issued visas. It may be assumed that the central VIS system will have to handle up to 70 million data sets very soon. This central system has to maintain a database which will be managed by a permanent EU management authority which will gather information from all Schengen countries. Member states will connect via their own national visa databases with the central system. Each visa application file will be stored for 5 years.

The project was first developed in 2004. Originally planned to be completed by the end of 2007, delays in establishing the legal basis for the program have pushed implementation into 2008. On June 18, 2007, the Justice and Home Affairs Council reached a political agreement on the legislative package on the VIS enabling the countries to use the database for visa issuance and verification of applicants and allowing the law enforcement authorities to consult the data under certain conditions, also considering data protection issues.

2.3 Electronic Passport

Over the last five years, the international community has placed a strong emphasis on improving standards to strengthen the reliability of travel documents. Perhaps the most well known of these initiatives has been the so-called e-passport, largely developed through a cooperative international effort of the International Standards Organisation (ISO) on request of the International Civil Aviation Organisation (ICAO). The purpose of a more secure biometrics based passport is to prevent passport fraud and terrorist travel by facilitating information sharing and identity verification. The e-passport is also meant to deter fraud by linking a person to one passport through the use of biometrics. The USA has adopted the new e-passport standards as a requirement of the US Visa Waiver Program (VWP), which specified that participating countries had to issue machine-readable e-Passports by October, 2005, followed by additional requirements one year later. The requirements to e-passports itself are defined by ICAO, a

UN organization representing more than 180 countries all over the world. As a matter of fact, the current developments are mainly driven by the US and the EU.

The EU requires that member states had to begin issuance of e-passports storing a facial image and an electronic copy of the Machine Readable Zones (MRZ) by August 2006, followed by the inclusion of fingerprints in e-Passports by June 2009.

The first instalment of technical specifications released by the European Commission was in February 2005, related to storing facial image data on a contactless chip protected by Basic Access Control (BAC) requiring the reading of the MRZ to unlock the data. The second set of specifications, issued in June 2006, require that the images of two fingerprints should be stored on the passport chip, protected by Extended Access Control (EAC). The use of fingerprints on the document is the key differentiator between the EU and other countries including the USA. EAC is a cryptographic protocol that prevents chip copying as well as unauthorized chip access.

The primary biometric identifier in all e-passports is the facial image of the holder, which is stored electronically in a format described in ISO/IEC 19794-5 and which is mandatory for all e-passports. Fingerprints are optional elements in the passports to be issued, but if a country decides to store them in the chip, it has been specified to store the two index fingers (as long as possible) in the image data format described in ISO/IEC 19794-4. The additional storage of template formats is optional.

The global e-passport system has the largest imaginable user group all over the world, potentially every passport holder. It is very likely that various inspection systems will be deployed in different countries. Data update during the passport validity period is not possible, because the chips are closed at the time of personalization of the passport.

The biometric interoperability of the data stored in the chips can be an issue if the data quality is not ensured in the enrollment and manufacturing process. For topics like template ageing and multi-biometric fusion including biographical data that can be read from a passport still some research is necessary.

It is recommended to use, at least for the enrollment of the fingerprint data, EFTS/F compliant equipment or scanners with properties as required in this standards. To ensure this, the ISO standard 19794-4 includes as an informative annex the EFTS/F requirements. The FBI does not certify single finger scanners to be compliant to EFTS/F, but currently the German Federal Office for Information Security (BSI) offers certifications according to the technical requirements taken from EFTS/F even for single finger scanners.

For border control processes (verification) there are no specifications available so far.

3 Standards

Where do the applicable standards come from? There are many national and international standardization bodies. The most important are: NIST, INCITS, FBI, ICAO, ISO, and CEN. In the following some of the most important standards are considered in more detail.

3.1 IAFIS-DOC-01078-7.1 CJIS-RS-0010

This standard is intended for criminal AFIS systems. IAFIS means Integrated Automated Fingerprint Identification System. In this standard, the Electronic Fingerprint Transmission Specification (EFTS) is published; the current version of this standard is V7.1. In the appendix F of this standard the IAFIS image quality specifications are given for palmprint and tenprint scanners, but unfortunately not for single finger scanners.

The FBI certifies scanners that comply with Appendix F requirements. A list of those scanners can be found in the Web at http://www.fbi.gov/hq/cjisd/iafis/cert.htm.

The German Federal Office for Information Security (BSI) also certifies compliance to the physical requirements defined in Appendix F. They do not limit the certification to scanner systems used in criminal application, but also certify single finger scanners.

3.2 FBI PIV specification 071006

This standard defines an image quality specification for single finger capture devices. It should be mentioned that the "primary application (of this standard) is to support subject authentication via one-to-one fingerprint matching in the United States government's Personal Identity Verification program". This standard has weaker requirements than EFTS Appendix F due to the different application case. The FBI also certifies scanners that comply with these requirements. See http://www.fbi.gov/hq/cjisd/iafis/cert. htm. This standard is intended to be used for fingerprint scanners that are used for verification purposes, not for identification and not for enrolment.

3.3 FIPS PUB 202-1

This standard defines the "Personal Identity Verification (PIV) of Federal Employees and Contractors". To this standard, there is the change notice 1 available. The standard defines the general framework for PIV, including biometric components.

3.4 NIST SP800-76-1

This standard defines the "Biometric Data Specification for Personal Identity Verification". It requires for enrolment data compliance to the EFTS Appendix F, for background checks the capturing of all ten fingers, rolled or flat, and for the storage on the PIV cards the capturing of the two flat index fingers, stored in minutiae template format. For verification applications compliance to the image quality specifications for single finger capture devices is required.

3.5 ANSI/NIST ITL 1-2007

This standard is published in a NIST special publication and contains the "American National Standard for Information Systems – Data Format for the Interchange of Fingerprint, Facial, & Other Biometric Information". In this standard all data formats are given that shall be used to ensure interoperability and exchangeability of captured biometric data. The standard has already been revised several times. Experiences applying the definitions and recommendations of this standard have been reused in many of the ISO standards of the 19794 standards family.

3.6 ISO/IEC 19794-2

This international standard on "Biometric Data Interchange Format: Finger Minutiae Data" also has a US version (ANSI INCITS 378-2004). The standard is applied in the Seafarers ID Cards and the plans for the Transport Workers ID Cards (TWIC) program.

3.7 ISO/IEC 19794-4

This international standard on "Biometric Data Interchange Formats: Finger Image Data" is used for electronic passports. In an informative annex, it refers to the EFTS/F specification of the FBI. The standard also has a US version (ANSI INCITS 381-2004).

3.8 ICAO Doc 9303

This is the key document for all machine readable travel documents including conventional as well as electronic passports, ID cards, and visas. It is referenced by ISO in the ISO/IEC 7501-1 standard. This ICAO document refers to ISO/IEC 19794-4 and contains all ICAO recommendations that shall be considered for travel documents. Fingerprint images are qualified as an optional feature as well as iris images, whereas the facial image is a mandatory feature for all electronic passports. If a country decides to use fingerprints, then the use of images is mandatory, templates can be additionally stored optionally. It is required to store images of the two index fingers. Requirements to inspection systems with respect to fingerprints are not given in this specification.

3.9 TC 224 WI 188:2005

This is a European standard specifying "Identification card systems – European Citizen Card – Part 2: Logical data structures and card services". This standard refers (considering the fingerprint) to ISO/IEC 19794-2 for the citizen card functions and to ICAO Doc 9303 for the travel document functions.

4 Requirements & Recommendations

Any project definition for large scale projects that plan to make us of fingerprint biometrics should consider the following aspects:

- Structure and size of the user group,
- Interoperability aspects,
- Reliability of the overall system, and
- Security aspects.

The user group can be open or closed, small or large (or something in between), there may be a need to enroll all persons, or the availability of fall-back authentication procedures. The size and the structure of a user group as well as the usage frequency have influences on the usability aspects that have to be considered. Can it be expected that in most cases experienced people use the system, or must it be that intuitive that anybody may use it without any training? The placement of a finger on a scanner might be considered to be a simple thing, but many project teams made the experiences that there a many different ways to misplace a finger on the scanner. Examples are putting the finger tips or the sides of the finger on the scanner, confusions of the left and right finger, or fear to put the finger on a scanner that is illuminated with red light due to an assumed similarity to a cooker. If older people of children have to be fingerprinted, a special treatment might be necessary. The throughput to be expected and required is also a factor of strong influence on the success of a project. Cheaper scanners often provide worse images than high quality devices, leading to higher false rejection rates (FRR). This can be addressed either by reducing the acceptance threshold, what would lead to higher false acceptance rates, a result that could be not acceptable in many cases, or by allowing some more trials, what would increase the time necessary per person.

Considering interoperability aspects it has to be determined if the planned system is monolithic considering scanners, feature extraction, and matching. Are there several systems or just one provider? Is the system controlled by one government or by a group of countries? Proprietary systems might have a better performance at the first look, but if a later extension has to be made this might be more complicated due to limited abilities of the one chosen technology provider. And, it might be intended not to allow monopoles at all. Furthermore, standards based biometric data, especially enrolment data, have a good chance of being usable for usage in successor systems. If all users have to be enrolled again, this is usually very expensive or not even feasible, and these costs can be avoided or at least limited. There might be a heterogeneous technological landscape, hopefully following all recommendations specified by applicable standards. It is possible that images or templates are intended to be stored. To ensure the highest possible level of interoperability two factors have to be taken into account. The first one is the technical interoperability which can be achieved by application of all relevant standards, especially considering data formats. The second factor is the performance interoperability which is determined mainly by the quality of the biometric data. The better the quality of the captured biometric data is, the better the performance of the system will be, considering false rejection as well as false access rates. Especially for enrolment data this statement is true. Data quality lost at the time of enrolment can never get back. So it is recommended to install quality assurance mechanisms especially for enrolment applications.

Reliability aspects should consider the usage frequency of the system (daily use, frequent use, infrequent use), an intended high throughput and/or high precision of the system, e.g., for border control or access control applications. The more infrequent a system is used the more ergonomic the application must be to give appropriate guidance to the customer. Bad guidance leads to inappropriate biometric data, something the system operator has to pay for with high false rejection rates. Furthermore, template ageing effects have to be considered if necessary. It may be assumed that during the ten years validity period of a passport the comparison performance will decrease. It is not known to which extent. But, fortunately, in the passport case it is exactly known how old the enrolment data and the person are. It is possible to use multi-modal technologies to get a fusion of different verifications, and to reach much better multi-modal results than those reachable with a single modality. This effect hopefully will be stronger than the template ageing effect. Generally spoken, it must be determined what can be done if an enrollment data update is not possible, and the planned validity of enrollment data should also be part of the consideration.

Some topics that should be in the focus of security aspect consideration for large scale biometric projects are spoof/liveliness/fake detection as well as general IT security aspects like data encryption, physical device protection, access restrictions for equipment that deals with biometric data, including databases. Not to forget data protection and privacy aspects. One of the most typical biometrics specific security aspects is the detection of fake or not living samples presented to the sensor, like gummy fingers, wood glue layers, or separated body parts. Such attacks to biometric systems always have to be considered, and possible impacts have to be analyzed especially for automated solutions, but also for semi-automated solutions, and sometimes even for staffed access control facilities. Data quality is not only important for the throughput of a system; image and/or template quality is essential for the overall security assessment of the entire system. People specifying a system that is based on fingerprints should also consider the differences between systems that rely on 1, 2, 4, 8, or 10 fingers, rolled or flat. Flat fingerprints fit for almost all needs in civil applications, but the distinctive power of four fingers is larger than that of one finger; and eight fingers can be captured in the same time as two fingers, providing much more, much more precise, and much more reliable data. This aspect is especially important for systems used in identification mode without a claimed identity given to the system.

To illustrate this with an example, the deployment of ID flats (i.e., four finger) scanners in border control systems has a lot of advantages compared with single finger scanners: Higher throughput, a lower false rejection rate, a lower failure to acquire rate, higher fake resistance, better usability. ID flats scanners are more expensive, but considering the overall system this might be superimposed by the positive effects.

5 Assessment

To give a short assessment at the end, the story is very short: **Garbage in = garbage out**. The higher the data quality of the captured data is, especially during enrolment, the better the system performance will be. Cheap solutions are almost never inexpensive. Cheaper technology may turn out to be suboptimal in terms of long-live cycle, recognition performance with respect to false acceptances as well as false rejections, and, probably most important, throughput of the overall system. Projects shall rely on applicable standards, but read them carefully before implementation. One should try to re-use experiences from similar projects that have been implemented before. It is useful to look ahead for a certain period, at least for 5, better for 10 years. It is always essential to consider privacy & data protection legislation, because user acceptance is one and probably the most important success criterion even for governmental projects.

References

[NIST]   National Institute for Standards and Technology. http://www.nist.gov

[FBI]   Federal Bureau of Investigations. http://www.fbi.gov

[CEN]   European Committee for Standardization. http://www.cen.eu

[BSI]   Bundesamt für Sicherheit in der Informationstechnik. http://www.bsi.bund.de/ zertifiz/tr/index.htm.

[ICAO]   International Civil Aviation Organization. http://mrtd.icao.int/

From the eCard-API-Framework Towards a Comprehensive eID-Framework for Europe

Detlef Hühnlein[1] · Manuel Bach[2]

[1]secunet Security Networks AG,
Sudetenstraße 16, 96247 Michelau, Germany
detlef.huehnlein@secunet.com

[2]Federal Office for Information Security (BSI)
Godesberger Allee 185-189, D-53175 Bonn, Germany
manuel.bach@bsi.bund.de

Abstract

The German eCard-strategy aims at harmonizing the various government projects which issue or use smart cards for authentication and signature purposes. Against this background the German government developed the eCard-API-Framework [eCard-TR] which aims at supporting arbitrary smart cards and facilitating the integration of them into various eID-applications. The present contribution provides a brief overview of the main features of the eCard-API-Framework, highlights current standardization efforts at CEN and ISO and provides an outlook how this approach might form the basis for a comprehensive eID-framework for Europe and beyond.

1 Introduction

The German eCard-strategy (cf. [Kowa07]) aims at harmonizing the various government projects, which issue or use smart cards for authentication and signature purposes. Within these projects there will be issued around 80 Million electronic health cards (eHC) [eHC] and in a second step about the same number of electronic ID (eID) cards which will comply to the forthcoming specification of the European Citizen Card standardized in [prCEN15480-1] and [prCEN15480-2]. These cards as well as all privately issued banking and signature cards shall smoothly interoperate with major public applications, like the German eTax-application (ELektronische STeuerERklärung, ELSTER) and various other eGovernment initiatives. As this comprises a very heterogeneous set of smart cards, this plan induces a major challenge for the related smart card middleware.

Against this background the Federal Office for Information Security (Bundesamt für Sicherheit in der Informationstechnik, BSI) developed a set of platform-independent interfaces - called the eCard-API-Framework [eCard-TR] - which aims at supporting arbitrary smart cards and facilitating the integration of them into existing and forthcoming eID-applications.

As there are similar requirements for handling electronic identities in other European countries, it is natural to think about applying the eCard-API-Framework for cross-border processes and in other countries as well.

N. Pohlmann, H. Reimer, W. Schneider (Editors): Securing Electronic Business Processes, Vieweg (2007), 276-286

The current paper provides a brief overview of the eCard-API-Framework (Section 2) and sketches possible path towards developing a comprehensive eID-framework for Europe and beyond (Section 3).

2 The eCard-API-Framework

This section provides a brief overview of the eCard-API-Framework as specified in [eCard-TR] and is structured as follows: Section 2.1 highlights the main features of the eCard-API-Framework. Section 2.2 provides an overview of the architecture of the framework. At the heart of the eCard-API-Framework are the Generic Card Services, which are addressed in Section 2.3. Finally Section 2.4 will provide an overview of possible deployment scenarios.

2.1 Main features

The main features of the eCard-API-Framework may be summarized as follows.

2.1.1 Truly generic card services

The eCard-API-Framework is build around a web-service based variant of the forthcoming [ISO24727-3]-interface. However instead of using the underlying so called "generic card interface" defined in [ISO24727-2], which in fact is – considering the range of existing and evolving European eID projects – neither generic nor sufficient, the eCard-API-Framework provides a generalization of both [ISO24727-2] and [ISO7816-15] which works with arbitrary smart cards, as the card-specific information is provided to the middleware in form of XML-based `CardInfo` files (cf. Section 2.3). These files allow to recognize the type of the card and map the generic [ISO24727-3]-calls to card-specific APDUs, even if – which is the case for most issued eID-cards – the card is not fully compliant to [ISO7816-15].

2.1.2 Platform-independent and scalable

As the eCard-API-Framework is a collection of web-service-interfaces, it is equally easy to support this interface in both Java- or .NET-based applications. Due to the web-service-interfaces it is furthermore trivially possible to scale from a local deployment on a single "client" machine to a fully distributed networked "server" environment. Hence it is possible to support not only the "Loyal-Stack" ([ISO24727-4], Section 5.2) but also the "Remote-Loyal-Stack" ([ISO24727-4], Section 5.4) and the "Remote-ICC-Stack" ([ISO24727-4], Section 5.6) using the same set of interfaces. Please refer to Section 2.4 for a more comprehensive discussion of possible deployment scenarios.

2.1.3 Support for and abstraction of various card terminal technologies

The eCard-API-Framework supports a wide range of existing and emerging card terminal technologies. Therefore it is possible to use local [PC/SC]-IFDs, networked [SICCT-v1.1]-terminals as well as proprietary RFID/MRTD-readers over the same interface. The Reader-Interface from a previous version of the eCard-API-Framework has recently been harmonized with the Card Transport Interface from the [Onom@topic]- project and has been included as "Interface-Device API" in [prCEN15480-3] and was recently submitted as contribution for [ISO24727-4].

2.1.4 Developer-friendly "high-level"-interfaces

While it is possible to use the very fine granular "low-level"-calls (e.g. for card services and other cryptographic functions) it is also possible to create and verify complex advanced electronic signatures in popular standard formats (e.g. XAdES or CMS) involving complex PKI-services with very simple API-calls. In a similar manner it is possible to perform complex card-to-card-authentication protocols with a single `Card2CardAuthenticate`-call with two parameters (`FromCard` and `ToCard`).

2.1.5 Aligned with major eID-standards and Microsoft's cryptographic architecture

In the design of the framework it was a major goal to align it with important eID- and related PKI-standards, such as [CEN14171], [CEN14890-2], [prCEN15480-1], [prCEN15480-2], [prCEN15480-3], [ETSI-101733], [ETSI-101903], [ETSI-102231], [ISO24727-1], [ISO24727-2], [ISO24727-3], [ISO24727-4], [OASIS-DSS], [PC/SC], [RFC2560], [RFC3161], [RFC3369], [SICCT-v1.1] and [XML-Enc]. Furthermore the framework was designed such that there are no negative interferences with Microsoft's cryptographic architecture [MS-CAPI] and the generic card services block neatly fits into the forthcoming Next Generation Cryptographic API [MS-CNG] and may be used to provide a truly generic "key storage provider".

2.1.6 May support higher Identity Management Layers

The eCard-API-Framework may form the basis for (federated) identity management solutions, like [CardSpace], [Higgins] and/or [Liberty]. As the eCard-API-Framework as well as all these approaches for (federated) identity management are built upon widely recognized web-service standards (WSDL etc.), it is possible to build a comprehensive eID-framework by combining the different layers (cf. Section 3).

2.2 Architecture

As depicted in Fig. 1 the eCard-API-Framework roughly consists of the following layers, whose functionality is briefly described in the following:

- Application-Layer
- Identity-Layer
- Authentication-Layer
- Terminal-Layer

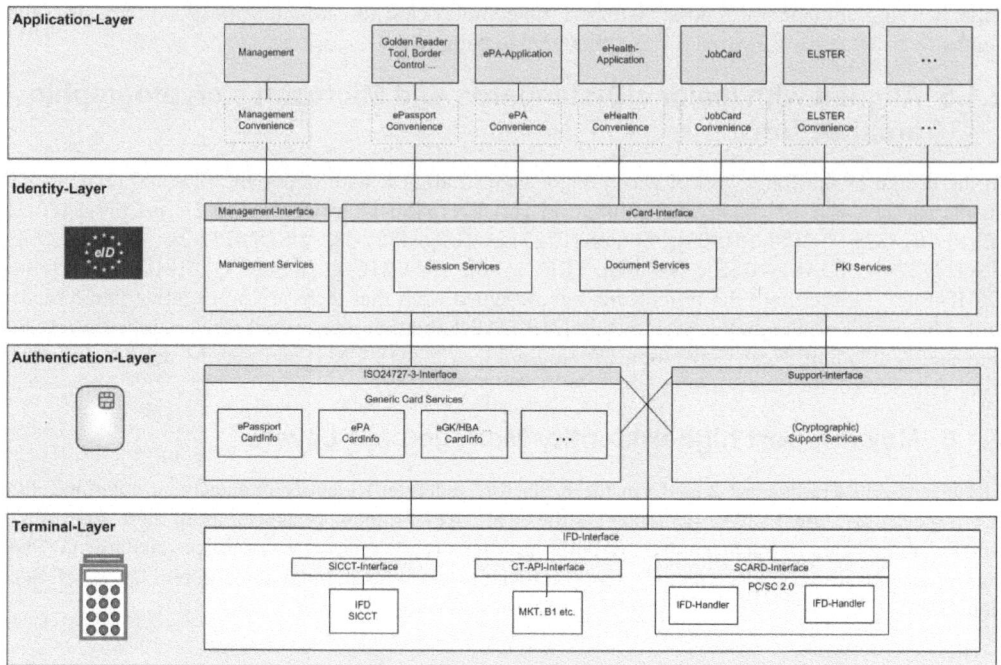

Fig. 1: eCard-API-Framework

2.2.1 Application-Layer

The Application-Layer may comprise different applications which access the services provided by the eCard-API-Framework in order to access eID-functions, secure electronic documents by means of (advanced) electronic signatures and/or encryption or to obtain access to some electronic service provided by a Service Provider.

2.2.2 Identity-Layer

The Identity-Layer provides functions to establish secure sessions (e.g. using [RFC2246]) and secure documents in various formats by means of (advanced) electronic signatures (e.g. according to [ETSI-101733] or [ETSI-101903]) and encryption (e.g. using [RFC3369] or [XML-Enc]). The functions for generating and verifying electronic signatures are closely aligned with the recently finalized standard [OASIS-DSS].

2.2.3 Authentication-Layer

The Authentication-Layer provides the basic authentication functionality using arbitrary smart cards. The authentication services are accessed using the "Service Access Interface" which is currently standardized in [ISO24727-3] and [prCEN15480-3]. In order to be able to use arbitrary identity tokens – especially tokens which fail to provide a standardized cryptographic information application according to [ISO7816-15] – the generic card services will use the XML-based `CardInfo`-structure introduced in [HüBa07] and currently discussed in CEN TC 224 WG 15 (cf. Section 2.3).

2.2.4 Terminal-Layer

The Terminal-Layer provides a homogeneous interface for arbitrary card terminals, which is currently standardized in [prCEN15480-3] and [ISO24727-4]. While the basic functions of this interface are similar to [PC/SC] this interface also allows to use more sophisticated interface devices according to [SICCT-v1.1] for example, which support multiple slots (for contact-based and/or contactless cards) as well as functional units (e.g. display, keypad, biometric sensors).

2.3 Generic Card Services

At the heart of the eCard-API-Framework is the generic card services block underneath the ISO24727-3-interface. This block is able to handle arbitrary eID-cards, since the necessary information to recognize some card type and to map the generic ISO24727-3-calls to card-specific APDUs is provided in an XML-based `CardInfo`-file, as outlined in Fig. 2.

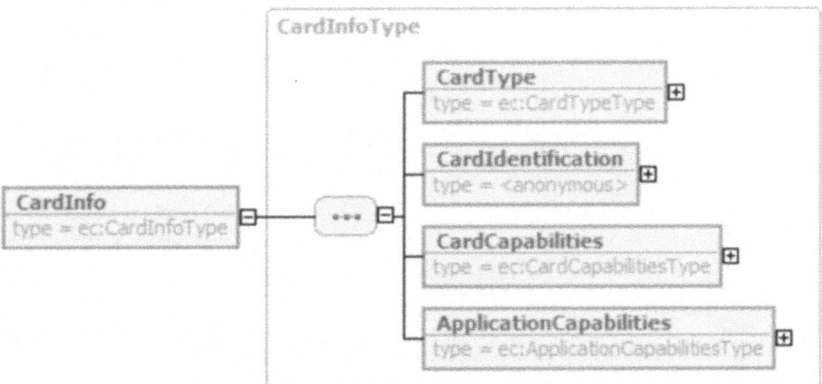

Fig. 2: `CardInfo`-Structure

The `CardInfo`-files roughly comprises of the following elements:

- `CardType` provides a unique identifier for the present (version of the) card type.
- `CardIdentification` comprises the necessary information to recognize the card type by a set of characteristic features (e.g. contents of the ATR/ATS and specific files on the card). As explained in Section 2.2 of [HüBa07] these data may be used to build a "decision tree" which is used to recognize the card type.
- `CardCapabilities` provide information concerning the capabilities of the specific card (e.g. basic card capabilities according to [ISO7816-4] as well as the cryptographic and biometric capabilities of the card).
- `ApplicationCapabilities` contain information concerning the personalization of the eID-card with card applications, keys (called Differential-Identities in [ISO24727-3]) and other data stored on the card (Data Structures for Interoperability (DSI) grouped in Data Sets according to [ISO24727-3]).

More details concerning these structures and the use of this information for mapping the generic [ISO24727-3]-calls to card-specific APDUs are provided in Section 2.3 of [HüBa07] and [eCard-TR].

2.4 Deployment Scenarios

In this section we briefly sketch some possible deployment scenarios of the eCard-API-Framework to demonstrate the flexibility of this approach.

2.4.1 Loyal-Stack

The simplest deployment scenario is the so called "Loyal-Stack" (cf. [ISO24727-4], Section 5.2) in which all layers of the eCard-API-Framework as depicted in Fig. 1 are deployed on a single machine. Besides the simplest case in which there is only one smart card accessed, the eCard-API-Framework is also able to handle more sophisticated Loyal-Stack scenarios. For example it is possible to support use cases for "Card-to-Card-Authentication" (cf. Fig. 3) or "Comfort Signature" (cf. Fig. 4), which are both (about to be) used in German eHealth-applications.

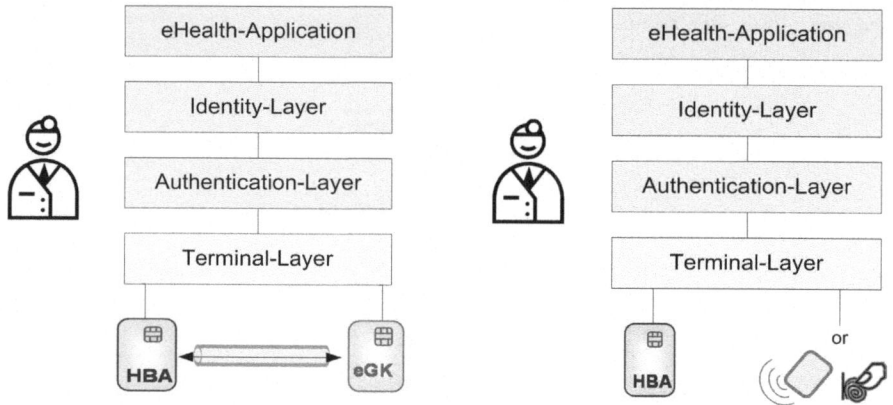

Fig. 3: Card-to-Card-Authentication   **Fig. 4:** Comfort Signature

For the first scenario it is possible to start an authentication between two cards using the complex protocols defined in [CEN14890-2] using a simple API call (`Card2CardAuthenticate`), which only specifies which keys on the cards are to be used for this authentication step.

For the sake of usability of qualified electronic signatures for power users (e.g. doctors, which issue hundreds of electronic prescriptions per day) it was proposed to activate the secure signature creation device once a day with the required six character signature PIN and perform the wilful act to sign a specific document with a more comfortable authentication mechanism in which a finger print is captured or an RFID-token is presented. Such deployment scenarios are easily supported by the eCard-API-Framework, because it is built around [ISO24727-3], which uses (an arbitrary Boolean combination of) Differential-Identities (DIDs) to protect resources.

2.4.2 Remote-Loyal-Stack

The "Remote-Loyal-Stack" (cf. [ISO24727-4], Section 5.4) is somewhat more complicated as the different layers are deployed on different machines. While the Identity-Layer (cf. Fig. 1) is present on both machines, the other layers may or may not be present depending on the specific application. In the following we will briefly highlight some popular examples for the "Remote-Loyal-Stack".

Similar to the local card-to-card-authentication (cf. Fig. 3) it is possible to perform the protocols defined in [CEN14890-2] over the internet. This may be used to handle electronic prescriptions in an internet-pharmacy (cf. Fig. 5) for example.

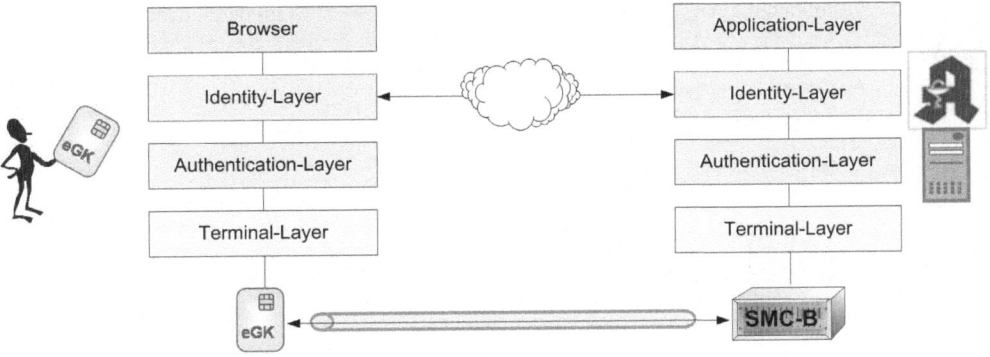

Fig. 5: Internet-Pharmacy

If an application (cf. Fig. 6) wants to sign invoices it does not necessarily need the Authentication- and Terminal-Layer on the local machine but it may use its Identity-Layer to connect to a Signature Server in order to get the invoices signed.

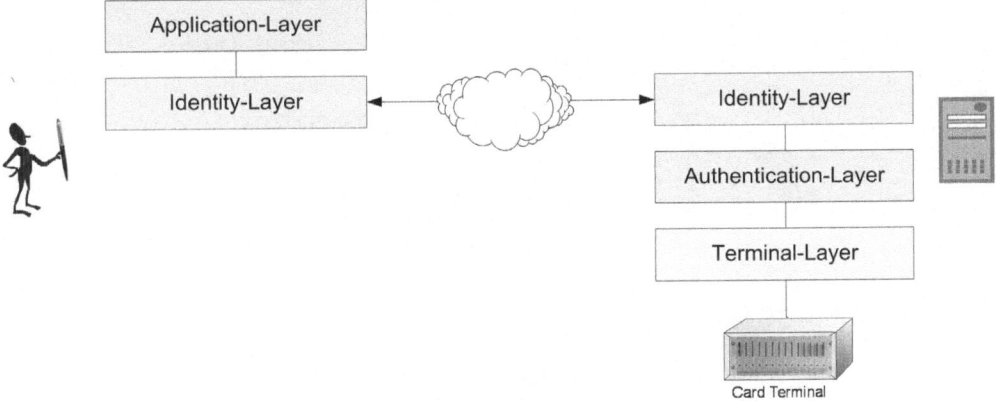

Fig. 6: Signature Server

On the other hand it would be possible to implement a "Remote-Loyal-Stack" scenario for web signing purposes (cf. Fig. 7) in which the application logic is present at the server but the signature generation uses the Authentication- and Terminal-Layer of the user's local machine.

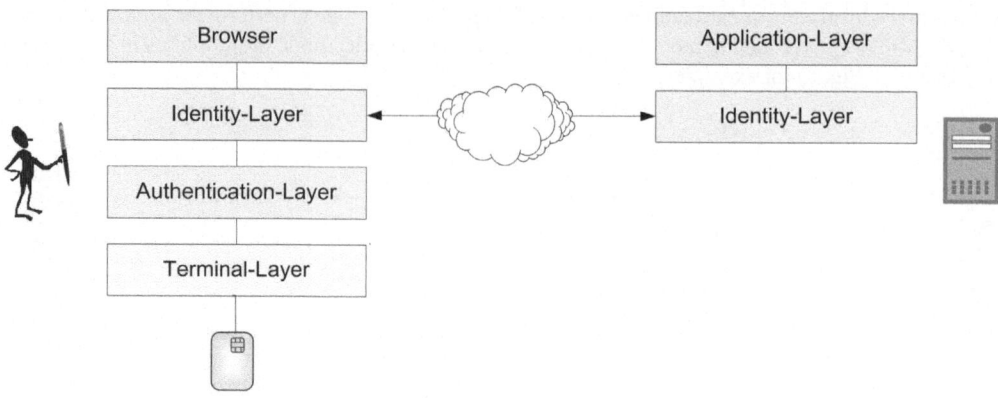

Fig. 7: Web-Signing

While it is not part of the current specification [eCard-TR] yet it would also be possible to support mobile signatures according to [ETSI-102204] (cf. Fig. 8) as an additional "Remote-Loyal-Stack" scenario with only moderate extensions.

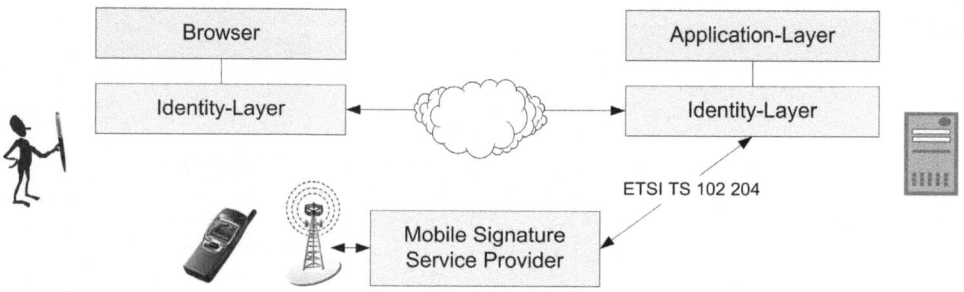

Fig. 8: Mobile Signature

2.4.3 Remote-ICC-Stack

Finally it is also possible to have the Authentication- and Terminal-Layer running on different machines in order to obtain the "Remote-ICC-Stack" (cf. [ISO24727-4], Section 5.6). As depicted in Fig. 8 this may be used for Card-Application Management Services (CAMS) as existing for the German eHealth-card [eHC].

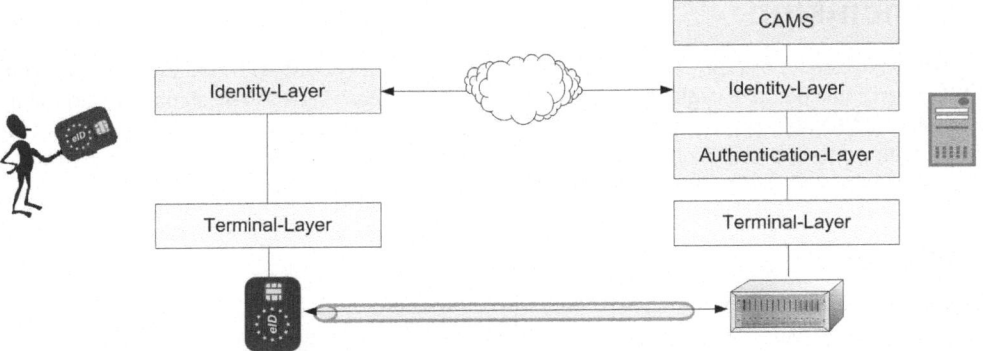

Fig. 9: Card-Application-Management

3 Towards a comprehensive eID-framework for Europe

With the Manchester Ministerial Declaration [ManDec05], the importance for interoperable identity management for our Information Society has been formally put on the political agenda of Europe and recognized as a priority and key enabling factor for our development. The declaration confirms the national autonomy in the issuance of national identity documents and electronic identities. Hence there may be various eIDs using different processes and technologies and hence providing different levels of trust. As the eIDs themselves may significantly differ from one domain to another, it is necessary to provide powerful middleware solutions, which are able to handle arbitrary eIDs and nevertheless provide common interfaces to applications which want to use eID services.

As the eCard-API-Framework [eCard-TR] is designed to support arbitrary smart cards (according to ISO/IEC 7816 and ISO/IEC 14443) and has been built on existing and emerging standards (cf. Section 2.1.5) it may well serve as starting point for the development of a comprehensive eID-framework for Europe. This development may be part of WP 5 of the forthcoming large scale eID-pilot "STORK" [Leym07]. While the eCard-API-Framework may obviously serve as reference architecture for the "Middleware Approach" in WP 5.2 it may also support the "Proxy Approach" in WP 5.3.

To use the eCard-API-Framework as basis for a common European eID-middleware it is only necessary to create appropriate `CardInfo`-files (cf. Fig. 2) for the smart card based eIDs in Europe (and provide appropriate drivers for non-smart-card-based eIDs if necessary).

In order to support the "Proxy Approach" the eCard-API-Framework may serve as basic web service framework for the secure exchange of data in cross border business processes. In this case the interoperability will entirely be handled by the Identity-Layer or an appropriate "Convenience Layer" on top of it. In order to support the different Identity-Management protocols used across Europe it may be necessary to provide different PlugIns for the generic `TC_API_Open`-function specified in [eCard-TR] and [ISO24727-4].

4 Conclusion

This paper provided a brief overview of the main features of the eCard-API-Framework [eCard-TR] and sketched some possible deployment scenarios. As this approach seems to be among the most comprehensive and flexible approaches for handling smart card based eIDs available today and is closely aligned with existing and emerging international standards we are confident that this approach will sooner or later provide a significant contribution to European eID-interoperability.

References

[CardSpace] Microsoft: *CardSpace*, via http://cardspace.netfx3.com/

[CEN14171] Comité européen de normalisation (CEN): *General guidelines for electronic signature verification*, CEN Workshop Agreement, May 2004, via ftp://ftp.cenorm.be/PUBLIC/CWAs/e-Europe/eSign/ cwa14171-00-2004-May.pdf

[CEN14890-2] Comité européen de normalisation (CEN): *Application Interface for smart cards used as Secure Signature Creation Devices – Part 2: Additional Services*, CEN Workshop Agreement, May 2004, via ftp://ftp.cenorm.be/PUBLIC/CWAs/e-Europe/eSign/cwa14890-02-2004-May.pdf

[prCEN15480-1] Comité européen de normalisation (CEN): *Identification card systems – European Citizen Card – Part 1: Physical, electrical and transport protocol characteristics*, prCEN/TS 15480-1, proposed Technical Standard, 2007

[prCEN15480-2] Comité européen de normalisation (CEN): *Identification card systems – European Citizen Card – Part 2: Logical data structures and card services*, prCEN/TS 15480-2, proposed Technical Standard, 2007

[prCEN15480-3] Comité européen de normalisation (CEN): *Identification card systems – European Citizen Card – Part 3: European Citizen Card Interoperability using an application interface*, prCEN/TS 15480-3, Working Draft, 2007

[eCard-TR] Federal Office for Information Security: *eCard-API-Framework – Technical Directive BSI 03112*, 2007

[eHC] gematik: *The Specification of the German Electronic Health Card eHC, Part 1: Commands, Algorithms and Functions of the COS Platform*, via http://www.gematik.de/upload/gematik_eGK_Specification_ Part1_e_V1_1_0_518.pdf, *Part 2: Applications and application-related Structures*, via http://www.gematik.de/upload/gematik_eGK_Specification_Part2_e_V1_1_1_516.pdf, *Part 3: Layout and Physical Properties*, vai http://www.gematik.de/upload/gematik_eGK_Specification_Part3_e_V1_1_0_514.pdf

[ETSI-101733] ETSI: *Electronic Signature Formats, Electronic Signatures and Infrastructures (ESI) – Technical Specification*, ETSI TS 101 733 V1.5.1, 2003-12, via http://portal.etsi.org/docbox/EC_Files/EC_Files/ ts_101733v010501p.pdf

[ETSI-101903] ETSI: *XML Advanced Electronic Signatures (XAdES)*, Technical Specification, TS 101 903 V1.2.2 (2004-04), via http://uri.etsi.org/01903/v1.2.2/ts_101903v010202p.pdf

[ETSI-102204] ETSI: *Mobile Signature Service - Web Service Interface*, Technical Specification TS 102 204 V1.1.4, via http://portal.etsi.org/docbox/EC_Files/EC_Files/ts_102204v010104p.pdf

[ETSI-102231] ETSI: *Provision of harmonized Trust Service Provider (TSP) status information*, Technical Specification TS 102 231, via http://portal.etsi.org/stfs/STF_HomePages/STF290/draft_ ts_102231v010201p&RGW.doc

[Higgins] Higgins Team: *Higgins Trust Framework Project Home*, via http://www.eclipse.org/higgins

[HüBa07] D. Hühnlein, M. Bach: *How to use ISO/IEC 24727-3 with arbitrary Smart Cards*, in C. Lambrinoudakis, G. Pernul, A.M. Tjoa (Eds.): TrustBus 2007, LNCS 4657, SS. 280–289, 2007

[ISO7816-4] ISO/IEC: *Identification cards – Integrated circuit cards – Part 4:Organization, security and commands for interchange*, ISO7816-4, Version 2005-01-15

[ISO7816-15] ISO/IEC: Information technology – Identification cards – Integrated circuit(s) cards with contacts – Part 15: Cryptographic information application, ISO/IEC 7816-15, 2003

[ISO24727-1] ISO/IEC: Identification Cards – Integrated Circuit Cards Programming In-terfaces – Part 1: Architecture, ISO/IEC 24727-1, Final Draft International Standard, 2006

[ISO24727-2] ISO/IEC: Identification Cards – Integrated Circuit Cards Programming In-terfaces – Part 2: Generic Card Interface, ISO/IEC 24727-3, Committee Draft, 2006

[ISO24727-3] ISO/IEC: Identification Cards – Integrated Circuit Cards Programming Interfaces – Part 3: Application Interface, ISO/IEC 24727-3, Committee Draft, 2006

[ISO24727-4] ISO/IEC: Identification Cards – Integrated Circuit Cards Programming Interface – Part 4: API Administration, ISO/IEC 24727-4, Working Draft, 2007

[Kowa07] B. Kowalski: *A survey of the eCard-Strategy of the German Federal Government*, (in German), Proceedings of BIOSIG 2007, GI Lecture Notes in Informatics, 2007

[Leym07] F. Leyman: *e-ID interoperability large scale pilot – STORK*, Talk at the EEMA-Conference "The European e-Identity Conference", Paris, June 2007

[Liberty] Liberty Alliance Project: *The Liberty Alliance*, via http://www.projectliberty.org/

[ManDec05] *Ministerial declaration*, approved unanimously on 24 November 2005, Manchester, United Kingdom, via http://archive.cabinetoffice.gov.uk/egov2005conference/documents/proceedings/pdf/051124declaration.pdf

[MS-CAPI] Microsoft Inc.: *Cryptography Reference (Microsoft CryptoAPI), Platform SDK: Security*, via http://msdn.microsoft.com/library/en-us/security/security/cryptography_reference.asp

[MS-CNG] Microsoft Inc.: *Cryptography API: Next Generation* http://msdn.microsoft.com/library/en-us/seccrypto/security/cryptography_api__next_generation.asp

[OASIS-DSS] OASIS: *Digital Signature Service Core Protocols, Elements, and Bindings*, Version 1.0, OASIS Standard, via http://docs.oasis-open.org/dss/v1.0/oasis-dss-core-spec-v1.0-os.pdf

[Onom@topic] M. Faher: *Onom@Topic – project*, presentation at Porvoo 9, May 2006, via http://porvoo9.gov.si/pdf/FRI_15_1000_MFaher_AXALTO_Porvoo9.pdf

[PC/SC] PC/SC Workgroup: *PC/SC Workgroup Specifications 1.0/2.0*, via http://pcscworkgroup.com

[RFC2246] T. Dierks, C. Allen: *The TLS Protocol – Version 1.0*, RFC2246, via http://www.ietf.org/rfc/rfc2246.txt

[RFC2560] M. Myers, R. Ankney, A. Malpani, S. Galperin, C. Adams: *X.509 Internet Public Key Infrastructure - Online Certificate Status Protocol – OCSP*, IETF RFC 2560, via http://www.ietf.org/rfc/rfc3161.txt

[RFC3161] C. Adams, P. Cain, D. Pinkas, R. Zuccherato: *Internet X.509 Public Key Infrastructure Time-Stamp Protocol (TSP)*. IETF RFC 3161, August 2001, via http://www.ietf.org/rfc/rfc3161.txt

[RFC3369] R. Housley: *Cryptographic Message Syntax (CMS)*, IETF RFC 3369., via http://www.ietf.org/rfc/rfc3369.txt

[SICCT-v1.1] TeleTrusT: *SICCT-Spezifikation*, Version 1.1.0, 2006-12-19, via http://www.teletrust.de/fileadmin/files/publikationen/Spezifikationen/SICCT_Spezifikation_1.10.pdf

[XML-Enc] W3C Recommendation: *XML Encryption Syntax and Processing*, 10. Dezember 2002, via http://www.w3.org/TR/xmlenc-core/

Making Digital Signatures Work across National Borders

Jon Ølnes[1] · Anette Andresen[2] · Leif Buene[2]
Olga Cerrato[1] · Håvard Grindheim[2]

[1]DNV Research & Innovation
Veritasveien 1, N-1322 Høvik, Norway
{jon.olnes | olga.troshkova.cerrato}@dnv.com

[2]DNV Industry
Veritasveien 1, N-1322 Høvik, Norway
{anette.andresen | leif.buene | havard.grindheim}@dnv.com

Abstract

Requirements for use of advanced electronic (i.e. digital) signatures are increasingly being raised. Today, the market for PKI-based electronic IDs (eID) is almost exclusively national, leaving international interoperability as a major issue. The main problem is not technical validation of eIDs and signatures, but rather how to assess and manage the risk related to their acceptance. This paper introduces a Validation Authority (VA) as a new, trusted role, providing the receiver of a digitally signed document with a single trust anchor. The VA provides one agreement and thus one liable party for validation of signatures, a single point of integration, and quality assessment of eIDs and signatures. Thus, the receiver is able to accept any digital signature with an assessed risk.

1 Introduction

Digital signature based on public key cryptography is the only available technology that fulfils the requirements for advanced electronic signatures as laid down in the EU Directive on electronic signatures [EU]; thus we use the term digital signature in this paper. A digital signature is supported by an electronic ID (eID) issued by a CA (Certificate Authority) in a PKI (Public Key Infrastructure). The eID market is primarily national. This causes serious problems when there is a need to exchange digitally signed documents across national borders. In Europe, electronic invoicing and electronic public procurement are two examples of activities that by necessity must work across national borders, and that also require digital signatures.

The ultimate interoperability requirements can be stated as:

- An eID holder shall be able to use the eID to sign a document towards any counterpart, even internationally. The eID holder independently selects the eID to use.
- The receiver (relying party, RP) of a signed document shall be able to accept signatures from all counterparts, regardless of the eID used by the counterpart. In an open market, the RP has no influence on a counterpart's selection of eID.

N. Pohlmann, H. Reimer, W. Schneider (Editors): Securing Electronic Business Processes, Vieweg (2007), 287-296

- A third party, receiving a document signed by other parties, shall be able to verify the signatures no matter the eIDs used by the other parties. One does not know at the time of signing who may need to verify signatures.

The RP role is clearly the one facing the complexity. The eID holder has one trusted party to rely on: the CA. The RP must rely on each and every CA used by its counterparts. To make this situation symmetric, this paper proposes to provide even the RP with a single trusted party to rely on: the Validation Authority (VA). In this paper, we introduce the VA as the trust anchor for the RP challenging the "PKI axiom" that only a CA can be a trust anchor.

We suggest implementing the interfaces towards a VA as Web Services since this is natively supported by most platforms and provide easy integration and good flexibility. Two services/interfaces have been designed: Signature verification and certificate validation. A request consists of either a signed document or a set of eIDs, indication of quality requirements, and a set of "respond with" parameters requesting information to be returned from the VA. The response contains overall validity and quality, validity and quality of all signatures and eIDs, and values for the respond with parameters.

2 DNV's Position and Role

DNV (Det Norske Veritas, http://www.dnv.com) is an independent foundation offering classification and certification services from offices in more than 100 countries. The maritime sector and the oil and gas industry are the main markets. DNV is also among the world's leading certification bodies for management systems (ISO 9000, ISO 14000, ISO 27001 and others), delivering services to all market sectors.

DNV seeks to extend its existing position as a supplier of trusted third party services to digital communication and service provisioning. A commercial version of a VA service along the lines described in this paper is currently being tested by pilot customers. For further information, see http://va.dnv.com.

3 The Challenges to the RP

The interoperability challenges are best described from the viewpoint of an RP as the receiver of a digitally signed document. The RP must check all signatures, handling:

- The relevant signature formats (PKCS#7, CMS, XML DSIG etc.) including all necessary modes (enveloped, enveloping, and independent) for multiple signatures.
- All necessary hash and crypto algorithms.
- The eIDs of all signers.

Processing of an eID consists of the following steps:

- Parsing and syntax checking of the eID certificate and its contents, including some semantic checking like use of certificate compared to allowed use (key usage settings) and presence of mandatory fields and critical extensions.
- Validation of the CA's signature on the eID certificate. This requires a trusted copy of the CA's own public key, either directly available, or obtained from further certificates in a certificate path.
- Checking that the eID is within its validity period, and that the eID is not revoked, i.e. declared invalid by the CA before the end of the validity period.

- Semantic processing of the eID content, extracting information that shall be used for presentation in a user interface or as parameters for further processing by programs. The name(s) in the eID and interpretation of naming attributes are particularly important.
- In the case of certificate paths, repeated processing for each certificate in the path.

Although the technical validation of signatures and eIDs has its challenges with respect to scaling (see [Ølnes1]), the real problem to the RP is:

- Assessment of the risk implied by accepting the signature (or an eID used for some other purpose), determined by the legal situation, the quality of the eID, the liability situation, and the trustworthiness of the CA.

4 The RP's Risk Situation

4.1 Liability and Law

A question which an RP always faces is to know with confidence the liability taken on by the CA, and what recourse, including which legal system, the RP has if the CA fails to fulfil its responsibility.

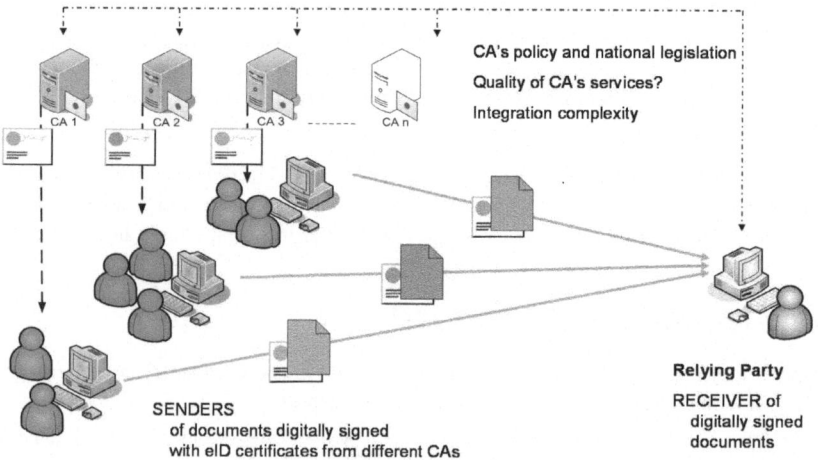

Figure 1: RP legal situation without a VA.

CA liability is described in certificate policies and is usually governed by the CA's national law. Additionally, agreements between the CA and RPs may control liability. In an international setting, certificate policies may be written in a foreign language and refer to foreign legislation with respect to the RP, and it is impossible for an RP to have agreements with all CAs on which it may want to rely. Thus, the RP is faced with an uncertain liability situation, which is usually not acceptable.

Note that trust structures (hierarchies, bridge-CAs, mutual cross-certification) do not solve the liability issue since the responsible entities for such structures (such as the Federal Bridge CA in the USA [FPKI]) do not take on any liability. Liability remains an issue between the RP and the individual CA.

4.2 Quality of eIDs and Digital Signatures

The fact that an RP is able to verify an eID issued by a particular CA (e.g. because the CA is in Microsoft's default list of CAs) is not a sufficient criteria for trusting a signature supported by the eID. Reasons for rejecting an eID may be that its quality is insufficient, lack of approval from appropriate authority, unacceptable legal conditions (liability or other issues), business conditions (unacceptable fee claimed by CA, CA is a competitor of the RP or otherwise not neutral etc.), or any other reason that the RP may come up with.

In addition to the quality of the eID, one should also verify sufficient quality of the digital signature: Hash algorithm and public key crypto algorithm and key size.

Liability is one aspect of the quality of the eID; the other two most important parameters being the registration procedure (protection against faked eIDs) and protection of the private key against misuse (use of smart cards etc. for high security). Quality is derived from the certificate policy but an RP cannot be expected to read the policy of all CAs, and the language and legislation issues mentioned above apply. Thus, an RP will have a hard time determining the quality of a digital signature on its own.

Approval status and membership in trust structures may be indicators of the eID quality.

4.3 Approval Status of eID and Signatures

An approval (registration, supervision, and accreditation) from a national authority may imply a particular legal standing of digital signatures and eIDs. This will typically also imply that certain quality criteria are fulfilled, as is the case for the qualified level in the EU (although requirements for qualified eIDs still vary between EU member states). In some cases, a particular status is indicated in the eIDs themselves, as for qualified certificates in the EU.

The EU Directive on electronic signatures gives a particular legal standing to qualified signatures, not to qualified eIDs. However, it is not uncommon to encounter situations where qualified eIDs are required on their own, e.g. for authentication.

Approval may be mediated through membership in trust structures, one example being cross-certification with the FBCA [FPKI] in the USA. Yet another alternative is a trust list distribution service for approved CAs [Certipost], [ETSI2].

However, determining the approval status of a particular signature or eID is in general not straightforward to an RP, and the RP may want to accept even non-approved signatures and eIDs. An explicit goal of the EU Directive on electronic signatures [EU] is to not unduly restrict the use of non-qualified signatures. In most cases acceptance or not of a certain eID is a risk management decision to be taken by the RP; exceptions being cases where transactions are subject to legislation posing specific requirements (e.g. only allows qualified signatures).

4.4 Other Aspects

The RP may want to add further considerations to its risk assessment. A.CA's nationality, financial status, reputation or other aspects may lead the RP to reject even a high quality CA; and the RP may explicitly decide to accept eIDs whose quality would normally be too low.

This situation may also be reversed: A CA may decide to (or be forced to for political or other reasons) prohibit use of its eIDs towards certain RPs. The policy of a CA may state allowed and/or prohibited applications of eIDs and signatures, and such policies should be obeyed.

5 Risk Management by use of a VA

5.1 Revising the Trust Model for the RP

The solution we propose to the challenges of the RP is to make the situation of the eID holder and the RP symmetric: both roles shall have one service provider as its trust anchor. The trust anchor for the RP is the Validation Authority (VA). This challenges present PKI practice where a CA is the only actor that can serve as a trust anchor; i.e. a trust decision must ultimately always be linked to a trusted CA. Contrary to this, we explicitly suggest that the VA shall be neutral and independent from any CA.

Upon trusting the VA, the RP is able to trust any CA that the VA handles. The VA may handle each CA individually, regardless of any trust structure that the CA may participate in. Certificate path discovery and validation are irrelevant (although the VA may use such processing internally) since there is no need to prove a path to a "trusted CA".

This trust model resembles a two-level hierarchy or use of a bridge-CA, but the VA does not issue certificates. It is an on-line service answering requests from RPs. An on-line VA may be able to make a business out of its services by providing real risk management services to the RP. The RP is provided with one-stop shopping for validation of digital signatures and eIDs: One point of trust, one agreement, one point of billing, one liable actor, and one integration.

5.2 Liability and Law

The VA service is based on agreements: One agreement between the VA and the RP (the customer), and agreements between the VA and the individual CAs. This transforms the legal situation from national law (of the different CAs) to contractual law. The complexity is not removed but rather outsourced to the VA, but only one agreement is needed with each CA. This is shown in Figure 2. The VA takes on a uniform liability for signatures and eIDs of a certain quality, regulated by the agreement between the RP and the VA.

The model relies on two further assumptions: The CAs must accept (or preferably even endorse) the model and the number of CAs must be manageable in order for the VA to obtain full coverage of all relevant CAs. The experience so far is that CAs react positively to the idea, as they may achieve both more widespread use of their eIDs (and thus a better service to their customers) and a more predictable risk situation due to the agreements-based model. Additionally, we propose to pay the CAs a certain percentage of the VA's income, proportionally to their shares of the VA's traffic.

The number of public CAs is not known but estimated to about 100[1] in Europe and in the order of several hundreds world-wide. The assumption is that there will be a consolidation rather than a proliferation in these numbers. However, it may be necessary to support even some non-public CAs such as corporate CAs issuing eIDs that may be accepted outside the company. These numbers are manageable to a VA.

---

1 This refers to the number of agreements necessary rather than the number of CAs. Certain systems (like the Norwegian Bank-ID) comprise many CAs but only one agreement is necessary in order to incorporate them.

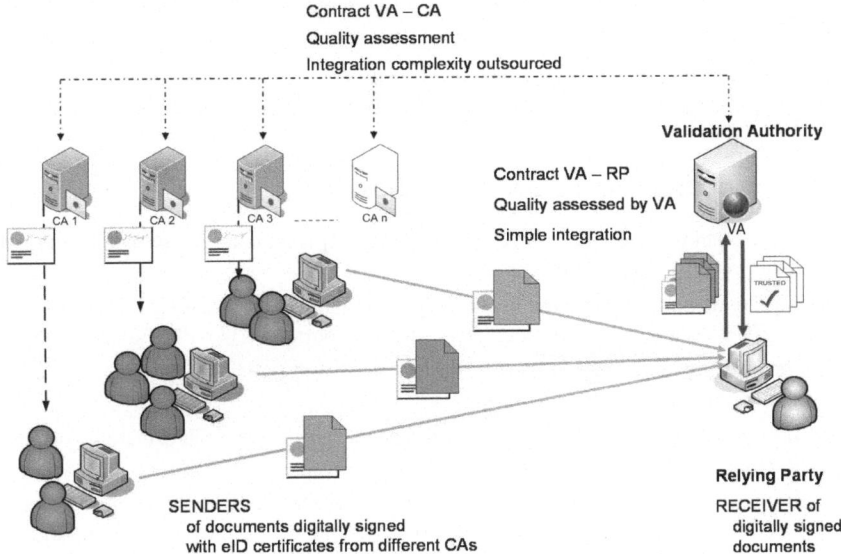

Figure 2: The Validation Authority as a trust anchor for the RP.

5.3 Quality Assessment

5.3.1 eID Quality

The quality of an eID is mainly described by the certificate policy. Some of the other aspects raised in 4.4 may also be considered when evaluating eID quality, such as the status of the actor running the CA, (financial status, market share, reputation etc.). Additionally, other documentation (certification practice statements, agreements with other actors etc.), and membership in hierarchies and cross-certification regimes may be studied.

A quality classification system applicable world-wide, i.e. taking US, Asian and other specifications into account, is under development at DNV. This will consider all initiatives mentioned in the ETSI study on international harmonization [ETSI1] plus several others such as Web Trust and T-scheme. Quality can be mediated as a profile with scores for individual parameters or as an overall (typically numerical) indicator. We agree with [Backhouse]: "With no common agreed method for rating the quality of digital certificates, trust in extra-domain certificates can only be slowly and expensively constructed through a small number of given models, such as cross-certification, bridge-CAs and cross-recognition, each of which has its own shortcomings."

A classification should include an "assurance level" to indicate to what degree an assessment of quality claimed by the certificate policy and other documentation versus actual operation has been done.

5.3.2 Approval Status

The formal approval status of eIDs and digital signatures, such as qualified eIDs and signatures, should be mediated from the VA to the RP. The suggestion is to divide quality classification into approved and non-approved levels. While in principle the approval status could be a matrix between eIDs/signatures and national rules, a more reasonable approach is to meditate whether or not an eID/signature is approved according to its own national law.

Note that the only method to assess that a digital signature is a qualified signature is to ensure that the CA's certificate policy demands use of a certified SSCD (Secure Signature Creation Device) according to CWA 14169 [CEN].

5.3.3 eID Classification in DNV's VA Service

The present scheme in use for DNV's VA services [Ølnes2] is an example of a rather simple system, applicable in this version primarily in Europe:

1. **Inadequate or non-determined level:** Very low confidence or assessment not possible, usually because a certificate policy does not exist. Many corporate PKIs will be placed in this category.

2. **Low level**: Low confidence in certificate but certificate policy exists or quality assessment is possible by other means.

3. **Medium non-approved level:** Medium confidence certificates with private key storage usually in software.

4. **Medium approved level:** Same quality as level 2 but certificate issuer is registered/approved by assigned inspectorate/authority according to applicable law to the CA. (Denmark, Sweden, and Norway are examples of countries where this level exists.)

5. **Qualified non-approved level:** Certificate quality is at or very close to qualified level but certificates are either not marked as qualified[2] or not registered/approved by assigned inspectorate/authority according to applicable law to the CA.

6. **Qualified approved level:** Certificates are marked as qualified and the CA is registered/approved by assigned inspectorate/authority according to applicable law to the CA. Hardware security token (smart card or similar) is not certified as SSCD.

7. **Qualified signature level:** Certificates are marked and registered as for level 5, and use of a certified SSCD according to CWA 14169 [CEN] is mandated. Thus, this level supports qualified signatures according to the EU Directive on electronic signatures [EU].

5.3.4 Signature Quality

The quality of a digital signature is determined by the eID and the quality of the cryptography used. In theory, the quality of the signer's entire environment should be considered but a VA can consider only the aspects that can be assessed from the signature itself. The formula used by DNV's VA services is:

$$Signature\ Quality = eID\ Quality + Hash\ Quality + Public\ Key\ Crypto\ Key\ Length\ Quality$$

This is amended by the rules: If any of the three elements is 0, signature quality is 0; if eID quality is 6, and each of the other two is 2 or higher, signature quality is 20. The value 20 thus specifies a qualified signature with acceptable cryptographic quality.

Values for cryptographic quality (hash and public key) are assigned as follows:
- Quality 0: Inadequate – should not be trusted.
- Quality 1: Marginal – reasonably secure for short term but not for high security.
- Quality 2: Trustworthy for approximately 5 years.

---

2 Note that only certificates issued to persons may be marked as qualified. Thus, this is the highest level that can be assigned to certificates issued to non-human entities.

- Quality 3-6: Increasing levels of security.

Assignment of values to algorithms (including key sizes) is done according to recommendations from NIST in USA [Burr]. European recommendations are aligned with NIST's work. For further information, see [Ølnes2].

5.3.5 RP Specific Policies

In addition to minimum quality levels, an RP is allowed to specify other aspects of its own validation policy, such as CAs that explicitly are trusted or not. At present, DNV's VA service does not support CA specific policies, i.e. exclusion of RPs according to specific criteria.

6 The VA Services

6.1 Web Services: Signature Verification, eID Validation

We clearly recommendation to implement VA services that plug directly into a service oriented architecture, i.e. Web Services using defined XML structures and the SOAP protocol. SCVP (Server-based Certificate Validation Protocol), under development by the IETF, could be an alternative for eID validation but client support for SCVP will not be readily available.

The XML should eventually be standardized. The schemas currently used for DNV's VA services are described in [Andresen]. A response from the VA is always signed. Requests may be signed. Communication is always on https with mutual SSL-authentication. The schemas are tailored to support asynchronous Web Services although only synchronous operation is offered at present (email interface to a VA Gateway (see 6.2) being an exception). Calls to the VA services can then be made at appropriate steps in the implementation of a workflow involving use of digitally signed documents, or eIDs used for any other purpose.

For DNV's VA services, a signature verification request consists of one signed document plus optional parameters requesting specific "respond with" parameters and signature and eID qualities above a specified level. The response contains an overall assertion status for the document (trusted, not trusted, indeterminate) and assertions for all signatures and eIDs. Quality of all signatures and eIDs is returned as well as values for "respond with" parameters.

The service should handle all signature formats (PKCS#7, CMS, XML DSIG, ETSI TS 101 733, ETSI TS 101 903 and possibly more), all cases of nested and independent signatures, and all necessary hash and crypto algorithms.

The certificate validation service is similar but with one or more eID certificate(s) as input parameter in addition to the "respond with" and quality requirements.

6.2 The VA Gateway

Sending the entire content of a signed document to the VA may reveal confidential information to the VA and since documents may be large, response from the VA may be slow due to the time needed to transmit the request. To cope with this, a VA Gateway has been implemented. The gateway is installed (software with or without separate hardware) in the RP's network and all VA requests are directed to the gateway. Here, signatures are extracted and the corresponding hash values computed from the document. Only signatures and hash values are sent to the VA; the content is disposed of as soon as the request has been sent. Figure 3 shows this setup, also showing that a direct call to the VA is allowed.

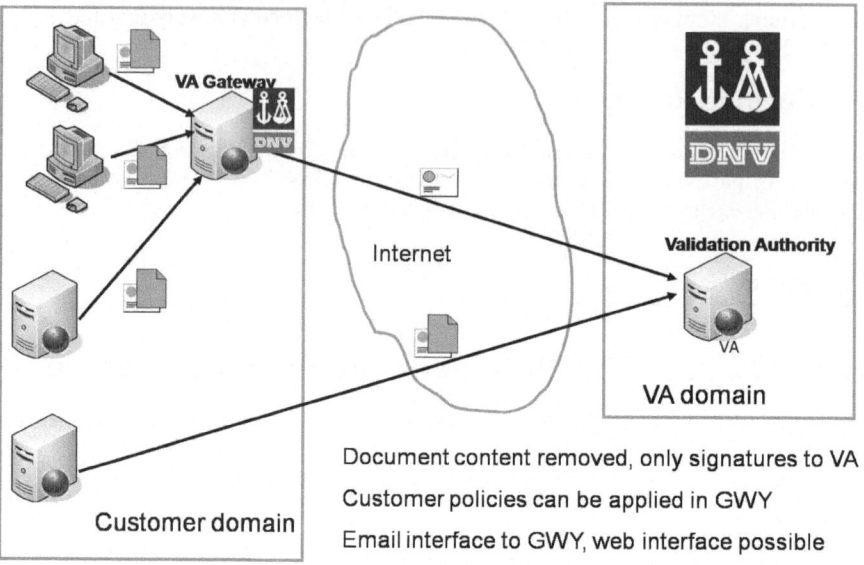

Figure 3: The VA Gateway.

Additionally, the VA Gateway may be used to enforce customer specific policies, e.g. ensure uniform quality requirements in all requests sent from the customer. An email interface is offered, where signed documents can be sent to the gateway as attachments; the response being attached to a response email.

7 Conclusion

International interoperability of digital signatures is difficult today, and the main problem is how a Relying Party (RP) can assess the risk related to a signature supported by an "arbitrary" eID. The legal situation (including liability and (national) approval status of the CA) and assessment of the quality of the digital signature and the eID are the main risk elements. Today, the relationship between an RP and a CA is governed by the CA's certificate policy and national law, unless an explicit agreement exists between the parties. In an international setting, this does not scale. Quality assessment is a difficult task to the RP.

An independent, trusted Validation Authority (VA) is proposed as a better solution to interoperability, and the paper shows how guidance in risk management can be provided by use of the VA as a one-stop shopping service for verification of digital signatures and eIDs. The RP has one agreement with the VA, controlling liability and providing the VA's assessment on quality. As important added values, the RP is provided with a single integration for validation, and the need for certificate path processing is removed, since the VA serves as an independent trust anchor for the RP.

References

[Andresen] Andresen, Anette: DNV VA XML Schema Description. Available from http://www.dnv.com/ict/va/ 2007

[Backhouse] Backhouse J., Hsu C., Tseng J., Baptista J.: A Question of Trust – An Economic Perspective on Quality Standards in the Certification Services Market. Communications of the ACM, Vol. 48 No 9, 2005.

[Burr]   Burr, Bill: NIST Cryptographic Standards Status Report. 5th Annual PKI R&D Workshop, NIST, Gaithersburgh, USA, 2006.

[CEN]   CEN: Secure Signature-Creation Devices EAL 4+. CWA 14169, 2002.

[Certipost] Certipost: Certification Practices Statement, European IDABC Bridge/Gateway CA for Public Administrations v2.0. EBGCA-DEL-015, 2005.

[ETSI1]   ETSI: Electronic Signatures and Infrastructures; International Harmonization of Policy Requirements for CAs Issuing Certificates. ETSI TR 102 040 v1.3.1, 2005.

[ETSI2]   ETSI: Electronic Signatures and Infrastructures; Provision of Harmonized Trust Service Provider Information. ETSI TS 102 231 v2.1.1, 2006.

[EU]   EU: Community Framework for Electronic Signatures. Directive 1999/93/EC of the European Parliament and of the Council, 1999.

[FPKI]   Federal PKI Policy Authority (FPKIPA): X.509 Certificate Policy for the Federal Bridge Certification Authority (FBCA) Version 2.1, 2006.

[Ølnes1]   Ølnes, Jon: PKI Interoperability by an Independent, Trusted Validation Authority. 5th Annual PKI R&D Workshop, NIST, Gaithersburgh, USA, 2006.

[Ølnes2]   Ølnes, Jon: DNV VA Quality Parameters, Certificate and Signature Quality. Available from http://www. dnv.com/ict/va/ 2007.

Financial Fraud Information Sharing

Sharon Boeyen

Entrust
sharon.boeyen@entrust.com

Abstract

The rate of fraudulent transactions in the financial services industry is increasing at an alarming rate. Fraudsters collaborate and share/sell information about successful incidents, providing a window of opportunity during which similar attempts may also succeed. The financial sector is attempting to combat fraud in a similar way, through the sharing of information about fraudulent incidents among themselves to help prevent or quickly close those windows of opportunity. To date, solutions have been based on proprietary tools and techniques, hampering the ability to share information quickly and effectively among organizations that may use disparate products and solutions. Standards work is now underway in the Internet Engineering Task Force (IETF) to standardize the information about fraudent financial transactions and standardize a format for the exchange of related information. Other industry initiatives have also been undertaken to try to move the sharing of information from its current state, with closed networks using proprietary solutions, to a more open standards, based environment. For example, the Open Fraud Intelligence Network (OFIN) is a recent initiative from Entrust that will provide a standards-based vendor-neutral network for the exchange of fraud data, tactics and behavior. Also the Financial Services Technology Consortium (FSTC) recently launched a fraud collaboration project focused on better collaboration tools for fighting fraud. That project also hopes to benefit from standards initiatives already underway. This paper focuses on the[THRAUD] standards activity underway in the IETF.

1 Introduction

Fraudulent online transactions are increasing at alarming rates. Financial institutions and merchants are unable to keep up with the increasing sophistication of criminal groups and rapid rate with which the perpetrators share information to facilitate ongoing fraud. Unlike the cooperation among the criminal organizations, banks and merchants work in relative isolation, responding to threats as they happen or are reported. They lack the tools and secure open networks necessary to facilitate information sharing to help reduce the likelihood of repeated fraud patterns succeeding at other banks or merchants.

Gartner Group recently estimated, "the cumulative financial losses stemming from phishing attacks rose to more than \$2.8 billion in 2006." While fewer victims report falling victim to scams, Gartner reported "the average [phishing related fraud] loss per victim nearly quintupled from \$257 to \$1,244 between 2005 and 2006 and attacks appear to be more targeted against relatively wealthy individuals."[1]

According to the Anti-Phishing Working Group (APWG), the number of unique phishing sites continues to increase at an astounding rate. In just one month, the number rose from nearly 35,000 (March, 2007) to 55,643 (April, 2007). Financial Services continue to be the most targeted industry sector at 92.5%.[2]

---

1 Phishing Attacks Leapfrog Despite Attempts to Stop Them, Gartner, Avivah Litan, November 1, 2006
2 Phishing Activity Trends for April 2007, Anti-Phishing Working Group, May 23, 2007, http://www.antiphishing.org/reports/apwg_report_april_2007.pdf

N. Pohlmann, H. Reimer, W. Schneider (Editors): Securing Electronic Business Processes, Vieweg (2007), 297-305

The Tower Group identifies increased risk of fraud as the top business driver for banking in 2007. The top strategic response for 2007 is to enhance fraud management policies and procedures and the top technology initiative is fraud detection and security technologies.[3]

Gartner recommends a layered approach for financial institutions and other e-commerce service providers to enhance security in their online channel to retain customers.[4] The layered approach integrates controls such as transaction anomaly detection with authentication techniques of varying strengths. Balancing security and convenience with cost, a risk based authentication scheme combined with a transaction anomaly detection system enables an adequate level of "trustability" in transactions.

In response, a number of consortia are addressing the need to cooperate and share information about fraudulent transactions and attempted fraudulent transactions. The APWG has been very active in this area. The Financial Services Technology Consortia (FSTC) has established a new project "Better Collaboration Tools for Fighting Fraud – Real-time Sharing of information for Fighting Fraud". This project will determine the feasibility and benefit of sharing models of fraudulent behavior, for better prediction and mitigation of fraud, and for better forensics investigation and prosecution support. The project plans to examine a number of ongoing standards and industry activities, including the IETF Internet Draft (ID) "How to Share Transaction Fraud (Thraud) Report Data" [THRAUD] and others. The goal of the FSTC project is to build upon existing capabilities and add significant value to the task of combating fraud occuring across communications channels and lines of business.

2 OATH and Transaction Fraud Information Sharing

The Initiative for Open AuTHentication (OATH) initiated a project in 2006 to promote standardization of a means to share transaction fraud report data, in conjunction with its activity on risk-based authentication. Risk-based authentication balances the conflicting goals of organizations to have stronger authentication without encroaching on the goodwill of their users. These same organizations have a strong requirement never to deny a genuine user access to services because of suspicion over the authentication. Risk-based authentication allows convenient authentication methods to only be used in low-risk situations but applies stronger authentication methods when the risk is higher. Access is denied only when it can be said with almost complete certainty that the subject is an impostor.

In the OATH Risk-based authentication architecture[5], the "risk evaluation and sharing component obtains information about fraud strategies in the broader community from a shared industry resource or Fraud Information Exchange Network, as well as fraud strategies it has already detected. Using this information, the component can make more informed decisions about the risk of fraudulent activity".

3 Banking Industry's Top 10 for 2007: Business Drivers, Strategic Responses, and Technology Priorities, Tower Group, Jim Eckenrode, January 2007
4 Tutorial on User Authentication and Fraud Detection, Gartner, Avivah Litan, June 2007
5 OATH Reference Architecture version 1.0 http://www.openauthentication.org/resources.asp

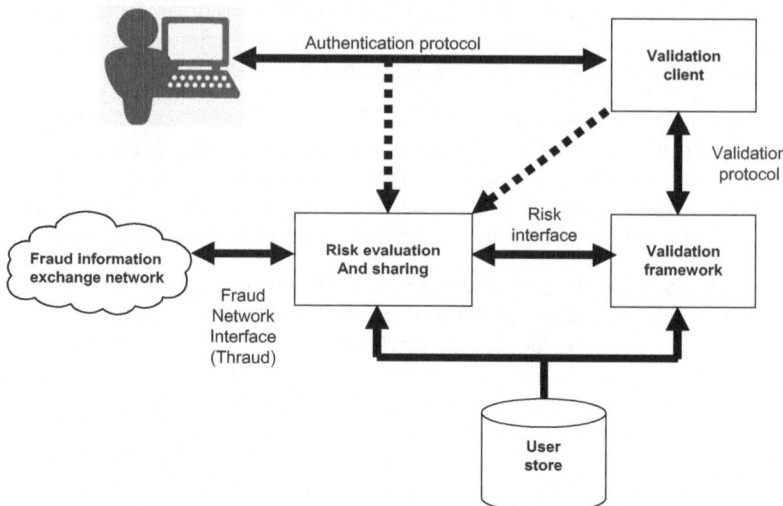

Figure 1: OATH Risk-based authentication architecture

Although there are a number of technologies in place that perform fraud detection and some networks that enable fraud information sharing, the existing tools were seen as either inadequate or proprietary. As a result, OATH undertook a task to specify a mechanism for the open sharing of Transaction Fraud (Thraud) report data. OATH does not itself produce standards and has submitted the resulting specification to the Internet Engineering Task Force (IETF) as an individual Internet Draft (ID). The goal is to eventually progress this specification as a standards track Request For Comment (RFC).

Rather than starting from scratch, [THRAUD] is a profile that extends some fields of a more general incident reporting specification. The general specification "The Incident Object Description Exchange Format" [IODEF] is a product of the Extended Incident Handling (inch) working group of the security area in the IETF. The specification has undergone extensive review and is, at the time of writing, in the hands of the Internet Engineering Steering Group (IESG) for approval and progression to RFC status. [IODEF] provides the basic outline for reporting incidents of all types, but does not include specific elements needed for Thraud reporting. The inch WG also produced "Extensions to the IODEF-Document Class for Phishing, Fraud, and Other Crimeware" [PHISHING], an IODEF profile that extends the reporting format to cover primarily the data specific to phishing attacks. However, since fraud incidents don't necessarily involve phishing, that specification is also inadequate for financial fraud requirements. OATH specifies [THRAUD] as a profile of [IODEF] including extensions specific to the sharing of financial transaction fraud data, following the same model as [PHISHING].

3 IODEF

As the foundation specification for [THRAUD], it is important to understand the report format specified in [IODEF] for incident reports. [IODEF] specifies an XML document format for representing computer security information commonly exchanged between Computer Security Incident Response Teams (CSIRTs), in order to enhance their operational capabilities.

The [IODEF] XML model has a single top level class, the IODEF-Document class. All IODEF-documents are instances of that class. An IODEF-Document is comprised of a single aggregate class, "Incident" and attributes that specify the IODEF version, the language of the document and optionally some processing instructions. More than one incident can be included in an IODEF document.

Table 1 outlines the mandatory and optional classes as well as mandatory and optional attributes associated with an instance of the IODEF Incident class.

Table 1: IODEF Incident Class Structure

Mandatory Class	Optional Class	Mandatory Attribute	Optional Attribute
IncidentID	AlternativeID	purpose	ext-purpose
ReportTime	RelatedActivity		lang
Assessment	DetectTime		restriction
	StartTime		
	EndTime		
	Description		
	Method		
	Contact		
	EventData		
	History		
	AdditionalData		

The mandatory classes and attributes of an IODEF incident report are outlined below:

- IncidentID is a string that uniquely identifies the incident within the context of the reporting organization.
- ReportTime is the time at which the incident was reported.
- Assessment describes the repercussions of the incident and includes a number of optional components. These components can specify the impact of the incident, including the severity (low, medium or high), an indication of whether the activity succeeded or failed, and indication of the category of malicious activity attempted (e.g. admin privileges, denial of service, file or database integrity etc). The language of the class must be included and the set of categories or types of malicious behaviour can be extended.
- purpose is an attribute that specifies the reason the IODEF-document was created. There are four values specified for this attribute as well as the ability to extend the set as needed. The defined values in IODEF can be used to indicate purposes such as trace-back, to request aid in mitigating the described activity, to comply with reporting requirements or for purposes described elsewhere in the report itself.

4 THRAUD

[THRAUD] builds upon the [IODEF] base with a focus on reporting and sharing information related to online fraud attacks targeted against customers of financial institutions and merchants.

The specification describes an open framework for the sharing of Thraud-activity-reports. A Thraud-activity-report conveys information related to specific fraud, or suspected fraud, incidents as well as fraudulent patterns of behaviour. Given that fraudsters share information very quickly and repeat successful patterns, the sharing of information about these events and behaviors can help prevent the same events from being successfully repeated at other institutions.

The framework includes a data format defined for information transfer. The same data format can be used to share information in a number of different models. For instance, a set of financial institutions and/or merchants may use the format to report incidents directly among themselves. In most deployments, however, it will be useful to have a central facility to which the financial institutions and merchants report incident information. That central facility might correlate those individual reports, possibly merge them with information gleaned from external sources of fraud behavior data and provide the financial institutions and merchants with "value-add" Thraud reports. Thus, the same format can be used for both inbound and outbound Thraud-activity-reports.

There are five types of fraudulent event types described and profiled within the single report format.

- Payment-event-reports convey information about the payee instructions in a fraudulent payment incident or attempt. For example the name, address and amount of the payment might be conveyed. This information may be valuable to other entities in preventing future fraudulent payment attempts to the same payee. Information about the target of the fraud (the entity whose funds were used to make the payment) is not disclosed in these reports.
- Transfer-event-reports convey information about the fraudulent transfer, or attempted transfer of funds from one account to another. Information about the destination of the transfer event is included in the report. This can include, for example, the bank, account and amount information. As with payment event reports, information about the target of the fraud (the account and account owner from which the funds transfer was initiated) is not disclosed in these reports.
- Identity-event-reports convey information about fraudulent impersonation or impersonation attempts. Information about the victim's identity may be included in a report of this type. For example, a victim's email address may be conveyed.
- Other-event-reports enable event types other than those listed above to be reported.
- Fraud-event-signature reports convey information about the behavior or sequence of events associated with a specific fraudulent event. For example, if a user logged from an unusual and risky IP address, immediately changed their password, then created a new bill payee and attempted to make a very large payment to that new payee, that sequence might be considered suspicious and a Fraud-event-signature report could be generated.

[THRAUD] builds upon [IODEF] in the following ways:

- Some classes that are optional in [IODEF] are mandated in Thraud-activity-reports;
- New classes are defined that are specific to financial transaction fraud incident report types;
- A fraud-event-signature-report format is defined for reporting the behavior associated with fraudulent events.

4.1 IODEF Classes Mandatory for THRAUD

As [THRAUD] is a profile of the IODEF data format, all classes and attributes that are mandatory for an IODEF-document are also mandatory for a THRAUD-report. In addition some of the classes that are optional in [IODEF] are mandatory for Thraud-reports. The Thraud profile also classifies some of the IODEF optional classes as "SHOULD", meaning that although not mandatory, these classes should be included in all Thraud reports. [THRAUD] also uses the [IODEF] extensibility mechanism to add some classes that are specific to financial fraud.

Table 2 illustrates the [IODEF] classes that are mandatory for THRAUD-reports and those that should be included in Thraud-reports of the various types. The "Event Report" column illustrates the content of a report of specific fraudulent transactions or attempted fraudulent transactions, including fraud payment, transfer, identity and other incidents. The "Event Signature Report" column illustrates the content of a report outlining suspicious behavior that may be associated with specific fraud events. "M" indicates the class is mandatory for inclusion in all THRAUD-reports of that type. "O" means [THRAUD] imposes no conditions on the use of the [IODEF] optional class for Thraud-reports.

Table 2: Thraud Mandatory IODEF Classes and Attributes

IODEF Class	Event Reports	Event Signature Report
IncidentID	M	M
AlternativeID	O	O
RelatedActivity	O	O
DetectTime	O	O
StartTime	O	O
EndTime	O	O
ReportTime	M	M
Description	O	O
Assessment	M ("Assessment.Impact" and "Assessment.Confidence" components are mandatory. Other components are optional.)	M ("Assessment.Impact" component is mandatory. Other components are optional.)
Method	O	M ("Method.Reference.ReferenceName", "Method.URL" and "Method.Description" components are mandatory for Thraud reports of this type. Other components are optional.)
Contact	M ("Contact.Email" and "Contact.ContactName" are mandatory. "Contact.Contact.ContactName", "Contact.Contact.Email" and "Contact.Contact. Telephone" components should also be included. Other components are optional.)	M ("Contact.Email" and "Contact.ContactName" are mandatory. Other components are optional.)
EventData	M ("Event.Data.DetectTime" and "EventData. AdditionalData" components are mandatory. "EventData.Flow.System.Service.Application", "EventData.Flow.System.Node.Address.vlan-num", "EventData.Flow.System.Node.Location" and "EventData.Flow.System.Node.NodeName" components should also be included. Other components are optional.)	M ("EventData.AdditionalData" component is mandatory.
History	O	O
AdditionalData	O	O

4.2 THRAUD Extensions to IODEF

[THRAUD] utilizes the base [IODEF] specification and extends it to facilitate reporting of financial fraud events. The information specific to the financial aspects of a fraud event are contained in the [IODEF] EventData class. That class definition includes a component "AdditionalData" that enables the extensibility needed to carry financial transaction fraud data. [THRAUD] extends the [IODEF] Incident class in two ways:

- The "purpose" attribute is extended with values specific to Thraud-activity-reports.
- The EventData.AdditionalData class is extended to include four new classes specific to financial fraud. These new classes are FraudEventPayment, FraudEventTransfer, FraudEventIdentity and FraudEventOther.

4.2.1 Purpose attribute

Three new values are added to the purpose attribute for the [IODEF] Incident class. These values are used to indicate the purpose of the current Thraud-activity-report:

- "Add" means the recipient should add this report to the corpus;
- "Delete" means the recipient should delete this report from the corpus; and
- "Modify" means the recipient should use the elements in the current report to replace corresponding elements in the corpus.

Each Thraud-activity-report must include the purpose attribute and must use one the three values listed above.

4.2.2 Fraud Event Payment Class

The FraudEventPayment class is used to report fraudulent payment, or attempted payment, of funds from a victim's account to a fraudster payee. The privacy of the victim is respected and only information about the fraudulent payee is revealed. The FraudEventPayment class has no attributes and is comprised of the following classes:

- PayeeName
- PostalAddress
- PayeeAmount

All classes are optional, however at least one must be included.

The PayeeName is a simple string. PostalAddress is a structured format for the specific components of an address. PayeeAmount includes a DECIMAL element representing the amount of the payment and the three letter currency code for the payment.

Sharing FraudEventPayment reports is intended to assist in the prevention of future fraudulent payments from other potential victim accounts to the same or similar payees.

4.2.3 Fraud Event Transfer Class

The FraudEventTransfer class is used to report fraudulent transfer, or attempted transfer, of funds from a victim's account to a fraudster's account. The privacy of the victim is respected and only information about the fraudster's destination account is revealed. The fraud event transfer class has no attributes and is comprised of the following classes:

- BankID
- AccountID
- AccountType
- TransferAmount

All classes are optional, however at least one must be included.

The BankID contains the destination bank routing transit ID or other financial institution ID. The AccountID is the primary account number of the destination account. AccountType indicates whether the fraudster's destination account is a brokerage, checking, corporate, mortgage, retirement or savings account. The TransferAmount shares a common syntax with PayeeAmount in the FraudEventPayment class definition.

Sharing FraudEventTransfer reports is intended to assist in the prevention of future fraudulent transfers from other potential victim accounts to the same fraudster destination account.

4.2.4 Fraud Event Identity Class

The FraudEventIdentity class is used to report fraudulent impersonation or attempted impersonation of a victim. Given the privacy issues associated with impersonation events, it is expected that very little information will be revealed. The Fraud-event-identity class has no attributes and is comprised of a single IdentityComponent class. IdentityComponent is defined as iodef:ExtensionType, enabling specific identity types to be added by any entity. [THRAUD] defines two types for this extension:

- EmailAddress
- UserID

Both types are defined as simple strings to facilitate easy integration with the systems from which the data would be extracted. A Fraud-event-identity report might include one or both of these identity types and/or some other identity type defined using the same extension capability.

Sharing FraudEventIdentity reports is intended to assist in the prevention of future fraudulent impersonations associated with the same identity information.

4.2.5 Fraud Event Other Class

The FraudEventOther class is used to report fraudulent events not covered by the specific classes defined above. The fraud event other class has no attributes and is comprised of the following classes:

- OtherEventType
- PayeeName
- Postal
- BankID
- AccountID
- AccountType
- PayeeAmount
- OtherEventDescription

The PayeeName, Postal, BankID, AccountID, AccountType, and PayeeAmount are as defined above. The OtherEventType is a string that classifies the event. OtherEventDescription is a free form string that includes a description of the specific event.

Sharing FraudEventTransfer reports is intended to assist in the prevention of future fraudulent impersonations associated with the same identity information.

4.3 Fraud Event Signature Report

The Fraud-event-signature-report describes behavior associated with fraudulent events (payee, transfer, identity and other) rather than the events themselves. None of the [THRAUD] extensions described in 4.2 are used in these reports. [IODEF] specifies all necessary components for these events. [THRAUD] does specify the required components and profiles their use for this report type. These include:

- purpose
- IncidentID

- ReportTime
- Assessment.Impact
- Method.Reference.ReferenceName
- Method.URL
- Method.Description
- Contact.Email
- Contact.ContactName

The IncidentID, ReportTime, Contact.Email and Contact.ContactName classes are as defined in [IO-DEF]. The value of the purpose attribute is "reporting" for these reports. The "severity" attribute must be included for the Assessment.Impact class. A name for the specific "signature" or behavior is contained in the Method.Reference.ReferenceName class. The Method.URL contains a value pointing to a brief description of the behavior. Note that this component is free form text and Thraud does not impose any particular syntax or language on the description. This enables the descriptions to be tailored to a particular deployment environment, community of participants etc. For example, the description might be formatted in such a way that a particular set of tools or products could automatically import it into the local environment as a "rule" to aid in the detection of attempted fraudulent activity.

5 Conclusion

With the rapid increase in fraudulent transactions and the sensitivity associated with the loss of trust in the financial institution/merchant by the victims of fraud, there is an increased willingness among institutions to quickly share information about fraudulent activity to try to reduce the likelihood of follow-on transactions by the same fraudsters. In order to be successful, the sharing of information in such a wide environment must use a standard structure and provide a common syntax and semantic for the data elements being exchanged. [THRAUD] provides the base for such a standard and benefits greatly from the fact that it profiles a more mature specification [IODEF] that is itself already in wide use for the exchange of incident reports of other types, including phishing attacks. With this common base, reporting of financial transaction fraud can be done using the same techniques, protocols and data elements as reports of other attacks and attempted attacks. With a standard fraud transaction report format, as provided by [THRAUD] and open vendor-neutral networks, such as OFIN, the sharing of information about fraudulent transactions can be much more effective than it is at the present time. Cooperation among financial institutions and merchants to share this information is critical to the fight against fraud and the prevention of fraudsters from repeating successful attacks against other victims.

References

[THRAUD] M'Raihi, David; Boeyen, Sharon; Grandcolas, Michael and Bajaj, Siddharth: How to Share Transaction Fraud (Thraud) Report Data. ftp://ftp.rfc-editor.org/in-notes/internet-drafts/draft-mraihi-inch-thraud-03.txt.

[IODEF] Danyliw, R; Meijer, J; and Demchenko, Y: The Incident Object Description Format. http://www.ietf.org/internet-drafts/draft-ietf-inch-iodef-13.txt.

[PHISHING] Cain, P. and Jevans, D.: Extensions to the IODEF-Document class for Phishing, Fraud, and other Crimeware: where applicable. http://www.ietf.org/internet-drafts/draft-cain-post-inch-phishingextns-01.txt.

Enterprise Key Management Infrastructure

Arshad Noor

CTO, StrongAuth, Inc.
arshad.noor@strongauth.com

Abstract

After two decades of securing the perimeter, companies are now recognizing that it is an insufficient deterrent to attackers of information systems infrastructure. As more breaches are disclosed and as IT-related losses continue to .rise, encryption of sensitive data across the enterprise is viewed as a necessity. Yet, the diverse nature of IT infrastructures makes it difficult to build and operate a cohesive encryption key-management strategy that balances security goals with costs.

The Organization for the Advancement of Structured Information Systems (OASIS) has created a Technical Committee – the Enterprise Key Management Infrastructure (EKMI) Technical committee (TC) – to address this challenge. While EKMI focuses on Public Key Infrastructure (PKI) and Symmetric Key Management Systems (SKMS), the TC is currently focused on SKMS-related activities. Participants on the TC are defining a platform-independent protocol to allow applications to request symmetric key-management services from an SKMS implementation, implementation, operations and audit guidelines for an SKMS and an interoperability test-suite for the protocol.

This paper describes the characteristics of an EKMI – more specifically, that of an SKMS – and how enterprises can take advantage of this protocol to protect sensitive information across the enterprise.

1 Introduction

With the availability of internet access to commercial entities and consumers, the world has witnessed a level of growth in Information Technology (IT) as never before. It is estimated that more than 1 Billion computers are currently connected to the internet, with more than 100M being added each year.

As companies race to take advantage of the productivity benefits and market advantages that low-cost computing and internet access offer, criminal elements also see an opportunity in the structural weaknesses that hyper-growth typically brings. An unprecedented number of breaches[1] have been disclosed in the US thanks to Computer Breach Disclosure laws in 38 states. The most recent breach was also one of the worst, having compromised 45 Million credit card numbers this year[2]. Even though companies have invested millions of dollars in perimeter defences – firewalls, intrusion detection/prevention, anti-virus, spam controls, etc. – they have been unable to prevent breaches to sensitive data within the heart of their systems.

There is recognition within specific industries that, while perimeter defences are necessary, they are an insufficient deterrent. The Payment Card Industry (PCI), a consortium of credit card companies such as Visa, MasterCard, American Express, Discover, etc., have mandated twelve (12) security controls

---

1 Privacy Rights Clearinghouse – http://www.privacyrights.org/ar/ChronDataBreaches.htm
2 Breach Disclosure by TJX – http://www.google.com/search?q=tjx+breach

N. Pohlmann, H. Reimer, W. Schneider (Editors): Securing Electronic Business Processes, Vieweg (2007), 306-312

within their Data Security Standard (DSS) for merchants and card-processors. Amongst the twelve is the requirement for encryption of credit card numbers during transport and when at-rest, accompanied with robust key-management practices[3].

The Health Insurance Portability and Accountability Act (HIPAA) federal regulation governing an aspect of the healthcare industry in the US does not explicitly mandate the use of encryption, but requires that patient data be secured during transport and at-rest[4].

The only safe harbour provided by most of the Computer Breach Disclosure laws in approximately 38 states of the US, is when the breached company in question has encrypted the sensitive data using appropriate encryption technology[5].

While Article 16 and 17 of the EU Directive (95/46/EC – Section VIII) focusing on "Confidentiality and Security of Processing" of sensitive data, do not explicitly call out for encryption, they require that implementers ensure that appropriate controls are in place when sensitive data is processed and stored on computers[6].

2 Requirements

Given this emphasis on maintaining confidentiality of sensitive data, enterprises are starting to recognize the need for encryption wherever that sensitive data resides. However, given the complexity of distributed computing in the 21st century, the task of encrypting sensitive data across the enterprise is not as simple is it might seem.

Multiple operating systems, databases, web-servers, application servers, laptops, Personal Digital Assistants (PDA), mobile telephones, flash drives, etc. are just some of the varied platforms and devices that enterprises must take into consideration in their encryption architecture.

It is possible to find an encryption solution for each of these devices and/or platforms in isolation; but the complexity and cost of managing multiple encryption and key-management silos is daunting to even the hardiest of IT Operations Managers. While organizations are focused on complying with regulations as quickly as possible, they are also trying to address the security problem at an optimal cost to the enterprise.

As a consequence, any encryption solution(s) must address these following requirements to be successful across the enterprise:

- It must allow the organization to define encryption policies centrally and ensure the consistent application of policy and protection of decryption keys;
- It must allow the organization to recover encrypted data (Ciphertext) even if the decryption key is unavailable on the device with the encrypted data;
- It must allow for secure sharing of information between computers without necessarily having to decrypt and re-encrypt data for each user sharing the data;

---

3 Payment Card Industry Data Security Standard – https://www.pcisecuritystandards.org/tech/
4 HIPAA Security Rule – http://www.cms.hhs.gov/SecurityStandard/01_Overview.asp#TopOfPage
5 California Breach Disclosure Law – http://info.sen.ca.gov/pub/01-02/bill/sen/sb_1351-1400/sb_1386_bill_20020926_chaptered.html
6 EU Directive 95/46/EC – http://eur-lex.europa.eu/smartapi/cgi/sga_doc?smartapi!celexapi!prod!CELEXnumdoc&lg=EN&numdoc=31995L0046&model=guichett

- It must allow for encryption/decryption of data even when the device is disconnected from the corporate network;
- It must allow for cryptographic algorithm and/or cryptographic device plug-ins to allow organizations to adopt newer cryptographic technologies without having to replace existing infrastructure;
- It must scale to handle internet-level loads while being redundant;
- It must leverage standards;

While it is possible to meet all these requirements through individual solutions for each platform and application, it defeats most organizations' goals of trying to achieve optimal Total Cost of Ownership (TCO) for IT assets. Not only do multiple encryption and key-management infrastructures raise costs due to duplication, but there is the potential that with many key-management infrastructures with potentially unique operational procedures on dissimilar platforms, security vulnerabilities could be introduced in the infrastructure through errors and omissions.

3 Enterprise Key Management Infrastructure (EKMI)

Recognizing the need for a standardized infrastructure for cryptographic key-management, the Organization for the Advancement of Structured Information Systems (OASIS) created a Technical Committee (TC) on Enterprise Key Management Infrastructure (EKMI)[7]. The goals of this TC are four-fold:

1. To standardize an XML-based, web-service protocol – Symmetric Key Services Markup Language (SKSML) – for requesting and receiving symmetric encryption key management services. The protocol is based on the royalty-free contributions of StrongAuth, Inc. a privately-owned company in Sunnyvale, California which created an open-source Symmetric Key Management System (SKMS) – StrongKey™ – to manage symmetric encryption keys across the enterprise[8];

2. To create Implementation and Operations Guidelines for EKMI, so that companies trying to address this problem have specific guidelines on how to architect, build and operate a secure EKMI;

3. In conjunction with members from Information System Audit and Control Association (ISACA). to create Audit Guidelines for how to audit EKMIs – specifically how to distinguish between secure and insecure EKMI implementations and operations;

4. To create an interoperability test-suite for the SKSML protocol to ensure compliance with OASIS standards;

An EKMI is defined as a collection of policies, procedures and technology to manage _all_ cryptographic keys within the enterprise. The keys may be symmetric encryption keys such as Triple-Data Encryption Standard (3DES), Advanced Encryption System (AES), Blowfish, etc. or asymmetric cryptographic keys such as RSA or Elliptic Curve (EC), etc.

While policies, procedures and technology is well standardized for asymmetric cryptographic keys with the body of knowledge known as Public Key Infrastructure (PKI) – mostly through standards created by the Internet Engineering Task Force's (IETF) Public Key Infrastructure X.509 Working Group (PKIX)[9] – similar policies, procedures and technology standards for the large-scale management of symmetric encryption keys do not exist.

---

7 OASIS EKMI TC: http://www.oasis-open.org/committees/tc_home.php?wg_abbrev=ekmi
8 StrongKey™ – http://www.strongkey.org
9 IETF PKIX – http://www.ietf.org/html.charters/pkix-charter.html

The International Standards Organization (ISO) has published standards such as ISO 11770-3:1999 Key management, while the American National Standards Institute (ANSI) has published documents such as X9.117 and X9.24 related to key-management. However, these standards primarily focus on financial sectors without addressing the general computing infrastructure of companies within and outside the financial sector.

The Institute of Electrical and Electronics Engineers (IEEE) has recently started a working group designated P1619.3, titled "Standard for Key Management Infrastructure for Cryptographic Protection of Stored Data" and whose scope is ".. an architecture for the key management infrastructure for cryptographic protection of stored data, describing interfaces, methods and algorithms."[10]

While the P1619.3 group has a more general focus than the ISO/ANSI standards, the group still restricts itself to key-management for storage devices such as disk-drives, tape-drives, SAN, NAS, etc., leaving the vast majority of applications fending for themselves between the application layer and the storage layer.

Consequently, the OASIS EKMI TC is focusing its energy on standardizing policies, procedures and technologies around Symmetric Key Management Systems (SKMS) while leveraging the vast body of work already standardized and defined by IETF PKIX, OASIS and the World Wide Web Consortium (W3C).

3.1 SKMS Architecture

Architected along the lines of the ubiquitous Domain Name Service (DNS), an SKMS consists of one or more centralized **Symmetric Key Services (SKS)** servers on the network, any number of clients using the **Symmetric Key Client Library (SKCL)** to request services from the SKS servers and an XML-based protocol for communication between the SKCL and the SKS servers, known as the **Symmetric Key Services Markup Language (SKSML)**.

The following graphic shows a high-level representation between a single SKS server and a single SKCL client. (Please note that the representation shown below is that of the open-source implementation, StrongKey™, which happens to be a Java2 Enterprise Edition (J2EE) application. It is possible for implementers of the SKSML protocol to architect a completely different solution that does not use J2EE or Java).

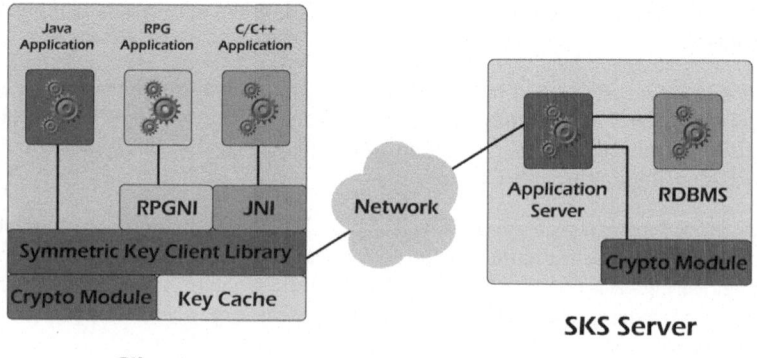

Figure 1: SKMS Architecture

10 IEEE P1619.3 – http://ieee-p1619.wetpaint.com/page/Key+Management+Subcommittee+PAR+Worksheet

Each SKS server consists of:

- a server-class computer running an operating system – typically Linux, UNIX or Windows – that has a compliant Java Virtual Machine (JVM) available for it;
- a relational database that serves as the storehouse for the symmetric encryption keys;
- a J2EE-compliant application server to respond to requests over the network, serving as the workhorse of the SKMS;
- a JCE-compliant cryptographic provider to perform the cryptographic operations of key-generation, key-protection, digital signing, verification, etc.;
- an optional, **but strongly recommended,** Hardware Security Module (HSM) or Trusted Platform Module (TPM) for securely storing the cryptographic keys that protect the database's contents;
- the SKS server software itself, consisting of an Enterprise Archive (EAR) and a Web Archive (WAR) file for the administration console, along with ancillary utilities;

Each SKCL client platform consists of:

- a client machine running an operating system – once again, typically, Linux, UNIX or Windows, but includes the OS/400 – that has a compliant Java Virtual Machine (JVM) available for it;
- a JCE-compliant cryptographic provider to perform the cryptographic operations of encryption, decryption, digital signing, verification, etc.;
- an optional, but highly recommended, Trusted Platform Module (TPM), smartcard or other USB-based cryptographic token for securely storing the cryptographic keys that protect the clients' authentication credentials;
- the SKCL software itself, consisting of an API callable by Java applications for communicating with the SKS server and performing cryptographic functions (non-Java applications have the option of either using a Java Native Interface (JNI) library to call the SKCL, or communicating with the SKS server directly using the SKSML protocol);

The SKSML protocol itself is extremely simple and consists of:

- a call from the client to request a symmetric key – new or existing – from the SKS server;
- a call from the client to request key-caching policy information from the SKS server;
- a response from the SKS server containing the symmetric key and the key's use-policy;
- a response from the SKS server containing the key-caching policy;
- a fault message from the SKS server, if either of the two calls do not succeed;

Given the sensitivity of the information managed within the SKMS, the architecture is predicated on an extraordinary level of security. (As with any security architecture, the controls and procedures in place at any specific implementation determine the degree of vulnerability the SKMS will have against attacks, so please don't assume these controls are bullet-proof and you can skimp on other aspects of security). The SKMS incorporates the following security features:

- all symmetric keys are generated using any number of compliant cryptographic providers, thus allowing sites to use whatever level of sophistication is desired for their implementation;
- all symmetric encryption keys are themselves, encrypted using multiple RSA asymmetric keys;
- all database records on the SKS server are digitally signed before storage, and verified upon retrieval to ensure their integrity hasn't been compromised;
- all administrative operations through the console are digitally signed and maintained in a history log for audit purposes, and verified upon retrieval;

- all administrative operations through the console require SSL/TLS-based client-authentication;
- only digitally signed client-requests are accepted by the SKS server from SKCL clients;
- only digitally signed responses from the SKS server are accepted by SKCL clients;
- all symmetric keys are transported, encrypted for the specific client making the request;
- all cached-keys on the client are digitally signed and encrypted on storage, decrypted and verified upon retrieval to ensure their integrity;
- all private-keys of the digital certificates can be stored on FIPS-certified cryptographic tokens ranging from software to smartcards, TPMs to HSMs to ensure their security;

3.2 Operations

Using the diagram shown earlier, when a client – be it a laptop, a DB application or an e-commerce web-server – needs a symmetric key to encrypt some information, it makes a request for a new symmetric key to the linked in SKCL (or directly to the SKS server if it has implemented the protocol itself).

The SKCL checks its key-cache to determine if it has any cached symmetric keys that are valid for use. If so, it retrieves the key, decrypts it, verifies its integrity, checks its key-use-policy (every symmetric key object has an encryption policy embedded in it, previously defined by the site Security Officer) and then hands the requesting application the symmetric key for use. If the application chooses not to use the SKCL for the actual encryption/decryption operations, it is expected to use the key in conformance with the embedded key-use-policy.

If any of the local checks result in no valid symmetric key being available for use, the SKCL creates a new symmetric-key request, digitally signs it with its authentication credentials, and sends the request to one of its pre-configured SKS servers as an OASIS Web Services Security (WSS)-compliant SOAP request. It is noteworthy to mention here, that since all requests and responses between the SKCL and the SKS servers are secured (digitally signed and encrypted) at the message-level, transport-level security (SSL/TLS or IPSec) is not required for the operations of the SKMS; plain old HTTP is sufficient. Administration console communications, however, do rely on mutually-authenticated SSL/TLS.

The SKS server, upon receiving such a request, verifies the authenticity and integrity of the request, determines the authorization and the symmetric-key policy in force for the requester (or the default policy), generates a new symmetric key based on this policy, assigns it a **Global Key-ID (GKID)**, escrows the key (which includes encrypting it with multiple RSA keys), encrypts the key with the requester's transport digital certificate, logs the transaction details (which includes digitally signing the transaction) and responds to the client with a WSS-compliant SOAP response.

The SKCL client, upon receiving the response, verifies the authenticity and integrity of the request, caches the secured object if so configured, decrypts the symmetric key and the embedded key-use-policy and returns it to the calling application. The calling application at this time may choose to have the SKCL perform the actual encryption or perform it, itself.

A similar process is repeated when a client application needs to decrypt a previously-encrypted object such as a file, directory of files, database record, etc. The application determines the GKID of the symmetric key it needs (which would have been previously stored with the encrypted ciphertext) and makes a request for this key to the SKCL. The SKCL checks to see if the requested key is in the key-cache. If it is, it goes through the standard security-checks and returns the symmetric key to the application; if not, it makes a request to the SKS server for this symmetric key. Upon receiving the request and after the standard security-checks, the SKS server responds with the symmetric key to the client. If the key does not exist for any reason, or the client is not authorized to receive the key, or for other error conditions, the SKS server returns a SOAP Fault to the requesting client.

It is noteworthy to mention, that given this operational infrastructure, it is feasible to use a unique symmetric key to encrypt every record in a database. With such an encryption policy, the breach of any key reduces the exposure of the database down to just a single record. This is in stark contrast to existing designs, where a single key typically encrypts an entire database or dataset, thus magnifying the loss associated with the loss of that single key.

3.3 Implementation

The construction of an SKMS will typically begin with the creation of a PKI – or procurement of PKI services – to manage the issuance of digital certificates to every client. *The architecture deliberately avoided the use of User-ID/Password for authentication because of their inability to prevent attacks against single-factor credentials.* The clients and servers in an SKMS use digital certificates for authentication, and secure storage & transport of symmetric keys within the infrastructure. (Notwithstanding the use of digital certificates, the administration console allows an Operations/Security officer to "deactivate" any client or server on the network without revoking the digital certificate of the affected entity).

Simultaneously, the application that will use the SKCL is modified to integrate the API, accommodate the encrypted data (ciphertext) and the GKID in its database. This raises a valid question of commercial off-the-shelf (COTS) software: how does one use the SKMS if a specific COTS at a site does not support it? Currently, we are at a stage of the SKMS' evolution, just as DNS and RDBMS were at their inception. Before the creation of these "abstraction" technologies, applications had to resolve hostname-IP addresses, and perform data management on their own. As DNS and RDBMS protocols and APIs became standards, application developers abandoned their proprietary implementations to adopt industry-standards- the monetary benefits were too good to ignore. It is anticipated that SKSML will be adopted faster than DNS and the RDBMS, because of the same benefits that would accrue to ISVs and also due to the regulatory and TCO pressures on IT organizations.

Multiple SKS servers are deployed, and encryption policies configured on the servers while digital certificates are issued to clients that will communicate with the servers. The applications are now ready to start requesting key-management services from the SKS servers. The SKMS transitions to Production status at this point, and traditional operational activities take over (backup, configuration management, DR, etc.).

4 Conclusion

While symmetric encryption has been in use for decades within general computing, we have reached a confluence of inflection points in technology, the Internet and in regulatory affairs, that require IT organizations to implement Symmetric Key Management Systems (SKMS) as independent infrastructures. Using the newly released open-source software – StrongKey™ – , and the soon-to-come Symmetric Key Services Markup Language (SKSML) standard from OASIS, IT organizations have another – and perhaps, one of the most effective – defense weapon in their arsenal against an increasingly hostile Internet.

Intrinsic Physical Unclonable Functions in Field Programmable Gate Arrays

Jorge Guajardo · Sandeep S. Kumar · Klaus Kursawe
Geert-Jan Schrijen · Pim Tuyls

Information and System Security Group
Philips Research Europe, Eindhoven, Netherland
{jorge.guajardo | sandeep.kumar | klaus.kursawe | geert.jan.schrijen | pim.tuyls}@philips.com

Abstract

In today's globalized economy, it has become standard business practice to include third party Intellectual Property (IP) into products. However, licensing IP to third parties forces IP vendors to ensure that they can generate revenue from their internally developed IP blocks. This is only guaranteed if designs are properly protected against theft, cloning, and grey market overproduction. In this paper, we describe a solution for the IP protection problem on Field Programmable Gate Arrays (FPGAs) based on the use of Physical Unclonable Functions (PUFs). Our solution includes optimizations at the protocol level, making the resulting protocols more efficient than previously proposed ones. In addition, we show how SRAM memory blocks present in current FPGAs can be used as a PUF. This leads to a solution which allows unique identification of FPGAs without requiring significant additional hardware resources, and to ensure code can only run on authorized platforms.

1 Introduction

Begining in the 1980s, there has been a continuos move towards outsourcing of non-key activities within companies. This is particularly true in the semiconductor industry where the costs of building a state-of-the-art high-volume CMOS digital logic fab range anywhere from 1 to 2 billion US dollars [Brun99], thus making it not cost-effective for single companies to build such a fab. This has led to the emergence of foundries, which can invest large amounts of capital and service several customers at one time. Parallel to this trend, IP developers have also recognized that IP developed in-house can be a source of additional revenue if licensed to external parties. The previous developments have led many companies to disclose internally developed IP to external parties and as a consequence to face the counterfeiting challenge. It is estimated that as much as 10% of all high tech products sold globally are counterfeit [KPMG05]. This translates into a conservative estimate of US$100 billion of global IT industry revenue lost due to counterfeiting [KPMG05]. The same paper advises to employ anti-counterfeiting technologies to mitigate the effects of counterfeiters. In this paper, we deal explicitly with one such technology and its implementation on Field Programmable Gate Arrays (FPGAs).

FPGAs are devices containing programmable logic blocks and programmable interconnect. The programmable blocks give an FPGA the ability to instantiate virtually any logic function whereas the programmable interconnect allows connecting different logic blocks in the FPGA. Since the mid 90s, FPGAs have steadily increased their logic resources. This has lead to an increasing number of im-

N. Pohlmann, H. Reimer, W. Schneider (Editors): Securing Electronic Business Processes, Vieweg (2007), 313-321

plementations and products using FPGAs. Most FPGAs in use today are volatile SRAM-based devices. This means that upon power-up, a configuration file or bitstream, stored in external non-volatile memory, needs to be loaded onto the FPGA providing it with the desired functionality. This flexibility is also the reason why FPGA designs can be easily copied. An attacker can easily tap the bus between non-volatile memory and FPGA on an authentic board, obtain the configuration file, copy it onto a different board, and obtain exactly the same functionality as in the original board. Such an attack is called a *cloning* attack and it results in counterfeited products.

From a security perspective, the counterfeiting threat can be best explained as an authentication problem. In general, we can identify the following security services required by different parties in the overall IP protection chain:

S1. Hardware IP authentication: a hardware design runs only on a specific hardware device, hence it can not be cloned.

S2. Hardware platform authentication: the hardware platform (FPGA) allows only authentic designs to execute.

S3. Complete design confidentiality: the intended design recipient (this could be the system integrator, the end user, etc.) has only access to the design as a black box (input/output behavior). No other party (in addition to the design developer) knows anything about the hardware IP.

S4. Secure hardware IP updating: given that there is already an authentic design running on the FPGA, the IP provider would like to update it and at a minimum keep all the security guarantees that the previous design kept.

S5. Design traceability: given an IP block, the designer can trace back who the intended recipient of the design was.

S6. User privacy: A design should not be linkable to the identity of the end-user

Using bitstream encryption with a key that is specific to a particular FPGA would provide the means to solve most of the problems. This observation is due to Kean [Kean02], who also proposes an associated protocol to support IP protection. The protocol is based on bitstream encryption using a key stored in non-volatile memory on the FPGA. By eavesdropping the bus between the external memory and the FPGA the attacker can only obtain an encrypted version of the design. As long as the secret key is securely stored on the FPGA, the attacker can not perform a successful cloning attack. One general problem with this solution is that there is no non-volatile memory on SRAM FPGAs to store a long-term key. In order to solve this problem two main solutions have been proposed: (i) some non-volatile memory such as flash is added to the FPGA or (ii) the FPGA stores a long-term key in a few hundred bits of dedicated RAM backed-up by an externally connected battery. Both solutions come with a price penalty and are therefore not very attractive. The second solution has the additional disadvantage that the battery has only a limited life time and that batteries can get damaged which shortens further their life-time. Both effects have as a consequence that the key and the design are lost after some time, rendering the overall IP block non-functional.

In this paper, we will focus on providing services S1, S2 and S3. In particular, we propose new and improved protocols for IP protection on FPGAs. We show that the protocols of [SiSc06] (which deals with S1 and S2), can be considerably simplified. We describe simplifications in terms of communication complexity, assumptions, and number of encryptions performed. In addition, our protocols provide privacy from the TTP. In other words, previous protocols allow the TTP to have access to the IP block exchanged between the IPP and the SYS. In practice, this might not be desirable from the IPP's point of view. The cost of TTP-privacy is a public-key (PK) based operation. The public-key operation does not affect the resource requirements of the FPGA implementation when compared to the work in [SiSc06].

This is achieved by performing the PK operation during the *online* phase of the protocol. Finally, we describe the implementation of an actual Physical Unclonable Function (PUF) on an FPGA which is *intrinsic* to the FPGA. Notice that this means that the PUF is already present on the FPGA and thus, it requires no modifications to the actual hardware. The actual implementation and analysis of this FPGA intrinsic PUF is described in detail in [GKST07].

2 Physical Unclonable Functions, Fuzzy Extractors and Helper Data Algorithms

Physical Unclonable Functions (PUFs), also referred to as Physically Random Functions, consist of inherently unclonable physical systems. PUFs are functions embedded in a separate physical structure or extracted from physical properties inherently present in a hardware device (intrinsic PUFs) that map challenges to responses (identifiers). They inherit their unclonability from the fact that they consist of many random components that are present in the manufacturing process and can not be controlled. When a stimulus is applied to the system, it reacts with a response. Such a pair of a stimulus C and a response R is called a *challenge-response pair* (CRP). In particular, a PUF is considered as a function that maps challenges to responses. In general, PUFs have three main properties:

- **Easy to evaluate**. It is easy and cheap to challenge the PUF and measure the response. This implies that the whole evaluation procedure can be carried out with minimal time delay and minimal cost.

- **Hard to characterize**. An attacker, who is in possession of the device containing the PUF can only obtain a negligible amount of knowledge about the PUF. Hence, he is unable to manufacture a device with similar properties. In other words, a realistic attacker (one who does not have infinite resources) cannot clone the PUF.

- **Tamper evidence**. Under a physical attack the PUF gets damaged to such an extent that its challenge-response behaviour changes substantially and the extracted identifiers are destroyed. In addition to the properties previously described, PUFs can be inseparably bound to the device. This means that any attempt to remove the PUF from the device leads to the destruction of the PUF (and/or the device). Hence, an attack aiming at removing the PUF will destroy the data being extracted from it.

PUFS can be used to generate unclonable identifiers and to generate and to securely store cryptographic keys in a device. The following assumptions are made on the PUF:

1. It is assumed that a response R_i (to a challenge C_i) gives only a negligible amount of information on another response R_j (to a different challenge C_j) with $i \neq j$.

2. Without having the corresponding PUF at hand, it is impossible to come up with the response R_i corresponding to a challenge C_i, except with negligible probability.

3. Extracting the data from the PUF is only possible by reading it in the "proper" way, i.e., when an attacker tries to investigate the PUF to obtain detailed information of its structure, the PUF is destroyed. In other words, the PUF's challenge-response behavior is changed substantially.

We distinguish between two different situations. First, we assume that there is a large number of challenge response pairs $C_i, R_i, i=1..., N$ available for the PUF; i.e. a strong PUF has so many challenge-response pairs such that an attack (performed during a limited amount of time) based on exhaustively measuring all responses only has a negligible probability of success. We refer to this case as strong PUFs. If the number of different CRPs N is rather small, we refer to it as a weak PUF; in the extreme case, a weak PUF may only have one challenge. Due to noise in the measurement process, the PUF responses may contain some errors, which need to be compensated and corrected. As PUF responses are noisy (as explained above) and may show statistical correlations, a Fuzzy Extractor or Helper Data Algorithm [LiTu03, DoRS04] is needed to extract usable data from the PUF responses. Informally, we need to implement two basic primitives: (i) *Information Reconciliation* or error correction and (ii) *Privacy Amplification* or randomness extraction. In order to implement those two primitives, helper data is generated during the *enrollment phase*, which happens once in the lifetime of the device in a trusted environment. Later, during the *reconstruction phase*, the data is reconstructed based on a noisy measurement and the helper data.

3 PUF Constructions

This section describes some known PUF constructions including: optical PUFs [PRTG02], silicon PUFs [GCDD02a] and coating PUFs [TSS+06]. Although coating PUFs are very cheap to produce they still need a small additional manufacturing step. For the FPGA protection, we use an intrinsic PUF (IPUF) [GKST07], i.e., a PUF that is inherently present in the device due to its manufacturing process and no additional hardware has to be added for embedding the PUF.

3.1 Optical PUFs and Silicon PUFs.

Pappu et al. [PRTG02] introduce the idea of a Physical One-Way Function. They use a bubble-filled transparent epoxy wafer and shine a laser beam through it leading to a response interference pattern. This kind of optical PUF is hard to use in the field because of the difficulty to have a tamper resistant measuring device. Gassend et al. introduce Silicon Physical Random Functions (SPUF) [GCDD02a] which use manufacturing process variations in ICs with identical masks to uniquely characterize each chip. The statistical delay variations of transistors and wires in the IC were used to create a parameterized self oscillating circuit to measure frequency which characterizes each IC. Silicon PUFs are very sensitive to environmental variations like temperature and voltage. Lim et al. [LLG+05] introduce *emph{arbiter based}* PUFs which use a differential structure and an arbiter to distinguish the difference in the delay between the paths. Gassend et al. [GCDD02b] also define a Controlled Physical Random Function (CPUF) which can only be accessed via an algorithm that is physically bound to the randomness source in an inseparable way. This control algorithm can be used to measure the PUF but also to protect a „weak" PUF from external attacks. Recently, Su et al. [SuHO07] present a custom built circuit array of cross-coupled NOR gate latches to uniquely identify an IC. Here, small transistor threshold voltage V_t differences that are caused due to process variations lead to a mismatch in the latch to store a 1 or a 0.

3.2 Coating PUFs

In [TSS+06], Tuyls et al. present coating PUFs in which an IC is covered with a protective matrix coating, doped with random dielectric particles at random locations. The IC also has a top metal layer with an array of sensors to measure the local capacitance of the coating matrix that is used to characterize the IC. The measurement circuit is integrated in the IC, making it a controlled PUF. It is shown in [TSS+06] that it is possible to extract up to three key bits from each sensor in the IC leading to approximately 600 bits per mm^2. A key observation in [TSS+06] is that the coating can be used to store keys (rather than as a CRP repository as in previous works) and that these keys are not stored in memory. Rather, whenever an application requires the key, the key is generated on the fly. This makes it much more difficult for an attacker to compromise key material in security applications. Finally, Tuyls et al. [TSS+06] show that active attacks on the coating can be easily detected, thus, making it a good countermeasure against probing attacks.

3.3 FPGA Intrinsic PUFs and SRAM Memories

The disadvantage of most of the previous approaches is the use of custom built circuits or the modification of the IC manufacturing process to generate a reliable PUF. In [GKST07], the authors approach the problem by identifying an *Intrinsic* PUF which is defined as a PUF already present in the device and that requires no modification to satisfy the security goals. We describe next how SRAM memories, which are widely available in almost every computing device including modern FPGAs, can be used as an Intrinsic PUF.

3.3.1 Basic Principles of SRAM PUFs

A CMOS SRAM cell is a six transistor device formed of two cross-coupled inverters and two access transistors connecting to the data bit-lines based on the word-line signal. The transistors forming the cross-coupled inverters are constructed particularly weak to allow driving them easily to 0 or 1 during a write process. Hence, these transistors are extremely sensitive to atomic level intrinsic fluctuations which are outside the control of the manufacturing process and independent of the transistor location on the chip (see [ChRA04]). In practice, SRAM cells are constructed with proper width/length ratios between the different transistors such that these fluctuations do not affect the reading and writing process under normal operation. However, during power-up, the cross-coupled inverters of a SRAM cell are not subject to any externally exerted signal. Therefore, any minor voltage difference that shows up on the transistors due to intrinsic parameter variations will tend toward a 0 or a 1 caused by the amplifying effect of each inverter acting on the output of the other inverter. Hence, with high probability, an SRAM cell will start in the same state upon power-up. On the other hand, different SRAM cells will behave randomly and independently from each other. In [GKST07], the authors consider as a challenge a range of memory locations within a SRAM memory block. The response are the start-up values at these locations. Notice also that SRAM-based PUFs produce a binary string as result of a measurement, in contrast to other PUFs, which have to go through a quantization process before obtaining a bit string from the measurement. This results in a reduction in the complexity of the measurement circuit. For our proof of concept, we use FPGAs which include dedicated RAM blocks. In order to be useful as a PUF, SRAM startup values should have good statistical properties and be robust over time, to temperature variations, and have good identification performance. These properties were studied in [GKST07]. Here we summarize their findings. Regarding robustness, the Hamming distance between bit strings from repeated measurements of the same SRAM block (intra-class measurements) should be small enough, such that errors between enrollment and authentication measurements can be corrected by an error correcting code admitting efficient decoding. In [GKST07], the authors compared the Hamming distance between a first measurement and repeated measurements of the same SRAM block carried over approximately two weeks. The experiment was done with four different RAM blocks, located in two different FPGAs. The measurements showed that less than 4% of the startup bit values change over time. Similarly, preliminary data indicates that measurements at temperatures ranging from -20°C to 80°C result in bit strings with maximum fractional Hamming distances of 12% when compared to a reference measurement performed at 20°C. Finally, we notice that intra-class Hamming distances of the SRAM startup values should remain small, even when other data has been written into the memory before the FPGA was restarted. In particular, it is important that the startup values are unaffected by aging and the use of the SRAM blocks to store data. The tests in [GKST07] indicate that storing zeros or ones into the memory has very little influence in the SRAM start-up values. The fractional Hamming distance between bit strings from an enrollment (reference) measurement and any of the other measurements does not exceed 4.5% in this test. The fractional Hamming distance between bit strings of different SRAM blocks and different FPGAs should be close to 50%, such that each FGPA can be uniquely identified. Reference [GKST07] investigated the distribution of Hamming distances between 8190-byte long strings derived from different SRAM blocks (inter-class distribution). The analysis shows that the inter-class fractional Hamming distance distribution closely matches a normal distribution with mean 49.97% and a standard deviation of 0.3%. The intra-class fractional Hamming distance distribution of startup bit strings has an average of 3.57% and a standard deviation of 0.13%.

3.3.2 On the Cost of Extracting a 128-bit Key

Due to the noisy nature of PUFs, a fuzzy extractor is required to provide error correction capabilities on the noisy measurements as well as privacy amplification to guarantee the uniform distribution of the final data. In general, we will need to choose an error correcting code, implement its decoding algorithm on the FPGA, and implement an appropriate hash function. In the following, we describe the choices that can be made to derive a 128-bit key, which can be used in combination with symmetric-key cryptography and the protocols proposed in Section 4.

The fuzzy extractor derives a key K from the SRAM startup bits by first correcting any errors present in the raw data stream coming from memory and then compressing and making the resulting string uniformly distributed with a universal hash function. The minimal amount of compression that needs to be applied by the hash function is expressed in the *secrecy rate* [ISS+06]. In [ISS+06], a method was presented for estimating this secrecy rate using a universal source coding algorithm called the Context-Tree Weighting Method. We have applied this method to the SRAM startup values. In repeated measurements of the same memory block, we find a secrecy rate of 0.76 bits per SRAM memory bit. That means that to derive a secret of size N, we need at least $1.32 N$ source bits, i.e., a secure 128 bit key requires 171 source bits to be fully random. In our experiments, the maximum number of errors that we have seen is about 12%. Thus, assume conservatively that we have a bit error probability of 0.15 and that we are willing to accept a failure rate of 10^{-6}. Since we are assuming that the errors are independent, a binary BCH [PeWe72] is a good candidate with N-bit code words and a minimum distance at least $d=2t+1$. Since we need to generate in the end at least 171 information bits, it becomes an optimization problem to choose the best code in terms of hardware resources, number of SRAM bits required, performance, etc. For example, using [511;19;t = 119]-BCH, we would need 9*511 = 4599 bits to generate 171 information bits. On the other hand, if we assume the error probability to be= 0.06 (i.e. assume that we only need to operate at 20°C), then we could use the binary [1023; 278; t = 102]-BCH code, which requires only 1023 bits of SRAM memory to generate 278 bits of information.

4 Offline HW/SW Authentication for FPGAs

In this section, we present two protocols to use the intrinsic PUF in an FPGA for IP protection. The first protocol assumes a trusted third party (TTP) that is allowed to see the IP block. Then, we introduce a protocol which provides total privacy, in the sense that not even the TTP has access to the IP block originating from the IP provider.

As done in the protocol in [SiSc06], we assume that the hardware manufacturer implements a security module on the FPGA. This security module includes a PUF and an AES decryption module, which allows to decrypt encrypted configuration files and/or other software IP blocks. However, in [SiSc06] there is no discussion about fuzzy extractors, which are required to deal with noise and extract randomness from a PUF. The protocol assumes secure and authenticated channels between all parties involved in the protocol during the enrollment and online phases. During the offline phase an unauthenticated public channel is assumed. Notice that the public channel allows the TTP to have access to *SW* since it is only encrypted with a PUF response, which is stored in the TTP database.

Finally, we assume, as implicitly done in [SiSc06], that the circuit used to obtain challenge-response pairs during the enrollment protocol is destroyed (e.g. by blowing fuses) after enrollment and that subsequently, given a challenge C_i the corresponding response R_i' is *only* available internally to the decryption circuit in the FPGA. Without, this assumption, anyone could access R_i and the protocols proposed (including those in [SiSc06]) would be completely broken.

4.1 HW/SW Authentication Protocols for FPGAs

In our protocols we write C_i to denote the PUF challenge *and* the corresponding helper data required to reconstruct the PUF response R_i from a noisy version R_i'.

We begin by describing how the combination of bitstream encryption and a key extracted from a PUF works in practice. It consists of the following steps: (i) loading the encrypted bitstream, (ii) challenging the PUF with a challenge C_i, (iii) measuring the PUF response R_i', (iv) retrieving the corresponding helper data from memory, (v) using a fuzzy extractor to extract the key K from R_i' using the helper data (vi) decrypting the bitstream, and finally (vii) configuring the FPGA.

During Enrollment, the hardware manufacturer (HWM) measures the PUF with all relevant inputs, and sends those inputs and the corresponding responses to the trusted third party. The system developer (SYS) sends the identity of the software and the hardware platform to the Trusted Third party, which asks the intellectual property provider (IPP) for the actual software. The TTP encrypts the software with a key matching the PUF in the hardware and sends the encrypted version with the appropriate challenge to the PUF back to the system developer. In addition, the block is authenticated with a MAC using an independent challenge to the PUF.

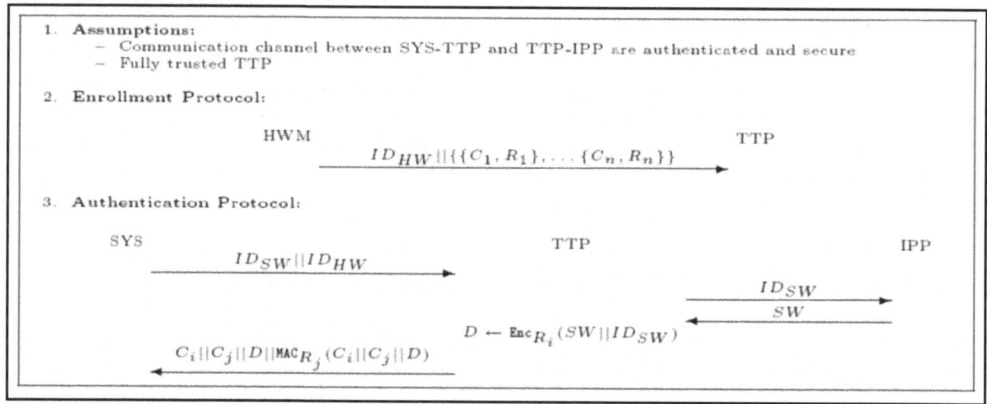

4.2 IP Protection Protocols Providing Code Confidentiality

In this section, we answer positively the question of whether it is possible to develop protocols with similar properties to the previous ones but without having the TTP have access to the software we want to protect. In the following, we do not assume any of the channels to be secure. However, we make the following assumptions: (1) the channels TTP-SYS, TTP-IPP, SYS-IPP are authentic (e.g. man-in-the-middle attacks are not possible), (2) it is possible to obtain the public-key of IPP (in an authenticated way) and use it for sending encrypted data to it, and (3) the TTP is "honest-but-curious". In other words, the TTP follows the protocol in an honest manner but tries to find out as much information as possible (i.e. he wants access to *SW*). The essential difference is that in this protocol, the intellectual property provider performs the encryption. By use of public key cryptography, we can assure that only the PUF knows the decryption key, even though the TTP still maintains the challenge response-lists.

5 Conclusion

In this paper, we describe efficient protocols for the IP-protection problem on FPGA code. In addition, we have also summarized existing PUF constructions. We pay particular attention to intrinsic PUFs as introduced in [GKST07]. This PUF construction is unique in the sense that it is intrinsic to FPGAs and thus, it does not require modification of the hardware or the manufacturing process to be used. We have tested this construction on FPGAs with embedded block RAM memories which are not reset at power-up. We have seen similar phenomena in ASICs and expect similar behavior on any other device which contains uninitialized SRAM memory. At present, we have identified other properties of SRAM memory, which have the potential to be used as a PUF-source. This will be investigated in future work. We will also explore in the future the exact complexity of implementing a fuzzy extractor on an FPGA. Finally, we notice that the unique identifiers derived from the PUFs could be useful for tracking purposes.

References

[Brun99]   Richard Bruner, Catching the Outsourcing Wave – the boom in semiconductor foundries serving fabless semiconductor companies – Industry Trend or Event. Electronic News, April 12, 1999.

[ChRA04] B. Cheng, S. Roy, and A. Asenov, "The impact of random doping effects on CMOS SRAM cell," in *European Solid State Circuits Conference*. Washington, DC, USA: IEEE Computer Society, 2004, pp. 219–222.

[DoRS04] Y. Dodis, M. Reyzin, and A. Smith, "Fuzzy extractors: How to generate strong keys from biometrics and other noisy data," in *Advances in Cryptology —- EUROCRYPT 2004*, ser. LNCS, C. Cachin and J. Camenisch, Eds., vol. 3027. Springer-Verlag, 2004, pp. 523–540.

[GCDD02a] B. Gassend, D. E. Clarke, M. van Dijk, and S. Devadas, "Silicon physical unknown functions," in *ACM Conference on Computer and Communications Security — CCS 2002*, V. Atluri, Ed. ACM, November 2002, pp. 148–160.

[GCDD02b] B. Gassend, D. Clarke, M. van Dijk, and S. Devadas, "Controlled Physical Random Functions," in *ACSAC '02: Proceedings of the 18th Annual Computer Security Applications Conference*. Washington, DC, USA: IEEE Computer Society, 2002, p. 149.

[GKST07] J. Guajardo, S. S. Kumar, G.-J. Schrijen, and P. Tuyls, "FPGA Intrinsic PUFs and Their Use for IP Protection," in *Cryptographic Hardware and Embedded Systems — CHES 2007*, ser. LNCS. Springer, To appear 2007.

[ISS+06] T. Ignatenko, G.J. Schrijen, B. Skoric, P. Tuyls, and F. Willems. "Estimating the Secrecy-Rate of Physical Unclonable Functions with the Context-Tree Weighting Method". In *IEEE International Symposium on Information Theory*, pp. 499-503, Seattle, USA, July 2006.

[Kean02] T. Kean, "Cryptographic rights management of FPGA intellectual property cores," in *ACM/SIGDA tenth international symposium on Field-programmable gate arrays — FPGA 2002*, ACM, 2002, pp. 113–118.

[KPMG05] KPMG Electronics, Software & Services and Alliance for Gray Market and Counterfeit Abatement, "Managing the Risks of Counterfeiting in the Information Technology Industry, White Paper," 2005.

[LiTu03] J.-P. M. G. Linnartz and P. Tuyls, "New Shielding Functions to Enhance Privacy and Prevent Misuse of Biometric Templates," in *Audio-and Video-Based Biometrie Person Authentication — AVBPA 2003*, ser. LNCS, J. Kittler and M. S. Nixon, Eds., vol. 2688. Springer, June 9-11, 2003, pp. 393–402.

[LLG+05] D. Lim, J. W. Lee, B. Gassend, G. E. Suh, M. van Dijk, and S. Devadas, "Extracting secret keys from integrated circuits," *IEEE Transactions on Very Large Scale Integration (VLSI) Systems*, vol. 13, no. 10, pp. 1200–1205, October 2005.

[PeWe72] W. W. Peterson and E. J. Weldon, Jr. Error-Correcting Codes. The MIT Press, second edition, 1972.

[PRTG02] R. S. Pappu, B. Recht, J. Taylor, and N. Gershenfeld, "Physical one-way functions," *Science*, vol. 297, no. 6, pp. 2026– 2030, 2002.

[SiSc06] E. Simpson and P. Schaumont, "Offline Hardware/Software Authentication for Reconfigurable Platforms," in *Cryptographic Hardware and Embedded Systems — CHES 2006*, ser. LNCS, L. Goubin and M. Matsui, Eds., vol. 4249. Springer, October 10-13, 2006, pp. 311–323.

[SuHO07] Y. Su, J. Holleman, and B. Otis, "A 1.6pJ/bit 96% Stable Chip-ID Generating Cicuit using Process Variations," in *ISSCC '07: IEEE International Solid-State Circuits Conference*. Washington, DC, USA: IEEE Computer Society, 2007, pp. 406–408.

[TSS+06] P. Tuyls, G.-J. Schrijen, B. Skoric, J. van Geloven, N. Verhaegh, and R. Wolters, "Read-Proof Hardware from Protective Coatings," in Cryptographic Hardware and Embedded Systems — CHES 2006, ser. LNCS, vol. 4249. Springer, October 10-13, 2006, pp. 369–383.

Security Evaluation and Testing – Past, Present and Future

Peter Fischer

Vizuri Ltd
1-9 Memel St.
London EC1Y 0UT
peter.fischer@vizuri.co.uk

Abstract

IT Security Evaluation started with the US DoD Trusted Computer Security Evaluation Criteria – commonly known as 'The Orange Book' – in 1983. This was the original and seminal work in this field. Even though it was based on research conducted in the late 1970s (The Bell-Lapadula Model), it remained the predominant standard for some 10 years until overtaken by the European IT Security Evaluation Criteria (ITSEC). The need for a common international standard drove the development of the Common Criteria, which has now been the predominant standard for 10 years.

CC has never penetrated the non-Defence marketplace and, with the growing interest in Information Security in relation to corporate governance, there is an increasing need for independent commercial assurance. In the UK this gap has been filled by the CSIA Claims Tested (CCT) Mark.

In the future it is expected that the trend will be towards holistic, through-life assurance, rather than a specific concentration on product evaluation, possibly in line with the evolving UK Assurance model.

1 The Past

1.1 The Beginning

The concept of structured security evaluation began in the US with the Trusted Computer Security Evaluation Criteria – the Orange Book – first published in 1983 and adopted as a Department of Defense Standard in 1985. This was the original and seminal work on the subject, and some of its tenets are still relevant, for example the security kernel and reference monitor concepts are an integral part of the Trusted Computing Initiative today.

Under TCSEC there were 6 levels of trust – C1, C2, B1, B2, B3 and A1 – each of which representing an increasing level of functionality and evaluation evidence. Actually, the levels were defined the other way around and reduced to reflect lower levels of trust – a problem which has plagued subsequent criteria definition processes.

The approach taken by TCSEC was based on the Bell-LaPadula Security Model, which was essentially a confidentiality model – but the 2 terms were virtually synonymous at that time, certainly within the defence and national security communities.

N. Pohlmann, H. Reimer, W. Schneider (Editors): Securing Electronic Business Processes, Vieweg (2007), 322-328

Perhaps because of the limited options for remote access, distributed systems and knowledge sharing in those dark days before the Internet, data and information flows within IT systems and networks were basic and simple, which encouraged the development of several data flow models, including the Biba Model, the Clark-Wilson Integrity Model and the Brewer and Nash (Chinese Wall) Model.

1.2 Evolution – the Road to Common Criteria

As the criteria in TCSEC were based on the Bell-LaPadula Model, itself the result of research undertaken during the 1970s, a number of interpretations of TCSEC (the Orange Book) were needed, eg to cover networked and distributed systems – these became known as the 'Rainbow Series'.

Despite its title, TCSEC was used to evaluate products – mainly operating systems, but later database management systems, etc. Evaluation was performed by the US National Computer Security Center (NCSC) and was restricted to (predominantly) US-owned vendors.

Opportunities for non-US vendors to get their products evaluated and certified against TCSEC were few. Although some evaluations against the criteria were undertaken by UK Evaluation Facilities (Admiral and Logica – now merged into LogicaCMG) and certified by CESG, these had no international recognition.

Consequently, a number of countries, including France, Germany and the UK (UK Confidence Levels) started to develop their own national evaluation criteria. In the late 1980s DGXIII of the European Commission brought together these 3 with the Netherlands, who were also doing some work in this area, and initiated work which led to the development of the European IT Security Evaluation Criteria (ITSEC), published in 1991.

ITSEC separated functionality requirements from assurance requirements, with 6 levels of the latter – E1 to E6. Functionality requirements were defined separately. Although it was envisaged that Functionality Classes would evolve with participation from the vendors, this vision was never realised.

By 1993 Canada had published its own criteria – CTCPEC. TCSEC was 10 years old, and based on research conducted between 1970 and 1980, and was beginning to strain at the seams. Initially, the US authorities – the National Security Agency (NSA) and the National Institute of Standards and Technology (NIST) – flirted with the development of new US Federal Criteria. However, pressure from the industry, who wanted and needed a single, internationally recognised evaluation and certification scheme, and recognising the success of ITSEC across Europe, negotiations between the US, Canadian and European authorities resulted in the development of the Common Criteria (CC). Common Criteria was enshrined as an ISO standard (ISO 15408) in 1999.

Common Criteria follows the ITSEC model of separating functionality from assurance. There are 7 levels of assurance (E1-E7) with certifications at E1 through E4 being recognised by all participating authorities and certifications at E1-E7 recognised within the European Community under the Common Criteria Recognition Arrangement (CCRA). National Security requirements are excluded from the recognition arrangement.

CC also allows for the development of Protection Profiles (PPs) which specify both functionality and assurance requirements for specific technology types. PPs are owned by the nation who registers them and are not automatically covered by the CCRA.

2 The Present (More or Less)

2.1 Common Criteria

Although CC was welcomed (rightly) as a major step forward on its introduction, 10 long years have passed. Regrettably, CC has not evolved adequately and some potentially serious problems have emerged, These include:

Static paradigm
CC evaluations are conducted against a specific version of a product in a specific configuration and on a specific platform. The configuration often does not represent common usage, the platform might be obsolescent and, because of the extended timescales of the evaluation, the version is often obsolescent by the time of certification.

Software development methods
Common criteria evaluations depend on the submission of evidence in a specific form, based on the waterfall method of software development. Whilst this was recognised as best practice 10+ years ago, other development methods are often preferred today. In these cases, documentation needs to be reverse engineered for the CC evaluation and presented as 'evidence' – even though it was not used in practice during design, development, implementation and testing.

Evaluation scope
The scope of a CC evaluation can be as broad or narrow as the developer wishes. Critical security functions can be excluded.

Common Criteria Recognition Arrangement (CCRA)
Over recent years there has been a move, especially within the US, to mandate the use of products evaluated against a specific PP. The prime example is Firewalls where almost all CC evaluations are conducted in the US against a US PP.

Products not Systems or Services
CC only applies to the evaluation of products. It does not cover integrated systems, although there has been work in the UK and Japan on 'interpreting' CC for use in evaluating systems. Neither can CC be used to assure IT security services

Recognition outside 'High Threat Club'
The original intention, especially from developers, was that the CCRA would open up the market for evaluated products to commerce and industry. However, with a few exceptions in the banking and finance sector, this has not happened. So, despite the national security exclusion in the CCRA, the main user community for CC certified products is defence and national security!

Cost and Timescales
CC is a time-consuming, bureaucratic process. Even at the lower levels of assurance (EAL2) the costs and timescales are seen as excessive. Procurers can rarely encourage or demand evaluation because it cannot be achieved within project timescales. And the costs tend to discourage all bar the major developers.

Although the Common Criteria is working to address these issues, this is, in the nature of multi-national standards, a slow process. Moreover, certain issues, such as recognition outside the national security community, are likely to be exceedingly difficult to resolve.

2.2 CSIA Claims Tested (CCT) Mark

The General IA Products and Services Initiative is a UK Government Committee, chaired by the Central Sponsor for Information Assurance (CSIA), with representation from a wide range of the UK public sector as well as industry and academia.

GIPSI members, especially those representing local government, health, education and criminal justice, expressed considerable concern over the lack of independently –assured, trusted products to assist them to satisfy their requirements to implement appropriate controls identified under ISO/IEC 17799 (now evolving into the ISO27000 series of standards).

As a direct result of this concern, in September 2005 Jim Murphy MP (then Minister for the Cabinet Office) launched a new scheme – the CSIA Claims Tested (CCT) Mark.

The CCT Mark Scheme provides a low assurance solution – broadly equivalent to Common Criteria EAL2 – by testing or validating claims by vendors of IA products and services. Claim sets are validated by the Scheme, e.g. to ensure that no important security functionality has been placed out of scope, and the testing is performed by independent test laboratories accredited to ISO 17025 by the UK Accreditation Service (UKAS). CCT Mark certification verifies that the product or service 'does what it says on the tin'.

3 The Future

At a conference hosted by CESG in 2004, stakeholders expressed the view that the availability of trusted products was only a part of the picture. What was needed, in addition, was authoritative information on secure implementation and configuration, assurance of the overall system or enterprise security and a broadening of scope from just development and installation to operational security management. The view was expressed strongly that information security professionals needed information and guidance to do their jobs, not labels.

These views have been taken forward, not just by the UK, and a new approach to assurance is starting to emerge.

The evolving model for security in the UK public sector is based on 4 principles – Intrinsic, Extrinsic, Implementation and Operation.

Intrinsic Assurance reflects the quality and rigour provided by the Developer, an issue not fully recognised by existing security evaluation criteria.

Extrinsic Assurance covers independent security evaluation and testing, i.e. the traditional focus of existing security evaluation criteria.

Implementation Assurance addresses issues such as secure architecture, design and configuration.

Operational Assurance includes issues such as patch and configuration management, regular penetration testing, protective monitoring and incident detection and response.

Whilst this is an excellent model, reflecting the real world and acknowledging the deficiencies of the past, delivery of the appropriate assurance mechanisms, criteria and schemes will be a major challenge. From personal experience adapting and modifying the Common Criteria methodology to address integrated systems has not been a trivial task and took several years to accomplish, even internally within the UK. Similarly, developing a test regime to cover IA services under the CCT Mark Scheme took nearly 2 years to refine and stabilise.

Over the past year or so, evaluation experts in a number of countries have been considering evaluation from first principles and looking at ways of building back into evaluation processes some of the intellectual input that Common Criteria's prescriptive approach has tended to reduce. Using existing evidence from development rather than requiring special documentation and focussing on the intrinsic and operational aspects of assurance could lead to a quicker and more cost- effective approach that is better attuned to today's requirements. But, this work is in its infancy and will take some time to evolve into a stable and re-usable methodology.

There remains both a need and a demand for basic assurance at the lower levels, i.e outside the 'High Threat Club' of Defence and National Security. The UK Cabinet Office has received enquiries and expressions of interest in the CCT Mark Scheme from government organisations in many countries including the United States, Canada, Sweden and Romania; NATO has also indicated an interest. At this stage it is the CCT Mark model – claims definition, independent testing, speed and low cost – which is attractive; there has been little or no discussion on mutual recognition or international standards.

On the *Operational Assurance* front there appears to be a change in focus by the national technical authorities, certainly in the UK, towards protective monitoring, intrusion detection and penetration testing. Again this is a recognition of the real world of IT security and is to be welcomed.

Penetration testing in particular is an important, if not essential, component of a good corporate governance and security profile. For example, a regular and frequent penetration testing schedule is required for compliance with ISO 27001 Control A.12.6 – Technical Vulnerability Management.

For many years there has been a single, recognised quality mark for penetration testing in the UK – the CHECK Scheme operated by CESG. However, this scheme is operated to service UK national security needs and, for a number of reasons, including restriction to UK nationals and a requirement to hold a UK security clearance, the CHECK Scheme is not appropriate for the wider public and private sector. Nevertheless, as the only independent quality mark scheme membership has been used as a differentiator, and even a requirement, for a number of customers outside the national security arena.

This indicates a need for a scheme which will provide a similar level of assurance in the quality of penetration testers, but is suitable for the wider marketplace. During 2007 two such schemes were launched in the UK, CREST and TigerScheme. The CREST Scheme is operated by CHECK Scheme service providers, whilst TigerScheme is run by an independent Management Committee with broad representation from end-users of the service and Government authorities.

4 Polishing the Crystal Ball

In the fast moving world of IT, which IT Security must keep pace with, forecasting is a mug's game. For example, even 10 years ago, who would have predicted the modern world of pervasive home computing, remote working, wireless, etc. Nonetheless, I shall make an attempt.

Whilst the need for product evaluation and testing will remain, it will become an increasingly small percentage of the total Information Assurance spectrum. System assurance and operational security management will become the main focus of IT security.

On the evaluation and testing front, Common Criteria will continue to be used to validate products, but these will increasingly be at the higher end of the assurance spectrum – EAL4 and higher – and evaluations will increasingly be against Protection Profiles. The CC marketplace will remain predominantly Defence and National Security, especially for the US and her allies, and the relevance of the CC Recognition Arrangement will become weaker.

Over time, there will be a move away from Common Criteria towards the evolving evidence-based assurance models, and from mutual recognition to bi- and multi-lateral recognition arrangements

At the lower (commercial) levels, the demand for independent and credible assurance will increase and the CCT Mark model, possibly with some modifications to reflect national priorities, will become the norm.

System security evaluation and testing will become the norm – Japan (Common Criteria) and the UK (CESG's Tailored Assurance Service) are currently leading the field in this area. In the longer term, as Information Assurance becomes more recognised as an essential part of business assuarnce and governance, security evaluation and testing will become more integrated into system testing, together with independent acceptance, load, stress and performance testing.

There will be a major growth in the area of operational IT security management, with Intrusion Detection and Prevention becoming as pervasive as Anti-Virus is today, both as products and services. Patch Management, Configuration Management and Penetration Testing will become standard practice, involving both in-house experts and service providers.

Until recently independent, professional qualifications in the important field of vulnerability assessment and penetration testing were the preserve of government national security organisations, but that is changing with, for example, the TigerScheme in the UK.

5 Conclusion

It is now recognised that product assurance alone is not sufficient – if indeed it ever was – and a more complete approach to IT security assurance is needed.

The new model – *Intrinsic, Extrinsic, Implementation, Operation* – appears to have merit, but as yet is unproven. Appropriate standards, criteria, processes and schemes will need to be put in place if this approach is to fulfil its potential.

Common Criteria has flattered to deceive and has not delivered assurance to meet the mainstream requirements. It is now dated and, although strenuous efforts are being made to update it, in the longer term it is likely to be superseded by evolving evidence-based assurance approaches, particularly for the Defence marketplace.

The gap at the lower end of the assurance spectrum has been met in the UK by the CSIA Claims Tested Scheme and this model is being investigated by a number of countries as a possible solution.

System security evaluation and testing will have a higher profile, and in time will be integrated with other system evaluation and testing processes.

Assurance throughout operation is an increasing focus, and this should be met by improved intrusion detection and intrusion prevention products and services. This will be supplemented by regular vulnerability and penetration testing.

References

Bell-LaPadula Model: *Secure Computer Systems: Mathematical foundations* (1973), *Secure Computer Systems: Unified Exposition and MULTICS Interpretation* (1976) MITR-2997 by David E. Bell and Leonard J LaPadula

Biba Integrity Model: *Integrity Considerations for Secure Computer Systems* MITR-3153 by K. J. Biba (1977)

Brewer and Nash Model: *The Chinese Wall Security Policy* by D. F. C Brewer and M. J. Nash (IEEE Symposium of Security and Privacy, 215-228 (1989)

Clark-Wilson Model: *A Comparison of Commercial and Military Computer Security Policies* by David D. Clark and David R. Wilson (1987 IEEE Symposium on Security and Privacy)

CSIA Claims Tested (CCT) Mark: *www.cctmark.gov.uk*

ITSEC: *Information Technology Security Evaluation Criteria (ITSEC): Preliminary harmonised Criteria* COM (90) 314, Version 1.2 (1991)

TCSEC: *Department of Defence Trusted Computer Security Evaluation Criteria* DoD 5200-28-STD (1985)

TigerScheme: *www.tigerscheme.org*

UKAS: *United Kingdom Accreditation Service – www.ukas.com*

Economics of
Security and
PKI Applications

Managing Information Security in Small and Medium Sized Enterprises: A Holistic Approach

Anas Tawileh · Jeremy Hilton · Stephen McIntosh

School of Computer Science, Cardiff University
5 The Parade, Cardiff CF24 3AA, UK
{m.a.tawileh | jeremy.hilton | s.b.mcintosh}@cs.cardiff.ac.uk

Abstract

Small to medium sized enterprises (SMEs) constitute a major part of the global economic activity. Due to the distinct characteristics of these enterprises, approaches to information security management that were mainly developed for larger organisations can not be feasibly applied in the context of SMEs. In this paper, we present some of the challenges impeding the implementation of information security management in SMEs. We propose a holistic approach based on Soft Systems Methodology to facilitate the development of security management systems within SMEs. The new approach acknowledges the limitations faced by SMEs and accounts for the systemic nature of the information security problem. We demonstrate the usefulness of our approach through a practical case study. The paper concludes with a brief summary of the findings and presents directions for future work.

1 Introduction

The Internet has been growing at a significant pace over the past few years. Both large and small-to-medium sized businesses invested substantial resources to create their presence on the global network. Increasingly, more information is created or converted into digital format, saved in different storage devices and transmitted over a plethora of interconnected networks. While the rapid growth of the Internet has changed the way we communicate, conduct business and achieve our goals, crime and security threats such as badware, spam, phishing and viruses have also increased, undermining users' trust and confidence in the Internet [HoHD02].

These threats can also result in major losses for companies around the world and impair the continued growth and utilization of the beneficial aspects of the Internet and the global Information Society. Such costs are incurred through loss of productivity, loss of business and damage to the organisation's "brand", and through the investments required for the protection of connected systems from attacks and misuse [CaMR04] [AsCH03].

The information security problem is characterized by complexity and interdependence. It contains a significant number of factors and elements that interrelate with each other. The presence of the human factor complicates the situation even further, as humans have free will, and will always act upon their own best interest [Jame96]. Moreover, the increasing reliance on the Internet in almost every business activity makes security a major concern on the agendas of many different stakeholders (individuals, businesses, governments, etc) [PaPo00] [TI3P03].

N. Pohlmann, H. Reimer, W. Schneider (Editors): Securing Electronic Business Processes, Vieweg (2007), 331-339

As security is a common concern among all stakeholders, combating information threats requires collaboration to ensure that the Internet is a secure medium which is needed for building a thriving information society. However, one of the challenges in reaching collaboration is that each group has a different position and approach to how to address security issues and deal with the potential trade-offs related to security and usability. Furthermore, different stakeholders possess different resources that they can invest in countering security threats. The gap between large and small-to-medium sized enterprises in the information security arena has been increasing substantially as a direct result of the scarcity of resources available to SMEs.

A significant element of any information security system are the costs associated with its design, development, implementation and decommissioning. Major investments need to be expended to build and maintain highly reliable, responsive and trustworthy information security systems [Ande01]. While very few would argue that information stored, processed and communicated in computer systems do not incur significant risks, the case for investing in appropriate security measures may still be difficult to justify [Lamp00]. It can be argued that the major reason behind the prioritisation of information security on corporate agendas in the past decade has been the increased and stringent regulatory compliance requirements imposed on commercial organisations. In addition, large businesses have developed a reasonable understanding of the consequences of poorly protected information systems. Consequently, larger proportions of business budgets have been allocated to improving the protection of the corporate digital assets.

While these investments and initiatives will certainly reduce the threats posed by the modern electronic marketplace, other aspects of the problem remain largely unaddressed. The complexity and interdependence of the security problems on the Internet seriously limit the effectiveness of any initiative undertaken within specific organisational or geographical contexts. Threats and attacks can originate from anywhere, without being bound to specific geographies or organisational borders [YeBU03].

Because of a serious lack of awareness of the negative consequences of information security issues and threats among small to medium sized enterprises (SMEs) [eCom00], added to the perception of less strict regulatory compliance requirements and the very high relative costs of securing digital information, the information and communications infrastructures within these firms remain highly unsecured and vulnerable [ABS03]. Increasingly, interconnectedness is becoming a major requirement for business communications. Large organisations rely on the services provided by many smaller partners and contractors spread across geographical borders. These smaller firms should be granted certain levels of access to the large organisations' information systems in order to deliver on their business contracts. By gaining access to the organisational information systems, partners and contractors are effectively becoming parts of the corporate network. Given the possibility for security threats and attacks to originate from any machine connected to the global network, SMEs act as the "weakest link" in the network. The weakest link in any network is an attractive point of entry for intruders to hack into the system and any network is as secure as its weakest link. This implies that for the global Internet to be properly secured, a more holistic approach should be taken, with special attention paid to the weakest link: SMEs.

In this paper, we present a new holistic approach to the management of information security in SMEs based on Soft Systems Methodology. Firstly, we will discuss the importance of the security problem within SMEs and why there is a need for a simple, holistic and low cost approach to security management. Afterwards, we introduce our approach to managing security in SMEs and explain the system development process. The application of the model in real world situations is then described through a practical case study and the paper concludes with a summary of the discussion and the areas that require further research.

1 Background

The problem of information security in SMEs cannot be solved only by raising awareness about the seriousness of its consequences. Within the UK, Government, in the form of the DTI, and industry organizations such as the Institute of Directors and the Confederation of British Industry, regularly publish general guidance for industry about the risks. However, many other factors are at play to complicate the situation even more; and the call for immediate action is vital. Even with appropriate awareness and complete understanding of the security issues, SMEs do not possess the required resources (human, monetary or technical) that should be invested to solve the problem. SMEs typically operate under very tight budgets; have seriously limited manpower and many needs competing for a very limited supply of resources, leading to information security being pushed down the priorities list. There is a negative feedback cycle at play here: less awareness of the information security problem pushes it down the priorities list, which in turn reduces the resources allocated to it, leading to even lower awareness (Fig. 1).

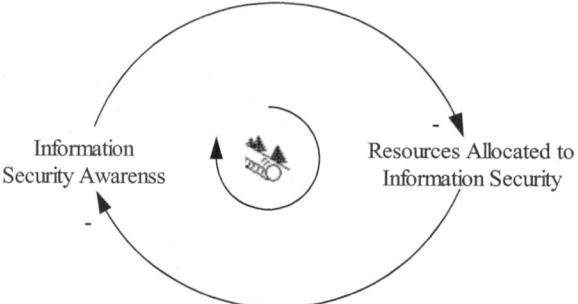

Fig. 1: Negative Feedback Loop of Information Security Awareness in SMEs

While the above mentioned problems do not usually occur in the context of large organisations, they certainly have a significant effect on the security problem within these firms. The interconnectedness of the Internet implies that even though these problems may be contained within smaller businesses, they have a substantial impact on other organisations as well. Most of the initiatives started in order to improve information security in large organisations had a local focus, assuming that the development of company-wide information and communications security infrastructure will enhance the security status across the organisation. This assumption ignores the essential fact that electronic attacks and security threats can originate from any place on the globe. An increased protection of the perimeter of the corporate network is not an effective option anymore due to the cross-border communication and collaboration requirements. Security should be approached with a holistic perspective that considers the interdependent and interconnected nature of modern global communications [ChCZ04].

Furthermore, because of the serious shortage of qualified technology professionals and expertise, information security is generally perceived as a high cost that should be justified well enough to be pursued [LaEl00]. Large and multinational organisations and conglomerates are struggling to get their own security budgets approved and allocated, even though the case they are making is quite appealing. With this perceived high cost of security, it will be over-optimistic to assume that large corporations will allocate sufficient resources to develop security outside their organisational borders.

To understand the scope of the information security problems within SMEs and how they might affect the information assurance status of the whole economy, the relative volume of business conducted by SMEs was compared against the overall economic activity in Europe and the United States. The Department of Trade and Industry (DTI) in the UK reported a total number of business enterprises of 4.3

million at the start of 2005. Small enterprises (defined as having 0–49 employees) constitute 99.3 % of this figure, while medium businesses (50–249 employees) represent 0.1 %. Only 0.1 % of all businesses in the UK fall into the large enterprises category (more than 250 employees) [Dti05].

Europe has, according to the Observatory of European SMEs, more than 19 million small or medium sized enterprises (using the same classification scheme mentioned above), comprising 99.8 % of all business enterprises in the continent. On the other hand, only 6,000 enterprises in Europe are large businesses [EuCo03]. In the United States, small and medium sized enterprises (those with fewer than 500 employees), constitute 99.7 % of all businesses [SBAo03].

Chris Anderson [Ande06] identified several reasons behind the proliferation of extreme market segmentation and niche creation witnessed in the last two decades. He claims that the Internet has radically changed the market dynamics of many major industries. The democratisation of production and distribution tools has placed significant power in the hands of small businesses and, to a certain degree, levelled the playing field for competition with larger corporations. This has led to the creation of a virtually unlimited number of micro market niches in almost every single industry. Small businesses are better fitted to satisfy the requirements of these micro niches, which in turn resulted in the significant growth of these businesses. The development of aggregators (websites that mediate transactions between consumers and producers in the world of unlimited choice [Ande06]) has lowered barriers to entry and supported the growth of new market entrants. Anderson argues that these trends will continue for many years to come. This would lead to further expansion of SMEs both in number and market share.

In addition to describing the forces behind the increasing proliferation of SMEs, Anderson's ideas draw attention to the projected growth in the information security problems in these organisations. Micro businesses established to satisfy the demands of the emerging tiny market niches do not possess adequate time, nor resources to actively tackle the issues of information security. Traditional approaches to information security cannot provide satisfactory solutions to the needs of these businesses. Most of the current approaches require considerable investments of time and resources, and demand high levels of technical expertise. Therefore, the "Long Tail" of the business information security market remains unaddressed. The next section presents a suggested holistic approach to tackle information security management in SMEs.

2 A Holistic Approach to Information Security

Several methodologies and standards were developed to address the increasingly important issues of information security (examples include CRAMM [Cram06] and ISO17799 [Iso05]). Some of these standards became mandatory requirements imposed by different regulatory compliance legislation. However, we argue that these approaches were not designed specifically with SMEs in mind. As a result, they require substantial technical expertise and significant investments. We propose a simple approach to information security management in SMEs that avoids the limitations of previous methods while acknowledging the systemic nature of the situation. The approach is based on the four main stages illustrated in Fig. 2.

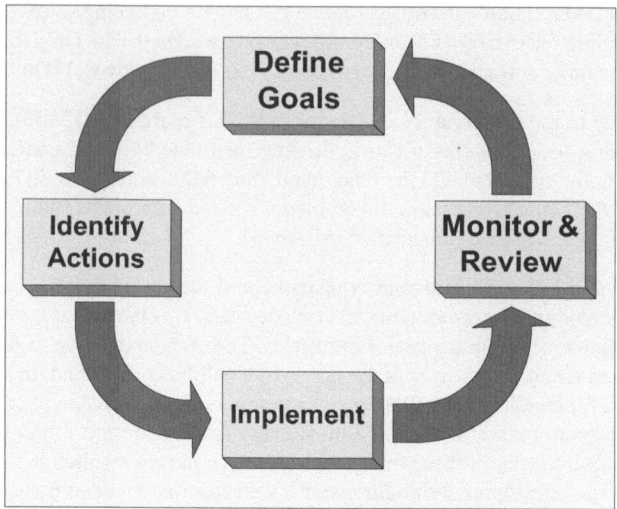

Fig. 2: Four Stages of the SME Security Management Process

Before any information security management system can be developed, the intended objectives of the system must be clearly defined and formulated. It is important to acknowledge at this stage the changing business environment in which SMEs usually operate. This will require the security objectives to adapt to match the new business requirements. Therefore, flexibility in defining and redefining goals with minimum resource requirements is critical to the success of the proposed approach. To define the requirements in a clear and unambiguous way, we propose the use of the Soft Systems Methodology (SSM). SSM was proposed by Peter Checkland as "a general problem solving approach appropriate to human activity systems" [Chec99].

SSM suggests an intellectual construct called a "Root Definition" (RD), which aims to provide a clear and unambiguous textual definition of the system to be modelled (in this case the information security management system). It provides a way to capture the essence (root) of the purpose to be served by this system [Chec99]. The Root Definition has 6 components, which can be memorised using the mnemonic (CATWOE). We have mapped these elements to match the purposes of information security management in SMEs and to facilitate the development process. The mapping is provided in Table 1.

Table 1: Elements of a Root Definition

Element	Original Description	SME Security
C	Customer of the system	In which organisation will the information security management system (ISMS) be implemented?
A	Actors in the system	Who will implement and maintain the ISMS?
T	The Transformation process that the system should undertake	What is the single most important objective to be achieved by the ISMS?
W	(Weltanschuuang) or Worldview upon which the system is based	How the company's security objectives will be achieved?
O	Owner of the system	Who is the owner of the organisation?
E	Environmental constraints	What are the constraints affecting the ISMS within the organisation?

3 Case Study

The following case study illustrates the process of capturing the goals of the information security management system in a small organisation. Firstly, the elements of the root definition should be defined by answering the questions posed in Table 1. While this may be a reversed order of deriving root definitions compared to the suggestions of SSM, (in the "pure" form of which it is argued that the CATWOE mnemonic should be used as a "quality" test of the Root Definition) it would significantly reduce the difficulty of developing these definitions[1]. This case study described the implementation of our holistic information security management approach at a small consultancy firm (3 employees) based in Germany. Table 2 provides Logiteca's answers to the CATWOE questions.

Table 2: Analysis of Logiteca's Requirements

Element	SME Security Question	Logiteca's Answer
C	In which organisation will the information security management system (ISMS) be implemented?	Logiteca.
A	Who will implement and maintain the ISMS?	Logiteca's staff members.
T	What is the single most important objective that should be supported by the ISMS?	Operate the business with reliable information appropriate to current business needs.
W	How this objective will be achieved?	Ensuring staff members understand and act on relevant security issues and that the company's information systems are established and operated in a manner appropriate to the importance of the information processed.
O	Who is the owner of the organisation?	Logiteca's general manager.
E	What are the constraints affecting the ISMS within the organisation?	Limited time, funds and staff.

Based on these answers, the root definition of the ISMS at Logiteca can be easily formulated as follows:

> *A general manager owned system, operated by Logiteca's staff members, to operate the business with reliable information appropriate to current business needs by ensuring staff members understand and act on relevant security issues and that Logiteca's information systems are established and operated in a manner appropriate to the importance of the information processed, while considering the limited time, funds and resources available.*

Once the security objectives are defined and captured appropriately in a root definition, the second step entails identifying actions that should be taken to achieve these goals. SSM proves to be an invaluable tool to perform such a task, as it provides a logical approach to the process of translating root definitions into a list of activities through a well defined modelling process. Based on the root definition presented above, a model of the intended ISMS was developed (Fig. 3) and the list of activities to be performed by Logiteca was derived. This list is reproduced in Table 3. After the required activities are identified, responsibilities can be assigned to determine who will be doing each activity and be accountable for that. The time frame for conducting each activity can also be determined and the performance measures defined.

---

1 We have for some years been using this approach with postgraduate students unfamiliar with SSM, to coach them in the development of Root Definitions.

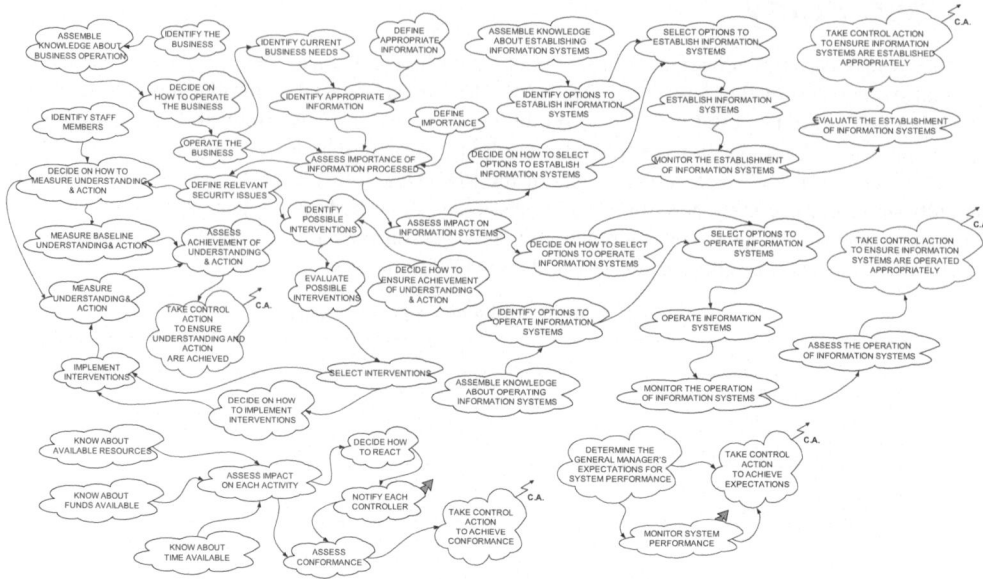

Fig. 3: Soft Systems Methodology Model for the ISMS at Logiteca

Table 3: List of Actions for Logiteca's ISMS

No	Action	Who	When	Measure
1	Define business information	Logiteca Staff		
2	Identify business information	Logiteca Staff		
3	Assess importance of business information	Logiteca Staff		
4	Define relevant security issues	Logiteca Staff		
5	Decide on how to measure security understanding and action	Outsourced		
6	Identify staff members	Logiteca Staff		
7	Measure baseline security understanding and action	Outsourced		
8	Identify possible interventions "awareness programs"	Logiteca Staff		
9	Decide on how to evaluate interventions	Logiteca Staff		
10	Evaluate possible interventions "awareness programs"	Logiteca Staff		
11	Select awareness program	Logiteca Staff		
12	Implement awareness program	Outsourced		
13	Measure security understanding and action	Outsourced		
14	Assess enhancement of security understanding and action	Logiteca Staff		
15	Take control action to ensure awareness and action are enhanced	Logiteca Staff		
16	Assess impact on information systems (IS)	Logiteca Staff		
17	Decide on how to select options to establish and operate IS	Logiteca Staff		
18	Assemble knowledge about available security technologies	Logiteca Staff		
19	Decide on how to evaluate security technologies	Logiteca Staff		
20	Evaluate security technologies	Logiteca Staff		
21	Select appropriate security technologies	Logiteca Staff		
22	Implement appropriate security technologies	Outsourced		
23	Monitor the establishment and operation of IS	Logiteca Staff		
24	Assess the establishment and operation of IS	Logiteca Staff		
25	Take control action to ensure IS are established and operated in a manner appropriate to the importance of information	Logiteca Staff		

The third stage of the ISMS development process becomes straightforward after the required activities are clearly identified, responsibilities and accountability assigned and time frames and performance measures set. Clarifying the actions to be performed enables management to make informed decisions about outsourcing specific tasks and the areas that require guidance from external parties. Logiteca has identified two security training programs. All staff members were enrolled in an introductory security awareness course targeted towards non-technical audiences, while the technology specialist was sent to a comprehensive information systems management course. The knowledge acquired by the technology specialist allowed him to undertake most of the technology implementation activities that led to a noticeable enhancement of the company's overall security posture.

In selecting how to measure enhancement in information protection after the implementation of the suggested actions, Logiteca decided to conduct an internal penetration testing procedure against its systems before and after the implementation. The company was able to demonstrate a 50% reduction in the vulnerabilities of its information systems. Interestingly, most of the eliminated vulnerabilities fall under the social engineering category.

Security management should be always perceived as a continuous process. In today's dynamic marketplace, it is no longer sufficient to implement excellent security measures without evaluating the changes in the business environment and requirements. This is particularly true in the case of SMEs. Small organisations are much more flexible than their larger counterparts, and they usually capitalise on this flexibility to enter different markets and adapt the way they perform their business.

The last stage is concerned with the changing nature of the business environment. It aims to adapt the ISMS implementation to respond to changes in the business requirements. When any major change necessitates a significant change in the company's ISMS, the same process described above can be followed to adapt the solution to satisfy the new needs.

4 Conclusions and Future Work

Much attention has been given to the problem of securing digital information in today's technology driven marketplace. Information collected, stored by, processed and communicated by organisations may be very sensitive and incur significant negative consequences if its integrity, confidentiality or availability is compromised. Organisations of all sizes are required to demonstrate due diligence in protecting information they possess. While large organisations have invested reasonably in increasing the standards of information security within their operations, small and medium sized enterprises face many challenges in pursuing enhanced levels of security.

In this paper, we presented some of the challenges impeding the development of information security within SMEs. These challenges contain, but are not limited to, tight budgets, limited human resources and constantly changing business environments. We proposed a holistic approach to managing information security in SMEs based on Soft Systems Methodology that acknowledges and addresses these challenges. This structured approach contains four stages: defining security goals of the enterprise, identifying actions, implementing actions and monitoring and reviewing the security implementation. We demonstrated the usefulness of the new approach through a practical case study. The case study illustrated the effectiveness of the approach in identifying the required actions to be taken and assigning responsibilities. These tasks were conducted within a very short period and with relatively low financial investments, proving the viability of our method for SMEs.

Future work will include the implementation of the approach on several other SMEs in different industries in order to evaluate its effectiveness on a larger scale. This should also include calculations of costs and manpower resources required for the implementation. In addition, adaptation and refinement of the approach to satisfy the requirements of different organisational settings should be pursued. Further guidance on particular security technologies relevant to SMEs and on applying the proposed method should be developed and tested.

References

[ABS03]   ABS, (2003). 8129.0 Business Use of Information Technology (2001 – 02). Canberra: Australian Bureau of Statistics.

[Ande01]   R. J. Anderson (2001). Why Information Security is Hard – An Economic Perspective, in Proceedings of the Seventeenth Computer Security Applications Conference, IEEE Computer Society Press (2001), pp 358–365.

[Ande06]   C. Anderson, 2006. The Long Tail: How Endless Choice is Creating Unlimited Demand. Random House Business Books, London, UK.

[AsCH03]   G. Ashish, J. Curtis & H. Halper (2003), Quantifying the financial impact of IT security breaches," Information Management & Computer Security, 11/2,74-83.

[CaMR04]   H. Cavusoglu, B. Mishra, and S. Raghunathan (2004), The effect of internet security breach announcements on market value: Capi-tal market reactions for breached firms and internet security developers. International Journal of Electronic Commerce, 9:69–104.

[ChCZ04]   Y. Chen, P. Chong & B. Zhang (2004), Cyber security management and e-government, Electronic Government, an International Journal 2004, Vol.1, No.3, pp. 316-327.

[Chec99]   Checkland, P. (1999) Systems Thinking, Systems Practice. Wiley, West Sussex, UK.

[Cram07]   CRAMM Risk Management Toolkit. http://www.cramm.com, accessed April 02, 2007..

[Dti05]   Department of Trade and Industry (dti), (2005). SME Statistics UK 2005: Statistical Press Release. http://www.sbs.gov.uk/SBS_Gov_files/researchandstats/SMEstats2005pr.pdf, accessed March 25, 2007.

[eCom00]   eCom-Adviser, (2000). SMEs: Australia's Business Backbone [Internet Web Site]. eCom- Adviser. http://host.ecomadviser.au, accessed March 25, 2007.

[EuCo03]   The European Commission, (2003). Observatory of European SMEs: SMEs in Europe 2003. http://ec.europa.eu/enterprise/enterprise_policy/analysis/doc/smes_observatory_2003_report7_en.pdf, accessed March 25, 2007.

[HoHD02]   A. Householder, K. Houle and C. Dougherty (2002), Computer attack trends challenge Internet security, IEEE Computer, Vol.35, No.4 (2002)5-7.

[Iso05]   ISO17799 Information technology – Security techniques – Code of practice for information security management.   http://www.iso.org/iso/en/prods-services/popstds/informationsecurity.html   accessed April 02, 2007.

[Jame96]   H. L. James (1996), Managing information systems security: a soft approach. Proceedings of the Information Systems Conference of New Zealand. IEEE Society Press.

[LaEl00]   L. Labuschagne & J. H. P. Eloff (2000). Electronic Commerce: The Information-Security Challenge, Information Management & Computer Security, Vol. 8, No. 3:154-57.

[Lamp00]   B. W. Lampson, (2000). Computer Security in the Real World. In Proceedings of the Annual Computer Security Applications Conference.

[PaPo00]   A. Papazafeiropoulou & A. Pouloudi (2000), The Government's Role in Improving Electronic Commerce Adoption. In H.R. Hansen et al., (Eds.) Proceedings of the European Conference on Information Systems 2000 vol. 1, (pp. 709-716). July 3-5. Vienna, Austria.

[SBAo03]   SBA Office of Advocacy, (2003). State Small Business Profile: UNITED STATES. http://www.sba.gov/advo/stats/profiles/03us.pdf, accessed March 25, 2007.

[TI3P03]   The Institute for Information Infrastructure Protection (The I3P) (2003), Cyber Security Research and Development Agenda.

[YeBU03]   V. Yegneswaran, P. Barford, & J. Ull-rich (2003), Internet intrusions: global characteristics and prevalence. InProc. ACMSIGMETRICS '03, pages 138-147.

EKIAS – Success Criteria
of PKI Implementations

Anja Beyer[5] · Sophie Hellmann[4] · Malte Hesse[2] · Friedrich Holl[1]
Peter Morcinek[1] · Sachar Paulus[3] · Helmut Reimer[4]

[1]FH Brandenburg
{holl | morcinek}@ fh-brandenburg.de
[2]Institute for Internet-Security, Gelsenkirchen
malte.hesse@internet-sicherheit.de
[3]SAP
sachar.paulus@sap.com
[4]TeleTrusT e.V.
{helmut.reimer | sophie.hellmann}@
[5]TU Ilmenau
anja.beyer@tu-ilmenau.de

Abstract

In the last months, FH Brandenburg and TeleTrusT have carried out the project called EKIAS to analyse success criteria of public key infrastructures and PKI implementations. The results are clear, and not surprising to experts. The top three insights are:

- sociological aspects have a higher influence than widely assumed,
- return on investment calculations are only effective if we also look at the targeted business processes and
- users will accept PKI applications only if well trained and supported during the ramp up phase.

The main recommendation for implementation projects is therefore as follows: to assure success focus on people and processes, the infrastructure itself must then follow.

1 The Project

The goal of the project named EKIAS, "Erfolgskriterien für Identifizierungs-, Authentifizierungs- und Signaturverfahren auf Basis asymmetrischer kryptographischer Verfahren", which translated in English approximately says "success criteria of methods for identification, authentication and signatures based on asymmetric cryptographic algorithms", is to find out when and why PKI projects are successful – and under which conditions they are deemed to fail. The project was sponsored by the German Ministry of Research to get indications where further research in the PKI area might be appropriate. It has been performed by the University of Applied Sciences of Brandenburg, Germany and TeleTrusT, a non-profit organization, with the help of further experts, notably from SAP and the Institute for Internet-Security, Gelsenkirchen, Germany.

To be able to tackle this complex topic in a more structured manner, we investigated the topic from three different angles: technological outlook, economical views and user resp. sociological aspects. Using an exhaustive literature scan, the potential future applications of technology have been assembled and

N. Pohlmann, H. Reimer, W. Schneider (Editors): Securing Electronic Business Processes, Vieweg (2007), 340-346

validated with a series of expert interviews. Topics include the development of biometrics and different forms of tokens as well as among others replacement procedures for outdated cryptographic algorithms. The economic aspects have been analyzed by researchers of the Department of Economics of Brandenburg University. Usage and usability insights were brought together in a two-step approach: in a first phase, we interviewed project members of successful PKI implementations and as a second step, we validated the results in a high-level workshop, bringing together experts, researchers, project leads as well as senior IT management.

In parallel, the project team performed several internal workshops to identify insights from the collected information and to deduce recommendations. As mentioned earlier, one of the expectations for the outcome of the project was where further promotion and support for PKI and applications using PKI is needed and where there might be additional innovation potential. The rest of this article will describe the results of the project as well as the recommendations of the project team.

2 Results

2.1 Technological outlook

Compared to other infrastructure technologies, PKI technology has a relatively long implementation cycle and high initial costs. To be successful in a business environment, we need to work with long usage cycles so that the initial investment can be amortized over time. One of the side requirements is therefore that the application context stays (more or less) the same during that same time period. A perfect example is the set of cryptographic parameters that are good enough for financial transactions over a certain period of time, e.g. for homebanking. Another key timing factor is the learning and customizing period, during which users must adopt specific behaviours to securely handle the keys and certificates, such as a new employee ID card.

On the other side, the success of technology is mainly dominated by an increasingly short-term oriented market. From this point of view, the assumption of a long term usage scenario is not very credible. Therefore the discussion on preserving the security of the underlying cryptographic algorithms seems esoteric. More specifically, exchanging algorithms and choosing key lengths for a long term usage will be simply overrun by the need of new form factors and new implementations of business processes in large portions of the market. Governmental applications, that need long term security such as electronic IDs and the archiving of specific documents on the contrary, could benefit from such an approach, since planning, implementation and usage cycles are much longer in the public sector than in companies. Conflicts will occur exactly where these two application areas will overlap, e.g. for tax related processes.

Another assumption that is often made implicitly is interoperability. In fact, there are a lot of applications of PKI technology that do not need to follow interoperability requirements. Examples are VPN solutions or software update processes. We call such applications "mono-process"; obviously, there is no need for interoperability, since PKI functionality can be successfully used in proprietary ways. In "multi-process" environments, i.e. where different processes are using the same security components based on PKI, interoperability is important. Examples here are secure e-mail and SSL. Nevertheless some standards "bootstrapping" is needed since if not, we may have competing de-facto standards – just look at S/MIME and PGP. For governmental applications, international aspects have to be considered; but for all other applications, the standards should be mainly driven by the market.

To be useful, PKI must be integrated into applications. There is not much standardization in this area. But not only algorithms must be interoperable, but implementations as well, this makes product development in the PKI area especially challenging. Even more is required in the application area of digital signatures: we need document interoperability, and we definitively question whether this ambitious goal can be reached by legal prescription. But we identified the biggest demand for interoperability in the area of key management. Often key management is considered as an integrated management capability of the PKI enabled solution, but IT managers complain about the heterogeneity and complexity in managing all these keys, both for mono-process and multi-process applications of PKI. Using the same keys in different applications or alternatively managing keys for different applications in one central management console is definitively a requirement.

Although we will discuss usage and usability requirements later in detail, there are some requirements for the technology related to usability: the user must not handle technical restrictions (as is mostly necessary today when looking at PKI applications) and trust decisions shall be taken over by technology whenever possible ("policy based decision making").

The usage of software keys and certificates should mid-term be replaced / complemented by hardware tokens. There is no trend towards one specific form factor, nor is there the need for such a "PKI device". Whether it will be a classical smart card, a USB token, a mobile phone, an MP3-player, digicams or PCs, or even electronic IDs, the form and usage scenario is not critical to the success of PKI as long as it is accepted by the user. What actually is going to be critical in our point of view is the integration with biometrics. There are two drivers: the comfort not requiring passwords in the consumer and business environment and the security for governmental applications. The acceptance by consumers and citizens will only be reached with a commodity application, such as e.g. the iPhone. Smart cards are still the most favorable choice when it comes to governmental applications, especially now with the option of contactless (RFID) usage. But then, tokens and smart cards shall then also support algorithm exchange for a long-term usage in G2C scenarios.

Finally, the new upcoming IT technologies such as service oriented architectures, smart items and ubiquitous devices will require new trust models which can only be delivered by using intelligent PKI implementations. But in any case, investing in PKI technology will only be successful when taking the user and his usability and economic requirements into account.

2.2 Economic insights

It is useful to look at the nature of the actors in PKI supported processes. We can distinguish three scenarios: subject-to-subject, such as e-mail communication or online tax reporting, subject-to-object, such as web browsing or self-service-applications in company intranets and object-to-object, such as payment clearing or automated stock ordering. The trend towards service orientation and the corresponding IT architectures will induce more object-to-object transactions, eventually even replacing subject-to-subject communications with intermediates not known at the beginning of the transaction. This will make new trust management processes necessary, which we don't yet understand fully today.

The nature and role of a stakeholder in the PKI environment can only be identified once we look at the processes and applications enabled by PKI. But looking at every single process and the impact of PKI on the economics thereof would be very tedious and complex. This is a standard discussion between infrastructure and business processes, e.g. take an e-mail infrastructure, nobody will deny the usefulness of an e-mail server, but computing the business benefit is actually only possible when looking at the multitude of business processes taking advantage of e-mail. The same is true for PKI: the business benefit of PKI as an infrastructure cannot be assigned to one or two specific processes, and this is the reason why a return on investment computation for a PKI project is relatively hard. But there is no other way: one needs to argue for the investment into basic technology that will enable new, better, faster business processes without exactly knowing the actual benefit. PKI is a business enabler (just like Identity Management and Service Oriented Architectures), and as such its benefit can only be demonstrated in the context of concrete business processes.

Looking closer, there are two financial motivations for using PKI: a. PKI allows to implement business processes electronically (such as e.g. digital invoices) and thereby reduces cost and b. PKI allows to standardize business processes (e.g. authentication in the context of business process outsourcing) and thereby to increase the effectiveness of selected business processes. Both motivations require knowledge of the costs of existing processes as well as of potential risks attached to digitized versions. But these numbers are often hidden in infrastructure investments and depend on variables difficult to estimate in general, moreover they are in most cases not comparable across companies, since the business processes are often tightly bound to the specific business case of a company. So if one wants to prove the success of PKI, one has either to perform very tedious and uncertain ROI calculations along the supported business processes. The alternative is to simply accept that PKI needs infrastructure investments and consequently that decision makers need to be convinced about the success of PKI without having an economical proof at hand.

Interestingly, there are a number of successful PKI implementations in use. Especially multinational organizations have deployed large-scale PKIs for their users. But in many cases it is not used to the full extend, a positive example is Siemens, where PKI delivers a central strong authentication for self services and thus IT service departments see the benefit of using this infrastructure for their purposes – that had been implemented beforehand.

The topic of „Return on Security Investment" (ROSI) is not directly related to PKI, but since it often plays a central role when discussing the economic value of security we shortly discuss it here. The problem with ROSI is that there is always the assumption that a potential damage with a certain probability actually occurs in the frequency described by the probability – theoretically. But since no one knows this, any investment into preventive measures are considered by management as opportunity costs. So ROSI does NOT help arguing in favor of PKI.

Since quantitative models don't work easily, let us try to express the benefit by qualitative means. One of the defining characteristics of PKI is the asymmetric nature of the protocols and algorithms. Practical experience shows that those who benefit from the usage of PKI often do not have to bear the cost, so that the benefit structure is asymmetric as well. Now remember that a cost-benefit transfer will not be possible at infrastructure level and that we need to switch to the business process level to be able to do this. And this works quite well in closed organizations – limited by the factors described above – but it is much more difficult to perform such a computation for cross-organizational processes. This is the reason why payment models resp. models for transferring the cost / benefit ratio – such as tested and tried by the Trust Centers – cannot work. We need to look at other factors that motivate to bear the „cost", which also includes change of behaviours, education or loss of control beyond pure product and project costs. A potential motivation might be compliance, i.e. the motivation of reducing the liability risk of executives. Therefore it might be an argument to use PKI to reduce liability on the service provider side, e.g. for homebanking. An argument against PKI nevertheless could be the slow down of innovation, since the investment cycles for PKI will be long.

We finally could try to prove that PKI improves information security. This is an important area, but there is little significant material available. The main reason is that the value of information is difficult to estimate (actually, one can only estimate the value of the integrity, the confidentiality and the availability of information) and that it is so difficult to quantify incidents and their potential impact. We would need the insurance sector to step up to this challenge, the remaining question is how long they will need until they have enough statistical data to perform simulations.

Summing up, PKI without an application, a supported or enabled business process is an infrastructure without any value. The value comes with the new, enabled processes. If there is no need for new processes (or for streamlining existing processes), there is no need for PKI. PKI is a business enabler, not a security technology, therefore PKI cannot be helped with ROSI. PKI needs to prove that a process is more costly without than with a public key infrastructure, and benefits will increase once the initial hurdle has been taken.

2.3 Usage requirements

First, let us look at the availability of products. Open source solutions make a large portion, in many cases we also find individual project implementations, integrated into core business processes. The market consolidates, and we have seen PKI infrastructure products vanishing. The market is still not commoditized, standard implementations are rare. Interoperability is still not at the level of customer's expectations, and especially the key management piece lacks standardization.

In the project lifecycle, PKI is clearly subordinate to higher project goals – such as the new business process support. An interesting observation though is the fact that PKI seem to be sensitive against external influences. We mean by this that requirements and conditions, that often may change during a project, may impact the success of the PKI project as whole. In most cases though, we have observed that the biggest issue is of political nature. Interestingly, the main reason is the trustworthiness of the new processes enabled by PKI: the new repeatable, policy-based trustworthiness means at the same time a restriction of the individual freedom and decision space of people participating in the process, they cannot manipulate the process any more, e.g. by sharing passwords. PKI centralizes trust decision making and assures a given business process. This is explicitly wanted by executives, but often difficult to realize because one needs to act against the interests of individuals. To put it another way: people feel heavily impacted in their freedom by the introduction of PKI.

Even worse: the use case for security is not understood by the average user, so he will not support additional activities or just even decisions he is ought to take. Their expectation is that the processes – and this is true both for consumer and enterprise usage – are secure by default and they do not need to contribute to make them secure – at least they don't consider securing a process to be their duty.

Therefore, the acceptance of PKI applications first and formost relies on the fact that trust decisions must be easy and transparent, and make sense in the context of the supported business process. There needs to be no decision to be taken without a business process in mind – what would be the value of saying "would you like to trust this certificate for everything"? Trust is always tied to a specific context, a transaction. Ideally, there are no decisions at all that have to be taken by the user and the alternatives are already cleared by the trust conditions of the business process.

Experienced PKI project leads reported to us that the workload for help desk activities for PKI is much higher than for standard IT projects. This should not be underestimated. Moreover it is critical to have well trained people at the hotline who do not give wrong recommendations ("it is ok to click "ok" now, even if it says in the manual you shouldn't do so"). Even worse: policy documents such as certificate practice statements are useless in practice "they are there for the lawyers".

The user ultimately needs a subjective feeling for security so that he accepts the new business process. This subjective feeling might well be different from the real security level. An experienced user feels more secure if he can take trust decisions himself, a novice would be overwhelmed and loose confidence. The real problems occur in that respect when implementing cross-organizational processes, since especially in this area trust decisions are not easy nor fully understood, even the responsibility for a specific IT component is often not clear. There are three main scenarios:

- The mass market (online shopping, home banking): the usability must be as easy and as cheap as possible. This could mean that PKI due to its complexity will never be used in that environment.

- The enterprise market: key criterion is as much flexibility as possible, different models for trust and user responsibility must be supported. Standardization is not a must, proprietary solutions often successful.

- The governmental market (ID cards, tax processes): standardization, together with high security and sustainability are key factors. Exchangeability of algorithms, the usage of biometrics and predefined trust decisions are absolutely necessary in this market.

These three markets have their own market dynamics. We learned that it is not very useful to compare them, especially with regards to usage requirements.

Regarding potential liability as a usage driver for PKI, we observe that qualified certificates are mostly not used today. In our view the "a priori" regulation is not realistic, we recommend to implement PKI solutions with their individual security levels and to wait for court decisions regarding the necessary security level of certificates. High security levels and the corresponding investment might be appropriate for some use cases, but not in general, and moreover, the liability has to be sorted out for the business process anyway.

Summing up, we need simple trust decisions for the user. We need to address the political issues about empowerment at an early stage, it is certainly wise to have change management experts in the project team. Don't invest into qualified certificates (except governmental applications), instead into more interoperability, especially for key management and integration into business processes. Simple, ad-hoc trust models (e.g. for "instant workgroups") must be developed, based on specific use cases and processes.

But there is one key learning you should take away for this section: Security consists of control and trust. If you reduce the people's ability to feel in control, you need to compensate with trust to maintain the security level overall.

3 Recommendations

We would like to express the following recommendations for the technical area:

- the ability to exchange algorithms – useful in the governmental scenarios – must also be implemented in tokens. Incentives for the hardware manufacturers to do so are needed.

- Key management will be a key PKI meta-application, which should not be realized individually for every process. Accordingly, one should foster the interoperability of key management.

- New infrastructure trends need trust modeling, such as Service Oriented Architectures.

Our recommendations for the economical part are:

- PKI has currently a negative image. One could carry out marketing campaigns to show the success PKI has already attained
- Forget about Return on Security Investment computation today. The methodologies need to be improved at first.
- Analyze current liability regulations and potential consequences for PKI applications in the B2B and B2C market

Our recommendations for the usage and project space are:

- Qualified certificates shall only be used in governmental applications, global ID cards shall be in focus for further interoperability
- Always consider sociological aspects when investigating a PKI project
- Investigate simple cooperational trust models ("instant worksgroups")

4   Conclusion

PKI is successful, no doubt. It has reached a wide adoption despite its complexity. But there are much more scenarios that could benefit from the use of PKI. Nevertheless, we need to change some aspects when working with PKI. It is a subtle topic, and especially integrating the technological, economical and sociological view will be key to success in the future.

References

The complete project report was in preparation during the writing of this article and can be obtained by requesting it via e-mail from the authors.

[EKIAS07] Project Homepage: "Erfolgskriterien für Identifizierungs-, Authentifizierungs- und Signaturverfahren auf Basis asymmetrischer kryptographischer Verfahren" with further information about the project: http://ekias.fh-brandenburg.de/

Embedded PKI in Industrial Facilities

Marcus Hanke

Siemens Enterprise Communications GmbH & Co. KG
Center of Competence Trusted Identity
marcus.hanke@siemens.com

Abstract

In addition to the traditional areas of use (employees or server identification), a public key infrastructure (PKI) can be integrated in industrial facilities. In this case, however, the characteristics of certificate enrolment and lifecycle management differ from those required for standard implementation. These differences are presented in this document together with potential use cases detailing certificate integration in industrial solutions.

1 Session Abstract

1.1 Introduction

Communication in industrial facilities is increasingly migrating from proprietary communication protocols to TCP/IP based communication, a trend that dramatically increases the potential for attacks. Depending on the sector in which they are deployed, machines are often used in vulnerable areas and security features must be implemented to prevent misuse. The ability to perform remote maintenance is a main customer and manufacturer requirement as this reduces the need for on-site service, which in turn cuts costs. Other security implications, such as ensuring integrity and authenticity, are also high priority.

1.2 Use cases and objectives

Since a PKI cannot be deployed without first looking at the final fields of application, potential use cases for industrial facilities must be analyzed prior to implementation. Generally speaking, a PKI can be manufacturer- or customer-driven. In the case of manufacturer-driven PKI, a manufacturer ensures that only authorized components can be combined or used to communicate with each other. This prevents third-party replacements from being used and ensures that only original equipment is deployed. It also allows manufacturers to implement a licensing infrastructure that permits the integration of components from other manufacturers at the respective facilities. Licensing also includes activation or deactivation of functions. This is already a common, state-of-the-art feature in software licensing. The certificate or signed license file specifies which functions are permitted.

Manufacturer-driven use cases include:

- Authorization of replacement parts
- Licensing
- Internal communication restrictions

N. Pohlmann, H. Reimer, W. Schneider (Editors): Securing Electronic Business Processes, Vieweg (2007), 347-354

The customer-driven approach is more public. It enables industrial facility customers to integrate their own PKI in their solutions or manufacturers to provide the necessary infrastructure. The PKI integration is transparent to the customer. The manufacturer communicates these features to the customer and provides interfaces for them to integrate their PKIs.

This is seen in traditional PKI use cases such as:

- Digital signature
- Authorization
- Encryption

The following are mostly standard use cases that require manufacturers of industrial facilities to implement a suitable solution.

- Remote access
- Digital signature of measurement data
- Code signing

In the case of digitally-signed measurement data, each instrument signs the data. This mechanism guarantees data integrity and enables data collectors to verify and identify the origin of data. A code signing mechanism ensures that a signature is required before any changes can be made on a machine. This authorization process guarantees that changes can only be made by authorized entities. If a firmware update or a new program is uploaded, the machines can verify that the code is authorized by checking the identity.

Potential fields of application include:

- Building services engineering
- Measurement instruments
- Automotive sector
- Control techniques
- Medical technology

The general objective is to increase security levels and avoid misuse of facilities. Standard PKI applications are used to enhance security features.

1.3 Security levels

A risk analysis must be performed to define security levels. Before this can be done, however, objectives must be defined. Unique authentication is one of the most important objectives. This may conflict with the selected implementation since a soft or hard token based solution must use passwords or PINs. This risk must either be accepted or suitable mechanisms implemented to reduce this risk.

The hard token based solution prevents keys from being copied as well as certificates and related private keys from being used several times on different machines. The following table displays major objectives and threats.

Table 1: Risk overview

Objective	Risk/threat	Measure
Distinct authentication	Copying keys Storing pins	Hard token
Secure remote access	Man in the middle	Certificate-based authentication
Eliminate unauthorized manipulation	Unauthorized manipulation of machines	Digital signature / code signing
Licensing	Copying licenses	Integration of machine-specific parameters

This table merely provides a brief overview and is not exhaustive. The threats are similar and in some cases a residual risk must be accepted. The integration of a hard token based solution can be compared with a hardware security module (HSM) for storing keys. The security level is defined by the certification of the selected smart card.

1.4 Architecture

The following architecture is designed for the manufacturer-driven approach. A standard mechanism can generally be used to integrate PKI functionality for openly communicated PKI integration. Manufacturers must provide options for integrating certificates.

First of all, the existing processes and requirements must be analyzed. These results can then be used to define restrictions.

1.4.1 Requirements

The following requirements must be met when a PKI is integrated in an industrial facility:
- Smooth integration in production processes
- No additional maintenance of machines due to PKI integration
- Certificate lifecycle management
- Avoidance of on-site service
- Unique identification
- No misuse of certificates or keys

Processing time is an important factor that should not be substantially affected by PKI integration. The optimum process step must therefore be identified for integration. Avoiding on-site service and maintenance is another important objective. On-site support is much more expensive and time consuming and should therefore be avoided. The PKI should be implemented in such a way that it can be handled easily by support. This especially applies to certificate lifecycle management and certificate status verification. Chapter 1.4.2 describes some restrictions that may occur as a result of this.

Ensuring unique identification and preventing misuse are complementary objectives. If keys can be used several times, unique identification is not possible. If they are used for defining data sources, as is the case for measurement devices, the copying of keys is a critical issue. Appropriate security mechanisms must therefore be implemented.

Certificate lifecycle management depends on the use case in question. In the manufacturer-driven approach, machines are not usually connected to the PKI. This makes lifecycle management almost impossible.

1.4.2 Limitations of PKI implementation

In the case of some requirements, certain system limitations are inherent. Over and above this, a PKI must already be taken into consideration when industrial facilities are designed. If this is not done, it will not be possible to implement certain features. This may be one of the main reasons why hard token solutions cannot be integrated in a system.

In case of smart card integration, hardware must be integrated together with the necessary access mechanism. The recommended implementation is to embed the chip as this prevents condensation and damage. Other aspects such as temperature level and air humidity should also be taken into consideration.

An additional limitation applies to the manufacturer-driven approach. Information regarding which certificate-based functions are implemented and how these functions are implemented is usually confidential. Furthermore, an industrial facility has no connection to the certification authority following initialization. This limits the options for certificate lifecycle management and validity checks. If the status of certificates needs to be verified, this can only be implemented using a certificate revocation list (CRL). Where CRL checks are mandatory, the CRL expiration date must be ignored, otherwise the result may prevent the system from functioning correctly. The same problem applies to certificate validation periods. It is therefore strongly recommended that you adopt a validation period based on the product lifecycle and add extra time.

This may affect security. Taking into account algorithm recommendations from institutions such as the Federal Office for Information Security (BSI) in Germany, there may be a conflict between the validation period and security requirements.

Preventing the misuse of certificates is a major issue that is almost impossible to solve when soft tokens are used. Although, mechanisms can be implemented to protect keys, they can still be identified if sufficient effort is applied. Chip theft is a residual risk with smart cards. Although using an initial password eliminates the need for storing a PIN or password on the machine, this may not be a viable solution for all scenarios.

If the manufacturer of the industrial facility communicates the PKI integration to a customer, this customer has no requirement to operate another PKI. The machines should therefore be connected to the existing PKI using enrolment protocols such as the Simple Certificate Enrolment Protocol (SCEP). Depending on the type of industrial facility, it should also be possible to integrate an HSM for increased key security.

1.4.3 Implementation

The following section concentrates on PKI integration performed by manufacturers. Other aspects are also relevant for servers and are not included in this document.

Prior to starting integration, the optimum process step for certificate enrolment must be identified. This is largely based on the requirement that throughput time is not increased. Furthermore, unique machine identifiers must already be available and part of a certificate. If the keys are stored on a smart card it should also be possible to generate these on the smart card.

For smart card integration, it is also important to define which functionality is required during normal operation to avoid software components that are only needed once. PKCS#11 is recommended as the smart card interface as this can be implemented in the most common use cases.

If you are planning to implement PKI functionality (such as smart cards) in your product, you must take this into consideration during the design phase. Depending on your specific requirements (such as environment or security needs), it may also make sense to implement your customized solution on the chip itself or integrate a cryptographic chip. If this is not included in the design phase, it may be difficult or impossible to integrate smart cards at a later date, as an interface will not be available.

Depending on the design phase, a soft token may be used as a compromise. Although an adequate mechanism is then required to protect the keys, this only increases the reengineering effort that potential hackers must invest before they can identify the keys. The residual risk of soft tokens being copied is much higher, and plans for a more secure solution (ideally based on smart cards) should be included in the product roadmap.

The following figure provides an abstract overview of the implemented architecture:

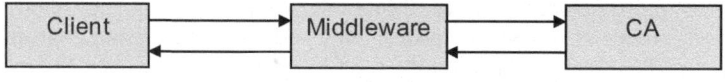

Fig. 1: Abstract architecture

A two-tier CA hierarchy is required for a licensing model. This allows the manufacturer to provide the licensed partner with a sub CA, which can be operated and integrated in the infrastructure.

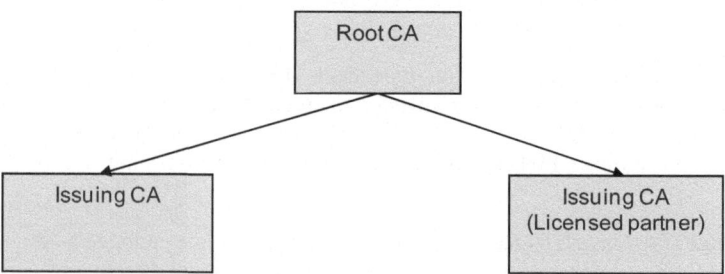

Fig. 2: CA hierarchy

The CA is implemented on a Linux system and is based on OpenSSL. To ensure that the solution is cost efficient, smart cards are used for storing CA keys. The CA keys from the sub CA were generated by an offline machine which was used as root CA. The soft token must be imported on the smart card. This enables the private key to be copied on several cards. Since cards may be stolen, only trustworthy people are provided with the PIN and the racks are locked. Siemens CardOS 4.3b [Siem07] was used as the smart card for storing CA keys. OpenSSL [Open07] uses the engine command to communicate with the smart card. Siemens HiPath SIcurity Card API 3.1 for Linux is used with the PCKS#11 libraries as middleware for the smart card.

The following packages were also used:

- PCSC-Lite [pcsc07]
- OpenSC [opsc07a]
- Libopensc [opsc07a]
- Lib P11 [opsc07b]
- Engine PKCS11 [opsc07c]

openssl.cnf is used for engine configuration during implementation. This is based on OpenSC documentation. [opsc07d] The following figure [hube07] provides an overview of the software stack:

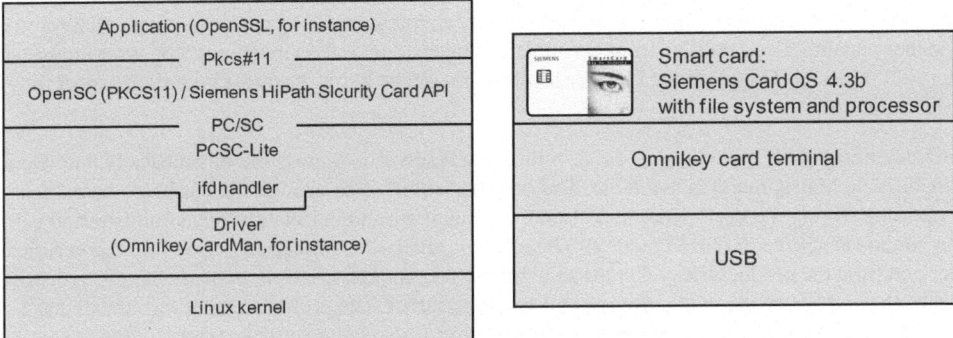

Fig. 3: Detailed software stack

The middleware comprises three components. The system on which the middleware runs is also used to initialize client systems. Once the facility has been initialized it can communicate with other components. This was identified as an ideal process step for PKI integration. The initialized system allows facility-specific identifiers to be read. The middleware initiates key generation at the facility. Keys can also be generated on the middleware system and then imported to the facility. Following key generation, a PKCS#10 request is prepared and sent to the CA from the middleware client. The middleware functions as a registration authority. The CA signs the request and forwards the certificate to the middleware which then installs the certificate on the client system and initiates a function test.

The underlying project uses certificates for client server authentication. In other words, the client site is a classic industrial facility and the server site is a standard computer system. At the certification authority will be PKCS#12-files generated to copy transfer (by file or network) ontoo the server site. This server certificates contain customer-specific information.

The OpenSSL CA also permits certificates to be revoked and CRLs to be generated.

If soft tokens are used by the client, mechanisms should be implemented on the server to prevent extensive misuse of certificates.

In cases where the manufacturer communicates the PKI integration to customers it is possible to provide security from very beginning. This is an option for initializing the system and enabling certificate enrollment processes with the customer's PKI. Where possible, facility customers can then connect their PKI to the server component and replace initial certificates with their own. This provides the basis for a distributed infrastructure with a high security level and strong authentication processes right from very beginning. Service technicians do not need specific PKI knowledge to configure the industrial facility.

2 Enrolment and Certificate Lifecycle Management

The initial enrollment of certificates is usually integrated in the production process with middleware component. This component has also implemented proprietary communication mechanisms. After this enrolment the further procedure depends on the implemented approach. In case that the PKI integration is used only for manufacturer internal processes then this will not be communicated to customers of industrial facilities. The final consequence can be that no Certificate Lifecycle Management can be implemented.

In order to avoid expired certificate in this approach the only possibility is to integrate a CA in the server. On this server some security mechanisms are needed to ensure the unique identification of the machines. In case that it was possible to duplicate the private key an integrated CA enables the manufacturer to exclude these unauthorized entities from enrollment. The residual risk is machines stop working because during key-renewal. Therefore the security level of the private key is the most important aspect for PKI implementations.

If an integration of PKI functions and CA in the central server is impossible this means that no Certificate Lifecycle Management is available. The only possibility is to change the hardware component of the machine storing the certificate. In addition, a manual enrollment via remote administration can be done but this is not the preferred method. Therefore normally the validation period of these certificates is derived from the product lifecycle plus an extra period. Another possible implementation is distributing the renewed certificate with software update of the server. The problem is that this update has to be installed before a certificate has expired. Therefore, this is also not a suitable solution.

A feasible approach is to implement at least a mixed mode. The initially generated certificates can be also used for internal use cases and for customer needs. This makes it possible to provide security out of the box. The first time when the system is set up and integrated in the infrastructure strong authentication is available. If the customer trusts the issuer of these certificates or uses a positive list of serial numbers than the next step can be the migration of these certificates to the customer's PKI. It is recommended to use a list of serial numbers otherwise it would be possible that misuse can occur.

In order to open the system for a customer's PKI additional efforts are needed. The best way is to use a central unit communicating with the industrial facilities. In this central server functions have to be implemented which allow a connection to standard CA communication protocols. The integration of enrollment protocols on industrial facilities will reduce the flexibility and a change in the enrolment protocol has to be implemented on all machines. To avoid this it is strongly recommended to use a central server as middleware. The selected method depends on the scenario in which the machines are used. If multiple measurement instruments are communication with a central server than the implementation of centralized enrolment agent – as the central server can be seen – is the best and flexible integration. On the other hand if only few machines are sold to one customers it might be better to implement the enrolment protocols on the machines itself.

Another advantage of the server implementation is that proprietary protocols can be integrated. Usually standard Protocols such as SCEP or CMP have to be available on server side to connect the CA. The server interacts then as a registration authority and request new certificates and cares for the enrollment. Based on this integration it must be possible to publish and distribute the CA certificate of the customer to the machines. Based on this mechanism certificate lifecycle management can be implemented.

The storage of the certificates on the machines is quite similar to the CA implementation. The software components can differ but the principle remains the same.

3 Conclusion

Using a PKI in industrial facilities opens up additional scenarios which in some cases may be derived from existing use cases. Prior to integration, an analysis should be performed to determine whether the PKI mechanisms are appropriate for solving existing problems. If a PKI is implemented, residual risks should be identified and communicated to the manufacturer. Despite this, implementing a PKI in industrial facilities is an interesting area that poses challenges not associated with more common PKIs.

PKI in industrial facilities cannot be used as general solution. Instead, it must fit specific requirements and ultimately increase levels of security.

The solution described here is only a starting point that needs to be adapted and developed to include certificate enrolment. Standard enrolment mechanisms are therefore required to reduce costs.

References

[hube07]   Online: http://sarwiki.informatik.hu-berlin.de/Smartcard_Based_Authentication, 2007-07-27

[open07]   Online: http://www.openssl.org/docs/apps/ca.html#, 2007-07-27

[opsc07a]   Online http://www.opensc-project.org/, 2007-07-27

[opsc07b]   Online http://www.opensc-project.org/libp11/, 2007-07-27

[opsc07c]   Online http://www.opensc-project.org/engine_pkcs11, 2007-07-27

[opsc07d]   Online http://www.opensc-project.org/engine_pkcs11/wiki/QuickStart, 2007-07-27

[pcsc07]   Online http://pcsclite.alioth.debian.org/, 2007-07-27

[Siem07]   Online: http://www.siemens.com/index.jsp?sdc_p=i1197281lmo1197281pHPcfs4u0z1&sdc_bcpath=
            1197281.s_4%2C&sdc_sid=16935067192&, 2007-07-27

SIM-enabled Open Mobile Payment System Based on Nation-wide PKI

Elena Trichina[1] · Konstantin Hyppönen[2] · Marko Hassinen[2]

[1]Spansion International Inc., Willi-Brandt-Allee 4
D-81829 Munich, Germany
Elena.Trichina@spansion.com

[2]University of Kuopio, Department of Computer Science, P.O.B. 1627
FI-70211 Kuopio, Finland
{Konstantin.Hypponen | Marko.Hassien}@uku.fi

Abstract

Many current mobile payment systems rely on mobile network operators for authentication, and lack adequate non-repudiation. In this work we describe a mobile payment system that uses a governmentally administered public-key infrastructure, namely, the Finnish Electronic Identity. FINEID cards store user credentials and private keys for authentication and digital signature, and upon user request can be issued as an application on a PKI-enabled SIM card which is used as a trusted module in our application. Using FINEID, our system authenticates persons, not customers of a certain bank, mobile network operator, or payment service provider. It also ensures non-repudiation, integrity and confidentiality of the messages related to the payment transactions. As the administration of the PKI system is the responsibility of the government, the system is very economical for both the service providers and the users. The proof-of-concept implementation, a system for purchasing train tickets, is done using freely available development tools and platforms. Implementing an open payment system based on a nation-wide PKI has proven to be feasible.

1 Introduction

Mobile payments are defined as wireless transactions of a monetary value from one party to another where a mobile device (e.g., a mobile phone, PDA, smartphone, etc.) is used in order to initialize, activate and/or confirm the payment [OnPi05, Karn04]. Mobile payments cannot be seen only as a "mobilization" of e-payments by providing a mobile interface to existing Internet payment procedures because the context (business models, players' relationships and roles) and capabilities (e.g., end device and communication technologies) are different. The obvious difference between mobile and other types of digital payments is that the customer and possibly the merchant use mobile devices in order to realize the transaction. This brings a new party, namely a mobile network operator (MNO) into the picture.

Traditionally payment service providers are financial institutions, such as banks and card issuers. They have experience in financial transactions and risk management and have established infrastructure and customer base. In a mobile payment context, mobile network operators are also natural candidates to offer payment services. They have customer base and some financial relationships with their customers via bills. Although a mobile device is only a medium by which payments may be carried out, its technical capabilities and security features may be of crucial importance, therefore device manufacturers also

N. Pohlmann, H. Reimer, W. Schneider (Editors): Securing Electronic Business Processes, Vieweg (2007), 355-366

have a role to play. Other players are newcomers and intermediaries, who can be competitors as well as enablers.

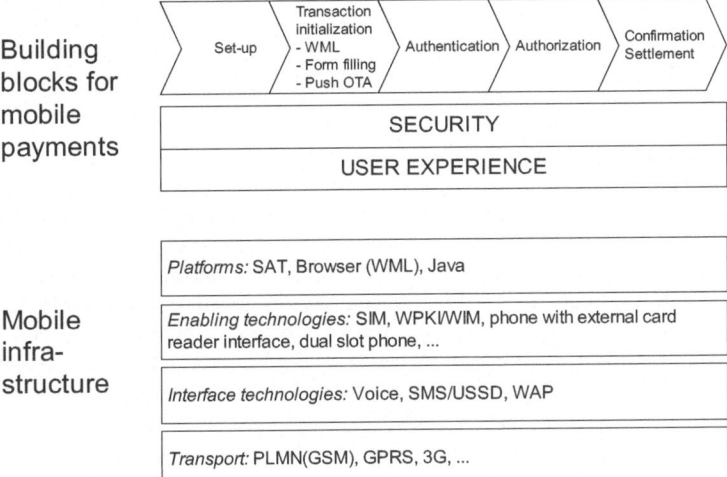

Fig. 1: Mobile Payments Building Blocks and Technologies

Figure 1 summarizes main building blocks of the mobile payment systems, and helps a reader to navigate among multiple communication, enabling and interface technologies and development platforms. For more details we refer to [KrPT02, Karn04, NLTL04, HaHT07].

Many issues have to be resolved before expecting mass adoption; such as standards, branding, legislation, finding profitable business models... Among issues to be resolved, security has a prominent role. Industrial consortia [MFS03] consider security as the basic requirement for mobile payments and financial services to be valid and adopted by all stakeholders. For customer proposition, both, technical and perceived levels of security should be high, so that customers do not suffer financial losses and that their *privacy* is protected (i.e., personal details are not disclosed to an unauthorized party). For business priorities, effective customer *authentication* (establishing customer's credentials) is cited as the most important element. It is mandated that in macro-payments (i.e., payments in excess of 10 euro) and in all mobile banking services strong authentication based on wireless public key infrastructure [WPKI01] and *non-repudiation* (i.e., binding parties to the transaction so that none of the involved parties can later deny the transaction details) based on digital certificates is necessary. It is also mandatory that transaction level security should be end-to-end, with message *integrity* (ensuring that payment data are not altered), *confidentiality* (protecting sensitive data from non-authorized parties), and authentication guaranteed.

Does the security level of existing mobile payment systems satisfy these requirements? A systematic summary of existing mobile payment solutions with respect to security functions can be found in [HaHT07]; papers [SaWi04, NLTL04] concentrate on security analysis of wireless communication, interface, and enabling technologies while [MaTu05] and [LiPW07] consider security issues from the merchants and customers point of view, respectively.

In almost all existing mobile payment procedures (for an encompassing survey see [Karn04]), the customer authentication is based on her mobile phone ID. A mobile device is considered as being highly personal, belonging to and being managed by the owner; and security of the transactions often relies on this perception. There is a reason for it as every GSM phone is equipped with a removable element called Subscriber Identity Module (SIM) which is a smart card, i.e., a tamper-resistant microprocessor chip card that contains identifiers, keys and algorithms that are required for a MNO to authenticate a subscriber. In existing procedures customer authentication is rested, essentially, with the network operators. The user authentication is based on the PIN code which is often done (unless the phone is "smart") once on power-on. Considering that most of the time the phones are "on", if they are lost or stolen there is no reliable customer authentication.

The payment authorization is usually based on a service-specific PIN that is issued during the registration with the payment service provider. While this gives a certain degree of assurance, the method is weak. Static PIN codes, especially if they are chosen by customers, can be easily guessed. The transaction details are captured in the SMS message which is sent in clear. SMS messages can be easily forged [MPF03], and thus cannot provide non-repudiation. Rarely more advanced security technologies are used; as a rule, mobile payment systems that use them are developed or controlled by financial institutions and are typically based on dual-slot mobile phones or phones with (external or built-in) card readers that accept bank-issued smart cards. These cards are used for customer authentication and for authorization of transactions according to bank procedures. Confidentiality and data integrity of payment transactions rely on transport-level security. Independent on what interactive technology is used – IVR (voice), SMS, USSD, or WAP – there is no guarantee of end-to-end security [SaWi04, NLTL04].

This paper describes an open PKI-based platform that facilitates development of a wide range of secure mobile payment applications. The platform provides an operator-agnostic technological solution to secure mobile payment transactions that can be utilized by financial institutions, mobile network operators and independent third parties. Our solution relies on today's handset technology and is based on existing standards, such as Short Message Services (SMS), and Wireless Application Protocol (WAP) [WAP03]. The proof-of-concept implementations are done entirely on open development platforms such as J2ME [ElYo03] and SATSA [JaCP04].

The proposed platform allows us to provide strong customer authentication, confidentiality, data integrity and privacy by employing public key cryptography and transaction certificates. What differentiates our system is that it utilizes existing (nowadays in Finland and some other European countries, but in a near future within the whole of EU) nation-wide PKI infrastructure which is independent from financial institutions, network operators and mobile payment solutions intermediaries but can be used by them all. Examples how this platform can be used for Out-of-Band payments (i.e., an extension of the traditional e-commerce scenario) and Proximity payment (which is wireless form of a traditional face to face payment scenarios) can be found in [HaHT07].

2 Public Key Cryptosystems

Three components comprise public key cryptosystems, as depicted in Fig. 2: public-key cryptography (PKC), public-key infrastructure (PKI), and personal security environment (PSE).

PKC is based on two keys, one for encryption and one for decryption. The keys are mathematically related so that a message encrypted with one key can only be decrypted with another one. The decryption key must be kept secret; it is called the private key. The corresponding encryption key, called the public key, can be published. The main property of PKC is that computing the private key from the corresponding public key is infeasible. The most widely used cryptographic algorithm is RSA [Schn96].

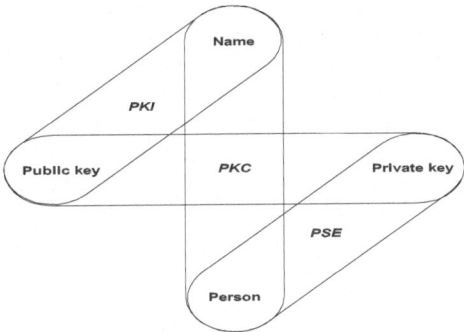

Fig. 2: Components of the Public Key Cryptosystem

Users are listed in a public directory with their public key. To communicate with the user A in private, one has to obtain A's public key from the directory, use it to encrypt the message, and send the encrypted message to A. Only A is able to decrypt this message, because only A has the decryption key. Furthermore, A can digitally *sign* a message by encrypting the (hash of the) message with her private key. The message together with its digital signature can be sent over an insecure channel. Anybody can verify that the message was indeed sent by A and has not been altered in a transmission, by looking up A's public key in the directory, encrypting the signature with this key and comparing the result with (the hash of) the original message.

Thus digital certificates and signatures ensure four security functions: authentication, confidentiality, data integrity and non-repudiation provided that there is a guarantee that the person who made the signature is the person who she claims to be. To protect the system from falsification, a *Public-Key Infrastructure* (PKI) must be set up for key distribution and management, with the following main components:

- The Certification Authority (CA) is responsible for issuing and revoking certificates for customers' public keys.
  - The Certificate contains a customer's public key and her personal details. It is digitally signed with the private key of the CA.
  - Customers of the PKI can validate digital signatures and their certificate paths from a known public key of a trusted CA.
- The Registration Authority (RA) provides a binding between the public keys and the entities of their holders.
- Repositories store and make available certificate directories and a certificate revocation list (CRL). Directory service providers maintain and update repositories.

Private keys must be kept in a *personal secure environment*. The WAP standardization body (see [http://www.wapforum.org]) devised a specification for secure provisioning and storage of the user's private and public key pairs and certificates, namely Wireless Identity Module [WIM01]. A SIM card seems to be the most suitable candidate for implementing WIM. Indeed, equipped with enough memory, 16- or 32-bit microprocessors, random number generators, cryptographic accelerators, and enhanced with tamper-resistant features, SIM cards are capable of processing public key computations securely and efficiently, and technology-driven standardization bodies put W/SIM forward as an approach combining SIM and WIM applications on one chip card [MeT02]. Bank consortia also explicitly state that WIM can be "integrated in the mobile device, such as ... a SIM-card based solution" [MFS03].

The issues of W/SIM *initialization* (equipping the card with the initial private-public key pairs and the root certificates) and of maintaining PKI remain. SIM cards are owned by the MNO; and the cost of establishing and maintaining PKI (i.e., providing services of certification and registration authorities, keeping and making available repositories of valid certificates and certificate revocation lists, etc.) is high, not mentioning an interoperability issue. We see the answer to the challenge in using a system supported by the government. In the public sector, government-issued identity cards have met reasonable public security objectives, but have been less successful in providing access to a wider range of services. There is no good reason why the population relying on, say, a public road infrastructure cannot rely on a governmentally administered nation-wide electronic identity and PKI for commercial mobile payments.

2.1 Finnish National PKI and FINEID cards

The Finnish Electronic Identity (FINEID) card along with the supporting infrastructure [PRCF04] is a system maintained by the Population Register Centre (PRC) of Finland. The FINEID card is a chip card in a bank-card format which displays the card holder's photo, data of birth, handwritten signature, date of issue. It is accepted as a valid ID in all EU countries. The chip on the card contains two Citizen Certificates: the authentication certificate of the card holder and the signature certificate of the card holder. Private keys of both certificates are generated by the card and stored exclusively in its protected memory. Additionally, the card contains the PRC's own CA certificate. The PRC maintains an online certificate directory (FINEID directory). The public keys of each user can be downloaded via a search with the appropriate criteria. The PRC maintains and updates a revocation list of invalid certificates which is also available from the FINEID directory. The local police station plays the role of a Registration Authority; the card holder must register the FINEID card in a local police station.

The current implementation of FINEID functionality on PKI-SIM cards is based on a platform developed by SmartTrust (see [http://www.smarttrust.com]) and works as depicted in Figure 3. A mobile subscription customer can request a FINEID-compatible PKI-SIM card from her MNO (at the moment, two operators in Finland issue such cards) and receives a card containing two private keys generated on-card. The keys are stored within a FINEID SAT applet used for customer authentication and signature. At this point, no public-key certificates corresponding to these keys exist. The certificates are produced and officially registered in the FINEID directory in the second step, when the customer registers her SIM card at a police station.

In order to authenticate a customer, the service provider sends an authentication request to the mobile network operator's authentication service. The operator sends a challenge to the customer's phone in an SMS message. The headers of the SMS message instruct the phone to forward the message to the SAT applet, which produces a response to the challenge. Before signing the challenge, the applet asks the user to enter her PIN code to access the private key. The response is sent back to the MNO in an SMS message. The operator checks the response and informs the service provider of the results of the authentication.

The advantage of the SmartTrust platform is in its compatibility with almost any GSM mobile phone and the availability of the required infrastructure. The system is supported by three mobile network operators in Finland. The drawback in the current approach is that authentication once again cannot be done without the participation of the MNO, and naturally, operators charge both customers and service providers for authentication. Apparently, this is a major barrier for joining the system: the system has been in place for almost two years, yet only a few service providers and fewer than 200 people use it. We argue that mobile network operators can be eliminated from the authentication process. In the proposed mobile payment system the SmartTrust platform is *not* employed.

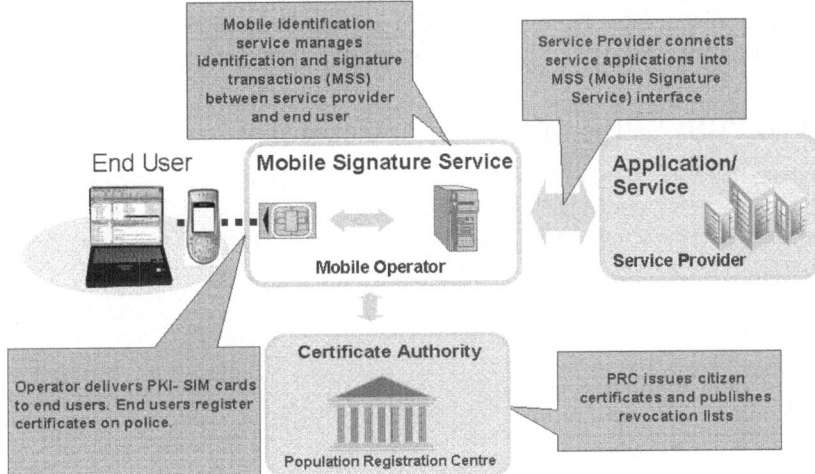

Fig. 3: Public Key platform currently implemented in Finland (as presented by R. Rauhala, Chairman of the HST Group)

3 Open Mobile Payment Platform based on FINEID

As a proof of concept, we designed and implemented a system for purchasing train tickets using a mobile phone which is based on FINEID-enabled SIM card, and which uses governmental PKI services directly. The overall system architecture is depicted in Figure 4 and includes a mobile payment *client* on the phone, an associated SIM-based *FINEID applet* for handling digital signatures and for user authentication, *simulation software* for a merchant, a bank, and an Open Certificate Status Protocol (OCSP) *server* which handles on-line certificate requests. We describe the execution flow within our system by phases in accordance with the steps of the payment procedure. Phases that occur in the mobile device and the SIM card are encircled.

3.1 Tools and implementation platform

The client software in the buyer's phone was implemented using J2ME (Java 2 Micro Edition). J2ME applications, called MIDlets, are run in a Java virtual machine. This facilitates the use of the Java sandbox security paradigm, enhancing the user perception of the security of the program. The client application was implemented using the Sun WTK (Wireless Toolkit) version 2.2 from Sun Microsystems. For connection to a SIM card with FINEID functionality we used the Security and Trust Services API (SATSA, JSR-177) [JaCP04]. This limits the functioning of the system to new mobile phone models which implement SATSA. However, this ensures that the system is not bound to a given mobile network operator infrastructure.

Implementing the communication between the mobile user and the merchant was done using the Web Services technology. Message exchange was implemented using SOAP (Simple Object Access Protocol), which is an XML-based technology for message exchange over HTTP. In J2ME there is an optional SOAP API that has been implemented in a number of devices available on the market today, such as the Nokia N91, which we used for testing our implementation. For communicating with a Web Service, stub classes are included in the MIDlet. Stubs are responsible for creating outgoing messages and parsing incoming messages. The WTK contains a stub creator utility that takes a WSDL (Web Service Definition Language) file or an URL as a parameter and creates the necessary stub classes.

3.2 Client Functionality

The user initiates the application by browsing merchant's website and requesting product options. Immediately, two certificates, one of the CA and another one of the OCSP server, are read from the local storage. This storage is the resource folder of the application's Java archive (JAR) file. RSA public keys are read from both certificates for later use.

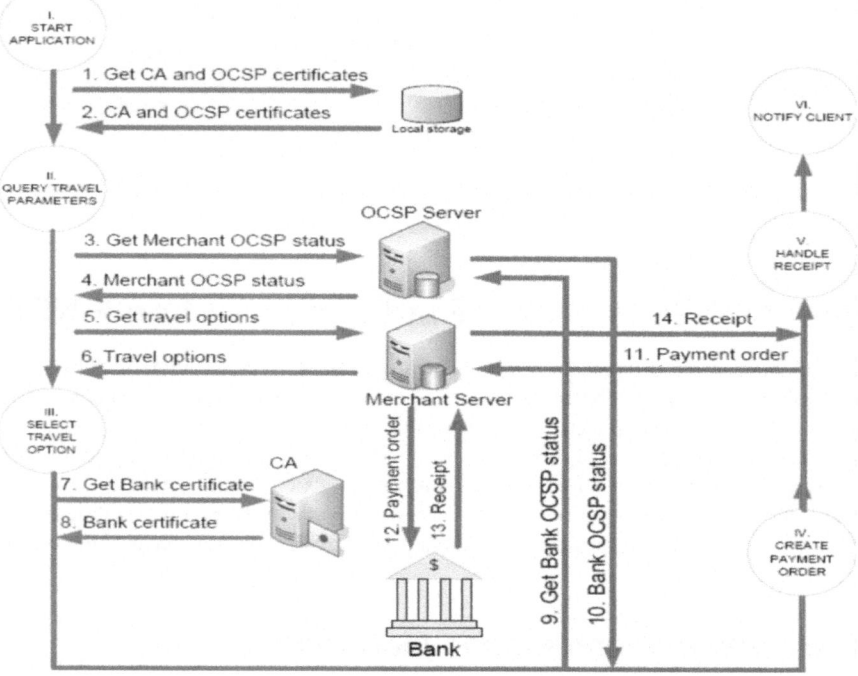

Fig. 4: Architecture of the mobile payment system with the emphasis on client SW

Phase I is the starting point of the transaction; the merchant's agent displays on the screen of the mobile phone a form where details of the journey (e.g., departure and destination, date and desired time) can be entered. Merchant's certificate is attached to the list of options. While the user is filling in the form fields, a separate thread sends an OCSP request querying the status of the merchant certificate to authenticate the merchant. Finally, the journey details entered by the user are submitted to the merchant.

In Phase II, the travel options received from the merchant are shown on the display as a list, and the user is prompted to select a journey. At the same time, two threads are started: one for retrieving the user's bank certificate and a subsequent thread for retrieving the OCSP status for that certificate. The user finalizes the details of the transaction in Phase III.

In Phase IV, the payment order message is created, digitally signed, and encrypted by the public key of the merchant for privacy. The user is prompted to enter the PIN code related to the signature certificate on her FINEID card, to sign the payment order. The merchant forwards the payment order to the bank and receives a (signed by the bank) receipt in Phase V. The merchant then forwards the receipt to the customer.

In Phase VI, the application decrypts the payment receipt generated by the bank. The bank's signature on the receipt is verified. The client also checks whether the receipt corresponds to the payment order sent in Phase IV and notifies the user of the result of the transaction.

Our current implementation supports only a single merchant, but it can be generalized by allowing the user to select a merchant in Phase 0. Available merchants can be queried from a central portal, and a response message would include instructions on what kind of user interface is to be generated for buying from a given merchant. The user interface would then be dynamically created according to these instructions, and subsequent messages would be directed straight to the right merchant. Similarly, if the user has more than one bank available for transaction settlement, she could be prompted to select the bank in Phase III. After the user has selected the desired bank, the bank certificate and subsequent OCSP status are retrieved before entering the next phase.

3.2.1 Cryptographic services

The J2ME environment does not contain classes for cryptographic processing. However, there is a package available from the Legion of Bouncy Castle [http://www.bouncycastle.org] that can be used in the J2ME environment. The package, commonly referred to as the Bouncy Castle Lightweight API, provides classes for encryption and decryption, calculating digests, and handling certificates, among others. For example, for digitally signing messages in various phases of the protocols, we used the classes `SHA1Digest` and `RSAEngine` available in the API. Since there are no ready-made tools for certificate signature verification in the Bouncy Castle, in our application a certificate is verified by calculating a hash of the `TBS` (To Be Signed) structure of the certificate and comparing the result with the decrypted signature of the certificate. Open Certificate Status Protocol (OCSP) [MMGA99] was used for obtaining certificate revocation status messages. The Bouncy Castle has a number of ready-made classes for creating OCSP requests. OCSP requests were sent using the HTTP protocol.

3.3 FINEID Applet

In our implementation, the payment order was generated from the filled in form by the client applet on the phone, after which the order was sent to the FINEID applet on the SIM card for creating its digital signature. It is important to note that the signature produced by the FINEID card is legally equivalent to the card holder's handwritten signature. Therefore, a signed combination of a product selection and a corresponding payment order constitutes a legally valid agreement between the customer and the merchant ensuring non-repudiation of a transaction.

We used the usual bankcard-sized FINEID card in our tests, because PKI-SIM cards currently deployed by Finnish mobile network operators do not allow direct communication between the phone software and the SIM card. This must be changed in order for our system to be fully functional. The environment that we used for testing our application is as follows. The client J2ME applet running in Sun WTK on the phone is implemented to communicate with the FINEID card using SATSA. However, this communication is forwarded by WTK to a bankcard-sized FINEID placed in a smartcard reader. We implemented a small mediator program which accepts commands arriving from WTK, sends them to the card, and forwards the card's responses back to WTK.

The functionality of the FINEID applet includes the computation of digital signatures, deciphering, and hashing. Access to the private keys is provided upon correct entry of the corresponding PIN codes which have to be different for authentication and for digital signature services. The user's public key certificates can be retrieved from the applet. The client applet on the phone sends requests to the FI-NEID applet using ENVELOPE APDUs (see [3GPP04] for the details on the messages format). The response is retrieved with the GET RESPONSE command. The functions of the FINEID applet are encoded in the INS bytes of APDUs.

3.4 Simulation Software for the Merchant and the Bank

The merchant server was implemented using the PHP script language. PHP is an interpreted language originally designed for implementing dynamic web pages. We considered using either Java Servlet technology or PHP. We found that while Java Servlets offer easier implementation of cryptographic computations, PHP with the NuSOAP library offer easier implementation of Web Services using SOAP (see [http://dietrich.ganx4.com/nusoap]). The package was used to create a single PHP script that has methods for handling the request messages sent by the J2ME client. Cryptographic processing in the PHP scripts was done using the PHP OpenSSL module.

The OCSP server was implemented as a Java Servlet. With servlets it is possible to use the broader API including the Java Cryptography Extensions (JCE) classes, which are not available in the Lightweight API for J2ME. A ready-made OCSP server package is also available from Novosec [http://sourceforge.net/projects/novosec-bc-ext].

Because FINEID certificates are not available for legal entities, we created our own Certification Authority to produce certificates for the merchant, the bank and the OCSP server in our simulation. The CA and OCSP certificates were included in the client JAR package so that the client could verify the certificates of other parties. The CA and all certificates were created using OpenSSL [http://www.openssl.org], and keys were created using JDK's keytool. A short Java program was used to extract the private keys for the bank and the merchant from the keystore. The certificates were converted to Privacy Enhanced Mail (PEM) format using OpenSSL, because the PHP OpenSSL module expects to have certificates in PEM format.

3.5 The Application Package and Deployment

The lightweight package of the Bouncy Castle has some classes which belong to system packages, for example, the `BigInteger` class in package `java.math`. The class loader does not allow such classes to be loaded, as they could be used to replace system package classes and thus would get more privileges than desired. Obfuscation is a method that renames classes to make the re-engineering of source code from class files more difficult. As classes that would otherwise conflict with system package names are also renamed, they can be used without the danger of being classified as system package classes. Obfuscation also removes unnecessary classes, which often makes the resulting JAR packages smaller. As the Bouncy Castle lightweight API has a lot of classes, the JAR package for our project is 587.4 K before obfuscation and 81.9 K after obfuscation. We used the `proguard` obfuscator.

Deploying a J2ME MIDlet into a device can be done in several ways. The application can be uploaded into the device using a cable, Bluetooth or IrDA, or it can be downloaded from the Internet using OTA (Over The Air) provisioning. For the end user the last option is by far the easiest to use. For our device testing we set up an OTA download page at http://katiska.uku.fi/~mhassine/OTA/MobileVR.html.

3.6 Performance and Bottlenecks

Computation speed was tested on a Nokia N91 phone. Retrieving connections that matched the search criteria from the server using GPRS communication took an average of 3.2 seconds. An average of 7.6 seconds was required to create and send the order message and to receive and verify the response message including time consumed by retrieving and verifying certificate information. In comparison, from our everyday experience we observe that in the face-to-face payment situation, the time needed for a customer to hand out the credit card, for the clerk to read the card and print out the receipt, and the customer to sign the receipt is over 20 seconds on the average for a small monetary value. With purchases worth more than 50 euros, the time needed to finalize a purchase is much longer as the terminal dials the bank to inquire whether the user has a sufficient balance to pay for the purchase. Paying with a credit card on the Internet is slower as it typically requires the user to type in the credit card number.

As the number of users of a mobile payment system increases, the number of payment requests becomes too large for a single server to handle. The number of payment servers can be increased with relative ease. As the payment system described in this paper relies on a single CA, the performance of the CA server can be restrictive because the CRL is needed by several parties in the protocol and hence would be downloaded very often, unless OCSP is used. As OCSP servers usually base their function on CRL lists, a single OCSP server can serve a large number of clients and needs to retrieve the CRL only whenever a new list is out. A number of OCSP servers can be set up to serve the clients of a single CA. This makes the OCSP approach very scalable in comparison with using a CA or an RA to distribute a CRL. Moreover, with high-density SIM cards (see the paper in this issue), an OCSP server can be implemented on the SIM card itself; the CRL updates can be done via push services from the CA.

4 Conclusion

We described a mobile payment system that uses a governmentally administered public-key infrastructure, namely, the Finnish Electronic Identity. Using FINEID, the system authenticates persons, not customers of a certain bank, mobile network operator, or payment service provider, and ensures non-repudiation, integrity and confidentiality of the payment transactions. As the administration of the PKI system is the responsibility of the government, the system is very economical for both the service providers and the users. The proof-of-concept implementation is done with freely available development tools in a way that ensures portability across different device platforms and demonstrates an open payment system to be feasible.

4.1 Turning the System into a Commercial Service

In order to launch the system described in this paper, a number of changes to the FINEID infrastructure are needed. The mobile network operators have to change the FINEID applet on SIM cards in such a way as to enable access to it from the authorized phone software. In the SIM card there must be an access control entry with a hash of the operator domain certificate. The implementation of SATSA on the mobile phone compares this hash with that of the certificate used for signing the J2ME mobile payment client applet. The J2ME applet is allowed to exchange messages with the FINEID applet only if the hashes match. This security mechanism is to be in place to ensure that the J2ME applet has not been tampered with.

The customer must also download and install a J2ME client program on her mobile phone in order to be able to use the proposed mobile payment system. The Population Register Centre currently issues certificates only to citizens. To make our system feasible, the PRC has to start issuing certificates to business entities, such as merchants and banks. In addition, it has to set up an OSCP server for checking the validity of certificates.

In order to support virtual POS payments, the merchant has to implement a web-service ready for processing mobile payments. To enable the protocol between the customer and the bank, the bank must implement the protocol and accept authentication with the FINEID card. At least one bank group in Finland (Osuuspankki) already supports authentication of its customers using FINEID cards. In order to support mobile payments with PKI-SIM cards, additional software must be implemented and deployed at the bank servers.

Another issue that has to be investigated is the standardization of the mobile phone as a payment card terminal. Because a SIM card is used for facilitating payments in our system, Europay-Mastercard-Visa (EMV) or similar standards might require the standardization of mobile phone keypads for entering payment-related PIN codes. As was already mentioned, at least one Finnish bank group accepts FINEID cards for the authentication of its customers. In other countries more strict standards may be in force.

4.2 Implementation on the level of the European Union

Many mobile payment systems can be extended to work seamlessly within several countries. To achieve this, the necessary infrastructure must be introduced, and contracts between mobile network operators may have to be established. Several European countries are implementing their eID (electronic identity) systems using PKI. On the European level, the European Commission has launched an interoperability action plan to obtain interoperable electronic identity management by 2010. When implemented, the plan will enable each member state to govern its own PKI-based eID system, while providing interoperability within the EU. Such an interoperable electronic identity can help create a pan-European mobile payment system based on electronic identity.

Clearly, building a national or a pan-European PKI-based mobile payment system requires support from the authorities: namely, it should be possible for the user to acquire a legally valid certificate on a SIM card. Currently, only in Finland and in Germany can one get such a legally valid certificate from a mobile network operator. In Finland, the certificate is signed by the Population Register Centre, while in Germany the mobile network operator acts as a certification authority if it has received an official license to do so. Both scenarios are acceptable in our mobile payment system, provided that the certificate directories are open.

An IST project SEMOPS [ViKa03], funded by the European Union, aims at creating a pan-European payment system. The project is based on the collaboration of banks and mobile network operators, with the objective to build a payment system that can deliver a variety of payment services to customers of participating banks and operators. The project is launching a pilot in Greece, Italy and Hungary to deliver interbank and cross-border payment services. The scope of our work is, however, somewhat different. SEMOPS aims at delivering an open and modular payment system that supports various security modules (including those based on public-key infrastructures). Our approach, being complementary to SEMOPS, aims at providing mobile payment services as a natural part of utilizing a national and in a near future pan-European identification infrastructure.

Governments have been granting means of identification for their citizens for centuries in forms of passports and other identification documents. An electronic identity is a natural continuation of such means of identification, and we believe that for many applications it will eventually replace existing paper documents. As banks start utilizing electronic identity as a means of authentication, the use of electronic IDs in payments will pave the way for mobile payments based on a European or even a worldwide electronic identity.

References

[ElYo03] Ellis, J., Young, M.: J2ME Web Services 1.0. Sun Microsystems, Inc., Santa Clara,CA, USA, 2003. http://www.jcp.org/en/jsr/detail?id=172

[HaHT07] Hassinen, Marko, Hypponen, Konstantin, Trichina, Elena: Utilizing Public Key Infrastructure in Mobile Payment Systems. In: Electron. Comm. Res. Appl. (2007). Available on-line at www.sciencedirect.com

[3GPP04] 3rd Generation Partnership Project, 3GPP TS 11.14: Specification of the SIM Application Toolkit (SAT) for Subscriber Identity Module – Mobile Equipment (SIM-ME) Interface, V8.17.0, Valbonne, France, 2004, http://www.3gpp.org/ftp/Specs/html-info/1114.htm

[JaCP04] Java Community Process, Security and Trust Services API (SATSA) for Java 2 Platform, Micro Edition, v. 1.0, Sun Microsystems, Inc., Santa Clara, USA,2004, http://www.jcp.org/en/jsr/detail?id=177

[Karn04] Karnouskos, Stamats: Mobile Payment: A Journey Through Existing Procedures and Standardization Initiatives, IEEE Communication Surveys, Vol. 6, No. 4, 2004, p. 44-66.

[KrPT02] Kreyer, Nina, Pousttchi Key, and Turowski, Klaus: Characteristics of Mobile Payment Procedures. M-Services, 2002. http://SunSITE.Informatik.RWTH-Aachen.DE/Publications/CEUR-WS/Vol-61/paper1.pdf

[LiPW06] Linck, K., Poutsttchi, K., Wiedemann, D.G.: Security Issues in Mobile Payment from the Customer View Point. In: Proc. 14th Int. European Conf. on Information Systems (ECIS), Goeteborg, Sweden, 2006.

[MaTu05] Mallat, N., and Tuunainen, V. K.: Merchant Adoption of Mobile Payment Systems. In: Proc. Int. Conf. on Mobile Business (ICMB'05), IEEE Computer Society, Washington DC, USA, 2005, p. 347-353.

[MeT02]   MeT Core Specification V.1.2, Mobile Electronic Transactions Ltd, 12-11-2002, http://www.mobile-transaction.org

[MFS03]   Mobey Forum White Paper on Mobile Financial Services, V.1.1, Mobey Forum 2003, http://www.mobeyforum.org

[MPF03]   Mobile Payment Forum: Risks and Threads Analysis and Security Best Practices. Mobile 2-Way Messaging Systems, 2003. http://www.mobilepaymentforum.org

[MMGA99] Myers, M, Malpani, A., Galperin, S., Adams, C.: X.509 Internet Public Key Infrastructure Online Certificate Status Protocol – OSCP. Network Working Group, Request for Comments 2560, 1999, http://tools.ietf.org/html/rfc2560

[NLTL04] Nambiar, Seema, Lu, Chang-Tien, Liang, Lily R.: Analysis of Payment Transaction Security in Mobile Commerce. In: Proc. IEEE, 2004. p. 475-480.

[OnPi05] Ondrus, Jan and Pigneur, Yves: A Disruption Analysis in the Mobile Payment Market, In Proc. 38th Hawaii Int. Conf. on System Sciences, IEEE, 2005, p. 1-10.

[PRCF04] Population Register Center of Finland: FINEID S1 – Electronic ID Application, v. 2.1, Helsinki, Finland, 2004, http://www.fineid.fi

[SaWi04] Misra Santosh K., Wickamasinghe, Nilmini: Security of a Mobile Commerce: A Trust Model. In: Electron. Comm. Research, 4, 2004, p. 359-372.

[Schn96] Schneier, Bruce: Applied Cryptography: Protocols, Algorithms, and Source Code in C, Second ed., John Wiley & Sons, NY, 1996.

[ViKa03] Vilmos, A, and Karnouskos, Stamatis: SEMOPS: Design of a New Payment Service. In: Proc. 14th Int. Conf. on Database and Expert Systems Applications, LNCS, vol. 2736, Springer, 2003, p. 865-869.

[WAP03]   WAP Architecture Specification, WAP Forum, 07-12-2001, http://www.wapforum.org

[WIM01]   Wireless Identity Module Specification, WAP Forum, 12-07-2001, http://www.wapforum.org

[WPKI01] Wireless Application Protocol Public Key Infrastructure Definition, WAP Forum, 24-04-2001, http://www.wapforum.org

Evidence Record Syntax – a new International Standard for Long-Term Archiving of Electronic Documents and Signed Data

Tobias Gondrom

Open Text Corporation,
Chair of IETF WG "Long-Term Archive and Notary Services"
tobias.gondrom@opentext.com

Abstract

In many scenarios, users need to be able to ensure and prove the existence and validity of data, especially digitally signed data, in a common and reproducible way over a long and possibly undetermined period of time. Especially in the light of the recent developments in crypto analysis around SHA-1 but also with the used public key algorithms and their parameters, it has been found that cryptographic algorithms are important but can not provide the whole solution. They must be applied in standardized data formats and concepts which take into account that some of the algorithms might get broken at a future point in time [1]. This has lead to the definition of a new standard to ensure the long-term security and integrity of data. This document explains the context and application of the recently by the IETF defined standard "Evidence Record Syntax (ERS)" [3] for the long-term conservation of digital signed documents and non-repudiation of their origin and integrity. It provides some technical background, reviews the mathematical concepts used in this new international standard and analyzes the process of signature conservation.

1 Introduction

Long-term non-repudiation of data and digitally signed data is an important aspect of standards, related to the Public-Key-Infrastructure (PKI). Standard mechanisms are needed to handle likely events, such as break of cryptographic algorithms, like e.g. SHA-1, the increase of the needed key-length of public key algorithms, compromise of private keys and the expiry of signer's public key certificate. The application of a single timestamp is not sufficient for this purpose [9].

Different approaches have been evaluated over the past years to enable the storage of digital signed documents without loosing the provability of the existence of the document and of the applied signatures after security algorithms like used public key algorithms become weak or broken. Some of the concepts rely on trusted third parties for storage; others involve the enveloping of the content with the signatures like the layers of an onion. Many of the concepts have been relying on some constructs of organizational trust-models to enable some reliability for possible law-cases and with this lack the possibility to unify these approaches on the international level. Or they base on concepts using multiple applied signatures that in many cases lack the performance and usability to apply those methods to huge amounts of signed documents.

N. Pohlmann, H. Reimer, W. Schneider (Editors): Securing Electronic Business Processes, Vieweg (2007), 367-375

The international standard defined by the working group LTANS (Long-term archiving and notary services) of the IETF defines a solution that is based on the use of public key cryptography, but has kept strictly in mind the later economic usability and interoperability of the solution for real-case scenarios. For this, economic aspects as performance and affordability have been combined with the mathematical waterproof concept.

2 Problem and Solution

Today in many countries the electronic signature based on hash- and public key-algorithms is recognized mostly as equal to the manual signature. In many cases such documents and the applied signatures are relevant for several years or even decades. Unfortunately untraceable manipulating of digital data is quite easier than with a piece of paper. So it is a necessary precondition that the underlying algorithms are not broken over the time the document is needed. This is something one cannot expect based on the current level of information and cryptanalysis.

Public-key-algorithms may become weak, key lengths may no longer be sufficient, or even the used hash-functions may be targets for an attack. And if one of these events occurs one can neither rely on the integrity of the document nor on the identity of its signer any longer.

This can be solved by resigning the data with newer (and stronger) algorithms and by thus creating various layers to protect the data with newer algorithms every time. The newly defined standard "Evidence Record Syntax" defines the way to apply these renewals in a highly performing and efficient way for large document volumes and with minimal usage of resources.

The solution developed is based on a combination of Merkle's hash trees and applied time-stamps. It has the ability to resign large volumes of documents without the need to apply for every single document an individual timestamp. And it allows verifying the integrity of the documents without knowledge of the other documents. Finally, it supports an infinite number of renewals

This opens the way to mathematically proof the integrity of every single document and the applied signatures for an unlimited time; and beyond the trust anchor of the Time Stamping Authority itself, it does not rely on the trust to a third party for storage. Last but not least the international standardization of the data format and protocols obviously enables the interoperability and easy independent verification with different applications.

3 Technical Details

3.1 Enhanced Timestamps

One basis of the concept of "Evidence Record Syntax" is Enhanced Time-Stamps, which refers not only to a single data object as ordinary time-stamps do, but to many data objects. An Enhanced Time-Stamp is a simple combination of hash trees, first described by Merkle [4] and a cryptographic timestamp. The leaves of the hash-tree are the hash values of the data objects. A time-stamp is requested only for the root value of the hash-tree. Obviously the deletion of any referred data objects does not influence the provability of the others. The hash-tree can be reduced to a few little sets of hash values, necessary to prove existence of a single data object or a data object group. These sets of hash values and the time-stamp yield the Enhanced Time-Stamp.

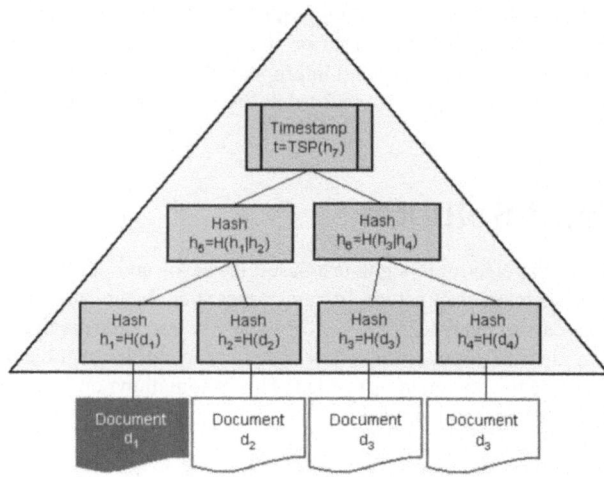

Figure 1: enhanced timestamp: hash tree with timestamp

To verify the Enhanced Time-Stamp for a data object d_i, the validation party only needs to follow the path from the hash of the required document up to the root recursively. You can calculate the chain of hashed values to the root and compare it to the original time-stamp. The following very simple example explains the concept:

1. To check the signature of data object d_1 the required path will be $d_1 \rightarrow h_1 \rightarrow h_5 \rightarrow t$
2. Hence, the mathematical recursive check must satisfy
   $$H(H(h_1|h_2)|h_6) = H(h_5|h_6) \in TSP$$

For the mathematical implementation it is important, that a Merkle hash tree can have an arbitrary number of child nodes, which extends the above computation.

3.2 Reduced enhanced timestamp

To reduce the amount of data needed for the verification of such an enhanced timestamp, a long-term archive service can reduce the hash tree to a small subset of data that will enable an independent verifier to follow the chain from one document up to the root node of the tree, the timestamp.

For this you can skip all the information of nodes not under the same father node for every level.

For this a set of hash values is completed with the ones required on the last recursion-level, given in the example of the previous chapter. At the very end of the list the hash value of the root node, the timestamp is located.

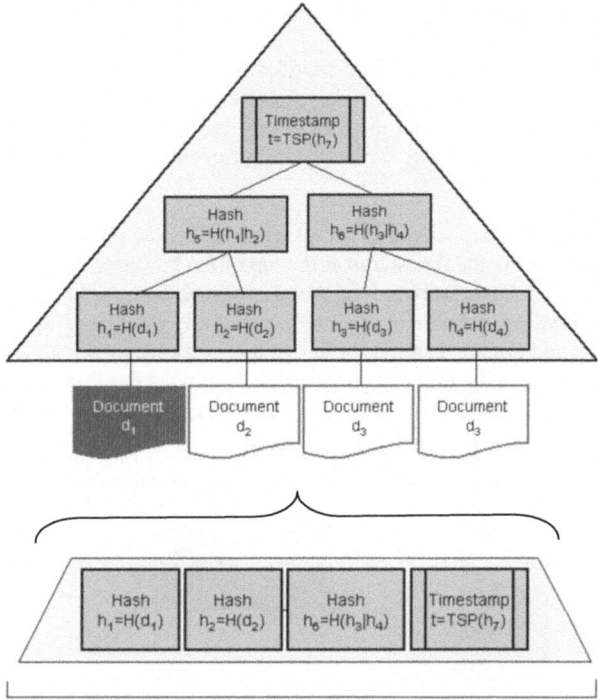

Figure 2: hash-tree and reduced hash-tree

3.3 Defined state upon entry of digital signed document in the system

To provide a defined state of security levels of used algorithms, documents that are stored to the system are time stamped initially. With this initial step it is not necessary to analyse the various formats (e.g. CMS [2]) and used algorithms in every single data object. But the system can rely on the well-known security parameters of the initially applied timestamps. Based on the well-defined security properties of the initial anchor a system can now resign the data whenever algorithms used in it become weak.

4 Security by Renewal

A system must cover two major cases where the applied methods might get weak and renewal is necessary. First, the used timestamps can become unreliable, in detail the used algorithm and/or their required key lengths are no longer effective or private keys might get compromised. Second, the used hash algorithm could be broken and reach a status of untrustworthy.

4.1 Renewal of Timestamps

At a future point in time one of the algorithms used in the timestamps may loose its required security criteria. This can either be if the used public-key-algorithms or their key-lengths are no longer reliable, or the hash-algorithms used within the timestamp itself is no longer conform to the criteria of hash-algorithms (collision-free, one-way function, etc.) or even if the private key of the time stamping authority is compromised.

If this happens (i.e. before this happens) it is necessary to renew the protection of the timestamp at the parent node of the hash tree. As the timestamp at the top of the hash tree contains the hash value representing the whole tree it is not necessary to load the represented documents themselves e.g. from media or to calculate new hash-values from them. A system can simply calculate a hash-value from the timestamp at the parent node and put this in a new hash tree that can be signed with a new timestamp and by thus be protected with newer and stronger timestamp algorithms. After this the valid and provable state of the complete system has been renewed with almost no effort in time or system resources.

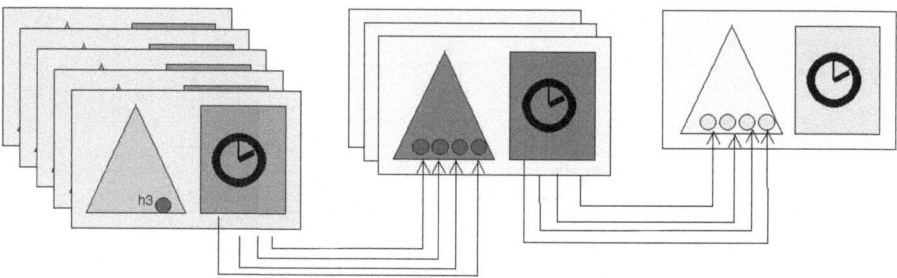

Figure 3: linked hash-trees after several timestamp renewals

4.2 Renewal of Hash trees

The second renewal operation has been separated from the first, as it may cost more resources than the very efficient "renewal of timestamps" and thus should only be run if needed. If the hash algorithm used for building up the hash tree looses its security properties, a system has to renew the complete hash trees. This can be a quite expensive operation, i.e. access to stored data to rehash with new algorithms to replace the old no longer reliable hash values. In this case, with one of the fundamentals of the signing process getting unreliable, it is obviously inevitable to rehash the already existing data with a new hash function. The "Evidence Record Syntax" still provides the benefit that a system does not need to renew every single document individually, but can again build hash trees (with basically unlimited height) and apply only one timestamp at the top. The result is again a renewed validity of the system of signed data. The next chapter will explain an approach to avoid the greater effort for this renewal technique.

4.2.1 Reliability by redundancy

To make a system more reliable, the IETF working group strongly recommends to support redundancy with the hash trees. E.g. build two hash trees, one based on SHA-512 and one on RIPEMD160. With this a system can decrease the risk further and gain time. So that, when one hash-algorithm is getting weak, it still has the other until it can complete the "renewal of hash-tree" for the complete set of documents.

4.2.2 Technical operation of hash tree renewal

In the incident that the hash-algorithm is losing its reliability it is not enough to only calculate a new hash value for the document. The system must also to take care of the already existing enhanced timestamps as they are required to provide a complete and unbroken chain beginning at the day the documents has been stored to the system. For this it is necessary to include the already existing reduced hash-trees together with the new hash value of the document in the new hash-tree (based on the new algorithm). This can be done by hashing the exiting reduced hash-trees, concatenating this value with the new hash value of the document, hashing this value again and using this as one of the leafs of the new enhanced timestamps / hash-tree.

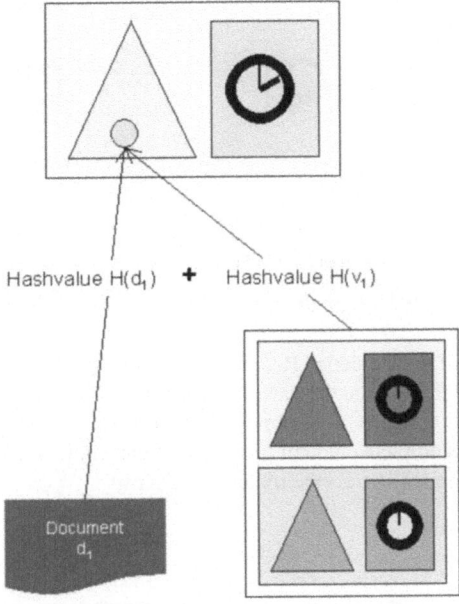

Figure 4: renewal of hashtree

5 Data

5.1 Data Format

The data structure of the standard "Evidence Record Syntax" has been defined in ASN.1, and an XML version [8] is at the moment in preparation. The data structure for enhanced timestamps and the format for verification data can be implemented in various other formats, too.

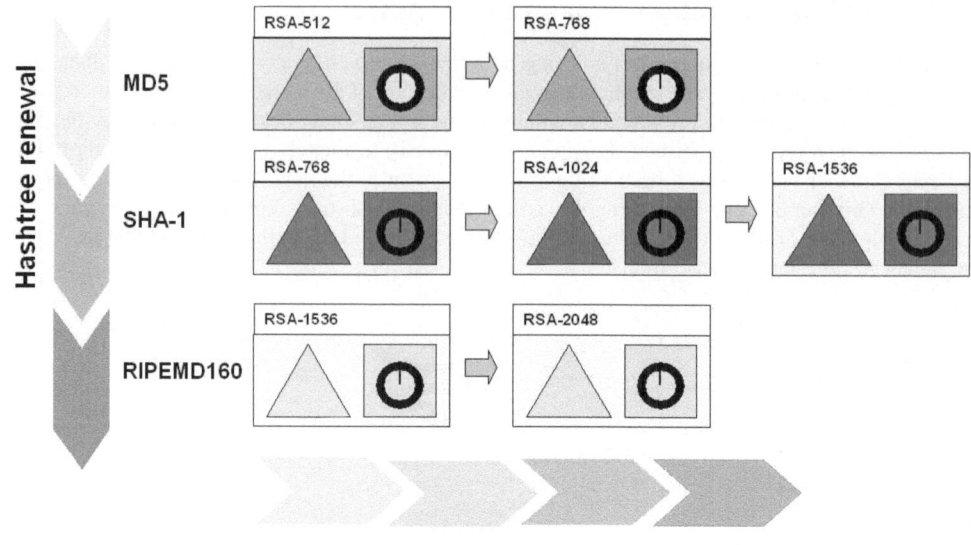

Timestamp renewal

Figure 5: example of development renewals of algorithms across time

The overall data structure of the Evidence Record is assembled from three core concepts: the enhanced timestamp, the timestamp renewal and the hash-tree renewal. The result is a list of enhanced timestamps each pointing to the following one in a chronological order and each linking from one (timestamp/hash tree) renewal to the next. A complete chain of proof across the whole time of the storage of the document can be provided and independently verified by any third party.

5.2 Verification

With the uniform anchor of the initial timestamp all documents stored can be handled and their signatures conserved based on their well-defined parameters without inspecting every individual signature of a document for its individual parameters.

Thus the verification [6] of the signatures within the document runs in two sequences. First, the point in time is evaluated up to which the signatures in the document were valid (i.e. until when you could rely on their algorithms). Second, using the Evidence Record, it can be proofed that the document and all applied signatures existed before that point in time and were not changed since then. As the system uses a unified view and mechanisms for all signed documents, the Evidence Records must of course fulfil the highest security requirements to not lower the value of signatures at some of the archived documents. For this reason it is strongly recommended to use qualified signatures from an accredited supplier for the Evidence Records. A system itself does not need to inspect the documents to conserve their integrity or signatures and documents can of course also be stored encrypted so that high levels of confidentiality can be achieved.

6 Conclusion

The feasibility and usefulness of the concept for the conservation of electronically signed documents has been proven and demonstrated in several real-case scenarios and environments. Additionally the concept also successfully passed a legal with test law-cases evaluated within a simulation-study with independent judges, attorneys and reviewers [9].

Today, the use of electronic workflows and archives is quite widespread for non-signed electronic documents. For electronically signed documents it is important, if not even critical, that a system can store them for an unlimited amount of time without loosing the provability of the applied digital signatures. As long as this had not been guaranteed and demonstrated, many scenarios could not fully move from the normal paper workflow to an electronic workflow. The new released international standard "Evidence Record Syntax" now enables many new long-term oriented scenarios requiring protection of document integrity for an unlimited time or using electronically signed documents instead of paper documents.

Excellent example cases, the working group has encountered in the past years, are scenarios from nearly any eGovernment, approval processes and integrity protection in health care, and other processes that are dependent on electronically signed documents.

At this time, the IETF working group is finalizing several further Internet Standards to define a protocol for access to long-term archive services [5] and provide best practices for required verification data [6], algorithm policies [7] and for implementation architecture.

Besides the already existing local implementations and applications of the Evidence Record Syntax, this standard will see its first global impact very soon when SHA-1 – as well as today used public key algorithms with shorter keys – will eventually be considered as insecure.

Evidence Records will then efficiently renew the cryptographic protection of the data we all signed and stored until today.

References

[1]   RFC 4810: Long-Term Archive Service Requirements, C. Wallace, U. Pordesch, R. Brandner

[2]   RFC 3369: Cryptographic Message Syntax (CMS), Network Working, RFC 3369, 2002.

[3]   T. Gondrom, R. Brandner, U. Pordesch: Evidence Record Syntax (ERS), May 2007, IETF

[4]   Merkle, R. Protocols for Public Key Cryptosystems, Proceedings of the 1980 IEEE Sympsium on Security and Privacy (Oakland, CA, USA, April 1980): pages 122-134

[5]   A. Jerman Blazic, P. Sylvester, C. Wallace: Long-term Archive Protocol (LTAP) draft-ietf-ltans-ltap-04, March 2007, IETF

[6]   T. Gondrom, S. Fischer-Dieskau: Verification Data, draft-ietf-ltans-validate-01, January 2007, IETF

[7]   T. Kunz, S. Okunick, U. Pordesch: Data Structure for Security Suitabilies of Cryptographic Algorithms (DSSC), draft-ietf-ltans-dssc-00.txt, June 2007, IETF

[8]   A. Jerman Blazic, S. Saljic, T. Gondrom: Extensible Markup Language Evidence Record Syntax, draft-ietf-ltans-xmlers-00.txt, February 2007, IETF

[9]   Rossnagel/Schmücker: Beweiskräftige elektronische Archivierung, Economica Verlag, 2005

[10]   Directive 1999/93/EC of the European Parliament and of the Council of 13 December 1999 on a Community famework for electronic signatures

[11]   SigG: Gesetz über Rahmenbedingungen für elektronische Signaturen und zur Änderung weiterer Vor-
         schriften. Bundesgesetzblatt Teil I 22: 876-84.

[12]   SigI: Bundesamt für die Sicherheit in der Informationstechnik (BSI): Signaturinteroperabilitätsspezi-
         fikationen, Abschnitt B5 Mehrfachsignaturen / Erneute Signatur, Version 1.2, 30.8.1999.

[13]   SigV: Verordnung zur elektronischen Signatur Entwurfs-Fassung zur Notifizierung aufgrund der Rich-
         tlinie 98/34/EG, August 2001

[14]   Rossnagel, A. / Hammer, V.: Kommentierung des § 18 SigV 1997, in Roßnagel (Hrsg.), Recht der Mul-
         timediadienste, 1999 ff.

PKI and Entitlement
– Key Information Security
Management Solutions for Business
and IT Compliance

Guido v. d. Heidt[1] · Reinhard Schoepf[2]

[1]Siemens AG
Corporate Information Office, CIO G IS
guido.von_der_heidt@siemens.com

[2] Former Chief Information Security Officer of Siemens AG
oscars@freenet.de

Abstract

Public Key Infrastructure (PKI) and Entitlement (Identity & Access Management) are considered core elements of Information Security Management which have been adopted by many organizations in public and private sectors.

In this paper we will derive on a strategic level how PKI and Entitlement can be deployed to meet IT needs of business and ensure compliance to regulatory and corporate policies.

In the second part we will describe how PKI and Entitlement solutions are successfully deployed at Siemens. The Siemens PKI and Entitlement infrastructure ranks among the largest private PKI and Entitlement implementations worldwide.

1 Introduction

Many public and private organizations have implemented Public Key Infrastructure (PKI) and Entitlement[1] solutions as core parts of their Information Security Management.

However, there are still concerns on the benefits and the business value of these technologies.

In this paper we will systematically derive on a strategic level how PKI and Entitlement can be deployed to meet IT needs of business and ensure compliance to regulatory and corporate (security) policies.

Business requirements such as

- enabling and optimizing of electronic business processes,
- efficiency and manageability of IT,
- security and privacy

---

1 In this paper Entitlement is used as generic term for Identity, Access and Session Management.

N. Pohlmann, H. Reimer, W. Schneider (Editors): Securing Electronic Business Processes, Vieweg (2007), 376-385

as well as compliance-related IT requirements by
- relevant laws for business management as Sarbanes-Oxley Act, etc.,
- data protection laws and
- e-discovery

demand an integrated security infrastructure instead of inhomogeneous application-specific "security silos".

PKI and Entitlement provide for this security infrastructure with efficient, unforgeable and auditable processes for managing identities and user credentials for authentication and authorization.

In the second part of the presentation we will show how PKI and Entitlement solutions are successfully deployed at Siemens Corporation. Siemens is a global powerhouse in electrical engineering and electronics with 475.000 employees and business operations in over 190 countries. With more than 320.000 users the Siemens PKI and Entitlement infrastructure ranks among the largest private PKI and Entitlement implementations worldwide.

Use cases will demonstrate how business and compliance requirements are met.

The paper is closed by a conclusion and perspective of future applications in this field.

2 Mapping of Business and Compliance-related IT Requirements to PKI and Entitlement

Why are PKI and Entitlement needed? Benefits and business value of those technologies can be demonstrated by mapping IT challenges to security mechanisms and describing an integrated security infrastructure based on PKI and Entitlement to provide these security functions.

2.1 Mapping Challenges and Requirements for IT to Information Security Management Functions

Analyzing and clustering today's challenges for IT among others, the following key requirements can be linked to PKI and Entitlement:
- Business Process Enabling
  - Enabling of electronic processes
  - Creating new ways to connect with customers and business partners
  - Realizing seamless and trustworthy electronic workflows
- Efficiency and Cost
  - Managing a reliable IT infrastructure at excellent cost-benefit ratio
  - Automation, reduction and simplification of manual processes
  - Efficient management of employees, business partners etc. in IT systems and applications
- Compliance
  - Operating IT and applications in accordance with legislation and company policies
  - Establishing secure and auditable IT (administration) processes
  - Policy-compliant management of users, resources and access rights

- Security & Privacy
  - Protection of corporate information and communication
  - Ensuring confidentiality, integrity and validity of data and business transactions
  - Securing access to network, IT systems and applications as well as securing physical access to locations and premises

Enabling electronic *Business Processes* means providing the necessary security functions for identifying the parties involved, protecting the data processed and ensuring validity of transactions. Thereby, simplified connections with customers and flexible integration of business partners are key success factors.

It is needless to say that *Efficiency and Cost* are primary objectives of every CIO. Next to the optimization of IT infrastructure operation, the efficient management of user accounts, credentials and access rights by automation and simplification is a crucial step to reduce cost.

Today, *Compliance* for IT is intensively discussed and achieving compliance to external and internal policies is a major challenge for IT governance. Besides reporting and auditing

- laws and regulations for business management such as Sarbanes-Oxley Act, KonTraG[2], HIPAA[3] or the US Federal Regulations (CFR) and
- data protection laws such as the European Data Protection Directive (95/46/EC), UK Data Protection Act or BDSG[4]

stipulate requirements for authenticating users, managing access rights and protecting information resources.

Protection of corporate information and communication, ensuring confidentiality, integrity and validity of data/transactions and securing access to network, IT systems, IT applications and buildings are classical *Security & Privacy* objectives.

These IT challenges can be mapped to 5 generic function blocks for information security management:

- Identity Management
- Authorization
- Authentication
- Encryption
- Digital Signatures

In conventional scenarios the required security functions are often provided on demand and tailored for the specific application or user group. This approach results in "security silos" with inhomogeneous technical solutions and management processes. *Identities* and *Authorizations* are managed in multiple user stores and application databases. For *Authentication,* various mechanisms like passwords, smart cards, one-time passwords, authentication tokens etc. are often deployed in parallel. This tool mix results in inconsistent security levels. In many cases *Encryption* is not adopted to the required extent or isolated solutions with different key management processes are used. If used at all, digital signatures are mostly implemented in a closed environment or for a single application.

---

2 „Gesetz zur Kontrolle und Transparenz im Unternehmensbereich", Germany.
3 Health Insurance Portability and Accountability Act, USA.
4 „Bundesdatenschutzgesetz", Germany.

PKI and Entitlement can provide an integrated security infrastructure on which applications and business processes can be built upon.

PKI provides a uniform platform to manage and use digital certificates for strong authentication, encryption of data at rest and during transport as well as non-repudiation of business transactions by (lawful) digital signatures. Strong registration processes ensure the binding of persons, functions/organizations and systems to electronic identities and thus provide a basis to meet compliance-related authentication and authorization requirements. A centralized key management with processes for key recovery is crucial for ensuring data confidentiality by encryption at one hand while also meeting e-discovery requirements on the other hand.

Entitlement provides infrastructure and processes to manage identities and authorizations in central stores/directories with automated provisioning/de-provisioning of user accounts in target applications. Access control based on groups, business roles and privileges simplifies management of authorizations and enables auditable processes for granting/withdrawing access rights. Services for single/reduced-sign-on reduce cost for managing user authentication in multiple applications and increase usability.

Figure 1 shows how the business and compliance challenges discussed above can be mapped to PKI and Entitlement.

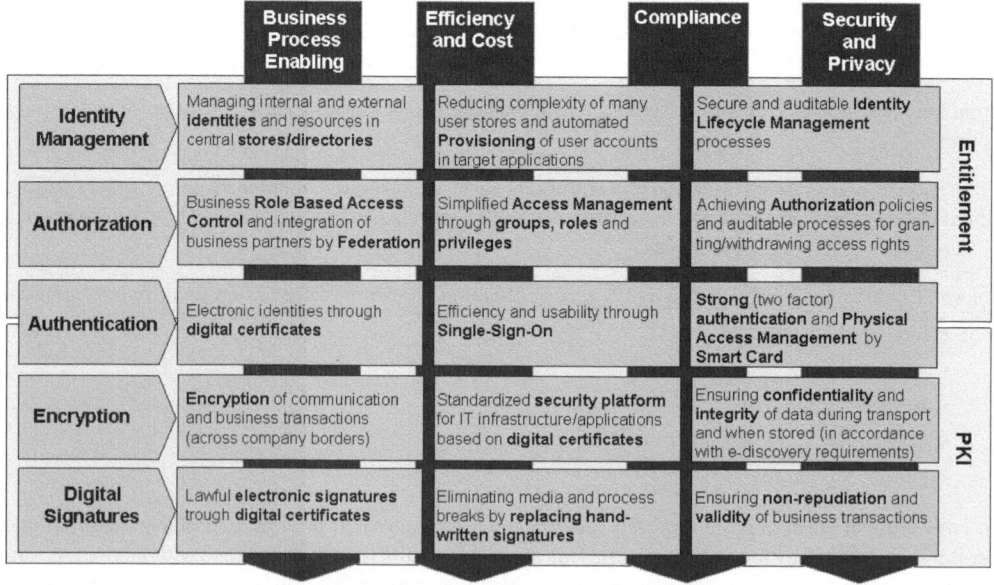

Figure 1: IT Requirements mapped to PKI and Entitlement

2.2 Architecture of a PKI and Entitlement Security Infrastructure

As shown in chapter 2.1, PKI and Entitlement can form an integrated security infrastructure to provide the information security management functions Identity Management, Authorization, Authentication, Encryption and Digital Signatures.

The following Figure 2 describes the architecture building blocks of such a integrated security infrastructure and the interaction of PKI and Entitlement functions.

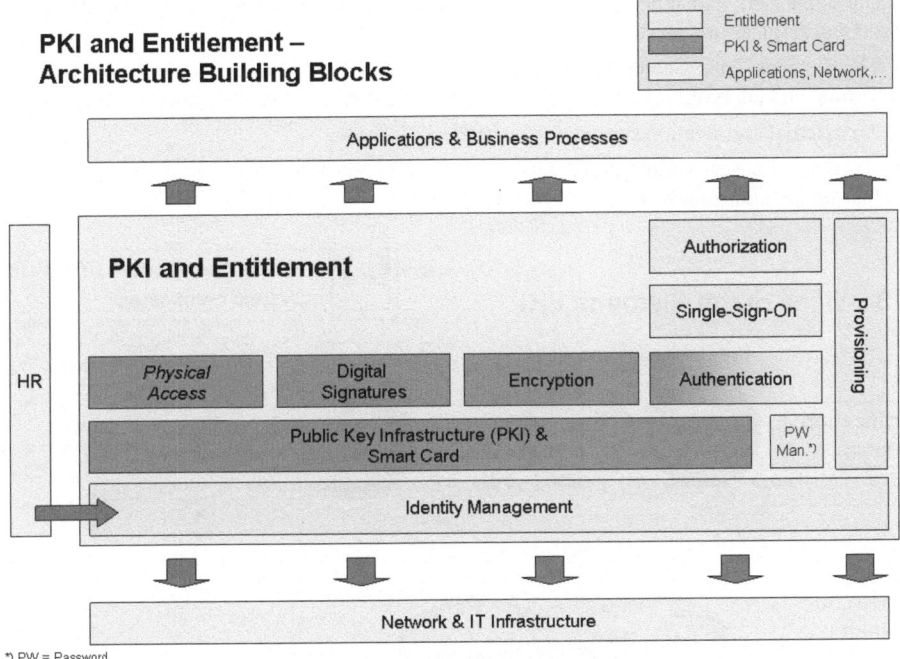

Figure 2: Architecture Building Blocks

3 Deployment of PKI and Entitlement at Siemens

Following the general business value description of PKI and Entitlement we would like to show how these technologies are successfully used within Siemens.

Siemens started the PKI and Identity Management program in 1997 by implementing the "Siemens Corporate Directory (SCD)" and launching an internal PKI for issuing multipurpose certificates and soft-PSEs[5] in 1998.

The Corporate Directory was mainly used as repository for communication data and for publishing PKI certificates. The initial PKI focused on secure e-mail.

---

5   File-based Personal Security Environment containing the private key.

Since then the initial PKI and the Corporate Directory have been further developed into a comprehensive enterprise security infrastructure for managing identities and authorizations as well as providing authentication, encryption and digital signature functions. A smart card based Corporate ID Card was implemented integrating PKI with physical access management. Siemens reported on the development of the PKI regularly at ISSE, see [Glae98], [vdH01] and [vdH03].

Today, the Siemens PKI and Entitlement infrastructure has more than 320.000 users worldwide and ranks among the largest private PKI and Entitlement implementations.

Within the PKI we distinguish between certification services for personalized entities such as employees, business partners and functions and certification services for impersonalized entities such as IT systems. Core services are, as shown in Figure 3:

- The Siemens Trust Center issuing multiple certificate types (on smart card) for authentication/ signing and encryption purposes for personalized entities and (web-)servers.
- An external certification service for internet web-servers.
- A certification service integrated with the Active Directory Forest providing machine certificates for domain controllers and client systems.

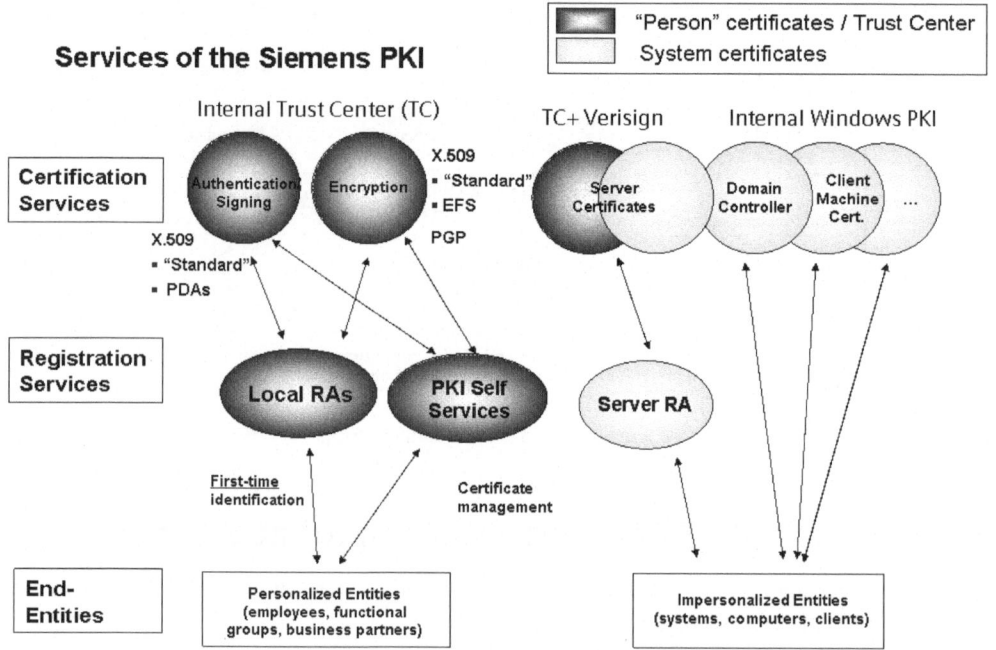

Figure 3: Services of the Siemens PKI

A company-wide network of Local Registration Authorities (LRAs) was set-up for the registration of end-users. Web-based PKI Self Services are deployed for the certificate lifecycle management. Registration of web-servers is provided by a dedicated Server Registration Authority.

The Identity Management system consisting of the Corporate Directory and Active Directory (AD) is closely linked to the PKI and provides the data of the entities within the registration process. The Corporate Directory is the source for all internal and external personalized entities, whereas the AD is the source for impersonalized systems. The Corporate Directory is automatically provisioned by the HR systems; for external business partners a self-registration interface is provided.

PKI user certificates are published in both the Corporate Directory and the AD. Furthermore, certificates are published in the Internet in an External Repository to give business partners and customers access to Siemens certificates.

The processes and system components of the PKI for personalized entities are illustrated in Figure 4.

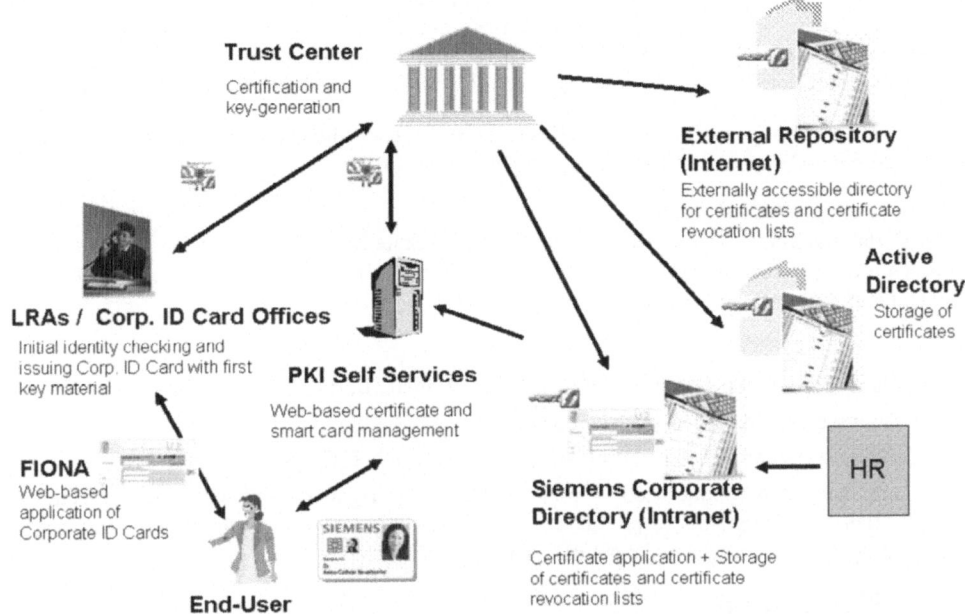

Figure 4: PKI for Personalized Entities

The PKI is used for the following fields of application:

- PC / domain login, (web-)single-sign-on, HTTPS/SSL, SAP login and session encryption
- Remote Intranet access, (W)LAN access, IPSec
- E-Mail encryption/signing, file/folder encryption
- Document signing, web-signing.

In addition to the Identity Management system a corporate Access and Session Management infrastructure has been implemented driven by the deployment of the enterprise-wide Global Intranet Portal and the Siemens Internet Portal. The Session Management provides Single-Sign-On for (primarily web-based) applications, in particular for all applications integrated in the Intranet / Internet Portal. Thereby, strong authentication with PKI provides full portal access whereas weak authentication with password gives restricted access only. The Access Management system takes on the assignment of identities to roles, groups and privileges and ensures an automated provisioning of users accounts, roles and access rights for the Intranet / Internet Portal, the Single-Sign-On system and further de-central Access Management systems of Siemens business units.

3.1 Siemens Use Cases for PKI and Entitlement

The following use cases indicate how business and IT compliance requirements are met through the integrated PKI and Entitlement infrastructure.

3.1.1 Strong Authentication / Single-Sign-On

Use Case – Global Intranet Portal
The Siemens Global Intranet Portal integrates more than 200 (web-)applications. An employee logging in to the Global Intranet Portal with the Siemens Corporate ID Card (smart card) is strongly authenticated to the Single-Sign-On (SSO) system and can access all other available applications without additional authentication. When logging in with password, the access to some applications e.g. HR applications is first rejected and will be only granted after an additional PKI-based authentication step.

The individual Portal view and the access rights of a user are controlled based on user roles in the Portal, in the Single-Sign-On system and in the target applications, cf. 3.1.4.

Use Case – Password Elimination
Besides Portal and Single-Sign-On system, PKI and Corporate ID Card are used for network authentication, login to PC / Windows domain, access to multiple web-applications not (yet) integrated in the Portal and login to several SAP systems

Benefits
- Reduction of login procedures, password management effort and related helpdesk calls
- Usability by smart card as single credential
- Central access and session control (single logout) by the SSO system
- Compliance to corporate security policies. Driven by legal requirements, data protection and IT security requirements corporate security policies require strong authentication for accessing confidential information and personal data.

3.1.2 E-Mail Security

Use Case – E-Mail Encryption
With more than 300.000 employees and contractors equipped with e-mail encryption, Siemens has established a corporate-wide infrastructure for secure communication. In order to facilitate and promote secure e-mail with external business partners Siemens is member of the "European Bridge-CA"[6]. For sending encrypted e-mails business partners and Siemens employees can (automatically) retrieve certificates form the Bridge-CA repository (which is connected with the Siemens External Repository). Furthermore the Brigde-CA provides a framework for establishing trust between public and private organisations.

Use Case – Electronic Pay Slip
More than 60.000 employees in Germany receive their monthly pay slip electronically via encrypted e-mail.

---

6 http://www.bridge-ca.org.

Benefits

- Security infrastructure for encryption/signing of e-mails within Siemens and with external business partners
- Electronic workflow for distributing pay slips instead of the former paper-based process with significant postage savings
- Easy-to-use solution by "built-in" encryption
- Compliance to corporate security policies which stipulate encryption of confidential and personal data

3.1.3 Digital Signatures

Use Case – Document signing at Siemens Medical
The products and solutions of Siemens Medical are subject to strict legal quality assurance requirements in engineering and production. Therefore, Siemens Medical deployed a digital signature solution for design and manufacturing documents, test reports, inspection sheets etc. A "Signature Server" provides a sophisticated workflow system supporting the complete process from creation over signing to archiving of a document. Thereby, the system allows defining signature fields, signers, representatives and signing sequences. Signers are informed by e-mail when a signature is required.

Benefit

- Electronic process for signing documents instead of former paper-based process. Replacement of hand-written signatures by electronic signatures.
- Reduction of process cost (printing, signing, distributing, scanning, archiving of documents) and reduced cycle times
- Usability by electronic workflow
- Compliance to regulations of US Food and Drug Administration (21 CFR Part 11)

3.1.4 User Provisioning / Role based Access Control

Use Case – Corporate Directory and Global Intranet Portal
After registration of a new employee in the HR system an entry in the Corporate Directory and user accounts in the Global Intranet Portal and the Single-Sign-On system are generarted automatically. Portal and SSO roles are assigned by a web-center and automatically provisioned by the Access Management system. All roles are automatically withdrawn and/or re-assigned in case of relocation or retirement of an employee.

Benefits

- Higher efficiency through automation of administrative processes
- Increased security by centralized and automated provisioning/de-provisioning of user accounts, roles and privileges
- Reduced license costs by automated de-activation of user accounts
- Reliable and auditable processes for granting/withdrawing access rights.

4 Conclusion

Efficient, reliable and auditable processes for the management of identities and their authentication and authorizations as well as the protection of confidentiality and integrity of data and business transactions are main challenges for information security management. PKI and Entitlement are leading technologies to meet these requirements and provide for an integrated security infrastructure.

The example of Siemens shows that the successful deployment of PKI and Entitlement in a global enterprise is possible. The Siemens PKI and Entitlement infrastructure contributes significantly to reduce complexity and process costs while usability and security are increased.

Key success factors are the continuous enabling and connection of IT infrastructures, applications and business process for and to PKI and Entitlement.

Main challenges for PKI and Entitlement are the integration of external partners and the use of PKI and Entitlement infrastructures across company borders.

In the field of PKI the processes, mechanisms and tools to establish trust between organizations, to access certificates of other PKIs and to equip partners having no PKI with digital certificates must still be improved.

Federation will simplify the management of business partners and their authorizations and will avoid the redundant registration in different Identity Management systems. From our point of view this will lead to the question of allocating responsibilities and establishing trust between federated Entitlement infrastructures similar to the trust between PKIs.

At last, we would like to encourage other companies and organizations to adopt PKI and Entitlement infrastructures and to support trustworthy internal and external business processes.

References

[Glae98] Glaeser, Martin: Strategy and Implementation of a PKI Rollout in an International Company. ISSE 1999.

[vdH01]   von der Heidt, Guido: Marhoefer, Michael; Oeser, Thomas: The Siemens PKI – Implementation and Evolution of a Large Scale Enterprise PKI. ISSE 2001.

[vdH03]   von der Heidt, Guido: The Siemens PKI – Implementation of PKI Self Services. Securing Electronic Business Processes, Highlights of the Information Security Solutions Europe 2003 Conference, Vieweg, 2004, S. 204 – 209.

Future Diffusion of PKI-Technology – A German Delphi Study

Michael Gaude

DaimlerChrysler AG, Sindelfingen, Germany
Vehicle Change Management
Michael.Gaude@DaimlerChrysler.com

Abstract

This article provides a contribution to innovation research in the field of electronic signatures, particularly to the future development of the aspects of diffusion throughout the IT-technology of the "Public Key Infrastructure" (PKI). In the modern Internet economy, PKI-technology is generally seen as the basis for obligatory authentication and safe communication. Nowadays, large scale enterprises in particular want to reach concensus concerning this security technology. In this article, the key factors for the future development of PKI are examined. The key factors will then be transferred into a diffusion model consisting of the primary PKI services, the secondary technologies, the process level, the user populations and the markets. Different qualities of a PKI will be distinguished. The qualified electronic signature, according to the German Electronic Signature Act (SigG), is also taken into account. With the results of a Delphi study by 69 experts, the PKI diffusion model will be filled and calibrated with real data. The study's board of participants consists of users, suppliers and scientists in the field of PKI. All participants are designated experts in their field and worked through the Delphi questionnaire twice, thereby judging, commenting and replenishing the study.

1 Introduction

Due to global competition, there is heavy pressure on the economic system and its protagonists to adapt its products and services to the quickly changing requirements of the worldwide markets. In light of this scenario, safe communication and agile electronic transactions between the participants of the development and supply chains are accorded a fundamental importance.

The basic IT technology for these demanding network transactions is the Public Key Infrastructure (PKI) [KaLP05]. A PKI can fulfill basic requirements concerning comprehensible and safe communication, as well as transactions. PKIs of the highest class allow the creation of so-called "qualified signatures" and, therefore, the origination of all types of proof-worthy documents. Moreover, a PKI is the basis for efficient authentication in open networks.

The use of PKI technologies and services is not widespread in German enterprises. Today only a very low distribution of the use of electronic signatures can be seen in business processes, at public authorities and at on the private level, as well. Nevertheless, many single PKI projects have been started [LMM+06] as well as bigger initiatives, like the already established German "Signaturbündnis". There is an uncertainty concerning the future dissemination and availability of PKI services among executive managers in Europe.

The analysis of relevant influencing factors based on the innovation theory is a green field in terms of the scientific based analysis of PKI-technology. This concerns the spreading and the adoption of PKI-

N. Pohlmann, H. Reimer, W. Schneider (Editors): Securing Electronic Business Processes, Vieweg (2007), 386-395

technology and particularly the extrapolation of the development of PKI into the future. The need for a technology forecast of PKI-technology is thus revealed, as well. This ought to concern Europe as well as the whole world.

This contribution provides a diffusion model for the future dissemination of the use of PKI-technology. This aims to theoretically and practically describe the process of diffusion of PKI-technology in the economic system, in the past and the future. The aim is to give decision-making advice for entering into PKI-technology and to provide a contribution to the theoretical analysis of PKI development.

The underlying parameters of the diffusion model are filled with estimated values by the instrument of a Delphi study. Based on a board of 69 German experts, several aspects of the future development and dissemination of the PKI-technology in Germany and Europe will be presented indicating the central research result of this contribution.

2 Explanation of PKI and Innovation Theory

2.1 PKI – Special Infrastructure for Electronic Signatures

The PKI-technology enables us to replace the personal signature (given by one's own hand) by an equivalent electronic signature. The possibility arises to replace almost all paper based and also all legally relevant documents and therefore to utilize all advantages of the virtualization [Heus04].

Table 1 defines three categories of the PKI-technology that are relevant for the Delphi study presented in this paper [LoOP05].

Table 1: Bundling of PKI-technology in three categories of different quality

Elements of PKI	Q-Sig Qualified signature	A-Sig Advanced signature	M-Sig Machine signature
Accreditation by German BNetzA	Yes, obligatory	Not necessary	Not necessary
Announcement against German BeNetzA	Yes, obligatory	Possible	Not necessary
Certificate Class 4	Yes, obligatory	Not necessary	Not necessary
Certificate Class 3	No	Yes	Not necessary
Owner: Natural persons	Yes, obligatory	Not necessary	Not necessary
Owner: Legal entity	No	Yes, possible	Yes, possible
Owner: Machine – Clients	No	No	Yes, possible
Owner: Machine – Server	No	No	Yes, possible
Owner: Services of Software (SOA)	No	No	Yes, possible
Storage of secure keys	Cert. smartcard	Softtoken or higher	Server
Registration	Cert. trusted Org., Official ID-Card	Trusted Org., email-ID	Prog.-ID, UID.
Proof of identity	PIN or Biometry	PIN or Biometry	-
CPS available	Yes, obligatory	Unstructured	Not necessary

A PKI allows the user to execute different services: registration of certificates, directory services, certificate checks, authentication in open networks, digital signature, encryption as well as time stamping. These basic services together with the technical surroundings and the accompanying legal regulations are called PKI-technology below.

2.2 PKI-Technology in Reflection of Innovation Research

With regard to PKI-technology the so called phase of invention, where new ideas are generated, has reached a high degree of performance. Those inventions are namely the development of the asymmetrical cryptography and the legal equality of personal and digital signature. In opposite to this the situation of the innovation shows generally an expandable level. Moreover, the development of the diffusion, or in other words the distribution of the PKI-technology into markets, is regarded as considerably low [PeOL05].

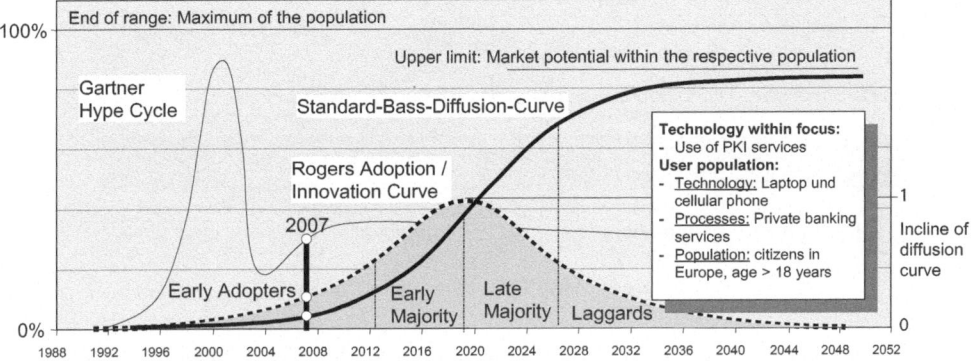

Figure 1: Hypothetical diffusion of PKI-services into banking processes.

It is called *adoption* when individuals decide to step into a technology and use it [MaPe85]. The aggregate analysis of many processes of adoption is described as *technology diffusion*, being described in the context of the diffusion theory. The most important dynamic model in this area is the so-called diffusion curve which describes the distribution of a technology over a specific period of time [Bass69, PuSr00]. This is illustrated by the fictitious example of the use of PKI in figure 1.

The gradient course of the Standard Bass Diffusion Curve leads to the Innovation Adoption Curve from Rogers [Roge95]. Finally the Technology Hype Cycle of the Gartner Group, which is based on subjective factors, has to be put into the period of early adopters of the PKI-technology's innovation curve. Thereafter, the PKI-technology is actually in the stage of "Climbing the Slope" [Whea06].

The diffusion theory represents a good basis for the preparation of a Delphi study. Moreover, the model is capable of expressing the special features of the PKI diffusion.

3 Evaluation of a PKI Diffusion Model

Chapter 3 presents the procedure of the PKI-Delphi study and its results. At first a theoretical model of the diffusion of the PKI technology is set up followed by the presentation of the research approach.

3.1 Conceptual Framework: T2D4 Diffusion Model

The T2D4 model describes the system of adoption and diffusion of the PKI-technology from a general viewpoint. It contains two technical levels: PKI categories and members of the PKI-value chain, furthermore, four diffusion subject levels: secondary technologies, business processes, user populations and economic sectors.

The model follows the assumption that the experts know the inner connections between different issues of PKI intuitively. The model describes defined cuts through the complex and dynamic scenario of the technology diffusion of the PKI.

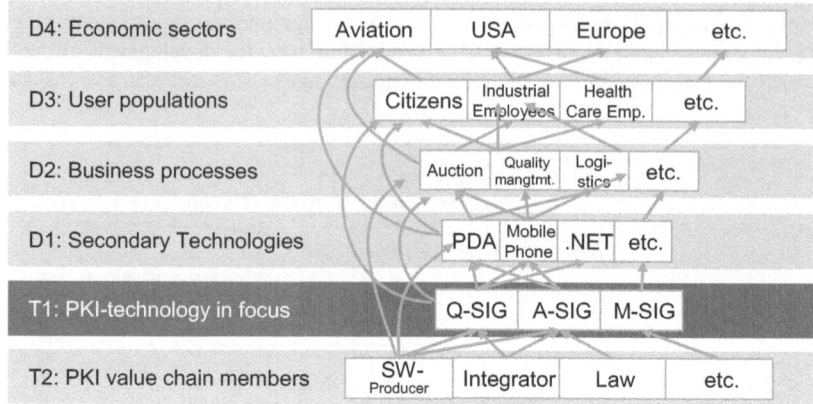

Figure 2: Model T2D4 of the PKI-Diffusion

It is posited that it is not necessary to ask for the respective causalities between the layers but to question the experts about snapshots of the effect system along these certain cutting layers (see Figure 2). From those an overall picture can be reconstructed that allows understanding the effective causalities between the layers.

3.2 The Approach: Progression of the PKI Delphi study

In order to forecast diffuse future facts from the field of PKI-technology, a certain research instrument, the so-called Delphi study, exists [Häde02]. In a multistage process of interviews experts are questioned about their personal assessments of developments in their respective expert areas. The total design method and the "Theory of Facets" describe how to break down a complex topic to a questionnaire with several simple multiple-choice questions [Häde02, Dill78].

The questionnaire of the PKI Delphi study is based on the PKI-T2D4-diffusion model. It is subdivided into a main study (chapters 1-6) with 243 questions and a deepening study (chapters 7-8) with 233 questions. More than 1700 comments and 73 new questions were given in the initial round one, allowing the experts to understand possible divergences between their own answers and the average results. The feedback rounds no. 2 and no. 3 aimed at providing an improvement concerning the quality of the content and the convergence of the experts´ opinions.

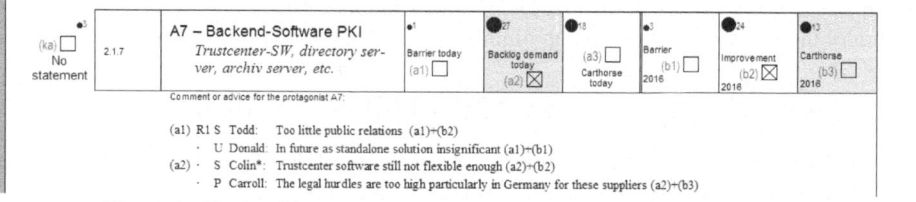

Figure 3: Clipping from the questionnaire of the 2nd round of the PKI-Delphi study

The medium of the questionnaire is a word document. **Figure 3** shows the presentation of a question about the members of the PKI value chain. In order to make a series of comments traceable, each participant gets a pseudonym, which can be found among the compendiums of comments in the feedback round.

The participants of the PKI-Delphi study recruit themselves with one third each from the professions science, users and technology provider. They are chosen experts with a distinct reputation in their field of work. It may be assumed that the experts of the Delphi study are adequately qualified, so that the results of the study can reach a solid level. The Delphi study was performed in three rounds between 03/05/2006 and 01/11/2006. 75 experts have personally confirmed their participation. In the end 69 experts fulfilled the study.

In this contribution the first results of the main study are published.

3.3 Results: Adoption and Diffusion of PKI-Technology

Among the five big topics of the main study, 110 questions can be found. Within those, 199 facet questions are defined containing all in all 925 answer choices. The average answer quota per question is numbered to 87%. That means that apart from 13% of the participants who selected the field "no comment" or who gave an invalid answer or no answer, all other participants gave a correct answer to the questions they had been confronted with. The loss rate in the feedback round was numbered on an average of 29%. That leads to the statement that all questions were processed twice with an average of 49 participants.

3.3.1 T2: Performance of Members of the PKI Value Chain

In chapter 2 of the questionnaire the participants of the study were asked for their opinion concerning 11 special members of the value chain of the PKI-technology. These questions aim at layer T2 of the diffusion model. Two facet-questions ask the participants' rating of the value chain member about its standing today (year 2006) and in future (year 2016).

The boxplots (see **Figure 4**) show the min/max values (brackets), the arithmetic average (in the centre of the box) and the median (gray point). Grey circles behind the boxplot show the number of votes for this category. Thin lines make it possible to pursue the ways of every single voice. The lines are encoded by colours (with regard to their length), so that unusual deviations can be identified easily.

International organisations (A1, rank 11 in 2016) are described as "sluggish" and "very slow" in the comments by the study participants. They are "by definition very active", but would not advance the topics from their "passive position", however. It is frequently pointed out that organisations like CEN, ETSI and W3C lack legal and procedural unification.

The *German legislator* (A3, rank 9 in 2016) is appreciated as a "forerunner" and seen in this role in future, too. The German Digital Signature Act (SigG) is described as "restrictive", particularly the obligations for supervision. Initiatives for more pragmatism in the design and interpretation of the laws (e.g. in the area of electronic invoice) would be blocked. The Digital Signature Act is mentioned positively because by this the construction of the trust centre infrastructure was advanced. Nevertheless, this law would not fulfil the current needs of the real business processes at the moment.

Software producers (A4-7) are generally advised in the comments of the participants to improve the user-friendliness of their products. The lack of consistency and low compatibility with each other are frequently called an "underlying evil".

In the target group of the *producer of mainstream-software* (A4, rank 5 in 2016), mainly producers of e-mail programmes and programmes for word processing are observed by comments. Reaching a critical mass was multiply annotated as an important aim.

It is advised to the *producers of enterprise software* (A5, rank 3 in 2016) to integrate the PKI-technology to the software product, so that the final user can use it "without thinking about it". The *backend software* (A7, rank 6 in 2016) gets respected as mature. Deficits are still seen, however, in the area of archival storage.

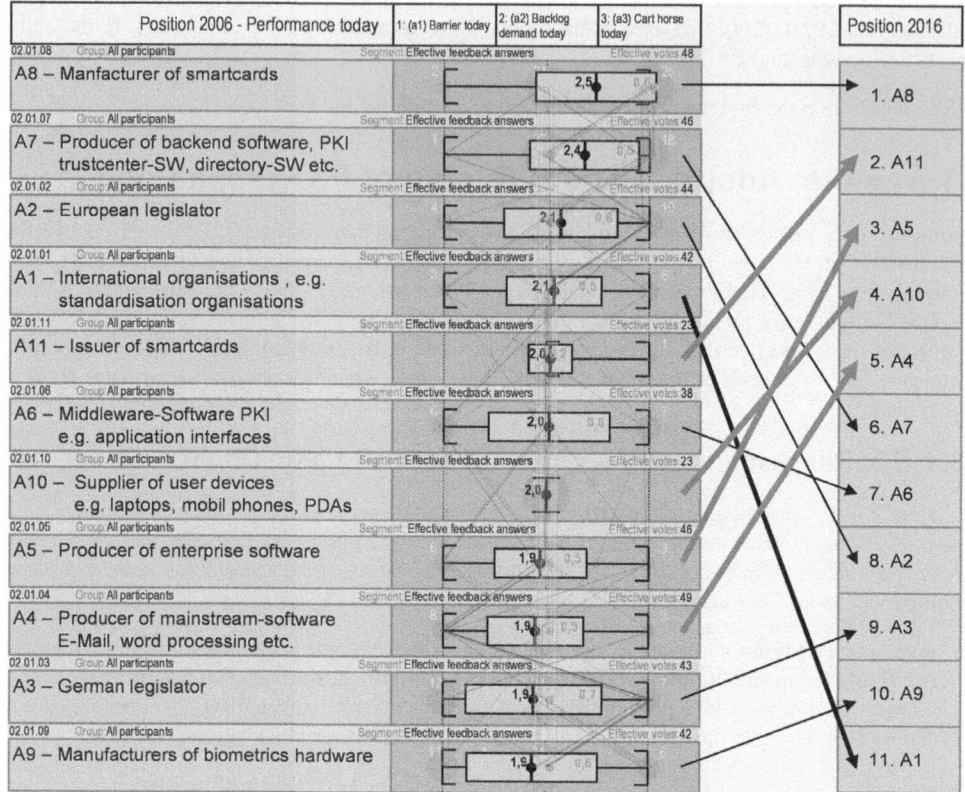

Figure 4: Position of the player in the value chain of the PKI-technology today and 2016

A difficult situation is certified to the *manufacturers of smartcards* (A8, rank 1 in 2016). On the one hand they are dependent on the existence of card readers, which could lead to the situation that the smart token or USB token will take a dominant role in future. On the other hand the manufacturers are dependent on the *issuer of smartcards* (A11, rank 2 in 2016) such as banks, certificate service providers or the government itself.

The issuer becomes ascribed a more important role at the distribution of the PKI only in the future. The issuers would primarily see their respective cards as one of the customer loyalty's instrument and therefore, it would have come to a number of spot solutions today. It is not forgotten that this group has already experiences in the area of PKI namely with HBCI and that it turned out that it is very hard to develop a cost-covering business model in the PKI area.

Manufacturers of biometrics hardware (A9, rank 1 in 2016) are confronted with the opinion that their technology has a "low reliability" and a "high failure rate". Positive votes consider the reached level "sufficiently reliable". Biometrics, as can be gathered from the comments, is decoupled of the question about the use of a PKI generally. Particularly governmental activities, such as the USA in the fight against terror or different projects with passports, become the strongest trigger for the use of biometrics and will be entirely thorough – at first without PKI.

The group of the *suppliers of user devices* (A10, rank 4 in 2016) is subdivided by the participant field into two groups: A10a: *Wireless carriers* and its partners for mobile telephones and A10b: *Manufacturers of PDAs and laptop computers*. A good "form factor" is ascribed to the TPM (Trusted Platform Module) and SIM (Subscriber Identity Module) cards. Having a great market volume, one more important reason appears why wireless carriers are considered as keyplayers in the future. Proprietary standards and concepts as well as missing integration of card readers are mentioned as obstacles of the PKI for spreading into the devices.

3.3.2 D1: Adoption by secondary Technologies

The participants of the study were questioned about their assessment of 20 special technologies in chapter 4. These questions are aiming at the level D1: "Secondary Technologies" of the T2D4 diffusion model. In a first facet question the study participants gave their judgement of today's potential of PKI for the respective technology (low, medium and high potential benefit). The second facet question refers to the integration of PKI in general in this technology in the year 2016 (barely, inferior or leading dissemination).

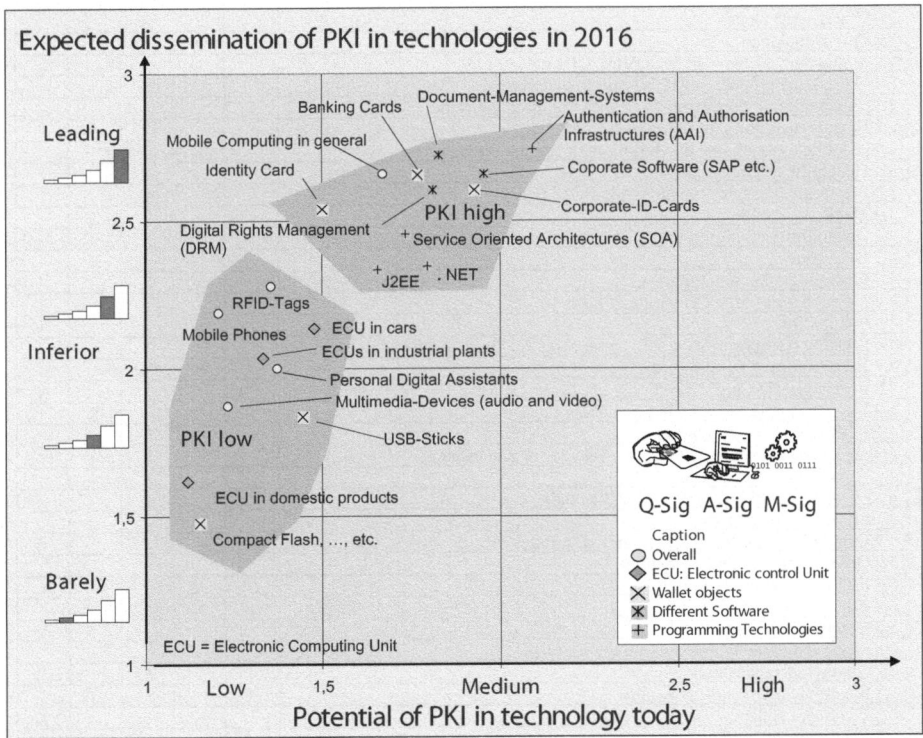

Figure 5: Overview of the potential today and the expected dissemination of PKI in technologies

Two clusters have been identified from the graphic cluster analysis of 2D representation of the average answers of both facet questions (see Figure 5): PKI low and PKI high.

3.3.3 D2: Advantages for Business Processes

A cluster analysis (see Table 2) on the basis of the average values and its standard deviations of the facet answer (1. PKI hinders the process, 2. No use effects to be watched, 3. Easy efficiencies, 4. Clear efficiencies, 5. There is nothing like PKI) subdivides the 42 most popular e-business processes into four areas with respectively clear statements concerning the use of a PKI and into two areas with comparatively disproportionate answer pictures.

Table 2: Overview of 42 processes and its affinity to the PKI-technology

	A1	B 1/2	A2	A3	B 3/4	A4
PKI almost indispensable / Superiority of PKI not clearly evident / Advantage of PKI / Slight benefit from PKI / Nonspecific benefit from PKI / PKI unhelpful						
1.1 Generally: Electronic correspondence; E-Mail				X		
1.2 Communication inside social associations			X			
2.1 Generally: Signing of contracts on the internet				X		
2.2 B2C – Auctions: Business to Consumer		X				
2.3 B2B – Auctions: Business to Business				X		
2.4 C2C – Auctions: Consumer to Consumer		X				
2.5 Stocktrading				X		
2.6 Insurance contracting				X		
2.7 Credit agreements				X		
2.8 Travel booking			X			
2.9 Media purchasing – Books, DVDs, CDs etc.	X					
2.10 Electronic products – MP3s, videos, pictures etc.	X					
2.11 Authorization purchasing – Tickets, bonus coupons etc.		X				
2.12 Catalogue selling	X					
2.13 Mobile transaction – purchasing with cellular phone etc.			X			
3.1 Generally: electronic invoice				X		
3.2 Electronic payment – paying with digital check				X		
3.3 Electronic money					X	
4.1 Generally: Activities in the „Virtual town-hall"				X		
4.2 E-Election					X	
4.3 Electronic official notifications				X		
4.4 E-Certificates – e.g. Certificate of birth						X
4.5 E-Cadastre						X
4.6 E-Bafög (Governmental credit agreements for German students)				X		
4.7 E-Tax return				X		
4.8 E-Personal ID-Card						X
4.9 Electronic governmental bid invitation					X	
4.10 E-Registration of vehicles				X		
4.11 E-Announcement of alienation (Vehicles or real estates)				X		
4.12 Electronic trade register				X		
4.13 Governmental registration of individuals				X		
4.14 E-Employment office	X					
5.1 Generally: Business Processes in Enterprises		X				
5.2 Order completion by e-Contract		X				
5.3 E-Order handling			X			
5.4 E-Delivery schedule			X			
5.5 E- recipe of goods	X					
5.6 Stock and capacity queries with the supplier	X					
5.7 Quality documentation				X		
5.8 Electronic transport supply note		X				
6.1 Electronic patients files						X
6.2 Electronic doctoral notice						X

It often happens that the benefit is divided unequally between the parties which are involved with the processes. This situation can lead into a blocking. A solution would be the compensation between the involved process parties. This must, however, be examined in each case.

3.3.4 D3: Diffusion into User Populations

The participants of the study were questioned about the assessment of 10 special user populations in chapter 6. The results of the respectively third facet question (distribution in 2016) are shown in Figure 6 as a rank representation within the answer categories of the facet question.

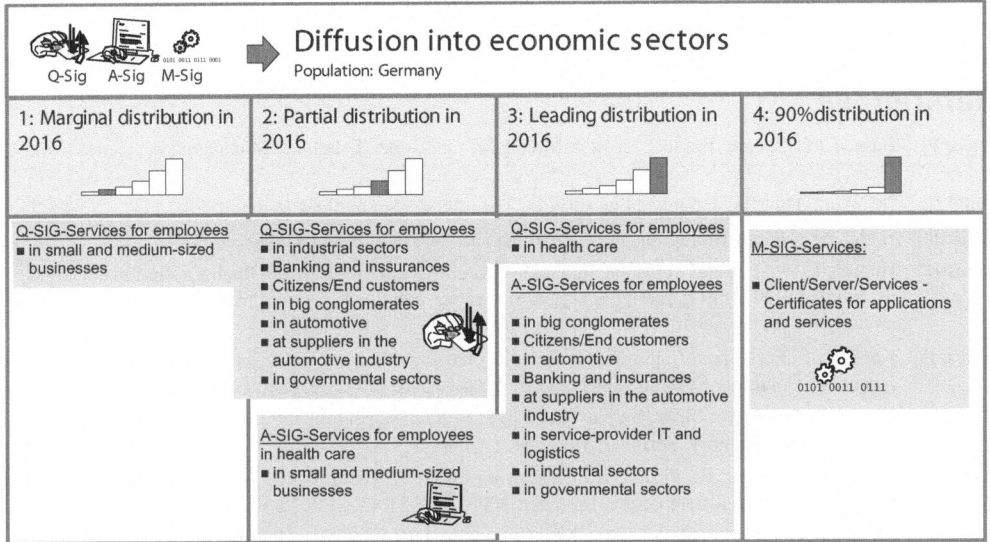

Figure 6: Diffusion of PKI-technology into economic sectors

It can be recognized that a leading role is ascribed to the area of "Health care" concerning the use of the qualified signature. The spread of the Q-Sig in other sectors, e.g. the area of citizen/end consumer, shows a comparatively low distribution.

3.3.5 D4: Dissemination into Markets and Branches

The participants of the study were questioned about the assessment of 17 business branches in chapter 6.2 of the questionnaire. The result suggests that the PKI will have found a leading spreading in pharma, financial services, aeronautics and automotive – on a basis of minimum A-Sig in 2016. At least a partially spreading is predicted for the branches chemistry, electronic, food, electrical engineering, engineering & tooling, printing, building, iron & metal, mining and ceramics (spreading intensity in a descending order).

4 Conclusion

A diffusion model of the PKI-technology was introduced consisting of the layers of secondary technologies, business processes, user populations and economic sectors. Three significant qualities of the electronic signature were defined and integrated into the model. By means of a Delphi study, the model parameters were described and afterwards filled in and judged by experts. The given results confirm the model construction.

Further steps within this research project will be the evaluation of the deepening study as well as the factor analysis of the whole survey. An extension of the diffusion model to additional socio-economic factors is planned, as well as the interpretation of the inner causalities between the given model layers.

Further areas of study can be identified in the quantitative research in order to capture real diffusion curves from the area of PKI. An extension of the study's underlying population towards European experts as well as a repetition of the Delphi study after an adequate period of time are research opportunities for further deepening the results.

References

[Bass69]   Bass, F.M.: A New product Growth Model for Consumer Durables, Management Science, Vol. 15, 1996, p. 215-227.

[Dill78]   Dillmann, D.: Mail and telephone surveys. The total design method, Wiley, 1978

[Häde02]   Häder, M.: Delphi-Befragungen – Ein Arbeitsbuch. Westdeutscher Verlag, 2002.

[Heus04]   Heusch, C.-A.: Die elektronische Signatur – Änderung des Bürgerlichen Rechts aufgrund der Signatur-Richtlinie (1999;93;EG) durch das Gesetz zur Anpassung der Formvorschriften des Privatrechts an den modernen Rechtsgeschäftsverkehr vom 13. Juli 2001, Tenea Verlag, 2004.

[KaLP05]   Katsikas, S. K.; Lopez, J.; Pernul, G.: Security, Trust and Privacy in Digital Business. In: International Journal of Computer Systems, Science & Engineering 10 (2005) 6, CRL Publishing, 2005.

[LMM+06] Lioy, A.; Marian, M.; Moltchanova, N.; Pala, M.: PKI past, present and future, in: International Journal of Information Security, Springer, Vol.5, Nr. 1, 2006, S. 18-29.

[LoOP05]   Lopez, J.; Oppliger, R.; Pernul, G.: Classifying Public Key Certificates, in: Chadwick, D.; Gansen Z. (Eds.): Public Key Infrastructure, Springer, 2005, p. 135-143.

[MaPe85]   Mahajan, V.; Peterson, R. A.: Models for Innovation Diffusion, Sage Publications Inc., 1985.

[PeOL05]   Pernul, G.; Opplinger, R.; Lopez, J.: Why have Public Key Infrastructures failed so far? In: Internet Research, 15 (2005) 5, p. 544-556.

[PuSr00]   Putsis, W. P.;Srinivasan, V.: Estimation techniques for macro diffusion models, in: Vijay M.; Muller, E; Wind Y. (Hrsg.): New Product Diffusion Models , Springer, 2000, p. 263-291.

[Roge95]   Rogers, E. M. : Diffusion of Innovations, 4. Edition, The Free Press, 1995.

[Whea06]   Wheatmann, Vic et al.: Hype Cycle for Information Security 2006, from: Gartner Inc., 2006.

Acknowledgements

I would like to gratefully acknowledge the support and advice of Prof. Dr. Günther Pernul from the University of Regensburg in planning and executing the PKI Delphi study.

The Introduction of Health Telematics in Germany

Dirk Drees

gematik –
Gesellschaft für Telematikanwendungen der Gesundheitskarte mbH
dirk.drees@gematik.de

Abstract

By enacting a law to modernize the statutory health insurance[1] the German government initiated a huge infrastructural telematics project: the introduction of a national electronic Health (eHealth) Card (in Germany it is known as the eGK). This microprocessor-based chipcard is an important element in the currently built infrastructure. Literally the card is the key to a health system data highway and to the applications already planned and waiting to be discovered. The primary intention of the German legislative authority is to enhance efficiency, quality and transparency of medical care. The solution is a patient based sector-spanning network with persistent information flow. The 15 top organizations of the national German health system undertook the difficult task to introduce the required infrastructure and therefore founded gematik – Gesellschaft für Telematikanwendungen der Gesundheitskarte mbH[2] in 2005.

1 Applications

The new smartcard is a building block on the road towards an overall modernisation of the German health system. It is the key to various applications which combined with the corresponding telematics infrastructure used for data communication will enhance the quality of medical care and also strengthen patients rights and responsibility. The applications can be divided into two types.

1.1 Mandatory Applications

Three applications are mandatory for all insured citizens[3]; the use of the personal insurance data on the card to legitimate medical care, the electronic Prescription (ePrescription) and the European Health Insurance Card (EHIC) on the backside of the German eHealth Card (limited to all statutory health insured).

- Personal Insurance Data
  The eHealth Card will replace the existing Health Insurance Card ("Krankenversichertenkarte – KVK") as a means of entitlement for health insurance which was introduced in 1994. Today a medical specialist is able to use the personal insurance data stored on the memory card to check validity of health insurance coverage. After checking, he can use this information for accounting.
  The eHealth Card will also contain a data set carrying the name of the insured, birth date, sex, address, health insurance number as well as personal insurance status.

---

1 Gesetz zur Modernisierung der gesetzlichen Krankenversicherung (GKV-Modernisierungsgesetz), § 291 SGB V – Krankenversichertenkarte
2 § 291 b SGB V – Gesellschaft für Telematik
3 § 291 a Abs. 2 Satz 1 und 2, SGB V – Elektronische Gesundheitskarte

N. Pohlmann, H. Reimer, W. Schneider (Editors): Securing Electronic Business Processes, Vieweg (2007), 396-400

- Electronic Prescription (ePrescription)
  The ePrescription is the first application useable with the eHealth Card that will reveal the technical advantages of telematics. Information will be available just in time for telematics participants. In the future a doctor will be able to transport and save a prescription on a server in the telematics infrastructure or directly on the smart card where it can be read and dispensed by a pharmacist. The electronic transportation of prescriptions will replace the recent procedure which is based on approximately 800.000.000 – 1.000.000.000 paper forms filled in by doctors and dispensed in a pharmacy [see Figure 1].

- European Health Insurance Card (EHIC)
  For all statutory insured citizens in Germany the eHealth Card will carry European Health Insurance information on its reverse side. This information ensures citizens travelling in Europe will get fast and unbureaucratic medical help without worrying about billing formalities. The EHIC is the connecting medical link between member states of the European Union.

1.2 Voluntary Applications

- Together with the mandatory applications like ePrescription the insured is free to choose voluntary applications useable with the eHealth Card[4]. Their approval is necessary to store e.g. emergency data information on the card or to set up a pharmaceutical therapy safety which will carry the pharmaceutical history of an insured.

- Emergency Data
  Normally a doctor doesn't have available information about a patient's general health status in an emergency situation. This will change with the emergency data set stored on the eHealth Card. Following the approval of the insured person a doctor can save a data set on the card about e.g. chronic diseases, pharmaceutical incompatibilities and allergies delivering important general information in critical situations for attending physicians.

- Pharmaceutical Therapy Safety
  This application represents an individual pharmaceutical history of an insured. As described for the emergency data set an approval by the insured is necessary to use this new application with the eHealth Card. A medical specialist prescribing a medicament can see what medicaments have already been prescribed and avoid a possible contra-indication. A pharmacist will also be able to store information in the pharmaceutical history.

- Discharge Letter
  This application will include e.g. findings, diagnoses, recommended therapies and therapy reports for fast data communication between attending medical specialists.

- Own Documentation by the Insured
  By using his eHealth Card an insured will be able to store e.g. courses of diseases, diabetes diary etc. to be understood as additional important information for medical specialists based on information given by the patient to complement his general medical status.

- Electronic Health Care Record
  Following approval of the insured and regulated by access rules, participants of health telematics like doctors, dentists, and medical specialists will be able to systematically store e.g. findings, diagnoses, therapy activities, therapy reports, radiographs and vaccinations to set up an individual patient's history delivering a broad and comprehensive insight to their medical condition.

---

4 § 291 a Abs. 3 Satz 1 bis 6, SGB V – Elektronische Gesundheitskarte

2 Unlimited Possibilities – Open Platform Basis

The new health telematics infrastructure represents an open platform that can be used by webservice providers as well as application providers. The prerequisites are that they have to meet the underlying specifications ensuring the high security level, interoperability and compatibility of the infrastructure. It will represent an interlinking potential of unlimited creativity. The internet is an example of the enormous possibilities. Within a few years it grew from an inconsiderable project amongst scientists to one of the most important information and communication platforms spanning economy, research, administration and private use. The market reacted fast, discovered the potential and offered numerous application solutions. Even today, with millions of interlinked computers and applications an end is not in sight. The same evolution is to be expected with the introduction of the health telematics, however with a higher safety level that cannot be attained by the internet.

2.1 Migration guarantees Success

The telematics infrastructure will interlink approximately 140.000 general practitioners (GPs), 55.000 dentists, 20.000 pharmacies, 2.200 hospitals and 270 health insurance companies [see Figure 1]. IT projects with such a revolutionary scope need to be gradually introduced to familiarize participants with the technical aspects and the applications to be used [see Figure 2].

With the new telematics infrastructure, existing IT solutions limited to local coverage in GPs, pharmacies, hospitals and health insurance companies will be transferred to a nationwide network. The medical care supply process as well as the participants in the process will be interlinked. The step-by-step introduction of the applications defined by the German Federal Ministry of Health will result in an increasing usage of health telematics, whose boundaries will not be reached just by the introduction of Electronic Health Care Records. Different migration steps are needed not only for testing the new technology but also to get used to changing workflows. Experiences taken from numerous IT projects worldwide showed that it is not realistic to run both – new technology and workflows – immediately accurate and smooth. There's no big button that, once pressed, will guarantee a faultless interaction between a gigantic network with extensive safety applications and network services, 80 million eHealth Cards and approximately 2 million Health Professional Cards (HPCs).

2.2 Testing the Infrastructure with first Applications

Business expertise has showed that the gradual migration is the key to a successful launch of a nationwide health telematics. Keeping that in mind, the first migration step is the substitution of the existing Health Insurance Card and its function as a verification of the entitlement to medical care, and the writing of electronic prescriptions. Necessary components and applications have to work precisely with the security measures in the infrastructure to form a viable system for all users. Additionally, migration is needed to test and understand the technology to avoid the possibility of delivering e.g. impracticable solutions. Laboratory tests can not substitute practicable field testing with thousands of users.

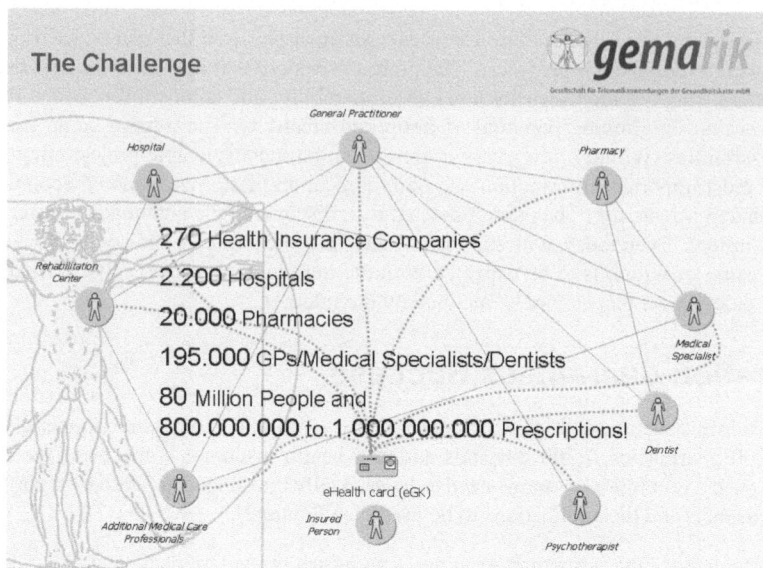

Figure 1: The Challenge of Cross-Sectoral Medical Care

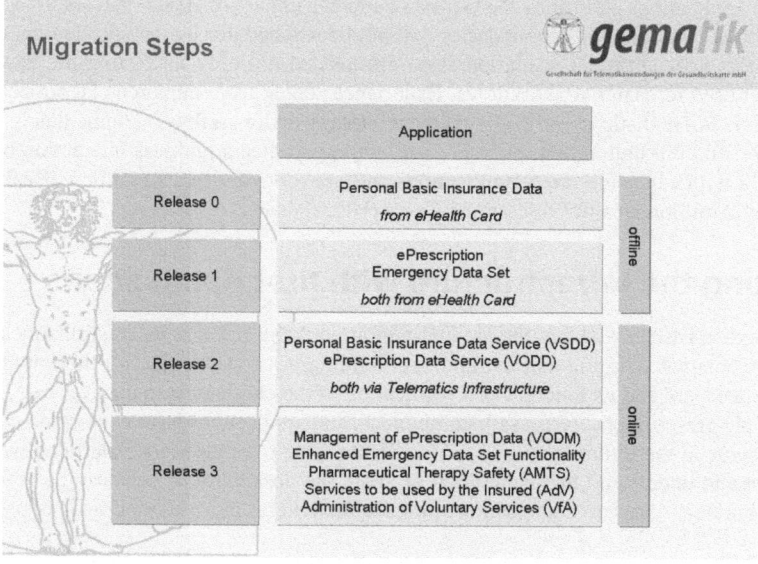

Figure 2: Migration Steps

3 Conclusion

The introduction of a telematics infrastructure as an open platform is an important step towards a modern efficient and transparent national health system symbolized by a patient's eHealth Card used for a never before known cross-sectoral medical care. The success will strongly depend on the expected advantages of telematics; enhancement of efficiency, quality and transparency of medical care. Furthermore, worries about safety and security of medical data transported via telematics must be credibly dispelled. All up-to-date security and safety measures have been implemented in the telematics infrastructure and the accessible applications to meet all requirements prescribed by law. Speaking of acceptance, use of the latest technology is just one important factor. Introducing a network with new workflows will not change the basics of medical care which is first and foremost formed by a respectable doctor-patient-relationship.

References

Fünftes Sozialgesetzbuch, § 291, § 291 a und b

Gesetz zur Modernisierung der gesetzlichen Krankenversicherung, 14.11.2003

The German Identity Card – Concepts and Applications

Andreas Reisen

Office of the Chief Information Officer,
Federal Ministry of the Interior, Germany
Andreas.Reisen@bmi.bund.de

Abstract

In future, biometric identifiers, an electronic authentication and optionally a qualified electronic signature will be included in the German identity card to establish a more reliable connection between the card and its holder and to enable citizens to prove their identity online. This facilitates a number of e-government and e-business applications. Thus, the citizens' identity card will become a key component of the identity management infrastructure in Germany.

1 Introduction

In recent decades, the German identity card has evolved from a national identity document which was mainly used for identity checks within the country into a European travel document. At the same time it has gained significance in the private sector.

An electronic identity card should give German citizens the possibility to complete legally binding on-line transactions and to provide reliable personal information (e.g. their age) electronically. To this end, an electronic authentication function should enable citizens to independently submit verified data from the card to third parties. At the holder's request, a qualified electronic signature can be added to the card to facilitate legal transactions which would otherwise require a handwritten signature. For example, citizens can use it for comfortable and flexible access to electronic administration services which for lack of legal validity could so far not be offered online or were available only to a limited extent. At the same time, the administration can allocate resources more efficiently and effectively if citizens increasingly use electronic channels. In addition, it is foreseen to integrate a digital bimetric photograph and fingerprints into the card to make identification more secure in the real world and to establish a more reliable connection between the card and its holder.

A detailed description of the concepts related to these functions will be given in Section 3. With these new functions the electronic identity card can be used for a variety of new applications, some of which will be presented in Section 4 (see below). The article will conclude with some thoughts on the future of government-issued eID cards and their use in further components of electronic identity management such as identity registers and citizens' portals.

N. Pohlmann, H. Reimer, W. Schneider (Editors): Securing Electronic Business Processes, Vieweg (2007), 401–404

2 Concepts

In addition to its traditional (visual) functions as a national identity document for German citizens and as a travel document for Schengen countries and certain other countries due to bilateral agreements, the electronic identity card will include new functions.

To establish a more reliable connection between the card and its holder, biometric data, namely a full face photograph and fingerprints of the left and right index finger, are planned to be stored on a chip. By electronically comparing this information with the data captured directly from the card user, the identity of the card user and the card holder can be established effectively and with a high level of certainty, which will make domestic controls and entry checks more reliable. To maintain compatibility with ICAO standards and thus the possibility to use the card's biometric function across Europe and the world, a contactless chip interface is to be provided. However, it will not be possible to store a template.

Unlike the biometric function, which is restricted to identification for sovereign purposes and may be accessed only via the EAC protocol and an appropriate certificate, the authentication function will be controlled exclusively by the citizen and will expressly be used also in connection with non-sovereign public- and private-sector procedures. Since citizens' trust is essential in this context, the authentication function is designed to meet users' needs, namely ease of use, transparency and the freedom to decide how one's personal data are used. To prevent phishing attacks, for example, it is crucial for users to be able to verify the identity of those requesting their personal data. For this reason, identity card data can be retrieved only with access certificates which specify who wants to read which data fields for which purpose. With this information, users can then decide whether to consent to the data transfer by entering their PIN. This creates greater transparency so that users can recognize the possible misuse of certificates.

At the same time, it should be considered whether the right of an individual to determine the use of his or her data would be strengthened if a requesting party's legitimate need for cardholder data is checked before an access certificate is issued. The authentication function is additionally protected by a PIN in case the card is lost. Lost or stolen cards can be blacklisted as no longer valid; parties wishing to retrieve data from an identity card will have to contact the list, and data from listed documents will be denied. For e-government and e-business providers the system has the advantage that they can rely on legally collected valid personal data for their transactions and thus have the possibility to seek legal remedy. This strengthens the binding character of online transactions and opens possibilities for new applications.

In addition to providing certain fine-grained and verified personal data online, citizens will be able to decide whether they want to use qualified electronic signatures which under German law would replace a handwritten signature. To this end, citizens may apply for the signature together with the identity card so that the document can be prepared accordingly. The signature will be activated upon delivery. Since the identity card is an affordable widely used identity document, and because it is unlikely that the majority of the population will use the signature function, adding it will be optional and at the applicant's expense.

3 Applications

The above-mentioned new functions can be used for a variety of new e-business, e-government and smart-card applications which will be presented in the following.

The lesson learned from the lack of widespread uptake for electronic signatures is that new technologies must be introduced together with applications which deliver real improvements for citizens. The learning and testing effort will be accepted only if it results in substantial benefits. Especially the authentication function must not only be easy to use to reduce the learning effort, it is also important that it can be used frequently so that it always brings new advantages and becomes familiar to the user. Since the average annual number of contacts between citizens and government is too low to produce such effects, the functions must be included in frequently used e-business and smart-card applications.

We identified the following fields of application for German e-government services:

- viewing and editing registry data, e.g. civil status, identity register, central register of traffic offenders;
- filing applications, e.g. to apply for a judicial order for payment or for a police clearance certificate;
- automatically filling out forms with registry data as a convenient service for citizens
- filing tax returns online (income tax, freelancers).

New Features of the German ID Card

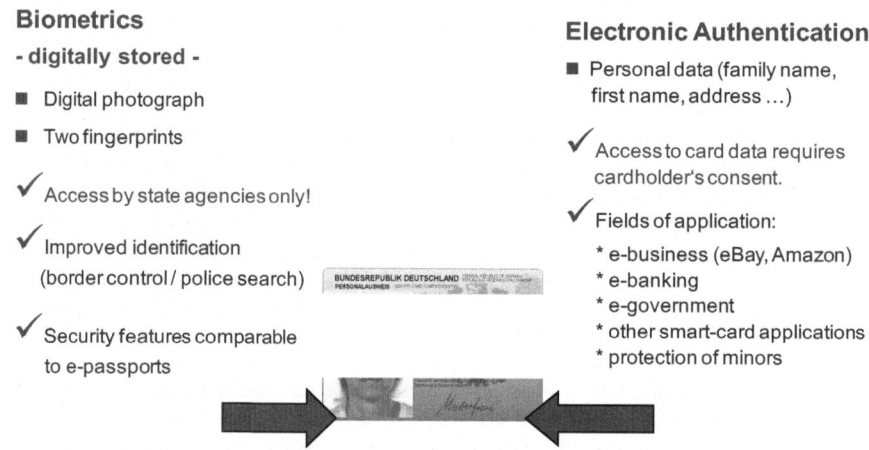

Biometrics
- digitally stored -

- Digital photograph
- Two fingerprints

✓ Access by state agencies only!

✓ Improved identification (border control / police search)

✓ Security features comparable to e-passports

Electronic Authentication

- Personal data (family name, first name, address …)

✓ Access to card data requires cardholder's consent.

✓ Fields of application:
  * e-business (eBay, Amazon)
  * e-banking
  * e-government
  * other smart-card applications
  * protection of minors

The following e-business and smart-card applications are conceivable:

- age verification to protect minors, prevention of addiction (online gambling), and classification of user groups, e.g. services for persons over 18 years, under 14 years, over 65 years, etc.;
- viewing, registering and cancelling contracts and relevant information (invoices);
- various online banking operations;
- opening accounts, e.g. for Internet auctions with verified personal data.

The examples show that the authentication function and the digital signature complement one another and may serve as a useful tool for numerous applications.

4 Conclusions

The electronic identity card featuring authentication and signature functions is a key component of the state's electronic identity management infrastructure. It covers several basic functions while providing a very high level of security.

Nevertheless, there are a number of additional functions which require that the identity card be embedded in further infrastructure components to develop new fields of application, notably the citizens' portals which provide additional personal data not stored on the identity card. Moreover, they confer rights on third parties and ensure that these rights are valid. The electronic identity card can be used to deliver a valid record of basic information for a citizens' portal or to create a citizens' portal account at a later date. Another field of application is identity registers. For administrative purposes, they provide other authorities and – to a limited extent – the private sector with identity information from the card. Consolidating public databases with these registers is also important for implementing the state's electronic identity management. Further components will have to be added to ensure the future interoperability of national eID infrastructures at European and global level.

References

[KüNa07]   Kügler, Dennis, Naumann, Ingo: Sicherheitsmechanismen für kontaktlose Chips im deutschen Reisepass – Ein Überblick über Sicherheitsmerkmale, Risiken, und Gegenmaßnahmen DuD 03/2007, S. 176

[Enge06]   Engel, Christian: Auf dem Weg zum elektronsichen Personalausweis DuD 04/2006, S. 207

Infrastructures for Identification and Identity Documents

Walter Landvogt

Bundesdruckerei GmbH
Systems House Solution Development
landvogt@bdr.de

Abstract

The introduction of the new German biometric passport on 1st of November 2005 has caused a change of the requirements for the technical systems at the local passport authorities and the computing departments of the city administration. The capturing of biometric information and the process of assuring the usability of biometric data for the verification process has led to a new technological standard for soft- and hardware equipment at the passport office and for the way of securely transferring the passport application data and biometric information to the central production facilities of Bundesdruckerei.

The legal framework clearly defines the conditions for the passport or identity document application process and the common level of security for the technical environment. However, the local administration bears responsibility for the concrete organization of the process and the kind and type of technical system.

1 Passport offices in Germany

From a total of 12.400 communities in Germany about 5.300 provide local administration services which run necessary local infrastructural tasks and services for the citizens. Smaller communities in the country side have – with respect to efficiency and costs – united to "Verwaltungsgemeinschaften" which share personnel, office facilities and services. A major service concerning the citizens of a community is the administration of the registration data and the enrolment and issuing of passports and identity documents. The two services a closely related, since they are typically based on a single software system that manages the registration database as well as the passport and identity document database. To provide a certain level of service for their citizens the 5.300 communities with administration services run about 7.500 citizen offices. Major cities like the capitol Berlin run about 50 citizen offices at which passport documents may be applied for and will be delivered to the applicant.

As the local administrations have to bear the cost of purchasing and maintenance for the technical equipment they make their own decision for a software product for registration and passport purposes and for the it-framework and organization which fits best to the cities budget and requirements. With respect to the number of citizens the figures of passport application cases vary. A city like Berlin manages about 4 million records and processes about 1.400 application cases a day with the help of about 250 PC desktop systems – one at each office counter. A small city with 20.000 inhabitants manages about 25.000 record sets and fills out 8 to 10 application forms at three to five office desks. The local responsibility and the wide range of different requirements concerning the performance of the software for registration and passport enrolment have led to a wide variety of systems and architectures in use.

N. Pohlmann, H. Reimer, W. Schneider (Editors): Securing Electronic Business Processes, Vieweg (2007), 405-410

2 The Application Process

Passports and identity documents are being manufactured at the central high security production facilities at Bundesdruckerei GmbH in Berlin. Every day 5.300 local passport authorities send up to 10.000 application records to the production server. Whereas in the past the passport data records had been mailed on paper formulas to Bundesdruckerei with the introduction of the biometric passport a change has taken place. Nowadays the electronic application process has become standard since the software systems being used at the local authorities have integrated standard software modules for the necessary digitalisation process for portrait photo and the applicant's signature. By 1st of November 2007 the electronic transfer of passport data via digital networks will be mandatory. With the introduction of fingerprints and the digital acquisition of the fingerprint image at the citizen office, there will be no paper based way to deliver the biometric information to the passport production.

2.1 Registration and Passport Application Software and Biometric Modules

Since the introduction of the new passport the software products were adapted to the new demands. At present there is a set of fourteen different software systems in use at the local passport offices. Due to the fact, that in the past citizen registration in detail was defined by federal law of the sixteen German states each software product had a regional focus. Even more, administration software often had been developed an operated by computing centres, which were part of the state administration and designed business processes to the needs of their regional customers. Thus infrastructures can be found, where the citizen offices of a state are connected to a mainframe host computer and a central database server. The citizen office runs personnel computer based desktop systems which connect via terminal software to the registration application. On the other hand personnel computer based registration applications were locally run at the desk of the citizen office sharing a local database server of the city.

The passport and identity document application process is above the registration data. For the application process a record set from the registration database is being taken and enriched by passport or identity document specific information like the physical height of the applicant or a portrait photo. In the near future two digital images of fingerprints are being added to the passport data set. For the registration software the mandatory digital application process and the acquisition of the fingerprint images increase the requirement to handle multimedia data formats: video streams are transmitted from the finger print scanner to the capturing module and digital images were acquired from a desktop scanner which converts the print-out of the photo shop or the photo cabin (see figure 1). In the past processing multimedia data was not very common for administration software and the software systems and databases were not prepared for managing it.

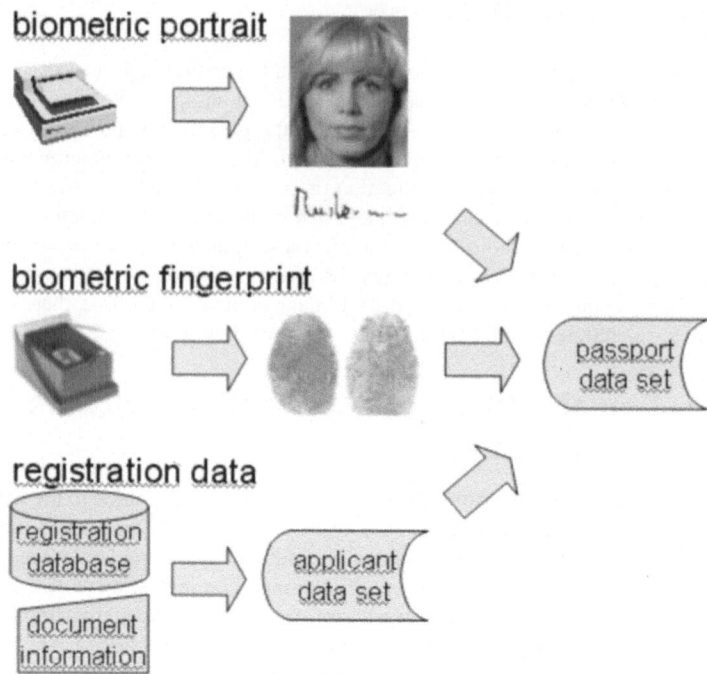

Figure 1: Composition of a record set for a biometric passport

To meet the challenge of capturing the applicant's biometric information the additional software and hardware modules were provided by Bundesdruckerei. Biometric software modules were distributed to the fourteen German manufacturers of registration software. The manufacturers had the task of integrating the software modules into their software framework. The biometric modules were designed to cover a broad variety of runtime environments such as typical WINDOW systems, database frameworks such as ADABAS NATURAL or even SAP Systems.

The passport photograph is captured via TWAIN as the standard PC image acquisition interface. For LINUX based registration software a module for the SANE interface is provided. To share the cost advantages of standard desktop equipment, common low cost image scanners can be used. Nowadays the image scanner is a standard hardware component on the office desk of the citizen office. As the image acquisition has to ensure a reproduction of the portrait photograph which is close to the original print out, the diverging colour processing performance of the scanners are adopted by a colour management component. The digitized photos are delivered to the registration software and for the life cycle of the passport document stored into the passport database. In addition to comply with the ICAO requirements the facial image is encoded in a DG2 pattern and added to the application data record ready for the transmission to the production server.

To get the clearance for the usability in a biometric verification scenario, the digitized image is passed to a software module which analyses the compliance with the ICAO standard for biometric photographs (see figure 2). As the evaluation of three dimensional facial characteristics on the basis of a two dimensional projection of the human face on a photograph is yet an unsolved algorithmic challenge the software detects basic deviations as the height and width of the face, the basic facial pose or the position of the eyes. As the algorithms employed in the software module reflect the state of the art for 2D face evaluation the performance of the module gives a valuable hint for the performance of future border verification. Since its introduction in spring 2006 the module shows reliability in judgement of about 90%. The module is in use in all the software of commercial registration and passport applications. As a fall back medium the employees in the citizen office use a face pattern on a transparency for a quick visual inspection.

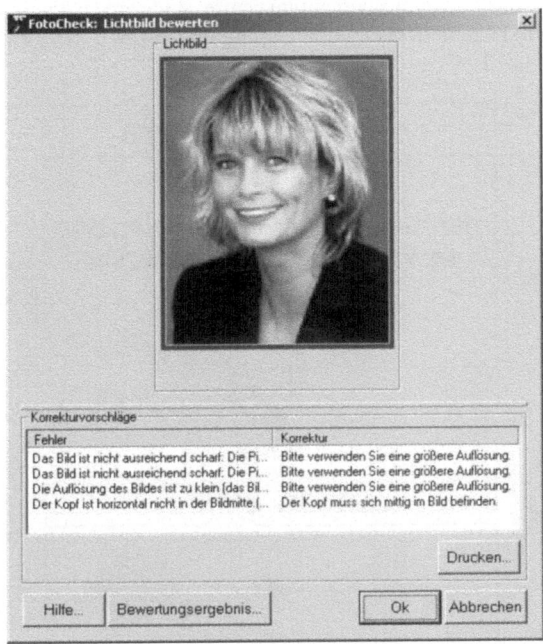

Figure 2: Software module for analysing the ICAO compliance rejecting a photograph due to deviation in facial pose

As photo capturing and ICAO evaluation has become a technology in practical use the fingerprint capturing will be delivered in the near future. At present the fingerprint scanner hardware is being sent to the citizen offices and up to the end of July 2007 every one of the 18.000 desktop systems at the citizen offices will be equipped with one of the two fingerprint scanner models certified by the Federal Office for Information Security (BSI). The fingerprint hardware connects via the USB 2.0 port to the local desktop computer. The life video stream data from the camera device inside the fingerprint scanner is transmitted to the driver module and a fingerprint image is extracted from the stream. The usability of the fingerprint image is qualified by the open source version of the NFIQ module and de facto standard of the U.S. American National Institute of Standards and Technology (NIST). The software module acquires three fingerprint images from an applicant and compares the images among each other on the basis of the open source BOZORTH algorithm of the NIST. The fingerprint with the highest combined quality value calculated from the match scores qualifies for being added to the application data record set. Two fingerprints each of one hand are encoded in a DG3 format ready for personalization on the passport chip.

The fingerprint acquisition process has been tested with 28 passport offices and with each commercial registration application. It turned out, that usability of the software and hardware has been rated comprehensible and easy to handle by the officers. The fingerprint software will be delivered up to mid September 07.

2.2 Challenges for the Infrastructure

The integration and the operation of multimedia equipment such as image and fingerprint scanners lead to new challenges for the standard commercial registration and passport software products. In the past, low performance networks sufficiently fulfilled the requirements of transmitting textual data from the citizen office to an application server in a computing centre. Wide area networks with transmission rates of 128 kbits/sec turn out to be a bottleneck for streaming fingerprint data or transmitting raw data from an image scanner (see figure 3).

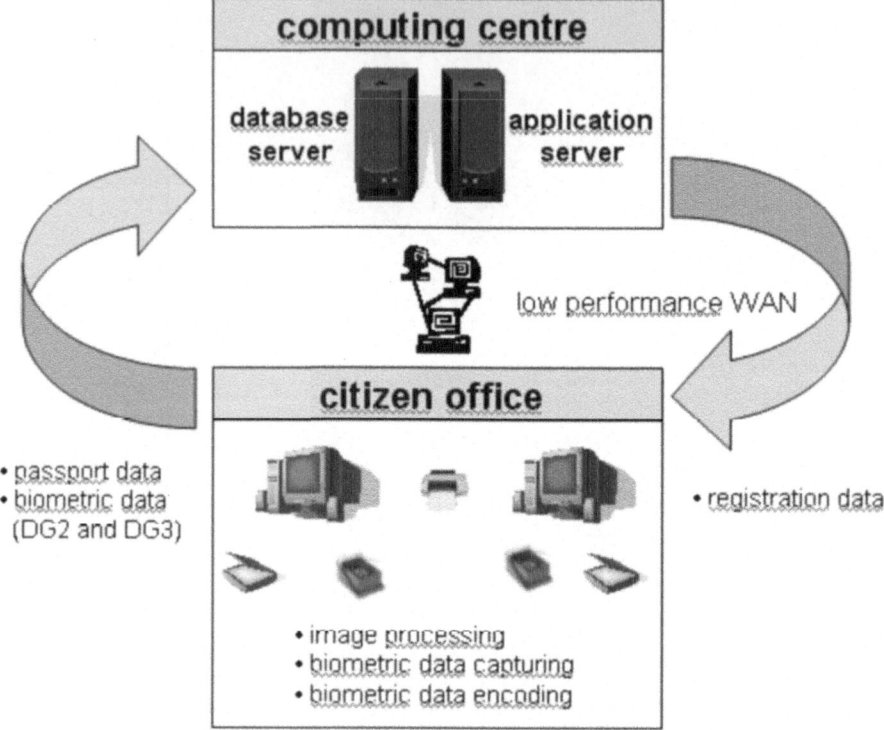

Figure 3: Critical Infrastructure with low performance WAN

The biometric software modules have been designed on the basis of a client/server architecture. The application interface on the server system evokes the biometric client module on the desktop computer in the citizen office. Image processing and biometric evaluation is performed in the client domain. Before transmitting the passport data to the application server the image data is compressed using the compression methods prescribed by the ICAO. With the chosen design, windows terminal server and CITRIX based systems can be supported.

2.3 Standards for data formats and data transmission

With biometric data included in a passport application record, requirements for data formats and safety requirements were redefined. Since standardization in the field of administration is a clear goal of the German government, the XPASS format has been defined on the basis of the XÖV framework (XML based information exchange in public administration) – an emerging standard for administration applications. The XPASS record set models passport data on the basis of XML schemes. The XPASS data model takes into account the requirements of the German identity card which in the near future will carry biometric data as well.

For safe transportation of the application data, the OSCI transport standard (version 1.2) has been developed. The passport records are signed with the private key of the passport authorities and encrypted with the public key of the production server. The passport records are stored within an OSCI transport container. A digital signature of the authorized OSCI client is attached, a handling protocol and the container is encrypted with the public key of the receiving OSCI exchange server.

About 1.800 OSCI clients are authorized to send passport data to the central production server. OSCI clients are being operated either by the local citizen office or by a computing centre performing as a service provider of a number of passport authorities. Authorization of passport authorities and transmission clients is assured by certificates edited by a designated certification authority as a sub-authority of the German administration public key infrastructure.

The standards for the passport data format and the transmission protocol as well as capturing process and quality requirements for the biometric data have been fixed in a government order which is the guideline for the suppliers of registration and passport enrolment software as well as for the manufacturer of the document. All involved hard- and software suppliers will have to provide certificates assuring that their products follow the safety and quality requirements of the government guideline.

3 Conclusion

The techniques for biometric data capturing and processing have been integrated in the commercial hard- and software products which are part of the passport enrolment process at the local authorities. The technical components have proven their usability in pilot studies with 28 citizen offices. The software was designed to meet the requirements widely differing runtime environments and with respect to performance considerations even in low performance networks. Thus all technical measures have been undertaken to guarantee the operability of passport authorities when on 1st of November 2007 the fingerprint is launched for the German passport.

The Security Infrastructure of the German Core Application in Public Transportation

Joseph Lutgen

Head of Security Management and Technology
VDV Kernapplikations GmbH&Co.KG
Kamekestraße 37-39, 50672 Cologne Germany
lutgen@vdv.de

Abstract

The following paper gives an overview of the goals and structure of the security management system of the German core application and considers arguments for and advantages of the implementation of a high security level system for public transport operators at a national level.

1 Background and Goals

The security infrastructure of the German core application is a shared, open and trustworthy platform for operators in public transportation and their customers, in all their various roles, which is organized and administered by the public transport industry itself and enables interoperability of the application from the view point of passengers as well as transport operators.

The primary goal of the security infrastructure and its management system is to systematically protect the production and business processes involved in electronic ticketing against intentional attacks as well as unexpected events. At the same time it must satisfy the expectation that the independence and security of individual organizations (e.g. transport operators, transport associations, customers, system operators and industry manufacturers or providers), all of which operate with differing interests in one or possibly several electronic ticketing systems, must be preserved.

The security infrastructure has its beginnings in 2002 within the framework of the core application project supported by the German Federal Ministry of Education and Research which was concluded successfully in 2005. From the very beginning the focus of the project was on interoperability and the creation of an open standard (to enable the establishment of a market for standard components and services for public transportation) with a high security level capable of economically integrating large as well as small transport operators on a nationwide level. General principles underlying the conception of the security system included:

- Ensure the integrity of communication and processes. Each entity shall have independent and decisive control over the integrity resp. confidentiality of all processes in which it is materially involved. All objects of value (e.g. transactions, products, entitlements) in the system shall posses a unique system wide identity. The unauthorized generation or modification and the unnoticed destruction of such objects within the system must be prevented.

N. Pohlmann, H. Reimer, W. Schneider (Editors): Securing Electronic Business Processes, Vieweg (2007), 411-418

- Establish traceability. The structure of the security system should enable the localization of sources of unauthorized or modified objects of value.
- Enable blocking or disabling of individual participants, components, products, cryptographic keys etc.
- Limit damage in the event that parts of the system are compromised and enable recovery.

During the conception a broad spectrum of requirements specific to electronic ticketing in public transportation concerning types of products (e.g. simple electronic tickets, stored value and automatic fare collection entitlements or combinations of these), technical characteristics of various front end systems (e.g. check-in/check-out or be-in/be-out systems) as well as various technical realizations of user media (e.g. smartcards and mobile phones) had to be regarded. Furthermore, no a priori assumptions were made on the existence of trust relationships between entities.

At the end of the core application project the "VDV Kernapplikations GmbH&Co.KG" was founded as issuer of the core application to administer central tender processes and to carry out various central duties including registration, security management, certification of components, administration of the specifications and further development of the core application. In the time following the core application project but before the conclusion of tender process for the implementation of the security management system in September 2006 a series of pilot projects in Saarbrücken, Schwäbisch-Hall and Hohenlohe as well as further work regarding the public key infrastructure and key management (see below) were carried out. The complete implementation and launch of all core security management processes were carried out in parallel with the introduction of the core application in the Rhein-Ruhr and Rhein-Sieg regions of Germany and were completed in December 2006.

Current developments focus on the introduction of the core application in further regions as well as the optimization of the flexibility, efficiency and user friendliness of the security management system.

2 Advantages of the security infrastructure for users

The advantages of the security management system for its users can best be illustrated by means of a cost-benefit analysis, which can only be indicated qualitatively in this paper. Such an analysis for public transportation systems is very complex and must account for investment, operating, replacement, adaptation and migration costs and operating risk. In particular, life cycle costs including losses due to successful attacks on the system, costs of adaptations to applications forced by the results of tender processes, costs for the parallel operation of systems as well as costs for decommissioning and disposal of the system must be regarded.

On the one hand, the dimensioning of the security infrastructure for a Germany wide deployment presupposes a high security level due to the corresponding attractiveness of such a system for attacks and fraud. On the other hand, precisely this dimensioning enables scale effects which justify the investment necessary to reach this security level. This security level and the distributed system concept made it possible to negotiate very good liability conditions from the service providers for the public transport operators with corresponding positive effects on operating risk and the pooling of risks and enable a very strong reduction in losses due to successful attacks.

The investment for the implementation of the security infrastructure and security management has already been made by the VDV Kernapplikations GmbH&Co.KG for the public transport sector and thus does not represent a cost or risk factor for an individual public transport operator in connection with the introduction of electronic ticketing on the basis of the core application. All users profit from the dimension of the system through the resulting degressive price scale for the products and services of the security management system. Furthermore, the operating, replacement and adaptation costs resulting from the security infrastructure can be clearly calculated due to the well defined durations and prices for all products and services of the security management system.

Since the security management and infrastructure are part of the open standard of the German core application, costs due to adaptations forced by the results of tender processes and for the parallel operation of systems can be reduced.

3 Anatomy of the security infrastructure

The German core application is based on a logical role model, in which the VDV Kernapplikations GmbH&Co.KG has the role of security management and the duties of registration and accreditation of organizations taking part in the core application. The technical operation of the security infrastructure is performed by an independent IT service provider who is contractually bound to offer these services at the specified conditions to all organizations accredited by the VDV Kernapplikations GmbH&Co.KG (public transport operators and manufacturers).

The VDV Kernapplikations GmbH&Co.KG owns the rights to the security management system and licenses external service providers to use the technology.

The security management system consists of the three primary parts (see **Figure 1**):
- Public Key Infrastructure (PKI),
- Key Management and
- Provision of Secure Application Modules (SAM).

The three parts are technically and contractually separated from each other, each part has its own ordering and delivery processes and their interfaces are completely documented.

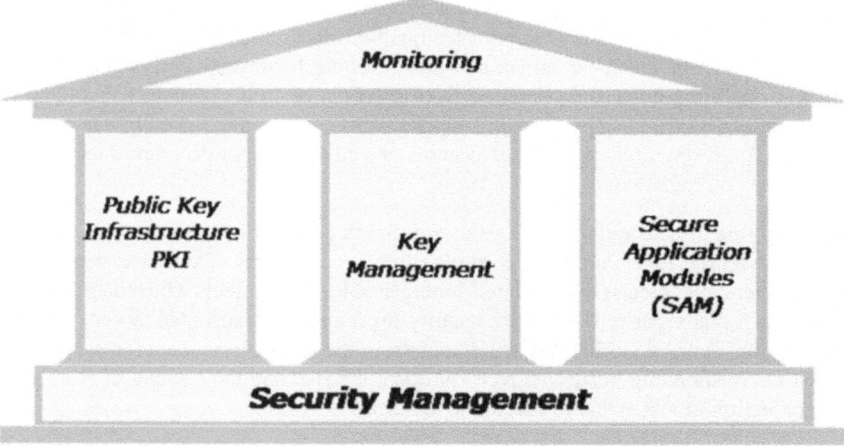

Figure 1 : Primary parts of the security infrastructure

3.1 Public Key Infrastructure

The VDV PKI uses a two-level structure, i.e. there is a Root Certification Authority (Root-CA), which is a kind of trust anchor for the entire system, and a level of 4 Subordinate Certification Authorities (Sub-CA's, see **Figure 2**). The Root-CA certifies the keys of the Sub-CA's, which in turn certify the keys of the individual components (SAM and User Media) and users. The Root-CA certifies that certain public keys indeed belong certain Sub-CA's which use these keys to certify that certain public keys belong to certain components or users and that they may only be used for certain purposes. Thus, using the known public key of the Root-CA, it is possible for any participant in the system to verify the authenticity and authorization of any public key in the system in a two-step procedure. The certified keys of the components and users are used e.g. to sign or encrypt data, but especially to perform authentications and session key agreement to set up secure communications channels between SAMs and User Media.

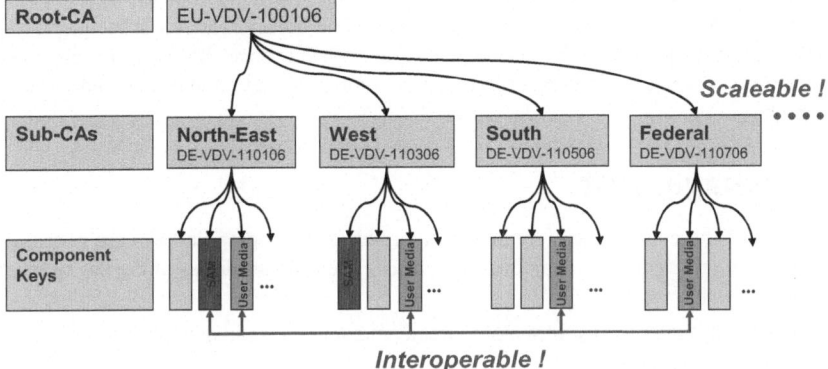

Figure 2 : Structure of the VDV PKI

The VDV PKI is a central service of the security management system, which enables other distributed services (e.g. key management). The VDV Kernapplikations GmbH&Co.KG commissioned T-Systems Enterprise Services to implement and operate the VDV PKI. Users intending to request certificates (e.g. manufacturers of SAMs or user media, public transport operators or key management service providers) close a standard contract directly with T-Systems.

During the implementation and launch of the PKI the VDV Kernapplikations GmbH&Co.KG granted specified personnel of T-Systems the authorization to carry out specified administrative duties. The primary duties of these "system administrators" are the technical issuance, transfer, extension and revocation of authorizations allowing users to request or revoke certificates for SAMs, user media and key management. Before an organization can be issued such an authorization it must be registered and approved by the VDV Kernapplikations GmbH&Co.KG. Assuming an organization has such an authorization it can then request and revoke certificates from a Sub-CA using the following interfaces:

- SOAP[1]-Interface,
- Bulk-Interface or
- Web-Interface.

---

1 SOAP = Simple Object Access Protocol

The SOAP-Interface allows the online request of single certificates. The user authenticates himself using a special certificate issued for this purpose, which can e.g. be installed in production equipment, and the communication with the Trust Center is encrypted using a hardware encryption device. Thus, this interface is well suited to automated real time requests during production (e.g. of user media).

In the case of the bulk-interface, requests are first collected offline and then sent in a file to the Trust Center for processing. The file must be signed by the user with a qualified signature and encrypted. The certificates are returned by the Trust Center to the user in the same way (signed and encrypted file). Various media can be used for the communication (e.g. Internet, file exchange server, exchange of data storage media).

The Web-Interface can be used to make single online requests. Since the information for the certificate has to be entered manually in a graphical user interface, this variant is not suited to automated mass processes, but rather to small numbers of requests, e.g. for the certificates needed by a public transport operator in connection with key management processes. The certificates can subsequently be downloaded directly. In order to access the system over the Web-Interface the users are equipped with a smartcard containing a specific certificate for authentication and encryption of the communication with the Trust Center.

3.2 Key Management

For the operation of the core application various symmetric cryptographic keys are necessary, which may be connected to organizations, components or roles. The primary duties of the key management in connection with these keys are:

- Import and archiving of keys from other already existent key management systems by authorized users;
- Processing of new key orders of authorized users as well as the secure generation and archiving of the keys in the key management system;
- Export of a key to its owner;
- Management of keys in SAMs including their secure loading and deletion and the alteration of usage limits;
- Administration of access rights of users to the key management systems;
- Revocation and ultimately secure deletion of keys from the key management systems at request of the key owner resp. as a result of a security relevant event.

The key management system of the core application is capable of supplying all participating organizations, in all their various roles and with all their various components, with the keys necessary according to the security concept of the system.

The keys may be divided into two groups according to whether their usage is relevant for many organizations or only for a single organization within the system. The so called „system keys" are used to secure the communication between possibly distinct organizations and are essential to the interoperability of the system. The organization specific keys are used to secure communications and to create transactions in which a single organization is both sender and receiver. They are essential for the assurance of independent and essential control of organizations over processes in which they have a stake. Due to the central nature of the system keys they are owned by the VDV Kernapplikations GmbH&Co.KG and are administered in the central key management system realized within the Trust Center of T-Systems. The organization specific keys on the other hand are owned by participating organizations (typically public transport operators) accredited by the VDV Kernapplikations GmbH&Co.KG and can either be administered in a similar fashion in the key management system of the VDV Kernapplikations GmbH&Co. KG or in an independent system.

3.3 Provision of Secure Application Modules

The security concept requires the employment of hardware based secure application modules (SAM) in the terminals of retailers and transport operators for sales and acceptance processes. The SAM enables

- the strict control over the confidentiality of cryptographic keys, the integrity of security relevant processes and the uniqueness of identifiers and cryptographic keys within the whole system;
- simpler processes for the initialization of terminals and
- the employment of less expensive terminals due to the reduced need for protective measures and terminal certifications.

In particular, the SAM was conceived to take care of all security relevant procedures having to do with the communication between terminals and user media resp. terminals and back office systems, which may be sorted according to the following five aspects:

- protection of the integrity of security relevant procedures and parameters,
- secure storage and usage of internal control parameters,
- secure key management,
- authorization of user media and stored entitlements as well as establishment of secure channels of communication between terminals and user media and
- establishment of secure channels of communication between terminal applications and back office systems.

The operation of acceptance terminals in the framework of the core application without a SAM is not allowed. Consequently, the provision of SAMs is an essential duty of the security management system of the core application. The production, delivery and distribution of SAMs specially configured for individual terminal operators is organized centrally by the VDV Kernapplikations GmbH&Co.KG and realized in the Trust Center of T-Systems as contracted service provider. For the actual procurement of SAMs public transport operators close standard contracts directly with the service provider. In particular, the service provider carries out the following duties:

- Receive and process SAM orders including the verification of the identity and authorization of the procurer (only accredited organizations with explicit authorization);
- Production of the SAMs according to the specifications of the German core application and the requirements of the security management of the VDV Kernapplikations GmbH&Co.KG;
- Employment of the standard interfaces to the VDV PKI and Key Management in order to obtain all the certificates and keys required for the specific configuration of the SAMs;
- Delivery of the SAMs directly to the procurer;
- Continued development and improvement of the SAM implementation.

These services are also provided to manufacturers of user media and terminals for production and test purposes. There are two levels of SAMs produced specifically for test purposes. The first level is a generic component equipped only with a standard set of keys in connection with the Test Suite of the German core application. In the second level, tailor made test configurations may be ordered. These contain only test identifiers and test keys, but are produced in exactly the same process as operational SAMs.

4 Security Level of the Security Infrastructure

In order to give an indication of the security level achieved by the system as a whole the following aspects are considered:

- the process of conception and specification of the system,
- the implemented technical measures,
- the implemented organizational measures and operational processes and
- requirements on the employed components.

The conception and specification of the system was based as far as possible on open and established standards and the resulting specification of the German core application, which forms the foundation of the security system, is itself an open standard and has been subjected to the continuous scrutiny of numerous experts and specialists, not only during the conception and specification phases, but also during the various phases of implementation and roll-out in projects.

Central to the secure operation of the infrastructure is the Trust Center operated by the service provider T-Systems in which the VDV PKI, Key Management and SAM Production are realized. The Trust Center is accredited according to the German law on qualified digital signatures and corresponding by-laws. The security concept of the Trust Center was sanctioned and approved by TÜV-IT, a testing laboratory accredited by the German Federal Network Agency.

The guidelines of the signature law place very high requirements on the archiving of paper documents and data backups as well as on the operation of applications in the Trust Center regarding the necessary organizational, technical and constructional measures to guarantee:

- Controlled entry and access (e.g. single person access gates, separation of duties, shared responsibility, use of smartcards for access),
- Protection against intrusion and unauthorized entry (e.g. alarm systems, intrusion resistant construction, multiply secured data safes, surveillance systems, motion detectors, securing of surroundings),
- Prevention of eaves-dropping (e.g. shielding against emission and absorption of electromagnetic radiation, use of offline systems, encrypted communication) as well as
- Fire prevention (e.g. early warning systems, fire alarm systems, gas flooding, fire-proof data safes).

Only personnel suitable according to Article 5, paragraph 4 of the German signature law may be employed in the Trust Center. All operational processes are subject to very strict organizational rules. The log files of the entry system are archived and evaluated regularly and are not accessible to the Trust Center personnel. Appropriate separations of duties in the production assure that the authorizations of individual operators and administrators are limited. Especially critical applications can only be started by 2 or more authorized individuals in cooperation.

A parallel backup system is operated in a separate fire area and backup copies are deposited in regular intervals in a secured archive on another site.

In addition to the operation of a digital signature solution according to the German signature law and the VDV PKI, the Trust Center also runs other applications including, for example, the backup system for the German Federal Network Agency, the Certification Authority for the Administration PKI of the German Federal Bureau of Security in Information Technology (BSI) and the European Bridge CA (EBCA). Consequently, the Trust Center is under the continual scrutiny and oversight of the German

Federal Network Agency and other institutions with the goal of maintaining the high security level. All of the Trust Center services mentioned here (including those for the German core application) are subjected to a single common security policy.

The SAM is implemented as a smartcard on a highly secure hardware platform[2] on the basis of an evaluated operating system[3]. The initialization of the SAMs is carried out in the secure environment of the Trust Center under the strictest protective measures.

By way of these standardized and documented security measures the user gains access to a comprehensible, consistently high security level within the framework of a standard contract.

5 Conclusion

The security infrastructure for the German core application in public transportation has set itself the goal of providing features and a level of security sufficient to exclude counterfeiting and fraud and at the same time to enable interoperability. The increased comfort and value to the customer stemming from the interoperability presumes the realization of a common infrastructure capable of supporting operations on a nationwide level. This required dimensioning of the system leads to the need for a uniformly high level of security. The important question is whether the necessary investments and costs of building and running such a system are justified by the added value and cost reducing effects for public transport operators. The very dimension of the system works to its advantage through the corresponding scale effects and reduction of investments through availability of standard components and services. The realization of the potentials for the customers and users will increase essentially with the number and coverage of core application projects launched in public transportation, and thus, for economic success it will be essential in the near future to maintain a rapid proliferation and acceptance of the standard.

References

[Acke07]   Ackermann, Till: Die VDV-Kernapplikation. In: Der Nahverkehr, 25. Jg. Nr. 4, 2007.

[BSI04]   Bundesamt für Sicherheit in der Informationstechnik: Risiken und Chancen des Einsatzes von RFID-Systemen, Bonn 2004.

[Fink06]   Finkenzeller, Klaus: RFID-Handbuch, 4. Aufl., München 2006

[Lutg04]   Lutgen, Joseph: Funktionsweise der Chipkarten in einer ÖPV-Anwendung. In: 14. SIT-SmartCard Workshop, Darmstadt 2004. Ed.: Struif, Bruno, 2004.

[Lutg07]   Lutgen, Joseph: Das Sicherheitssystem hinter der VDV-Kernapplikation: Voraussetzungen, Methoden und Ziele. In: Der Nahverkehr, 25. Jg. Nr. 5, S. 44-47.

[RaEf02]   Rankl, Wolfgang und Effing, Wolfgang: Handbuch der Chipkarten, 4. Aufl., München, 2002.

---

2 The hardware has been evaluated to the level EAL5+ according to Commen Criteria with reference to the Protection Profile BSI PP-0002.

3 It is required that the operating system has been evaluated to at least the level EAL4+ according to the Common Criteria.

Applications of Citizen Portals

Hannes Ziegler

T-Systems Enterprise Services GmbH
hannes.ziegler@t-systems.com

Abstract

The EU Directive on services in the single market has been resolved. It should contribute to making the European Union into the most competitive and dynamic economic area in the world by 2010. The implementation of this Directive within a very short period of only three years will lead in Germany to enormous changes in all administrative areas. The key elements of the Services Directive (EU-SD) are administrative simplification, the creation of standard contact partners for the support of the service providers in all processes and formalities for the access to the single services market and for the exercise of service activity as well as the fully electronic handling of all processes and formalities. The Services Directive is a major support for the further development of the e-government strategy of the Federal state of Baden-Württemberg and fits perfectly into the overall total strategy of the one stop government. An important role in this respect is the securing of the access and the data through suitable mechanisms.

1 Introduction

With the globalisation of the markets the location of competition has extended from a rather local or regional level to the global level. Municipalities, regions and countries are therefore eager to increase the attraction of their location. An important factor for a location is the friendliness of the administration towards citizens and corporations. Today clear signs of reform in all administrative areas are recognisable with regard to, for example, the increase of effectiveness, efficiency and the citizen friendliness of the administration. This process of change for the public sector is a dominating subject not only in Germany but also worldwide. The so-called Lisbon strategy foresees the support of economic growth, the creation of workplaces and the strengthening of the social environment. By 2010 the EU should be the most competitive and dynamic knowledge-based economic region in the world.

The subject of competition is strengthened by the Directive of the European Parliament and the Council which came into force in December 2006 concerning services in the single market (EU services Directive) (EU-SD). It should reduce bureaucratic obstacles and promote the cross-border trade in services, which in the view of the Commission is still subject to a large number of limitations. In particular small and medium-sized companies should in future be able to use the single market without restrictions. The hitherto existing limitations of the freedom of establishment of service providers and the free trade in services should be abolished; these include in particular the complexity, the lengthiness and lack of legal certainty of the administrative processes.

In future it will be made simpler for the service providers to establish themselves in another EU member state or to enjoy the free trade in services. Furthermore, the Directive in accordance with the Lisbon strategy should promote economic growth and contribute to the creation of workplaces. In order to achieve the objective of free trade in services, the principle of country of origin should apply, administrative processes should be made more effective, approval processes should be streamlined and other-

N. Pohlmann, H. Reimer, W. Schneider (Editors): Securing Electronic Business Processes, Vieweg (2007), 419-426

wise general bureaucratic obstacles should be reduced. In this respect a major role will be played by the simplification of administration through electronic processes.

The individual implementation obligations are addressed to all state levels as well as those with state approved legal authorities. In the Federal Republic of Germany these concern the Federal government, the states and the municipalities as well as also chambers and other institutions (for example pension insurance providers) as well as the corresponding institutions in the other EU member states. All these authorities must implement a large number of complex organisational, reporting and auditing tasks. Above all the volume of information and communication between public administrations will increase within the EU, in order, for example to exchange data from companies and employees from abroad. Furthermore, contact offices ("standard contact partners") must be set up for foreign providers / companies.

The regulations of the EU Services Directive require from all administrations in Germany an optimal and smooth cooperation over all areas of competence, which cannot be guaranteed without performant standardised information and communications technology. This is all the more important since it appears in the meantime that the Directive concerns not only foreign but also domestic providers due to the ban on discrimination. Furthermore, it is becoming increasingly clearer that the Directive is very often interpreted in such a way that it concerns not only the establishment of a business but should also include the whole life cycle of the service provider. As a result of this expanded application the probable "case numbers" in the Federal Republic of Germany would increase by more than 10 times.

2 Key elements of the Directive

The objective of the Directive is the creation of a legal framework which guarantees the freedom for establishment and the free trade in services between the member states. In paragraph 33 of the preliminary remarks the services included in the Directive are described in detail. Service providers are considered to be all individuals with the nationality of a member state and all legal entities which exercise a service activity in a member state. Article 4 regulates the details for this definition.

Key elements of the EU Services Directive are the simpflication of administration (chapter II), freedom of establishment (chapter III), free trade of services (chapter IV), quality of the services (chapter V) and the administrative cooperation (chapter VI). The regulations in chapters II, III and VI are of particular importance for the municipalities. A summary of the most important requirements is given below.

3 Summary of important regulations

3.1 Chapter II – Simplification of administration

Article 5
determines that the member states should examine and if appropriate simplify the processes and formalities which are valid for the exercise of a service activity.

Article 6
determines that certain processes and formalities must be handled via standard contact partners. These include in particular declarations, announcements or the application for approvals from competent authorities, including the application for entries into registers, professional lists or data banks as well as the registration with trade associations or organisations.

Article 7

Determines the right to information. The member states must thereby ensure that a large volume of information is easily accessible via the standard contact partner. This includes information on processes, formalities, competent authorities, registers and data banks, legal assistance, associations and organisations.

Article 8

regulates the electronic process handling whereby all processes and formalities must be able to be handled "at a distance" without problem and also electronically via the standard contact partner or at the appropriate authorities.

3.2 Chapter III – Freedom of establishment

Article 13

determines approval processes and formalities. These must be clear, known in advance and presented in such a manner that an objective handling of the applications is guaranteed. If an application is not answered within a period to be determined, the approval is deemed to have been granted.

Article 15

has the objective of examining all approval requirements and of eliminating those which are not valid. The member states must change their legal and administration regulations in such a way that they correspond to the new regulations.

3.3 Chapter VI – Administrative cooperation

Article 28

determines the official assistance of the member states amongst each other. These should take measures which are required for an effective cooperation in respect of the control of service providers and their services. Furthermore, it must be ensured that the registers in which the service providers are entered and which can be consulted by the competent authorities in the sovereign area can also be consulted by all competent authorities in the member states.

The European administrations should be able to cooperate better with regard to the control of the service providers As an instrument for this a single market information system, the so-called Internal Market Information System (IMI), will be introduced within three years. As an information and communications platform IMI should enable the exchange between the authorities of the member states. According to the Federal Ministry of Economics it will require substantial capacities to develop such an IT supported system, in order to, for example, check the details of foreign service providers or to supervise German service providers abroad. IMI should enable one to find a competent authority in another member state. Moreover, it should make available for the authorities a large number of already formulated questions, which frequently arise during the cooperation between the member states. It should take care of the periods for the answering of queries and be available in 21 languages.

3.4 Standard contact partners

Articles 6, 7, 8 and 11 of the EU services Directive determine primarily the tasks and activities of the standard contact partner. This should function as a contact agency through which the service providers can handle all the necessary processes and formalities. In this respect it should be a supporting agency which informs, advises but also initiates and / or handles the processes itself. An expert report drawn up at the beginning of 2006 by the German Academy for Administration Sciences in Speyer on the subject of the standard contact partners (scp) comes to the conclusion that the following functions and tasks will accrue to the scp:

- The area of activity of the scp will include the handling of all processes and formalities, and not only approval processes, but, for example also the processes for subsequent control.
- The scp will carry out the function of an agency which will support the service provider and will function as an intermediary or as a contact point to the competent authorities.
- From a functional point of view the agency will thus extend further than that of a contact point required only to receive and transfer further applications or documentation.
- The scp must not, however, necessarily assume the function of a competent agency; the differentiation is important: the scp can be a competent agency but is not obliged to be so.
- On the basis of the supporting function of the scp there results the task of ensuring the fast and uncomplicated completion of all steps in the process versus the competent authorities in favour of the service provider as the "process partner". This obligation is limited with regard to the competence of the authorities responsible for the carrying out of the process and the decision; the scp has therefore no legal authority versus the competent authorities.

With regard to the electronic handling of processes in accordance with Article 8 of the EU Services Directive the expert report comes to the conclusion that in this respect the member states are obliged to enable for the service providers a process handling which is both cross-border ("from a distance") as well as electronically. Accordingly the scp must communicate securely with all institutions involved in the provision of services within the framework of the EU Services Directive and also with those without access to an administrative network.

According to the expert report there exists in accordance with Article 11 of the EU Services Directive an obligation for the scp to also be able to transfer approvals in addition to receiving information. The creation of the scp does not affect the distribution of competences of the existing authorities and institutions in the Federal Republic, but it becomes clear that a networking of many of the agencies involved will be necessary. A specific number of scp per administrative unit is not proscribed, but the Directive foresees, however, that from the point of view of the service provider the one and the same contact partner must be responsible for the total period of the process.

In a further expert report the Research Institute for Public Administration in Speyer has examined the matter of which administrative levels can potentially be considered. In accordance with this report the creation of a completely new authority cannot be taken into consideration for constitutional reasons. The integration of the scp at the level of the administrative district and cities independent of administrative districts is on the other hand view by the experts as a meaningful variant. At the same time an integration of the scp is thinkable also at the state level. From a legal point of view it would be possible to integrate them into the chambers of commerce, which consider themselves to be fully competent in this respect and which can present the arguments of their closeness to the economy as well as the existence of a wide trans-national contact network.

In a joint opinion the municipal associations also request that in principle the municipal administrations should be appointed as scp due to their experience and competence. As proof of this it is mentioned that the municipalities already function today as the contact partners for service partners from both home and abroad and, for example, with regard to trade applications transfer data to various organisations, for example, to chambers of commerce, emission protection authorities, the Federal Agency for Labour, professional associations or also the trade registers.

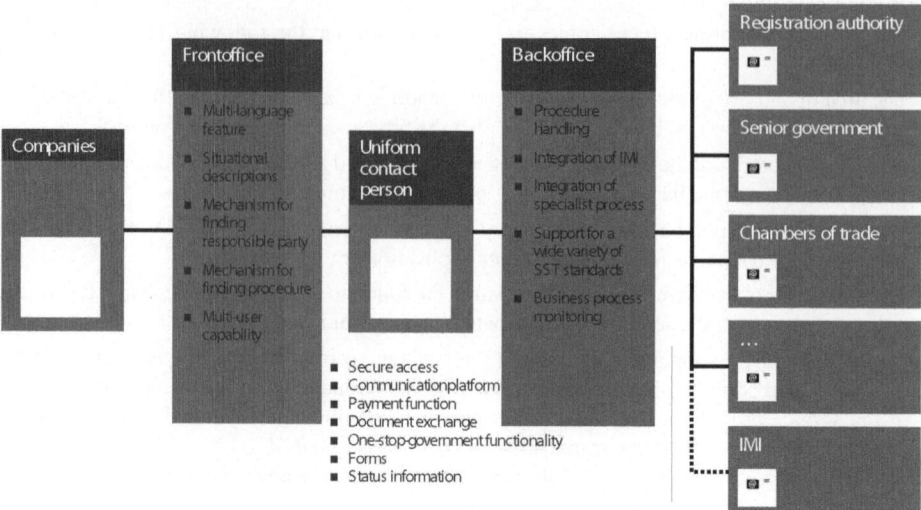

Figure 1: European Service Directive – Functions

4 Implementation of the EU Service Directive

As a reaction to the EU Service Directive the heads of government of the Federation and the Länder extended in June 2007 the Germany Online (GOL) action plan. The leadership in this project has been assumed by the states of Baden-Württemberg and Schleswig-Holstein with the cooperation of the German Administrative Districts Council and the Federal Government. In this respect Baden-Württemberg is taking on a leadership role for good reason. In the past important bases were created with T-Systems as the service provider and which can now serve as a technical basis for the implementation of the EU Services Directive. Baden-Württemberg and T- Systems have developed jointly prototypes which received much attention. This is based on components such as the competence finder (z-finder) which have been in effective operation successfully since many years. The following diagram shows the components of the framework architecture. Important elements of the one-stop government are the identity management and the document storage.

Figure 2: EU-Services Directive Service Framework

4.1 One government and document repository in the "service-bw.de" portal

In its e-government strategy Baden-Württemberg is pursuing also the objective of close state-municipality cooperation within the context of which as many online services and content should be made available as possible. In this respect the "service-bw" service portal will play an important role with its development functions, particularly with regard to the one stop government. A strong motivation for the further development of the one stop government is the handling requirement which results from the implementation of the EU Service Directive. This stipulates that all processes and formalities which are necessary in order to provide a service must be able to be handled without problems electronically and independent of the location. The Services Directive is therefore a major support for further development, but also fits in smoothly into the overall total strategy of the one stop government. In this respect the objective is to make available the functionalities required for the implementation of the EU Services Directive in such a way that the greatest possible additional value can result therefrom for the administration and the citizens. The target is a one stop government with a document repository as the basic support function. The implementation of the EU Services Directive will result in a high processing requirement for the further development of the one stop government and the document repository.

From the point of view of the citizen there are various questions with regard to the context of the one stop government:

- What happens if as the result of a fire in the home diplomas, documents or contracts are destroyed?
- Can I as an IT layman also use electronic receipts, invoices and other important documents without them being endangered by viruses, spy software etc. on my home computer?
- Who can take note of all the user codes, passwords or secret numbers?
- Who can I rely on?

In order to prepare an adequate solution for these a document repository was designed in service-bw, which is gradually being developed further. Already today the following functionalities are available:

- Input of electronic documents
- Provision of stored documents with expiry date monitoring (when the document expires, the citizen receives the information by email)
- Deposit of personal data (e.g. name, address, date of birth, telephone number, email address) and their use as a secure data exchange with authorities, which offer portal services (one stop government).

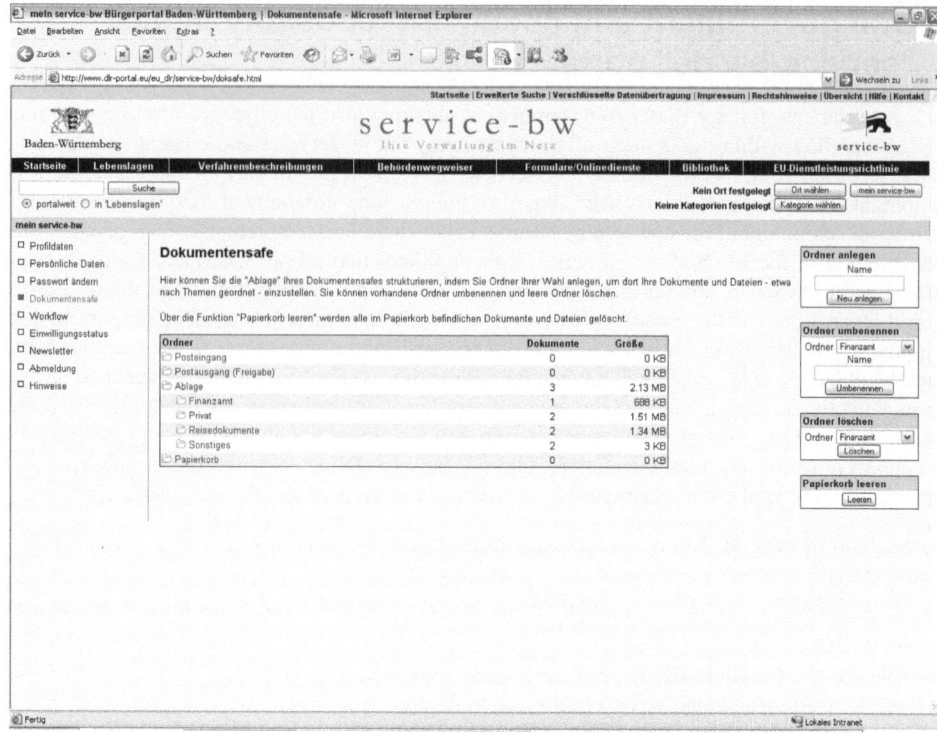

Figure 3: Personal data repository

These functionalities should be extended. In this respect the security of the access and the data plays above all a major role. To date the combination of an easy <u>and</u> secure access to administrative services was a problem for their acceptance. Now help appears to be in sight. In 2008 the roll-out of the new electronic personal identity card (eic) should start in Germany. A key characteristic is the possibility of the online authentification. The requirements of e-government and e-business are therefore taken into consideration, which require a new type of secure electronic identification.

Together with BSI and the state of Baden-Württemberg the authentification functionality should be checked in a practice test in combination with the document repository.

The diagram below shows the process scheme as the integration of the electronic personal identity card.

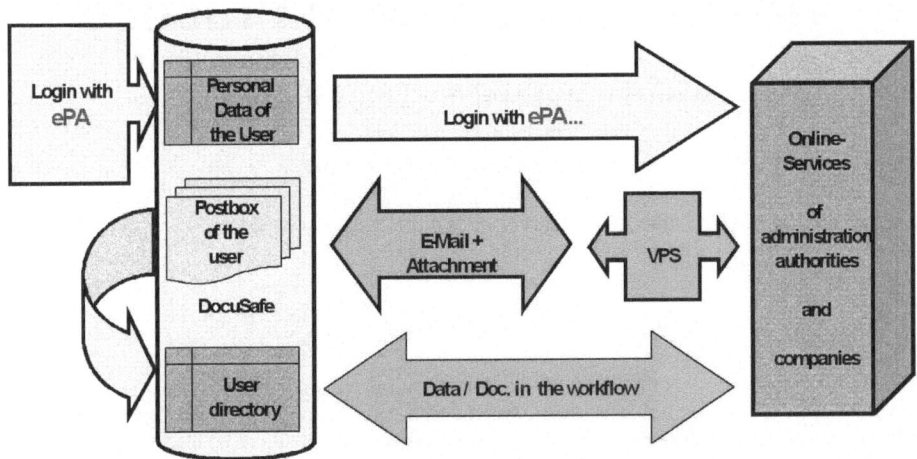

Figure 4: Managing secure access to personal data repositories

5 Conclusion

For the implementation of the EU Services Directive many currently discussed challenges must be solved in e-government. Proven strategies such as one stop government, process orientation or the life situation principle are obtaining real attention within the federalism reform and the necessary internal administrative interfaces between the federal government, the states and the municipalities. On the basis of components, which have already been proven in practice, T-Systems is developing jointly with Baden-Württemberg a framework architecture, which supports the one stop government strategy over and above the requirements of the Services Directive. With the planned introduction of the electronic personal identity card a medium will in future be available overall, which solves the challenge of secure access through the authentification function. At the same time there exists with the document repository an application scenario, which offers a practical use to the functionalities of the electronic personal identity card. One winner is thus clear: the citizen!

References

[EU-SD]   DIRECTIVE 2006/123/EC OF THE EUROPEAN PARLIAMENT AND OF THE COUNCIL of 12 December 2006 on services in the internal market

[DOL]   Press announcement: German administration should be more attractive for entrepreneurs: heads of government extend Germany Online action plan, Berlin June 15, 2007

Virtual Post Office in Practice

Wilhelm Weisweber · Frank Planitzer

Deutsche Rentenversicherung Bund[1]
Ruhrstraße 2, D-10709 Berlin
{Dr.Wilhelm.Weisweber | Frank.Planitzer}@drv-bund.de

Abstract

The Virtual Post Office (VPS)[2] is the core element of the infrastructure component for data security of the reference architecture for IT systems of federal authorities. The VPS supports applications with cryptographic as well as communication services. Thus it is the basis for information processing without cross-media transfer as well as for secure and legally compliant communication. At the Deutsche Rentenversicherung Bund (DRV Bund) the VPS is part of a Service Oriented Architecture (SOA) based infrastructure. It was integrated into the business processes and is operated under heavy load and real conditions. Within the German Pension Insurance the DRV Bund has taken the responsibility for the VPS and is hosting a service for the verification of certificates for all federal authorities. The DRV Bund is a strategic partner of the Federal Office for Information Security and is member of the advisory board for the VPS client for citizens. This article describes the operation concepts and scenarios with regard to the VPS as well as the standards based infrastructure of the DRV Bund.

1 Introduction

The DRV Bund is the biggest carrier of the German Pension Insurance. The core business is the payment of pensions (legal and voluntary insurance), the funding of rehabilitation services as well as the support of the old age provision. Table 1 presents some actual data and facts:

Table 1: Data and Facts about the Deutsche Rentenversicherung Bund (Year 2005)

Insured Persons	Approx. 24,7 Million
Pensioners	Approx. 8,5 Million
Employers	Approx. 3,3 Million
Stock of Pensions	Approx. 9,76 Million
Application Forms for Pensions	Approx. 642.000
Application Forms for Rehabilitation Services	Approx. 620.000
Employees	Approx. 27.000
Inbound Mail	Approx. 60.000 Daily
Outbound Mail	Approx. 80.000 Daily

Within the initiative "Bund Online 2005" of the Federal Ministry of the Interior the DRV Bund has obliged itself to provide all suitable services online via Internet. The basis for that is a continuous

---

1 "Deutsche Rentenversicherung Bund" is translated into "German Federal Pension Insurance". In this paper we will keep the German term and use the abbreviation DRV Bund.
2 "Virtual Post Office" is the translation of the German term „Virtuelle Poststelle". In the following the abbreviation VPS will be used. Another translation is "Virtual Mail Room".

N. Pohlmann, H. Reimer, W. Schneider (Editors): Securing Electronic Business Processes, Vieweg (2007), 427-436

processing of information without cross-media transfer and secure electronic communication with customers and external partners:

- G2C: customers (pensioners, ensured persons and rehabilitation patients)
- G2B: employers, health and other insurance companies
- G2G: courts and other government authorities

The Virtual Post Office (VPS) provides cryptographic functions and an infrastructure for secure and legally compliant electronic communication.

2 The Virtual Post Office

The Virtual Post Office (VPS, see [VPS]) is the core element of the infrastructure component for data security of the reference architecture of the Standards and Architecture of E-Government Applications (SAGA, see [SAGA]) of the KBSt[3]. It provides services for cryptographic functions and secure electronic communication. Federal authorities can use the VPS within a framework agreement of the Federal Office for Information Security without additional license costs. The following Figure 1 shows the architecture of the VPS.

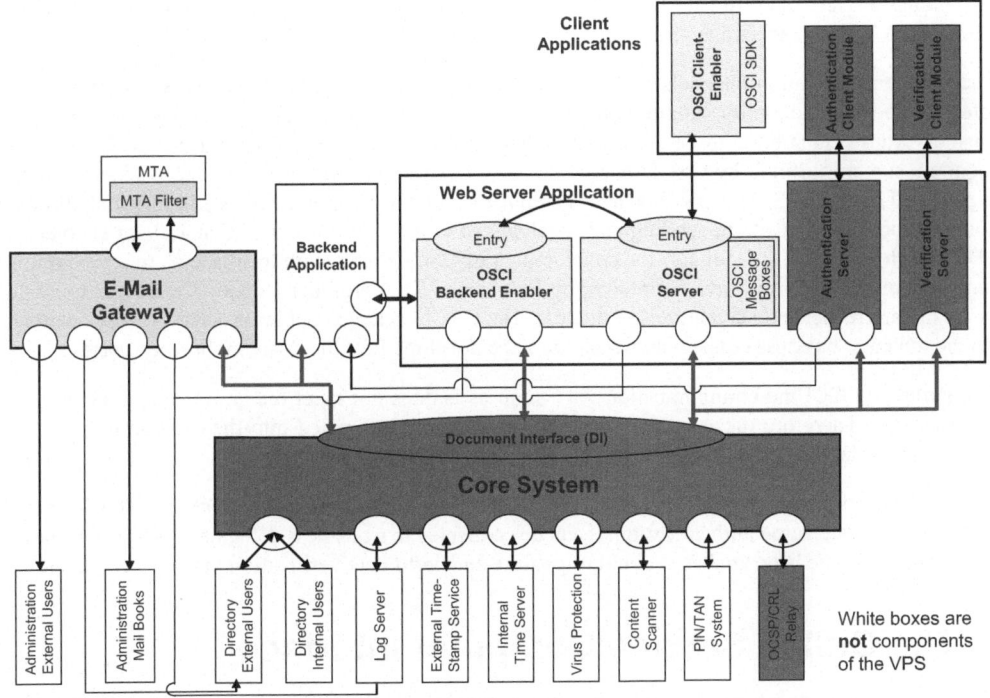

Figure 1: Components of the Virtual Post Office (VPS)

---

3 KBSt is the abbreviation for „Koordinierungs- und Beratungsstelle der Bundesregierung für Informationstechnik in der Bundesverwaltung" which means "Coordination and Consulting Office of the Federal Government for IT in Federal Authorities".

The VPS is composed of client and server components. The client components consist of software developments kits (SDK) from which corresponding components for accessing the server functionality can be developed. The server components are an authentication and verification server, the core system, an e-mail gateway as well as an infrastructure for secure communication via the Online Service Computer Interface (OSCI, see following section).

The core system of the VPS relieves all persons involved from developing complex and error-prone cryptographic services like

- advanced signatures (software signatures)
- qualified batch signatures
- verification of signatures
- encryption and decryption
- timestamp and verification of timestamps
- verification of certificates

Qualified batch signatures are applied to documents with the help of the NetSigner which is part of the core system. In order to achieve this one or more card readers are connected to the core system server. The verification of certificates is realized with the help of the OCSP/CRL relay which accesses the corresponding services of certificate authorities (CA). The core system is used by the other server components of the VPS or backend applications via the XML based document interface (DI).

The two communication channels supported are e-mail and OSCI. Both have to ensure authenticity, integrity and confidentiality. Additionally the communication and all process actions especially the business transactions have to be legally compliant, i.e. traceable, provable and not deniable. These requirements are fulfilled by OSCI. The complete infrastructure (server, client and backend enabler) is provided by the VPS. The OSCI enabler components are based upon the OSCI library and allow for composition, decomposition, sending and receiving of OSCI messages. The OSCI client enabler is a SDK which additionally facilitates the development of OSCI clients with local access to cryptographic functions provided by the Java Cryptography Extension (JCE) provider Bouncy Castle and to a wide range of card readers and signature smart cards. The OSCI backend enabler is a server component and can be linked to business connectors which are to be developed for the different business cases.

In contrast to OSCI the communication via e-mail as is does not meet the above mentioned security requirements. Therefore the e-mail gateway is transparently integrated into the existing e-mail infrastructure in order to access the cryptographic functions of the core system.

The authentication and verification server provide services for (external) applications. The former allows for certificate based authentication. It can be connected to a business delegate which is to be developed if needed. The latter makes available signature and certificate verification via the core system.

3 The Online Service Computer Interface

The VPS provides an infrastructure for the communication via the Online Service Computer Interface (OSCI, see [OSCI]) and is a mandatory standard of SAGA. It references the open standards SOAP, XML encryption and signature and realizes a secure, legally compliant, synchronous or asynchronous exchange of information. The OSCI specification distinguishes between a transport protocol (OSCI-A) and content data (OSCI-B or XÖV[4]). OSCI-A guarantees authenticity, integrity, confidentiality and le-

---

4 XÖV stands for „XML in der öffentlichen Verwaltung" which means „XML in public administration".

gal compliance[5] of a message during transport. It is independent of business requirements and provides containers for content data and unstructured attachments.

In contrast to e-mail OSCI content data is structured by XML and other than OSCI-A depends on business requirements. The content data is generated by specific XML schema definitions which are standardized for different business cases.[6]

Figuratively speaking OSCI can be regarded as registered mail with acknowledgement of the addressee. An OSCI message is wrapped with two envelopes (see the following Figure 2).

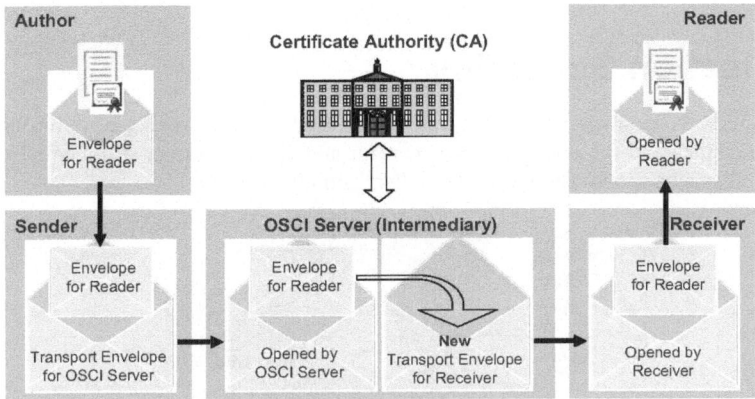

Figure 2: OSCI Principle of the Double Envelope

The author of a message creates an electronic document (OSCI content data) which is signed by the author and encrypted with the public key of the reader. This inner envelope together with a docket is handed over to the sender which is an OSCI client or backend component. The docket contains the addressee data, instructions for further message processing and all certificates involved. The OSCI sender assembles the envelope and the docket to an OSCI message which is signed by the sender and encrypted with the public key of the OSCI server. This outer envelope is sent to the OSCI server which opens it (decryption) and checks the signature of the sender. At this point all certificates noted on the docket are verified and all results are recorded. The docket is timestamped and sent back as acknowledgement for the sender. After that the OSCI message consisting of the inner envelope and the docket is signed by the OSCI server and encrypted with the public key of the receiver. Now there are two possible situations. If the addressed receiver is an

- OSCI client, the message is stored in the corresponding message box for the receiver of the OSCI server. In order to process the content data the client has to fetch the message from the server (asynchronous processing). The client authenticates itself by its private authentication or encryption key. The client is developed on the basis of the OSCI client enabler and may be integrated into a business application.
- OSCI backend, to which the message is directly transmitted. Via a business connector the content data is processed synchronously and fully automatically without cross-media transfer by the corresponding business application. The business connector is to be realized on the basis of the OSCI backend enabler of the VPS.

---

5 Legally compliant (traceable, provable and not deniable) not only means the documentation of the message exchange and business transactions but the transmitted information also has to be usable in court proceedings.
6 For actual OSCI-B (XÖV) specifications see [OSCI].

The OSCI receiver (client or backend) opens the outer envelope (decryption) and checks the signature of the OSCI server. Optionally the docket is analyzed. After that the inner envelope is passed on to the reader who is able to decrypt the content data for further processing with the help of his private key.

In every step during OSCI transport authenticity, integrity and confidentiality of the OSCI message and content data are guaranteed. The docket ensures the traceability of all process actions and business transactions. Because the inner envelope is never opened by any OSCI component (sender, server or receiver) an end-to-end encryption of the content data is realized. Thus the OSCI server may be operated by a third party.

4 Application Scenarios

The VPS supports the business processes of the DRV Bund, i.e. the existing e-mail infrastructure, the business applications and the document management and archive system with central cryptographic services as well as with secure and legally compliant communication.

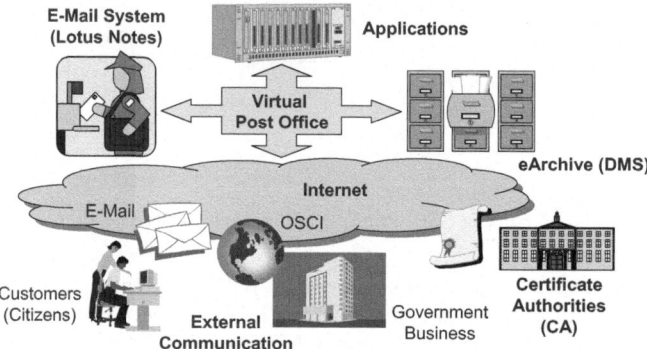

Figure 3: Application Scenarios of the Deutsche Rentenversicherung Bund

Figure 3 illustrates the use cases of the DRV Bund. The VPS supports the electronic communication with external partners via e-mail or OSCI and provides cryptographic functions like signature and encryption for business applications. Thus a fully automatic processing of documents without cross-media transfer is enabled. External partners are customers (citizens, pensioners, insured persons or rehabilitation patients), business partners (employees, health and other insurance companies) as well as other public and certificate authorities.

The DRV Bund communicates with external partners via e-mail or OSCI. Because e-mail is widespread the emphasis for the communication with customers is put on e-mail and with business partners or public authorities on OSCI. In order to send messages to customers a combination of both is aimed at. In this case an OSCI message is deposited in the OSCI message box of the customer first. In parallel an e-mail is sent to him that a new OSCI message can be picked up. This presupposes that an appropriate OSCI client is publicly available.

Incoming electronic messages or their attachments are logged (legal compliance). If necessary they are decrypted (confidentiality) and their signatures verified. The latter ascertains that the corresponding documents are unchanged (integrity), that the sender is identified (authenticity) and that the certificate is valid and not cancelled. The results are attached to the message before it is passed on to the responsible person.

Outbound electronic messages do only leave the DRV Bund via the VPS. They have to be signed either qualified or advanced. A message can be attached with a personal (qualified) signature only locally with the help of a card reader and a smart card. A signature with the software certificate of the DRV Bund (advanced signature) is provided as a central service of the VPS core system. The signed message is encrypted with the public key of the addressee. All outgoing messages are logged.

Legal regulations require that invoice documents are archived for six years and other documents of administrative procedures even much longer. In order to keep their legal evidence they are signed in a qualified way by the core system component NetSigner when they are archived. For this personal but pseudonymized signature smart cards are used. For applications and notifications of customers advanced signatures are sufficient.

The validity of a certificate is limited in time or it may otherwise become invalid. Another point is that because IT is permanently developing the hash and encryption algorithms which are used for signatures are becoming more and more insecure. Thus the signatures of archived documents have to be renewed regularly. Additionally the results of the signature and certificate verification have to be archived and signed together with the document.

5 E-Mail vs. OSCI

As mentioned in section 3 an OSCI message can be regarded as a registered mail with acknowledgement of the addressee whereas e-mail is comparable with a letter or even a postcard. In the following the pros and cons are outlined.

5.1 Pros and Cons of E-Mail

The main advantage of e-mail is that it is an established medium for communication and widespread. Clients are available for different operating systems which can be used for the communication with customers and other external partners with only a few efforts. E-mail is suitable for processes which are initiated inhouse, e.g. sending pension approval notifications or other information.

The main disadvantage is that e-mail is not suitable for fully automatic processing. Even if an inbound e-mail is decrypted and its signature is verified by the e-mail gateway of the VPS it has to be manually forwarded to the responsible person. The automatic reception and processing of inbound e-mails by a business application is difficult to handle. For outbound e-mails it cannot be guaranteed that the addressee will receive the message. The best case then is a returning mail but it cannot be decrypted because the private key of the addressee is not available. The worst case is that there is no reaction at all. In times of frequent changes of the e-mail provider this is not unusual. The good news is that the confidentiality is preserved.

In order to deal with signed and encrypted messages the customers need a plug-in for their e-mail client. The first experiences show that even IT professionals are not very familiar with this technology. In this case support is difficult because many tools of different providers are used. An additional obstacle occurs when a vendor does not adhere to the standards.

5.2 Pros and Cons of OSCI

In contrast to e-mail OSCI is XML structured. This is a good prerequisite for automatic processing without cross-media transfer. This makes OSCI suitable for processes which are initiated by customers or external partners.

Customers can transparently use an OSCI client with fully integrated cryptographic functionality on the basis of the OSCI client enabler. The client supports a wide range of card readers and smart cards for signature and encryption. The handling of such clients is similar to e-mail clients. Besides asynchronous client-client communication also synchronous client-backend connections with request and optional direct response are possible. If the receiver is a backend the message can automatically be routed to the internal business processes.

Outbound OSCI messages are sent in combination with an e-mail which informs the addressee that a new message is available such that the customer can connect to the OSCI server and fetch the message.

The main disadvantage of OSCI is that it is a relatively new national standard and not widespread. In addition to an e-mail client customers have to install an OSCI client and for each use case, i.e. specification of OSCI content data a separate client is needed.

6 IT Infrastructure of the DRV Bund

The IT infrastructure of the DRV Bund is based on a Service-Oriented Architecture (SOA). An extract of the system architecture around the VPS is shown in the following Figure 4.

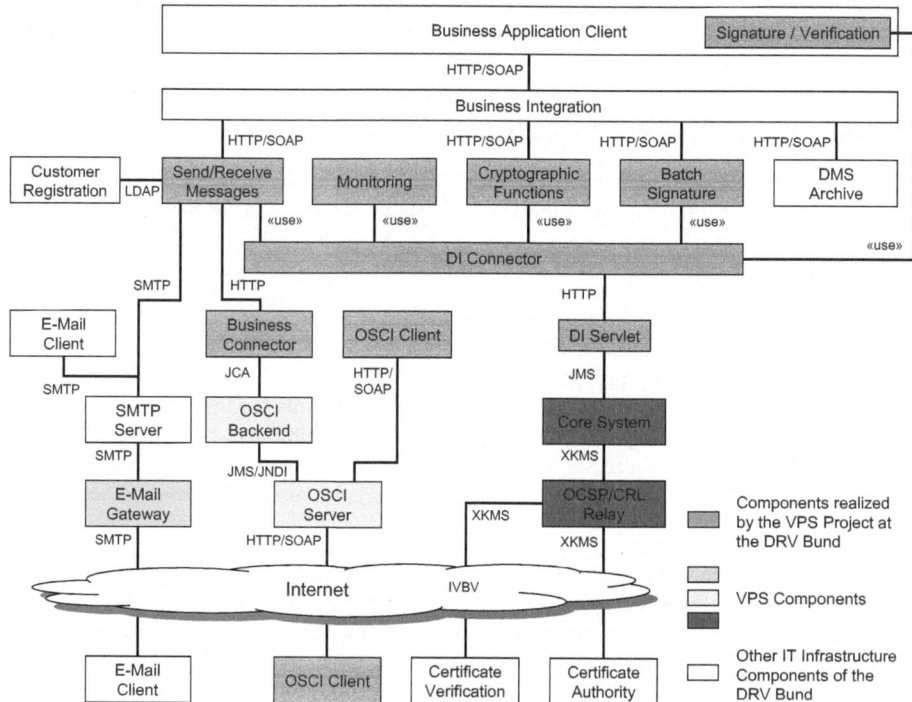

Figure 4: Extract of the SOA-based IT Infrastructure of the DRV Bund

The foundations of the system architecture are among others the standards of the

- Standards and Architecture of E-Government Applications (SAGA), see [SAGA]
- World Wide Web Consortium (W3C), see www.w3c.org
- Internet Engineering Taskforce (IETF), see www.ietf.org
- Organisation for the Advancement of Structured Information (OASIS), see www.oasis-open.org
- Web Services Interoperability Organization (WS-I), see www.ws-i.org
- Object Management Group (OMG), see www.omg.org
- International Organization for Standardization (ISO), see www.iso.org
- Open Service Oriented Architecture Collaboration (OSOA), see www.osoa.org
- Java Community Process (JCP), see www.jcp.org, especially the Java Enterprise Edition (Java EE), see java.sun.com/javaee

The first basic components of SAGA which have been integrated into the infrastructure were the VPS, a document management and archive system (DMS) and a content management system (CMS)[7]. The VPS and the CMS are provided by the Federal Office for Information Security and can be used by federal authorities within a framework agreement without additional license costs. The DMS has been realized by the DRV Bund and provides a standard web service interface (SOAP) in order to digitize and archive documents in a legally compliant way.

According to the generic security concept of the VPS their components are located in a separate highly secured network area.[8] The OCSP/CRL relay of the VPS is hosted for all federal authorities in order to provide a certificate verification service. It can be accessed via Internet and the Interconnection Network of Federal Authorities (IVBV)[9].

Since the year 2005 the DRV Bund has been providing services as an announced certificate authority (CA) and distributes ISIS-MTT compliant smart cards with signature, encryption and authentication certificates as identity cards to its employees.

The VPS team of the DRV Bund has realized different services on the basis of the VPS and has integrated them into the SOA-based IT infrastructure:

- Connector to the core system via the document interface (DI). It encapsulates the XML of the DI and the connection to the core system. Because it is difficult for the JMS protocol to overcome network boundaries a servlet has been developed in order to provide a HTTP connection to the core system.
- Component for signature and verification on the basis of the OSCI client enabler. It can be embedded into applications and supports the use of a wide range of card readers and smart cards. Cryptographic functions are supplied locally by the JCE provider Bouncy Castle. Certificates are verified with the help of the core system via the DI connector (see above).
- Web service for the use of cryptographic functions by business applications. The functions of the core system are used via the DI connector (see above).
- Web service for qualified batch signatures. This service is used by the DMS and archive component. The NetSigner of the core system is used via the DI connector (see above).

---

7 The content management system is not displayed in Figure 4 because it is not relevant in the context of this document. The name of this component is "Government Site Builder (GSB)" (see [SAGA], section A.5).
8 The generic security concept of the VPS is described in [GenSec] and [SecVPS].
9 IVBV is the abbreviation for „Informationsverbund der Bundesverwaltung".

- Web service for sending and receiving electronic messages, i.e. e-mails or OSCI messages (e-message). Before a customer can communicate electronically with the DRV Bund he has to register at a remote directory service. In order to send a message the address and public encryption certificate of the addressee is looked up first. Subsequently the message is signed with the software signature certificate of the DRV Bund and encrypted with the public certificate of the addressee. For that the signature and encryption functions of the core system are used via the DI connector (see above). The last step is to generate the electronic message and send it via OSCI (business connector and backend) or e-mail according to the choice of the customer. In case of OSCI a supplementary e-mail is sent in order to inform the addressee that a new OSCI message is available.

- Generic OSCI client based on the OSCI client enabler. It is suitable for different use cases (OSCI content data or arbitrary valid XML documents). From the XML Schema Definitions (XSD) valid OSCI content data, the Graphical User Interface (GUI) as well as the business objects are generated. The client can be used by customers, external (business or government) partners as well as internal users. The VPS team is member of the advisory board for the OSCI client for citizens which is realized by the Federal Administration Office (BVA)[10] and the Federal Physical and Technical Institute (PTB)[11].

- Business connector on the basis of the OSCI backend enabler. Business applications use this component via the web service e-message (see above) in order to send and receive OSCI messages. Inbound messages are automatically be routed to the internal business processes without cross-media transfer.

- Monitoring tool in order to check the availability of the OCSP/CRL relay.

The following Table 2 shows the number of usages of the above mentioned VPS services.

Table 2: Number of VPS Service Uses (July 2007)

Application Form Processing	Approx. 7.500 Signatures/Day
Orders to the Payment Counter	Approx. 7.500 Signatures/Day
DMS and Archiving	Approx. 120.000 Signatures/Day (Batch Signatures)
Business Processes	Approx. 90.000 Certificate Verifications/Day
Customer Notification	Approx. 30 Electronic Notifications/Day[12]

The infrastructure is available for external partners via Internet and uses external services:

- Customers exchange electronic messages, i.e. e-mail or OSCI messages with a standard e-mail client with signature and encryption plug-in or with an OSCI client, respectively.

- Business or government partners communicate via OSCI. Inbound messages are automatically delivered to the internal business processes without cross-media transfer.

- Federal authorities connect to the OCSP/CRL relay via Internet or the Interconnection Network of Federal Authorities (IVBV) in order to verify certificates.

- The OCSP/CRL relay makes requests to public certificate authorities (CA), i.e. inquires the OCSP responder or downloads CRL lists. The signed responses are verified.

---

10 BVA is the abbreviation for „Bundesverwaltungsamt".
11 PTB is the abbreviation for „Physikalisch-Technische Bundesanstalt".
12 The number of customer notifications seems to be low. The reason is that a customer who wants to communicate electronically with the German Pension Insurance can only be registered when he owns a signature smart card. The low degree of distribution leads to a low usage of electronic communication (compare to section 7).

7 Conclusion

The Deutsche Rentenversicherung Bund (DRV Bund) has started to set up a SOA-based IT infrastructure which is based on international standards. The basic component of SAGA for data security (VPS) has been successfully integrated into the business processes and is operated under heavy load and real conditions. The first practical experiences have shown that the large-scale operation of central infrastructure components like the VPS is a challenge. Of course special solutions perform better but centralised solutions are much easier to handle. The DRV Bund is one of the biggest users of the VPS in Germany. In order to meet the requirements and to achieve a good compromise the VPS infrastructure has been adapted and expanded. As a strategic partner of the Federal Office for Information Security the improvements directly affect new releases of the basic component for data security. It has proved its value and remains a strategic component of the IT infrastructure of the DRV Bund.

Another point to mention is the low public distribution of signature smart cards. Signature and encryption are an indispensable precondition for realizing electronic business processes without cross-media transfer. For this an extensive spreading of corresponding smart cards is crucial which only can be achieved if they are available for a acceptable price. This may be the case in the near future because the Federal Government plans to introduce identity and health smart cards which are prepared for signatures. Additionally some banks distribute cash cards with signature function and business companies corresponding identity cards to their employees.

References

[EGov]   Federal Office for Information Security: Secure E-Government, www.bsi.de/english/topics/egov/
            index_en.htm

[EGovM]   Federal Office for Information Security: E-Government Manual, www.bsi.de/english/topics/egov/
            3_en.htm

[GenSec]   Sönke Maseberg, Christian Mrugalla, Matthias Intemann: Datensicherheit, In: BundOnline 2005 – Die
            Virtuelle Poststelle des Bundes und ihr generisches Sicherheitskonzept, Datenschutz und Datensicher-
            heit 28 (2004) 11, pp. 660-664, www.bsi.de/fachthem/egov/download/6_VPS_GenSiko.pdf

[OSCI]   OSCI-Leitstelle: Online Service Computer Interface, www.osci.de

[SAGA]   Federal Office for Information Security: SAGA – Standards and Architectures for E-Government Ap-
            plications, KBSt Publication Series, ISSN 0179-7263, Vol 59, Dec 2003, www.bsi.de/english/topics/
            egov/download/5_SAGA2_en.pdf

[SecCom]   Federal Office for Information Security: Secure Communication in E-Government, www.bsi.de/english/
            topics/egov/download/4_SiKomm_en.pdf

[SecVPS]   bremen online services GmbH & Co. KG, datenschutz nord GmbH: Generisches Sicherheitskonzept
            für die Kern- und Webkomponenten der Virtuellen Poststelle, Sept 2004, www.bsi.de/fachthem/egov/
            download/VPS_SiKo_1_0.pdf

[VPS]   Federal Office for Information Security: The Virtual Post Office, www.bsi.de/english/topics/egov/
            vps_en.htm

Index

A

B

F

G

M

N

O

P

Understanding IT

Martin Ruckert
Understanding MP3
Syntax, Semantics, Mathematics, and Algorithms
2005. xiv, 250 pp. Softc. EUR 39,90   ISBN 978-3-528-05905-7

ISO Standard MPEG 1 Layer 1, 2, 3 and MPEG 2.5 - Audio Compression - Digital Filters - Psychoacoustics - Discrete Cosine Transform - Bitstream Decoding - Huffman Coding - Low Frequency Extensions

MPEG audio coding became popular under the name MP3. It is now the most important means of delivering high quality audio over the internet and will play the lead role in digital movie sound as well as in digital audio broadcast. This book explains the ideas, the concepts, and the implementation of MP3. Reading it requires no special prerequisites, but still, the book is detailed enough to include a fully executable highly efficient MP3 decoding engine. Not only understandable but even enjoyable.

Klaus D. Niemann
From Enterprise Architecture to IT Governance
Elements of Effective IT Management
2006. xii, 232 pp. with 89 figs. and Online-Service. Softc. EUR 56,90
ISBN 978-3-8348-0198-2

Enterprise Architecture: Significance, Creation and Approach - How does Architecture Management work? - Analyses and Key Figures - IT Development Planning - Costs - Significance and Benefits for IT Governance

This book shows its readers how to achieve the goal of genuine IT governance. The key here is the successful development of enterprise architecture as the necessary foundation. With its capacity to span and integrate business procedures, IT applications and IT infrastructure, enterprise architecture opens these areas up to analysis and makes them rich sources of critical data. Enterprise architecture thereby rises to the status of a crucial management information system for the CIO.

vieweg
Abraham-Lincoln-Straße 46
65189 Wiesbaden
Fax 0611.7878-400
www.vieweg.de

Stand 1.7.2007. Änderungen vorbehalten.
Erhältlich im Buchhandel oder im Verlag.

W